HUMAN
RESOURCES
MANAGEMENT

HUMAN RESOURCES MANAGEMENT

Third Edition

P D GERBER • P S NEL • P S VAN DYK

International Thomson Publishing (Southern Africa) (Pty) Ltd

I ⓣ P   An International Thomson Publishing Company

Johannesburg • London • New York • Bonn • Boston • Madrid • Melbourne • Mexico City •
Paris • Singapore • Tokyo • Toronto • Albany, NY • Belmont, CA • Cincinnati, OH • Detroit, MI

ISBN 1 86864 036 1

Previously published by Southern Book Publishers (Pty) Ltd
First edition, first impression 1987
Second edition, first impression 1992
Second edition, second impression 1993
Second edition, third impression 1994
Third edition, first impression 1995
Third edition, second impression 1995

Published by ITP/Southern
Third edition, third impression 1996

Cover design by McMurray Graphic Productions
Set in 10 on 12 pt Plantin
Typesetting and reproduction by PG&A, Ottery, Cape
Printed and bound by
National Book Printers, Drukkery Street, Goodwood, Western Cape

Published by
International Thomson Publishing (Southern Africa) (Pty) Ltd
PO Box 2459
Halfway House
1685
South Africa

*This edition is dedicated to Riëtte
Suzanne and Stephan van Dyk*

Pieter S van Dyk

Preface

Now that this third edition has been finalised and one can view the entire effort in retrospect, one becomes increasingly aware of the dynamic nature of this field of study and the pro-activeness it requires of human resources management practitioners.

When we began work on this revised edition we were still in the old South Africa, with the authors "feeling their way" into the new South Africa and anticipating the influence a new government would have on the management of human resources. We have incorporated this influence in as far as it was possible and to a large extent there is concord between our efforts and what is happening in the new South Africa. We specifically refer to affirmative action, training and development and industrial relations. While writing this preface, all the media have been full of reports about strikes and new industrial relations legislation. Affirmative action has been superimposed on every human resources management process and it will require great prudence on the part of human resources practitioners to ensure that sound management practices are followed in all respects.

We wish to express our gratitude to all those people and institutions who have contributed positive commentary towards the improvement of the previous edition, as well as to the colleagues who have routed specific feedback through Southern Book Publishers. We also thank our own colleagues in the Department of Business Economics at UNISA for their positive input, and finally Southern Book Publishers, particularly Leanne Martini and Joey Kriek.

The thought we wish to leave with you is that our country's human resources are our only competitive advantage and can become even more so through the application of sound human resources management practices.

Contents

Part 2: HUMAN RESOURCES PROVISIONING   63

Chapter 16: Motivation   318

Chapter 17: Leadership in organisations   341

Part 4: HUMAN RESOURCES DEVELOPMENT 457

Chapter 21: Employee development: training principles and legislation 459

Part 1

General introduction

Introduction to human resources management	Chapter 1
Human resources management: historical development and *status quo* in South Africa	Chapter 2
A systems approach to human resources management	Chapter 3

Overview of Part 1: General introduction

AIM

To provide the student or reader with an overview of the study field of human resources management in order to develop a need for, interest in and scientific approach to the study of this applied behavioural science.

PRINCIPAL STUDY OBJECTIVES

Chapter 1: Introduction to human resources management. To offer the student or reader insight into the importance of human resources for economic and employee welfare in a national economy.

Chapter 2: Human resources management: historical development and *status quo* in South Africa. To provide the student or reader with an overview of the historical development of this applied behavioural science and the state of art in South Africa.

Chapter 3: A systems approach to human resources management. To broaden the student's or reader's comprehension of the systems approach as it applies to human resources and to show its application in an organisational context.

Chapter 1

Introduction to human resources management

P.S. van Dyk

STUDY OBJECTIVES

After studying this chapter, you should be able to:
- Weigh up the concepts of human resources management and personnel management against each other;
- Give an overview of the human resources function within the organisation;
- Define the sphere of responsibility of human resources management;
- Explain the study lay-out of this book.

1.1 INTRODUCTION

It is rightly said that labour (human resources) is the only resource in an organisation that reacts when acted upon. This means that with the exception of human resources, all resources of an organisation are static. Other resources derive their dynamic character from human resources.

In the South African context, the efficient and effective management and utilisation of human resources cannot be overemphasised. South Africa has a shortage of skilled and professional human resources, and its labour market is characterised by an imbalance between skilled and unskilled human resources. Coupled with this, South Africa also has a very low productivity ratio that inhibits natural growth in employment opportunities. As successful human resources management plays a key role in rectifying this situation, it should be given its rightful place in the management of an organisation.

In this introductory chapter, the following relevant aspects are examined:
- The contribution that scientifically based human resources management can make to the success of the South African national economy as a whole;

- Micro-aspects of human resources management such as definition of concepts, the role and functions of human resources management and the organisational structure of the human resources management department;
- The lay-out of this book.

1.2 THE RELATION BETWEEN HUMAN RESOURCES MANAGEMENT AT ORGANISATIONAL LEVEL AND ECONOMIC PROSPERITY

1.2.1 General

> It is important for the author to offer you, whether you are a student, human resources manager, other functional manager or interested party, a general overview of the important contribution that South Africa's human resources can make in the creation of a new South Africa.

Stephane Gavelli, director of the *World Competitiveness Project*, emphasises what he calls the role of the "softer side of competitiveness" in the creation of a competitive environment:

The softer side of competitiveness reflects the shift towards a knowledge-based economy. In the industrialized world today, only 15% of the active population physically touches a product. The other 85% are adding value through the creation, the management and the transfer of information. As a result, the human dimension of competitiveness has become a key success factor in a modern economy.

The World Competitiveness Organization aims at comparing countries all over the world with regard to their competitive position. Only countries that fulfil certain requirements are included in the survey. In 1992, South Africa was included for the first time, under the so-called Group II countries known as "newly industrialized economies". In 1992, South Africa was placed eighth among the Group II countries on the basis of its performance with regard to eight general *competitiveness factors*, i.e.:

- National economic strength;
- Internationalisation;
- Government;
- Finances;
- Infrastructure;
- Management;
- Science and technology;
- People.

In his "executive summary", Valchanges (1992:23) describes South Africa's position as follows:

4

FIGURE 1.1: South Africa's competitive position among Group II countries in 1992

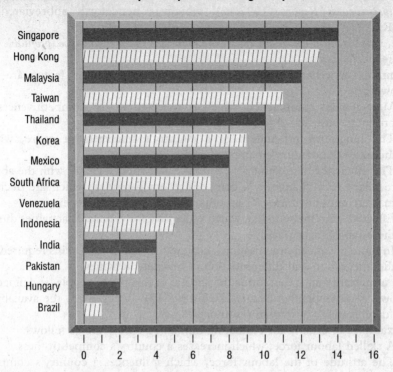

Source: World Competitiveness Report (1992:12)

Of the newcomers this year, South Africa ranks 8th, followed by Venezuela. Financial services and science and technology efforts have achieved the best rankings for South Africa. However, the challenge facing South Africa is to spread its competence, skills and educational basis among the population. This need is reflected in its being ranked last in the people factor.

Subsequently, a national competitiveness balance sheet is drawn up for each country. This ranks each country in terms of the eight competitive factors in its particular group and also gives reasons why a country has a specific ranking.

The term "country competitiveness" refers to a country's ability to create and maintain long-term added value in comparison with its competitors.

As the subject of study is management in general and specifically human resources management, South Africa's position in comparison with other newly industrialised economies is of particular importance.

Management as a competitive factor is defined as follows by the *World Competitiveness Report* (1992:12), which is henceforth abbreviated to WCR:

> . . . *the extent to which enterprises are managed in an innovative, profitable and responsible manner.*

Examples of criteria for evaluating the competitiveness factor are the following:

- Management competence, which is reflected in the competitiveness of products with regard to price and quality;
- The long-term orientation of a country's management cadre, which increases the country's competitiveness over time;
- The efficiency of a country's economic activities, together with the ability to adapt to a change in a competitive environment, which are decisive management attributes for an organisation's competitiveness;
- Effective entrepreneurship, which is decisive for economic activities during the establishment phase;
- In more advanced organisations, corporate management skills required for the integration and differentiation of business activities.

The important factor that forms the subject of this book, people, is defined as follows as a competitive factor (WCR 1992:12): "People . . . the availability and qualifications of human resources."

Examples of criteria for evaluating human resources are as follows:

- A skilled labour force, which increases a country's competitiveness.
- The attitude of the labour force, which influences a country's competitiveness.
- Competitiveness, which tends to increase the expectations of employees with regard to quality of life.

During 1992 and the first half of 1993, South Africa lost its competitive position and was placed eleventh among 15 Group II countries. Its evaluation on the basis of the eight competitiveness factors is indicated in table 1.1 (WCR 1993: Summary).

TABLE 1.1: South Africa's competitive position 1992–93

Factor	1992	1993
1. Infrastructure	7	5 (+2)
2. Finances	8	6 (+2)
3. Management	7	7 (0)
4. Science and technology	5	7 (−2)
5. Domestic economic strength	12	11 (+1)
6. Internationalisation	10	13 (−3)
7. Government	10	14 (−4)
8. People	14	14 (0)

Source: Adapted from WCR 1992 and 1993

> South Africa maintains a ranking of 14 from 1992 for the extent to which its human resources assist competitiveness. Of all the report's major criteria, the people factor ranks at the bottom. (Valchanges 1992:23)

This state of affairs is hardly a compliment for the management of human resources in South African organisations.

We then take a look at the *World Competitive Report's* evaluation of the human factor. The content of this book (both its first and second editions) is an attempt at a more scientific yet pragmatic approach to the management of human resources in Southern African organisations. No country in Africa, with the exception of South Africa, was included in the *World Competitiveness Report*, and it may thus be said that the same or an even worse state of affairs prevails in the rest of Africa.

TABLE 1.2: South Africa's national competitiveness balance sheet, 1993

MANAGEMENT			
Assets	**Ranking**	**Liabilities**	**Ranking**
Criteria		*Criteria*	
Overall productivity	4	Company profits	14
Labour productivity	4	Intercultural understanding	15
Compensation levels	3	International experience	15
Size of industrial corporations	3	Senior management	15
Size of service companies	1	Labour relations	15
Labour turnover	1		
Product reliability	3		
Social responsibility	4		
HUMAN RESOURCES			
Growth in labour force	4	Population composition structure	15
Female labour force	3	Labour force percentage	15
Unemployment among the youth	2	Employment percentage	13
Secondary school enrolment	3	Growth in employment	14
		Skilled labour	14
		Competent senior managers	13
		Equal rights	15
		"Brain drain"	15
		The education system	14
		Compulsory schooling	13
		Computer literacy	14
		Economic literacy	14
		Employee motivation	15
		Alcohol and drug abuse	15
		Community values	14

Source: Adapted from WCR 1993

The ranking reflects South Africa's performance with regard to each criterion in comparison with the rest of the Group II countries. It appears that the liabilities exceed the assets: this state of affairs is worrying and requires human resources management interventions both on a macro and an organisational level.

The challenge is in your hands!

1.2.2 How can human resources management contribute towards improving this state of affairs in a new South Africa?

South Africa was placed last or second last in practically all the criteria on the liability side of the human resources balance sheet. Human resources management interventions on both a national and organisational level can, if effectively managed, change the situation to a large extent. A new South Africa requires:

- A highly skilled worker corps;
- A motivated worker corps;
- A satisfied worker corps;
- A worker corps that is free from discrimination based on race, sex or religious conviction.

The question then arises how this may be brought about. Some thoughts in this regard are given here:

- The creation of a highly skilled worker corps is primarily a matter of national education. From secondary school level onwards, schooling should take into account the needs and demands of the labour market. In other words, it must be practically oriented.
- Uniform standards must be set and standardised national curricula must be developed for all occupations.
- At an organisational level, management must attempt to develop in-house training programmes in such a way that an increase in productivity is a clearly recognisable output.
- Programmes for uplifting the underprivileged must be developed. This refers to human resources development interventions such as programmes to address:
  — Literacy
  — Basic mathematical skills
  — Computer literacy
  — Economic literacy
  — Health education programmes in respect of AIDS, hygiene, alcohol and drug abuse. (These aspects will be discussed later.)
- Sound management practices and particularly sound human resources management practices can relieve many of the existing problems. A motivated and satisfied worker corps can only exist if sound human resources management practices are adhered to.

- The technology used by an organisation is also decisive for the improvement of the competitive position of both organisations and a country as a whole. Management must decide what is best for uplifting the organisation and the national economy as a whole. The link between the technology used and productivity is obvious. This aspect is discussed in chapter 24.
- Finally, but certainly most importantly in a new South Africa: organisations should pay particular attention to the implementation of an affirmative action policy and programmes, as well as to the philosophy of life-long learning. This aspect is discussed in detail in chapter 10.

The words of Peter Wrighton, Chairman of the Premier Group (Wrighton 1993) are a good summary of the above:

It is then the third category, "people", which will pose the greatest challenge! This is of course the most important category as "people" make all the other things happen. Let me remind you that we came bottom in this category. It is important that we analyse why this is so, because in the final analysis it is the quality of people which determines a country's competitiveness: skilled, motivated people are the factors upon which success depends, before machines and money.

The key to South Africa's success lies in creating an environment where people strive to do their best, where opportunities are equally distributed, where initiative is encouraged—business can't run an economy, but we can create the conditions for success.

The role of the human resources manager discussed in the following section of this chapter is thus of cardinal importance.

1.3 THE TERM "HUMAN RESOURCES MANAGEMENT"

1.3.1 General

The exact meaning of terms used in the field of human resources, for example personnel management, the personnel function, human resources management and personnel administration, are not always clear. To avoid confusion and uncertainty about the exact meaning of important terms in the field of human resources, they are explained in more detail in this part of the chapter.

1.3.2 Clarification of concepts

Holley and Jennings (1987:4) provide a general definition of the concept of human resources management in the following words:

Human resources management refers to activities, policies, beliefs and the general function that relates to employees or the personnel department.

They describe the elements contained in the abovementioned definition as follows:

- *Human resources activities:* examples are activities carried out by the human resources department such as the training of a group of employees or a recruitment campaign.

9

- *Human resources policy:* these are formalised official guidelines with regard to the manner in which personnel matters should be carried out.
- *Human resources beliefs:* these may be described as strong convictions on the part of executive personnel with regard to people as employees. These beliefs or convictions are one of the most important elements of organisational culture.
- *Human resources management function:* a function is a group of unique activities such as carrying out a job analysis, drawing up a job description, and carrying out a salary and wage survey to create a remuneration structure for an organisation. The human resources management function indicates all human resources management activities within an organisation.
- *Human resources department:* this is the physical place where employees charged with carrying out human resources management activities are found.
- *Human resources official:* employees, irrespective of their appointments, who deal with the execution of human resources activities, such as a human resources manager, training official or recruitment agent.

The British Institute for Personnel Management defines the concept of "personnel management" as follows:

Personnel management is that part of management concerned with people at work and with their relationships within an enterprise. Its aim is to bring together and develop into an effective organisation the men and women who make up an enterprise and, having regard for the well-being of the individual and of working groups, to enable them to make their best contribution to its success. (Graham and Bennett 1993:157)

According to the aforementioned institute, personnel management is concerned with the development and application of the following policies:
- Human resources planning, recruitment, selection, placement and termination of service;
- Education, training and career development;
- Conditions of service and remuneration standards;
- Formal and informal communication and consultation by the representatives of employers and employees at all levels of the organisation;
- Negotiations and the application of agreements regarding wages and working conditions;
- Procedures for the prevention and avoidance of disputes.

Finally, personnel management is concerned with the human and social implications of internal changes in the activities of organisations, as well as with the social and economic implications of change within the community of the organisation.

The most important differentiation that must be made is between the terms *personnel management* and *human resources management*.

To obtain clarity on this difference, Hall and Goodale (1986:8) ask the question given in the box.

Personnel management or human resource management?

In many organizations titles like personnel department, personnel director, and personnel manager are common. Traditional books about personnel management concentrate on how programs for selection, training, compensation, and career planning are designed by members of the personnel department, and their audience is students who plan to specialize in personnel management. We have chosen to use the term human resource management for two major reasons. First, we view it as a process much broader than designing personnel programs; it also involves strategic planning and implementation. Second, the expanded definition of human resource management includes responsibilities that can only be assumed by line managers. Therefore, our audience is not only students who wish to become human resource professionals, but also business students who plan to become line managers.

The authors of this book share the view of Hall and Goodale, and our agreement with this view will become clear during the course of this book.

Graham and Bennett (1993:159–160) refer to the following similarities and differences between the concepts of *personnel management* and *human resources management*:

- Personnel management is practical, useful and instrumental, and is generally concerned with the administration and implementation of human resources management policy. Human resources management, on the other hand, is concerned with strategic aspects and involves the total development of human resources within the organisation.
- Human resources management is concerned with the broader implications of the management of change and not only with the effects of change on work in practice.
- Human resources management aspects are an important input for organisational development.
- Personnel management is both reactive and diagnostic in nature. Thus, for example, it *reacts* to changes in labour legislation, labour market conditions, trade union actions and environmental influences. Human resources management, on the other hand, is *prescriptive* in nature and concerned with strategies, the introduction of new activities and the development of new ideas.
- Human resources management determines the general policy for employment relations within the organisation. Its task is thus to develop a *culture* within an organisation that promotes employee relations and cooperation. Personnel management, on the other hand, is criticised because it is primarily concerned with the enforcement of company rules and regulations among employees rather than with bringing about loyalty and commitment to company goals.

11

- Personnel management has short-term perspectives, while human resources management has long-term perspectives and attempts to integrate all human aspects of the organisation into a coherent whole, thus encouraging individual employees to have an attitude that strives for high performance.

Human resources management as an applied management science is closely related to a sister science, industrial psychology.

From an industrial psychology perspective, human resources management may be regarded as the implementation of policies, customs and procedures with regard to the human being as an employee on the basis of psychological principles.

Graham and Bennett (1993:158) put it as follows:

Its purpose is not to make effective use of people at work and develop satisfactory relationships among them but to motivate them by providing them with jobs that are satisfying in themselves (if it is practically possible) and by offering them financial and other rewards.

To emphasise the psychological basis of human resources management, it is appropriate to redefine it as a management strategy related to one of the means of production of the organisation, i.e. its labour. From this perspective, human resources management consists of three general functions:

- Human resources utilisation, which includes recruitment, selection, transfers, promotion, appraisal, training and development;
- Motivation of the human resources factor, which includes work design, remuneration, fringe benefits, counselling, participation and equal rights;
- Protection of the human resources factor, which includes working conditions, welfare services, safety and the formalisation of policy regarding the assurance of employee interests after retirement.

A clear distinction must also be made between human resources management and the management of people.

- Every functional manager—each departmental head, foreman and supervisor—is responsible for the management of the staff. This means that every manager must provide guidelines for his or her immediate subordinates. He or she must set objectives with and for them; delegate responsibility to them; measure their performance and provide them with feedback and must encourage underachievers to improve—in short, must motivate immediate subordinates to do their best, and provide opportunities for them to make optimal use of their skills. This responsibility forms part of human resources utilisation.
- On the other hand, human resources management, like marketing and purchasing, is a specialised function that provides back-up services for other managers in the organisation, to enable them also to make optimal use of their subordinates.

The approach followed in this book is expressed in the definition of Hall and Goodale (1986:6):

. . . Human resources management . . . the process through which an optimal fit is achieved among the employee, job, organization, and environment so that employees reach their desired level of satisfaction and performance and the organization meets its goals.

This description is revolutionary in the field of human resources management, but is very important, as the authors refer here to *organisational effectiveness* as well as *organisational efficiency*, both of which will be discussed in this chapter.

Since the foregoing definition is a far more pragmatic approach than the traditional references that have been quoted above, for the purposes of this book it will be further elaborated upon. The discussion that follows refers to figure 1.2.

FIGURE 1.2: Components of human resources management

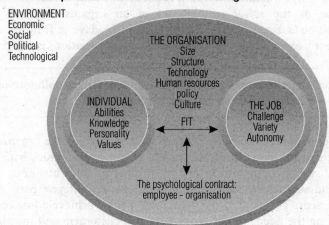

Source: Adapted from Hall and Goodale (1986:4)

It is clear from figure 1.1 that there are four important components implied in the definition given by Hall and Goodale, namely:

- The external environment;
- The organisation;
- The work itself; and
- The individual or employee.

Nowadays the focus of human resources management lies in the integration of the human resources management strategy into the global strategy of the organisation. This approach has been needed for a long time, since human resources are the only dynamic production factor an organisation has.

(a) The external environment

Every organisation exists inside an external environment that consists of four primary sub-environments, namely:

13

- The economic environment;
- The social environment;
- The political environment;
- The technological environment.

The *economic environment* must surely be the most important from a free market (capitalistic) point of view. In the general literature the economic environment is taken to mean the external influences that have an effect on an organisation, such as:

- The availability of capital;
- The current interest rates;
- The rate of inflation;
- The strength (or weakness) of the competitors of the organisation;
- The level of employment (whether it is above or below average).

The influence of the *social environment* of an organisation has been underestimated to a large extent in the past. Nowadays it features much more prominently as far as the top management of organisations is concerned.

Just consider the influence of the "Green Movement" on pollution and the subsequent reaction of top management.

The social environment is shaped by the society in which the organisation features. Potential customers and employees of the organisation, with their attitudes and values concerning work, products, and business, their educational and skill levels, and their expectations, are integral parts of the social environment. To prosper, the organisation must achieve a fine balance between meeting the needs of the employees and customers and meeting its own organisational goals.

The *political environment* is particularly important in the present South African context. Every organisation is run according to laws and regulations, whether they originate at central, provincial or local levels. These laws and regulations influence any organisation from its external environment, no matter what the nature of the business is.

In South Africa, labour legislation and expected affirmative action, as well as laws and regulations with regard to training and development, are currently of particular importance to the management of local organisations.

Now, more than ever before, the *technological environment* has an influence on management philosophy, not only in South Africa, but in the whole African context, since there is a positive correlation between the technology in use and the productivity of a community (see chapter 24).

Technology essentially means the way in which an organisation changes the inputs (raw materials in whatever form is available) into outputs (products or services) by means of an ongoing process.

> South African organisations (i.e. their management cadre) are, however, restricted in their ability to make optimal use of the country's raw materials because of the limited skills available on the South African labour market.

(b) The organisation

Before going on to discuss the role that the organisation plays in this regard, cognisance must first be taken of what constitutes an organisation. Schein (1980:15) says that:

> *An organization is the planned co-ordination of the activities of a number of people for the achievement of some common explicit purpose or goal, through division of labor and function, and through a hierarchy of authority and responsibility.*

According to Hall and Goodale (1986:5), an organisation has a number of characteristics. One obvious characteristic is *size*; some people have strong preferences about the size of the organisation they want to join. Organisations also differ in their *structure*. Some are hierarchical while others are structured according to certain functional preferences. Another key characteristic of organisations is the *technology* used, which governs how work is done; this determines the profiles that employees must match. The organisation's human resources policies show its orientation towards people and play a major part in attracting and satisfying employees. Finally, the *culture* of the organisation is of particular importance. This indicates the way in which things are done in an organisation and is also known as the personality of the organisation. For the success of an organisation it is particularly important that the individual employee's personality and the "personality" of the organisation are in tune with one another. A mismatch can hamper the attainment of both personal and organisational goals.

(c) The work (job) itself

An individual employee joins an organisation by virtue of his or her potential for reaching personal goals in that organisation by supplying work and work potential (see chapter 4). The basic motivation of a person (employee) in this context is that he or she sees the opportunity of satisfying his or her *intrinsic* and *extrinsic* needs (see chapter 16).

Hall and Goodale (1986:6) comment in this regard that:

> *Among the key characteristics of jobs that directly affect employee performance and satisfaction are the degrees of* challenge, variety, *and* autonomy *they offer to employees. Challenge is the level of difficulty of a job's tasks and activities. Variety refers to the number of different tasks and activities included in the job, and autonomy is the extent to which an employee works independently on a job.*

15

(d) The individual employee

The last, but undeniably the most important component in Hall and Goodale's conceptualisation (figure 1.2) is the individual in an organisation.

> Please note that the term "employee" is used not only to mean the employee at a low level—even though people in the management of an organisation and who are responsible for its functioning normally dissociate themselves from this designation.

Hall and Goodale (1986:6) describe the individual in an organisation in the accompanying box.

> Finally, each individual brings a unique combination of attributes to an employer. Some personal characteristics that cause people to succeed or fail on a job are their abilities, knowledge, personality, values, and expectations. Abilities and knowledge determine an employee's potential to perform specific jobs successfully. Personality, values and expectations are related to an individual's preference for different kinds of jobs and organizations and therefore determine the choice of a specific job or employer.

Hall and Goodale's approach now falls into line with that of the authors. As you get further into the book, the similarity will become more obvious.

The aspects mentioned are discussed in chapter 4 under the management of the psychological contract, the component that the authors of this book have added to Hall and Goodale's model.

1.4 THE ROLE AND FUNCTIONS OF HUMAN RESOURCES MANAGEMENT WITHIN THE ORGANISATION

1.4.1 General

We are of the opinion that human resources management is a staff function, with the aim of helping other functional managers apply and utilise the most important production factor, *human resources*, as effectively as possible within the organisation. The people in an organisation essentially determine how successfully the other means of production will be applied. With this fact in mind, human resources management as an organisational function is defined as stated in the box.

> Human resources management is a purposeful action of the human resources department aimed at assisting functional managers in the optimal application and utilisation of the human resources under their control, in accordance with official organisational policy as well as human resources management policy and application in practice, in order to achieve the goals of the organisation.

1.4.2 The development and maintenance of human resources management objectives

Like any other organisational function, the human resources department requires focal points or objectives to direct the diverse nature of the activities to be carried out. Three general human resources management objectives are universally accepted in this regard (see Holley and Jennings 1983:6–7).

Objective 1: To establish the belief that the human resources of an organisation consist of unique individuals who can make a meaningful impact on the success of the organisation.

This objective is usually reflected in the human resources vision or mission of an organisation. The vision of Toyota South Africa is a good example of this.

**TOYOTA SA MARKETING
HUMAN RESOURCES DIVISION**
Vision
1. To unlock and unfold human potential;
2. To strategically align the organisation for change.

You might reason that this objective is an obvious one in modern organisations. This is, however, not the case: many organisations in South Africa, seen from a multi-cultural point of view, still disregard this important principle. Employees are still treated as "machines" and their contribution is regarded as unimportant for the success of the organisation. The contemporary view that the human being is the most important asset of an organisation is relatively new. The general acceptance of this principle does, however, give rise to individual employees having an optimally positive attitude towards performance.

Objective 2: Establishing how employees and organisations can adapt to each other to the advantage of both parties.

This objective is linked to the first objective. If employees are unique components of organisational success (see figure 1.6), modern organisations should react in a flexible manner and adapt to the diverse needs of employees. The days of one policy for all employees are over. The divergence of individual employee needs may be seen in the conditions of service of modern organisations (see chapter 13). Mutual adaptation of needs is also discussed in chapter 4.

Objective 3: The support by human resources managers of other line and staff managers in the execution of their tasks related to human resources management and the management of people.

The main theme of this book is to highlight the contribution to organisational success made by the human resources management function as well as the role of other managers in this regard. Figure 1.3 embodies this approach.

17

At the end of each chapter, an attempt will be made to highlight the application of the relevant theories in increasing the performance inclination of employees.

1.5 THE HUMAN RESOURCES MANAGEMENT FUNCTION WITHIN THE ORGANISATION

Within the organisational framework of the organisation the human resources function manifests itself as a human resources department. The human resources function of an organisation refers to a number of functions carried out in order to achieve the goals of an organisation. The human resources function is carried out by a human resources department responsible for the organisation's human resources management activities. The department also gives *advice* and *assistance* to the rest of the organisation.

The human resources function is therefore a *staff function* aimed at providing the organisation with labour, and giving it specialised human resources services to help it to achieve its goals. The human resources function should be flexible by implication, and the physical embodiment of this function depends on the nature of the organisation in terms of its size, product(s), service(s) and geographical location. The human resources function includes the following:

- Human resources provisioning, comprising human resources planning, recruitment, selection, placement, induction and career management.
- Human resources maintenance, comprising the determination of conditions of service, remuneration structures, record keeping, personnel turnover, settlement of disputes, advisory services, employer-employee relations, social responsibility, affirmative action and performance assessment.
- Human resources development, comprising training and development as its most important activities.

1.6 RESPONSIBILITIES AND FUNCTIONS OF THE HUMAN RESOURCES MANAGEMENT FUNCTION OR DEPARTMENT

1.6.1 General

The human resources management function in an organisation aims at producing certain *outputs* in order to achieve the organisation's goals. The responsibilities of the human resources function and the conditions for its success will briefly be dealt with in the following section.

1.6.2 Responsibilities of the human resources management department

The responsibilities of the human resources management department can probably best be outlined as follows (adapted from Graham and Bennett 1993:158):

- Carrying out wage and salary surveys to ensure that the organisation's wage and salary levels are in line with those of other related organisations.
- The development of incentive schemes such as compensation systems to increase employee efficiency.
- Implementing first-class pension schemes and advising employees with regard to their pension and other privileges.
- Maintaining personnel details and statistics.
- Preparing accurate job descriptions and other recruitment aids.
- Implementing health and safety regulations, accident prevention and first-aid facilities.
- Management training, development and succession planning.
- Employee communication, i.e. sending out important information to employees through newsletters, notice boards and information sessions.

1.6.3 The function of the human resources manager
Theoretically, three functions may be distinguished:
- A service function;
- A control function;
- An advisory function.

The *service function* incorporates the everyday tasks of a personnel department such as recruitment, selection, remuneration, training and health and safety activities. The *control function* is more strategic in nature and incorporates activities such as:
- An analysis of key human resources management outputs such as labour turnover, productivity, absenteeism, resignations;
- The recommendation of appropriate corrective action by line managers, such as training and development, dismissals and transfers.

The *advisory function* is associated with the expert advice given by the human resources department regarding human resources policy and procedures with regard to matters such as:
- Which employees are ready for promotion;
- How a grievance procedure should be carried out;
- How service contracts, health and safety regulations should be carried out.

From the above it thus appears that the human resources manager must be a *diplomat* in the sense that he or she must act as a mediator between management and the employee, between management and management, and between various groups of employees. This role is of particular importance in contemporary South African organisations.

The human resources manager must also be a *diagnostician* who collects information, interprets it for various parties and prescribes the best solutions.

Finally, Graham and Bennett (1993:163) are of the following opinion:

Thus a human resources manager has to be an effective planner, analyst, team worker and communicator, capable of presenting proposals and arguing a case at all levels within the organisation—from the board room to the employees' workplaces.

1.7 THE PLACE OF THE HUMAN RESOURCES MANAGEMENT FUNCTION IN AN ORGANISATION

1.7.1 General

The human resources management function is responsible for rendering a personnel service to both line and staff functions in an organisation. This function belongs to a department or section, which in turn forms an integral part of the total structure of the organisation.

1.7.2 A typical structure for a human resources management department within an organisation

A typical human resources management department with its different human resources management functions may be represented as shown in figure 1.3.

FIGURE 1.3: The place of the human resources management function in an organisation

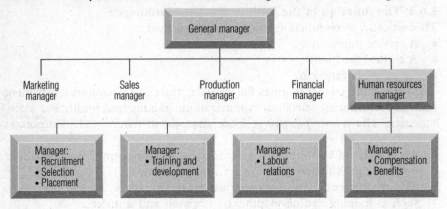

A further subdivision of the organisational structure according to figure 1.3 indicates that the human resources management function consists of various subfunctions. Each organisation will organise its human resources function in such a way that it will satisfy the unique requirements of the organisation.

The previously mentioned concept is merely the point of view of the authors. A further distinction must be made between line, functional and staff authority.

- *Line authority* is the authority vested in managers to give their subordinates orders that they are expected to carry out. In other words, line authority is the direct authority of any manager/supervisor over immediate subordinates. For example, the general manager has line authority over heads of departments who have line authority over employees in their sections, and so forth. Line authority gives the human resources department the right to issue enforceable orders to its functionaries on any matter dealt with by the human resources department.
- *Functional authority* gives the human resources manager the right to issue enforceable instructions on human resources matters throughout the

organisation, in order to fulfil duties and responsibilities outside his or her own department. The authority to ensure that human resources policy, regulations and procedures are correctly applied is an example of this functional authority.

- *Staff authority* is only advisory and cannot be enforced. A functionary of the department may, for example, advise a supervisor how to reprimand an employee who is regularly late for work.

Figure 1.4 illustrates the functional and staff authority of a human resources manager.

FIGURE 1.4: The functional and staff authority of the human resources department

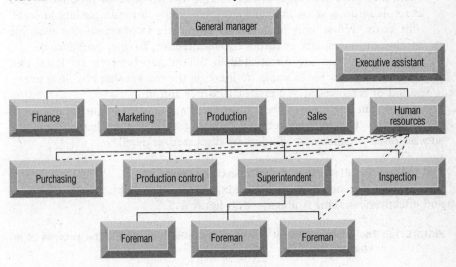

The dotted lines indicate the staff authority of the human resources department with regard to other line and staff functions. It is clear that the human resources manager may exercise functional authority over human resources matters throughout the organisation. Orders issued from the human resources department to the production department, for example on personnel matters, are binding and must be executed by the production department. Staff authority, however, means that the human resources manager may give advice but cannot enforce it. For instance, he or she cannot force a foreman to treat an underachieving factory worker in a specific way.

1.8 HUMAN RESOURCES MANAGEMENT AND THE SUCCESS OF THE ORGANISATION

1.8.1 General

The success of an organisation means the extent to which it succeeds in achieving its organisational goals, as measured against specific set standards of achievement. According to the systems approach to organisations,

organisations have multiple goals. To be successful, they must therefore work towards the optimal achievement of multiple goals.

1.8.2 Multiple goals in an organisation

The goals of an organisation are usually divided into three broad categories: long-, medium- and short-term goals.

- *Long-term goals* focus on the organisation's ability to adapt to changes in the economic situation, technological development, social responsibilities, statutory and political responsibilities, human resources requirements, etc.
- *Short-term goals* are set, measurable goals with regard to production (for example returns, sales, market share); efficiency (for example labour costs, unit costs, refuse and waste); and employee satisfaction (for example morale, attitudes, labour turnover, absenteeism, fatigue, grievances).
- *Medium-term goals* are formulated to fill the gap between set long- and short-term goals, for example, to increase the market share by 30% over a period of three years, at a rate of 10% per annum.

A question that might arise is how this relates to the study of human resources management. The relation between human resources management and the success of an organisation will now be discussed in detail.

1.8.3 The cornerstones of organisational success

The success of an organisation is based on two cornerstones, namely efficiency and effectiveness. This is illustrated in figure 1.5.

FIGURE 1.5: The relation between efficiency and effectiveness and the success of an organisation

As may be seen from figure 1.5, the success of an organisation is the result of its efficiency and effectiveness. In simple terms the efficiency of an organisation means *doing things the right way* and is closely related to ratios. Examples of ratios are the input-output ratios of individual employees, sections and departments; in other words, the *cost-effectiveness ratios* in the production process and other processes within the organisation. The efficiency of an organisation also refers to the nature and quality of the interpersonal intergroup, and intragroup relationships within the organisation.

Beer (1980:29) defines organisational efficiency as stated in the accompanying box.

22

> [Organisational efficiency] may be defined as the extent of fit between the internal components of the social system. The more congruity exists between these components the more the organization will function smoothly, with relatively little dissatisfaction on the part of organization members.

The definition of Beer (as adapted by the authors of this book) has many implications: among other things it requires thorough *internal* management of the organisation.

Effectiveness means *doing the right things*, which is primarily determined by setting goals for the organisation. These goals are not set in isolation, but are directly linked to the demand for an organisation's product or service. A study of this demand must also be based on the system's approach with particular attention to the background of the organisation's suprasystem. Only thorough identification and analysis of the needs of groups interested in the organisation will enable top management to interpret the demand correctly, and formulate goals for the organisation accordingly.

Beer (1980:39) has the following view with regard to organisational effectiveness:

> *Effectiveness may be defined as the extent of fit between the organization's environment and all the internal components of the social system. The more congruity exists between the internal social system components and the environment, the more the organization is likely to exchange favorably with its environment.*

Beer (1980:40) places organisational success in perspective as follows (adapted by the current authors):

> *Organizational health (success) may be defined as the capacity of an organization to engage in ongoing self-examination aimed at identifying incongruities between social systems components and developing plans for needed change in strategy (environment), structure, process, people, culture and the dominant coalition. Such a healthy organization is likely to maintain organizational efficiency and effectiveness in the long term.*

If organisational managers carry out the tasks assigned to them in an effective manner and set aside organisational politics, they should be able to transform their organisations in the interests of their employees and shareholders and to the benefit of South Africa.

REMEMBER:
- Management in South Africa is rated last among Group II countries by the WCR.
- Senior human resources management is rated last among Group II countries.

However, these goals (and therefore the success of the organisation) cannot be achieved of their own accord. Goals cannot be achieved without the necessary resources. Resources such as capital, raw materials and machinery are static and can only take on a dynamic character through the intervention of the labour resources (i.e. human resources). For this reason there is a causal relationship between the success of an organisation and the utilisation of its resources, in particular human resources, which activates the other resources. Therefore it seems essential that human resources management be studied from a management point of view, especially in the light of the purpose of human resources management, namely to provide the organisation with a more efficient and effective worker corps. Every organisation's worker corps consists of individual workers, groups, and management. In this respect the task of human resources management may be defined as follows:

> Human resources management implies the proactive creation, maintenance and development of individual and group efficiency and effectiveness in order to improve individual and group performance (output).

The integration of this with the concept of the success of the organisation is illustrated in figure 1.6.

Figure 1.6 clearly shows that organisational success is the result of interaction between a number of variables. As mentioned, an organisation cannot be successful unless it accurately identifies the demand for the product or service within its external environment (effectiveness of the organisation). An organisation may accurately identify and define the demand for its product or service, and yet not be successful if it does not "do things in the right way" (efficiency). This is illustrated in the following example.

Suppose the management of an organisation determined, on the basis of their strategic planning and market research, that there was a great demand for a less expensive version of a popular bicycle for children, and decided to produce it. They supplied according to demand, and sales forecasts were topped within a short period. Within the course of a few months the organisation's management learnt from the media and through complaints from their outlets that their version of the bicycle had been responsible for many injuries among children using it. A thorough internal investigation found that the strength of the metal used for the bicycle was in accordance with the predetermined standards, but that the quality maintained during the assembly process was poor. As a result of these incidents the demand for this particular bicycle dropped sharply, and the organisation also became less successful with regard to the other products they marketed. Upon further investigation it was found that, for various reasons, the motivation of production personnel was very low, which resulted in a negative attitude

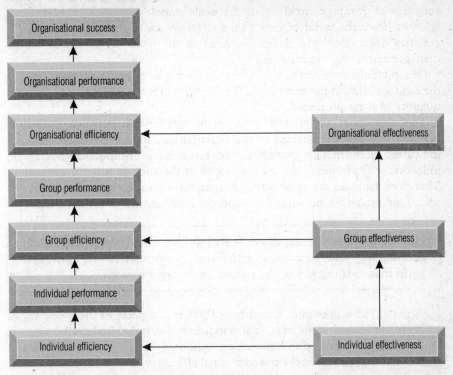

towards their work and the organisation and its goals. In other words, although the management of the organisation was doing "the right thing", they were not doing it "in the right way".

This example may also be approached from the point of view of the effectiveness of the organisation. Suppose the demand for that particular bicycle had indeed been identified, but the price was set so high that the greatest portion of the market (parents) could not afford it despite the fact that it was an example of exceptionally fine workmanship. In this case the organisation would not have been successful either, as they were not "doing the right thing" even though they were "doing it in the right way".

Figure 1.6 also shows that the efficiency of the organisation depends on group performance. Organisations consist of groups of employees, and employees are grouped on the basis of joint activities at work. For this reason organisations have different departments such as production, marketing and personnel, based on a functional approach. This implies that groups (whether departments, divisions, sections or plants) produce the organisation's product or render its service according to the demand as identified with a view to the effectiveness of the organisation. Group performance, however, is the result of group efficiency and effectiveness. Group effectiveness refers to the extent to which groups "do the right things". In this the extent to which the formal activities of groups coincide with the goals pursued by the organisation is relevant (from the point of view of the effectiveness of the organisation), i.e. are they doing the right things in terms of the goals set for them by the management of the organisation?

Group efficiency refers to the extent to which groups carry out their tasks in the right way (i.e. in the most cost-effective way). This includes the quality and quantity of work produced.

The next point to be dealt with is the relationship between individual performance and the success of the organisation. Figure 1.7 illustrates that individual performance (which is the result of individual efficiency and individual effectiveness) is the cornerstone of the success of an organisation. Therefore the main responsibility of human resources management lies in this area. One might ask how human resources management is involved here.

> Human resources management is mainly concerned with establishing, maintaining and improving individual performance, as individual performance is the key to the success of an organisation.

Figure 1.7 also illustrates a number of different aspects of the efficiency of an organisation and its success. It also indicates that individual performance is the result of the interaction between an unlimited number of the elements of both individual effectiveness and individual efficiency. From this point of view individual performance may be regarded as the cornerstone of the efficiency of an organisation and its success.

1.8.4 Conclusion
The above clearly shows that human resources management has an important role in establishing more successful organisations. Ensuring excellent individual performance largely depends on the application of sound human resources management principles. Furthermore, it is obvious that human resources management should be regarded as a scientific process to be implemented in full, and that every effort should be made to avoid focusing on only certain aspects of the process. In other words, it requires a holistic approach.

1.9 THE FOCUS AND STRUCTURE OF THIS BOOK
1.9.1 General
The focus in this book is on human resources management from two viewpoints, namely:
- A macro-approach, which means that the management of labour as a resource is dealt with in broad terms from the point of view of national human resources management in South Africa;

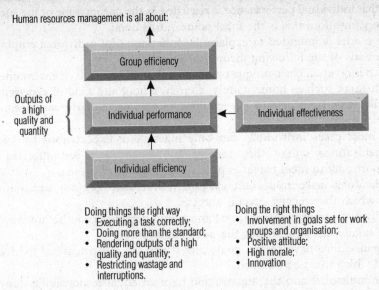

A micro-approach, where the focus primarily falls on the individual employee and the principles and techniques used by human resources management to improve the performance of individuals in organisations. Other than in this chapter, the micro-viewpoint is discussed first.

> The emphasis of this book falls mainly on the micro-component, i.e. the human being as an employee. However, as the authors' approach to this book is from a management point of view, it is essential that the macro-component, i.e. labour as a production factor, should also get its fair share. For this reason attention is paid to the nature and composition of the South African labour market and other relevant aspects. The micro-component will be discussed according to a model of the functioning of the individual as an employee within the context of the organisation, as well as the scientific application of the human resources management processes and principles that may increase or reduce the individual's functioning.

1.9.2 A human resources management model of the individual as an employee

A step-by-step human resources management model of the individual as an employee is set out in chapter 3. This is used to highlight those human resources management processes and principles that affect the individual as an employee, in an attempt to provide a visual representation of the variables that have a positive or negative effect on individual performance. The reader will recall that individual performance is regarded as the cornerstone of the success of an organisation; this is the focal point of this book.

The model is intended to explain the functioning of individual employees on the basis of the following theoretical principles;

- Each individual has a unique personality that is the result of environmental influences such as home, family, church, school and field of experience.
- Individuals have certain expectations in life, particularly with regard to their career.
- In most cases individuals can only meet these expectations by joining organisations where they receive an income and are afforded the opportunity to meet career expectations or to satisfy needs.
- Individuals make inputs (energy, expertise, knowledge) into organisations, for which they receive certain outputs.
- Individuals translate their expectations into personal goals before they join the organisation, or during the negotiation process.
- Organisations have certain goals with which the individual has to identify and which must be pursued.
- The individual and the organisation have an equal responsibility towards each other for the achievement of both sets of goals (the psychological contract).
- At work the individual functions in three environments, namely the job content, the job context, and the external environment.
- In simple terms, the job content environment is the work a person does or the job he holds. It relates to Maslow's higher-order needs and Herzberg's motivators. Theoretically this environment has the following dimensions, among others: the degree of challenge in the work, the nature of the work, utilisation of training, knowledge and skills, goals and significance of the job, job satisfaction, feedback on the execution of the task (recognition), task standards and guidelines, and so on. These are dealt with in human resources management processes such as human resources planning, recruitment, selection, training and development.
- The job context environment may be described as the task environment within which an individual functions, that is the organisation, the work group, other groups, leadership, etc., and which has an effect on individual employees' functioning within an organisation. Theoretically it relates to Herzberg's hygiene factors and Maslow's lower-order needs, and includes the following: leadership style, organisation structures and personnel policies, work conditions, service benefits, career planning, quality of work life, etc.
- The external environment represents factors outside the organisation that affect personal functioning. Theoretically this environment includes the following: the effect of technological acceleration on individual employees, the effect of social and other groups outside the organisation to which the

employee belongs, such as labour unions, on his or her participation in the organisation, the current economic climate and so on.

- According to the systems approach to organisations and the functioning of individual employees, these three environments always exert an influence on individual employees. These influences may be positive or negative.
- The individual employee constantly compares personal progress with personal goal achievement in a particular organisation, and the extent of progress determines his or her attitude towards the organisation.
- Individual employees' attitudes determine their personal functioning, i.e. it affects the way they identify with goals related to their job, their group and the formal organisation.
- The sum total of individual employee outputs forms the basis of group efficiency, which in turn is the cornerstone of group performance.
- Group performance is the basis of the efficiency of an organisation, which is directly related to the success of the organisation.

1.9.3 The structure of the book
The book is presented in five parts and 25 chapters:
Part 1: General introduction
Part 2: The provision of human resources
Part 3: The maintenance of human resources
Part 4: The development of human resources
Part 5: Human resources management in South Africa: *quo vadis?*

1.10 CONCLUSION
This chapter discussed South Africa's relative position with regard to human resources management by comparing it to that of other countries. Attention was also given to the theoretical principles, points of departure and conceptual base of this applied science. From the discussion it appears that individual employee performance is the basic building block of organisational success; this is then also the primary focal point of this book. Apart from the other relevant aspects contained in this chapter, it is essential that note should be taken of the structure and focus of the book, as this will be of help in studying and understanding it.

Questions
1. Explain the difference between human resources management and personnel management.
2. Draw an organisational chart of an organisation that you know of. Use this chart to explain the different authority relationships that the human resources department has with the rest of the organisation.
3. Write an essay to demonstrate the critical relationship between strategic planning and efficient human resources management.
4. Write an essay (± 500 words) on the individual employee as the basic cornerstone of success in an organisation.

Sources

Beer, M. 1980. *Organization change and development: a systems view.* Goodyear, Santa Monica, California.

Gavelli, S. 1992, 1993. *World competitiveness report.* EMF Foundation, Geneva, Switzerland.

Graham, H.T. & Bennett, R. 1993. *Human resources management.* M & E Handbook Series, London.

Hall, D.T. & Goodale, J.G. 1986. *Human resources management: strategy, design and implementation.* Scott, Foresman, Glenview, Illinois.

Holley, W.H. & Jennings, K.M. 1983, 1987. *Personnel management: functions and issues.* Dryden, New York.

Schein, F.H. 1980. *Organizational psychology.* Prentice-Hall, Englewood Cliffs, New Jersey.

Valchanges in Gavelli, S. 1992, 1993. *World competitiveness report.* EMF Foundation, Geneva, Switzerland.

Wrighton, P. 1993. Reply to Stephane Gavelli's speech about South Africa's competitiveness. Sandton Sun, March.

Chapter 2

Human resources management: historical development and *status quo* in South Africa

P.S. van Dyk

STUDY OBJECTIVES

After studying this chapter, you should be able to:
- Describe the historical course of development of human resources management;
- Motivate in a simple manner the reason for the existence of the Institute of Personnel Management;
- Explain in detail the role and objectives of the Board for Personnel Practice;
- Pragmatically explain the behavioural code for personnel practitioners.

2.1 INTRODUCTION

In informed circles, it is often stated that problems with people as employees began just before the Industrial Revolution, when cottage industries became so large that owners were obliged to employ "strange" people in addition to family members. This was the beginning of the problem with which contemporary managers still have to contend today, i.e. *how does an employer or manager motivate an employee or subordinate to perform in an optimal manner?*

In this chapter, brief attention is given to:
- An historical perspective of the course of development of the applied behavioural science of human resources management;
- The *status quo* of human resources management in South Africa.

The aim of this chapter is to orientate the newcomer to human resources management with regard to the origin, development, application and career practices in South Africa of this applied behavioural science.

> REMEMBER:
> South Africa's competitive factor "people" was rated 15th among the 15 Group II countries by the WCR in 1992.

2.2 THE END OF THE PREVIOUS CENTURY

At the end of the previous century, there was a large-scale influx of workers to the manufacturing industry. This forced "management" to decide on some management practice to accommodate the new generation of "employees".

In this case, the human resources managemement question (Bendix 1956:254) dealt with the following:

- The relative position of management as compared with employees;
- The obligations of management towards employees.

The general management practice during this period was based on the principle of "social Darwinism", i.e.: *survival of the fittest*.

The application of this scientific principle to human resources management amounted to the following:

. . . the weak (the employees) were thought to have lost the struggle for dominance and so were expected to submit to the successful competitors (the managers).

This management philosophy, which was associated with strict religious convictions, is illustrated by the following utterance (Litwack 1962:67):

The rights and interests of human labouring man will be protected and cared for, not by labour agitators, but by the Christian men to whom God in his infinite wisdom has given the control of the property interests of the country.

This management philosophy was strengthened by state and judicial practices which amounted to the business world of the time being responsible for its own welfare.

Despite the above, there was no consensus among the management cadre of organisations about the best management philosophy regarding human resources management practice. In fact, there were two dominant approaches:

- The commodity approach
- The so-called paternalistic or social welfare approach.

Litwack (1962:64) reports the following in this regard:

Under the commodity approach, employees represented a factor of production to be performed as cheaply as possible and discarded when no longer useful. The human factor was at best irrelevant in employment decisions. Some employers, for example, viewed employees' desire for education as harmful, spoiling these people for the realities of hard work.

The paternalistic or social welfare approach was based on strong moral grounds, closely linked to social Darwinism. Many organisations employed so-called "welfare secretaries". Paternalism or fatherly protection of employees took the form of company services, schools, shops and company housing. It has been said that this paternalistic approach was used to manipulate employees through kindness. Another opinion is that a paternalistic policy was followed because employers thought that employees could not think for themselves, and were unable to plan for the future and to arrange their own affairs.

With regard to the welfare function, Rowntree (Farnham 1990:21) has the following to say:

As representatives of the employees it is the duty of the social helpers to be constantly in touch with them, to gain their confidence, to voice any grievances they may have either individually or collectively, to give effect to any reasonable desire they may show for recreative clubs, educational classes, etc. and to give advice in matters concerning them personally.

During the period 1910 to 1930 (Holley and Jennings 1987:27), two movements arose which began to bring employers to the realisation that employees are people with unique capabilities. The two movements can be described as the psychological reform approach and the effectiveness approach.

The *psychological reform approach* amounts to the fact that, in as far as is possible, every person wants to be a normal human being, but is at the same time also an employee. It was realised that people have certain needs with regard to family, work and justice, and that the human being is creative. Successful managers realised that workers are complicated beings as a result of their intelligence and thus susceptible to stress in the work environment.

The *effectiveness approach* is the second approach of this era, which motivated management to realise that the employee is a unique being. One distinctive development that arose from this movement is Taylor's well-known scientific management approach. Taylor stated that, if an employee is not performing well, this was not the employee's fault but that of management. In 1937, Taylor published his famous book, *The principles of scientific management*.

The publicity obtained with the abovementioned two approaches stimulated research with regard to personnel affairs. Among other things, research was conducted about subjects such as personnel services, recruitment and selection, training, salaries and wages. Two professional personnel journals were also published in this era: *Personnel* and *Journal of Personnel Research*. Many of the research articles that appeared in these journals dealt with the association between employee characteristics and work performance. Research dealt with aspects such as hair colour, weight and height, weight profiles, sex, marital status, and ethnic and religious background. Personnel departments were established in about 1912.

The outbreak of the First World War emphasised the importance of the personnel function as an essential organisational activity. The demand for products increased tremendously. Many employees were drafted into the armed forces, which led to the remaining employees getting far more attention from the management cadre. People as employees became so important for the company that legislation was introduced in the USA to force companies to establish personnel departments to ensure efficient functioning in the production of weaponry and implements of war.

Furthermore, the American government established a committee called "Committee on Classification of Personnel" to determine soldiers' capabilities and to allocate them in accordance with the job requirements of the various military tasks. The personnel techniques that arose from this exercise were later adapted for industry. These wartime efforts also changed the dominant management philosophy with regard to the personnel function.

During the build-up to the Second World War, personnel management took another leap forward with its establishment as a full-fledged organisational function.

Niven in Farnham (1990:23) defines personnel management in this era as follows:

Personnel management is that part of the management function which is primarily concerned with the human relationships within an organisation. Its objective is the maintenance of these relationships on a basis which, by consideration of the well-being of the individual, enables all these engaged in the undertaking to make their maximum personal contribution to the effective working of that undertaking.

Niven uses the word "undertaking" when referring to a company or organisation, and his reference to "effective working" is derived from the building blocks of organisational success discussed in chapter 1.

2.3 HUMAN RESOURCES MANAGEMENT AS A PROFESSION
2.3.1 General
Human resources management as a functional area within the management sciences is a relatively new discipline. The first professional personnel organisation, the Boston Managers' Association, was founded in 1912 (Gerber 1985:1). The first manual on the subject, *Personnel administration* by O. Tead and H.C. Metcalf, appeared in 1920. In the USA, human resources management was only recognised as a profession in 1946—if obtaining a professional diploma or degree is a valid measure—when the School of Industrial and Labor Relations at the University of Cornell awarded the first personnel diploma.

In Germany, the University of Stuttgart began to offer human resources management as a subject in 1946. The University of South Africa (UNISA) has been offering Business Economics as a subject for the BCom degree since 1955 and, among other things, this subject covers human resources management. The Institute of Personnel Management was founded in 1946 as a professional body for human resources managers in South Africa.

Although human resources management has only been formally recognised as an independent discipline for a relatively short time, its roots go back as far as 1700 BC. The Babylonian Hammurabi Code laid down 285 laws which, to a large extent, concur with certain management practices still valid today. These laws made provision for the family and for labour. Even the custom of sealing a legal contract with an official seal dates from this period. After the Second World War, personnel or human resources management increased in importance.

This already formed the basis for minimum wages and incentive wage plans. The first principles of modern industrial training in apprenticeship programmes and of employee benefit plans originated during this era.

2.3.2 The *status quo* of human resources management in South Africa

The current situation regarding human resources management in South Africa will now be examined.

2.3.2.1 *The Institute of Personnel Management of Southern Africa*

The information in this section is reproduced with the permission of IPM (SA).

The IPM is an organisation dedicated to the human resources profession and is committed to the effective management and development of human potential, in accordance with its values statement.

It provides effective leadership, appropriate knowledge and technology and the opportunity to network.

Effectiveness is measured by: quality of output, growth of and participation by its membership and its contribution to the nation.

Hence IPM aims to influence and assist in the development and utilisation of human resources in South Africa in the interests of the South African community as a whole, including the promotion and development of the highest standards of competence and ethical conduct amongst the members of the Institute.

To achieve the above, the goals of IPM include:

- To promote the professional development of members and other interested persons.
- To actively cooperate and liaise with organisations on relevant human resources issues and with professional human resources management locally and internationally.
- To play a leading role in the field of promoting effective affirmative action strategies.
- To supply specialised, formal and professional training to members and to see that provision is made for professional education.
- To provide and disseminate specific, applicable and current information on developments and trends in the field of human resources management and in the Institute.

- To assist the human resources practitioner and profession in playing a strategic role in the areas of social investment, quality of work life, unemployment, etc.
- To provide an appropriate infrastructure that includes a sound organisational structure and a healthy financial resource base to implement and manage the above goals.

2.3.2.2 Membership categories and numbers

The membership of the IPM can be subdivided into two main categories: members with voting rights and members without voting rights.

- Members with voting rights consist of the following sub-categories:
  — Honorary fellows numbering 47;
  — Fellows numbering 58;
  — Members numbering 6 633;
  — Associates numbering 219.
- Members without voting rights are the following:
  — Students;
  — Affiliates;
  — Group affiliates.

Allocation to a specific category or sub-category is determined by qualifications and experience.

2.3.3 The South African Board for Personnel Practice

2.3.3.1 General

The South African Board for Personnel Practice was established on 15 October 1982, but restructured in 1993. The Board serves as an instrument of the IPM to place professional practitioners of human resources management in organisations on a professional footing and to expand their sphere of influence in organisations (South African Board for Personnel Practice 1993:1).

The mission of the Board appears in the accompanying box:

Mission

To establish, conduct and maintain a high standard of professionalism and ethical behaviour in personnel practice.

The philosophy that underlies the reason for the existence of the Board is to enable those involved in personnel practice to make a meaningful contribution:

- To the organisation, its management and utilisation of human resources;
- To the individual, in the fulfilment of his or her potential;
- To the broader society, in its striving for a better quality of life.

The Board follows this declared strategy:

To promote, guide and influence the development of the personnel profession; to set standards of competence for the education, training and conduct of those who practise the profession; to give the parties involved advice about the development and acquisition of such skills; and to evaluate their attainment.

The Board formulates its objectives as follows:

- To promote the profession of personnel practice in South Africa;
- To promote the standard of education and training of persons in personnel practice and to give recognition to the education and training that is a prerequisite for registration in terms of the charter;
- To promote liaison in the fields of education and training;
- To advise the Minister of Manpower, or any other person, on any matters within the framework of the charter;
- To communicate to the Minister of Manpower information with regard to matters of public interest that has been acquired by the Board in the execution of its functions in terms of the charter;
- To exercise control over all matters regarding the standard of the professional conduct of persons in personnel practice, who are voluntarily registered in terms of the Board's charter.

Every profession is characterised by a special behavioural code for its members. Personnel managers are no exception; the behavioural code of the Board for Personnel Practice is as follows.

A registered person shall:

- As far as responsibility to his or her employer, employee, client and profession is concerned, place public interest first, at the service of society;
- Behave in such a way that the dignity, esteem and good name of the profession is honoured;
- Carry out his or her duty towards the employer, employee or client to the best of his or her abilities;
- Not accept work for which he or she is inadequately trained or has insufficient experience;
- Not recruit or attract professional employment in an improper manner;
- Not advertise professional services in a self-praising manner or in any other way that undermines the dignity of the profession;
- Not compete for work in an unethical manner;
- Neither maliciously nor recklessly, whether directly or indirectly, damage the good name, prospects or interests of any other person or organisation;
- Not make public any information regarding any person or organisation which should not be made public and which is encountered when practising the profession. (In a court of law, professional secrecy will only be violated under protest in accordance with a directive from the presiding officer of the court);
- At all times and under all circumstances that affect personnel practice, act in accordance with the regulations as prescribed by the Board.

37

2.3.3.2 Registration categories

In terms of the Board's charter, a person is registered on one of the following levels:

- Personnel practitioner (general or specialist);
- Associate personnel practitioner (general or specialist);
- Candidate personnel practitioner;
- Candidate associate personnel practitioner.

The registration requirements for the abovementioned levels are as follows:

- Personnel practitioner: a four-year qualification, accredited by the Board, in a discipline or disciplines relevant to the field of personnel practice, plus two years practical training in and experience of personnel work as a registered candidate under supervision of an approved mentor who will endorse the final application for registration (a candidateship); *or* another combination of appropriate qualifications and relevant practical training that is regarded as being of an equal standard by the Board, and that is acceptable to the Board. Under certain circumstances, the Board may give permission for a Board examination to be taken.
- Associate personnel practitioner: a three-year qualification after matric, accredited by the Board, in a discipline or disciplines relevant to the field of personnel practice, plus two years practical training in and experience of personnel work as a registered candidate under supervision of an approved mentor who will endorse the final application for registration (a candidateship); *or* another combination of appropriate qualifications and relevant practical training that is acceptable to the Board.
- Candidate personnel practitioner or candidate associate personnel practitioner: a candidateship programme of two years duration, the aim of which is to promote and structure the development of prospective professional personnel experts. The practical experience thus acquired by the individual is evaluated by a mentor and by the Board in the light of registration requirements set by the Board.

The following human resources functions are applicable to registration in any of the above categories:

- Human resources provision: this includes human resources planning, recruitment, selection, placement, transfers, promotions and dismissals.
- Training and development: this includes induction, training, management development and career planning.
- Human resources utilisation: this includes performance appraisal, productivity and motivation.
- Industrial welfare: this includes safety, health, welfare services, housing, recreation and advice.
- Organisational development: this includes organisational structure, job design and organisational personnel planning.
- Industrial relations: this includes communication, negotiation, consultation, agreements, grievances and disciplinary procedures.

- Remuneration: this includes job analysis, job evaluation, salary and wage structuring, fringe benefit schemes and incentive systems.
- Administration: this includes personnel records, statistics about personnel and information processing.
- Research: this includes the analysis of information, systems development, investigations, surveys and applied personnel research.
- Management: this includes planning, organising, directing and controlling the personnel function and coordination with other functions.

More information can be obtained at the address in the accompanying box.

The Registrar
South African Board for Personnel Practice
P.O. Box 31390
BRAAMFONTEIN 2017

Telephone (011) 642-7272

2.4 CONCLUSION

The above gives a brief historical overview of the course of development of human resources management. Today the human resources management function is certainly one of the most essential functions for South African organisations for placing the new South Africa on a winning road.

Questions

1. Describe the course of development of human resources management in not more than 500 words.
2. Motivate why it is essential to professionalise the human resources profession.
3. What guidelines will you take into account before approaching a human resources consultant for advice?

Sources

Bendix, R. 1956. *Work and authority in industry.* University of California Press, Berkeley.
Farnham, D. 1990. *Personnel in context.* Wimbledon, London.
Gerber, P.D. 1985. "Mannekragbestuurstegnieke in perspektief". Unpublished inaugural speech. UNISA.
Holley, W.H. & Jennings, K.M. 1987. *Personnel/human resources management: contributions and activities.* Dryden Press, Chicago & New York.
IPM (Institute for Personnel Management of Southern Africa). Brochure, Johannesburg.
Litwack, L. 1962. *The American labor movement.* Prentice-Hall, Englewood Cliffs, New Jersey.
South African Board for Personnel Practice 1993. *Bekendstelling van die Raad se riglyne vir registrasie.* Johannesburg.

Chapter 3

A systems approach to human resources management

P.S. van Dyk

STUDY OBJECTIVES

After studying this chapter, you should be able to:

- Give a schematic explanation of the systems approach to the management of an organisation;
- Theoretically describe the systems approach to human resources management;
- Explain the functioning of the employee as a system in its own right;
- Describe the environments within which individuals find themselves as employees in organisations;
- List the variables that act on the employee from various environments;
- Schematically set out the model for studying this book.

3.1 INTRODUCTION

We shall discuss the systems approach to human resources management in broad terms in this chapter. Attention will first be given to the definition of a system, and to the characteristics of a system. Then reasons will be provided as to why an organisation may be regarded as an open system. The model that is the focal point of this book will be provided against this background. We shall use this model as a point of departure for a discussion on the individual employee as a system in its own right. This will be followed by a brief discussion on human resources management processes affecting individual employees. The effect of these human resources management processes on individual employees will be explained throughout in terms of the model.

3.2 THE SYSTEMS APPROACH

The question arises: "What is a system?" A system is simply a number of interdependent components that form a whole and work together with a view to attaining a common goal. Thus, for example, you as a person are also a system in your own right (a biological system) and you come into daily contact with various types of systems:

- When you travel to work in the morning by car, bus or train, you are part of a mechanical system;
- When you are at work, you are in a social system;
- When you come home in the evenings, you are in a micro-social economic system, i.e. your family.

In the literature, a distinction is made between a closed and an open system. A system is **closed** when it is self-sustaining and independent of external stimuli or input. An example is the development of a test-tube baby from conception (fertilisation) until it is implanted in the womb of a woman. An **open** system, on the other hand, requires certain input or stimuli from elsewhere, known in technical terms as the environment. According to Cronje *et al.* (1994:28), a system is open if:

- It is dependent on the environment in which it operates;
- The environment depends on it;
- There is interaction between the system and the environment.

Diagrammatically, an open system can be represented as in figure 3.1.

FIGURE 3.1: The basic elements of a system

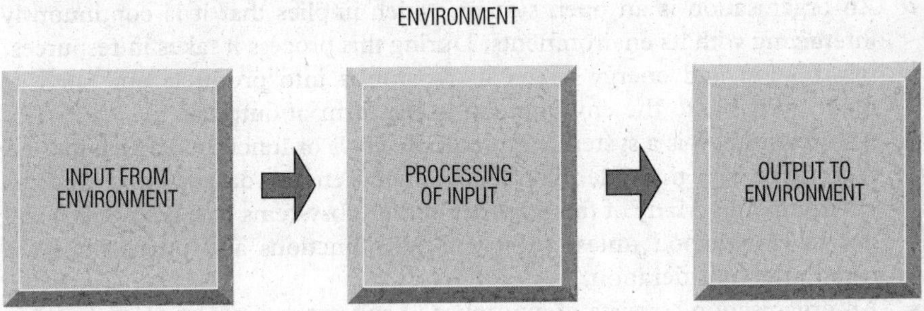

ENVIRONMENT

INPUT FROM ENVIRONMENT → PROCESSING OF INPUT → OUTPUT TO ENVIRONMENT

Source: Cronje *et al.* (1994:30)

The system takes *inputs* from its environment (which represents a larger system), processes them and returns them to the environment in another form as output.

3.2.1 The most important characteristics of a system

Most authors identify the general characteristics in their work on the systems approach to organisations. Characteristics discussed in this section are largely based on the work of Katz and Kahn (1966), who are regarded as pioneers in this field.

- Energy intake: The first characteristic of an open system is that an organisation as a system is dependent on the intake of energy to activate the functioning process. Energy includes resources and information. Energy intake may also be described as the input process.
- Throughput process: All open systems transform the energy at their disposal by means of some throughput system. This throughput process differs from one organisation to the next, but it remains essential for the functioning of a system.
- Output process: Each open system has an output process for the very reason that it has an input process and a throughput process. Output may be regarded as the dependent variable in a system. Outputs usually take the form of finished products, services, and so on.
- A system as a cycle of events: The product released by means of the output process provides a source of energy for the repetition of the cycle of events. In a profit-seeking organisation making use of resources to produce a product, monetary returns are used to procure more resources for a repetition of the process.
- Mutual dependence: The components of a system are dependent on one another. If a change should take place in one part of the system, this will influence all the other components of the system, either directly or indirectly.

3.2.2 The organisation as an open system
Edgar Schein (1980:228–29) defines an open system as follows:
- An organisation is an open system, which implies that it is continuously interacting with its environments. During this process it takes in resources, information and energy which it transforms into products and services made available to the environment in the form of outputs.
- An organisation is a system with multiple goals or functions, which implies that there are multiple interactions between an organisation and its environments. Many of the activities of the subsystems (see next point) will not be understood unless these multiple functions and interactions are taken into consideration.
- An organisation consists of a number of subsystems in a state of dynamic interaction. It is becoming increasingly important to analyse the behaviour (functioning) of these subsystems when focusing on the concept of the organisation, instead of describing individual behaviour.
- Change in one subsystem is followed by changes in other subsystems because the subsystems in an organisation are interdependent.
- An organisation functions in a dynamic environment which consists of other subsystems differing in scope. The environment makes certain demands on an organisation, which inhibit it in certain respects. Therefore thorough investigation of environmental problems and restrictions is essential to understand the overall functioning of an organisation.

- The multiple connections between an organisation and its environments complicate the delimitation of the boundaries of an organisation.

In the light of this, the organisation can be represented as an open system as shown in figure 3.2.

Figure 3.2 shows the organisation from a systems perspective on the basis of the principles of organisational success discussed in chapter 1. The reason for the existence of the organisation lies in the needs present in the organisation's external environment. For this reason it is essential that the organisation should undertake environmental scanning to identify *opportunities* and *threats* in its external environment and to formulate its strategy accordingly. Even if an organisation identifies its needs, it will not automatically be successful, unless the external infrastructure is such that it favours the satisfaction of needs (or goal achievement).

> There is a great need for water to start agricultural production in the Sahara desert. However, there is no external infrastructure at all. Such an attempt would thus be doomed to failure from the start.

The external infrastructure of each organisation is unique, as is the nature of its activities. These aspects, which may be regarded as conditions for success and can be classified as external success factors, are the inputs that activate the functioning of the organisation.

As discussed in chapter 1, organisational efficiency refers to the internal functioning of an organisation, and according to Beer there must be an optimal fit between the external environment and the internal components of the organisation as a system. The present authors refer to the internal components as the *internal infrastructure* that is used in the organisation's transformation process to render desirable output. They may also be regarded as internal success factors or prerequisites for efficiency.

As far as organisational success is concerned, a distinction must be made between short-, medium- and long-term success. This distinction will become clear during the course of the discussion below.

It was mentioned elsewhere that, according to the systems approach, an organisation strives for multiple objectives. The writers are of the opinion that these objectives can be divided into two main categories, i.e. tangible outputs and non-tangible outputs. The former refers to what organisations primarily pursue, i.e. profits, return on investment and an increased market share, while non-tangible outputs generally refer to the quality of work-life of the organisation's worker corps. This includes aspects such as morale, grievances and job satisfaction.

For organisational success, management should set measurable objectives for those outputs and the attainment thereof should be measured by a set performance standard.

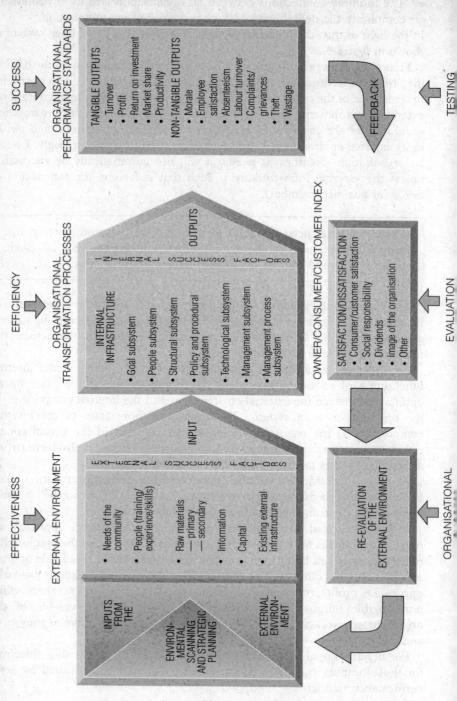

FIGURE 3.2: The systems approach and organisational success

SUCCESS

ORGANISATIONAL PERFORMANCE STANDARDS

TANGIBLE OUTPUTS
- Turnover
- Profit
- Return on investment
- Market share
- Productivity

NON-TANGIBLE OUTPUTS
- Morale
- Employee satisfaction
- Absenteeism
- Labour turnover
- Complaints/ grievances
- Theft
- Wastage

FEEDBACK

TESTING

EFFICIENCY

ORGANISATIONAL TRANSFORMATION PROCESSES

INTERNAL INFRASTRUCTURE
- Goal subsystem
- People subsystem
- Structural subsystem
- Policy and procedural subsystem
- Technological subsystem
- Management subsystem
- Management process subsystem

INTERNAL SUCCESS FACTORS OUTPUTS

OWNER/CONSUMER/CUSTOMER INDEX

SATISFACTION/DISSATISFACTION
- Consumer/customer satisfaction
- Social responsibility
- Dividends
- Image of the organisation
- Other

EVALUATION

EFFECTIVENESS

EXTERNAL ENVIRONMENT

- Needs of the community
- People (training/ experience/skills)
- Raw materials
  — primary
  — secondary
- Information
- Capital
- Existing external infrastructure

EXTERNAL SUCCESS FACTORS INPUT

INPUTS FROM THE

ENVIRON- MENTAL SCANNING AND STRATEGIC PLANNING

EXTERNAL ENVIRON- MENT

RE-EVALUATION OF THE EXTERNAL ENVIRONMENT

ORGANISATIONAL

44

The dilemma is that management is generally orientated towards the attainment of tangible outputs, and if it is kept in mind that tangible outputs are produced by the people in the organisation (who represent non-tangible outputs), goal achievement generally takes place at the cost of the human element.

An organisation that pursues tangible outputs at the cost of the human element (quality of work-life), will only be successful in the short term, as human resources, particularly in modern organisations, do not tolerate exploitation.

An organisation will be successful in the medium term if there is a balance between management's focus on both types of outputs.

An organisation will only be successful in the long term if the owners, consumers and other stake-holders are consistently satisfied with the outcomes such as dividends and product reliability, which they receive from the organisation.

This double feedback loop, i.e. performance standards and owner/consumer satisfaction, is known in contemporary management as the cybernetic principle, which is a characteristic of the organisation as a social system. The aforementioned thus has important implications for human resources management and organisational success.

3.2.3 Conclusion

The above clearly demonstrates the necessity for an understanding of a system and its characteristics. An organisation must be managed in accordance with the characteristics of the systems approach if it is to be successful. The organisation as such consists of a number of subsystems including human resources management as a functional subsystem. Furthermore, an organisation consists of other types of subsystems such as groups and individuals. The individual may be regarded as the smallest subsystem within the organisation.

3.3 A SYSTEMS MODEL FOR STUDYING HUMAN RESOURCES MANAGEMENT

3.3.1 General

A systems model (see figure 3.3) is presented in this section and may be used for reference when studying the information in this book. This model has two main purposes:

- In the first place it focuses on the employee as a subsystem within the organisation as a system, with specific reference to the inputs which an employee brings into an organisation, the throughput process, and the outputs produced by employees. This topic is discussed at length in paragraph 3.3.2.

- In the second place it focuses on those human resources management processes aimed at the management, maintenance and development of an employee as a subsystem within an organisation. The purpose of these human resources management processes is to obtain optimal utilisation of the employee, as well as optimal outputs. There is a detailed discussion of this topic in paragraph 3.3.3. This also provides the reader with a frame of reference when studying the information in this book.

3.3.2 The employee as a subsystem within the organisation

The individual employee is the smallest system within the organisation as a system. As can be deduced from the systems approach to organisations, there is a critical relationship between inputs, outputs and throughputs in the organisation. As is the case with an organisation, individuals as a system also have certain inputs with which they join an organisation and which they release as long as they are part of the organisation. These inputs are released mainly during the throughput phase where they are utilised and transformed by general and human resources management processes. The quality of application of these processes determines the individual employee's outputs. These phenomena will become clearer during the course of this discussion.

3.3.2.1 *The input process of individual employee functioning within the organisation*

The input process of individual functioning is discussed at length in chapter 4, but a few clarifying remarks are deemed necessary at this stage:
- Each employee has a unique personality, and employee's personalities differ from one another. These differences mean that employees are not the same and do not necessarily experience the same needs at the same times. An employee's personality is the result of numerous variables which have affected him or her since birth. These variables include aspects such as the personal environment in which the child grew up, the culture to which it was exposed, and its needs which, in turn, are the result of numerous other factors. (This topic is discussed in detail in the next chapter.)
- Individuals' personality and needs constitute the basis of their expectations of their job and of life in general. Because individuals have different personalities they also have different expectations in life. This may be observed in the way in which individuals pursue their personal goals in an organisation.
- Individuals set certain personal goals they wish to achieve in life, on the basis of their unique personalities, needs and expectations. To satisfy these needs and expectations and achieve these goals, individuals have to work and earn money. Therefore individuals join organisations with the sole purpose of achieving their personal goals, as this results in need satisfaction. Individuals' personal goals, in turn, motivate them to behave in certain

ways in the organisation. This behaviour is personal and is aimed at satisfying individuals' own needs and goals, irrespective of the group with which they identify. Therefore individuals continuously interact with the organisation where they are employed in order to achieve their personal goals.

- Before an individual joins an organisation, a psychological negotiation process takes place, which takes the form of a psychological contract between the individual and the organisation. During this negotiation process, the individual states his or her expectations and personal goals, and the organisation similarly states its expectations and goals. If this negotiation process results in an agreement, the individual is employed and joins the organisation as an employee. (This topic is discussed in detail in chapter 4.)

An employee's personal goals, together with his or her aptitude, qualifications, ability, experience and potential, constitute the input process of individual functioning within the context of the organisation. This input phase is indicated on the left-hand side of the model in figure 3.3.

3.3.2.2 The throughput process of individual employee functioning within the organisation

We may say that individuals with unique personalities join organisations with certain expectations, and formulate personal goals on the basis of a negotiation process resulting in a psychological contract. They try to achieve their personal goals while also pursuing the goals of the organisation.

There are three environments that exert an influence on employee functioning within the organisation. These environments are the job content environment, the job context environment and the external environment.

(a) The job content environment

The job content environment may also be referred to as the psychological work environment, and may thus be regarded as the most significant environment in terms of its relation to individual performance as the basic cornerstone of success in the organisation. The job content environment is related to the psychological satisfaction experienced by the employee while doing the job for which he or she applied and was appointed. This is related to man's cognitive, affective and conative functions. The *cognitive* function refers to the stimulus value of the job, that is the extent to which it creates interest. The *affective* function refers to the emotional aspect, the employee's feeling/ attitude/inclination towards the job as such. The *conative* function refers to the volition aspect of man. It therefore seems that the job content environment refers to interpersonal job satisfaction.

Different authors use different terms for these concepts; however, what is important is that they concur to a large extent on the elements present in the job content environment and exerting an influence on the employee's inclination to perform.

One definition that may be closely related to what we term the job content environment, concerns Herzberg's so-called motivators. Hodgetts (1979:273) summarises this as follows:

Herzberg found that factors relating to the job itself can have a positive effect on job satisfaction and result in increased output. He called these motivators or satisfiers and identified them as the work itself, recognition, advancement, the possibility of growth, responsibility, and achievement.

Ford's (1969:124) viewpoint should also be mentioned in this respect. He emphasises job characteristics rather than individual differences: jobs with opportunities for achievement, recognition, responsibility, promotion and growth in competence are jobs that will promote motivation and job satisfaction. Turner and Lawrence (in Wanous 1974:616) identify six attributes that jobs need to have (job content environment), namely variety, autonomy, compulsory and optional interaction, required knowledge and skills, and responsibility.

In view of the aforementioned, an employee's job content environment consists of five important elements, i.e. the nature of the job, job guidelines and goals, utilisation, status and recognition, and development. These elements will now be briefly discussed:

- *Nature of the job:* The nature of the job means what the job entails. Does it afford the employee the opportunity to utilise his or her abilities to their full potential? Does the employee find the opportunity for self-actualisation in the job? Does he or she have the opportunity to be creative and use initiative? Is the job interesting and in line with what he or she wants to do? Is there the opportunity for independent decision making? Does the job offer variety? The human resources management processes discussed in paragraph 3.3.3 must address these questions if the organisation is to ensure motivated employee behaviour.

- *Job guidelines and goals:* This element entails directing an employee's work behaviour in accordance with the goals of the organisation. An important element often neglected is linking job goals to the goals of the organisation. Human resources management processes related to the job content environment need to answer the following questions: Do employees know what they have to do? Do they know how to do it? Do they know why they are doing it? Is there a logical relation between what employees do and the goals of the organisation? Do employees know what is expected of them? Do they know what they are accountable for and what standards they are to maintain? Job guidelines and goals not only enable the employee to assess his or her activities within the functioning of the organisation, but they also spell out how he or she should attempt to achieve personal goals.

- *Utilisation:* Vroom (1966:143) states that the self-actualisation need identified by Maslow is represented by the opportunity people are given to utilise their capabilities. We distinguish between qualitative and quantitative utilisation, however. *Quantitative utilisation* refers to the amount of time an employee actually spends on the job daily, whereas *qualitative utilisation* refers to the utilisation of an employee's potential such as intelligence, skills and qualifications. Over- and under-utilisation may occur in both instances. Questions to be addressed in this respect in order to ensure optimal employee functioning are: Are employees busy every day all day? Is the extent of an employee's job such that he or she can cope with what has to be done? Are employees utilised according to their abilities, qualifications, experience and training?

- *Status and recognition:* There is a causal relation between the type of job an employee has and the status enjoyed. Vroom (1966:41) describes it as follows:

  The job is a description or a tag which marks the person, both at his place of employment and in the world outside.

  Status in this respect refers to the job content status, which means the relative status value linked to a job within a specific organisation by the organisation itself and by other employees of the organisation. *Recognition* in this respect comes from two sources. Firstly it refers to the respect an employee enjoys among colleagues at the organisation, which is the result of the status value of the job, and secondly it is the recognition an organisation affords an employee for good performance. The most critical question to be addressed by human resources management processes in this respect, is whether employees are proud of their jobs, as this is the best indication of the status and recognition they themselves give to the job.

- *Development:* Modern work life is characterised by technological and other changes placing increasing demands and pressure on employees. When employees are unable to meet changed job expectations/ requirements, they become superfluous and redundant. In this respect development refers to development possibilities within a job/position for a specific employee, with reference to the employee's personal growth and personal goals. In our opinion, development has a number of dimensions applicable to any work situation within any organisation. Human resources management processes must assess the opportunities for training and development, whether the training offered is applicable to the execution of tasks and whether the work an employee is doing at present is preparing him or her for a higher position; i.e. whether there is career preparation.

Individual employee performance is the cornerstone of success in an organisation and takes place mainly in carrying out tasks given by the organisation. The extent to which employees experience psychological or interpersonal job satisfaction within the job content environment determines to a large extent the quality and quantity of these employees' outputs.

49

(b) The job context environment

The second environment that has an extremely important influence on the throughput process is the employee's job context environment within the organisation. This environment contains two important factors:

- The leadership element in the job context environment consists of the employee's superiors, and the management cadre within the organisation. The leadership element determines numerous aspects of the job content, for example the nature of the job. Therefore the leadership element has a significant effect on the employee's job content environment.
- Those elements that Herzberg terms the hygiene factors (discussed in detail in chapter 16) are primarily satisfiers of lower order needs that include physiological, safety and social needs. According to Herzberg, examples of hygiene factors are salaries, promotion policy and fringe benefits. These hygiene factors are an essential prerequisite for motivation to pursue the goals of the organisation, mainly because they are related to job content factors that can only come into prominence once job context aspects are such that lower order needs are reasonably satisfied, so that the employee will look for the opportunity to satisfy his or her higher order needs within the job.

We regard all the influences exerted on an employee because of his or her presence in the organisation, with the exception of the job content and external influences, as job context influences affecting the employee in the job context environment. Porter *et al.* (1975:211) emphasise the significance of these influences on individual employee behaviour as follows:

Among the many influences on the work behavior of individuals in organizational settings, none is more important or more pervasive than the design of the organization itself. By "organization design" we mean primarily the particular arrangements of the structural factors that constitute the basic form and nature of the organization.

In our opinion the job context environment refers to the interpersonal as well as the intragroup job satisfaction individual employees experience because of their membership of an organisation. An employee derives interpersonal job satisfaction through interaction with peers, superiors, subordinates and clients in the execution of the job. Schein (1980:88) calls this an employee's interaction context. In other words, interpersonal job satisfaction refers to satisfaction experienced by an employee within the context of the formal organisation, i.e. within the formal execution of his or her tasks.

Intragroup satisfaction refers to the satisfaction an employee experiences through membership of informal groups.

Because humans are social beings, they will always try to establish informal interaction. Within the context of Maslow's theory, man is a social being and needs to belong to a group and be accepted by the group. When a social need becomes dominant, a person will strive to establish favourable relationships with other persons. The need for social interaction may be satisfied in the work situation to a large extent, but it is very difficult to develop strategies that would translate this need into an incentive for improved performance.

We regard the following elements that can have either a positive or a negative effect on the individual employee's functioning and his or her inclination to perform as important within the job context environment: organisational climate, management philosophy, leadership style, structure and personnel policy, working conditions and interpersonal and group relations.

- *Organisational culture:* We define the concept of organisational culture simply as "the manner in which things are done in the organisation". It is also known as the personality of the organisation. Irrespective of what it is called, the culture of an organisation develops over time and employees are often not even aware of its existence. Organisational culture is, however, of particular importance to management because it helps them understand how employees feel about their work.

  Culture involves general assumptions about the manner in which work should be done, appropriate goals for the organisation as a whole and for departments within the organisation, and personal goals for employees. It is particularly the latter that makes the nature of the psychological contract (discussed in chapter 4) of special importance in the pursuit of organisational success.

- *Organisational climate:* In our opinion, organisational climate is an all-encompassing concept that could be regarded as the result of all the elements contained in the job context environment. For example, the climate within a specific organisation is the result of the management philosophy of that organisation as shown in the style of management practised in the organisation. In this respect human resources management processes should be directed at monitoring the outputs of the organisation such as labour turnover, absenteeism, grievances, complaints and productivity, as there is a correlation between these variables and organisational climate.

- *Management philosophy:* The origin of management philosophy lies in the assumptions people make in respect of others, and the way in which they perceive and interact with others. Irrespective of whether they are aware of it or not, people's social behaviour is based on the way in which they believe other people behave. Managers as human beings do not differ from other human beings. All managers direct their behaviour and actions according to the way they believe others (employees) behave. Human resources management processes must use management and organisational development to determine the prevailing management philosophy and its effect on the work behaviour of the worker corps, and to change this philosophy if necessary.

- *Leadership style:* In our opinion, leadership style is the way in which management philosophy manifests itself in practice. Huse and Bodich

(1977:482) emphasise the important relation between leadership style and employee outputs:

> There is no doubt that managerial leadership and supervision have an important impact on the motivation, commitment, adaptability and satisfaction of employees.

Leadership is discussed at length in chapter 17. The human resources manager must ensure that the leadership of the management cadre in the work situation is sound, as leadership behaviour has a significant effect on the functioning of individual employees.

- *Structures and personnel policy:* It is generally accepted that the structures of an organisation are related to the management style of its management cadre. Mintzberg (1983:2) states that the structures of an organisation may be defined as the sum total of the way in which its labour is divided into specified tasks, and the degree of coordination achieved between these tasks. Gibson *et al.* (1976:38) emphasise the importance of culture to organisational behaviour. They state that the purpose of management is to bring about an effective organisation. There are various examples of the way in which management may use structures in order to achieve desirable results. For example, management may design compensation systems, especially bonus systems, to promote performance and goal achievement; they may implement job specialisation to promote closer supervision to counteract deviations, etc. It is clear that all these aspects are related to human resources management processes. Personnel policy is a result of human resources management as a subsystem within an organisation. Therefore personnel policy has a direct influence on employee functioning. Examples of this influence are the effects of the compensation policy of the organisation, its promotion policy and its labour relations policy on the individual employee. Numerous human resources management processes use these means to retain employees.

- *Working conditions:* Working conditions are created by the interaction of employees with their physical work environment. It is that environment which impinges on employees' senses and which is related to their lower order needs, which in turn affect their physiological functioning. Various sub-elements of working conditions should be distinguished.

  — The first sub-element is the physical working conditions. Backer (1979:41) states the following in this respect:

    > This aspect refers to the amount of work and the availability of facilities such as production machinery and protective clothing, and to aspects of the physical environment in which the employee works, such as ventilation, lighting and space.

  There are thus two important considerations in the physical work environment, i.e. aids and the physical work environment *per se*. Aids refer to the equipment and appliances at the employee's disposal for the execution of a task, irrespective of its nature. What is important is the extent to which these aids enable employees to function effectively. The physical work environment *per se* refers to the attractiveness of the work environment—the aesthetic element and other aspects involved in the physical execution of tasks.

— The second sub-element is the psychological working conditions. According to our view, this refers to the psychological effect of work pressure on individuals and groups. Psychological working conditions also include the psychological expectations of employees in the psychological contract in respect of their working conditions as compared to what they actually experience.

— The last sub-element is the physical layout of the job, which refers to the neatness, organisation, convenience, attractiveness, and stimulus value of an employee's personal micro work environment. This affects the employee's physical interaction with these work aids and this interaction affects physical and sensory functions.

It seems clear, therefore, that human resources management processes are faced with a number of problems which may affect employee functioning within the job context environment.

● *Interpersonal and group relations:* In our opinion interpersonal and group relations are a subsection of working conditions and more specifically social working conditions. Milton (1981:196) defines interpersonal relations as "the whole range of human conduct between individuals who interact as they are involved in relationships of communicating, cooperating, changing, problem solving and motivation".

In these relationships, each employee tries to influence and adapt the behaviour of other employees in order to satisfy his or her own needs. Therefore we should take a brief look at the role of the individual employee within the group context.

An organisation depends on groups for the achievement of its goals, therefore it is organised accordingly. Continuous interaction is a characteristic of groups within an organisation. The ideal state for each group is one of harmonious cooperation in order to achieve the goals of the organisation. In practice, however, groups are continuously in a state of conflict, mainly because they are often competing with one another. If this competition does not coincide with or follow the direction of the goals of the organisation, it will adversely affect the organisation. Competition should be in line with the goals of the organisation and this means that group objectives need to be associated with these goals, bearing in mind that groups as subsystems of the organisation have their own goals. In addition to the formal groups and the reasons they compete on a formal basis, there are informal groups within an organisation and these probably have the strongest influence on formal groups. Informal group formation determines group functioning and sets informal group goals which may either help or hinder the achievement of the goals of the organisation. Interpersonal and group relations present a great challenge for human resources management because of their effect on the functioning of an organisation.

To summarise, individual motivation, and therefore individual performance, is either positively or negatively affected by the individual's job context environment. The philosophy of the management cadre or the leadership element determines to a large extent the nature and content of the influencing process within the job context. The leadership style of the management cadre in an organisation is a primary factor influencing employee functioning and performance. Structure and policies within an organisation must be such that they will not only promote the achievement goals of the organisation, but enhance the achievement of individual goals within the framework of the psychological contract. Physical, psychological and social working conditions are important in any organisation. In this book we regard these conditions as even more important than is generally maintained among theorists. The quality of interpersonal and group relationships is equally important in view of the significant effect it has on the achievement of employee goals and the goals of the organisation.

However beneficial individual employees' job content environment may be to individual performances, influences from the job context environment, together with the external environment, are jointly responsible for their motivation and performance. The last environment in the throughput process of human resources management is the individual employee's external environment.

(c) The external environment
We shall discuss the external environment exerting an influence on individual employee functioning in broad terms only. The term external environment refers to areas outside the organisation that affect employees via the organisation, as well as areas within the organisation that affect individual employees. We refer specifically to the effect of labour demand and supply on an employee's period of service with a particular organisation. For example, an employee may be unhappy with his or her job content and job context environments in an organisation, but is forced to stay with that organisation because of labour market conditions. Such an employee will probably do just enough work not to be dismissed. In this respect the economic conditions of South African organisations and the entire country are very relevant, as well as the effects of these conditions on individual employees. For example, the state of the economy has a direct effect on employees' compensation packages. Furthermore, technological change plays an important part. Owing to the lack of skilled employees in the Republic, organisations are sometimes forced to mechanise and this often leads to unemployment. These factors have an indirect effect on employees' performance inclinations.

Figure 3.3 indicates the three environments, i.e. an employee's job content environment, job context environment and external environment, as illustrated on the left-hand side of the model. The dotted line indicates the psychological contract, with specific reference to the extent to which an employee progresses towards the achievement of personal goals. The solid line at the top of the model is also related to the process of comparison mentioned above, with specific reference to the opportunity an employee perceives in an organisation to achieve personal goals while at the same time pursuing the goals of the organisation. If the opportunity is provided, the employee will integrate personal goals with the goals of the organisation, which will serve as a foundation for motivated employee behaviour. (This topic is dealt with at length in chapter 16.) The extent to which personal goals coincide with the goals of the organisation determines the employee's inclination to perform. This inclination has a direct bearing on the employee's real outputs in terms of efficiency and effectiveness, which ultimately determine the success of the employee.

Attention will now be paid to those human resources management processes which may have a positive or negative effect on the employee's functioning within the three environments and which are representative of the layout of this book.

3.3.3 Human resources management processes directed at employee functioning within the organisation

The input, throughput and output processes of an employee as a subsystem within an organisation have been discussed on the basis of a systems model of employee functioning. The next section will focus on those human resources management processes directed at improving individual employee functioning. This discussion will follow the systems approach towards human resources management, with reference to figure 3.3.

(a) Human resources management input processes
An employee joins an organisation with certain inputs (also see chapter 4). A number of management processes may be classified as human resources management input processes as they are directed at ensuring that the right employee holds the right job at the right time in order to contribute towards the functioning of the organisation by means of the throughput process. Figure 3.3 illustrates that these processes are related to ensuring that the right quality and quantity of employee inputs are released within the job context environment. These human resources management input processes are human resources planning, recruitment, selection, placement and induction, technology, training, and intrinsic motivation:
- *Human resources planning:* The human resources planning process is discussed in detail in chapter 5. An organisation must conduct human resources planning according to the nature and composition of the labour

FIGURE 3.3: A systems model of the employee as a subsystem, and human resources management processes affecting the individual employee

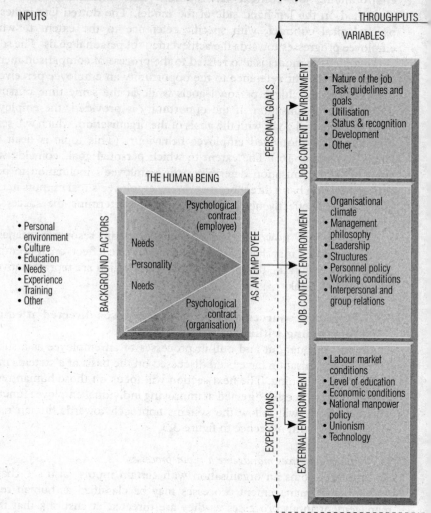

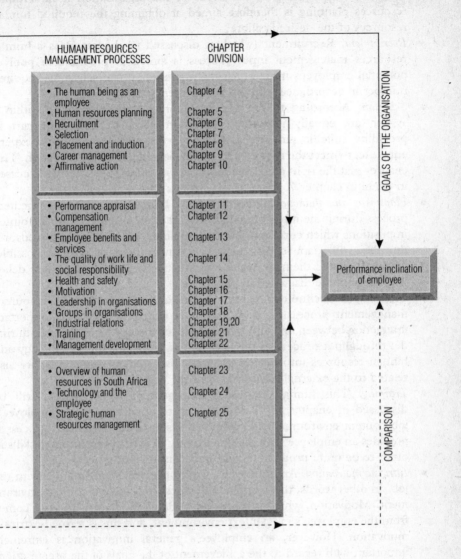

HUMAN RESOURCES
MANAGEMENT PROCESSES

CHAPTER
DIVISION

- The human being as an employee
- Human resources planning
- Recruitment
- Selection
- Placement and induction
- Career management
- Affirmative action

Chapter 4

Chapter 5
Chapter 6
Chapter 7
Chapter 8
Chapter 9
Chapter 10

- Performance appraisal
- Compensation management
- Employee benefits and services
- The quality of work life and social responsibility
- Health and safety
- Motivation
- Leadership in organisations
- Groups in organisations
- Industrial relations
- Training
- Management development

Chapter 11
Chapter 12

Chapter 13

Chapter 14

Chapter 15
Chapter 16
Chapter 17
Chapter 18
Chapter 19,20
Chapter 21
Chapter 22

- Overview of human resources in South Africa
- Technology and the employee
- Strategic human resources management

Chapter 23

Chapter 24

Chapter 25

GOALS OF THE ORGANISATION

Performance inclination of employee

COMPARISON

market, and according to the needs of the organisation itself. Human resources planning is therefore aimed at obtaining the required human resources of the desired calibre.

- *Recruitment:* Recruitment (which is discussed in chapter 6) as a human resources management input process is aimed at providing a pool of potential employees from which the organisation can select the required number in accordance with job requirements.
- *Selection:* According to the systems approach all subsystems within a system are equally important. Selection plays an important part in providing suitable employees who have the aptitude, abilities, experience, etc. to meet the requirements of the job and of the organisation. This ensures that the right employee inputs are obtained. Selection is discussed in detail in chapter 7.
- *Placement and induction:* Placement as a human resources management process during the input phase ensures that new employees are appointed in positions which correspond to their abilities, whereas induction ensures that they will adapt in their new work environment as soon as possible. This will enable them to become productive without unnecessary delay. These topics are discussed in chapter 8.
- *Technology:* Technology cannot be regarded as a human resources management process as such, but it is added to show the important interaction between an employee and the technology he or she uses during the throughput process in the job content environment. Technology and human resources information systems, discussed in chapter 24, are also related to the external environment of the organisation.
- *Training:* This human resources management input process will be discussed in chapter 21. Training is more applicable to an employee's job content environment. As a human resources management process it provides an employee with the opportunity to extend and improve skills in order to be more productive during the throughput process.
- *Intrinsic motivation:* An employee's will to perform stems mainly from the job. In other words, this stimulation comes from the job content environment. Motivation, which is discussed in detail in chapter 16, also comes from the employee's job context environment, and this is termed extrinsic motivation. However, an employee's general motivation is extremely important with regard to the achievement of the goals of the organisation.

In our opinion the effective implementation and application of these human resources management processes will ensure the optimal utilisation of the inputs with which employees join an organisation during the throughput phase of employee functioning.

(b) Human resources management throughput processes
The human resources management throughput processes are related to an employee's functioning in his or her job context environment. This entails

numerous processes. The main purpose of these processes is to maintain the human resources of the organisation during the throughput phase of employee functioning.

- *Development* (discussed in detail in chapter 22): This human resources management throughput process is aimed at preparing employees for further career development and progress.
- *Career development* (chapter 9): Career development as a human resources management process has a significant effect on an employee's duration of service with an organisation. It is also closely related to the process of comparison discussed in chapter 4.
- *Extrinsic motivation* (chapter 16): Extrinsic motivation refers to motivational factors affecting the employee from the work environment outside the job content environment. This includes factors such as working conditions, leadership, and compensation.
- *Leadership* (chapter 17): Although it is impossible to say which human resources management process has the most profound effect on employee functioning during the throughput phase, leadership is certainly one of the most important influencing factors.
- *Quality of work life and social responsibility* (chapter 14): The responsibility of an organisation towards its employees is strongly emphasised today. Quality of work life programmes and the involvement of an organisation in social responsibility affects employees' duration of service with that organisation.
- *Labour relations* (chapters 19 and 20): The effect of current relationships between management and the labour force causes problems in many an organisation. Labour relations are becoming increasingly important, not only for human resources management, but for the management of the entire organisation. Labour relations are discussed in this book in view of the relevance and importance of the subject. We discuss labour relations from a human resources management point of view.
- *Performance appraisal* (chapter 11): The importance of performance appraisal as a human resources management process in the throughput phase cannot be overemphasised. It is essential to the psychological contract as discussed in chapter 4, that performance appraisal provides employees with formal feedback on their functioning within the job content and job context environments.
- *Compensation management* (chapter 12): Theorists do not concur on the effect of compensation on employee attitudes. Our opinion is that it plays an extremely important part in employees' inclination to perform as well as in their actual performance during the throughput phase.
- *Employee benefits and services:* The benefits and services employees enjoy on the basis of their membership of an organisation are related to compensation administration. Their importance will become clear in chapter 13.

- *Health and safety* (chapter 15): Employee health and safety within the context of the organisation tie in with quality of work life and social responsibility. The importance of this human resources management throughput process is illustrated by the fact that organisations are forced by legislation to pay attention to health and safety.

An aspect that is as important as the management of an employee's input and throughput processes within the job content environment, is the positive influence of human resources management throughput processes on functioning within the job context environment. Every single human resources management process makes a positive contribution towards employee functioning, if it is effectively implemented.

(c) The effect of the external environment on employee functioning
Although the external environment falls outside the job context, it has an indirect and a direct effect on employee functioning within the organisation. For example, the state of a country's economy affects labour demand and supply: an over-supply of labour often forces employees to stay with an organisation even if the job content environment and the job context environment are not suited to their needs and preferences. Similarly, the rate of technological change has an effect on employees. (These topics are dealt with in chapters 22 and 23.)

(d) The management of the output process of employee functioning
As stated in paragraph 3.3.2, the extent to which employees progress towards the achievement of personal goals owing to the impact of human resources management processes, determines their will to perform. This in turn determines employees' outputs.

3.4 CONCLUSION

This chapter is aimed at giving an overall idea of the systems approach to human resources management. We have discussed the systems approach as such, the characteristics of the systems approach and the organisation as a system. To promote understanding, a systems model of employee functioning has been developed and discussed, and we have dealt with the employee's environments during the input, throughput and output processes. Problems affecting employee functioning within the job content environment, the job context environment and the external environment, were dealt with in broad terms. Human resources management processes influencing the employee within these environments were listed and placed within the model as a frame of reference to facilitate the study of this book.

Questions

1. List and discuss the characteristics of a system.
2. In about 500 words, give a practical explanation of the organisation as a system.

3. Critically discuss the input process of individual employee functioning within an organisation.
4. Which variables influence the employee in the throughput process? Critically discuss these variables.
5. Distinguish between the three environments in which the employee functions within an organisation. Discuss the influence of each environment on the employee's functioning.
6. What is the connection between management philosophy and leadership style?

Sources

Backer, W. 1979. 'n Kritiese evaluering van die motiveringshigiëneteorie van Herzberg. TIMS, Pretoria.

Beer, M. 1980. Organization change and development: a systems view. Goodyear, Santa Monica, California.

Cronje, G.J. de J., Neuland, E.W., Hugo, W.M.J. & Van Reenen, M.J. (eds.) 1994. Inleiding tot die bestuurswese. Southern Book Publishers, Halfway House.

Ford. R.N. 1969. Motivation through the work itself. American Management Association, New York.

Gibson, J.L., Ivancevich, J.M. & Donnelly, J.H. 1976. Organizations: behavior, structure, processes. Business Publications, Dallas, Texas.

Hodgetts, R.M. 1979. Management, theory, process and practice. Saunders, Philadelphia.

Huse, E.F. & Bowditch, J.L. 1977. Behavior in organizations: a systems approach to managing. Addison-Wesley, Boston, Massachusetts.

Katz, D. & Kahn, R. 1966. The social psychology of organizations. Wiley, New York.

Milton, C.R. 1981. Human behavior in organizations: three levels of behavior. Prentice-Hall, Englewood Cliffs, New Jersey.

Mintzberg, H. 1983, 1992. Structures in fives: designing effective organizations. Prentice-Hall, Englewood Cliffs, New Jersey.

Porter, W.W., Lawler, E.E. & Hackman, J.R. 1975. Behavior in organizations. McGraw-Hill, New York.

Schein, F.H. 1980. Organizational psychology. Prentice-Hall, Englewood Cliffs, New Jersey.

Vroom, V.H. 1966. Work and motivation. Wiley, New York.

Wanous, J.P. 1974. Individual differences and reactions to job characteristics. Journal of Applied Psychology, vol. 59, no. 5, pp. 616–22.

Part 2

Human resources provisioning

The human being as an employee	Chapter 4
Human resources planning	Chapter 5
Recruitment	Chapter 6
Selection	Chapter 7
Placement and induction	Chapter 8
Career management	Chapter 9

Overview of Part 2: Human resources provisioning

AIM

To describe the theory underlying human resources provisioning to the student or reader in a pragmatic manner in order to establish a basis for the scientific application among those who practise this sub-field of human resources management.

PRINCIPAL STUDY OBJECTIVES

Chapter 4: The human being as an employee. To instil in the student or reader an understanding of the human being as an employee within an organisational context so that he or she can explain employee behaviour within this context.

Chapter 5: Human resources planning. To instil in the student or reader an understanding of human resources planning as the first and activating step of the human resources management process so that he or she can apply its principles in practice.

Chapter 6: Recruitment. To instil in the student or reader an understanding of the recruitment principles that are generally adhered to in practice, so that he or she can effectively apply recruitment within an organisational context.

Chapter 7: Selection. To instil in the student or reader an understanding of the selection principles so that he or she can strictly apply them within an organisational context.

Chapter 8: Placement and induction. To instil in the student or reader an understanding of the importance of the effect that placement and induction have on individual employee performance so that he or she can apply it in practice.

Chapter 9: Career management. To instil in the student or reader the importance of the effect of career management on individual employee performance so that he or she can apply it in practice.

Chapter 4

The human being as an employee

P.S. van Dyk

STUDY OBJECTIVES

After studying this chapter, you should be able to:

- Explain the concept of personality in theory;
- Pragmatically describe the psychological contract between the employee and the organisation;
- Explain the author's view of "motivation" from a personal framework of reference;
- Describe the attachment to and involvement in the goals of an organisation from personal experience.

4.1 INTRODUCTION

This chapter focuses on the individual as an employee. In other words, the essence of this chapter is the inputs with which an individual joins an organisation as an employee. We also refer to the input phase of human resources management as conceptualised and discussed in broad terms in chapter 3. Discussions in this chapter will be presented in accordance with figure 4.3. As each employee has a unique personality, this aspect is dealt with briefly without giving too much psychological detail. Nevertheless, the emphasis in this chapter falls on the psychological contract, and the personal expectations and goals with which an individual joins an organisation as an employee. As motivated employee behaviour (which underlies individual performance attitudes) is only possible when personal goals are integrated with the goals of an organisation, attention is also given to this.

In the model, the human being as an employee appears on the left, with the input phase. The success of an employee depends primarily on himself or herself. You should therefore study this chapter very well before continuing with the others.

4.2 THE INDIVIDUAL EMPLOYEE AS A HUMAN BEING

Personality is certainly one of the most exhaustively researched concepts in the field of behavioural science. The relation between employee behaviour and personality requires knowledge and insight on the part of superiors to enable them effectively to guide their subordinates in their pursuit of the goals of the organisation. Glueck (1979:34) defines personality as a characteristic way in which a person thinks and acts in an effort to adapt to his or her environment. This includes personal characteristics, values, motives, genetic factors, attitudes, emotional reactivity, abilities, self-image and intelligence. It also includes a person's discernible behavioural patterns.

According to Gibson *et al.* (1976:98), cultural and social factors have a significant effect on personality. They state that psychologists agree on the following generalisations about the concept of personality:

- Personality is an organised whole, otherwise the individual will have no meaning.
- Personality seems to be organised into patterns. These patterns can be observed and measured to a certain extent.
- Although personality has a biological basis, its particular development is a product of social and cultural environments.
- Personality has superficial aspects such as attitude towards taking the lead, sentiments towards authority and others.
- Personality involves both common and unique characteristics. People differ from each other in certain respects, and show similarities in other respects.

In view of this, personality can be defined as follows:

An individual's personality is a relatively stable set of characteristics, tendencies, and temperaments that have been significantly formed by inheritance and by social, cultural, and environmental factors. This set of variables determines the communalities and differences in the behaviour of the individual.

It has been shown that *hereditary factors* do play a role in the shaping of personality, but that this role differs from one characteristic to the next. Heredity usually plays a more significant role in temperament than in values and ideals. *Culture*, however, has a major effect on the shaping of personality. Gibson et al. (1976:99) explain this effect as follows:

We do not clearly recognize the impact of culture in shaping our personalities. It happens gradually, and usually there is no alternative but to accept the culture. The stable functioning of a society requires that there be shared patterns of behavior among its members and that there is some basis for knowing how to behave in certain situations. To ensure this, the society institutionalizes various patterns of behavior. The institutionalization of some patterns of behavior means that most members of a culture will have certain common personality characteristics.

This description poses many challenges for the management of people and human resources. A diversified worker corps requires a more scientific human resources management practice than a homogeneous worker corps. The South African labour market is not only characterised by wide national diversity, but also by international diversity. This state of affairs results in human resources policies and practices having to be based on well-considered scientific principles (particularly in view of affirmative action).

Gibson *et al.* (1976:99) conceptualise the influence of variables on personality as in figure 4.1.

FIGURE 4.1: Major factors affecting personality

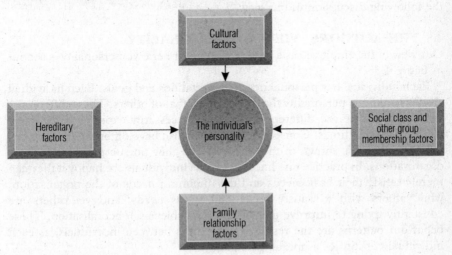

Source: Gibson *et al.* (1976:99)

Social class is also important in the shaping of personalities. The environment in which a person grows up largely determines what he or she will learn about life. Social class affects a person's self-perception, perception of others and perception of work, authority and money. Such things as the nature of people's expectations of others, the way in which they try to achieve satisfaction, the way in which they express their feelings and solve emotional conflict, are acquired within interpersonal contexts. A key factor in this respect is the parent-child relationship which serves as a model of behaviour patterns for the child, and a frame of reference for its future.

The relation between an individual's personality and individual behaviour is shown in figure 4.2.

This simple conceptualisation shows that the situations in which people are involved from time to time affect their perception of these situations, which in turn determines their behaviour (employee behaviour) in the execution of a task or job.

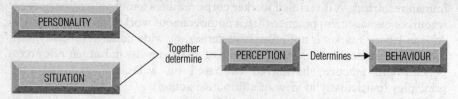

When one considers the factors contributing to the shaping of personality (as set out in figure 4.1), it seems that superiors within organisations have very little control over these factors. The significance of this will become clear in the following discussion of our view.

4.3 THE AUTHORS' VIEW OF PERSONALITY

Our view of the employee as a person with his or her own personality is set out in figure 4.3.

Each individual has personal needs, expectations and goals. Each individual also has a unique personality that differs from that of others. These differences mean that people are different and do not necessarily experience the same needs at specific times. Consequently, people also have different expectations in life, and this is shown in the way in which they pursue personal goals in organisations. In practice one finds that some individuals are happy if they can merely satisfy their basic needs and the minimum needs of the organisation, while others wish to satisfy social and status needs, and yet others are constantly trying to improve themselves and achieve self-actualisation. These behaviour patterns are the result of differences between individuals, as each individual constitutes a unique personality.

> An individual's personality forms the basis of the expectations and personal goals with which he or she joins an organisation.

Personality is known to be the result of many factors, of which the most dominant are those shown in figure 4.3.

An individual's personality is primarily the result of his or her *personal environment* from the day of birth until the day of joining the particular organisation with which he or she has entered into a psychological contract. Through personal environment an individual is exposed to a certain *culture* in terms of which he or she is educated. This culture influences the person through a process of socialisation during which certain behaviour patterns, values, attitudes and views of humanity are acquired.

Individuals acquire certain *personal qualities* such as skills, training, experience and ability within their personal environment, whereas the personal quality "aptitude" is a congenital characteristic, the full realisation

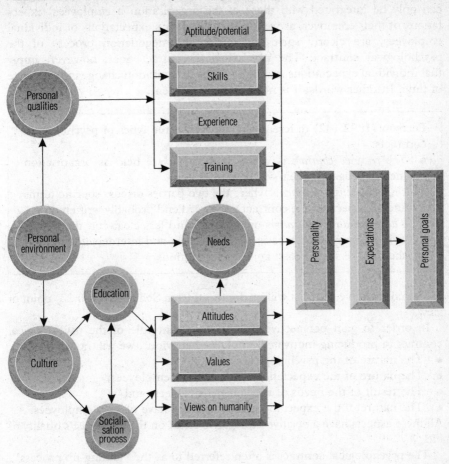

of which is the result of their personal environment. As chapter 16 refers to human needs it should be mentioned that certain needs are congenital (physiological needs) while others are acquired. In addition, it is characteristic of human beings that needs develop in the course of time and change in accordance with levels of development. All these factors together shape the personality of a person who has certain expectations of life and work, which are transformed into the personal goals with which the person joins an organisation.

4.4 THE PSYCHOLOGICAL CONTRACT BETWEEN THE HUMAN BEING AS AN EMPLOYEE AND THE ORGANISATION (MANAGEMENT) AS EMPLOYER

Individual performance is the result of motivated employee behaviour. It is a known fact that motivated employee behavior may be best achieved by integrating personal goals with the goals of the organisation. Personal goals can only be integrated with those of the organisation if employees' expectations of their employer, as well as the employer's expectations of individual employees, are clearly spelt out during the negotiation process of the psychological contract. The psychological contract does, however, imply that individual expectations and those of the organisation change in the course of time. In other words, it is not a static agreement.

> Pearson (1992:142) differentiates between three types of psychological contracts:
> - *The coercive contract* is where individuals are held as organisation members against their will (e.g. in prison).
> - *The calculative contract* is where the two parties discuss specific terms and all aspects of the contract are agreed and probably written down.
> - *The cooperative contract* is open-ended and less clear-cut, the parties to it operating on the basis of mutual trust and interdependence and sharing the same broad goals and intentions.

The cooperative contract will be discussed from Schein's (1980:23) point of view.

In order to gain perspective on the important role of the psychological contract in producing motivated employee behaviour, we will now deal with:
- The nature of the psychological contract;
- The nature of the expectations of individual employees;
- The result of the needs of individual employees; and
- The nature of the expectations organisations have of their employees.

All these aspects have a positive or negative effect on the employee's quality of life.

The psychological contract is often referred to as the "joining-up process". The ineffective execution of this contract may result in numerous problems for the organisation, such as:
- Dissatisfaction with the work;
- Low productivity;
- Poor attitude towards the organisation;
- Low morale;
- Increased labour turnover;
- Increased conflicts and tension.

When individuals join an organisation they have certain expectations about promotion opportunities, salary, status, office and decor, the amount of challenging work as opposed to the amount of boring work—things they expect to receive. They also have expectations about their technical skills, time and energy, involvement, communication skills, supervisory skills and so on—things they expect to give.

70

The organisation (represented by management) also has certain expectations about what it will receive from the employee (in the same way as the employee expects to receive things from the organisation), as well as expectations about what it can offer the employee, examples of which are similar to what the employee expects to receive.

These two sets of expectations may therefore either correspond with or differ from each other. The psychological contract also differs from legal and labour agreements. In reality it could contain an indefinite number of items even though the employee may only be aware of a few expectations about his or her most pressing needs.

The employee of the 90s

The world and organisations are becoming ever more complex as the end of the 20th century approaches. However, the world and organisations consist of people. This poses the question: How do modern employees look and what are their expectations?

The American Association for Training and Development (McLaglan 1989:50) identifies four changes in the labour force that necessitate new human resources management practices and interventions. (Certain similarities in the population composition of the USA and South Africa also make these aspects applicable to this country.)

- The workforce of the 90s will be far more diverse. In the USA it will be more female and non-white than male and white. Literacy will spread and multinational employees will enter organisations to a larger extent.
- In this decade, more people will do "knowledge" work that requires judgement, flexibility and personal commitment rather than subordination to policies and procedures.
- A further change in the expectations of employees is related to a shift in value system. The employee of the 90s increasingly expects and demands meaningful work and involvement at work. Employees will regard their skills as resources to be utilised. They will have access to more information than they require to carry out their tasks through technology rather than hierarchy. They expect to be involved in decision-making and to share in the prosperity of the organisation that they are helping to create.
- There is a shift in the nature of the psychological contract between the employer and the employee. Merit will replace loyalty. In this decade, organisations will have to *earn* the right to utilise the skills of employees. (This particularly applies in South Africa, given the composition of the labour market and an upswing in economic activity.)

Kotter (1976:93), who is a pioneer in this sphere, identifies the following types of expectations:

- The first group of expectations represents what an individual expects to receive from an organisation and what the organisation expects to give the individual. In other words, for each item on the list an individual has expectations of what the organisation will offer and what he or she will receive. Similarly, the organisation has expectations of what it will offer or give the individual in that area:
  — a meaningful job;
  — opportunities for personal development;
  — interesting work that will generate curiosity and excitement on the part of the individual;
  — challenging work;
  — authority and responsibility at work;
  — recognition and approval for work of a high standard;
  — status and prestige at work;
  — friendly people and equality in the work group;
  — compensation;
  — the extent to which the environment is structured, for example general practices, discipline or regimentation;
  — security at work;
  — promotion possibilities;
  — the amount and frequency of feedback and assessment.

- The second group of expectations includes what an individual expects to offer an organisation and what the organisation expects to receive from employees. In other words, for each item on the list the individual has an expectation of what he or she is willing or able to offer or give the organisation. Similarly, the organisation has certain expectations of what it will receive from the individual in that area:
  — the ability to execute tasks that are not socially related and that require a certain degree of technical knowledge and skills;
  — the ability to learn to execute various aspects of a job in the work situation;
  — the ability to invent new methods of task performance and the ability to solve problems;
  — the ability to state an opinion effectively and convincingly;
  — the ability to work productively with groups of people;
  — the ability to present well-organised and clear reports orally or in writing;
  — the ability to supervise and guide others in their work;
  — the ability to make good, responsible decisions without assistance;
  — the ability to plan and organise his or her own work as well as the work of other employees;
  — the ability to use time and energy to the benefit of the organisation;

- the ability to accept instructions/requirements from the organisation that are incompatible with personal prerogatives;
- social interaction with other employees outside the working environment;
- conforming to the norms of the organisation applicable to the job in areas not directly related to the job;
- self-study outside normal working hours;
- maintaining a good public image of the organisation;
- accepting the organisation's values and goals as own values and goals; and
- the ability to realise what has to be done and to take the appropriate steps.

The psychological contract may contain an infinite number of items. More important than these items, however, is an understanding of the nature of the psychological contract, and the communication of these mutual expectations.

Porter (1975:109) refers to the psychological contract as the "dynamics of organisation-individual interactions" and conceptualises it as in figure 4.4.

FIGURE 4.4: The dynamics of organisation-individual interaction

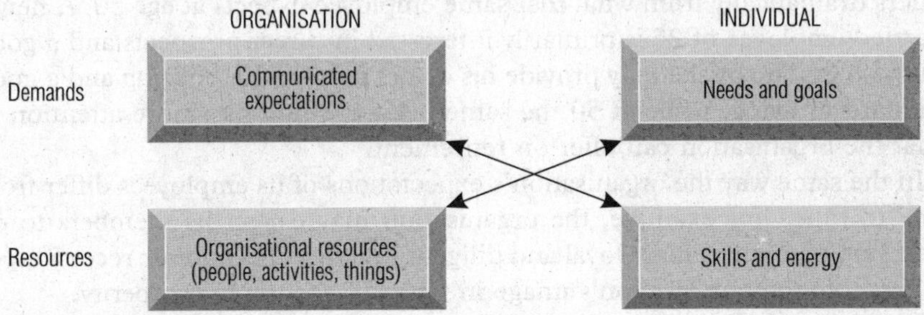

Source: Porter *et al.* (1975:109)

As indicated by the arrows in figure 4.4, the different requirements of the individual and the organisation represent a tapping of common resources. In other words, the communicated expectations of the organisation make demands on the skills and energy of individuals, while the satisfaction of individuals' needs depends on certain resources of the organisation. It seems obvious that if a working relationship is to be developed and maintained between the individual and the organisation, both parties will have to respond to mutual expectations and needs.

Schein (1970:77) makes the following remarks about the importance of the psychological contract:

By way of conclusion, I would like to underline the importance of the psychological contract as a major variable of analysis. It is my central hypothesis that whether a person is working effectively, whether he generates commitment, loyalty, and enthusiasm for the organization and its goals, and whether he obtains satisfaction from his work, depends to a large measure on two conditions: (1) the degree to which his own expectations of what the organization will provide him and what he owes the organization match what the organization's are of what it will give and get; (2) assuming there is agreement on expectations, what actually is to be exchanged—money in exchange for time at work; social-need satisfaction and security in exchange for work and loyalty; opportunities for self-actualization and challenging work in exchange for high productivity, quality work and creative effort in the service of organizational goals; or various combinations of these and other things. Ultimately the relationship between the individual and organization is interactive, unfolding through mutual bargaining to establish a workable psychological contract. We cannot understand the psychological dynamics if we look only to the individual's motivations or only to organizational conditions and practices. The two interact in a complex fashion, requiring us to develop theories and research approaches which can deal with systems and interdependent phenomena.

The psychological contract is dynamic and changes in the course of time. This change takes place in accordance with changed needs of both the individual employee and the organisation.

What an employee expects of an organisation or the employer at age 25 differs dramatically from what that same employee expects at age 50. A newly married employee of 25 is primarily interested in career prospects and a good salary so that he or she may provide his or her family with housing and a good standard of living, while at 50 the same person would pay more attention to what the organisation can offer on retirement.

In the same way the organisation's expectations of its employees differ from time to time. For example, the organisation may expect its members to do their very best and remain loyal and diligent in times of economic recession, or to promote the organisation's image in times of economic prosperity.

In most cases, the needs of employees starting a career revolve around "self-testing". Employees would like to determine whether they have all the skills needed to do the job for which they are appointed. Therefore they expect organisations to provide them with challenges to test their skills and knowledge in terms of goal achievement. This is where the problem of conflicting goals comes to the fore. In theory employees are usually disappointed if they are kept in meaningless training programmes for too long, or if they are occupied with tasks that bear no relation to the primary goals of the organisation. In such cases neither the organisation nor the individual employee is in a position to determine the employee's actual abilities in terms of the goal achievement of the organisation, and this results in a feeling of uncertainty.

During a later phase of employees' work life, their needs and expectations move into an area where they may feel that they are contributing to the organisation, and where they are enabled to develop in their area of speciality. At this stage employees expect the organisation to acknowledge their contributions. Most employees reach this position in the middle of their career, usually when they are at their most productive and consequently also expect the most recognition and remuneration. At a later stage, when the employee is doing less crucial work, his or her need for security increases and expectations in the psychological contract change to not wanting to be sidelined or sent on early retirement. Retired employees often complain that the psychological contract has been broken because they could still make a positive contribution to the organisation.

4.5 THE INTEGRATION OF PERSONAL GOALS WITH THOSE OF THE ORGANISATION

Both the expectations of the employee and the manager are, among other things, the result of what they have learnt from others of prevailing traditions and norms and of previous experience. As needs and other external factors change, expectations also change, and this gives the psychological contract a dynamic character that requires constant renegotiation. Although the psychological contract is unwritten, it remains the critical determinant of the work behaviour of employees.

The question then arises how the psychological contract can contribute to the process of motivation. In the following section, this important aspect is explained.

Individuals as employees have certain personal goals that are the result of the expectations contained in the psychological contract. In keeping with the nature and content of the psychological contract, it is also clear that organisations expect certain things from their employees. The individual and the organisation are thus in constant interaction with one another, with the aim of attaining their mutual goals.

An individual employee enters an organisation with a certain set of needs. If the organisation has an organisational climate that promotes need satisfaction, an employee should show positive employee behaviour. If such a climate is not present, employees will tend to subordinate organisational goals to their personal goals for need satisfaction.

It should thus be clear that there is a critical link between the successful integration of personal goals and the goals of the organisation, as well as organisational success.

4.6 ATTACHMENT TO THE ORGANISATION AND INVOLVE-MENT WITH THE GOALS OF THE ORGANISATION

An employee's behaviour within an organisation may be regarded as the function of his or her perception of the content of the psychological contract entered into with the organisation. Organisations expect their employees to accept the goals allocated to them, and to be motivated to achieve these goals. On the other hand, individual employees expect the organisation to fulfil its part of the contract too. Steers (1977:113) has the following view of the results of this interaction:

The results of this interaction can be seen as leading to two equally important outcomes: (1) an individual's desire to maintain his membership in a particular organization (termed here attachment); and (2) an individual's desire to perform on the job and contribute to organizational goal attainment.

An organisation can only expect its employees to be attached to the organisation and to be involved with their personal goals if it fulfils the following commitments:

- It must be able to attract (recruit) the workers required and retain them. This involves not only the recruitment, selection, employment and induction of workers, but ensuring that individual employees receive sufficient compensation, commensurate with their individual contribution and need satisfaction, in order to retain them.
- The organisation must also be able to ensure that each employee executes the tasks allocated to him or her. This implies that employees should not merely do their work, but should do it with responsibility.
- A third requirement, which is often neglected and which is not formally included in individual employees' goals, but which does promote the goal achievement of the organisation, is innovation and spontaneous cooperation on the part of employees.

Organisations must ensure that employees become involved and give their spontaneous cooperation.

The recruitment and maintenance of the required human resources are related to attachment to organisations. In other words, it has to do with *why* an individual joins a particular organisation, and *what* motivates him or her to stay with that organisation.

The second and third commitments on the part of the organisation, to ensure that employees are responsible and that their behaviour is spontaneous and innovative, are related to the quality of employee functioning or their performance level. Steers (1977:115) says:

In the study of human behavior as it relates to organizational effectiveness, employee attachment and performance emerge as the key variables to be examined. Although structure, technology and environment contribute to and often constrain effectiveness, such variables are largely overshadowed by the role of employee behavior. If employees are not motivated to remain with and contribute to an organization, questions of effectiveness become academic.

This quotation substantiates the approach followed in this book. Therefore it seems necessary to take a closer look at the concepts of attachment and involvement, as applied to organisations.

4.6.1 Employees' attachment to the organisation

Attachment to organisations may be divided into two components. The first is formal attachment. This refers to methods to reduce labour turnover, absenteeism and other forms of withdrawal from the work environment, and to increase time spent at work. A simple statement that employees are attached to organisations does not necessarily imply that they are strongly drawn to the organisation, nor that they have positive feelings about the organisation, but involves only the question of why they retain their membership of organisations. The second component, namely involvement, is discussed in paragraph 4.6.3.

At this point one might well ask why individuals retain their membership of organisations. In general, it may be said that organisations can expect employees to be attached to them and less prone to withdrawal if the employees experience *job satisfaction*. This is related to the variables contained in the job content and job context environments.

From the literature (see Steers 1977:116 among others), the following reasons may be given why employees remain with a particular organisation:

- Environmental factors, for example compensation and promotion policy and the size of the organisation;
- Factors within the employee's immediate work environment, for example supervision and interpersonal and group relationships;
- Job content factors; and
- Personal factors.

Without going into detail it should be noted that, in theory, the employee's perception of these factors or sources will determine whether he or she will withdraw from the organisation permanently (which means labour turnover) or temporarily (for example absenteeism).

Another question arising at this stage is how it affects the success of an organisation if individuals terminate their membership of organisations permanently or temporarily. According to Steers (1977:120), withdrawal (in particular permanent withdrawal) often has specific consequences for organisations and eventually for their efficiency. Many studies claim that increased labour turnover often leads to the employment of more administrative personnel in proportion to production personnel. It can also have a negative effect on innovation and creativity. Labour turnover gives rise to undesirable outputs and is directly related to the success or failure of organisations. On the other hand, organisations do benefit from getting rid of unproductive workers. Some labour turnover is desirable as it ensures that new workers with new ideas join the organisation, thus preventing stagnation.

The withdrawal of performance-inclined employees, in particular, poses a difficult problem for management.

Successful organisations are characterised by performance-inclined, innovative and creative employees. The "price" that an organisation has to pay for the withdrawal of such an employee is irrecoverable. It is therefore a challenge to human resources management to retain such successful employees as well as less successful employees and to develop them further to the advantage of the organisation and its stake-holders.

4.6.2 Involvement with the organisation

Involvement, the second component of attachment, represents a state where individuals feel strongly drawn to the objectives, values and goals of their employer. In other words, it goes much deeper than mere membership of an organisation, in the sense that it makes goal achievement possible by ensuring a positive attitude towards the organisation, as well as the willingness to make a bigger effort on behalf of the organisation.

Involvement in organisations and organisational goal achievement indicates the nature of the individual employee's relationship with the organisation. A performance-oriented employee generally shows the following work behaviour:

- A strong desire to remain a member of the organisation;
- A willingness to do more than is expected for the sake of the organisation;
- A definite acceptance of the organisational culture and goals.

Involvement refers to an active relationship between employee and employer, where the employee is willing to make sacrifices in pursuit of the employer's goals. One might now ask how increased involvement with organisations would affect the success of the organisation, or in different terms, what is the result of real involvement in organisations? Steers (1977:122) is of the opinion that involvement is closely related to at least four effectiveness variables which we will briefly discuss:

- *Increased attendance:* Employees who are deeply involved with the objectives and values of an organisation are more inclined to increase their participation in the activities of the organisation. In general, their attendance will only be prevented by events such as illness. With employees such as these, voluntary absenteeism will be lower than with employees who are less involved.
- *Employee retention:* A second variable related to increased attendance is reduced labour turnover (employee retention). This implies that employees who feel committed to an organisation have a strong desire to stay with that organisation, so that they may continue their contribution to goal achievement with which they identify.
- *Work involvement:* Increased identification with and belief in the goals of the organisation will increase employees' involvement in their work, as work is the key mechanism by which individuals contribute to the achievement of the goals of the organisation.
- *Increased effort:* This variable implies that individuals who are deeply involved will be willing to make a bigger effort on behalf of the organisation. In some cases such increased efforts will result in outstanding achievement.

4.6.3 Summary

In this chapter we have attempted to explain why individuals join a particular organisation and what motivates them to stay with that organisation.

Organisations must therefore not only recruit, employ, and induct new individuals, but also ensure that they are attached to the organisation and in particular that they become involved in the pursuit of the goals of the organisation. Employees will feel attached to or involved with organisations if factors such as their immediate work environment, job content and so on are satisfactory. This will result in fewer resignations and reduced absenteeism with the resultant positive effect on the success of the organisation. Involvement also means that employees will identify with the overall goals of the organisation, and they will consequently make a bigger effort in their pursuit of the goals of the organisation.

4.7 CONCLUSION

This chapter dealt with the individual employee as a human being with a unique personality and his or her individual needs, expectations and personal goals. A person joins and enters into a psychological contract with an organisation on the basis of his or her personal needs and goals. Both the individual employee and the organisation have certain expectations that must be met in order to uphold this contract. The integration of personal goals with the goals of the organisation seems to be the best way to uphold this contract. This provides the basis for motivated employee behaviour, which is essential to the success of the organisation. Attachment to organisations and involvement with the goals of the organisation greatly contribute to the success of the organisation. In other words, the inputs with which an employee joins an organisation must be utilised by that organisation in order to achieve optimal employee functioning.

Questions

1. How do you understand the concept of personality?
2. Critically discuss the authors' view of personality.
3. In not more than 500 words, explain what you understand by the psychological contract.
4. One of the key factors in individual motivation is achieving personal goals. Critically discuss this statement.
5. What do you understand by attachment to organisations?
6. Critically discuss Steers' views on involvement with the goals of the organisation.

Sources

Gibson, J.L., Ivancevich, J.M. & Donnelly, J.H. 1976. *Organizations: behavior, structure, process*. Business Publications, Dallas, Texas.

Kotter, J.P. 1976. The psychological contract: managing the joining-up process. *California Management Reviews*, vol. xv, no. 3, pp. 91–9.

McLaglan, P. 1989. *Training and Development Journal*, September, pp. 50–1.

Pearson, G. 1992. *The competitive organisation*. McGraw-Hill, Berkshire.

Porter, L.W., Lawler, E.E. & Hackman, J.R. 1975. *Behavior in organizations*. McGraw-Hill, New York.

Schein, E.H. 1980. *Organizational psychology*. Prentice-Hall, Englewood Cliffs, New Jersey.

Steers, R.M. 1977. *Organizational effectiveness: a behavioral view*. Goodyear, Santa Monica, California.

Chapter 5

Human resources planning

P.D. Gerber

STUDY OBJECTIVES

After studying this chapter, you should be able to:

• Describe the concept of job analysis in a practical manner;
• Differentiate between a job description and a job specification;
• Schematically explain the steps in the human resources planning process;
• Describe human resources planning as a component of the provision process using a theoretical frame of reference.

5.1 INTRODUCTION

The successful continued existence of an organisation is based on the degree to which it is able to obtain the most suitable employees, particularly in South Africa, where the labour market is characterised by an imbalance: a dire shortage of skilled and professional people on the one hand, and an over-supply of unskilled and semi-skilled workers on the other.

To become competitive, South Africa must correct this imbalance, but this can only take place in the long term. In the meantime, organisations within an extremely competitive labour market environment must attempt to retain employees in order to be competitive and successful themselves. This requires a thorough human resources planning process that can provide organisations with a competitive advantage over other organisations.

In this chapter, attention is given to:

• The concepts that underlie human resources planning;
• A theoretical view of the human resources planning process;
• An applied human resources planning model.

Human resources planning forms the first step in the human resources provision process. The total process can be shown as in figure 5.1.

The concepts underlying human resources planning, i.e. job analysis, job specification and job description, are now discussed.

5.2 TERMINOLOGY EXPLANATION

The nature of the job that the individual must carry out within the organisation forms the basis of all the activities of human resources management. Before any decisions can be taken with regard to the number and types of individuals necessary to carry out a job, one first has to look at the job itself.

Any job involves:
- The content, consisting of tasks, functions, responsibilities, behaviour and obligations;
- Qualifications necessary for the job, which include skills, abilities and experience;
- Output and compensation, i.e. salaries, promotion and intrinsic job satisfaction.

The design of the job presupposes that the job content is integrated with the skills, abilities, interests and qualifications necessary to carry out the job successfully and with the compensation received by the employee. The following basic approaches can be followed during job design (Leap and Crino 1993:157):
- *Job simplification:* This means that the job is divided into smaller units so that lower skilled and paid employees can carry out the lesser jobs.
- *Job rotation:* Employees take turns in carrying out certain jobs. Job rotation makes provision for more flexible job allocations, reduces monotony and boredom, and makes it possible to distribute unpleasant jobs.
- *Job enlargement:* This is the opposite of job simplification. Job enlargement combines simple tasks into a meaningful job that can be carried out by one employee. The principle that applies is that "whole" jobs eliminate monotony and give more meaning to the work.
- *Job enrichment:* The responsibility of the employees is increased by giving them more autonomy and greater control. This is done on a vertical level, i.e. they are expected not only to see that the production process is carried out, but also, for example, that raw materials for the production process are ordered and quality control is carried out.

The job design has a definite influence on the employees' propensity to perform and thus on the organisation and organisational effectiveness (Armstrong 1988:183). In view of this, and against the background of a definition of the nature of a job and of job design, it is necessary to pay more detailed attention to the information required to describe a specific job. This process is known as job analysis.

FIGURE 5.1: Principal learning components of human resources planning

HUMAN RESOURCES PLANNING

JOB SPECIFICATION
DESCRIPTION
STEPS

JOB DESCRIPTION
JOB IDENTIFICATION
TASK SUMMARY
RELATIONS, ETC.
AUTHORITY & STANDARDS
WORK CIRCUMSTANCES

JOB ANALYSIS

Concepts
Usages
The process
Methods

General techniques
Specialised techniques

Factors affecting HRP
HRP process

Present situation
HRP estimate
Implementation programme
HRP audit
A pragmatic model

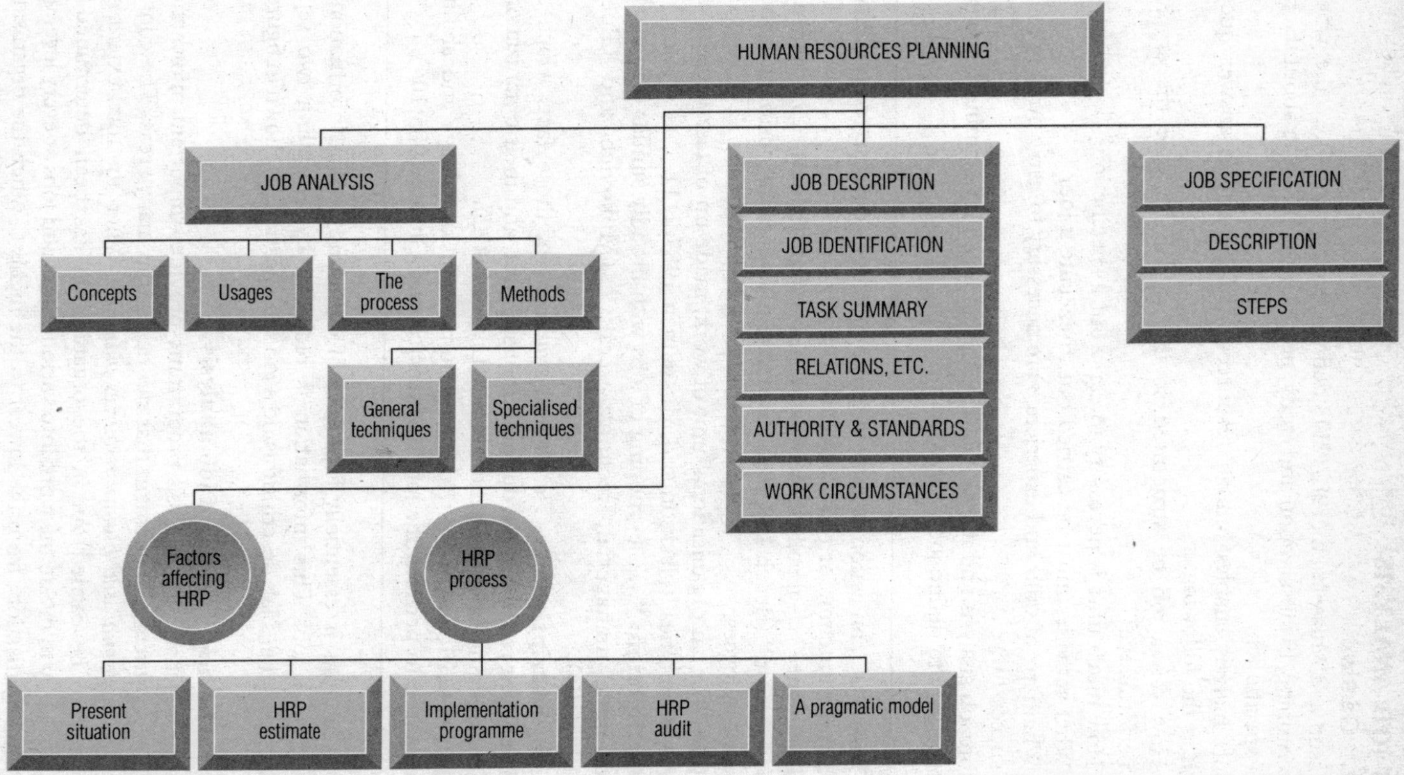

5.3 JOB ANALYSIS

5.3.1 General

Jackson and Musselman (1987:211) define job analysis as ". . . the process of determining, by observation and study, pertinent information about the nature of a specific job."

Job analysis enables human resources management to answer questions such as the following:

- How can a job be structured so that it will increase the employee's performance?
- How much time is necessary to carry out a specific job?
- What activities must be carried out to execute a job?
- What type of skills and experience are necessary to carry out a specific job successfully?

Before job analysis and its associated techniques can be examined, however, it is necessary to define job analysis terms.

Task: ". . . an action or related group of actions designed to produce a definite outcome or result" (Beach 1985:97).

Position: ". . . a collection of tasks and responsibilities . . . assigned to one person" (Beach 1985:97). There are thus as many positions as there are employees.

Job: ". . . an organisational unit of work, made up of tasks, duties and responsibilities" (Jackson and Musselman 1987:211).

Occupation: ". . . a grouping of jobs with broadly similar content, for example managerial, technical, crafts" (Milkovich and Glueck 1985:104).

Job description: ". . . a written statement of those facts which are important regarding the duties, responsibilities, and their organizational and operational interrelationships" (Livy 1988:72).

Job specification: ". . . the minimum skills, knowledge and abilities required to perform the job" (Milkovich and Glueck 1985:104).

Job analysis is essentially a process of obtaining certain information with regard to a job. This information is recorded by compiling two separate documents, i.e. a job description and a job specification, as shown in figure 5.2.

5.3.2 The applications of job analysis

A comprehensive job analysis programme provides important information to human resources management that can be used in many areas. These include:

- *Organisational and human resources planning:* When the total extent of the work to be carried out in the organisation has been determined, it is necessary to divide the work into various tasks and jobs at every level within the organisation, from the lowest to the highest. When the organisational

FIGURE 5.2: Job analysis

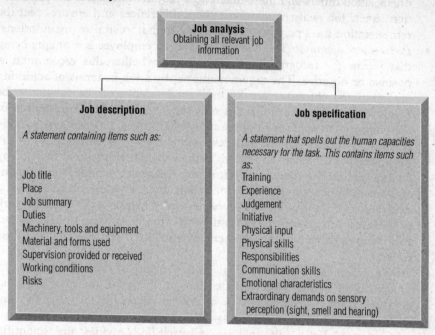

structure is developed, the tasks are combined into meaningful units according to their distinctiveness and are then classified into jobs. Job analysis plays an important role here, as it helps to create the correct number and types of jobs, and to determine the necessary job specification (i.e. qualifications) for each job. Job analysis is thus an essential element for effective human resources planning.

- *Recruitment, selection and placement:* To place an employee in a job effectively requires an accurate job specification, i.e. a description of the knowledge and skills that employees must have to be able to carry out these tasks successfully. This requires that the skills and interests of employees must be matched with the requirements of the job. Comprehensive job information is thus essential.
- *Training and development:* Comprehensive job information is very valuable for those who must administer training and development programmes. It helps them determine the content of the courses, so that the necessary qualifications for each job can be determined. The success of an organisation is based on the ability of its personnel to successfully carry out the jobs assigned to them. Job analysis information provides the necessary inputs so that programmes can be designed that will enable employees to successfully carry out their jobs.
- *Remuneration:* This depends on the contribution of a particular job to the attainment of organisational objectives. The importance of jobs in an

organisation differs and these differences require differences in remuneration levels. Job analysis points out these differences and ensures that the remuneration for a particular job is equal to that in similar organisations.

- *Performance appraisal:* The human being as an employee is a unique being that yearns for recognition—irrespective of whether this recognition is positive or negative. The requirements set by a job in terms of achieving organisational objectives can be used to develop accurate standards for employee performance which not only reflect the current contribution of the employee to achieving organisational objectives, but can also provide reasons for further training and development, or even dismissal.
- *Safety and health:* Safety and health in the work situation are influenced by factors such as the correct lay-out of the workplace, standard equipment and other physical conditions. Information about what the job entails and a description of the type of employee necessary help to establish safe work procedures. Job analysis provides the opportunity to bring unhealthy and restricting or dangerous environmental factors such as noise, heat and dust to light.
- *Career planning:* The individual joins an organisation with certain preconceived career expectations that are part of the psychological contract. Career advancement is of special psychological value for any normal employee and is directly associated with an employee's attitude to performance. Valid job analysis information provides the scientific framework within which meaningful career management can take place.

The applications for the information obtained through job analysis are illustrated in figure 5.3.

5.3.3 The job analysis process
Successfully carrying out the job analysis process requires a number of logical steps. These steps are summarised as follows by Livy (1988:63):

Step 1: The organisation as a whole is analysed according to job analysis principles. This step is important because it provides an overall picture of the work activities that will be carried out in the organisation.

Step 2: This step involves decisions about the manner in which the information to be obtained from the job analysis will be utilised.

Step 3: The selection of jobs to be analysed is decided on.

Step 4: The analysis of the selected jobs in accordance with job analysis principles and techniques. Information is obtained with regard to the nature of the job, the desired employee behaviour and the characteristics of the employee who would successfully fill the job.

Step 5: The information obtained in step 4 is used to draw up a job description. It details the most important elements for carrying out the job.

Step 6: The job specification is compiled. It fully stipulates the minimum skills, knowledge and abilities required for successfully carrying out a job.

FIGURE 5.3: Applications for job analysis information

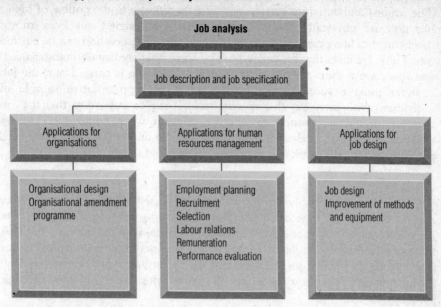

Source: Milkovich and Glueck (1985:105)

Step 7: With the information obtained in steps 1 to 6, the task of job design is embarked upon. Job design indicates how the elements, obligations and tasks of a job must be combined to obtain optimal employee performance and job satisfaction.

Step 8: The last step involves the continuous evaluation of the job to ensure that the job description and specification are in accordance with modern technology.

5.3.4 Methods of job analysis

Methods of job analysis can be classified into two main groupings: general techniques and specialised techniques. These two approaches are now briefly discussed.

5.3.4.1 *General techniques*

It is possible to use any of the four techniques now discussed in combination. Although this is very expensive and time-consuming, all four techniques may be used simultaneously to do a comprehensive job analysis. If a more specialised job analysis is required, or if a quantifiable score is needed, the job analyser will have to make use of more specialised techniques, such as those discussed in paragraph 5.3.4.2.

Observation

The actions and activities carried out by an employee in the course of his or her task are physically observed. Tasks that are carried out by a motor mechanic or a filing clerk are examples where direct observation can be carried out. These are tasks that are carried out by hand, that are usually standardised, and that have a short activity cycle. When observation is carried out, the job analyser must ensure that he or she covers a representative sample of individuals who carry out this specific task. It is also important that the job analyser should be trained to observe relevant work behaviour. During observation, the job analyser must ensure that he or she is as unobtrusive as possible, so that the work can continue unhindered.

The interview

The interview is probably the most commonly used job analysis technique, and is often used together with the observation technique. During the interview, the job analyser can communicate directly with the incumbent. This has two advantages: the job analyser can ask the incumbents questions about how exactly they carry out the task; and the incumbents can be reassured by the job analyser about how the latter will use the information obtained through job analysis.

During the interview, a structured set of questions is usually used, so that the answers of the individual incumbents or groups of employees can be compared with each other. Interviews may be conducted with a single incumbent, a group of individuals or a supervisor who has sufficient knowledge of the job.

The interview has one important disadvantage: erroneous information can easily be presented in this manner. This will particularly be the case if an incumbent is under the impression that the job analyser wants to use the interview to determine remuneration levels. An incumbent may then provide erroneous information in an attempt to increase the remuneration. To eliminate this problem, interviews should be conducted with more than one incumbent. The interview must also be well planned, meaningful questions must be asked, and it must be ensured at all times that the communication between the incumbent and the job analyser is accurate.

> Information obtained through an interview must be supplemented and further refined through observation and questionnaires.

Questionnaires

The structured questionnaire asks specific questions with regard to the job, job requirements, work circumstances and equipment. An unstructured questionnaire will, for example, ask the incumbent to describe the task in his or her own words. Whether the questionnaire should contain structured or unstructured questions depends on the competence and articulateness of the incumbents.

When using the questionnaire, it is important that the job analyser should keep the following in mind:

- Explain to the incumbent what the questionnaire is used for.
- Make the questions short, clear and factual.
- The questionnaire should be as concise as possible.
- Test the questionnaire before it is given to incumbents. (This gives the analyser an opportunity to make changes before the questionnaire is used in its final form.)

The questionnaire is probably the cheapest way of doing job analyses. It is also an effective method to obtain a large quantity of information within a short time.

Incumbent's diary/logbook

Incumbents may be using a diary/logbook to record the job duties, frequency of the duties and times when the duties are carried out. Such a diary/logbook can provide the job analyser with valuable information, particularly where it is difficult for him or her to observe the incumbent while carrying out the task. This is particularly true of high-level jobs such as those of scientists, senior executive officers and engineers.

In practice it happens that incumbents are slow or even irresponsible, and fail to update the diaries/logbooks daily. This means that the information obtained from this source is not always as reliable as it should be.

5.3.4.2 Specialised techniques

In specialised techniques, systematic and quantitative procedures are used to obtain information with regard to job duties and the skills, knowledge and abilities necessary for a specialised job. The specialised techniques mentioned here are functional job analysis, the position analysis questionnaire, and the management positions description questionnaire.

Functional job analysis

This technique is generally used in the public sector to describe the nature of jobs, to draw up job descriptions, and to provide details of job specifications. Functional job analysis is based on acceptance of the fact that all jobs presuppose that there are relations between data, people and things, and that these relations can be arranged by the job analyser in terms of their complexity. The simplest relation is one in which someone receives an instruction. The most complex relation is one in which the role of mentor or adviser is played. Figure 5.4 gives an example of such a functional job analysis.

The position analysis questionnaire (PAQ)

The position analysis questionnaire was developed by the University of Purdue in the USA and consists of 194 items. It is the job analyser's task to

FIGURE 5.4: Functional job analysis

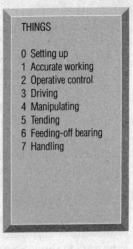

DATA	PEOPLE	THINGS
0 Synthesising	0 Acting as mentor	0 Setting up
1 Coordinating	1 Negotiating	1 Accurate working
2 Analysing	2 Giving instructions	2 Operative control
3 Setting up	3 Supervising	3 Driving
4 Processing	4 Turning away	4 Manipulating
5 Copying	5 Persuading	5 Tending
6 Comparing	6 Signalling	6 Feeding-off bearing
	7 Rendering service	7 Handling
	8 Taking instructions/ rendering assistance	

Source: Adapted from Fine and Wiley (1973)

decide whether a certain item is essential for carrying out a specialised task. The 194 items are divided into six categories:

- *Information input:* How does the incumbent obtain information?
- *Intellectual processes:* What decision-making, planning and reasoning ability is necessary to do the work?
- *Relations with people:* What type of relations with other people are necessary for the work?
- *Job contacts:* In which physical and social context is the work carried out?
- *Other characteristics of the work,* for example activities, working conditions.

A point allocation for each task is done on the basis of the following:

- Decision making;
- Communication;
- Social responsibilities;
- The execution of skilled activities;
- Physical activities;
- Control over vehicles or equipment;
- Processing of information.

The most important advantage of this technique is that it is widely used and researched. There are also few differences when various job analysers analyse the same job. The greatest disadvantage of this technique, on the other hand, is the large number of items that have to be considered and the fact that the process is time-consuming. The fact that the technique mainly focuses on similarities between jobs, while for some applications of job analysis data (for example with regard to remuneration) it is necessary to pay attention to both similarities and differences between jobs, has also been criticised (Milkovich and Glueck 1985:113).

Management positions description questionnaire (MPDQ)
Because managerial jobs differ widely from industry to industry and particularly with regard to hierarchical levels, the job analyser is subjected to particular demands when he or she undertakes the analysis of managerial jobs. The management positions description questionnaire contains 208 items, divided into ten groups:
- General information;
- Decision-making;
- Planning and organising;
- Supervision and control;
- Counselling and innovation;
- Contacts;
- Monitoring of business indicators;
- General evaluation;
- Expertise;
- Organisational chart.

The answers given by the incumbents (managers) are used to bring job descriptions up to date, to do career planning for managers, to evaluate management performance appraisal tasks, and to develop new job analysis methods.

The most important disadvantage of this technique is its high cost. Studies have indicated that before such a system begins to pay for the effort, time and expense spent on it, about a year is spent developing and administering the content. In addition, there is the cost of computerisation and consultation (Milkovich and Glueck 1985:113).

5.3.5 Job description
The job description is, as already mentioned, the written document in which is spelled out what the incumbent does, how he or she does it, and under what circumstances the task is carried out. A typical job description should contain information on the following:
- Job identification;
- Task summary;
- Relations, responsibilities and duties;
- Authority and job standards;
- Work circumstances.

These aspects are now briefly discussed:
- *The job identification:* This specifically refers to the job title or job designation, such as sales manager or cashier. The job status is also indicated, together with the date on which the job description was compiled, and the name of the person who compiled the job description.

Space must be left for the approval of the job description by a senior manager. The job identification often also provides information with regard to the remuneration associated with the job.

- *The job summary:* This provides a list of the most important functions or activities of a specialised post. It must be as specific as possible, since it must provide information that will be used in drawing up a job specification (what type of employee is required to fill the job, what training is necessary for the incumbent, and how the incumbent will be evaluated).

- *Relations, responsibilities and duties: Relations* indicate the incumbent's relations with others within and outside the organisation, for example to whom he or she reports, whom he or she supervises, with whom he or she works and with whom he or she must liaise outside the organisation (trade union representatives, recruitment agencies, personnel consultants, etc.).

  As far as the *responsibilities* and *duties* of the job are concerned, it is desirable first to spell out the most important duties and then to define each duty in detail.

- *Authority and job standards:* The incumbent's *authority* limits must be clearly spelled out here. This includes his or her decision-making powers, supervision of other employees and budget limitations.

  Job standards state how the employee is expected to carry out each of the main duties and responsibilities spelled out in the job description.

- *Work circumstances:* The job description should indicate any special work circumstances for the job, for example the noise level, heat and other risk factors such as the placement of equipment.

Finally, some remarks about the writing of the job description. The job description should be *clearly* compiled so that the task can be carried out without referring to other job descriptions. *Specific* definition is necessary to indicate the following:

- The nature of the work;
- The degree of complexity;
- The skills required;
- The extent to which problems are standardised;
- The responsibility of each employee in each phase of the work;
- The degree of and types of responsibility.

5.3.6 Job specifications

The job specification is developed from the job description, and must provide the answer to the question of which personal skills and experience are necessary for the effective execution of a certain task. The job specification thus also provides clear guidelines for recruitment and selection.

Job specifications can make use of the judgement of supervisors or human resources managers to determine which requirements with regard to training, intelligence, skills, etc. are necessary for a certain task.

Job specifications based on statistical analyses are far more objective, but also more difficult to compile. Basically, a statistical relationship between a forecast measure of personal skills such as intelligence or manual dexterity, and a measure of task effectiveness, for example performance, is determined by the supervisor. Dessler (1984:99) defines this process in five steps:

- A job is analysed and a decision is made on how to measure task performance.
- Personal skills are then selected. These skills are used as performance predictors.
- The candidates are tested for these skills.
- The candidates' task performance is then measured.
- A statistical analysis is carried out to test the relationship between personal skills (such as manual dexterity) and task performance.

5.3.7 Conclusion

Management must ensure that each individual employee has a separate, clearly demarcated job with special tasks and duties in order to attain objectives in a coordinated manner.

In this section, it is pointed out that the nature of the work plays an important role in the management of human resources. Job design and job analysis are discussed as two important aids to determine the nature of the work and the demands it makes on the employee. Special attention is paid to job analysis as a procedure to determine what the job entails and the kind of individuals to be employed.

How can the filling of vacancies be planned? It can be decided to wait until a vacancy does arise, and then to fill it as effectively as possible. Such an approach is probably successful in a small organisation. Larger organisations, on the other hand, require forecasting and planning. This is discussed in the following section.

5.4 THE HUMAN RESOURCES PLANNING PROCESS
5.4.1 General

The simplest definition of human resources planning is the process through which it can be ensured that the correct number of employees, of the right kind, in the right place and at the right time are available to the organisation.

Armstrong (1988:205) supplements this definition and regards human resources planning as consisting of six associated activities, i.e.:

- Demand forecasting;
- Supply forecasting;
- Forecasting requirements;
- Productivity and cost analyses;
- Action plans;
- Budgeting and control.

From the aforementioned descriptions it is clear that human resources planning is a continuous process that must be constantly adapted as circumstances within and outside the organisation change. In addition, human resources planning requires a detailed analysis of current and future circumstances to ensure that the organisation has the right number of employees with the right skills to be able to do the work when required to do so. Ultimately, a balance must be found between the organisation's need for productive employees and the employees' need for personal job and career satisfaction.

Milkovich and Boudreau (1988:313) define human resources planning as follows:

> . . . the process that estimates the future demands for employees, both in quality and quantity, compares the expected demand with the current work force; and determines the employee shortages or surpluses based on the organization's strategies and objectives.

From this it is clear that human resources planning is an integral part of the overall strategy of the organisation.

In simple terms, human resources planning involves a series of activities that can be illustrated as in figure 5.5.

FIGURE 5.5: Human resources planning activities

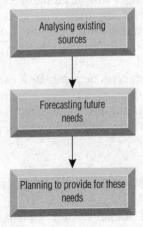

It must be emphasised that human resources planning is an activity undertaken at the top management level of an organisation. It is often a sophisticated process that is carried out with the aid of computer and mathematical models. It is thus only the human resources specialist who is normally directly involved in the formulation of the human resources plan of the organisation.

Systematic human resources planning as an important factor only began to receive recognition fairly recently. Traditionally, it was accepted by management that personnel could be recruited whenever vacancies occurred. Beach

(1985:110) provides important reasons why human resources planning should take place on a continuous basis:

- Human resources planning is essential for determining future human resources needs.
- Human resources planning enables the organisation to adapt to changes in markets, competitors, technology, products and government regulations. Such changes often generate changes in job content, skill requirements and the number and type of employees required.

> Because of the knowledge explosion and technological acceleration, it is expected that by the last part of this decade, a job will be done in an entirely different manner every three years.

- Human resources planning is an important component of strategic planning.
- Human resources planning provides important information for the design and implementation of activities such as recruitment, selection, training, transfers, promotions and dismissal of personnel.

5.4.2 Factors that influence human resources planning

Human resources planning is influenced by various factors. These factors can be internal or external, as shown in figure 5.6.

FIGURE 5.6: Factors that influence human resources planning

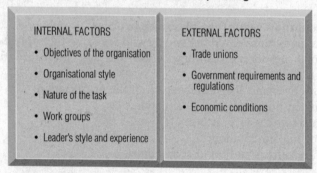

Source: Ivancevich and Glueck (1986:135)

Human resources planning is closely related to the objectives of the organisation. If growth is one of the organisational objectives, human resources planning will have to be prepared to provide sufficient personnel in the case of, for example, diversification. This implies effective planning for additional employment. A need for unskilled employees will not necessarily have to be planned for in advance, but because highly skilled marketing personnel will probably have to go through a training period, their employment will require more planning. In the same way, the management philosophy and the nature of the work will exercise an important influence on human resources planning. Work groups and their functioning influence human resources planning because the replacement of individual members of a work group, for example, requires that the group dynamics be taken into account. The mutual interaction of work groups must also be taken into account. The style of the leader or supervisor and his or her experience is another important factor that must be considered during human resources planning. How the leader will guide and handle the employees will ultimately determine how many employees will be necessary to carry out the task and, very important, how often these employees will have to be replaced.

The external factors that can exercise an influence on human resources planning include: firstly, trade unions which can set certain requirements with regard to the number and type of employees for a specific task. Secondly, the government may set requirements or regulations which, for example, determine that only employees with special training can be allowed to carry out a specific task. Finally, labour market conditions and the economic climate can exercise an important influence on planning for employment.

Finally, it must not be forgotten that the employment needs of an organisation have their origin in strategic decisions made by its top management. The top management combines economic, technological and market forecasts with planning in respect of investment, and then calculates with the assistance of human resources management how many employees with specific skills will be necessary to carry out the tasks.

5.4.3 The human resources planning process
Although organisations can differ widely with regard to the sophistication with which human resources planning is carried out, there are five general components in the process:
- The objectives and the strategic plan of the organisation;
- The current human resources situation;
- Human resources forecasting;
- Plans for implementation;
- Human resources audit and adaptations.

5.4.3.1 *The objectives and the strategic plan of the organisation*
As has already been mentioned, human resources planning forms part of the global strategic planning of the organisation. This implies that human resources management cannot plan in advance, unless it has sufficient information with regard to aspects such as possible expansion in the activities of the organisation, marketing of new products, development of new markets, new plants, etc.

We might well ask how far in advance planning should take place to make provision for sufficient human resources. Various factors must be taken into account here. In the first place, the overall strategic plan of the organisation will provide important information or inputs. Secondly, the nature of the organisation and the type of product will play an important role. An organisation such as Eskom or Telkom will do long-term planning for periods of 10 or 20 years. This type of organisation is, however, the exception: in most cases, planning takes place for periods of one to three years. In most cases, short-term forecasts can be linked to trends such as population growth and economic indicators. Other organisations, such as shops that sell ladies' clothing, must do short-term planning to take fashion changes into account.

Human resources planning is generally done for a period of one year. Planning for periods longer than a year considerably increases the risk.

At a strategic level, provision should be made for succession planning. This involves preparing specific candidates (current employees) to replace existing incumbents when they are transferred or promoted, or when they retire. It is important to develop an accurate profile of the requirements to fill specific jobs, to select the candidates who meet the requirements or have the necessary potential, and then to take the necessary steps to prepare such candidates for filling the expected vacancy by, among other things, sending him or her on training and development programmes.

Figure 5.7 is an example of a typical succession planning chart.

FIGURE 5.7: Succession planning chart

Promotability coding system

* Requires considerable development

** Only slight development necessary

*** Immediately ready for promotion

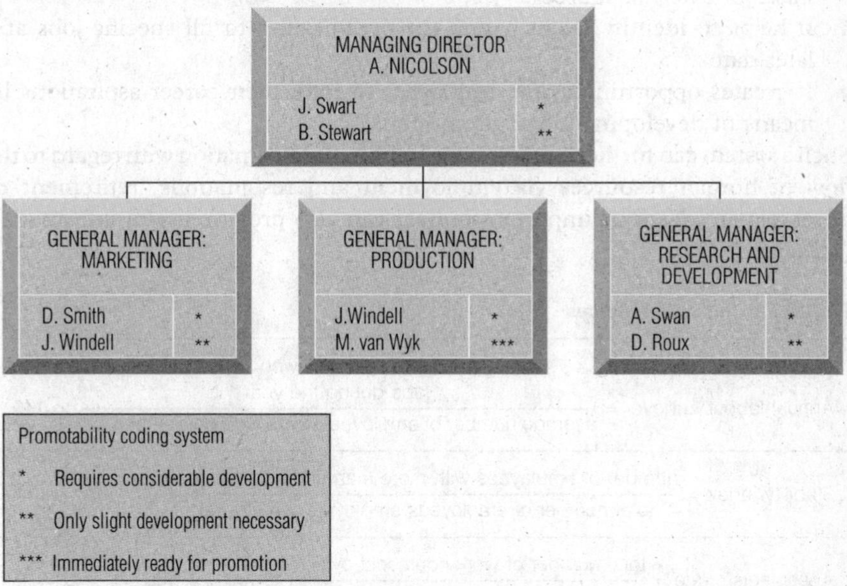

5.4.3.2 The current human resources situation

The second step in the human resources planning process is an inventory of the people currently in the employ of the organisation. This survey is often referred to as a skills inventory or a human resources information system. Such a skills inventory constantly supplies up-to-date information with regard to the qualifications of selected categories of employees, such as technical or professional staff. In turn, a human resources information system will provide information with regard to all the employees in the service of the organisation, from unskilled employees to top management.

A skills inventory will, among other things, contain the following particulars:
- Personal information such as name, date of birth and sex;
- Training, for example diplomas or degrees obtained or special training courses completed;
- Service record—current job, salary scale, previous employers;
- Performances and potential—results of performance evaluation, appraisal centre evaluation;
- Career prospects—personal plans for training, specific tasks, placement.

The skills inventory strives for the following:
- It makes a comparison between what is required in the human resources forecast and the skills currently available in the organisation. The skills bank provides an indication of the extent to which the existing personnel can be developed by means of training, upgrading and special attempts at development to be able to meet future needs, and whether use should be made of external sources.
- It helps to identify talent within the organisation to fill specific jobs at a later date.
- It creates opportunities for employees to fulfil their career aspirations by means of development and promotions.

Such a system can furthermore provide important information with regard to the flow of human resources via employment and resignations, retirement or retrenchment. Various important indices can also provide useful information (see table 5.1).

TABLE 5.1: Important indices

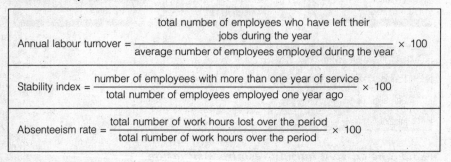

$$\text{Annual labour turnover} = \frac{\text{total number of employees who have left their jobs during the year}}{\text{average number of employees employed during the year}} \times 100$$

$$\text{Stability index} = \frac{\text{number of employees with more than one year of service}}{\text{total number of employees employed one year ago}} \times 100$$

$$\text{Absenteeism rate} = \frac{\text{total number of work hours lost over the period}}{\text{total number of work hours over the period}} \times 100$$

Important additional information can include salary budgets, performance evaluation data and data on skills that are available but are not being used.

5.4.3.3 Human resources forecasting

Human resources forecasting involves establishing the future demand for employees with certain skills, as well as an estimate of the supply of employees who will be available. This supply consists of two groups of employees: those who are currently employed by the organisation and who will still be available at the end of a specific period, and external candidates who must be appointed. The figure for the latter is obtained by subtracting the number of employees who are internally available from the projected demand. If the figure is positive, employees will have to be recruited. If the figure is negative, some of the existing employees will have to be dismissed.

The demand forecast is extrapolated from the information obtained in step 1 in paragraph 5.3.1, where information about expected sales, the number of units produced, the number of clients, possible new plants, etc. is collected.

The forecast of the future need can be influenced by various factors. The most important factor is the strategic plan of the organisation. Other factors, both internal and external, should also be taken into consideration.

Internal factors include:
- The age structure of the labour force;
- How long the employees stay with the organisation on average;
- Productivity;
- Absenteeism;
- Overtime.

External factors include:
- Skills available in the labour market;
- Competitors in the labour market;
- Accelerated technology;
- New work patterns/attitudes;
- Current remuneration levels;
- The extent to which affirmative action may in future become enforceable in South African organisations.

Milkovich and Boudreau (1988:317) propose a model according to which human resources forecasting can be carried out through a demand and supply analysis in three phases.

Phase 1: Demand analysis. During this phase, an internal analysis is made of the marketing, financial, operational and technological plans of the organisation, and the need for human resources is determined.

Phase 2: Supply analysis. During this phase, the following aspects are analysed:
- The effectiveness of the existing recruitment programme(s);
- Turnover patterns such as promotions, transfers, demotions, retrenchments, retirements and resignations;
- The external labour market to determine the external supply of potential employees.

99

FIGURE 5.8: Human resources forecasting through demand and supply analysis

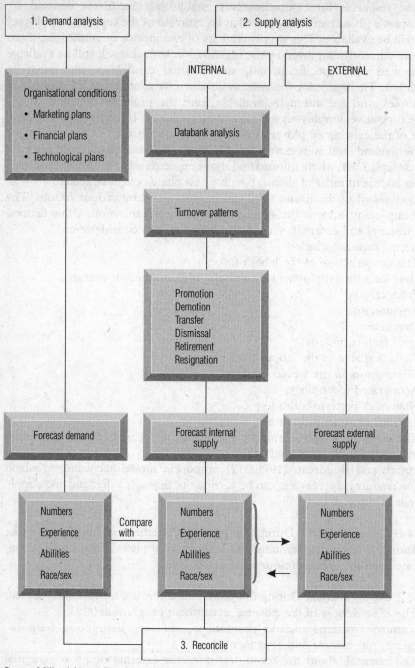

Source: Milkovich and Boudreau (1988:314)

Phase 3: Reconciliation. The demand forecast is compared with the supply forecast with regard to the number of employees, experience, skills, race and sex.

The techniques available for human resources forecasting vary from subjective estimates to highly sophisticated quantitative models. The techniques can be grouped according to three approaches:

- *The "top-to-bottom" approach:* This implies that top management does all the human resources forecasting.
- *The "bottom-to-top" approach:* This implies that units or departments do their own human resources forecasting.
- *A combination of the two approaches* is also possible.

The approach in which top management does the forecasting is probably the one used most often. Four techniques can be used for this purpose:

- *The expert approach technique* is probably the simplest way to do human resources forecasting. The expert is asked to make an estimate of human resources needs based on his or her own experience or intuition. This technique can, however, be refined by making use of the Delphi technique, in which the opinions of a group of experts are used. The Delphi technique involves the intensive questioning of every expert to obtain the required information. The experts are purposely not brought into contact with one another, to ensure that each gives his or her independent opinion. After the information supplied by each of the experts has been processed, the average figure is determined. The experts are then asked once again to make their estimates against the background of the average figure. The new average will then serve as the forecasting figure.
- *The trend projection technique:* By using this technique, a forecast is developed based on a relationship (in the past) between a factor related to employment and employment itself, for example sales figures and the number of employees required. This is a relatively cheap way of forecasting employment needs and is often used.

  A considerable number of quantitative analyses may be necessary to indicate the relationship between changes in economic indicators and necessary changes in human resources. In some types of organisation, the total number of employees is not directly proportional to the production volume. Thus an oil refinery may require just as many employees when it runs at 80% capacity as it would when running at full capacity. During forecasting, this must be carefully taken into account.
- *The tendency projection technique* is based on the relationship between a single factor (such as sales figures) and employment. The more sophisticated approaches simultaneously take into account multiple factors such as sales, gross national product and discretionary income, to name but a few. To be able to do this, models are used in which these variables are simulated.

  An example of such a model is the Markov chain analysis. This involves the development of a matrix through which various forecasts can be done.

Markov analyses are used to determine the time a person would take to master a post if he or she were employed at various levels in the organisation. Thus it can be statistically determined how an employee's career progress will take place.

- *The unit forecasting technique:* A unit may consist of a department, a project team or a group of employees. They use the "bottom-to-top" approach. The members of the unit provide their own information for forecasting the future demand to top management. Top management then makes use of the information obtained from the various units to make a global forecast. The advantage of this method is that the unit manager, together with his or her unit, is probably best equipped to judge or to make optimal use of the available human resources, and to decide whether the demand for the product or service will be the same in future. The accuracy of the forecasts is probably enhanced by the in-depth knowledge that units have of their own, smaller departments.

5.4.3.4 *The implementation programme*

Implementation requires that human resources planning be transformed into action steps. If, for example, forecasts show that there will be a shortage of trained artisans, plans will have to be put into action to train existing personnel in time, or to recruit others. The implementation of such plans naturally has a direct influence on other activities such as recruitment, selection, placement, performance evaluation, career planning, promotions, transfers, dismissals, retirements, training, development, motivation and remuneration. As each of these activities is discussed in detail elsewhere in this book, this discussion will only briefly touch on the most important implementation actions and how they affect each of these activities.

When a shortage of, for example, artisans is expected, management must identify potentially good sources of supply and then use the correct recruitment method. The selection programme must be scientifically designed. In the same way, placement must be done in such a way that individual job preferences and qualifications tally with the needs of the organisation.

Performance appraisal has two uses, i.e. to enable management to take decisions about salary increases, promotions, transfers and dismissals, and to provide information about the development of employees.

Career development focuses on individual career training and self-analysis, plus planned opportunities and development activities.

Because organisations are constantly changing, there is personnel movement within the organisation: promotions, transfers, dismissals and retirements.

As technology changes, new products are placed on the market, re-organisation of personnel takes place and promotions are made, the need for well-designed training and development programmes arises. This encompasses programmes such as on-the-job training, in-house training, coaching and the attendance at formal courses and seminars, to name but a few examples.

The entire system of motivation, leadership and remuneration contributes towards the proper execution of the human resources plan. If remuneration is inadequate, the organisation will find it difficult to attract suitable personnel. If there are problems with the type of leadership within the organisation—for example where employees perceive themselves as being treated in an autocratic and arbitrary manner—the organisation will also find it difficult to satisfy its human resources needs.

5.4.3.5 Human resources audit

The human resources audit differs from human resources forecasting in the sense that human resources forecasting looks at the future, while human resources audits are concerned with the present.

A human resources audit (Milkovich and Boudreau 1988:320) can be described as:

> . . . a systematic formal experience designed to measure the costs and benefits of the total human resources programme and to compare its effectiveness and efficiency with the organization's past performance, the performance of comparable effective enterprises, and the enterprise's objectives.

Important activities that must be carried out by the human resources audit include: first, the current quality of the existing employees must be investigated with the aim of improving the quality of the employees over a certain period. Job analysis can be used for this purpose. Secondly, attention must be paid to the skills inventory—the level of proficiency of the employees. Thirdly, the human resources audit must take labour turnover into account. This also includes replacement schedules, which are concerned with dismissal, strikes, etc. Finally, the human resources audit must take note of the internal movements of employees, such as transfers and promotions.

A human resources audit creates the opportunity to make the necessary changes and adaptations to the human resources planning process.

5.5 AN APPLIED APPROACH TO HUMAN RESOURCES PLANNING

5.5.1 Introduction

Human resources planning aims at providing an organisation, by means of a scientific process, with the necessary human resources, according to specific job requirements, when and where necessary.

The advantages associated with such a process are, among others:

- A human resources budget can be accurately forecast for certain periods according to such a process.
- The necessary recruitment actions can be launched in good time.
- Succession planning can be carried out according to objective information.
- Personnel development planning is facilitated.

5.5.2 The human resources planning process

The process is shown in figure 5.9 and explained step by step. The example used is the development of a human resources planning process for a faculty of a tertiary institution.

FIGURE 5.9: Human resources planning process

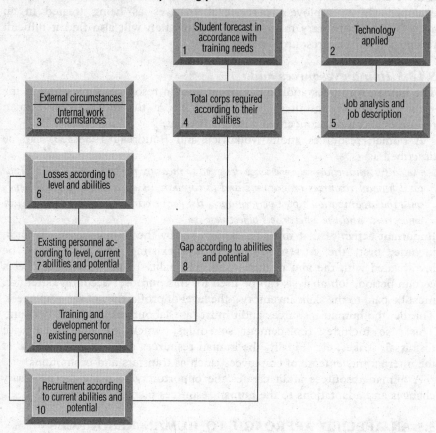

Source: Wolvaardt and Van Dyk (1993:2)

- The process begins in block 1. On a demographic basis, it is calculated how many students the faculty can expect in each of the following 10 years. The numbers are integrated with the institutions own statistics to see how many will be enrolled for each of the courses in the faculty in each year. These figures are centrally calculated in the faculty and passed on to the' departments for improvement and use in their planning process, as the rest of the process takes place per department.
- Block 3 is also done by the faculty for and in cooperation with each department. Here the working conditions and the supply/demand situation

outside the university are investigated and the department's appeal to academics is determined. The aim is both to estimate the possible losses to the outside and to investigate the possibility of attracting new people from outside. The block is divided to indicate that the external circumstances are out of the faculties control, but that various possibilities with regard to how things look within the university can be followed up.

- Block 3 is an independent point of departure and goes over into block 6, where it is individually calculated how many academics the university is expected to lose. This takes place on the basis of the information in block 7 which states how many people of each type are in the academic departments. If there is a 10% loss of cost accountants, and there are 20 of them, then the loss will be two as opposed to a loss of one if there are only 10 of them. In the same way the loss of tax experts may be 25%, which gives another result again.

  Note that the department itself can determine which categories will be used. It is, for example, possible to work by job level, or by age.

- Block 7 is the "database" which, within the department, refers to a list of the various categories and how many people there are in each. A page is allocated to each of the 10 years to be planned for. On the first page, the current numbers are filled in. The numbers for the following year are filled in by subtracting losses (according to blocks 3 and 6), adding (according to block 10) and shifting (according to 9).

- In block 10 it is determined how many people will be recruited in each category. The categories must be multi-dimensional to indicate potential, as given in table 5.2.

TABLE 5.2: Tax experts

Age	RANK							
	Lecturer		Senior lecturer		Associate professor		Professor	
Younger than 30								
30–39								
40 and older								
	High	Low	High	Low	High	Low	High	Low
	POTENTIAL							

Sometimes, for example, lecturers must be recruited only to act as markers and to remain markers. In such cases the potential for further development does not need to be high. This can apply at various job levels. These figures are carried over to the page that represents the condition at the beginning of the following year.

- Block 9 shows the shifting of staff between categories. The result of this is taken over to the page that gives the projected condition for the beginning of the following year.
- For each of the following 10 years, a page is calculated in the same manner: starting condition in the various categories minus losses plus recruitment and shifting of existing staff due to personal development or due to decline or stagnation.

> A department has two ways in which to improve the personnel matrix: recruitment and personnel development. It is especially the latter which provides many possibilities. Recruitment can also be methodically addressed with a long-term view.

- Block 2 indicates the educational model and technology from which the job descriptions in block 5 flow. A department that writes programs to mark the work of students and provides it to the students on disk at the beginning of the year, has quite different job descriptions from one that corrects large numbers of assignments.
- In block 4, the student numbers are added up according to their year courses and the technology used to determine how many lecturers are required in each category in the given year. This is carried over to block 8, where the input of block 7 for the same year is also added. A desired personnel matrix and a forecast personnel matrix are thus combined to give a gap matrix which is useful for recruitment and personnel development.
- Each department decides for itself how this must take place: whether planning is to take place for 10 years or five, what the categories will be, whether it first wants to calculate the desired personnel matrix for the tenth year and work backwards, or whether it wants to work forward from the present, etc.

5.6 CONCLUSION

The first step in the human resources provision process, i.e. human resources planning, was discussed in this chapter. The focus was on job analysis. Now that the organisation's need for human resources has been determined, the following chapter deals with the next step in the provision process, i.e. the recruitment of suitable personnel to fulfil these needs.

Questions

1. Fully discuss how job descriptions differ from job specifications.
2. How do you see the role that the human resources planning process plays in the total human resources strategy?
3. Contrast and compare the general and specialised methods of job analysis.

Sources

Armstrong, M. 1988. *A handbook of personnel management practice*. 3rd edition. Kogan Page, London.

Adams, R.H. 1989. Management, analysis and planning for skill development in the 90s, *Advanced Management Journal*, vol. 54, Autumn, pp. 34–40.

Beach, D.S. 1985. *The management of people at work*. 5th edition. Macmillan, New York.

Dessler, G. 1984. *Personnel management: modern concepts and techniques*. 3rd edition. Reston, Virginia.

Fine, S.A. & Wiley, W.W. 1973. *An introduction to functional job analysis: a scaling of selected tasks from the social welfare field*. W.E. Upjohn Institute for Employee Research, Kalamazoo, Michigan.

Ivancevich, J.M. & Glueck, W.F. 1986. *Foundations of personnel/human resources management*. Business Publications, Plano, Texas.

Jackson, J.H. & Musselman, V.A. 1987. *Business: contemporary concepts and practices*. 9th edition, Prentice-Hall, Englewood Cliffs, New Jersey.

Leap, T.L. & Crino, M.D. 1993. *Personnel/human resources management*. Macmillan, New York.

Livy, B. 1988. *Corporate personnel management*. Pitman, London.

Milkovich, G.T. & Boudreau, J.W. 1988. *Personnel/human resources management*. Business Publications, Plano, Texas.

Milkovich, G.T. & Glueck, W.F. 1985. *Personnel/human resource management: a diagnostic approach*. 9th edition, Business Publications, Plano, Texas.

Wolvaardt, J.S. & Van Dyk, P.S. 1993. 'n Menslikehulpbronbeplanningstelsel vir 'n tersiêre instelling. Unpublished Report, UNISA, Pretoria.

Chapter 6

Recruitment

P.D. Gerber

STUDY OBJECTIVES

After studying this chapter, you should be able to:

- Differentiate in a logical manner between the various factors that influence recruitment;
- Weigh up the external and internal sources of recruitment against each other;
- Formulate a recruitment policy in practical terms;
- Evaluate the potential employee's perception of recruitment;
- Explain in a practical manner how you would evaluate a recruitment programme.

6.1 INTRODUCTION

The South African labour market is characterised by an oversupply of unskilled and semi-skilled labour and a great shortage of technically qualified and professional human resources. This is one of the main reasons for the low productivity rate of South African organisations. South African organisations do not have adequately qualified human resources to be competitive in the international market environment.

One great shortage is skilled management. When comparing the South African span of management with that of First World countries (table 6.1), it becomes clear why productivity is so low.

TABLE 6.1: The spread of management

USA	Britain	Japan	Germany	RSA (1987)	RSA (2000)
1:7	1:10	1:10	1:9	1:42	1:100

Source: Manning (1988:7–9)

In the same way, the human resources composition in organisations does not promote productivity (see table 6.2).

TABLE 6.2: Labour force relations: South Africa vs First World countries

	Managerial personnel	Highly skilled	Semi-skilled	Unskilled
South Africa	2%	9%	35%	54%
First World	7%	33%	40%	20%

Source: Manning (1988:7–9)

One may well ask: What does the above have to do with recruitment?

If it is already difficult for organisations to obtain human resources of adequate quality now, how much more difficult will it be in a time of economic upswing? It is thus implied that in future there will be stiff competition between organisations to attract the best workers. Only a proactive approach to recruitment can save organisations from this predicament in the future.

6.2 RECRUITMENT: A GENERAL OVERVIEW
6.2.1 General
As a second step in the process of providing human resources, the place of recruitment can be represented as shown in figure 6.1.

FIGURE 6.1: Principal learning components of recruitment

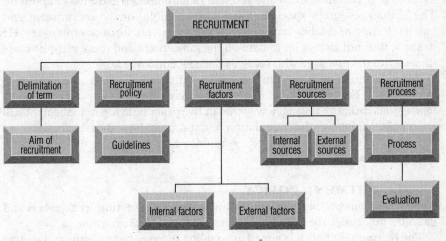

6.2.2 Recruitment planning
Milkovich and Boudreau (1988:361) define recruitment as follows:

   . . . activities to identify and attract a pool of candidates for changes in employment status, from which some will later be selected to receive offers.

109

Recruitment aims at encouraging those applicants who have the skills and qualifications necessary to meet the organisation's needs, to apply for employment.

Recruitment is a two-way process in the sense that, just as organisations are searching for potential applicants, applicants are also searching for suitable organisations. The following conditions must be met for this meeting between the organisation and the applicant to take place:

- There must be a common communication medium (the organisation advertises in the medium read by the employment seeker).
- The applicant must be able to find a match between his or her characteristics and the requirements of the job.
- The applicant must be motivated to apply.

To remain competitive, a company should have an effective recruitment programme to ensure that suitable and qualified applicants are attracted.

The following steps should be followed to establish an effective recruitment function within an organisation:

- A recruitment policy must be formulated.
- An analysis of the factors that influence recruitment must be made.
- The various sources of recruitment must be investigated.
- A choice must be made between the various recruitment techniques.
- The recruitment programme must be audited.

Recruitment is an expensive process. For this reason it is important that it should be handled in a scientific manner to make it as cost-effective as possible. The mutual cooperation between line and staff functionaries is extremely important. The human resources specialist who is responsible for the recruitment and initial selection of candidates is normally not the superior of new employees. He or she is thus not always up to date on the job content and there must be close liaison with the manager who receives the new employees.

When formulating a recruitment policy, affirmative action must be taken into account. For example, an organisation may adopt a policy of changing its managerial structure in such a way that in five years time top management will be representative of the population composition. Another example is to increase the percentage of women in middle management by 5% per annum over the following three years.

6.3 RECRUITMENT POLICY

The recruitment policy spells out the objectives of the recruitment process and provides guidelines for carrying out the recruitment programme.

The recruitment policy is aimed at enabling management to attract the most competent individuals for every task, and to fill the job with the best qualified applicant. Questions that may arise in the formulation of a recruitment policy include:

- Can someone from within the organisation be promoted?
- Will family members of existing employees be employed?

- Will handicapped people be employed?
- Will people over 65 be employed?
- Will there be cooperation with other employers?
- Will affirmative action be taken into account?

It is also important to determine who will be responsible for carrying out the recruitment function. The smaller the organisation, the more probable it will be that recruitment will be handled by the line manager, and that it will take place in a fairly informal manner. The larger the organisation, the more probable it will be that the human resources manager will carry out this function. In the case of a very large organisation, this function will probably be carried out by a recruitment specialist.

6.4 FACTORS THAT INFLUENCE RECRUITMENT

6.4.1 General

Whether the potential employee will respond to recruitment depends on various factors, which may be internal or external. External factors are government or trade union limitations and the general condition of the labour market. Internal factors are aspects such as organisational influences, which include both strategy and recruitment, as well as specific criteria for the recruitment of candidates. To this can be added the likes and dislikes of potential candidates. These factors are discussed separately.

6.4.2 Guidelines for recruitment

- Human resources planning and forecasting should precede any recruitment action.
- Comprehensive job analyses are a prerequisite for ensuring that attempts at recruitment are non-discriminatory and that they take place in accordance with job-related factors.
- Full job specifications (the minimum qualities required of the applicant) must be created to ensure an accurate match.
- Sources and methods of recruitment must be adapted to each organisation.
- Both the negative and the positive aspects of the job must be made known to the applicant (realistic job preview).
- Recruitment must take place in accordance with the needs (continuously and not only annually).

6.4.3 External factors

As mentioned, external factors are government or trade union limitations and the labour market.

Government or trade union limitations

Government legislation and regulations must be taken into account when a recruitment programme is compiled. In a country such as the USA, equal rights legislation plays an important role in this regard. Government agencies can even control the sources of recruitment, advertisements and details of the applicants to determine whether equal rights legislation is being adhered to. In terms of these regulations, specifications are even given with regard to which questions may be put to potential candidates during the recruitment interviews.

> Equal rights indicate the ability of an organisation to appoint a person free from any discrimination (sex, race, religion, age, experience).
> Equal rights legislation will become a reality in the new South Africa.

In the USA, some trade unions determine in their contract that recruitment should be limited to that trade union's recruitment centre. This transfers the function of recruitment of trade union members to the trade union itself. In South Africa, this process has as yet not been taken that far.

Labour market conditions
Labour market conditions are probably the most important factor that must be taken into account when a recruitment programme is compiled. If there is an oversupply of the skills required, informal recruitment will probably be sufficient to attract enough candidates. If, however, there is a state of full employment, an intensive recruitment programme will be necessary to attract candidates. The employer can obtain details about the state of the labour market from various sources, such as indices of employment or reports from the Department of Manpower.

> ### Definition of a labour market
> A labour market is a place where demand and supply factors are expressed in the exchange of labour between two parties, the one (employee) who offers labour and the other (employer) who requires and wants labour. This exchange takes place in various types of labour markets, where in many cases there are various intermediaries who act with the aim of facilitating the necessary labour market transactions.

Source: Van Dyk *et al.* (1992:37)

Labour market conditions in South Africa can be described as chaotic, as figure 6.2 confirms.

The question arises how this imbalance can be redressed.

From the imbalance it becomes clear that there must be some innovation or remodelling within the labour force if South Africa wants to remain competitive in any way in the year 2000 and beyond. This innovation or remodelling process can, however, not take place within the South African

112

FIGURE 6.2: The imbalance in the South African labour market

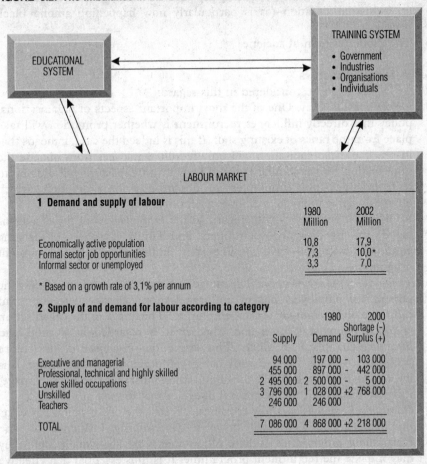

EDUCATIONAL SYSTEM

TRAINING SYSTEM
- Government
- Industries
- Organisations
- Individuals

LABOUR MARKET

1 Demand and supply of labour

	1980 Million	2002 Million
Economically active population	10,8	17,9
Formal sector job opportunities	7,3	10,0*
Informal sector or unemployed	3,3	7,0

* Based on a growth rate of 3,1% per annum

2 Supply of and demand for labour according to category

	1980 Supply	Demand	2000 Shortage (-) Surplus (+)
Executive and managerial	94 000	197 000	- 103 000
Professional, technical and highly skilled	455 000	897 000	- 442 000
Lower skilled occupations	2 495 000	2 500 000	- 5 000
Unskilled	3 796 000	1 028 000	+2 768 000
Teachers	246 000	246 000	
TOTAL	**7 086 000**	**4 868 000**	**+2 218 000**

Source: President's Council (1987:PR.1)

context without taking into account the cultural and motivational differences between the various population groups which form part of the South African labour market, or which will enter it. To redress the imbalance, there must not only be quantitative growth in the labour force, but important qualitative shifts must also take place. The qualitative characteristics of a labour force are, according to Spies (1989:7), measured in terms of the average levels of education and training of its participants. There are, however, also other factors that influence the quality of a country's labour force. Within the South African context, the following factors are of particular importance for the remodelling of the labour force:
- Cultural differences (particularly their variety and divergence in South Africa);
- Population ageing (especially in the case of whites);

- Rural to urban migration, which places a traditionally rural community in an industrial situation (as is particularly now happening among black people);
- The modernisation of societies.

6.4.4 Internal factors

Three factors must be considered in this regard:

- *Organisational policy:* One of the most important aspects of organisational policy that directly influences recruitment is whether promotion will take place from the ranks of existing staff. If this is indeed the case, it means that in practice the organisation will only recruit employees from outside the organisation for the joining ranks. The point of departure will thus be to offer existing, loyal employees an opportunity for promotion, which obviously helps to create a feeling of security.

  Organisational policy with regard to the employment of the disadvantaged, the handicapped, pensioners and family members of existing employees will also have an important influence on the recruitment programme.
- *The image of the organisation:* The image that the public, and specifically the prospective employee, has of an organisation can have an important influence on its ability to recruit employees. The image of the organisation is based on what it does and whether it is regarded as a good and advantageous place to work. The larger the organisation, the more probable it will be that it already has a well developed public image. It is important to note that, while the organisation must build up its own image, it is also influenced by the general image of that branch of industry.
- *Recruitment requirements:* The requirements that the organisation has of its prospective employees will have a determining influence on the recruitment programme. If these requirements are abnormally high, they may impede the recruitment programme. It is thus essential that effective job analysis, job descriptions and job specifications should be used to lay down realistic requirements for the job incumbent, so that the recruitment programme can be meaningfully launched.

If accurate information is available with regard to the job requirements, the remuneration and the direction in which the organisation is moving, both the candidate and the organisation can make a better judgement of whether the job and the candidate's own needs and abilities will match.

6.5 RECRUITMENT SOURCES

6.5.1 Internal sources

Internal sources indicate that the organisation will turn inward when recruiting candidates for vacant posts. The sources that can be used in this way are:
- Present employees;
- Job advertisements;

- Personnel records;
- Skills inventories.

These will now be discussed in more detail.

Present employees

The employee corps currently employed by the organisation is in most cases the most important source of candidates for vacancies. That this source is becoming ever more important is illustrated by the fact that a very large percentage of all management posts are filled by way of promotion or transfer of existing personnel.

There are certain advantages and disadvantages in the use of present employees to fill specific vacancies.

The advantages are:
- Employees see this as a reward for their commitment and loyal service, which in turn can exercise a positive influence on employees' morale and future performance.
- The promotion of present employees can increase loyalty towards the organisation; employees obtain recognition for their performance.
- Existing employees have a better perspective when long-term decisions must be taken, as they have grown with the organisation over a longer period.
- Because they have been in the service of the organisation for a long time, the knowledge and abilities of internal personnel can be more accurately evaluated than those of a person appointed from outside.
- The cost of training and orientation of existing personnel is lower than for employees appointed from outside.

The disadvantages are:
- There may be a danger of "inbreeding", as there will be fewer opportunities for new employees with new ideas and innovations to join the organisation.
- If existing employees apply for promotion and do not succeed, this may have a negative influence on the morale if outsiders are indeed appointed.
- A vacancy may well be filled by the transfer or promotion of a current member of staff, but if there is to be a net addition to the total labour force, someone from outside will have to be appointed.

Job advertisements

Vacant jobs are advertised on bulletin boards within the organisation, or existing employees are periodically informed about vacancies. Full particulars of the available job are given and interested parties are invited to apply.

Personnel records

By investigating personnel records (including application forms), information can be obtained about employees currently in jobs that are below their qualifications, abilities and skills. This can also serve to identify employees who have the potential for further training and development, or who already have the right background to fill certain vacancies.

Skills inventories

Skills inventories consist of all the personal information of employees: their qualifications, potential, skills, performance, promotion and experience. Such a system is usually computerised. With the aid of a computer program, the job requirements can be evaluated against potential and the most suitable person for a certain job identified.

6.5.2 External sources

Depending on the nature of the vacancies, managerial policy and labour market trends, there are certain external sources that can be used by the organisation.

Employment agencies

These agencies act as intermediaries between the employer and prospective employee. The employer notifies the agency about vacancies. The agency then recruits the applicants and sometimes also undertakes the selection. When an appointment is made, the fees for this service are paid to the agency.

Head hunting

Another service that an employment agency can render is the recruitment of managers and high-level professional staff. This is usually done when the agency knows about candidates with special skills and the potential successfully to fill certain managerial positions. The agency then personally approaches such a candidate with an offer from a specific organisation. Usually such a candidate has already been successfully employed by a competitive organisation, but is lured by an attractive offer.

Walk-ins

It does happen from time to time that prospective employees approach an organisation and enquire about possible vacancies. It also happens that an employee applies for a job by sending a completed application form to the organisation in expectation of future vacancies. For employers, this is a useful way of recruiting applicants from outside, especially in the case of low-paid jobs.

Referrals

Employees already in the service of the organisation communicate information about vacancies to family and acquaintances. This method is responsible for filling a considerable percentage of jobs in an organisation, because it is a relatively cheap form of recruitment. In addition, current employees do not want to embarrass themselves by recruiting unsuitable candidates; they therefore recommend useful people.

Professional associations

Professional associations for employees such as engineers, scientists and accountants create opportunities and make their services available to have their members placed in jobs. In practice, these associations offer employers and their members the opportunity to meet each other at their conventions, and often to negotiate about job offers. The professional publications of these associations are also a popular medium for advertising vacancies.

Advertisements

Advertisements in newspapers, magazines and professional journals are an important recruitment method. In fact, this is recognised as the most widely used recruitment method. Advertisements do not only reach the unemployed job seeker, but also attract those looking for better job opportunities. When an organisation wants to advertise a vacancy, it is very important to think about the medium to be used. The choice is between radio, television and press advertisements. The second important point is to pay attention to the wording of the advertisement.

The advertisement should be specific in its content, as it is aimed at a certain target audience, i.e. those who meet the criteria for the job. The aim of the advertisement should be to obtain as wide a response as possible from suitable candidates.

The following are guidelines for the design of an advertisement (Stafford 1990:191):

- The job title must stand out prominently.
- A brief job description must be provided and people must be invited to apply.
- There must be an indication of the type of person required and the special characteristics, capacities, talents, skills and qualifications must be specified.
- In certain cases, information about compensation may be mentioned. Additional conditions of service such as a company car and leave arrangements must be mentioned.
- It must be specified how to apply and to whom applications should be addressed.
- A name or names of references who can be contacted must be clearly requested.
- The closing date for applications must appear prominently.
- The name, address and telephone number of the organisation must be prominently mentioned.
- The organisational logo must form part of the total design.
- Advertisement lay-out techniques must be such that they will draw the attention of a job seeker.

FIGURE 6.3: Advertisement for a professional person through the medium of a professional journal

ABB Powertech is South Africa's largest power electrical engineering group, based in Pretoria West. The Company is engaged in the supply of a wide range of power electrical equipment, including power, distribution and instrument transformers, high-voltage switchgear and relays. We also contract to supply and erect indoor and outdoor sub-stations as well as power generation and reactive power correction equipment.

Senior Personnel Officer

This challenging position calls for a degree-calibre individual with at least 4 years' Personnel and Industrial Relations experience, preferably gained in the steel and engineering industries. Diplomates or registered personnel practitioners will also be considered.

Reporting to the General Manager, the incumbent will assume responsibility for the Human Resources function at the Distribution Transformers Division situated in Rosslyn. The emphasis will be on Industrial Relations and key performance areas will include: ● personnel administration ● recruitment and selection ● policies and procedures ● labour disputes ● grievance and disciplinary hearings and ● compliance with Industrial Relations legislation.

It is essential that candidates must have well-developed communication and interpersonal skills and the ability to interface effectively with people at all levels. Bilingualism is preferred.

The Company offers a negotiable salary and normal company benefits.

Interested applicants should please telephone the Personnel Manager, Lionel Vester, on (012) 318-9911 ext. 9710 or submit a detailed CV to him at PO Box 691, Pretoria 0001.

ABB Powertech
Human Resources Division
ASEA BROWN BOVERI

FIGURE 6.4: Advertisement for a semi-skilled worker through the medium of the organisation's bulletin board

ABC SHOE FACTORY

WANTED

1. Female workers as packers

2. Wage: standard minimum wage for the industry

3. Fringe benefits: normal

4. To start: as soon as possible

5. Contact person: Mrs Recruitment at Extension 007

Timber Sales Representative

The Hardwoods Marketing Division of Hans Merensky Holdings, situated at Alrode, require the services of an experienced timber representative to accept responsibility for the sales of eucalyptus sawtimber.

This position, reporting to the Marketing Manager Hardwoods, would ideally suit a bilingual person with a timber technology diploma or equivalent qualification with several years of proven timber sales experience.

The Company offers a competitive salary, a company car and generous fringe benefits which include an annual bonus, pension and medical schemes.

Applicants should contact Mrs P Van Schoor at (011) 482-1770 or write to: The Group Human Resources Manager, P O Box 52288, Saxonwold 2132, or fax a CV to (011) 726-8600.

HM

HANS MERENSKY HOLDINGS (PTY) LTD.

Costs are an important consideration, and these should be taken into account at all times. The status of the job will determine to a large extent how much should be spent on the advertisement.

Figure 6.3 is an example of an advertisement that meets the above guidelines.

The objective of recruitment is to attract candidates who will possibly accept an offer of work. In this process, the employer may be tempted to follow the so-called *"flypaper" approach* of only listing the most attractive aspects of the job in question in the advertisement. A *marketing approach*, on the other hand, involves determining the needs of a special target group to offer career opportunities in such a way that they address these needs. Such approaches reflect the aim of filling jobs rather than attracting applicants who will best meet the job requirements. The focus should rather be on an accurate

119

description of the job and the organisation, including negative aspects. This approach is called the *realistic job preview*. An example is a film company that clearly indicates in its advertisement that the job involves strict supervision, is repetitive in nature and sometimes requires the applicant to deal with unpleasant and rude clients.

Accurate recruitment messages have the following advantages, according to Milkovich and Boudreau (1988:377):

- They grant applicants an opportunity not to apply if they feel that their interests and qualifications do not meet the stated requirements.
- Realistic information scales down the applicant's expectations.
- Realistic information helps applicants develop better strategies to cope with work problems.
- Applicants can develop a more positive attitude towards employers who provide honest and complete information.

Finally, the timing of the recruitment message is very important. Long waiting times between the placing of the advertisement and the final job offer may contribute towards applicants losing interest and withdrawing from the pool of candidates.

Campus recruitment

Educational institutions such as schools, colleges, technikons and universities are an important source where candidates can be recruited for jobs, particularly people who can be trained for management posts. These sources provide professional and technical employees. The candidates are usually recruited during the final year of their training by arranging open days on campuses.

The campus recruiter has two important functions, i.e. to screen prospective candidates and to attempt to attract the right candidates to the organisation. Applicants who impress the recruiter are invited to visit the organisation to give them an opportunity to find out about the working conditions there. This visit should be arranged in such a way that the prospective applicant will retain a favourable impression of the organisation.

6.6 THE RECRUITMENT PROCESS

Before a recruitment process begins, a study can be done of the factors that will probably contribute towards attracting or discouraging the right candidates. This involves an analysis of the strong and weak points of the organisation as an employer. It includes aspects such as the national or local reputation of the organisation, remuneration, fringe benefits and working conditions, opportunities for training and development, career opportunities and the location of the office or plant. These factors should be compared with those of competitors, so that those that look like selling points can be incorporated in a marketing plan. The positive aspects that will most appeal to prospective candidates can be emphasised in the recruitment strategy. In a certain sense candidates sell themselves when they apply, but at the same time they buy what the organisation has to offer.

Livy (1988:100) proposes the following steps for the recruitment process:

- Obtain approval for an appointment in accordance with the human resources budget and level of appointment.
- Update job descriptions and job specifications and confirm these.
- Choose the most suitable recruitment medium.
- Develop the recruitment advertisement.
- Place the advertisement in the most suitable communication medium.
- Set a closing date for responses.
- Evaluate the applications.
- Compile a short list of candidates for a preliminary interview.
- Choose the candidates on the basis of the job description and job specification criteria.
- Notify the successful and unsuccessful candidates and thank them for their interest.

The impact of an advertisement will partially depend on timing and on whether the advertisement was correctly positioned, which determines the number of readers reached on a certain day, week or specific time of year.

The response to an advertisement can be measured in terms of the number and quality of the candidates who apply. The refinement or sophistication of the subsequent selection process cannot make up for a poor short list of candidates. The recruitment process must thus strive towards compiling the best possible short list of candidates. At the same time, the recruitment process must be cost effective. This in itself requires that a careful analysis be made of recruitment campaigns. A formula that can be applied appears in the accompanying box.

$$\text{Cost of recruitment campaign} = \frac{\text{recruitment costs}}{\text{number of people employed}}$$

6.7 THE EVALUATION OF THE RECRUITMENT PROGRAMME

In most cases, recruitment is an expensive process. The cost of recruitment does not only include the direct costs associated with the salary of the recruiter and the various methods used, but also the time spent by operational personnel in this process.

Each organisation should carefully evaluate the cost of recruitment. The organisation can calculate the cost of each recruitment method separately and then compare it with the advantages that such a system gives. Such advantages can be analysed in terms of a measure, such as acceptance of offers. It can thus be determined that some methods provide a high percentage of qualified applicants, for example referrals from existing employees, but that this method does not provide sufficient applicants to meet the needs of the organisation.

It is important to note that a single recruitment method will rarely yield enough applicants to meet all the needs, particularly those of larger organisations. The organisations are then in most cases obliged to make use of alternative methods, even if the first method is the most cost effective.

When the cost effectiveness of the various recruitment methods is weighed up, it must be kept in mind that factors such as external conditions, the time required to fill vacancies, the nature of the work and the individual characteristics of the applicant and recruiter can all contribute towards cost effectiveness. Stoops (1982:102) further points out that information from previous recruitment activities is the best source for obtaining cost advantages, but that these data are usually either not fully kept, or are not readily available at all.

The evaluation programme consists of two components:

- The evaluation of the effectiveness of the recruiters themselves;
- The evaluation of the recruitment sources.

The effectiveness of the recruiters can be measured by quantifying a certain target and measuring how well the recruiters have succeeded in attaining this goal, for example by counting how many appointments could be made for 30 expected vacancies for clerical personnel. An evaluation of the recruitment sources can be done in several ways. In the case of campus recruitment, for example, the number of acceptances of job offers can be divided by the number of campus interviews to calculate the cost per recruitment at each campus.

The evaluation of the recruitment programme ultimately shows the suitability of the applicants for the jobs, given the money spent. Suitability can be measured as follows (Leap and Crino 1993:217–18):

- The percentage of total applicants who qualify for the job;
- The number of qualified applicants in relation to the number of jobs available;
- The quality of the subsequent performance of the new appointees;
- The total turnover rate for new appointees and the rate at the recruitment source;
- The cost of recruitment to measure the effectiveness of the overall process, as well as the various methods used.

Another important dimension in measuring the success of the recruitment strategy is the extent to which the pool of applicants is representative of the community or labour market. The composition of the pool of applicants should offer an opportunity for participation to all types of individuals.

6.8 THE POTENTIAL EMPLOYEE'S PERCEPTION OF RECRUITMENT

6.8.1 General

Up to this stage, recruitment was looked at from the point of view of the organisation. However, the appointment of employees involves a mutual evaluation process. To accept a job at a new organisation is an important decision for any individual who considers his or her career important. In the same way, it is important for the management of an organisation to employ a person with the right skills and personal attitude. During the recruitment process, there is thus a mutual evaluation which is essentially the psychological contract discussed in chapter 4.

To carry out an effective recruitment campaign, an employer must take note of the manner in which a potential applicant will proceed when looking for a suitable job, and what must be taken into account when a job offer is evaluated.

When an applicant is searching for a suitable job, an attempt will be made to obtain as much information as possible with regard to potential employers. It is important that the employer should know about the ways in which the potential employee obtains this information. For example, the employer must be aware of the fact that the prospective employee acquires a lot of job information in an informal manner, for example through family or friends who are already working for the organisation. Job information is also often obtained through incidental enquiries (walk-ins). A knowledge of how the applicant obtains job information can be important for the employer with a view to the formulation of its recruitment strategy. It is also interesting to note that the higher the job is in the job hierarchy of the organisation, the more enthusiastically the applicant will attempt to obtain job information.

The evaluation of job offers by a potential employee consists of two steps. First, the job seeker makes a career choice: he or she decides what type of work he or she would like to do. His or her career choice is influenced by psychological, economic and social factors. Psychological factors in career choice involve the job seeker's needs, aspirations and future expectations. Economic factors require little explanation: the job seeker wants to find out whether the job has sufficient economic advantages. Social factors indicate the role that the family, the educational system and the group play in the career choice. Secondly, the job seeker wants to exercise a choice with regard to the specific organisation which he or she wants to join. In this choice, he or she will to a large extent be influenced by information about and knowledge of the organisation.

6.8.2 The manner in which applicants look for a certain job

Most job seekers obtain job information in an informal manner. Friends and family are the most common source of information, and the direct application (walk-ins) is the second most popular form (Milkovich and Boudreau 1988:364). The nature of the job plays an important role here. Applicants for management posts and clerical posts are more inclined to consult a private employment agency than low-level workers.

Milkovich and Boudreau (1988:365) identify three categories of job seekers:
• Those who obtain as many interviews and job offers as possible, and then rationally decide on the best offer on the basis of their own criteria.

- Those who accept the first offer they get, and believe that all organisations are equally good.
- Those who get a good offer (which they like a lot) and then, just to satisfy themselves, obtain another offer to compare and ensure that the first offer is indeed the best.

6.8.3 The choice of a career and an organisation

Just as an organisation demands certain things from an applicant it wants to employ, most applicants also have preferences for a specific job. Thus a student of engineering who has recently completed his or her studies may choose a job near the coast with a compensation package of R50 000 in preference to one on the Highveld with a higher compensation package. It is unlikely that all the expectations of an applicant can be met. Like the organisation, he or she must often be prepared to make a compromise with regard to the ideal they had in mind.

A career choice involves two steps. *Firstly*, the individual makes a choice at school or shortly thereafter with regard to the occupation he or she wishes to work in. *Secondly*, he or she makes a choice with regard to the organisation where he or she wants to practise this occupation. Career choices are influenced by individual preferences, the realities of the labour market, the structural limitations of an organisation and the individual's socialisation and identification with an organisation. In addition, the choice of a career is influenced by the person's needs and aspirations. The family, educational system and groups can also play an important role in this regard.

The selection of an organisation offering the chosen occupation is the next step. Various alternatives are possible here. The first job seeker may receive various job offers from which to choose. Particular attention will be paid to the minimum level of compensation that will make the job offer acceptable. This is called the "reserve wage" of organisations. On the other hand there is a compensating model, in which the advantages of various job offers are set off against each other, for example a low starting salary against the possibility of rapid promotion, or an unattractive area or city against a high compensation package.

6.9 CONCLUSION

In this chapter, recruitment was explained as an important function in the process of providing human resources. Among other things, attention was paid to the formulation of recruitment policy, the factors that influence recruitment, the sources from which employees can be recruited, and the evaluation of the recruitment programme. Finally, attention was paid to the potential employee's perception of recruitment. Each of these aspects forms an important component of the recruitment process. Management should pay attention to each one separately and in detail to place recruitment on a scientific basis.

Once the recruitment process has been finalised, the following step in the provisioning process can be addressed, i.e. the selection of applicants.

Questions

1. Explain how you would set about formulating a recruitment policy for an organisation.
2. Contrast the internal and external factors that influence recruitment.
3. What sources of recruitment would you use to fill a vacancy for secretary to a marketing manager?
4. Why is it important to take into account the potential employee's perception of the recruitment practices of an organisation? Discuss.

Sources

Leap, T.L. & Crino, M.D. 1993. *Personnel human resource management*. Macmillan, New York.

Livy, B. 1988. *Corporate personnel management*. Pitman, London.

Manning, P. 1988. In Van Dyk, P.S. 1990. "Opleidings- en ontwikkelingsuitdagings vir Suid-Afrika: 'n bestuursbenadering." Unpublished inaugural address, UNISA, Pretoria.

Milkovich, G.T. & Boudreau, J.W. 1988. *Personnel human resource management*. 5th edition. Business Publications, Plano, Texas.

RSA, President's Council. 1987. *Report of the committee for economic affairs on a strategy for job creation and labour-intensive development*. Government Printer, Pretoria.

Spies, P.H. 1989. Mannekragaanbod en -aanvraag in die RSA tot die jaar 2020. Paper delivered at the SA Defence Force Symposium. 8 June. Pretoria.

Stoops, R. 1982. Recruitment strategy. *Personnel Journal*, February, p. 102.

Van Dyk *et al.* 1992. *Management: a multi-disciplinary approach to human resources development*. Southern, Halfway House.

Chapter 7

Selection

P.D. Gerber

STUDY OBJECTIVES
After studying this chapter, you should be able to:
- Practically demonstrate the factors that influence the selection decision;
- Sequentially describe the various steps in the selection process;
- Theoretically contrast the various selection strategies;
- Practically evaluate the selection process.

7.1 INTRODUCTION

Because of the great shortage of professional, highly skilled and technically trained people in the South African labour market (see figure 6.1), organisations must pay particular attention to the important step of selection in the process of providing human resources. Should a potential employee not fit into the culture of an organisation, such a candidate should not be employed because productivity may suffer.

However, the above is contrary to affirmative action. This dilemma will be addressed in chapter 10.

In this chapter, attention will be paid to the theory underlying the selection process. The following aspects are examined:
- Factors that influence the selection decision;
- The selection process;
- Selection strategies;
- The evaluation of the selection process.

FIGURE 7.1: Principal learning components of selection

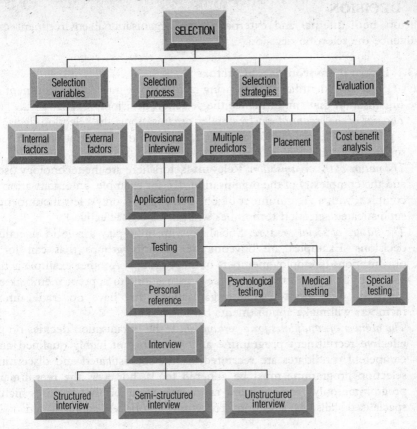

7.2 SELECTION: A DEFINITION

Selection involves the choice, from a pool of candidates, of the most suitable candidate who, according to the judgement of the selection panel, best meets the given job requirements. The decision to appoint a certain candidate to a post thus rests on the assumption that the person will function successfully in the job. An appointment is made after the individual potential of the candidates and the specific job requirements have been weighed up against each other. The same principles also apply to the appointment of new employees in entry jobs, to transfers and to the promotion of candidates to higher posts.

Selection is defined by Livy (1988:107) as:

. . . a process of job matching, and must begin with a description of the jobs to be done and the identification of personal qualities necessary for the field of candidates by progressively eliminating those who do not measure up to the specifications.

127

7.3 FACTORS THAT INFLUENCE THE SELECTION DECISION

Factors both internal and external to the organisational environment can influence the selection decision.

7.3.1 Internal environmental factors

Livy (1988:107) identifies the following factors in the internal environment of the organisation that can influence the selection decision:

- *The size of the organisation*: In smaller organisations, the selection decision is probably taken in an informal way. The larger the organisation, the more sophisticated the selection process.
- *The nature of the organisation*: Relevant factors here are the technology used and the complexity of the organisation. (If, for example, an organisation is complex, with a great number of jobs that each has only a few incumbents, sophisticated selection techniques will not be cost effective.)
- *The nature of social pressure*: Social pressure may play a role in selection decisions. Examples are boycotts by minority groups that can force organisations to employ members of these groups. Another example is the role of trade unions, that can force organisations to appoint members on the basis of seniority, while organisations that have no trade union members will make appointments based on skills.
- *The number of candidates for a certain job*: If the organisation decides on an effective recruitment programme and a number of highly qualified and competent candidates are recruited, a very sophisticated and discerning selection programme must be adhered to. If, however, the recruitment programme only provides a few candidates for a job that requires highly specialised skills, the selection programme can be less sophisticated.

7.3.2 External environmental factors

Factors in the external environment may include:

- *The nature of the labour market*: The labour market from which the organisation must draw its employees to fill vacancies is influenced by labour market conditions that affect the country as a whole. In addition, labour market conditions in a city or region also play an important role. In turn, the labour market is influenced by the working conditions offered by the organisation, the content of the job itself and the general public image of the organisation.

  The labour market can be analysed by using the selection ratio as expressed in the accompanying box.

$$\text{Selection ratio} = \frac{\text{number of applicants selected}}{\text{number of applicants available for selection}}$$

If there are many applicants, for example a selection ratio of 1:2, the organisation can be selective in its choice for appointment. If, however, the ratio is 1:1, the selection process will be short and unsophisticated because there are few applicants to choose from.

- *Trade unions*: A trade union can influence an organisation's selection process in various overt or covert ways. Employees who belong to a trade union can, according to the trade union contract, make certain demands regarding employment, training and remuneration.
- *Government regulations*: The government may stipulate regulations that can influence the selection decisions of organisations. Influx control in urban areas used to be one example. This aspect will probably develop into a particularly sensitive issue in a new dispensation for South Africa.

The decision to appoint a certain candidate according to the requirements of the job description and job specifications must be based on human resources management principles and practice, if management wants to ensure individual employee performance.

> Party politics, organisational politics, discrimination and nepotism must as far as possible be avoided by means of the selection process. Appointments should only be made on the basis of the match between a candidate's potential and the job requirements, irrespective of race, sex, colour or religion.

7.4 THE SELECTION PROCESS

7.4.1 Introduction

The selection process consists of a number of steps that do not necessarily have to be carried out in a certain order: it will differ from organisation to organisation. In figure 7.2, the steps that can be followed in a selection process are theoretically presented.

7.4.2 The provisional selection interview

The provisional selection interview mainly serves the purpose of saving time and costs in the actual selection process. This interview usually only lasts ten minutes. During this time, it is determined whether the applicant has the necessary minimum qualifications, training, interest, etc. for the job. The interviewer will also briefly explain the availability of jobs and the minimum requirements set for every available job.

In practice it may happen that an applicant arrives at an organisation to offer his or her services. The organisation should lay down specific minimum standards for employment in advance. During the short interview, the applicant is weighed up against these measures. During the provisional interview, a first impression can be formed of the general appearance and personality of the applicant. If it should appear during the provisional

FIGURE 7.2: Steps in the selection process

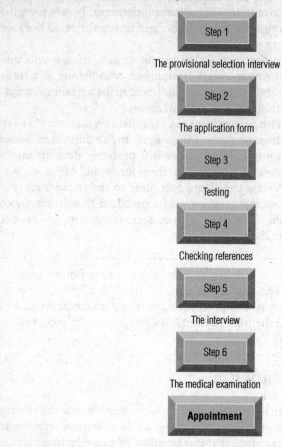

Step 1

The provisional selection interview

Step 2

The application form

Step 3

Testing

Step 4

Checking references

Step 5

The interview

Step 6

The medical examination

Appointment

interview that the minimum requirements of the organisation and the qualifications and interests of the applicant correspond, the applicant can go on to the following step in the selection process, i.e. the completion of a formal application form.

7.4.3 The application form

From the completed application form, information is obtained with regard to the training, experience and personal characteristics of the applicant. The application form can be designed for various types of jobs, for example for weekly wage earners, clerical personnel and for managerial or professional jobs. What is important, though, is that the application forms should be designed to meet the requirements of the organisation in question. This means that, if there is certain information that is important to the organisation, the application form should make provision for this. An example of this is an engineering company that wants to obtain special information about an applicant's previous experience and leaves sufficient space for this on the application form, so that projects in which the applicant was involved can be indicated. Figure 7.3 is an example of an application form used at a financial institution.

The weighted application form is designed to be used as a selection mechanism. In the weighted application form, an attempt is made to determine a link between the characteristics of the applicant and success in the job. The weighted application form (Milkovich and Boudreau 1988:413) evaluates the information on the application form by allocating scores for the answers to every question. The scores for each question are multiplied by a weighting factor that reflects the importance of the question in the forecasting of work performance. The weighted scores are then added up to give the total score for each applicant. The typical approach is to divide existing job incumbents into categories (for example high, average and low) based on certain criteria of success, for example performance measured by production records or supervisor evaluation, or high versus low absenteeism. The characteristics of high and low performers are then analysed. In the case of many characteristics for a specific organisation, there may be no difference in criterion scores for age or educational level, but possibly for experience. A weight is then allocated for the degree of difference, for example 0 for no difference, ± 1 for a small difference and ± 2 for a large difference. These weights are then added up for all applicants. The one with the highest score is employed. The compilation of such a weighted application form takes quite some time (about 100 hours), which is why it should only be used for jobs with a large number of incumbents. In such a process it may be found that certain items are better predictors of success than others.

Weighted application forms can be usefully applied to predict such diverse factors as creativity, mechanical insight, scientific and engineering performance, and labour turnover. These prediction factors may differ from job to job and occupation to occupation. In some jobs, for example, age is a good predictor of success; in others it plays no role at all. In spite of everything that can be achieved with the weighted application form, research proves that the usual aptitude tests can give the same or even better results at a lower cost.

7.4.4 The selection methods
7.4.4.1 General
The testing of candidates generally falls under the following broad categories:
- Psychological tests;
- Medical tests;
- Specially designed tests for managerial personnel.

In this section, attention is given to the various types of tests, their validity and reliability, problems experienced with their use and guidelines for their use.

FIGURE 7.3: Application form for a financial institution

Application for employment

TRUST BANK
The Trust Bank of Africa Limited · Registered Commercial Bank

Important: Applicants should complete this form in own handwriting. An applicant making a false statement will be liable to immediate dismissal. This application will be treated in strict confidence.

Tick the applicable space.

A. Position(s) for which you are applying or direction in which you are interested _____

_____

B. Personal details

1. Full names and surname (Mr/Mrs/Miss): _____

   Home address: _____   Postal address: _____

   _____   _____

   _____   _____

   Telephone number: Home: _____   Work: _____

2. Date of birth: _____   Place of birth: _____

3. Identity number: _____   Nationality: _____ Since: _____

4. Marital status

   Married ☐   Spouse's full names: _____

   Is your spouse employed: Yes ☐ No ☐   If yes, state Employer: _____

                                           Position: _____

   Unmarried ☐   Next of kin: Name: _____
                                                        (Initials and surname)
   Divorced ☐   Occupation: _____

   Widow/ ☐   Relationship: _____
   Widower
                                           Address: _____

                                           _____

                                           _____

5. Dependants:

   Children: Number _____   Ages: _____

   Other dependants: _____

C. Financial details

1. Do you have any debts? Yes ☐ No ☐   If yes, state amount: To whom?

                                         (i) _____   (i) _____

                                         (ii) _____   (ii) _____

                                         (iii) _____   (iii) _____

2. Do you have a home loan? Yes ☐ No ☐   If yes, state
                                           Balance outstanding: _____

                                           Present value of property: _____

                                           Monthly instalment: _____

   Are you presently occupying the property?   Yes ☐ No ☐

3. Are you standing surety for anyone? Yes ☐ No ☐

   If yes, state details (nature, amount, expiry date of surety): _____

4. Have you ever been in financial trouble? Yes ☐ No ☐

   If yes, state details (nature, amount, date): _____

   _____

5. Have you ever been found guilty of a criminal offence? Yes ☐ No ☐

   If yes, state details (nature, details, date): _____

   _____

D. General information

1. Do you have any relative who is a TrustBank employee? [Yes] [No]

   If yes, state name and surname of relative: _____

   Branch where employed: _____ Relationship: _____

2. Do you know any TrustBank employee(s)? [Yes] [No]

   If yes, state name and surname of official: _____

   Branch where employed: _____

3. Home language: _____ Other language: _____

4. Religion: _____

5. What are your main extramural activities and/or hobbies? _____

   _____

6. To which clubs, organisations or associations do you belong? _____

   _____

7. Do you possess a driver's licence? [Yes] [No]   If yes, state type: _____

   Has licence been endorsed? [Yes] [No]

   If yes, state details: _____

E. Education

1. **Schooling**

Name of school	Highest standard Passed	When/Date

Subjects with % /symbols	

2. **Highest education (Professional/Academic)**

Institution/Establishment	Courses passed	Date	Major subjects

3. **If currently studying, state details**

Institution/Establishment	Study field	Date started	Completing date

Subjects passed		Present subjects	

4. **Are you interested in further study?** [Yes] [No]

   If yes, state details: _____

   _____

   _____

   _____

   _____

   _____

133

F. Experience and remuneration

1. Present employer

Name and tel. number	From Month/Year	Position and/or title	Fringe benefits and other remuneration	Basic salary

2. Previous employers

Name and tel. number	From Month/Year	To Month/Year	Position and/or Title	Reason for leaving employ	Monthly Remuneration

If more space is needed, use separate page

3. Military service

Type Unit/Reserve	Originally From	To	Rank	Future liabilities

4. Why do you wish to leave your current employer? _____

5. Have you ever been dismissed?   Yes No

If yes, state details: _____

6. Why are you applying for a position at TrustBank? _____

7. Remuneration required? (Salary plus benefits) _____

8. When can you commence duties? _____

9. Would you object to our: Contacting your previous employers for a reference? Yes No

Contacting your present employer for a reference? Yes No

10. Please supply details of at least two persons from whom references may be obtained (not relatives — preferably present or former superiors)

Initials and surname	Address	Occupation	Relationship	Tel. no.

11. Would you be prepared to:

11.1 Accept transfers?   Yes No

If no, state reasons _____

11.2 Promote TrustBank services anywhere?   Yes No

If no, state reasons _____

11.3 Work after hours?   Yes No

If no, state reasons _____

11.4 Attend training classes before or after hours? Yes No

If no, state reasons _____

134

G. Health statement

1. What is your present state of health? _____

2. (a) What is your height (without shoes)? _____ cm   (b) Your weight according to scale (clothed) _____ kg
   (b) How long has your weight been stable? _____

3. Have you during the past 5 years:

   3.1 Consulted a doctor or a specialist? .... [Yes] [No]

   3.2 Undergone X-rays, ECGs or other special examinations? .... [Yes] [No]

   3.3 Received medical advice or undergone treatment or operations? .... [Yes] [No]

   If yes, state full particulars _____

4. Do you have any sight (vision), hearing or speech disorder? If yes, state full details _____ [Yes] [No]

5. **Habits**

   5.1 What and how much do you smoke per day? _____

   5.2 What kind and quantity of alcoholic liquor do you consume per day? _____ per week? _____

   5.3 Were you ever a heavy alcohol consumer or an alcoholic? .... [Yes] [No]

   If yes, state full details _____

6. Have you, or have you ever had, any of the following:-
   (If yes, state full details of each instance in the schedule below.)

   6.1 Any disorder of the heart, eg. rheumatic fever, heart murmur, coronary artery disease, chest pain, shortness of breath or palpitations? [Yes] [No]

   6.2 High blood pressure or disease of the blood vessels or circulatory disorder? [Yes] [No]

   6.3 Any respiratory or lung trouble, e.g. asthma, bronchitis, persistent cough, tuberculosis? [Yes] [No]

   6.4 Any disorder of the digestive system, gall-bladder or liver, e.g. actual or suspected gastric or duodenal ulcer, recurrent indigestion or hiatus hernia? [Yes] [No]

   6.5 Disease or disorder of kidney, bladder or reproductive organs, e.g. albumin in urine, stones, prostatitis or venereal disease? [Yes] [No]

   6.6 Any nervous or mental complaint, e.g. epilepsy, blackouts, paralysis, anxiety state or depression? [Yes] [No]

   6.7 Eye, ear, nose or throat disorder, e.g. defective vision, ear discharge, recurrent tonsillitis? [Yes] [No]

   6.8 Disorder or disease of muscles, bones, joints, limbs, spine, e.g. rheumatism, arthritis, gout, slipped disc or other back trouble? [Yes] [No]

   6.9 Diabetes, sugar in urine, thyroid or other glandular or blood disorder? [Yes] [No]

   6.10 Cancer, growth or tumour of any kind? [Yes] [No]

   6.11 Any other illness, disorder, operation, disability or accident? [Yes] [No]

Question No.	Nature and duration of complaint or symptoms	Date	Name and address of attending doctor or hospital	When did you last have symptoms?

7. **For female applicants**

   7.1 Are you pregnant? [Yes] [No]   If yes, state expected date of birth _____

   7.2 When was your last child born _____

8. **Family history**

8.1		If living State of health. If health is not good state reason and age	If dead Age at death	Cause of death
	Father			
	Mother			
	Number of brothers			
	Number of sisters			

   8.2 If not already stated: has any close blood relative had diabetes, heart disease, high blood pressure, mental illness, porphyria or hereditary disease? If yes, state full details [Yes] [No]

9. Are you easily susceptible to any ailment, however slight? [Yes] [No]

   If yes, state full details _____

10. State the name and address of your regular medical attendant and state how long he has been your doctor _____

I declare that the above information is true and correct and will form the basis of my appointment to the staff and admission to the Bankorp Pension Fund and/or Group Schemes. I confirm that the Trustees of the Pension Fund and Group Life Scheme will at any time in their discretion have the right to cancel my membership of the Fund/Scheme should it come to light that such membership was granted due to an oversight or misrepresentation, and I understand that I am liable to summary dismissal should I have supplied false and incorrect information.

Signed at _____ on this _____ day of _____ 19__

| **For office use:** |
| 1. Refer to general guidelines on medical requirements, if necessary. |
| 2. Arrange for doctor to complete confidential medical report (P17) if necessary. |

Signature of applicant
Any further information on the application may be attached.

T. 22 (8/85)   0067 (8/85)

Source: By courtesy of Trust Bank.

7.4.4.2 *Types of test*

Performance tests

Performance tests have been designed to determine to what extent the applicant is already able to do what is expected in the job advertised. Thus a prospective mechanic may be asked to repair the gearbox of a car within a certain time, a programmer may be expected to explain how a certain computer program has been developed, or a typist may be expected to type a letter in a certain time without exceeding a permissible percentage of mistakes.

Intelligence tests

Intelligence tests are designed to determine the intellectual ability of the applicant. Although the intelligence test can be useful for selecting individuals, for example for training, high intelligence is not in itself a valid predictor of success in the work situation. Intelligence tests do, however, help to ensure that only applicants who meet the minimum intelligence requirements for a job will be considered for employment.

Aptitude tests

Aptitude tests measure the ability to learn a specific task. Some of these tests can measure a multitude of skills such as clerical speed, verbal ability, abstract reasoning ability, mechanical aptitude, numerical skill, an understanding of spatial relationships and spelling and sentence construction. Specific aptitude tests measure the skills that are necessary to carry out a specific task, such as mechanical skill for the prospective car mechanic.

Interest tests

Interest tests are designed to determine the direction of interest, particularly of school leavers. A person may have the intelligence and aptitude (i.e. ability) to master a certain type of work cognitively, but if the person is not interested in that specific work, the chances for individual job performance are low.

> How many people do you know who have changed work, to do something other than that for which they were initially trained or educated?

Interest tests have been developed to determine to what extent the skills required for carrying out a certain job are present or latent in the candidate's personal make-up.

Personality tests

Employee success primarily depends on the extent to which an individual's personality matches the organisational culture. It is thus of particular importance that management should specify personality testing as a selection

136

criterion because, although it is expensive, it will be to the advantage of long-term organisational success.

The most common personality tests in use in South African organisations are:
- the 16PF;
- the Rorschach blotting index.

Psychological tests

The use of psychological tests must be justified on moral and ethical grounds because of its effect on the candidate. It is therefore of the utmost importance that –
- testing should be done by registered practitioners;
- the validity of the tests used and their reliability should already have been statistically proven.

Validity is the extent to which a psychological test measures the psychological constructs that it is supposed to measure.

Reliability indicates the statistical correlation in the results of tests that measure certain psychological constructs, when the tests are used again after a certain time.

Skills tests

Tests to measure intellectual skills include general reading, spelling and mathematical tests, specific job skill tests or job knowledge tests (for example the use of specific word-processing programs) and general job samples (use of multiple job skills). These tests are very popular in practice. In the USA it is estimated that about 50% of all organisations make use of skills tests (Fuchberg 1990:131).

In a developing country such as South Africa, the use of these types of tests should take a prominent place. The reading and mathematical abilities of applicants, and particularly minimum requirements, are without doubt important.

Physical and motor skills

There are three broad categories of information with regard to physical and motor skills:
- Information about height and weight;
- Information about motor skills such as hand-eye coordination and manual skill;
- Information about illnesses such as cancer and diabetes, as well as handicaps such as poor sight and hearing.

Employers should ensure that no decision is made not to employ the applicant unless the information proves beyond all doubt that the person will be unsuitable for properly carrying out the necessary job function.

Medical tests

Tests can determine whether an individual has a tendency towards serious illnesses. The testing of individuals' body fluids, such as blood and urine, is carried out. Tests for AIDS are also gaining in importance. Important guidelines for tests of this nature are as follows:

- If such tests are done, all employees must be tested – there must be no exceptions.
- Provision must be made for follow-up tests.
- Applicants must be warned beforehand that tests will be done (also for drugs).
- Applicants must be reassured with regard to the confidentiality of the test results.

The use of all psychometric tests and techniques is controlled by law. The Medical, Dental and Supplementary Health Services Profession Act (No. 56 of 1974), as amended, controls the training and registration of persons who are authorised to practise the profession of psychologist in South Africa. It controls the supervision and use of psychological tests and techniques in the labour field.

The right to use tests is granted under the following conditions:

- Only an individual may register, not an organisation.
- Registration as a personnel practitioner or personnel technician at the SA Board for Personnel Practice does not give the individual involved any right to use the tests.
- The National Institute for Personnel Research and the Institute for Psychological and Edumetrical Research of the Human Sciences Research Council sell tests to registered test users. However, these bodies do not register people as psychologists, psychometrists, psychotechnicians or A-test users.

Assessment centres

The use of assessment centres is a popular method for obtaining information with regard to applicants for supervisory and managerial jobs.

An assessment centre is a central physical location where applicants come together to have their participation in job-related exercises evaluated by trained observers. The principal idea is to evaluate managerial applicants over a period of time (1 to 2$^1/_2$ days) by observing (and later evaluating) their behavior across a series of selected exercises or work samples.

Source: Leap and Crino (1993:279)

The applicants take part in in-basket exercises, leaderless work groups, computer simulations and role play, which require the skills similar to those needed for successful execution of the actual tasks.

Various methods of evaluation are used, such as interviewing, objective testing, role play and management games. A panel of line managers usually acts as evaluators. They can, however, be replaced by consultants or outsiders who are trained in operating assessment centres. The assessment centre is aimed at the tasks that must be carried out within the organisation.

The assessment centre enables the organisation to formulate decisions with regard to the following:

- The qualifications for certain jobs;
- The promotability of applicants;
- How candidates function in a group situation;
- The type of training and development programmes that are necessary to develop the desired work behaviour of candidates;
- How well candidates do in observing, evaluating and reporting on the performance of other candidates.

Conclusion
The responsibility for the employment of personnel has traditionally been shared by the human resources management department and the manager of the department in which the individual is to work. Two alternatives to this process have recently been developed in the USA:

- An employer can hire a part of, or the entire staff from an employee hiring company. These employees are not temporarily employed, but are full-time, long-term personnel. The hiring company carries out all personnel functions such as recruitment, selection, the keeping of records and remuneration.
- Team employment, where work teams accept responsibility for the recruitment, selection and employment of a new team member. This process may differ from organisation to organisation, and the responsibility of a team may vary from the initial selection only to the whole process including recruitment and final employment.

7.4.4.3 *The validity and reliability of tests*
To control the validity of a test, the following question must be asked: "What does this test test?" It must be kept in mind that a test evaluates only a sample of a person's behaviour, and it must be ensured that the correct test is used for this purpose. The ideal is for performance in the test to serve as a valid predictor of future performance in the work situation.

When testing for selection, there are two ways of determining the validity of a test: criterion validity and content validity. Criterion validity means that an individual who performs well in the test will also perform well in the work situation. Content validity assumes that the test content is a sample of the job content. The behaviour required in the work situation, which is critical for job success, should thus be built into the test.

Reliability indicates consistency; in other words, the same test scores are obtained by the same test persons when they are retested with the same or an equivalent test. The reliability of the test can thus be determined by testing the same people at various times and comparing the test results with each other.

7.4.4.4 *Some guidelines for the use of tests*
The following guidelines for the effective use of tests in the selection process must be followed:

- Tests should not be used as the only selection technique, but should be supplementary to the interview and referrals. It must be kept in mind that tests are not infallible and that they often rather indicate which candidates will not be successful in the job.
- Use the right tests for the job for which selections are made. The tests must thus be checked for validity and particularly for validity within the organisation in which they are to be used. Ensure that the tests are to the point.
- First use the tests on current employees before approving them for general use. Thus it can be ensured that the tests are practically relevant and meaningful.
- Analyse the existing employment and promotion standards. The primary aim of the tests must be to predict success in the work situation as accurately as possible.
- Make use of the advice of competent consultants in the development of tests that meet the needs of the organisation.
- Use trained psychologists or industrial psychologists to administer the tests.
- Carry out testing in a private, quiet and well-ventilated area, where the lighting is good. Also ensure that the various applicants take the tests under the same conditions.
- Test results must be regarded as strictly confidential.

7.4.5 Personal references
The method by which references are controlled and the type of information requested may differ from organisation to organisation. During telephone enquiries or interviews with the employee's previous employer or supervisor, specific information can be obtained about the applicant's previous job performance. Because the application form does not give all the necessary information regarding an applicant, following up references is often the only other source that can provide specific information about job performance.

Information that appears on the application form can be checked by following up references. It is particularly important to note the correctness of data such as the periods of employment with previous employers, the salaries earned, responsibilities and educational background.

It is important to establish how the employee has performed in his or her previous jobs. This may serve as a point of departure for making an estimate of future job behaviour.

Studies indicate that a large percentage (up to 90%) of previous employers report favourably on former employees (Klatt et al. 1985:212) and that there is some doubt about the value to be attached to such reports. It would therefore be desirable to obtain as many objective facts as possible about the applicant's job performance, such as sales figures and production figures. This task can be facilitated when formal job analyses with clear job specifications accompany the reference. The applicant is then evaluated according to the job specification.

7.4.6 The interview
7.4.6.1 Introduction
The interview is the most important hurdle that must be overcome during the selection process. During the interview, the interviewer is granted the opportunity to learn a great deal about the applicant's background, experience and interests. It also gives the applicant an opportunity to ask questions about the job or the organisation. The interview is thus the step in the selection process where face to face communication takes place, and where impressions are formed of the personality, values and attitude to life of the applicant. The applicant also obtains an impression of the interviewer and the organisation.

The various techniques used in the interview situation will now be examined in detail, after which some guidelines will be given that must be taken into account during interviewing.

7.4.6.2 Interview techniques
The employment interview can take three forms:
- The structured interview;
- The semi-structured interview;
- The unstructured interview.

Although information is obtained during each type of interview through asking and answering questions, the difference lies in the interviewer's approach to the interview, the type of information required and the nature of the interview situation.
- *The structured interview*: During this interview, the interviewer makes use of a previously compiled list of questions to obtain certain information from the applicants. The interviewer can even ask the questions in a certain order. The response of each applicant to each question is recorded. The structured interview leaves little room for adaptation to the interview situation, as the applicant is afforded little opportunity to expand on answers.
- *The semi-structured interview*: In this case, only the most important questions are compiled in advance. This thus leaves room for flexibility

141

in the type of questions asked. The interviewer can ask questions about aspects that require deeper investigation. Because the structure is not so rigid, it is more difficult to recall the detailed content of interviews. This type of interview serves a dual purpose, i.e. to collect factual information and to allow scope for asking additional questions to gain deeper insight into certain aspects.

- *The unstructured interview*: During the unstructured interview, the interviewer is free to adapt questions during the course of the interview. The interview requires little or no preparation. Care must be taken, however, that the unstructured interview does not deviate so far that the interviewer no longer succeeds in collecting facts on which an objective evaluation of the various candidates can be based. On the other hand, the unstructured interview can enable the interviewer to ask those questions that may help to make a delicate distinction between candidates of almost the same quality. The unstructured interview may begin by asking the applicant to tell more about himself or herself. Then further questions can be asked.

When weighing up the three types of interview against each other, it becomes clear that the more structured the interview, the more reliable the information obtained.

7.4.6.3 *Guidelines for successful interviewing*
A number of guidelines that can be used to increase the effectiveness of interviewing are proposed by Milkovich and Boudreau (1988:415):

- Ensure that interviewers are trained for their task.
- The interview must be conducted at a suitable venue, where privacy is ensured. The facilities must be clean, well lit and comfortable, so that the applicant is left with a favourable impression of the organisation.
- Plan the interview and formulate its objectives and the questions to be asked.
- Thoroughly study the relevant job description before the interview.
- Study the information that appears on the candidate's application form.
- Ensure that the interviewer is both objective and unbiased.
- Put the applicant at ease by making a few general remarks about the job and the organisation.
- Encourage the applicant to speak by asking pertinent questions and listening attentively.
- Leave sufficient time for the interview, but without wasting time.
- Keep control of the interview. Avoid domineering behaviour, but direct the interview towards attaining the initial objectives.
- Conclude the interview in a friendly manner.
- Write down the facts gained during the interview as soon as possible.
- Follow-up work: Check the accuracy of the information gained during the interview. Find out which interviewers are better than others, and where and how interviewing can be improved.

7.4.7 The medical examination

The medical examination is regarded by most organisations as the last step in the selection process. The medical examination is carried out to eliminate applicants whose physical condition does not meet certain standards. However, if there are many applicants, for example when recruiting for the defence force, medical examinations will take place immediately after the recruitment stage.

The medical examination is particularly aimed at protecting the employer against later claims from a medical aid and prevents absenteeism.

The medical examination usually determines the following:

- General state of health, as determined by checking blood pressure, allergies and the presence or absence of illnesses such as tuberculosis;
- Specific illnesses, as determined by testing for AIDS and cardio-vascular problems.

7.5 SELECTION STRATEGIES

To make a final choice between the applicants for a specific job, a selection strategy must be decided on in advance, which will take into account certain important concepts. Here we refer to multiple predictors, placement and cost benefit analysis.

Multiple predictors

In a case where more than one predictor of success in the work situation or more than one selection technique are to be used, it must be decided what combination will be used to take the selection decision. There are three approaches to this problem, i.e. the multiple obstacle approach, the compensating approach and a combination of these two methods.

- *The multiple obstacle approach* means that each selection aid is regarded as an obstacle that the applicant must overcome before he or she can progress to the following step. Thus the candidate must go through each of the selection steps – from the provisional selection to the final step, i.e. the medical examination. If the candidate fails any of these steps, he or she is rejected.
- *The compensating approach*: The applicant is not automatically rejected if he or she fails one of the steps of the selection process. The applicant can make up for a low score in one of the steps by achieving an above average score in another. For example, an applicant who communicates badly will do poorly during the interview, but may compensate for this with a high score in a performance test. He or she is then not automatically withdrawn from the selection process, but is allowed to complete the entire process. At the end, the applicant is then weighed up against the other applicants.
- *The combined approach*: The process begins with the multiple obstacle approach and ends with the compensating approach. The multiple obstacle method can, for example, be used up to the level where tests are

conducted, because certain tests must be passed for entry into certain jobs. Those who fail one of these selection steps are automatically eliminated from the selection process. During the steps after testing, the compensating method can be used, with the applicants being allowed to complete the selection process. The final choice can then be made from this group of applicants.

Placement

While selection is the process in which someone is selected to fill a specific job, placement is a wider process in which an applicant is considered for more than one job. The placement strategy will thus take into account the applicant's interests, skills and knowledge. If the applicant is not regarded as suitable for a certain job, he or she will be considered for others.

As opposed to the selection process, the placement strategy makes particular sense under tight labour market conditions. A larger organisation with a more diversified job structure can also use the placement strategy to reduce the costs of recruitment and selection.

Cost benefit analysis

During the selection process, two types of cost must be taken into account. Firstly, there is the cost of filling a job (this includes recruitment, testing and interviewing). Secondly, there are the potential costs that may result from a wrong selection decision. These include aspects such as the cost of terminating service, the cost of selecting another employee, and low productivity.

These costs will vary, depending on the employment standards set during the selection process. It may be assumed that at a certain point the total costs will increase as the employment standards rise. It is thus important that the selection techniques and standards are periodically reviewed to ensure that they are still cost effective.

One method of determining which selection technique would be most suitable is to check which specific methods have brought successful candidates, and what the cost of these methods would be. Ivancevich and Glueck (1986:217) analyse the seven steps in the selection process and the costs that may be allocated to each step.

From figure 7.4 it becomes clear that it is particularly during the interview and testing that costs must be strictly controlled. Cost benefit analyses should thus focus on these two components.

The selection of managers

It is obvious that the selection process and the aids used will vary, depending on the type of person to be employed. It is thus essential that the job be studied in detail before appointing someone to it.

Although successful managers may have above average intelligence, drive, judgement and managerial skills, criteria must be determined that the candidate for a certain job must meet. Such criteria may be derived from the performance standards of existing managerial personnel and from future needs.

These criteria must be determined in advance, as managerial tasks differ according to management level, the function and the industry.

FIGURE 7.4: The selection process and the cost of each step

METHOD	COST
1. Provisional interview	Minimal
2. Application form	Minimal
3. Interview	Time used x cost
4. Testing	R5 - R1 000
5. Checking references	R100
6. Medical examination	R100
7. Selection decision	Nil

When a choice must be made between candidates for a managerial job, the focus must be on behaviour and not only on test scores or general impressions. For example, it is difficult to choose between candidate A who is of medium intelligence, highly motivated, has average verbal skills and can work hard, and candidate B who obtains a high test score with regard to intelligence and motivation, has low verbal skills and an average capacity for hard work. In such a case, the organisation will have to be guided by criteria that indicated success in the past to make a meaningful choice between the two candidates. Once again, attention will have to be paid to the requirements of the vacant job.

Generally, tests are not often used to fill managerial jobs. Following up references about the job performance of the applicant can make a valuable contribution towards the final selection decision. However, the interview is the selection mechanism that is most commonly used to fill managerial jobs.

7.6 THE EVALUATION OF THE SELECTION PROCESS

It is not easy to develop a scale on which the success of the selection process can be measured. One of the most important scales is the job performance of the recently appointed employee. However, the job performance does not depend on the effectiveness of the selection process, which makes objective evaluation difficult. When job performance is analysed after an appointment has been made, factors such as supervisor evaluation, attendance records and productivity must be taken into account. These indicators can then be compared with the forecasts made during the selection process.

The decision to appoint a candidate is based on the expectation of management that the candidate will be able to function at a certain job level.

Klatt *et al.* (1985:222) propose several areas on which to focus and in which questions must be asked to evaluate the selection process in a systematic manner. They include the following:

- Has a well defined selection policy been developed?
- Why are the current employment standards being used? How are they related to actual performance in the job?
- Are accurate records being kept of the reasons why each candidate has been rejected?
- What percentage of applicants has been employed?
- What contribution does each step in the selection process make towards the entire programme?
- How much does each of the steps in the selection process cost?
- Has every selection tool been properly validated?
- What percentage of the newly appointed employees is dismissed during the trial period?
- Can the selection process be successfully defended in court?
- Is there a correlation between the degree of success in the job and the predictions made during selection?
- Is there an exit interview to determine how well employees and jobs were matched?

Despite the fact that it is difficult to establish measures for the success of the selection process, each organisation should seriously attempt to evaluate the effectiveness of the selection process. The aim must be to direct the selection process in such a way that the right sort and quality of employees are attracted, as explained in human resources planning. Regular audits, research and experiments with selection techniques are thus essential.

7.7 CONCLUSION

An effective selection programme should be preceded by a thorough job analysis, careful human resources planning and a purposeful recruitment programme. During the selection process, an attempt is being made to appoint employees who will succeed in attaining preset performance standards in certain jobs.

In this chapter, the various steps of the selection process were comprehensively discussed. These steps include the provisional selection interview, the application form, testing, following up references and the interview.

Each step in the selection process and the various selection strategies were discussed. The importance of preset performance measures in each job was specifically pointed out. The selection process then selects the candidate with the expectation that the applicant's job performance in the new job will match the preset performance measures. It was also made clear that it is essential to determine regularly by means of evaluation whether the selection process did indeed produce the candidates specified in the human resources planning process. Important concepts such as multiple indicators, placement and cost benefit analysis were discussed in the section on selection strategies.

The strategy for selecting managers was also examined. Particular attention was paid to the use of assessment centres as a selection technique for this group of employees.

Now that the selection process has been finalised, the last steps in the provisioning process, i.e. placement and induction, are discussed in the following chapter.

Questions

1. What factors would you regard as the most important to influence the selection decision?
2. Contrast and compare the various interviewing techniques with which you are familiar.
3. Which selection strategy would you choose when appointing a human resources manager in a group of chain stores? Discuss.

Sources

Ivancevich, J.M. & Glueck, W.F. 1986. *Foundations of personnel/human resource management.* 3rd edition. Reston, Virginia.

Klatt, L.A., Murdick, R.G. & Schuster, F.E. 1985. *Human resource management.* Charles E. Merrill, Columbus, Ohio.

Leap, T.L. & Crino, M.D. 1993. *Personnel/human resource management.* 2nd edition. Macmillan, New York.

Livy, B. 1988. *Corporate personnel management.* Pitman, London.

Milkovich, G.T. & Boudreau, J.W. 1988. *Personnel/human resource management.* 5th edition. Business Publications, Plano, Texas.

Chapter 8

Placement and induction

P.D. Gerber

STUDY OBJECTIVES

After studying this chapter, you should be able to:
- Differentiate between various placement strategies;
- Demonstrate the various components of an induction programme;
- Explain the objectives of an induction programme;
- Evaluate an induction programme.

8.1 PLACEMENT

8.1.1 Introduction

Placement and induction are essentially the last steps in the human resources provisioning process, although this may not appear to be so from the overview given at the beginning of part 2 of this book. Career management is a continuous process that must already be initiated during placement. For this reason it features as the last step in the human resources provisioning process as detailed in the overview.

Placement is the process through which individuals are appointed to jobs within organisations. The placement process also has to do with the movement of individuals within the organisation in the sense of promotions, transfers and terminations of service. However, it is primarily a follow-up to the selection process: selected applicants are now appointed (most of them in entry ranks).

The most important difference between the placement process and the selection process is that the former has to do with the internal labour market, i.e. with people already employed by the organisation, while selection is mainly aimed at the external labour market. Selection takes place on the basis of a

FIGURE 8.1: Principal learning components of placement and induction

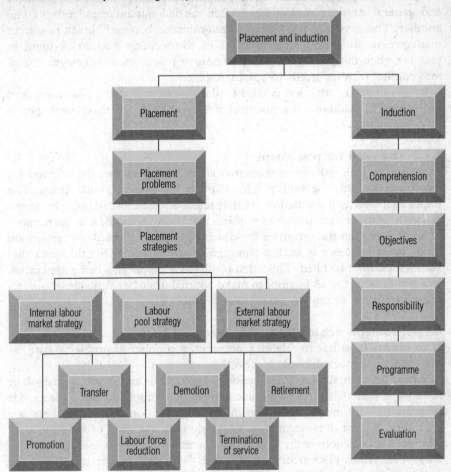

forecast of the candidate's expected future performance. Placement is based on additional information such as the employee's performance since appointment, the individual's own preferences for career development, how he or she sees the status of the current job, opportunities for promotion within the organisation, and opportunities to change jobs. Successful placement thus involves a careful combination of the employer's need to fill a post and the employee's career motivation. For this reason, placement can be defined as:

> *The process by which the newcomer/transferred employee/promoted employee is placed in a certain job for optimal individual and organisational goal achievement in accordance with the individual's own potential and needs.*

Placement practices should be seen in association with general organisational strategy, with the aim of effectively controlling the general flow of labour. It is

149

true, however, that human resources planning, placement policy and practices and general strategic planning are often carried out independently of one another. This may lead to a lack of communication between human resources management and line management. This shortcoming becomes evident in practice when the placement policy of human resources management comes into conflict with the needs of line management.

In this chapter, attention is paid to the theory underlying placement and induction. In addition, the practical implementation of these strategies is investigated.

8.1.2 The need for placement

In a country with a dynamic economy, it often happens that the demand for employees exceeds the supply. This is often the case in South Africa. The implications of such a situation are that selection is almost impossible, as the rationale of the selection process requires that there should be a larger number of applicants than the vacancies for which people are selected. At certain job levels there is currently such a shortage of employees in South Africa that vacancies cannot be filled. This often results in all applicants being appointed, which means that in an attempt to make optimal use of its available labour, an organisation has to rely on the process of placement.

8.1.3 Problems arising from the placement process

If an organisation has to rely on placement, a number of problems arise, as placement is a more difficult process than selection.

Where the compilation of a selection programme is aimed at a special job or at most at jobs that are of a similar nature, the compilation of a placement programme encompasses all jobs in the organisation for which there are vacancies. Where, for example, a job analysis in the case of selection only involves a specific job, in the case of placement a job analysis must be made of all jobs for which placement is considered. (This may be compared with the problem of the career guidance official – if he or she is to give proper guidance, the official must be familiar with all possible jobs and measures for testing the abilities involved.)

This problem worsens when testing or measuring forms part of the placement procedure. It is, for example, difficult to determine where there is the best match between the abilities of the applicant and the requirements for successful job execution with regard to the various vacant jobs. This means that it is not always possible to make a judgement about the specific vacancy that will best suit a specific applicant.

This problem often results in a need for differential placement in organisations. Differential placement requires measures (tests) that are able to measure differentially. Unfortunately, the supply of differential psychological tests and measures is limited. Consequently, a test battery consisting of scientifically validated, independent tests must often be compiled. The process of establishing a test battery with differential abilities is more complex and difficult than the normal compilation of a selection battery.

8.1.4 Placement strategy

A placement strategy is a technique that human resources management and line management can use to regulate the interaction between the internal and the external labour market to place the right employee in the right job.

Wallace *et al.* (1982:263) identify three placement strategies, i.e. the internal labour market strategy, the labour pool strategy and the external labour market strategy. In practice, it is unlikely that an organisation will use any of the three strategies in their pure form; a combination of the three is often the best solution.

The internal labour market strategy
This strategy is mostly suitable for employment at the joining rank. The initial selection decision has been based at filling only a certain entry job. Applicants who have the potential to fill a vacancy higher up in the organisation are not considered for such jobs. As vacancies occur higher up in the hierarchy, individuals can be promoted or transferred from other job hierarchies within the organisation.

The individual's upward movement in the organisation is strictly controlled by policy. Such a policy structures the internal labour market in such a way that promotions, transfers, dismissals and termination of service take place in an orderly manner.

Burgess (1989:469) defines a job family as follows:
. . . jobs involving work of the same nature but requiring different skill and responsibility levels.
A job family can be diagrammatically represented as in figure 8.2.

An important *advantage* of the internal labour market strategy is that special opportunities for promotion are available to employees simply because they are already employed by the organisation. Special mechanisms are put in place to identify and develop skills to fill vacancies higher up in the hierarchy. The long-term advantage of the internal labour market strategy is the greater loyalty, commitment and career orientation of employees who know that promotion is possible and that their interests are being looked after as far as this is possible for management.

The most important *disadvantage* of this strategy is the inability of the organisation to make immediate use of the services of individuals who apply for jobs above the entry level. In addition, the individual is expected to move through all the levels of the organisation, although he or she may already be competent to accept responsibility for a job at a much higher hierarchical level.

The labour pool strategy
The difference between the internal labour market strategy and the labour pool strategy is that according to the latter, individuals are appointed to a pool

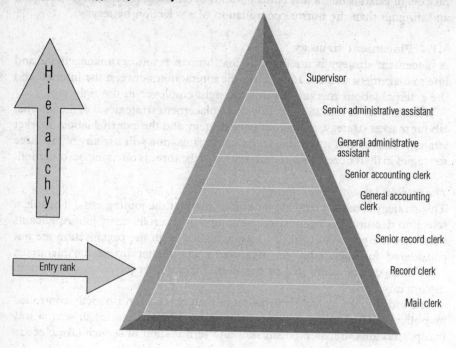

of entry ranks. If the individual is appointed in such a pool, it is accepted that he or she meets the minimum requirements for appointment. The person is then temporarily appointed to various jobs until the supervisor or line manager has a permanent job in which the employee can be placed. The individual can then be promoted through the job family in the usual way, or he or she can return to the labour pool.

The labour pool strategy grants a measure of flexibility that the internal labour strategy does not offer. The organisation has the opportunity of building up its own source of "temporary" employees who can be used in times of high labour turnover or absenteeism. In addition, the cost of poor initial selection decisions is limited to a minimum, as the work behaviour of these "temporary" employees can be observed before they are permanently appointed in a job. The biggest disadvantage of the labour pool strategy is the high cost of maintaining a pool of employees from which appointments can be made.

The external labour market strategy

This strategy not only aims at appointing employees in entry ranks but in any rank and any job. No provision is made for promotion or for internal shifts within the organisation. Individuals are recruited externally and "kept" for each job. With no chance of promotion, neither management nor the employee has any reason for career planning. This strategy places strong emphasis on the recruitment function. A constant flow of applicants is ensured to fill the jobs of employees who leave the organisation because there are no opportunities for promotion within the organisation. This is a short-sighted policy. External standards for employment, compensation and the treatment of employees may be adhered to, but at the cost of the effective utilisation of the labour available within the organisation.

The external labour market strategy can be usefully applied under certain circumstances, particularly by organisations with a relatively flat organisational structure with few opportunities for promotion or upward mobility within the existing, limited job structure. There is often not much room for promotion in the medical and scientific professions because of the limited job structure. The external labour market strategy is also practical when an industry is stagnating and organisations experience a declining demand for their products, which results in declining employment figures. Under such circumstances there will be few opportunities for promotion or upward movement within the organisational hierarchy.

8.1.5 The implementation of placement strategies

There are various methods of implementing placement strategies. Some of these are well-known techniques such as promotion, transfer, labour force reduction, demotion, termination of service or retirement.

Promotion

Promotion involves a change of job and a shift to a higher organisational level. The higher level implies a new job title, more authority and responsibility and, in most cases, a larger salary. Promotion can take place within a certain job family, for example from salesperson to sales manager, or between job families, for example from typist to training officer.

Promotion is generally viewed as being to the advantage of both the organisation and the individual who is being promoted. A promotion affords the organisation the opportunity of utilising the general experience of the individual in a more important job. Promotion affords the individual an opportunity for personal growth, increased status and compensation.

It is important to ensure that the process of promotion is effectively implemented. Some of the means in current use for promoting individuals are management development programmes, assessment centres, career management programmes and performance appraisal.

Transfer

Transfer is regarded as the lateral or horizontal movement of an individual within the internal labour market. This movement is not associated with a change in the level of skill, responsibility, status or compensation.

Transfer as a placement mechanism may be considered for a number of reasons:

- To man a new department or to fill a specific job;
- To improve the training of the transferred individual in the interests of the organisation;
- To eliminate or reduce personality conflicts within a department;
- To comply with an employee's request to be trained in a certain department or for a specific job;
- To re-open blocked promotion lines.

A transfer may take place between job families, or on a geographical basis where the transfer takes place at the initiative of the employer. Care must be taken to prevent the employee regarding it as a form of demotion. When the transfer is initiated by the employee, the basic reason is often to improve his or her position. Motivational problems are thus seldom experienced in the latter case.

In the case of geographical transfers, the employees in question are compensated for the inconvenience often associated with such shifts, such as salary differentials, the cost of living which differs noticeably from area to area, housing subsidies to compensate for the expense of finding another residence in the new area, the cost of transporting furniture and resettling.

Labour force reduction

Labour force reductions are usually considered for financial reasons. A typical example is the motor industry, which must dismiss some of its assembly-line workers when economic conditions are poor, due to the low demand for its products. Such labour force reductions may be temporary, for a specific period (especially if there is a seasonal demand for a product) or semi-permanent until the state of the economy improves.

Labour force reduction has an inhibiting effect on the functioning of the internal labour market because employees who have the potential of progressing within the job hierarchy leave the service of the organisation either temporarily or permanently. The administration of labour force reduction requires that management draw up rules beforehand on how to go about reducing the labour force if necessary. For example, attention must be paid to who will be dismissed first, what the position is with regard to status, seniority and skills when it comes to dismissal, and the rights of employees when the labour force is reduced.

Demotion

Demotion is the opposite of promotion and involves a downward movement in the job hierarchy as regards skill, responsibility, status and compensation. Demotion takes place on an individual basis, and in most cases has a negative effect on the individual, because it is often the result of poor job performance. The demotion process must be carried out as carefully as possible. The demoted person experiences embarrassment as a result of a decrease in status, and probably a drop in motivation to give of his or her best. Demotion is often camouflaged as a transfer when a supervisor wishes to get rid in a subtle manner of an employee whose job performance is not as desired.

The following are necessary for carrying out a successful demotion procedure:

- Criteria for demotion must be specified and incorporated into the human resources management policy and procedures.
- Criteria for demotion should be uniformly applied to all employees.
- Promotions and transfers should be carefully monitored so that they do not serve as cover-ups for demotions.
- Managers, supervisors and employees should be regularly informed when upward, downward and lateral movements are under discussion.

Termination of service

Termination of service may take two forms, i.e. *voluntary resignation* by the employee or *dismissal*, which may be the result of unsatisfactory job performance, misconduct or shortcomings in the qualifications necessary to carry out the job effectively. Forced resignation is a form of dismissal where the employee is granted the opportunity to obtain other employment before being dismissed. The employee is then spared the embarrassment of dismissal.

Although termination of service is a process that sometimes takes place naturally within an organisation and should be accepted as such by management, the timing and conditions for termination of service can create problems. Management must thus be constantly aware of and prepared for termination of service, and take the opportunity to arrange and manage the placement programme.

Particular attention must be paid to the requirements as contained in the Labour Relations Act (see chapter 20).

The *termination of service interview* is a useful aid in identifying the problems that give rise to voluntary resignation. To avoid emotional responses, a questionnaire should be sent 30 to 90 days after termination of service to the employee who resigned. In this questionnaire, relevant questions may be asked to attempt to establish the reasons for termination of service.

Retirement

As is the case with promotion, transfer, labour force reduction and termination of service, the retirement of employees must be managed in an orderly fashion, as it forms an important part of the placement strategy. For the employer, the retirement of an employee means that a placement decision must be taken with regard to a replacement for the job. For the outgoing employee, it means the end of his or her career, terminating the relationship with the organisation and the job held, and entering a new period of adaptation, which is usually an emotional step.

When an employee is retiring, management should pay attention to the following steps:

- Plans must be made beforehand for orderly succession to fill the job.
- There must be communication and advice to meet the needs of the outgoing employee.
- Attention must be paid to gradual retirement options such as reduced work time to facilitate the transition to retirement, and job modification to allow reduced work time for the job.

8.1.6 Conclusion

The placement process requires competent management to ensure that employees are optimally used within the organisation. The various placement strategies discussed help to control the flow of human resources within the organisation, and to make a contribution towards the development of internal human resources. The strategies under discussion were those of promotion, transfer, labour force reduction, termination of service and retirement. Each of these strategies can make an important and unique contribution towards the process of placing the right individual in the right job and ensuring optimal individual performance orientation.

Once the necessary preparations have been made for placing the right person in the right job, induction follows. This is the final step in the human resources provisioning process, during which the person is taken into the organisation or is oriented in the job.

8.2 INDUCTION
8.2.1 Introduction

Induction is defined by Hall and Goodale (1986:275) as the process through which a new employee learns how to function efficiently within a new organisational culture by obtaining the information, values and behavioural skills associated with his or her new role in the organisation.

Ivancevich and Glueck (1986:448) regard induction as the human resources management activity that introduces new employees to the organisation and to the employee's tasks, superiors and work group.

The first few days in a new job are of vital importance for both the employee and the employer. The employee must immediately feel part of the organisation, associate himself or herself with the goals of the organisation, and experience a positive disposition and attitude towards the job. Only then can the task be addressed in a positive manner. Induction can make an important contribution in this regard.

The employee and the job that he or she holds will determine how sophisticated the induction programme will be. Thus managers will have to follow a more detailed induction programme than ordinary clerical personnel. The manager's induction programme will include things such as an introduction to the business philosophy of the organisation, how to inform new employees about their tasks, work groups, supervisor leadership relation, working conditions and policy. New clerical employees, on the other hand, will be informed about their jobs, meet their colleagues and supervisors and receive information about working conditions and the discipline of the organisation. Part-time employees will probably undergo a much shorter and less intensive induction.

The climate of the organisation also determines what the induction programme will look like and what attention it will receive. A newer employee who has recently left school will probably undergo a far more intensive induction programme than an employee who already has ten years experience in a similar organisation.

With these few introductory remarks about induction made, attention can now be given to aspects such as the objectives of induction, who should accept responsibility for this function, how an induction programme works, and the course such a programme should follow.

8.2.2 The objectives of induction

An effective induction programme can make an important contribution towards attaining the following objectives:

- To make a new employee more rapidly productive: When a new employee joins an organisation, he or she is unfamiliar with the way in which the work must be done, how the organisation functions and how to act to fit into the organisation effectively. It usually takes a while before the new employee is as productive as his or her colleagues who have been working for the organisation for some time. An effective induction programme can contribute much towards enabling the new employee to reach production standards more rapidly and to reduce the cost of employment.

- To reduce fear and insecurity: When they join an organisation, most new employees experience a degree of fear about whether they will succeed in the job, as a result of insecurity about the requirements of the new job. This is a normal reaction. Tactful behaviour on the part of existing employees can eliminate the new employee's initial insecurity and fear, so that he or she can address the new task with a positive attitude.

- The reduction of labour turnover: Labour turnover is particularly high during the first phase of the employee's period of service. If, during this time, the employee is allowed to build up negative feelings towards the task – a feeling that he or she cannot make a positive contribution to the organisation, insecurity or frustration – this can induce the person to leave the service of the organisation. An effective induction programme can make a positive contribution towards limiting labour turnover to a minimum during the initial phase of the new employee's career.

- Helping to create realistic employee expectations: Employees who have gone through a long training period, for example professional people such as attorneys and doctors, learn during their training exactly what to expect once they begin their actual task. This is not the case for most types of work, however. During the induction programme, new employees must be taught exactly what the organisation expects of them and what they in turn can expect from the organisation. Here the induction programme can make an important contribution towards toning down expectations and basing them on reality.

- Creating job satisfaction and a positive attitude towards the employer: The induction programme can contribute much towards the immediate development of a positive attitude towards the employer and job satisfaction on the part of the new employee. If, during induction, the employee finds that the employer takes an interest in him or her, wants to make the job climate pleasant, wants to see to it that he or she is a happy employee and is being treated with dignity, all this can contribute towards fostering a positive attitude in the employee.
- Saving the time of supervisors and colleagues: Employees who do not undergo an effective induction programme may feel insecure with regard to what is expected of them and how the task must be carried out. It would take their colleagues or supervisors some time to correct this problem; the new employee will now have to ask the supervisor and colleagues questions that could have been answered during the induction programme and that can mean a waste of time.

8.2.3 Who is responsible for the induction programme?

Induction is carried out on two, clearly distinguishable levels in the organisation:

- General orientation with regard to the organisation, where subjects of general interest are discussed with all new employees.
- Departmental and job orientation, in which subjects unique to the new employee's specific task and the department in which he or she will be working are discussed.

The responsibility for induction is usually divided between the human resources department and the new employee's immediate supervisor or manager. The responsibilities of the human resources department and those of the supervisor or manager can, however, be clearly separated. The human resources department is responsible for:

- The initiation and coordination of both levels of induction;
- The training of line management in the procedures for departmental and job orientation;
- General induction within the organisation;
- Following up the initial induction of the new employee.

The supervisor or manager is responsible for the orientation of the new employee with regard to the new task and the section or department in which he or she will be working. While some organisations make use of the so-called "buddy" system, in which job orientation is carried out by one of the existing employees, it is very important that such a helpmate should be carefully chosen and properly trained to fulfil his or her responsibility effectively.

8.2.4 The induction programme

The induction programme must be designed so that it will meet the needs of both the organisation and the new employee. The needs of the organisation are aimed at making a profit, which means that the organisation wants the new employee to make a productive contribution to profit-making as soon as possible. New employees, on the other hand, are more interested in compensation, benefits and conditions of employment. Particular care must be taken that a healthy balance is maintained between the needs of the organisation and those of the new employee.

An induction programme that provides a general orientation with regard to the activities of the organisation can include the following:

- *An overview of the organisation*: An historical overview of the formation of the organisation, its goals, norms, standards and philosophy; the organisational structure; products and services; the job environment;
- *An overview of policy and procedures*: How to communicate; how to get the product/service to the consumer; management philosophy;
- *Compensation*: Salaries and salary scales; overtime pay; bonuses; leave pay; how payment takes place;
- *Fringe benefits*: Insurance, medical benefits; unemployment insurance; leave; retirement benefits; cafeteria and recreation facilities;
- *Safety*: Health and emergency clinics; safety measures for the prevention of accidents; reporting of accidents; use of alcohol and drugs during working hours; the use of safety equipment;
- *Labour relations*: Employee rights and responsibilities; employee organisations; employment conditions; grievance procedures; discipline; communication channels; termination of service;
- *Facilities*: Cafeteria services; parking; rest rooms; stock;
- *Economic factors*: The cost of theft, absenteeism, accidents, starting work late, equipment and labour; profit margins.

An induction programme that wants to orientate new employees specifically with regard to the task will include the following:

- *Functions of the department/section*: Objectives; organisational structure; activities in department/section; relation of functions to other departments/sections; relation of tasks to each other within the department/section;
- *Tasks and responsibilities*: Detailed explanation of the task based on job description; explanation of the importance of the task; explanation of performance standards; working hours and overtime; forms, records and reports to be completed; obtaining and maintaining tools; explanation of general problems in the work situation;
- *Policy, procedures, rules and regulations*: Rules unique to the task; safety requirements and accident prevention; reporting of accidents; reporting for

159

service; rest periods and lunch times; private use of the telephone; stock requests; public relations;

- *Viewing of the workplace*: Rest rooms; first aid facilities; reporting for service; lockers; approved entrances and exits; stock room and maintenance department;
- *Introduction to employees*: Introduction to colleagues in the department/section; introduction to employees in other departments/sections.

As well as oral induction, it is desirable to provide a new employee with written material in the form of a manual to support the oral programme. This written document should not only supply essential information, but also include items such as the organisational chart, the organisational policy, a procedural guide, the telephone numbers of key personnel and a copy of the newsletter.

Finally, it can be pointed out that it is often advisable to present the induction programme in short sessions (not longer than two hours). It is difficult for new employees to take in all the information in one long session.

8.2.5 Following up and evaluating the induction programme

It is very important that the manager should regularly find out how the new employee is coping. The manager should be available to answer any questions on the part of the new employee and to pay attention to his or her problems.

A feedback system can be designed on the basis of an objective management programme, for example to provide follow-up twice during the first week of service and at least once a week in the following two or three weeks. Such a technique can enable management to compile a follow-up schedule so that a comprehensive record of how the new person has been integrated into the job can be established within a month.

An important source of feedback about the induction programme is the new employee himself or herself. This feedback can be obtained by asking the new employee to fill in a questionnaire, holding in-depth interviews with randomly chosen new employees, or holding group discussion sessions with new employees who are already established in their jobs. These methods are useful in helping the organisation determine how successful its induction is. The methods can also supply useful information about specific adaptations needed in the induction programme.

8.2.6 Conclusion

Induction programmes are established to introduce new employees to their role as employees, to the organisation and to their colleagues. In small organisations, this task is mainly carried out by the supervisor, but in larger organisations the human resources department plays an important role in integrating the new employee into the organisation. As was indicated in the previous sections, the induction programme can take various forms, depending on the needs of the organisation and the new employee. Attention was given to the formal induction programme and the individual items covered by such a programme. Particular attention was also paid to the responsibilities of human resources management and the supervisors or managers with regard to the induction programme. Finally, the importance of following up and evaluating the induction programme was emphasised.

Questions

1. Contrast and evaluate the various placement strategies with which you are familiar.
2. Explain how you would go about implementing the various placement strategies.
3. Why is it so important to expose employees to a proper induction programme? Discuss.
4. How would you go about developing an induction programme? Fully discuss the steps.

Sources

Burgess, L.R. 1989. *Compensation administration*. Merrill, Columbus, Ohio.

Hall, D.T. & Goodale, J.G. 1986. *Human resource management*. Scott, Foresman, Illinois.

Ivancevich, J.M. & Glueck, W.F. 1986. *Foundations of personnel/human resource management*. 3rd edition. Business Publications, Plano, Texas.

Wallace, M.J., Crandall, N.F. & Fay, C.H. 1982. *Administering human resources*. Random House, New York.

Chapter 9

Career management

P.S. Nel

STUDY OBJECTIVES

After studying this chapter, you should be able to:
- Distinguish between training, development and career management;
- Explain why personality traits are important in making a career choice;
- Motivate why the various career and life stages are important in career planning;
- Distinguish between career planning and career development;
- Explain the importance of the Guidance and Placement Act in career development;
- Differentiate between career directions and methods;
- Explain the importance of retirement as the last phase of career development.

9.1 INTRODUCTION

Figure 3.1 (chapter 3) shows that career management is part of the throughput process and occurs in the job context environment. The interaction of career management in the various environments is seen from figure 9.1 to have a direct influence on the development, status and recognition of workers in the job content environment. In the job context environment it has an influence on management philosophy, leadership, working conditions and intergroup and intragroup relations. In the external environment, career management is directly influenced by the national human resources policy, technology and economic conditions in South Africa.

FIGURE 9.1: Principal learning components of career management

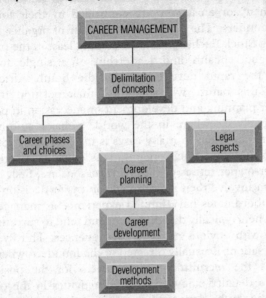

It is to the advantage of any organisation to retain productive employees for as long as possible. In chapters 21 and 22 we explain that training and development make employees more productive in an organisation. A further means, closely linked to training and development, is for the organisation to invite employees to treat their relationship with their employer as a career. Ideally there should be sufficient opportunities and promotion possibilities to enable employees to remain with their employer for the duration of their working life.

The long-term interests of employees should be protected by the organisation and, on the other hand, employees should be encouraged to grow and realise their full potential for the benefit of the organisation. If the career planning and development of employees is effective, they will realise their full potential and will probably be prepared to remain with their present employer till retirement.

Countries such as Japan and Taiwan believe in the principle of life-long employment.

Succession planning in an organisation is essential to ensure that suitably qualified and experienced employees are available when vacancies arise and to fill human resources needs that result from the growth and reorientation of the organisation in the economic environment in which it operates. Employee succession and filling of new jobs—particularly management jobs—are therefore essential for the survival of any organisation.

Career management has become a crucial issue in South Africa and one reason is that many organisations are controlled by their founders or the families of the founders. The success of a number of organisations listed on the Johannesburg Stock Exchange is attributed, at least in the public mind, to the continued good health and leadership of a single founder-owner. However, with the rapid development of the South African economy, organisations of this nature will jeopardise their position if they do not implement career planning and development or succession in posts. In South Africa, and probably elsewhere in the world, a major stumbling block to effective career management in many cases is the personality of the founder-owner of the organisation. Such organisations could face serious problems when the founder-owner retires or dies. The reasons are, first, that such men or women seldom involve their subordinates in major decision-making, with the result that subordinates have limited experience as managers. Secondly, these founder-owners typically dislike dissent and tend to surround themselves with "yes-men", with obvious negative consequences. Thirdly, communication in the organisations is usually directed to the founder-owners themselves. This complicates the recruitment of outsiders for the position of chief executive, since a detailed knowledge of all activities in the organisation is essential if the job is to be done well.

Scores of small and medium-sized organisations in South Africa are in this position and they will suffer losses if the founder-owner should die suddenly. The same applies, albeit to a lesser extent, to some large public organisations in South Africa, where there are often no written prescriptions for career management: arrangements are made at the whim of the chief executive.

In South Africa, large organisations that fall into this category should draw up five-year career management plans, medium-sized organisations should draw up three-year plans and small organisations should plan to implement career management within a year.

In a small organisation, the chief executive should consider recruiting at least one young executive who can be developed into his or her successor. In many cases such a young person might be a son, daughter or other relative. The founder-owner should assign specific responsibilities to such a successor and should involve him or her in all major decisions. This means that the founder-owners may have to fight the natural instinct to make all significant decisions themselves, even though this is the way they have been operating in the past and how they achieved their success. If they neglect to do so, the plan to groom a successor will probably fail, because responsibility without authority is a major source of frustration and causes people to contemplate resigning or to lose their motivation to excel.

If the organisation cannot support two heads, the chief executive should at least maintain an excellent record and reporting system so that any successor should be able to assume responsibility swiftly if necessary (for example, if the chief executive dies or retires suddenly because of serious illness).

164

Career management is now discussed in more detail.

A *career* can be defined as a series of jobs that follow a hierarchy of levels or degrees of difficulty, responsibility and status (Graham and Bennett 1993:389).

Career planning may be defined as the process by which an individual analyses his or her work situation, specifies his or her career goals and plans various means to achieve these goals.

To plan a career, an employee must set certain career priorities, evaluate the behaviour and attitude of other people who have successfully achieved such a career, choose a type of work that makes use of his or her strong points, undergo the necessary training, and where possible get a good mentor to guide him or her. The individual must then regularly monitor his or her progress against the goals that have been set, investigate shortcomings and, where necessary, replan.

A *career path*, according to Mondy and Noe (1987:336) can be seen as flexible lines of progression from the organisation's point of view, through which an employee typically moves in his or her career. By following an established career path, the employee participates in career development with the assistance of the organisation.

Career development is defined as a formal approach taken by the organisation to ensure that employees with proper qualifications and experience are available when they are needed by the organisation.

An important question is: Who is responsible for career planning and development? The answer is: It normally requires effort from three sources— the organisation itself, the employee's immediate manager and the employee.

- *The organisation's responsibilities:* An organisation cannot and should not bear the sole responsibility for planning and developing an employee's career. The organisation has to furnish career opportunities for its employees and advise employees about the various career paths that are available in that organisation to enable them to achieve their career goals. The human resources department is generally responsible for relaying this information to employees and informing staff when new jobs are created and old ones are phased out. The human resources department therefore needs to work closely with individual employees and their superiors to ensure that their career goals are realistic and are followed within the constraints of the organisation.

- *The employee's immediate superior:* This person, although he or she is not expected to be a professional counsellor, can and should take part in facilitating his or her immediate subordinates' career planning. The superior should act as communicator, counsellor, appraiser, coach and mentor, ensuring that the subordinate employee gets the information necessary for furthering his or her career. It is unfortunate that many superiors do not see it as part of their duties to assist in the career development of their subordinates. Either they do not know how to go about

165

it or they see every subordinate as a potential threat to their own position, so they give no assistance, and they may even exert a negative influence.

- *The individual employee:* The final responsibility for career planning and development rests with individual employees because they know what they want from their career and how hard they are prepared to work.

Successful career planning and development is therefore a joint effort by the individual employee, his or her immediate superior and the organisation: the employee does the planning, the immediate superior provides the resources and the organisation provides the means and structure for development.

The rest of this chapter is devoted to the importance of career management, career choices employees should make, the various career stages of employees, legislation that assists employers with career choices for employees in South Africa, a more detailed analysis of career planning and development itself, and a practical five-step approach that employers and employees can use for career management.

9.2 THE IMPORTANCE OF CAREER MANAGEMENT TO EMPLOYERS AND EMPLOYEES

For the organisation the major purpose of career management is to match the employee's needs, abilities and goals with the current or future needs of the organisation. This is intended to ensure that the organisation places the right employee in the right place at the right time and so offer the employee the opportunity of achieving personal fulfilment in the job. Matching the employee with the job is the first step, which entails matching the employee's potential with the requirements of the job, and the employee's needs with the job reward, as discussed in the chapters on recruitment and selection.

There are a number of reasons for implementing career management in organisations:

- Being given the ability to advance increases the quality of work life of employees. Employees wish to have control over their own careers, and the new generation of younger employees wants greater job satisfaction and more career options.
- It is necessary today for organisations to avoid obsolescence by encouraging employees to learn new skills. This is because rapid changes in technology and changes in consumer demand cause skills to become outdated. With career development programmes, employees can gain new skills when their old skills are no longer in demand.
- Career management reduces staff turnover in the organisation. Employees experience less frustration and greater job satisfaction because they know they can advance in the organisation.
- When employees' specific talents have been identified, they are given the opportunity through career planning to perform better and to be placed in jobs that fit their ambitions and personal talents.

Career management integrates the objectives of the individual and the organisation in such a way that both will gain. The employee will experience satisfaction and personal development, while there will be increased productivity and creativity within the organisation. The end result of career management is an organisation staffed by committed employees who are well trained and productive.

9.3 CAREER STAGES AND CHOICES

South Africa has a vast unskilled and semi-skilled population and small numbers of qualified personnel. Organisations therefore need to identify skills and talents quickly and embark on effective career development programmes, so that employees can contribute to the productivity of the organisation. In South Africa special attention is paid to identifying the talents and skills of employees and assisting them with career planning, in terms of the Guidance and Placement Act (which is discussed in the next section). The National Institute of Personnel Research and the Human Sciences Research Council do research into the aptitudes, career choices, personalities, and so on, of employees. The various needs and the career and life stages of employees need to be taken into account when career planning and development programmes are being designed. Employees also need to analyse how a career choice should be made and developed.

FIGURE 9.2: The relationship between people's most important needs and their career and life stages

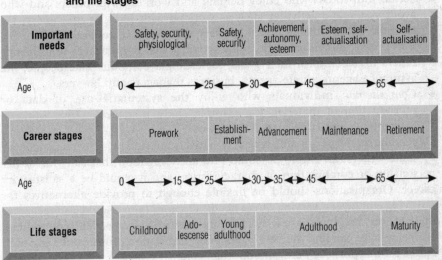

Source: Adapted from Ivancevich & Glueck (1986:523–7)

Figure 9.2 shows that all people go through different but interrelated stages in their lives and careers. Depending on the state they have reached in their

167

lives and their careers, they have different needs. This should be borne in mind when careers are planned and developed. Most people prepare for an occupation in some formal educational institution like a high school, and then take a first job. They will eventually move to other jobs within the same organisation or join other organisations. Although the stages may vary, most employees go through all the stages indicated in figure 9.2.

Analysis of the various career and life stages of people shows that the most important decision a person makes is what career to follow. It is generally accepted that what employees accomplish and derive from their career will depend on the congruence between their personality and the job environment. Each individual resembles one of six personality types to some extent, and people choose their occupations in accordance with their personality, in order to follow a career that generally matches it. People sometimes have a combination of these personality characteristics. The personality types are:

- *Realistic:* individuals who prefer activities involving the use of machinery or tools; for example artisans, tool and die makers, farmers, engineers and carpenters.
- *Investigative:* individuals who are analytical, curious, methodical and precise; for example medical technologists, teachers, biologists and astronomers.
- *Artistic:* people who strive for self-expression, are non-conformist, original and introspective; for example artists, musicians, photographers, sculptors and actors.
- *Social:* individuals who enjoy helping and working with others and who avoid systematic activities such as working with tools or machinery; for example police officers, social workers and guidance counsellors.
- *Enterprising*: individuals who enjoy activities that permit them to influence others to accomplish their goals; for example computer salespeople, life assurance agents, estate agents, business managers and lawyers.
- *Conventional*: individuals who enjoy the systematic use of data or reproduction of material; for example credit managers, office workers, accountants and supermarket managers.

Depending on the personality type, alternatively referred to as "career anchors" by some writers, an employee could find an occupation that suits his or her personality or combination of characteristics, and it would be a satisfactory career. Organisations should be flexible enough to provide alternatives for satisfying employees' varying career needs. Organisations should also recognise that not every employee is or wants to be the enterprising type. With counselling, each employee can find the best career path. Legislation promulgated in South Africa for this purpose plays an important role.

9.4 THE GUIDANCE AND PLACEMENT ACT
The Guidance and Placement Act (Act 62 of 1981) provides for the establishment and control of guidance and placement centres and advisory

employment boards, as well as for the registration and control of private employment offices.

Since this chapter primarily deals with career management, we shall give more attention to guidance than to placement.

Guidance and placement centres are established in terms of the Act. These centres may be established in any area for any work-seekers. The functions of the officials of these centres are described below.

They guide work-seekers in their choice of occupation by collecting and disseminating information, which includes vocational information and advice to work-seekers. This is similar to the vocational guidance supplied to school leavers.

These centres provide services in the form of interviews and IQ, aptitude and personality tests. Tests are also administered to determine reasons for a work-seeker's preference for or rejection of a particular job.

These services are rendered by the Directorate of Career Services and Placement of the Department of Manpower, which operates the **centres for career services and placement**. There are 17 of these centres at present. They usually have the services of a vocational counsellor whom work-seekers may consult. All work-seekers can also consult *Career guide*, which is published by the Department of Manpower to provide information about job opportunities in the labour market. A meaningful choice of career requires much knowledge about the nature, working conditions and training requirements of the various careers. Other information is also available, such as Careers 2000 exhibitions, written replies to career enquiries and participation in radio and television programmes.

Apart from the actions mentioned, according to the *1990 Annual Report* of the Department of Manpower (1991:92–4) the Directorate distributed the following pamphlets, newsletters and information brochures during 1990:

- Newsletter to school leavers about available services and information about unusual careers, bursaries, training courses, etc.
- Pamphlet about the career adjustment service to employers and employees in the Civil Service.
- Pamphlet about the bursary scheme for the handicapped of the National Readjustment Committee and Careers Council.
- Pamphlet about career services for use during the Careers 2000 exhibitions and for distribution to schools.
- Internal newsletters to career counsellors and placement officers.

These actions by the Directorate of Career Services and Placement are an attempt to enable work-seekers to match their personal talents and aptitudes to jobs that are available in the market and in so doing to make better career choices. Centres keep a register of work-seekers listing particulars such as address, age and area for employment, and try to place them in employment.

Centres also assist employers in the selection of suitable staff. Employers can make use of the Department of Manpower's regional offices where the guidance and placement centres are located, and where professional vocational counsellors will assist them. The tests that are used are based on job analyses and other information from the employer, and all candidates are interviewed by the counsellor. A report is submitted to the employer to assist him or her in the selection of a suitable employee.

These services, provided by guidance and placement centres throughout South Africa, can be of great help to human resources managers, particularly of smaller businesses that do not have specialised assistance such as psychometrists to guide employees and place them in the right jobs.

Career rehabilitation information is also distributed by the Department of Manpower in its quarterly publication, *Rehabilitation in SA*, which appears every year in March, June, September and December. The aim of this publication is to promote career rehabilitation, to bring handicapped people as a valuable and supplementary human resource to the attention of society, to eliminate prejudice against the handicapped on the part of employers, and to promote the employment of handicapped people. People and organisations involved with the handicapped and their rehabilitation can submit articles for publication or subscribe to the magazine. This service originated from the *HSRC/NTB investigation: Training and placement of the handicapped person* in 1989, which brought this question into focus.

There were four issues of *Rehabilitation in SA* during 1990, with a print run of 7 000 per edition. This publication is held in high regard by professional people and is used in universities in the training of students.

A professional service, provided free of charge to all work-seekers in South Africa, facilitates better career choices and placements by recording work-seekers' qualifications, aptitudes, personalities and interests. With these details placement service officials can place work-seekers in the best available posts. Recommendations are made to the work-seeker, with whom the final decision on a career or job then rests. Once the work-seeker has decided on a job, he or she is sent to the employer with an introduction card.

In terms of the Guidance and Placement Act information about young work-seekers can also be obtained from schools, in particular about pupils over the age of 15 who are no longer compelled to attend school. In fact the guidance and placement service is primarily aimed at juvenile work-seekers.

The Act also provides for the establishment of **advisory employment boards.** These boards deal with the employment, welfare and supervision of work-seekers.

The Act also has jurisdiction over **private employment offices.** These offices are subject to the terms of the Act if they levy charges for finding work for a work-seeker or staff for an employer. Such private offices have to be registered in terms of the Act. Their records have to be kept for a minimum of three years. The Act stipulates the fees that may be charged by these employment offices. Personnel agencies throughout South Africa fall under the jurisdiction of the Act, which makes provisions for stringent control of their activities in order to eliminate abuse by employees or employers.

The Guidance and Placement Act was thus promulgated to formalise career guidance in South Africa. It provides an orderly means of promoting the job choices of particularly juvenile work-seekers who have just left school. Private employment offices cater for the needs, career guidance and counselling of professionals and adults who are already in employment, but who are looking for jobs that may suit them better.

In 1981 the National Manpower Commission undertook an investigation into high-level human resources. The result was a request to the Director-General of Manpower to make provision for the coordination of information, recruitment, selection, placement and career planning. In 1985 the National Committee for Coordination of Career Services was established to do so. It is therefore clear that the authorities are intent on providing career services for South Africa's economically active population.

9.5 CAREER PLANNING

9.5.1 Career planning by the individual

We have stated that career planning is a process whereby an individual sets career goals and identifies the means to achieve them. The responsibility for career planning rests primarily with the individual, but he or she will need support from superiors and the organisation in general. Career planning begins with understanding oneself: each individual needs to identify his or her personality characteristics, as described above. Career planning is as important to a new job-seeker as to an adult worker already in employment. Adult workers planning their careers need to establish their present life stage and career stage (figure 9.2). As a person progresses through life, his or her priorities usually change. People also have different priorities in different life and career stages.

By introspection individuals should decide what kind of person they are, what skills they possess, their values and interests, likes and dislikes, and strengths and weaknesses. They should draw up a balance sheet listing their strengths on the left-hand side and weaknesses on the right. It may be necessary to make several lists because such repetition forces a person to discover more about his or her characteristics. On the basis of these lists a person might decide on a career in, say, a technical field instead of in the arts or management.

According to Mondy and Noe (1987:342), the employee should identify job opportunities in his or her organisation by asking:

- What are my prospects for promotion and transfer from my present job?
- What positions have my peers reached within the last year or two?
- What are the compensation ranges for various jobs in the organisation?
- Which division in the organisation has the fastest growth and therefore provides the best promotion opportunities? The employee might even consider changing jobs and accepting a lower grade job in the organisation to obtain a position that is an avenue for moving up faster in the organisation.

171

Employees should also study trends in the economy, for example where there are human resources shortages in various skills, what technology developments are taking place and how government policy could shape the future job market. In South Africa there is a particular shortage of managerial talent and technically competent artisans, as discussed in chapter 23. These issues should be taken into consideration when career decisions are made and opportunities investigated.

The next step, after job trends and specific opportunities in the employment market have been analysed, is to set goals in terms of the personal strengths, weaknesses, interests and values identified. Then short-term, medium-term and long-term goals must be set in order to monitor growth in the chosen career. Goals should be consistent with a person's capabilities and compatible with his or her self-image, because unrealistic goals lead to frustration and disillusionment.

Once the goals have been set, the employee needs to prepare a plan to meet them. In drawing up this plan the employee needs to have discussions with superiors in the organisation and with members of the human resources department. They will assist him or her to implement the plan.

9.5.2 Career planning by the organisation

If an organisation is to be successful, it needs to ensure that sufficient numbers of qualified employees are available when vacancies occur or expansion takes place. Recruitment and selection is one means of ensuring this; on the other hand, an organisation can implement training and development and have recourse to promotion from within to achieve this goal. What is essential is that people must be groomed for posts, and planning must be instituted so that the right people are available for vacant positions when other people retire or resign or when the organisation expands. This process is a technique that outlines specific progression from one job to another by employees according to the goals and needs of the organisation. It includes plans for a sequence of development activities which will give an individual job experience enabling him or her to step into more advanced jobs in the future. The major aim of career planning programmes, therefore, is to ensure that the goals of the organisation are smoothly achieved through the utilisation of human resources.

Numerous authors believe that organisations should do career planning to make employees' career goals realistic. If an employee's career expectations are unrealistically high because of poor career planning, the result will be disappointment, reduced commitment and diminished performance. There will probably be increased labour turnover as well. The primary aim of career planning is therefore not necessarily to lay out a career plan, but to help employees acquire the skills that are essential for the planning of their own careers.

To help employees with their career planning, employers should make information available about jobs and should create career options; they should help employees to set realistic career goals and to plan their careers. This can be done by the employee's immediate superior, and guidance and counselling can be provided by the human resources department. Career path information for each job should be based on historical trends in the organisation. Such information is useful to employees in a number of ways. First, it indicates to them how their job relates to other jobs; secondly, it might suggest career alternatives; thirdly, it indicates educational and experience requirements for effecting a career change; and lastly, it shows how various work groups fit together.

Employers traditionally developed career paths for upward mobility because if a person could not move upward he or she had to leave the organisation. Today enlightened organisations recognise that not everybody wants to follow a vertical career path and become the top executive: career paths can be developed with lateral, diagonal and even downward career progression (for example as a person nears retirement). In other words, when an employee's career is planned, the career path can be built in accordance with his or her goals, ensuring that the employee's job satisfaction remains of paramount importance. If the organisation synchronises its career planning activities with the career planning of the individual, the result is bound to be a positive response on the part of employees, and the organisation will have sufficiently qualified and motivated staff when vacancies occur.

9.6 CAREER DEVELOPMENT

As we have mentioned, career development is a formal approach by the organisation to ensure that employees with proper qualifications and experience are available when needed. To realise this goal, the organisation needs to support career development and be committed to it. Its policy must be to make resources available for promotion of the career development plans of employees. The human resources department should control and coordinate all career development programmes, and provide information, tools and guidance so that employees can implement their development activities. The immediate superior of the employee is of cardinal importance in providing support, advice and feedback, but the employee is ultimately responsible for his or her own career development.

Employees proceed from one job to another in a certain sequence. It is generally accepted that the right sequence of jobs contributes materially to career development. In the first place career development starts with the job itself. Each day the employee faces different challenges and different tasks to be mastered. What is learned at work often has a greater influence than formally planned development activities. Secondly, different jobs demand different skills: a supervisor needs human relations skills, and a training specialist needs teaching skills and technical knowledge. Development can take place when a person is assigned a job for which he or she has not yet developed the necessary skills, and he or she would learn the skills while doing the job. Thirdly, a transfer might help an employee to acquire the skills and knowledge needed for a further promotion. Fourthly, a rational sequence of job assignments can reduce the time required for an employee to develop the necessary skills for a chosen target job. If particular jobs teach particular skills, a series of job assignments should be selected that will provide the best means of development over the course of an employee's career.

Career development programmes can use both formal and informal means. Informal means would, for example, be on-the-job training or off-the-job training, but within the organisation. Alternatively, the trainee can participate in off-the-job programmes away from the organisation, for example seminars and short courses provided by technikons, universities and the Institute of Personnel Management. If employees want to be successful in their career, they must be on the constant lookout for the best career opportunities. In addition, they must keep their options open; not waste time working for a manager who procrastinates; ensure that they are vital subordinates to a proactive superior; strive for exposure and visibility in the organisation; be prepared to present themselves when jobs become vacant; leave the organisation if their career development slows down too much; be ready to resign if necessary; and not let success in their present job jeopardise their career plan, because it would reduce their upward mobility.

By taking such action employees may ensure that their career plans are not unduly hindered. However, the organisation also has a role to play in employees' career development: performance appraisal has to be done regularly and various other human resources tasks need to be performed, such as promotions, transfers, lay-offs and retirement planning.

9.6.1 Career development for retirement

Career development for retirement is the last logical step in the career management process. In South Africa employees retire anywhere between 55 and 65, depending on the organisation. For many, retirement is a bitter experience because many organisations do not prepare employees for it. Some employees look forward to retirement as the culmination of their career, providing an opportunity to relax. Yet often it is a disappointment and a bore. Where life was once busy and full of incident it has become dull and unexciting. Furthermore retirees sometimes struggle to maintain their sense of identity and self-worth without a fulfilling job. Organisations need to devote attention to this stage of career development, and start by asking the following questions:

- When does the employee plan to retire?
- Who is considering early retirement?
- What does the employee plan to do during retirement?
- Will he or she attempt a second career outside the organisation?
- Can the organisation assist him or her in preparing for such a career?
- Can the retiree be approached by the organisation to help new employees to learn the job?

It is obvious that organisations need to answer these questions to prepare employees for their retirement.

The human resources department, in particular, should provide counselling for those about to retire, helping them to accept their reduced role, to live a less structured life and to make adaptations in their family and community life. Other subjects for counselling are how the pension scheme operates and how lump sum payments will be made, how leisure time can be spent, health issues, accommodation arrangements, financial arrangements and investments. Counselling should smooth the way for employees who are retiring, and they should come to understand that this is the culmination of their career development.

9.6.2 Career development methods

There are a number of methods used in carrying out career development. The most important are outlined below. (Training and development methods are discussed in chapter 21.)

- *Performance appraisal*: The organisation can use performance appraisal as a valuable tool for career development, because the strengths and weaknesses of employees are assessed.
- *Workshops*: Through workshops lasting two or three days, employees can be actively assisted with the planning and development of their careers.
- *Career counselling*: The human resources department or outsiders can assist employees by counselling them on their careers.
- *Tailor-made materials*: Some organisations provide material that has been specifically developed to assist employees in their career development and planning, for example company brochures showing future plans and expansion. Assessment centre material is devised which portrays a specific organisation's activities and needs.
- *Management by objectives*: This could be an excellent means of assisting employees with career development, because superiors and subordinates jointly agree on ways to achieve the organisation's goals, while also taking employees' personal goals into account. When goals are not achieved, new development needs may be identified and included in employees' career development.

9.7 A PRACTICAL APPROACH TO CAREER MANAGEMENT

As already stated, employee career development is the joint responsibility of the employee and employer. If there is to be sound employee career development, a structured strategy should be followed. A practical five-step strategy that employers can use to ensure effective career development in their organisations is given below.

Step 1: Match the goals of the individual with those of the organisation
It is essential that each employee involves himself or herself in a career planning exercise to determine what he or she wants to do now and in the

future. This means that the organisation must also have very clearly defined strategic and tactical plans, that is, that careful *organisational planning* is undertaken.

In addition, the employer should undertake *human resources planning*, which will indicate exactly what the demand will be for particular employees in the organisation at any particular time, and whether there will be sufficient people to meet the demand. Job analysis is also important, because it indicates what the personal requirements are for a job and what the job entails. It is then easy to determine whether a specific employee is capable of doing a particular job. Recruitment and selection are also easier if career planning is done because employers are able to fill specific vacancies internally. Career development will identify internal staff when capable outside employees cannot be recruited. The reward system could motivate employees to develop themselves in a particular direction. It can also gauge how successful an employee's career development programme has been. Performance appraisal also plays a role in employee career development in that it can be used to determine an employee's development potential.

An individual who is already in the employ of the organisation must go through a specific procedure related to his or her career before he or she can participate in career development. The steps are as follows, and the employer should help the employee with each step:

- *Self-assessment*: Employees must develop a personal profile of their unique attributes. This will help them to recognise their skills or lack of skills.
- *Work values:* Employees need to crystallise their perception of the work environment, that is, whether they are equipped to be in a position of power, whether they seek and receive recognition, and whether they are working towards becoming an expert or are inclined to provide service only.
- *How to decide on a career:* Employees must be taught how to decide scientifically on a career. The employer should provide exercises and case studies and expose employees to the decision-making process.
- *Connection workshop:* At such a workshop, which lasts approximately three days, employees are made aware of the organisation's labour needs. They review all the issues previously mentioned, including the needs of the organisation, to decide on a particular job. Once they have decided on a job, they should be given an opportunity to discuss the job with an incumbent to confirm that their perception is in line with the reality of the job. The discussion with an incumbent is important to dispel any misgivings an employee may have about the chosen job.
- *Discussion with the relevant supervisor or manager:* It is imperative that the employee has in-depth discussions with the relevant supervisor or manager to ensure that he or she understands the environment within which the job is to be performed. From the discussion the employee will gain essential information about the job.

Supervisors and managers should be trained to counsel subordinates. This is usually an unfamiliar role to them. However, good managers concern themselves with the careers of their subordinates, knowing that they will get the credit when their subordinates succeed.

- *Writing the individual development plan*: By this stage an employee should have sufficient information on the career he or she plans to follow. A career development plan should be drawn up in conjunction with the relevant section head and the human resources department, outlining as precisely as possible how it should unfold. The matching process between the needs and goals of the individual and those of the organisation is then completed. This means that the employee and employer have reached consensus as to what should happen and how and when it should take place to equip the employee for a rewarding career.

Step 2: Link career development with the human resources department and with management

Management, and particularly the human resources department, need to ensure that all key supervisors and managers are fully conversant with the career development programmes in the organisation and actively support them. Top management could circulate a letter expressing support of career development and praising supervisors and managers who direct such programmes. Such support is essential if career development programmes are to succeed in an organisation.

Career development should fit in with the organisation's management system to ensure that career development programmes do not clash with the organisation's long-term philosophy, strategy and goals.

Step 3: Link career development with environmental trends and values

The whole process of career development needs to be refined in terms of future trends. The organisation's goals, production methods and demographic shifts should be considered.

It is commonly accepted that technological changes occur so rapidly today that an employee's skills (particularly among artisans) should be comprehensively updated every five years if he or she is to remain abreast of technological developments. (Technological innovation is discussed in chapter 24.) These factors should be taken into account in career development. Employees should start working on a bridging qualification long before it is actually required, so that they can adjust their career and move to a more suitable job if necessary. It may be necessary, for example, to put some employees on flexitime so that they can undertake part-time study in case they need to change their job.

Step 4: Have regular communication between the employer and employees

All affected parties should communicate regularly on the drawing up of career development plans and should be kept up to date on the actual progress made.

These parties are the human resources department, heads of sections and departments, trade union representatives and the affected employees. Interactive meetings should be held where career development plans are updated, and employees should receive feedback on their progress.

Should employees discover that their career development takes place at a faster pace than their actual progress in the organisation, consideration should be given to lateral moves within the organisation. If upward movement is out of the question and the employee insists on it, he or she should be assisted by the employer to find alternative employment either in another plant or in a different organisation. This is important since a major impediment in the career development path of an employee could lead to frustration and a decrease in productivity.

Step 5: The employer's responsibilities in effective career development for employees
The employer's commitment to career development should be evident in the creation of opportunities and provision of the means required by an employee to carry out his or her career development. The participation of employers should be apparent in the following areas:

- *Periodic review of employees' progress:* Not merely performance appraisal or merit assessment, but an evaluation of employees' career development progress.
- *Self-study:* Opportunities should be provided for employees for self-study within and outside the organisation, and company-sponsored training programmes should be arranged. These programmes should aim to enhance an employee's potential.
- *Support teams:* The employer should encourage the formation of teams of employees who have similar career development plans, as this provides them with moral support and a feeling of cohesiveness. These teams should be allowed to meet, say, once a month and discuss common problems, and where necessary, refer these to the employer. Such a system will ensure that employees maintain their desired rate of career development.
- *Counselling:* The employer should provide a regular counselling service to all employees who are involved in career development. Counselling should be individual and problems identified should be diagnosed so that recommendations can be made to solve them. This task should be undertaken jointly by the human resources department and the relevant supervisor or manager, depending on the type of problem being experienced.

9.8 CONCLUSION
There is a close relationship between training and development and career development, since training and development are means that enable employees to achieve their own career goals. It is also of cardinal importance, however, that

employees know what they want and how they want to spend their working lives. They need to plan their career in terms of their own talents and limitations. If people know their personality traits and apply themselves to improving their attitudes and skills, they will make a success of their career. People's career stages normally run parallel to their life stages, according to their individual needs. Bearing this in mind they ought to be able to plan their career development.

In South Africa specific efforts are made in the guidance and placement of work-seekers. The Guidance and Placement Act provides, through various centres, for vocational guidance and testing to guide work-seekers into jobs that suit their talents.

Career planning and development need to be painstaking if an employee is to gain the maximum benefit from his or her endeavours. Career management by organisations should be broad enough to meet the specific career needs of individuals, yet specific enough to afford employees flexible job experience. It has happened that various methods such as management by objectives, job enrichment and organisation development have become ends in themselves. This generates more resistance than results; consequently career development has sometimes resulted in negative responses and unrealistic job expectations by many employees.

Effective career management holds the following advantages for employees: an awareness of their skills, abilities and weaknesses; an awareness of their needs, values and goals; realistic job and career opportunities to match their abilities and needs. The organisation, on the other hand, benefits from the more effective use of its current work-force, reduced absenteeism, lower staff turnover, improved morale among employees, diminished obsolescence and a better image among work-seekers.

Employee career development therefore plays an important role in an organisation's survival strategy, particularly if there is total commitment to success, because it is a joint employer-employee responsibility. Successful career development meets the goals of both employees and employers.

Questions

1. Describe the relationship between training and development and career development.
2. What is the difference between career planning and career development?
3. What benefits do you see from managing your own career? Discuss.
4. What can you do to manage your own career effectively?
5. Who should be responsible for managing an employee's career—the individual or the organisation? Discuss critically.
6. What are your career goals? Draw up a balance sheet of your strengths and weaknesses and decide whether you are in the right job at present.
7. Describe the most important stages of a person's work life according to figure 9.2. Do you find these conclusions realistic?

8. Do you think it is important to do career planning for retirement? Draw up a plan for your own retirement.
9. What can you learn from examining your own career path as developed for you by the organisation?
10. In the light of the rapid changes facing South Africa after the election of April 1994, in which circumstances can change virtually overnight, does career planning still make sense, given affirmative action programmes and staff shortages in many organisations? Discuss.

Sources

Department of Manpower. *Careers guide.*

Department of Manpower. *Rehabilitation in SA.*

Department of Manpower. 1991. *Report of the Director-General for the year ended 31 December 1990.* (RP 51/1991). Government Printer, Pretoria.

Graham, H.T. & Bennett, R. 1993. *Human resources management.* Business Handbooks, London.

Human Sciences Research Council. 1989. *HSRC/NTB investigation: training and placement of the handicapped person.* HSRC Publishers, Pretoria.

Ivancevich, J.M. & Glueck, W.F. 1986. *Foundations of personnel/ human resource management.* 3rd edition. Business Publications, Plano, Texas.

Mondy, R.W. & Noe, R.M. 1987. *Personnel: the management of human resources.* 3rd edition. Allyn & Bacon, Boston.

South Africa (Republic). *Guidance and Placement Act No. 62 of 1981.* Government Printer, Pretoria.

Part 3

The maintenance of human resources

Affirmative action	Chapter 10
Performance appraisal	Chapter 11
Compensation management	Chapter 12
Employee benefits and services	Chapter 13
The quality of work life and social responsibility	Chapter 14
Health and safety	Chapter 15
Motivation	Chapter 16
Leadership in organisations	Chapter 17
Groups in organisations	Chapter 18
Industrial relations: The role of the human resources manager in industrial relations	Chapter 19
Industrial relations: South Africa's industrial relations system	Chapter 20

Overview of Part 3: The maintenance of human resources

AIM

To describe to the student or reader the theory underlying human resources maintenance in a pragmatic manner in order to establish a basis for scientific application among those who practise this sub-field of human resources management.

PRINCIPAL STUDY OBJECTIVES

Chapter 10: Affirmative action. To instil in the student or reader the importance of affirmative action in a new South Africa and to demonstrate its application within the organisational context.

Chapter 11: Performance appraisal. To instil in the student or reader the importance of performance appraisal and its important influence on individual performance orientation in order to promote its scientific application in an organisational context.

Chapter 12: Compensation management. To instil in the student or reader the nature and essence of compensation management so that the determination of compensation in an organisational context takes place in accordance with scientific principles.

Chapter 13: Employee benefits and services. To instil in the student or reader the importance of employee benefits and services as an extrinsic motivating factor so that they can be scientifically managed within an organisational context.

Chapter 14: The quality of work life and social responsibility. To instil in the student or reader the importance of the quality of work life and social responsibility to enable him or her to practise them in an organisational context in accordance with certain guidelines.

Chapter 15: Health and safety. To instil in the student or reader the importance of health and safety in the workplace in order to ensure sound work practice.

Chapter 16: Motivation. To instil in the student or reader an understanding of the motivational variables that may have a positive or negative effect on individual performance orientation so that it can be scientifically managed within an organisational context.

Chapter 17: Leadership in organisations. To instil in the student or reader an understanding of the importance of leadership in the achievement of organisational objectives so that he or she can apply this knowledge in practice.

Chapter 18: Groups in organisations. To instil in the student or reader an understanding of the important contribution of groups to organisational success so that he or she can apply the principles of group dynamics in an organisational context.

Chapter 19: Industrial relations: the role of the human resources manager in industrial relations. To demonstrate to the student or reader the important role played by the human resources manager in sound industrial relations practice in an organisational context in order to establish a scientific practice of application.

Chapter 20: Industrial relations: South Africa's industrial relations system. To instil in the student or reader an understanding of how the South African industrial relations system works so that a sound basis for its application can be established.

Chapter 10

Affirmative action: theory and practice for the new South Africa

P.S. Nel

STUDY OBJECTIVES

After studying this chapter, you should be able to:

- Define the concept "affirmative action" in practical terms;
- Contrast affirmative action and equal employment opportunities;
- Describe the application of affirmative action in Europe, America and certain African countries;
- Explain the difference between affirmative action in South Africa and other countries;
- Explain the terminology, principles and relevance of an affirmative action programme in South Africa;
- Compile an affirmative action programme in theory;
- List the obstacles in the way of implementing such a programme.

10.1 INTRODUCTION

After decades of apartheid legislation and its application in South Africa, there is now an intense discussion about correcting historical inequalities and about the most effective way in which this may be implemented and managed.

Drake International (1993:4) remarks:

Five years ago, the concept of "affirmative action" was something which US companies operating in South Africa were forced to adopt as signatories to the Sullivan Code. Today the issue of affirmative action is seen as an important tool to counteract the inequities of apartheid legislation. Many companies have identified affirmative action as the most important human resource priority.

183

FIGURE 10.1: Principal learning components of affirmative action

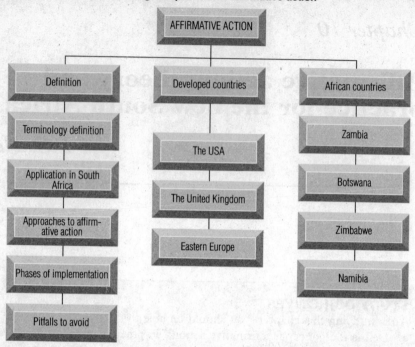

Many organisations are already implementing affirmative action programmes. Nevertheless there is some confusion about what affirmative action really is and how its implementation should be managed.

Many countries have been experimenting with affirmative action programmes for years, and have come far in solving problems associated with this process. There is, for example, the American system of affirmative action, but South African circumstances are radically different to those in the USA. Consequently experts on the subject maintain that similar programmes could not be instituted in South Africa. Little attention has, however, been given to the experiences of other African countries such as Zambia and Namibia, which attempt to apply affirmative action programmes. For South Africa it is nevertheless essential to study other countries' interpretations of affirmative action, which are discussed later in this chapter.

One of the problems about affirmative action in South Africa is a lack of properly defined concepts and terms. Various views are analysed and evaluated below.

10.2 WHAT IS AFFIRMATIVE ACTION?

Maphai (1993:6) has the following opinion of affirmative action:

In South Africa, affirmative action carries both narrow and wide connotations. At both levels, there is a great deal of confusion. The narrow conception involves the recruitment of groups, previously discriminated against, into positions of common, though not exclusive, sites of affirmative action. Traditionally, narrow affirmative action seldom rises beyond tinkering.

However, the broad concept is also confusing. Some people regard affirmative action as an instrument of national reconstruction or even transformation. Some expect affirmative action to eliminate or at least reduce all the inequalities of past discrimination. Others, in turn, regard it as a strategy to fight poverty. In general, however, it appears that affirmative action for South Africa is seen as an instrument of reconstruction and not only as a superficial adaptation of the system.

The narrow concept is primarily, but not exclusively, expressed by the private sector, while the broad concept would be impossible without government intervention and authority. To a large extent, government authority guarantees the success of government-driven affirmative action.

The broad concept of affirmative action poses some problems when it comes to terminology. In general, affirmative action indicates extraordinary measures designed to correct the inequalities of the past, particularly if these arose from purposeful government policy. Superficially viewed, it thus has the unpleasant connotation of race and sex, which appears to repeat some of the negative elements of the apartheid era. For this reason proponents of non-racism have spent some time pointing out to critics that affirmative action will disappear as soon as the inequalities of the past have been eliminated.

According to Maphai (1993:6), however, affirmative action in the broad context should be seen as a general government method to promote democracy. The concept should thus be regarded in its narrow context, as the broad context promotes a lack of clarity on the subject. This means that for affirmative action to have any relevance in South Africa, organisations will mainly have to concentrate on the narrow concept and on temporary preferential treatment. The broad context will have to be applied at government level to place the country as a whole on a non-racial and equal democratic basis.

The exclusion in the past of women and black people from authority and influence in the country was both wrong and unacceptable. For this reason, affirmative action must immediately be instituted by applying the broad approach as an interim measure. This means that the new government will have to address general inequalities, reconstruction, poverty, etc. at a national level.

However, affirmative action should not become an obsession with numbers and quotas according to sex and race. Such a situation can easily be regarded as tokenism, which may have an adverse influence on the country in the long term. Ultimately, the number of black people on the management council of an organisation should not merely reflect a numerical relation; rather, their creditworthiness and appointment must contribute towards the broader mission and objectives of the organisation.

An attempt at national level to eliminate all poverty and social problems through affirmative action would be a mistake. The reason is that affirmative action and the upliftment of disadvantaged communities are mutually dependent, but not identical. The one is a temporary measure, while the other is continuous.

In view of the above, Njuguna (1992:1) describes affirmative action as follows:

> My definition of affirmative action in the workplace is adopting management styles conducive to racial integration, and developing attitudes that enhance racial coexistence, racial tolerance and racial acceptance.

This definition clearly reflects the narrow approach to affirmative action.

Moerdyk (1992:1) is of the opinion that affirmative action consists of positive steps to correct historical inequalities by means of training and development opportunities, both in the work environment and in the wider community.

Joubert (1992:1) says:

> If we see affirmative action merely as the replacement of white labour with black labour to redress inequality and injustices we have no chance of improving South Africa's competitiveness. If, however, we assess South Africa's skills profile in the context of leading developing and even developed countries of the world and determine what must be done at an international, national, company and individual level to improve our skills base, we will be on the road to improvement and success.

Affirmative action is therefore necessary to redress the social injustices of the past. Affirmative action should create opportunities through which people, irrespective of race or sex, can make technological, entrepreneurial, management and leadership skills available to meet the country's needs.

The position of the ANC/COSATU alliance on affirmative action is defined in a speech by Naidoo (1994:2):

> Our position is very clear—we are not advocating racism in reverse, neither are we calling for a scenario which will lead to declining growth and productivity levels or the lowering of competency standards . . . This is why affirmative action must be linked to broader restructuring of the economy and in particular education and training . . . Equal employment measures on their own are not enough, neither is the assertion that education measures can meet broad equitable objectives.

Irrespective of other views, the broad approach therefore also plays a role in South Africa's future.

10.3 TERMINOLOGY DEFINITION

South Africa can only have effective affirmative action if the concept is accurately defined, so that politicians, government sectors, semi-government sectors, the private sector and particularly line and human resources managers clearly understand their role and obligations in this regard, thus eliminating misunderstandings.

To avoid the problems experienced by the USA and other countries, a distinction must be made between compulsory and voluntary affirmative action.

Various programmes are already being applied in South Africa, but currently everything that organisations do in the field of human resources is being regarded as affirmative action. For example, the question may be asked: Is the social responsibility of an organisation part of its affirmative action programme, or do the projects being carried out merely reflect general human resources practices in the rest of the world?

If affirmative action is defined as measures to eliminate the negative consequences of past discrimination, the priority of the various affirmative actions must be determined.

It is also essential to determine what can be classified as affirmative action. The view of Louw (1992) is discussed below:

- *The all-encompassing approach.* The term "affirmative action" is used to indicate all attempts at eliminating the negative consequences of past discrimination. The modern approach in the USA and some other countries is that the aim of these actions is to establish equal opportunities for all, but that this is not possible before certain reverse discrimination measures or measures for preferential treatment have been instituted. The aim, however, remains the establishment of equal opportunities. This view reflects the broad approach to affirmative action.

- *The legal approach.* Laws are promulgated to make equal opportunities compulsory. Such laws usually stipulate certain quotas and time schedules. However, the empirical measurement of equal opportunities is difficult, which is why the laws actually pose a normative goal which must be measured against certain numerical requirements. This is therefore a narrow approach to affirmative action.

  In this regard, Ivancevich (1992:82) remarks as follows:
  - Equal opportunities are legally compulsory; affirmative action is voluntary.
  - Equal opportunities are neutral; affirmative action gives preference to individuals on the basis of certain characteristics.
  - Equal opportunities are preventive; affirmative action is promotive because members of protected groups enjoy preference.
  - Equal opportunities are a permanent obligation; affirmative action is a temporary measure.

- *The neutral approach.* This approach implies that one group (favoured in the past) must help another group (disadvantaged in the past), even at the expense of the first group, because this is "right".

  Louw (1992:55) indicates that where the problem is of national proportions and not associated with one group, a joint effort must be made to correct it to everyone's advantage. In this case affirmative action has a neutral meaning, as it cannot be related to any specific group.

187

Affirmative action not only applies to the consequences of former apartheid legislation in South Africa, but also to all spheres in which there are abnormalities. This includes aspects such as unemployment, human resources shortages and imbalances in the economy.

Ivancevich (1992:82) proposes that affirmative action should be defined as "those actions appropriate to overcome the effects of past or present practices, policies, or other barriers to equal employment opportunity". He regards as controversial the interpretation of affirmative action that accords groups previously discriminated against preferential treatment with regard to recruitment, selection, promotion and development. Various pressure groups in South Africa would, however, like to see this controversial approach established as a permanent human resources management practice, while it is recognised, accepted and applied worldwide as only a temporary measure. Later on in this chapter, the negative effect of this approach is discussed, as are the consequences for various countries where it has been applied.

In overcoming South Africa's problems, affirmative action, which includes the promotion of equality, skills development and job creation, should thus be applied as a coordinated but only temporary process until equal opportunities for all are a reality.

10.4 APPLICATION OF BROAD AFFIRMATIVE ACTION IN SOUTH AFRICA

Politicians and businesspeople point out that the promotion of equality by means of affirmative action has become a priority for the new government of South Africa since April 1994.

Promotion of equality means that all people must be regarded as equal as far as citizenship, social and moral convictions, job opportunities, promotion and the law are concerned. This may be regarded as a prerequisite for equal opportunities.

The civil service is targeted as the first place where the new government will enforce equal opportunities and therefore the promotion of equality.

The promotion of equality may become a legal requirement that organisations must meet within a certain time, while the private sector can decide for itself what affirmative action to take. The success of any programme to promote equality in South Africa will depend on the priority accorded the development of people.

Human resources development is already enjoying much attention in South Africa, and not necessarily because of possible future legislative pressure. It is normal human resources practice in organisations that proactively approach their future.

188

Unemployment is one of the greatest problems currently facing South Africa. If it is not overcome soon, South Africa is heading for disaster. According to informed observers, up to 40% of South Africa's economically active population was unemployed at the beginning of 1994, and by 1999 some 10 million people may be unemployed (see chapter 23). This is a fundamental aspect of labour economics that must be addressed by affirmative action. If the government and private sector do not cooperate in relieving the problem soon, socio-economic circumstances may deteriorate to such an extent that a revolution or even a total collapse of the national economy may follow.

Unemployment in the private sector can only be relieved by strategic planning in every organisation. Trade union officials already demand from large organisations that pay excessive dividends to shareholders to spend part of this profit on job creation (Golding 1990:38).

In 1993, 54% of the country's economically active population was unskilled, 35% were skilled and 11% were highly skilled or in management positions— this is partially the cause of unemployment (see chapters 21 and 23).

However, South Africa's unemployment problem cannot be easily eliminated. A high economic growth rate and an extensive national educational policy are prerequisites for an economic revival. Skills development is also of vital importance. Although it is difficult to determine accurate numbers, there is clearly a great backlog in teaching qualifications and skills in the South African labour market.

Various strategies and mechanisms (e.g. taxes and the application of the RDP) for the redistribution of wealth have been proposed, and this may become a national priority. Whatever the various arguments, only time will tell to what extent the redistribution of wealth can relieve unemployment, if at all.

South Africa's productivity is so low that it will have to become an absolute priority if South African organisations are to compete in international markets. Even the redistribution of wealth will hold no long-term advantage without increased productivity.

All the above aspects must receive attention because the economy has numerous interdependent components. Affirmative action must be aimed at "correcting" the entire system, and not only parts of the system. In this context, readers are referred to the government's reconstruction and development programme (RDP), which is discussed in chapter 21.

10.5 APPROACHES TO AFFIRMATIVE ACTION IN SOUTH AFRICA

10.5.1 Guidelines

Any party in the country that is in a position to promulgate legislation must first make a study of other countries' practices and experiences to identify the positive and negative potential of affirmative action. Secondly, the realities of the South African macro-environment, including unemployment, violence and illiteracy, must be carefully researched before ideological considerations and social pressure become motivators for affirmative action.

During an SABC television debate in 1991 on the promotion of equality in South Africa, Dr Walter Williams from the USA made two important remarks to Saki Matozoma of the ANC. First, the onus is on the ANC to prove that indiscriminately (and thus generally) applied affirmative action has been successful in any country in the world. Secondly, a study of affirmative action in the USA must take into account that the USA is a rich country that can finance its mistakes, while South Africa is a poor country that cannot afford to make mistakes. The necessity of studying the experiences of other countries is therefore clear.

Louw (1992:64–8) proposes various guidelines for effective affirmative action in organisations:

- The promotion of equality should not be regarded as the only form of affirmative action. The problems that such a short-sighted approach creates may be greater than the solutions it offers.
- Economic growth may not be disregarded as in other African countries, where affirmative action was indiscriminately applied.
- Correct terminology must be created for an accurate definition of the action required, to prevent terminological misunderstandings from hampering the system (as happened in the USA).
- A quota system according to which black people who may be unqualified are placed in jobs must be avoided. This leads to unproductivity and tokenism.

A quota system determines numerical objectives for various races and sexes in organisations and the civil service in order to reflect the population composition of the country in its labour force. In the USA, repeated attempts are made to link target dates to this quota system.

- Quotas cannot be established according to the composition of society, as a large part of the black population is illiterate and works in rural areas. If quotas are indeed considered, they must be drawn up according to supply.
- Whites are mobile and can leave the country relatively easily. This may lead to a drain of skilled human resources that South Africa cannot afford.
- The emphasis of promoting equality should initially be placed on education and training, and only later on equal representation in the labour force.
- The private sector should not be forced to take steps that are unproductive or uneconomical, as the entire country will suffer the consequences.
- The process of affirmative action should be a long-term project, with training and development as a first priority.

190

- The economic and demographic problems in South Africa are so serious that they must enjoy priority above the promotion of equality, otherwise a cycle of problems may result that could make the country ungovernable. Hence the assertion that affirmative action should be regarded as a global term and not as synonymous with the promotion of equality.
- The white community is at present the main source of skilled human resources, and given the shortage of such people, the country cannot afford not to make full use of this resource.
- Many sectors in South Africa are already undertaking credible steps towards promoting equality, and this trend must be encouraged and not undervalued.
- The business sector will obviously be affected by the decisions the new government takes, and this influences strategic planning. Although government policy is still vague, certain conclusions can be drawn that may serve as guidelines for strategic planning in the business sector. Organisations must cooperate in training and developing potential black management candidates. Thus the problem of poaching can be limited and the business sector can offer effective training for black managers.
- In view of the shortage of skilled human resources in South Africa, it is essential that special selection instruments be developed.
- It must be accepted that the promotion of equality is not a short-term strategy, but an ideal that can only be realised over a long period.

The realities in South Africa must therefore be thoroughly taken into account. Mphelo *et al.* (1991:24) describe this as follows:

Any data relating to South African conditions would have to be analysed with due regard to the continuing shortage of highly skilled, especially technical labour, which will bedevil our ability as South Africans to establish a non-discriminatory society.

10.5.2 Organisational growth through affirmative action

The career progression programme of the Chamber of Mines to bring about more rapid development for various people shows how growth can be brought about by affirmative action. Aspects that must be taken into account include the strategic business plan, marketing, the need for affirmative action in the organisation, the acquisition of skills and peer group evaluation of the affirmative action.

What is of vital importance, however, is how to determine the need for an affirmative action programme.

Unfortunately there are organisations that merely pay lip service to affirmative action without any meaningful change. To avoid this, top management must be informed and also encouraged to implement a programme of affirmative action. Proposals on how the process can be tabled and carried out, include the following:
- Top management must be responsible for affirmative action. Active steps must be taken.

- Timing is vital. The possibility of nationalisation, a recession, a shortage of skilled persons, and ideas on alternatives that can be implemented in the organisation can make decision-makers aware of the problem.
- Thorough preparation is necessary. For example, contact can be made with successful organisations such as South African Breweries and Total. This will ensure that everyone involved will understand that affirmative action will result in higher productivity and will therefore be to the advantage of the organisation.
- It must be identified where the organisation intends to be in a number of years so that realistic objectives can be set.
- It must be determined where the organisation is in the market environment at present, and where it wants to be. This will indicate how many black people and women must be appointed in management positions.
- Plans must spell out the organisation's need for training and qualified people, so that a budget can be tabled that also reflects the cost savings that may arise from affirmative action.
- Factors that will either support or disrupt the plans for affirmative action must be identified. It must be determined how to solve problems and how to implement affirmative action to everyone's advantage.
- The entire plan for affirmative action must be clearly and accurately formulated and presented to top management, which will take the decision whether to implement it or not. It will take time to filter through to line managers and other operational people, who will apply the plan daily.
- People who initiate affirmative action can expect not to get the credit for the long-term advantages obtained: other people will reap the fruits of their labour.

Once planning has been completed and top management has approved affirmative action, the strategy must be immediately implemented to make it effective.

10.6 AFFIRMATIVE ACTION IN DEVELOPED COUNTRIES
10.6.1 The USA

There are essential differences between circumstances here and in the USA, but South Africa can learn a lot from the American experience. The USA was the first country to make affirmative action as an anti-discriminatory measure compulsory by law.

Discrimination had been common for a long time, particularly in the Southern States of the USA, but in 1941 President Roosevelt began to dismantle it in earnest. In 1957, the Civil Rights Act declared any measure designed to deny someone the vote illegal.

In 1961, President Kennedy declared that specific affirmative action should be taken to counteract discrimination. President Johnson defined in more detail what was meant by affirmative action; to a large extent this coincides with the current broad approach to affirmative action in the Western world.

The Civil Rights Act of 1957 was amended in 1964 to make discrimination based on race, sex, colour, religious belief or national origin by both private and public employers illegal. This law may be regarded as the origin of modern affirmative action legislation.

The sensitive aspect of affirmative action is the stipulation of quotas. In practice, the difference between a quota and a target is vague in the USA. An anomaly in legislation in 1978 made universities a unique case in the implementation of affirmative action. Capaldi (1985:41) explains how Alan Bakke sued the University of California in 1978 on the grounds of the university's quota system for admission. In its judgement, the court prohibited the use of quotas at any university that had accepted a voluntary programme of affirmative action and that had not previously been found guilty of discrimination.

Schmitt and Noe (1986:71) provide the most important stipulation of the Civil Rights Act, Title VII, which spells out equal opportunities as follows:

It shall be an unlawful employment practice for an employer . . . to fail or refuse to hire or discharge any individual, or otherwise to discriminate against any individual with respect to his compensation, terms, conditions, or privileges of employment, because of such individual's race, color, religion, sex or national origin . . .

However, Sowell (1983:200) also says: "While affirmative action results were impressive in gross terms, a finer breakdown shows disturbing counter-productive trends." In his opinion, these counterproductive results include the following:

- The least privileged black people are even worse off with affirmative action than before, while the more privileged black people rapidly increase their economic status.
- Reverse discrimination takes place because the demand for qualified black people is higher than the demand for qualified white people. In 1980, graduated black couples earned more than graduated white couples.

According to Reynolds *et al.* (1982), another important argument is that so-called window dressing (the appointment of incompetent candidates of whom little or no work is expected) is encouraged by legislation, thus hampering affirmative action.

10.6.2 The United Kingdom
The United Kingdom does not have an official policy of affirmative action: British labour legislation is based on the principle of voluntary involvement. Jenkins and Solomos (1987:211) have the following to say in this regard:

In the sphere of discrimination in employment, a further difficulty can be discerned in the tradition of voluntarism which has, for a long time now, characterised British industrial relations.

Rhodes and Braham (1987:192) indicate that the definition of equal opportunities is open to various interpretations. Thus it may be regarded as an anti-discrimination measure as well as an order to apply affirmative action.

Another factor in the British system that cannot be disregarded is that there are few migrant workers in the United Kingdom. Workers from Africa and Asia only make up a fraction of the working class in the United Kingdom.

In their research on equality, Rhodes and Braham (1987:201) also point out that unemployment levels are high. Under such circumstances, equality comes second, and the result is that black workers in particular have the highest unemployment rate in the United Kingdom.

10.6.3 Eastern Europe

Turgeon (1990:155–65) mentions an interesting example of affirmative action on behalf of European gypsies after the Second World War, which saved many gypsies in Eastern Europe from extinction.

The violent expansionism of Hitler before and during the Second World War brought most of the continent of Europe under German rule. Hitler wanted to remove the gypsies from Europe, and thousands were killed. Romania is the only country which, during the war and while under German rule, erected its own concentration camps for gypsies. This saved many from certain death. Countries such as Bohemia, Moravia and Hungary, on the other hand, handed over their gypsies to Hitler, thus ensuring their death.

After the war, numerous gypsies found themselves in what was then the Soviet Union, where extensive informal affirmative action was later launched. In East Germany and Czechoslovakia, which had the greatest gypsy populations, they were provided with jobs and housing, while large-scale efforts were also made to give them greater access to education and medical services. The improved medical services reduced infant mortality, causing a population explosion among gypsies. In 1985, 80% of all children in orphanages were those of gypsies.

Affirmative action in socialist countries such as the former Soviet Union never became an official policy for ideological reasons. In a system based on equality for all, there could be no policy actively promoting one group. Gitelman (1990:184–5) does, however, point out that ethnicity created serious problems for socialist leaders. During the 1920s the Soviet regime was already confronted with sensitive questions such as: "Do equal opportunities eliminate inequality?"

In view of this, certain employers in South Africa think that affirmative action failed in Eastern Europe and that South Africa should follow another approach. Naidoo (1994:4) points out:

Employers often tend to refer to the failed experiences of Eastern Europe and Russia to back up the argument in favour of market domination in training and skills requirements. We are perhaps more aware of these failures than business and have learnt from those mistakes. Unlike Eastern Europe, we are not planning on a skills surplus without jobs. Our entire strategy is geared to linking training to job creation, mobility and growth.

194

Both the reconstruction and development programme (RDP) and the education and training programme of the ANC aim to effect these changes.

It is thus clear that the context in which affirmative action takes place and the way in which it is applied largely contribute to its success or failure. South Africa can definitely learn from the experiences of Europe and America to avoid the same mistakes.

10.7 AFFIRMATIVE ACTION IN AFRICAN COUNTRIES

Affirmative action in a number of African countries can offer interesting guidelines for South Africa.

10.7.1 Zambia

According to Alfred (1991:8–9), Zambia took various steps shortly after independence in an attempt to correct the after-effects of imperialism:

- Partial nationalisation was applied: 51% of the shares of the 30 largest multinational organisations were taken over by the state.
- Whites were replaced with blacks in almost all jobs (under a policy of Zambianism).
- Jobs were created for black people.
- Black education was improved.

According to Alfred (1991:9–10), the results were as follows:

- Zambia, which had once been the bread basket of Africa, became an empty basket.
- Education concentrated on academic subjects, with the result that there is now a dire shortage of many practical skills such as those of mechanics.
- Under the policy of Zambianism, many people were placed in jobs for which they were incompetent, with the result that supervision today is particularly poor and many senior employees cannot adapt to attempts at industrialisation.

With the above in mind, Zambian business leaders have the following advice for South Africa (Alfred 1991:11):

- Do not try to reform too rapidly.
- Remember that not everything can be corrected at once.
- Organisations must resist the demands of black employees to be promoted too quickly.
- Black managers must master both the social and the technical aspects of promotion in order to be successful; this usually takes time.

The conclusion is therefore that Zambia attempted to achieve too much too quickly with its policy of socialism and affirmative action, and that recovery is difficult because almost the entire economy was destroyed. The recovery in Zambia at present (1994) is slow but sure and will probably accelerate in the near future.

10.7.2 Botswana

This country is internationally regarded as an African miracle. Martins (1990:62-3) made the following interesting findings:

- Botswana has a modern economy and a stable government, which encourages economic growth and consequently attracts foreign investors more easily than other African countries.
- The country did not follow a policy of "blacks in white jobs" and is very dependent on highly skilled, expensive foreign human resources.
- Although education was a high priority with the government after independence, it now has very low priority. There is a dire need for training because the rapid economic growth created a great demand for skilled human resources.

No official affirmative action programme was followed, yet Botswana's economic growth during the past years has been one of the highest in Africa and even in the world. It is therefore clear that the economic, political and human resources needs, as well as the businesses of a country, must be handled with great care to provide optimal benefits to the country's citizens. If this is not done, affirmative action can do a country more harm than good.

10.7.3 Zimbabwe

Unlike most African countries, Zimbabwe never launched an official affirmative action programme (Hofmeyr and Whata 1991:13), but steps were taken directly after independence to eliminate inequalities in the public sector. The private sector was largely permitted voluntarily to adapt to the changing environment. However, in 1980 President Mugabe warned the private sector to launch affirmative action programmes and spelled out an informal policy in this regard.

Alfred (1991:13) maintains, however, that because of the country's socialist policy, too much state money was spent on uneconomic social projects, which impoverished the country. One of the first laws after independence, for example, introduced minimum wages, which can be interpreted as affirmative action. Hofmeyr and Whata (1991:15-16) also indicate that the rapid promotion of black people in the private sector enjoyed high priority with the government to place economic power in black hands. The government's attempt at correcting the imbalance of the labour composition in the private sector was the closest that Zimbabwe ever came to a policy of affirmative action.

As far as Zimbabwe's private sector is concerned, Louw (1992:23) speculates that the government was initially afraid of drastically reforming the business community and that at a later stage the economy was too poor to withstand a formal affirmative action policy. Moreover, training and empowerment are such long-term processes that Zimbabwe is only now (1994-95) beginning to reap the fruits with a definite economic recovery.

According to Alfred (1991:16) and Hofmeyr and Whata (1991:20–1), the advice of Zimbabwean government officials and the business community to South Africa on the subject of affirmative action is the following, which makes a lot of sense in retrospect:

- Black people in management jobs want to know that they are there because of their qualifications and abilities.
- The attitude of top management to affirmative action in general and the promotion of black managers in particular is decisive for the success of the process.
- Window dressing does not promote the productivity of business organisations or the interests of the black community.
- A well-planned strategy of affirmative action should be followed in order to resist pressure from the community and the government to implement unworkable measures.
- Business organisations must be proactive if compulsory affirmative action is expected in South Africa, as well as if government pressure without legal sanction is expected, in order to give legitimacy to the attempts made by business organisations.
- Decisions must be based on business principles and not political rhetoric.
- The human resources management departments of organisations will be first to experience the pressure to promote black people. They must therefore be trained for this at an early stage.
- Voluntary affirmative action must be launched before it is legally enforced.

10.7.4 Namibia
Namibia's legislation on affirmative action is particularly important to South Africa, according to Hugo (1993:49), especially to "observers who have sought cues in anticipating possible outcomes in a future South Africa".

Namibian legislation may possibly serve as a blueprint for South Africa, as it is the most recent example on which South Africa's future policy can be based.

The International Labour Organisation (1991:113) states the following:

By virtue of their history, the issue of equality of opportunity and treatment is one to which the Namibians are particularly sensitive. Consequently, Article 23 of the Constitution, entitled "Apartheid and Affirmative Action", provides for parliament to enact legislation to facilitate the advancement of those "socially, economically or educationally disadvantaged" as a result of past laws or practices.

The Constitution describes affirmative action as the legislative competence of the government to correct almost anything that is wrong in society as a result of apartheid.

Namibia has published a draft law governing affirmative action in employment, but this has not yet been promulgated into law by parliament, and may still be scrapped as a result of the experience of other African countries. Nevertheless it may influence legislation in South Africa. Swanepoel (1993:1) explains it as follows:

According to this proposal employers employing more than 25 persons will be legally required to draw up and implement affirmative action programmes . . . The Namibian government has taken a decision at the 31st meeting of Cabinet (held on 14 September 1993) to prepare and implement an affirmative action policy, and a 12-month deadline has been set for the preparation of laws and for setting up a commission to run them.

Namibia's Ministry of Labour and Manpower Development set up this commission to implement affirmative action in three phases over a period of 12 months. These will take place as follows (Minney 1993:1–2):

- *Phase one will entail research, which will include workshops and consultations with management and labour.*
- *Phase two will consist of drawing up and passing the relevant laws and regulations as well as the preparing of manuals and training of staff.*
- *Phase three will entail the appointment of a commission to oversee the implementation of the "statutory affirmative action policy".*

Namibian organisations and human resources managers must therefore (Thompson 1992:57):

- Put various processes in operation to inform employees and their representatives and to consult on affirmative action programmes.
- Analyse the composition of the labour force to determine how various groups are represented in various job categories.
- Evaluate existing human resources practices to identify people being discriminated against and groups that are being excluded.
- Amend or eliminate human resources management practices that discriminate against certain people or exclude them from certain groups.
- Make provision for people with physical or other handicaps.
- Employers with more than 50 employees must institute special training programmes or schemes to ensure that people in certain prescribed groups attain skills and qualifications, are recruited by employers and progress in their careers.
- In recruitment give preference to the disadvantaged and promote qualified people from groups previously discriminated against.
- Set quantifiable objectives.
- Determine a time schedule for achieving each objective.
- Design internal procedures or processes to monitor and evaluate the implementation of the affirmative action programme.
- Allocate the final responsibility for the affirmative action programme to a senior manager.

Swanepoel (1993:2) sums up the question of affirmative action as follows:

The challenge facing Namibian (and South African) employers is therefore not so much to merely design and implement affirmative action programmes, but more to formulate and implement comprehensive and sophisticated "total employment strategies" which can facilitate empowerment.

10.8 PHASES FOR THE IMPLEMENTATION OF AFFIRMATIVE ACTION

A practical programme for affirmative action is proposed in *Die Suid-Afrikaan* (1993:49). The principles for human resources managers contained in this programme are based on the experience of hundreds of organisations in the USA, Europe, other African countries and elsewhere. Organisations can profitably use the logical series of steps to initiate and implement an affirmative action programme.

The proposed programme should not, however, be mechanically applied, as the order of steps, period and phases of implementation, as well as management styles and personalities differ from organisation to organisation and influence implementation. Socio-economic and political circumstances also play a role.

It would appear that 18 months are the optimal period for the effective implementation of an affirmative action programme. This includes the critical preparation phase during which a meaningful programme is designed.

No organisation is too small or too large to implement affirmative action. *Die Suid-Afrikaan* (1993:40) states:

Even the mini enterprise engaged in home based sorting of mail or printed material can, by deciding to pro-actively employ disabled persons, make a specific contribution. The same applies to informal and small enterprises with only 3 to 10 employees . . . yet our phased program framework is probably more relevant to medium and large enterprise than to micro-businesses.

It is clear that organisations not for gain and even government organisations can also implement an affirmative action programme. Table 10.1 shows the proposed programme with its various phases.

The proposed affirmative action programme can be extended to include the education and training of black or female employees so that they can progress in the organisation. Table 10.2 indicates the elements of such a programme.

From the above it is clear that all areas of human resources management must be involved in applying a comprehensive affirmative action programme in an organisation to bring about equal opportunities and the elimination of historical discrimination.

Ferndale (1993:27) points out that it is of vital importance to change the culture of the organisation (organisational climate):

The business culture should be transformed in such a way that it tolerates differences and should be supportive of AA. What is therefore needed is a fundamental change of the culture of the organisation so as to reflect the diverse nature of the values, norms, needs and aspirations of its workforce.

The attitudes and values of employees must be reformed so that they accept change and realise that diversity is a fact and an advantage in South Africa. Apartheid has had a deep and adverse effect on people, through which thoughtless racial bias has become the norm among most whites. This

TABLE 10.1: Proposed affirmative action programme

Programme phases and elements	Duration in months
A PREPARATORY PHASES	
1 Awareness of need; organisation out of step; internal tensions; external criticism; lone-voice proposals not backed by top management	—
2 Pre-assessment of internal situation: *ad hoc* or more systematic; initiative sometimes crisis-triggered	1–2
3 Top-level commitment to non-discrimination with respect to blacks, women and other disadvantaged	3
4 Preparation of a systematic programme with specific targets (by in-house human resources specialists, external consultants or a management task group)	3–5
5 Securing commitment at middle management level	4–5
6 Comparing plans with those of other organisations	5
7 Formal commitment to programme:	
• Announcement or launch;	
• Establishment of monitoring committee	6
B IMPLEMENTATION PHASES	
8 Adjusting the recruitment process	7–9
9 Internal sensitising at all levels and in all sections	7–10
10 Negotiation with unions (if applicable) or staff associations	8–10
11 Supplementary training of black staff	8+
12 Adjustment of promotion and advancement system	9+
13 Determining other areas for equalisation and black or female involvement:	
• Social development or support;	
• Education and training (e.g. bursaries, literacy programmes);	
• Work atmosphere;	
• Recreation and interpersonal contact	10+
14 Fine-tune monitoring system; regular board and executive feedback	10+
15 Refinement of the programme in the light of problems and ongoing performance evaluation	12+
16 Expansion of the programme to reach all relevant groups effectively	12+
17 Internal and external promotion of the programme	13–16
18 Sharing of experience with other organisations	13–17
19 Preparation of first major audit, including internal discussion by monitoring committee	16/17
20 Release of first annual programme audit with top-level response and confirmation of commitment	18

Source: Die Suid-Afrikaan (1993:40)

attitude, whether unknowing and subtle or intentional and aggressive, must be eliminated. What is more, many whites have become accustomed to the privileges of apartheid. Such people feel threatened by affirmative action and may attempt to undermine it. It is therefore important to grant whites the opportunity to discuss their fears and expectations with facilitators, as this may relieve their doubts about affirmative action.

TABLE 10.2: Comprehensive education and training programme for black or female employees

Adult literacy
Run in-house programmes
Encourage external (part-time or *ad hoc*) courses
Subsidise correspondence or self-study courses

Apprenticeships
Support completion of formal programmes
Start new types of in-house programmes
Assist those using external programmes

Correspondence studies
Facilitate university or technikon studies
Encourage and facilitate other correspondence courses
Offer self-study management courses with or without internal mentoring

After-hours studies
Support part-time university studies, e.g. by time off, fee sharing, study leave
Part-time technikon studies
Other private courses
Short-term after-hours courses

Study leave or training secondments
Offer a year's or semester's full-time study leave with or without fee payment
Full course bursary or study leave
Secondment for external internship
Transfer for internal internship

Facilitate *ad hoc* attendance of external conferences
Specific and job-related
Specific, but of broader relevance
General-interest workshops
Career-enhancing conferences

Provide internal team-building training
For colleagues at same level or section
For same division or project
Related to social-development needs
Leadership training
For staff and relatives to strengthen contacts

Arrange mentoring
To familiarise people inside department
For skills training
For management apprenticeships
Special external mentors

Other types of training (internal or external)
Business peer-group contacts
Senior management training
Career development interviews

General staff sensitising on
Affirmative action strategy
New recruitment strategies
Advancement prospects
Inter-staff relations

Source: Die Suid-Afrikaan (1993:42)

Such discussions can confirm the following:
- The reasons for change;
- Abilities will not be compromised;
- The country needs more skilled workers for economic growth, which will be to everyone's advantage;
- The present management pool is not large enough to satisfy the demand for managers;
- Affirmative action is only there to correct the inequalities caused by apartheid;
- Affirmative action is only an interim process;
- White middle managers may even be promoted to make space for black managers who have to be promoted.

To make affirmative action succeed in South Africa requires a macro-approach. According to Naidoo (1994:3):

> Our education and training policy calls for the need to introduce curricula aimed at literacy and numeracy training and development of our people's ability to think critically. We must also move away from the notion that university education is more advanced than other forms of training and education. In fact a major shortcoming of university education was its purely academic focus while ignoring scientific and technological skills development.
>
> We are looking at three pillars of human resource development—training, adult basic education and women workers. Existing structures for training are limited in their perspective and scope to meet training requirements essential for economic growth.

It is clear that the success of affirmative action in South Africa depends on an overall strategic plan and synchronisation of all involved, meaning the entire spectrum of politicians, the state, semi-state organisations, the private sector, trade unions and individual employers.

Figure 10.2 is a proposed strategy for the implementation of affirmative action.

10.9 PITFALLS TO BE AVOIDED

An affirmative action programme is decided upon in the boardroom of an organisation, but it is implemented on the shop floor. There are often large gaps between the conceptualisation and daily implementation of the programme. According to Human (1993:34), a common problem is the following:

> To start with, many organisations commit themselves to affirmative action policies without really knowing what they are committing themselves to! Affirmative action is a pro-active development tool to assist with the creation of, inter alia, greater equal employment opportunity. It is a process which should be integrated and holistic, involving the entire organisation and all of its actors. It should not just be a series of ad hoc training programmes for blacks and diversity programmes for whites. These programmes are important, but are no more than one aspect of what often involves a fairly major restructuring of how human resources are recruited, promoted, and developed.

For affirmative action to be successful, top and line management must take responsibility, but Human (1993:34) maintains that this responsibility is often delegated:

> Too often in organisations responsibility for AA is "relegated" to the Human Resources or Personnel Department which is often only too ready to take over this area. This tendency is highly problematic for a number of reasons. Most importantly, by taking on responsibility for the AA programme the department is, to put it crudely, setting itself up for failure. Successful AA depends on the line managers' willingness to recruit, develop, and promote formerly excluded groups—which the human resources department cannot do. Line managers are only too

FIGURE 10.2: Strategic development of an affirmative action plan

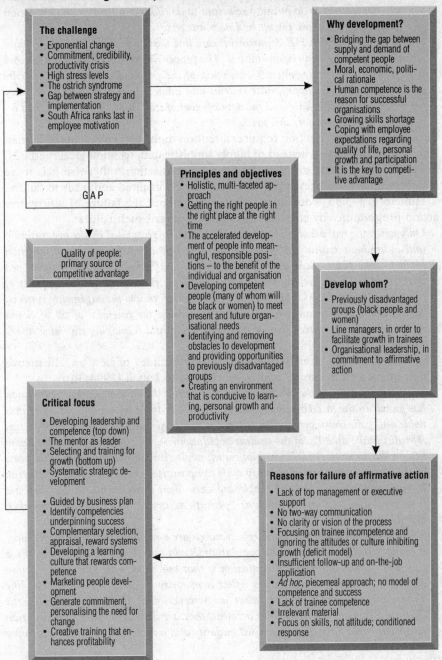

The challenge
- Exponential change
- Commitment, credibility, productivity crisis
- High stress levels
- The ostrich syndrome
- Gap between strategy and implementation
- South Africa ranks last in employee motivation

GAP

Quality of people: primary source of competitive advantage

Principles and objectives
- Holistic, multi-faceted approach
- Getting the right people in the right place at the right time
- The accelerated development of people into meaningful, responsible positions – to the benefit of the individual and organisation
- Developing competent people (many of whom will be black or women) to meet present and future organisational needs
- Identifying and removing obstacles to development and providing opportunities to previously disadvantaged groups
- Creating an environment that is conducive to learning, personal growth and productivity

Why development?
- Bridging the gap between supply and demand of competent people
- Moral, economic, political rationale
- Human competence is the reason for successful organisations
- Growing skills shortage
- Coping with employee expectations regarding quality of life, personal growth and participation
- It is the key to competitive advantage

Develop whom?
- Previously disadvantaged groups (black people and women)
- Line managers, in order to facilitate growth in trainees
- Organisational leadership, in commitment to affirmative action

Critical focus
- Developing leadership and competence (top down)
- The mentor as leader
- Selecting and training for growth (bottom up)
- Systematic strategic development
- Guided by business plan
- Identify competencies underpinning success
- Complementary selection, appraisal, reward systems
- Developing a learning culture that rewards competence
- Marketing people development
- Generate commitment, personalising the need for change
- Creative training that enhances profitability

Reasons for failure of affirmative action
- Lack of top management or executive support
- No two-way communication
- No clarity or vision of the process
- Focusing on trainee incompetence and ignoring the attitudes or culture inhibiting growth (deficit model)
- Insufficient follow-up and on-the-job application
- *Ad hoc*, piecemeal approach; no model of competence and success
- Lack of trainee competence
- Irrelevant material
- Focus on skills, not attitude; conditioned response

Source: Van Niekerk and Charlton (1994:183)

203

willing to let the HR department take over an area of their job which they are often not only not trained to do but also reluctant to do. This can lead to an abrogation of responsibility for development by line managers.

The tension between HR departments and line managers thus often results from a confusion of roles and responsibilities. The proper role of HR departments in AA is to support line management's ownership of the people-development process by providing, inter alia, appropriate systems and advice. Line managers play a key role in on-the-job coaching and the development of staff; they should be trained in, and held accountable for, this area.

Successful affirmative action requires attention to the basic elements of human resources management instead of highly sophisticated, technological methods. People must be made more useful for the organisation, otherwise it is mere tokenism or window dressing, which is politically inspired and leads to failure.

Human (1993:35) concludes her thoughts about the failure of affirmative action programmes by emphasising ways to prevent such failure:

Only when the real benefits of affirmative action are recognised by the organisation and individuals within the organisation, will true development and integration begin to take place. Seen as a "necessary evil", affirmative action remains just that. Seen as a pro-active mechanism for the recruitment and development of competent individuals and for professionalising people-management systems, affirmative action becomes a method of optimising the potential of all of South Africa's human resources and of truly respecting and managing diversity in the process.

The Western Cape already offers us some examples of how an affirmative action quota system can go wrong. According to Ismail (1994:30),

. . . the University of the Western Cape boasts that the African student population has grown in the last 10 years to make up 40% of those on campus. It all sounds noble and politically correct. But when does the preferential treatment stop—when Africans make up 80% of the student population? . . . Coloured matriculants who live on the doorstep of UWC cannot get in, while African students from other parts of the country are allowed to study with comparative ease. Also when it comes to bursary allocations, coloured people are very often unsuccessful, unless they are from rural areas. Comments such as "perhaps we are not black enough" are often heard.

The reply is usually that although coloureds are a majority in the Western Cape, it makes absolute sense that the population should be reflected in all spheres of life . . . The "politically correct" deduction is that one expects an affirmative action approach to ensure that Africans reflect a majority in all spheres in regions like Transvaal and Natal. The concern is, however, that if the differences in the Western Cape are not taken into account, they are destined to lead to a situation where one could have a marginalised majority and a minority of Africans receiving priority treatment.

The question of training must also be handled with care, as Naidoo (1994:5) points out with reference to a 1993 survey by *Die Suid-Afrikaan*:

. . . the underlying motives for affirmative action are mostly still governed by fear and guilt rather than a desire to succeed in the long term. The survey points out that employment equity and affirmative action have become to a large extent public relations exercises and window dressing.

The survey further points out that although there has been a general shift towards greater training and development expenditure for blacks, most companies lack clearly articulated training strategies. Compared to international norms for training and development expenditure of 6 to 8% of total remuneration, companies are only spending an average of 1,5% of employment cost.

Now clearly these indicators, also backed by COSATU and the ANC's own research [in 1993] point to a lack of understanding of employment equity and affirmative action [in South Africa]. Unless there is clarity among employers and some direction, corporate initiatives may be rendered inaccurate and could result in similar failures as the United States.

Organisations that attempt to find a "quick fix" solution have to contend with the following problems:

- There is a gap between strategic planning and the implementation of affirmative action.
- People do not know how to implement affirmative action.
- Insufficient human resources planning renders the implementation of affirmative action impossible.
- A negative attitude causes people to remain unempowered because a culture of recognition of control maintains the *status quo.*
- There is a lack of two-way communication.
- Formal but obsolete training methods are maintained.
- Line management does not accept ownership of and responsibility for the affirmative action programme.
- There is a lack of personal commitment in terms of time and energy, as well as a lack of leadership and cooperation on the part of top management.
- Trainers are incompetent because they have an inadequate understanding of the dynamics of individual and organisational change.
- The programme lacks a goal and clear objectives, which impede its execution.

Experiments with affirmative action conducted by other countries indicate the following important lessons, which are internationally valid and must therefore be taken into account:

- There is no universal, custom-made affirmative action programme. Each programme must be based on the unique national and organisational needs in a country.
- Attitudes dating from colonial or apartheid times must change and this is a time-consuming process.
- There must be a simultaneous strategy to correct structural and other inequalities at a national level. This includes health, literacy, employment,

education, housing, land ownership and agriculture. It represents the broad approach to affirmative action which must be initiated by the state.

- Affirmative action must focus on attempts to promote a relatively small group of people to positions of competence in the economic system.
- Successful affirmative action depends on economic growth and an underlying attitude that recognises the value of people.
- Attitude changes are a complex process that people at all levels within the organisation must undergo, i.e. top management, trainers and trainees.
- Programmes should not only be operated by the state, but also by a variety of organisations, institutes, universities and non-government organisations.
- Affirmative action should only be used to eliminate clearly defined inequalities in a society.
- Programmes must be both political and economic and should not be forced on a country and its people as instruments of control.
- Targets should be set instead of strict quotas, as it is of critical importance that people should be held responsible and accountable. There must thus be compensation for organisations that implement affirmative action and punishment for those that do not.
- Affirmative action must be regarded as an investment in the future of people and their competencies, instead of as a punitive measure or one that forces people to give up something.
- The state must establish incentive measures to encourage the implementation of affirmative action, for example tax rebates for organisations that apply it and serious tax increases for those that do not.
- Change must take place through legislation, at an organisational level, in people and between people, otherwise affirmative action will not be effective.

It is clear that a holistic and integrated approach to affirmative action, taking into account the needs and logic prevalent in South Africa, is essential to ensure that it remains executable and meaningful. For this reason, attention is next given to the effect of affirmative action on human resources practices.

10.10 AFFIRMATIVE ACTION AND SOUND HUMAN RESOURCES PRACTICES

Affirmative action has far-reaching consequences for the human resources practices of organisations. For this reason, people's perception of the effect of affirmative action, organisational politics and the culture of the organisation must be thoroughly studied before an affirmative action programme is instituted.

"Culture-free" recruitment and selection procedures are vital for appointing the right people to the right jobs. Without this, the appointment of certain people in an organisation may be regarded as tokenism or window dressing (see chapters 6 and 7).

Human resources planning and affirmative action go hand in hand. Any organisation striving to implement affirmative action will have to make it part of its strategic planning. It is obvious that the organisation will have to be well informed about affirmative action before organisational strategy is formulated, followed by human resources strategy.

The Sullivan Code is a point of departure for organisations that want to launch a social responsibility programme and want to support it with affirmative action. In-depth attention must, however, also be given to social investment as a broader concept of affirmative action (see chapter 14).

Compulsory quotas must be avoided, as this may impede the availability and utilisation of competent people. This may hamper organisational success and the attainment of the organisation's objectives (see chapter 25).

As far as labour relations are concerned, indefensible preferential treatment and the appointment of people in jobs for which they are not qualified may lead to unfair labour practices. All legislation regarding human resources management should, however, be strictly implemented (see chapters 19 and 20).

Both compensation and promotion must be based on competence, provided that there are equal opportunities because the inequalities of the past have been eliminated by affirmative action.

10.11 CONCLUSION

In this chapter it was said that the aim of affirmative action is to raise the quality of life of disadvantaged communities in South Africa, thus enabling them to compete on an equal footing.

A true improvement in the quality of life of a population cannot, however, be brought about by merely redistributing wealth, but rather by creating it. To make this possible, businesses must be both cost-effective and competitive. Affirmative action should therefore not hamper effectiveness, but rather increase it. This is only possible if an integrated strategy for affirmative action is followed.

Affirmative action involves all the aspects that must be addressed to bring about ultimate equality. This includes economic growth, increasing productivity, the redistribution of wealth, reducing population growth and promoting equality. To avoid reverse discrimination, affirmative steps must be discontinued as soon as equality has been attained.

Successful affirmative action requires positive intervention by top management: it does not happen by itself. Organisations must regard affirmative action as a method of achieving organisational success and plan it as such. This means that objectives and time schedules must be formulated. A detailed and integrated approach to affirmative action is unavoidable.

The entire organisation must be engaged in affirmative action and consultation about it. An affirmative action manager must be appointed, but the responsibility for the daily implementation of affirmative action must ultimately lie with line management and not with human resources management. The organisational culture must change so that affirmative action in planning, support structures, recruitment, selection and the development of human resources is carried out as part of the total organisational strategy.

Finally one of the most important requirements for the success of affirmative action appears to be that organisations must cooperate in devising strategies and training programmes for attaining equality in the workplace. This is also crucial for gaining legitimacy and acceptance by the international community. The mistakes of the past must be corrected, but in such a way that the objective always remains correction and not the permanent promotion of one group at the expense of another.

Questions

1. What is affirmative action? Discuss existing approaches and how they can be successfully implemented in South Africa.
2. Describe the difference in the elements for a successful affirmative action programme for the disadvantaged as opposed to one for managers in South African organisations.
3. Compare affirmative action in African countries with the way in which it is applied in South Africa.
4. Compare affirmative action in the USA with that in South Africa. Are there similarities? Can overseas models be applied here? Give a critical evaluation.
5. How can tokenism and window dressing in the affirmative action programmes of South African organisations be avoided? Focus particularly on the negative consequences.
6. Will a quota system of affirmative action in South Africa succeed? Critically discuss your view.
7. Compile an affirmative action policy for your organisation in order to promote employee empowerment and equal job opportunities.
8. Draw a comparison between the contents of affirmative action programmes that should be implemented in future in the public and private sectors. Should they differ? Thoroughly motivate your approach.
9. Compile an affirmative action programme for the rapid, effective and productive application of the potential of disadvantaged employees in an organisation.
10. Affirmative action can mean short-term costs to obtain long-term advantages. How can South African organisations effectively overcome this dilemma in times of economic stagnation and recession?

Sources

Alfred, M. 1991. *Africa survey, August 1991*. The manpower brief, Norwood.
Capaldi, N. 1985. *Out of order*. Prometheus, Buffalo, New York.
Die Suid-Afrikaan. 1993. Special focus: affirmative action in action. May/June, no. 44.
Drake International. 1993. *Affirmative action guide*. Sandton.
Ferndale, U. 1993. A broad brush approach to affirmative action. *People Dynamics*. October, vol. 11, no. 12, pp. 25–8.

Gitelman, Z. 1990. The politics of ethnicity and affirmative action in the Soviet Union. In M.L. Wyzan (ed.) *The political economy of ethnic discrimination and affirmative action*. Praeger, New York.

Golding, M. 1990. A changing world in the 1990s. *IPB Journal*, no. 9(2), pp. 35–8.

Hofmeyr, K. & Whata, P. 1991. Black advancement in Zimbabwe: some lessons for South Africa. *IPB Journal*, no. 9(10), pp. 21–31.

Hugo, P. 1993. The South African debate on affirmative action: learning cues from India, Malaysia and post-independence Africa. *Politeia*, 12 no. 2, pp. 43–54.

Human, L. 1993. *Affirmative action and the development of people*. Juta, Cape Town.

International Labour Organisation. 1991. *Social and Labour Bulletin of Namibia*. Windhoek, Namibia.

Ismail, A. 1994. Preferential affirmative action: Cape controversy. *People Dynamics*. February, vol. 12, no. 3, pp. 24–30.

Ivancevich, J.M. 1992. *Human resource management: foundations of personnel*. 5th edition. Irwin, Homewood, Illinois.

Jenkins, R. & Solomos, J. 1987. Equal opportunity and the limits of the law: some themes. In R. Jenkins & J. Solomos (eds) *Racism and equal opportunity policies in the 1980s*. Cambridge University Press, Cambridge.

Joubert, D. 1992. Affirmative action is the solution to South Africa's skills crisis. Paper.

Louw, A.A. 1992. Regstellende aksies in Suid-Afrikaanse verband: 'n makro-studie. Unpublished B.Com.Hons. Research Essay. Rand Afrikaans University, Johannesburg.

Maphai, V.T. 1993. One phrase, two distinct concepts. In *Die Suid-Afrikaan*, Special focus: affirmative action in action. May/June, no. 44, pp. 6–8.

Martins, P. 1990. Botswana: a management training and development laboratory. *Human Resources Management*, 6 (annual), pp. 62–6.

Minney, T. 1993. Affirmative action policy on the way. *The Namibian*, vol. 3, no. 255, pp. 1–2.

Moerdyk, A. 1992. Affirmative action and the implication on assessment methods. Paper.

Mphelo, C., Grealy, P. & Trollip, T. 1991. Discrimination and the new South Africa. *IPB Journal*, vol. 9, no. 5, pp. 21–6.

Naidoo, J. 1994. Affirmative action and the new South Africa: what social dialogue? Speech given at congress on affirmative action, Indaba Hotel, 10 February.

Njuguna, M. 1992. A Kenyan case study: focusing on a country where affirmative action has been introduced. Paper. Juta, Cape Town.

Reynolds, L.G., Masters, S.H. & Moser, C.H. 1982. *Readings in labour economics and labour relations*. Prentice-Hall, Englewood Cliffs, New Jersey.

Rhodes, E. & Braham, P. 1987. Equal opportunity and high levels of unemployment. In R. Jenkins & J. Solomos (eds) *Racism and equal opportunity policies in the 1980s*. Cambridge University Press, Cambridge.

Schmitt, N. & Noe, R.A. 1986. Personnel selection and equal employment opportunity. In C.L. Cooper & I.T. Robertson (eds) *International review of industrial and organisational psychology*. Wiley, Chichester.

Sowell, T. 1983. *The economics of politics and race*. Quill, New York.

Swanepoel, B.J. 1993. Aspects of employee empowerment and affirmative action in Namibia: research results and some questions South African managers may ponder on. EBM Research Congress.

Thompson, C. 1992. Affirmative action: Namibian portents. *Employment Law*, vol. 8, no. 3, pp. 56–8.

Turgeon, L. 1990. Discrimination against and affirmative action for gypsies in Eastern Europe. In M.L. Wyzan (ed.) *The political economy of ethnic discrimination and affirmative action*. Praeger, New York.

Van Niekerk, N. & Charlton, C. 1994. *Affirmative action from strategy to implementation*. Van Schaik, Pretoria.

Chapter 11

Performance appraisal

P.D. Gerber

STUDY OBJECTIVES

After studying this chapter, you should be able to:
- Motivate the usefulness of performance appraisal;
- Differentiate between various performance appraisal techniques;
- Identify problems experienced during performance appraisal;
- Explain the importance of the feedback process in performance appraisal.

11.1 INTRODUCTION

The appraisal of an employee's performance or task execution is a sensitive matter that must be handled with great care by managers and supervisors. The results of such an appraisal are directly related to the intrinsic motivation of the employee, his or her self-image and status among fellow employees. The application of performance appraisal in a scientific manner can have a great effect on the individual performance orientation of employees.

Among other things, this chapter pays attention to:
- Performance appraisal;
- The aim of performance appraisal;
- By whom it is applied;
- Applications and techniques;
- Feedback of performance appraisal results.

11.2 DELIMITATION OF CONCEPTS

Appraisal is defined by Ivancevich and Glueck (1986:277) as the human resources management activity that is used to establish the degree to which an individual carries out his or her work effectively.

FIGURE 11.1: Principal learning components of performance appraisal

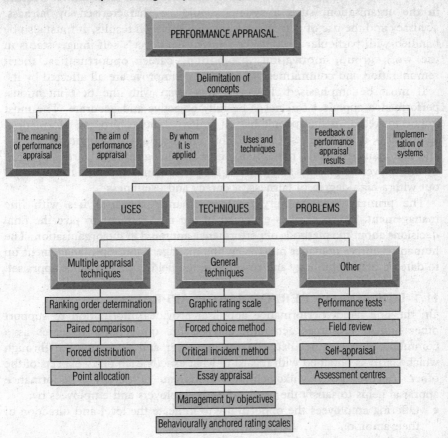

Brown (1988:6) sees it as the process of evaluation and documentation of personnel performance in order to make a judgement that leads to decisions. Among other things, these decisions relate to feedback about professional development, the appraisal of individual and group training needs, establishing who should be promoted, the taking of remuneration decisions and the selection of new personnel.

Leap and Orino (1993:331) regard it as a process through which the quantitative aspects of an employee's work performance are evaluated.

The appraisal of the performance of individuals and organisations is a basic task of management. It is important that the performance appraisal system measure the performance climate and that the remuneration system reward this performance reasonably and fairly. It may thus be said that performance appraisal and remuneration have a direct influence on the motivation of employees to achieve organisational goals.

As performance appraisal is an activity that determines an employee's future in the organisation, such a system should be characterised by fairness, accuracy and the use of correct performance appraisal results. It must also be handled with particular circumspection. An employee's self-image, status in the work group, motivation, promotion, career opportunities, merit remuneration and commitment to perform or improve are all affected by it.

It must be emphasised, however, that even with the best intentions, performance appraisal can never be fully objective and accurate. The most important reason is that people have a limited ability to process information. In addition, it must be remembered that organisations are political in nature and that many decisions, particularly those involving appraisal, are influenced by this. Nevertheless, it is still possible for performance appraisal to be carried out with a high degree of fairness, accuracy and usefulness.

The primary responsibility for performance appraisal lies with line management. However, it is expected of top management to take the final decisions about the methods of performance appraisal in the organisation. The human resources manager must keep line managers and top management up to date on new technology and research in the field of performance appraisal.

11.3 THE AIM OF PERFORMANCE APPRAISAL

On the one hand, performance appraisal provides information to support other human resources activities, and on the other hand it serves as a communication channel between the employer and the employee through which clarity is obtained with regard to what exactly each party expects of the other. According to Milkovich and Boudreau (1988:187), performance appraisal helps to satisfy the needs of both employers and employees by:

- Offering employees the opportunity to indicate the level and direction of their ambition;
- Offering managers the opportunity to show an interest in employee development;
- Identifying areas where specific training is needed;
- Encouraging employees who have tried hard to perform well;
- Communicating dissatisfaction on the part of the employee and employee performance that is unacceptable to the employer.

11.4 WHAT MUST BE EVALUATED?

Performance appraisal can evaluate the behaviour of employees (how the employees carry out their work), results (how well the employees have met the job requirements) or a combination of these. It is possible to measure some of these results. Milkovich and Boudreau (1988:189) use the example of supermarkets that make use of computerised sales points that record each till entry by each employee during each shift. This information can be used to measure the speed and accuracy of sales clerks as well as the volume of items they handle. However, other results are not so easily measured. These same clerks may pack shelves, greet customers, train new employees, keep sales points clean, etc. Not one of these results is reflected by the computerised sales point. It is therefore important to evaluate both results and behaviour. Behaviour shows whether poor results are the consequence of insufficient skills, poor attempts on the part of the employee or circumstances beyond the control of employees.

The criteria against which performance is measured should meet the following requirements:

- The criteria must be linked to the goals of the organisation. If, for example, the organisation aims at increasing market penetration, output data on sales figures and customer satisfaction will be important in performance appraisal.
- The criteria must be linked to the job. Job analysis and job descriptions form the basis for the development of measuring instruments. Performance standards should be attainable and, as far as possible, measurable.
- The criteria must take employee needs into account. Employees are interested in how the employer experiences their performance, but also want to know what their future with the employer will bring. Feedback about performance provides information about an employee's potential for promotion or further development, but also offers employees an opportunity to communicate about how they feel about their work, work groups and their interest in further training or promotion.

It must be emphasised that success in the work situation depends on various factors. It is therefore necessary not only to set multiple criteria for the appraisal process, but also to weight the criteria because some are more important than others. For example, a salesperson may be evaluated on both the number of visits to customers and on sales. The relative importance of these two criteria may be determined by negotiations between the employer and the salesperson.

11.5 WHO CARRIES OUT PERFORMANCE APPRAISAL?

Performance appraisal should be carried out by superiors who have the best knowledge of employees' job performance and who are able to observe employees' job behaviour daily:

- *The immediate supervisor* should have a general overview of the employee's daily job performance because he or she works closely with the employee. The most important disadvantages of the immediate supervisor as the only judge are those of personal prejudice, personality clashes or friendships that might hinder objective appraisal.
- *Higher-level supervisors* can complement the immediate supervisor's appraisal. This can eliminate some prejudices. It can also help to assure employees that their promotion or salary increase does not depend exclusively on the judgement of their immediate supervisor.
- *Multiple supervisors*: It may be advantageous to obtain an appraisal from some or all of the supervisors who come into contact with a certain

employee. This is particularly valuable where employees carry out their task in various departments or environments. Thus employees can be evaluated by one supervisor with regard to technical skills and by another with regard to communication skills.

- *Appraisal by subordinates* may be useful for evaluating skills such as the ability to communicate, the delegation of tasks, the dissemination of information, the solution of personal disputes and the ability to work together with fellow employees. This information can, in turn, be valuable for management development, promotion decisions and the allocation of work loads. These appraisals are used to supplement other sources of performance appraisal.
- *Self-appraisal* requires the employee to evaluate his or her own performance. The value of self-appraisal is doubtful, however. The differences between self- and supervisor appraisal may provide a useful basis for an in-depth discussion about the employee's job performance.

11.6 THE USES OF PERFORMANCE APPRAISAL

The appraisal of employees is important because it indicates how effectively they execute their tasks. Performance appraisal also provides important information about the following:

- *Performance improvement*: Feedback about performance offers the employee, management and the human resources specialist the opportunity to take the appropriate steps to improve performance.
- *Remuneration adjustments*: Performance appraisal helps management to decide which employees qualify for salary adjustments.
- *Placement decisions*: Promotions, transfers and demotions are based on performance or expected performance. Promotion is often a reward for good performance.
- *Training*: Poor performance may indicate the need for training. Good performance indicates potential that should be developed further.
- *Career planning*: Feedback about performance provides important guidelines for specific career directions that can be investigated.
- *Shortcomings in the provisioning process*: Performance appraisal can give a good indication of how effective the employment practice of the organisation is.
- *Inaccurate information*: Poor performance may indicate erroneous job analysis information, faulty human resources plans or other aspects of the human resources management information system. If erroneous information is used to support decisions, wrong appointments and training may follow.
- *Faulty task design*: Poor performance may be the result of poorly designed tasks. Performance appraisal can make an important contribution towards identifying this weakness.
- *External factors*: It may happen that performance is influenced by factors outside the job context, such as family, health, financial or other personal

problems. Performance appraisal may help to identify these factors and enable management to give the employee the necessary support.

It is interesting to note that Klatt *et al.* (1985:413) are of the opinion that there is a trend away from the traditional skills-oriented performance appraisal to a more positive motivation-oriented approach. This trend originated with Drucker and McGregor, who advocate a more participatory, motivation-oriented approach that will theoretically lead to higher performance levels.

11.7 POTENTIAL PROBLEMS WITH PERFORMANCE APPRAISAL

Various factors may contribute towards performance appraisal not being effective. In general, these factors may be linked to the performance appraisal system itself, as well as to the person who carries out the appraisal.

11.7.1 The design of the performance appraisal system

Performance appraisal systems may be poorly designed and cause operational problems. This may mean that the criteria for appraisal have been poorly constructed, or that the technique itself is cumbersome, or that the system has more form than substance. In addition, the system may lose its value if the criteria are based on activities rather than on output results, or on personality characteristics rather than on performance. Another important shortcoming is that many performance appraisal systems take a long time to create a comprehensive written analysis. Finally, a serious problem is that some performance appraisal techniques are not used consistently within an organisation. Not only should top management see to it that they are used, but it should also give active support and attention to the application of performance appraisal.

11.7.2 The evaluator

Even in the case of a well-designed performance appraisal technique, its injudicious use by a poorly trained performance evaluator may lead to failure in its application. Poor training of evaluators leads to various problems in the process of performance appraisal. These include:

- *The halo effect* occurs when an evaluator bases his or her appraisal on an overall impression, which may be positive or negative. An example would be a performance evaluator who believes that an untidy person always has a low intelligence quotient. He or she may then subjectively appraise someone who does not always have a neat appearance in a negative manner. Klatt *et al.* (1985:412) state "Halo error occurs when the evaluator allows his or her assessment on one trait or characteristic to influence the assessment of the same person on other traits or characteristics."
- *Performance appraisal standards*: If we look at the perceptual differences that may arise through the use of words to evaluate employees, one can see why

problems with performance standards may be experienced. Words that can be interpreted in various ways are "good", "adequate", "satisfactory", "excellent", etc. What does it mean, for example, to say that the performance of the employee must be "good" to render a "satisfactory" result? It is thus essential that the meaning of each term used by evaluators in appraising performance should be exactly defined.

- *The central tendency problem*: Evaluators often tend to avoid high and low appraisals and to group their appraisals around the average on a scale. This may be because of a lack of detailed performance data, or simply because it is easier to evaluate everyone around the middle of the scale than to explain extreme appraisals.

- *Strictness or leniency*: Performance appraisal requires from the performance evaluator an objective decision based on performance criteria. Not only is it difficult for any person to make an objective judgement, but it is equally difficult consistently to maintain this level of judgement.

- *The recency of a problem*: It is normal for evaluators to forget old events and to remember more recent behaviour. It then happens that an employee is actually appraised on his or her behaviour during the past month instead of on the average of the past six months. This problem can be overcome by using a technique such as the critical incident method, management by objectives or irregular but scheduled performance appraisal sessions.

- *Personal prejudice*: The prejudices of performance evaluators may influence their appraisal of employees. Performance appraisal techniques such as forced choice and management by objectives do, however, partially eliminate this problem. By clearly defining the dimensions that are evaluated and defining what is meant by terms such as "good" and "excellent", the problem can also be overcome to a large extent. Proper training of performance evaluators also makes an important contribution towards limiting this problem.

11.8 PERFORMANCE APPRAISAL TECHNIQUES
11.8.1 General
Performance appraisal requires performance standards by which performance can be measured. These standards must be accurately determined and must be directly related to the work output required for a certain job. The standards may under no circumstances be arbitrarily determined. Job analysis provides the necessary information to establish proper performance standards. These standards must be defined in the form of performance measures that constitute the criteria for appraisal.

In general, there are three categories of performance appraisal methods or techniques: individual appraisal methods, multiple performance appraisal methods and other methods that cannot be classified under these two categories. Attention will now be given to each of these categories.

FIGURE 11.2: A typical graphic rating scale

Name _____	Department _____	Date _____

	Out-standing	Good	Satis-factory	Fair	Unsatis-factory
Quantity of work Volume of acceptable work under normal conditions Comments:	☐	☐	☐	☐	☐
Quality of work Thoroughness, neatness and accuracy of work Comments:	☐	☐	☐	☐	☐
Knowledge of job Clear understanding of the facts or factors pertinent to the job Comments:	☐	☐	☐	☐	☐
Personal qualities Personality, appearance, sociability, leadership, integrity Comments:	☐	☐	☐	☐	☐
Cooperation Ability and willingness to work with associates, supervisors, and subordinates toward common goals Comments:	☐	☐	☐	☐	☐
Dependability Conscientious, thorough, accurate, reliable with respect to attendance, lunch periods, reliefs, etc. Comments:	☐	☐	☐	☐	☐
Initiative Earnestness in seeking increased responsibilities. Self-starting, unafraid to proceed alone? Comments:	☐	☐	☐	☐	☐

11.8.2 Individual appraisal methods

These are methods by which employees are individually appraised, without being directly compared to other employees. The most important methods of individual performance appraisal are discussed below.

Graphic rating scale

The graphic rating scale is the most commonly used performance appraisal technique. The performance evaluator receives a list of characteristics according to which he or she must evaluate employees. A typical graphic rating scale is shown in figure 11.2. The appraisal can also be quantified, for example on a scale of 1 to 9.

The forced choice method

With the forced choice method, the performance evaluator must choose between statements that best describe the employee being evaluated. The items are usually grouped in categories such as learning ability, performance and interpersonal relations. A typical example of the forced choice method is shown in figure 11.3.

FIGURE 11.3: Example of the forced choice method

Out of each set of five statements, check the one that best describes the employee and the one that is least descriptive of the employee:

		Best	Least
1.	Would be very difficult to replace		
	Very valuable in a new operation		
	Alert to new opportunities for the company		
	Good for routine supervisory job		
	Tends to delegate things that will not reflect credit on him/her		
2.	Not willing to make decisions unless he/she has very complete information		
	Lets difficulties get him/her down		
	Makes snap judgements about people		
	Tries to run things his/her own way		
	Has not demonstrated up to now that he/she has the ability to		

Source: Klatt *et al.* (1985:421)

The critical incident method

For this technique, a list of very effective and ineffective behaviour of the employee during the appraisal period is prepared by the supervisor. This information (critical incidents) is then combined in categories that may vary, depending on the job. At the end of the period in which performance appraisal is done, all these incidents are evaluated. This method eliminates prejudice with regard to the most recent behaviour. In addition, the evaluator is able to make a positive or negative appraisal by using specific examples of behaviour. Finally, the critical incident method is very useful for providing work-related feedback to employees. Performance evaluators must, however, be constantly encouraged to record these critical incidents so that a complete set of information with regard to employee behaviour is available at the end of the period under review.

Figure 11.4 is an example of this method.

FIGURE 11.4: Critical incidents for a plant manager

DUTIES	TARGET	CRITICAL INCIDENTS
Schedules the production for the plant	Full utilisation of plant personnel and machinery; orders must be delivered on time	Installed new production scheduling system. Reduced late orders by 10% in comparison with last month. Increased plant utilisation by 20% in comparison with last month.
Controls stock acquisition and inventory	Reduce inventory costs but ensure that sufficient stock is available	Let stock storage costs rise by 15% last month; an average 15% increase in surplus spares ordered in comparison with last year
Controls the maintenance of machinery and equipment	No production stoppages due to faulty machinery	Installed new preventative maintenance system for the plant. Prevented an incident of machine failure by tracing a faulty component

The essay appraisal

For this technique, the performance evaluator is requested to write down the good and bad points of the employee's behaviour. Another version of this method is the so-called checklist method in which the performance evaluator chooses words or statements that, in his or her opinion, best describe the employee's performance or characteristics. This process can be refined by allocating weights to the various items on the checklist, depending on the importance of each item. This is known as the weighted checklist, which is used to quantify the appraisal so that a total performance score can be calculated for each employee.

Management by objectives

An important characteristic of a management by objectives programme is that the discussions on performance appraisal concentrate on results. Because performance evaluators are in most cases exposed to antagonism because of their appraisal function, management by objectives offers supervisors an opportunity to formulate objectives together with the subordinates, and to measure performance against these objectives. (This technique is discussed in detail in chapter 22.) Ivancevich and Glueck (1986:303) identify the following short-comings of management by objectives as a performance appraisal technique:

- Too many objectives are set, which may cause confusion;
- Management by objectives may be forced on organisations where objective goals are difficult to determine;
- The inability to relate the results of management by objectives to remuneration;
- Too much emphasis on the short term;
- The failure to train supervisors in the management by objectives process;
- Adaptation of the initial objectives is frequently neglected;
- Management by objectives is used as a rigid control mechanism that intimidates rather than motivates.

Behaviourally anchored rating scales

Behaviourally anchored rating scales were developed by Smith and Kendall to reduce or eliminate the bias of subjective performance measures. The behaviourally anchored rating scale uses critical incidents to serve as anchor statements on a scale. The behaviourally anchored scale:

- Usually contains between six and ten performance dimensions.
- The dimensions are usually anchored by positive or negative critical incidents.
- Each employee is appraised according to the dimensions.
- Feedback is then provided by using the terms on the performance appraisal form.

The steps in the development of behaviourally anchored rating scales are:

- Supervisors of a group of employees who carry out the same type of work are requested to identify the general categories of activities of which the work consists.
- The same supervisors generate a set of critical incidents that represent actual examples of very good and very poor performance.
- Every member of a second, independent group of supervisors then evaluates every incident against the criterion of good or poor and identifies the dimension to which each incident belongs.

- The designer then identifies the set of incidents that is systematically associated with the original performance dimension by the second group.
- The resulting set of performance dimensions, each with a set of orderly and scaled incidents, is known as behaviourally anchored rating scales— BARS). Figure 11.5 gives an example.

FIGURE 11.5: Behaviourally anchored rating scale for the performance dimension "knowledge and judgement" for a cashier at a chain store

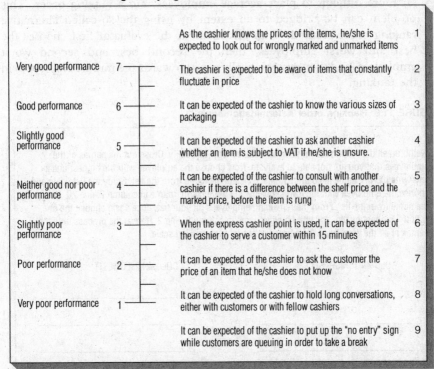

The use of behaviourally anchored rating scales has been further refined in the following:

- Behavioural observation scales (BOS), which require the observer to perceive the frequency of behaviour.
- Behavioural discrimination scales (BDS) also require the appraisal of the frequency of behaviour, but the actual frequency is compared to the frequency of opportunities to show the behaviour and the frequency at each performance level. This method thus focuses on the appraisal of performance constancy.

11.8.3 Multiple performance appraisal methods

Multiple performance appraisal methods involve techniques by which an employee's performance is compared to that of others, as opposed to individual performance appraisal methods which rate each employee individually. Multiple performance appraisal includes the following:

- *Ranking order determination*: This method requires the evaluator to rank employees from the highest to the lowest in terms of a global criterion. Ranking order determination becomes difficult if a large group must be evaluated: more than 20 people are very difficult to handle in this manner. It is quite easy, of course, to identify the best and worst employee, but it is far more difficult to place average employees into a ranking order. This problem can be bridged to an extent by using the so-called alternative ranking order method. With this method, the evaluator first chooses the best and worst employees, then the second best and second worst employees, and then systematically works towards the middle employees in the ranking.

FIGURE 11.6: Ranking order determination scale

Weigh up all the employees on your list in terms of their quality. Cross out the names of the employees that you are not able to evaluate. Now choose the employee with the highest quality and write his/her name in column 1, line 1. Delete the name from the list. Study the list again and choose the employee with the lowest quality and write his/her name in column 2, line 20. Delete the name from the list. From the remaining employees on your list, once again choose the one with the highest quality and write his/her name in column 2, line 2. Repeat the process until the names of all the employees have been written into the ranking scale.

COLUMN 1 (HIGHEST)   COLUMN 2 (LOWEST)

1 _____   11 _____

2 _____   12 _____

3 _____   13 _____

4 _____   14 _____

5 _____   15 _____

6 _____   16 _____

7 _____   17 _____

8 _____   18 _____

9 _____   19 _____

10 _____   20 _____

- *Paired comparison*: In paired comparison, the names of the people being evaluated appear on a sheet of paper in a previously determined order, so that each person can be compared with each other person on the list. The criterion according to which each person is evaluated against every other person is his or her overall ability to carry out a task. The number of times that a person is preferred to his or her colleagues is recorded and determines his or her position in the ranking order of appraisal. Figure 11.7 serves as an example.

FIGURE 11.7: Rating of workers by paired comparison

FOR THE CHARACTERISTIC "QUALITY OF WORK"

As compared with:	A Anton	B Ben	C Charl	D Deon	E Ernst
A Anton		+	+	−	−
B Ben	−		−	−	−
C Charl	−	+		+	−
D Deon	+	+	−		+
E Ernst	+	+	+	−	

Ben gets the highest ranking

FOR THE CHARACTERISTIC "CREATIVITY"

As compared with:	A Anton	B Ben	C Charl	D Deon	E Ernst
A Anton		−	−	−	−
B Ben	+		−	+	+
C Charl	+	+		−	+
D Deon	+	−	+		−
E Ernst	+	−	−	+	

Anton gets the highest ranking

Note: "+" means "better than"; "−" means "worse than". For each table the plus signs in each column must be added up to obtain the employee with the highest ranking.

- *Forced distribution*: With this method, the evaluator is asked to rate employees in fixed categories, for example by placing 10% of the employees in the weakest group, 20% in a low average, 40% in an average, 20% in a high average and 10% in the highest group. This helps to overcome problems with high appraisals and to eliminate the central tendency problem.

  The *point allocation technique* is a variation of forced distribution. In this case each evaluator is given a number of points per employee in the group to be evaluated. The total number of points for all the employees being evaluated may not exceed the number of points per employee, multiplied by the number of employees being evaluated. Points are allocated in this way according to a previously determined criterion.

11.8.4 Other performance appraisal methods

- *Performance tests*: The design of a performance test based on the content of the work may serve as a point of departure for an appraisal. An example are tests taken by artisans who, for example, have to take apart and reassemble a gearbox within a given time.
- *The field review method*: With this method, a competent representative of the human resources department is allocated to assist supervisors with performance appraisal. The human resources specialist obtains specific information about the performance of the employee to be evaluated from his or her immediate supervisor and then prepares an appraisal based on this information. This appraisal is then sent to the supervisor for his or her changes and approval, and for discussion with the employee who was evaluated. This type of appraisal aims at achieving more objectivity through the mediation of a person who is not daily and directly involved with the employee whose performance is being evaluated.
- *Self-appraisal*: It may be useful for employees to assess their own performance, particularly if the aim of such an appraisal is primarily the promotion of self-development. The danger of self-appraisal is mainly that employees tend to estimate their own performance higher than an objective evaluator would. The use of this method therefore requires particularly good judgement.
- *Assessment centres*: The assessment centre was developed as an aid in identifying management talent. The assessment centre subjects selected employees to in-depth interviews, psychological tests, personal background studies, appraisal by other employees who attend the assessment centre, group discussions, appraisal by psychologists or managers and simulated work exercises to determine future potential. The simulated work exercises include in-basket exercises, case studies, leadership exercises, decision-making exercises and employee observation. The aim of the assessment centre is to collect information about the individual's behaviour in the work situation. (Assessment centres are discussed in detail in chapter 22.)

  The results of all the components of the assessment centre programme can be extremely valuable in management development and placement decisions.

11.9 THE IMPLEMENTATION OF A PERFORMANCE APPRAISAL SYSTEM

Various important considerations must be taken into account during the implementation of a performance appraisal system.

The frequency at which performance appraisal should take place depends on various factors. Performance appraisal should be linked to the remuneration cycle. If increases are considered annually, it makes sense to carry out performance appraisals before increases are granted, if such increases are partially or entirely granted on merit.

Performance appraisal may be based on a job cycle with appraisal taking place upon completion of a specific project.

Performance appraisal may also take place more often, particularly in the case of lower-level jobs, while management jobs require a longer appraisal period because the actions and decisions of managers cannot be fully evaluated in a relatively short period.

It is important to have performance appraisal in an environment in which there are equal opportunities. Decisions about promotion, resignation, bonus payments, etc. should be based on objective and effective performance appraisal. The documentation should objectively compare employees according to defensible, job-related criteria, and should substantiate the superiority of the promoted employee to those who have not been promoted. The same applies to decisions regarding dismissal: documentation should confirm that the employee can no longer maintain the minimum job performance standards, or could never achieve them. Leap and Orino (1993:335) rightly state:

> *An appraisal system that can provide objective and valid information on defensible, job-related criteria, that compares the performance of employees with one another or with established, mutually agreed-upon standards, will meet the requirements of an equal employment opportunity environment.*

11.10 FEEDBACK ON PERFORMANCE APPRAISAL RESULTS
11.10.1 General
After completion of the performance appraisal, the result should be discussed with the employee. Feedback in the performance appraisal process means that employees will be provided with an objective appraisal of the current situation to let them know how their performance can be improved. The performance appraisal interview provides an excellent opportunity to sum up the performance of the past year by pointing out incidents of success or failure. It is important to note that feedback is most effective when it takes place immediately or as soon as possible after the appraisal.

Feedback may be either negative or positive. Each of these requires a specific approach that is now discussed.

11.10.2 Negative feedback
In cases in which the performance does not meet the expectations, the task of providing feedback may be thankless, but it must be done. If, however, negative feedback is not correctly handled, it may be counter-productive and lead to poorer rather than better performance in future. This is confirmed by Schuler (1981:238), who quotes the findings of a study carried out at General Electric:

- Criticism has a negative effect on the achievement of goals.
- The average subordinate reacted defensively to criticism during the performance appraisal interview.
- Defensiveness that arises from critical appraisal resulted in poorer performance.
- The disturbing effect of repeated criticism in successive appraisals was greater among those who already had a poor self-image based on previous feedback.
- The average employee placed himself or herself on the 77th percentile during prior self-appraisal.
- Only 2 out of 92 participants in the study estimated their own performance to be lower than average.

When performance evaluators provide feedback to employees, a clear distinction must therefore be made between criticism and feedback. *Criticism* indicates an appraisal with reference to good or poor. *Feedback* is descriptive and provides the subordinate with information that can be used for self-appraisal.

11.10.3 Effective or positive feedback
Effective or positive feedback has various characteristics, including:
- Effective feedback is specific rather than general.
- It focuses on behaviour rather than on the person.
- It takes the needs of the receiver of the feedback into account.
- It is aimed at behaviour about which the receiver can do something.
- Feedback is more effective when it is requested than when it is forced on a person.
- Effective feedback involves the sharing of information rather than giving advice.
- It involves effective timing.
- It contains only the amount of information the receiver can use, rather than the amount the evaluator could impart.
- Effective feedback involves what was said or done and how, but not why.
- It is checked to ensure clear communication.

In the performance appraisal interview, feedback can be provided in a number of ways:
- *The tell-and-sell approach*, in which the employee's performance is reviewed and an attempt is made to persuade him or her to perform better.
- *The tell-and-listen approach*, which offers the employee the opportunity to provide reasons and excuses, and to express defensive feelings.
- *The problem-solving approach*, which identifies problems that have an adverse effect on employee performance. Training, coaching or advice are used in an attempt to eliminate these shortcomings by setting new goals.

No matter which of these approaches is used, Brown (1988:60) states that it is important to keep the following in mind:

- Emphasise the positive aspects of the employee's performance.
- Communicate to the employee that the appraisal session is there to improve performance and not to discipline.
- Keep the performance review session private, with the minimum disturbance.
- Review the performance at least once a year, and more often in the case of new employees or employees who are doing poorly.
- Keep the criticism specific and not vague or generalised.
- Focus criticism on performance and not on personality characteristics.
- Remain calm and do not argue with the person being appraised.
- Identify specific actions that the employee can carry out to improve performance.
- Emphasise the performance evaluator's willingness to support the employee's attempts to improve performance.
- End the performance appraisal session by emphasising the positive aspects of the employee's performance.

11.11 CONCLUSION

From the above it should be clear that performance appraisal is a critical human resources management activity. The aim of performance appraisal should be to provide an accurate picture of employees' performance and what can be expected of them. To be able to do this, performance standards against which work performance can be measured must first be set. The criteria used for work standards must be based on job-related aspects that can best indicate how the job can be successfully carried out. Real performance must be appraised as objectively as possible at all times.

A wide variety of performance appraisal techniques have been discussed, enabling the human resources manager to choose those that, in his or her opinion, will best succeed in appraising work performance in the most objective manner. It is important that the human resources manager should choose techniques that can rate past performance while also anticipating future performance.

The importance of providing employees with feedback after the performance appraisal has been spelled out. Employees must be given a realistic overview of their job performance. They must be made aware of the positive aspects of their job performance, but also be informed in a positive manner about where their performance falls short. It is particularly important to correct the unsatisfactory part of the work performance through training and guidance.

Performance appraisal provides extremely important feedback to the human resources management process. Human resources management should realise that poor job performance, particularly if it is widespread, may be a manifestation of problems in the application of human resources management, which may have an adverse effect on the individual performance attitude of employees.

Questions

1. Describe how you would carry out a performance appraisal interview.
2. How do the results of performance appraisal affect the other human resources management activities?
3. Discuss the uses of performance appraisal.
4. Discuss and contrast the various performance appraisal techniques known to you.

Sources

Brown, R.D. 1988. *Performance appraisal as a tool for staff development*. Jossey-Bass, San Francisco.

Ivancevich, J.M. & Glueck, W.F. 1986. *Foundations of personnel/human resource management*. 3rd edition. Business Publications, Plano, Texas.

Klatt, L.A., Murdick, R.G. & Schuster, F.E. 1985. *Human resource management*. Charles E. Merrill, Columbus, Ohio.

Leap, T.L. & Orino, M.D. 1993. *Personnel/human resource management*. 2nd edition. Macmillan, New York.

Milkovich, G.T. & Boudreau, J.W. 1988. *Personnel/human resource management*. 5th edition. Business Publications, Plano, Texas.

Schuler, R.S. 1981. *Personnel and human resource management*. West, St Paul, Minnesota.

Chapter 12

Compensation management

P.D. Gerber and
P.S. van Dyk

STUDY OBJECTIVES
After studying this chapter, you should be able to:
- Identify the components of a compensation system;
- Differentiate between non-quantitative and quantitative methods of job evaluation;
- Differentiate between the various job evaluation systems;
- Design a theoretical compensation structure.

12.1 INTRODUCTION

The basic question of compensation theory is: Why are employees paid? The answer is very simple: Employees are paid to *motivate* them to work.

There is much speculation among academics and practitioners about the real influence of money as a motivator.

In the opinion of the present authors, money as a motivator is particularly important in South Africa, where the great majority of the labour force comes from the lowest socio-economic levels of society, where money as compensation is required for mere survival. To understand the influence of compensation on motivation requires a knowledge of motivation theories, which are discussed in chapter 16. Here it will suffice, however, to give the view of Smit *et al.* (1992:341) (see accompanying box).

Money as a motivator

Almost all the motivation theories discussed in chapter 16 accept that money exercises a certain influence on the performance of people.

The monetary reward received by employees is a package consisting of salaries or wages and fringe benefits such as medical aid schemes, insurance, holiday bonuses, sick leave and housing schemes. The following becomes apparent from the motivation theories:

- The lower-order needs in Maslow's theory can be satisfied by money.
- Herzberg's hygiene factors can be satisfied by money, although Herzberg says that the motivators cannot be satisfied by money.
- The expectation theory assumes that money can satisfy a variety of needs. The theory holds that, if employees perceive that good performance will result in good remuneration, money can serve as a motivator.
- The reinforcement theory portrays money as a reward that can be used to strengthen positive job performance.

Money thus undoubtedly plays a role in motivation, but researchers agree that a reward system must meet certain requirements:

- Employees must be convinced that high remuneration is the result of high performance.
- Employees must know that rewards other than money are also associated with high performance.
- Maslow's lower-order needs and Herzberg's hygiene factors must be satisfied.
- Employees' rewards must be comparable to rewards paid for similar work by the organisation and by other organisations.

    Too low rewards can have considerable negative results. If an individual is dissatisfied with his or her remuneration, this may result in lower performance, strikes, theft and grievances. Dissatisfaction and the need for more money will also motivate the individual to look for other work. Symptoms of too low remuneration in the workplace manifest themselves, among other things, in an increase in absenteeism, high staff turnover and a poor organisational climate.

- Various people have various needs that they satisfy in various ways. In as far as possible, the remuneration system of an organisation must make provision for this.

Source: Smit *et al.* (1992:325)

Most strikes in South Africa have compensation-related causes.

This chapter pays attention to the following important aspects:
- The components of compensation management;
- Job evaluation;

- Compensable factors;
- Compensation systems;
- Salary surveys;
- The design of a compensation structure.

FIGURE 12.1: Principal learning components of compensation management

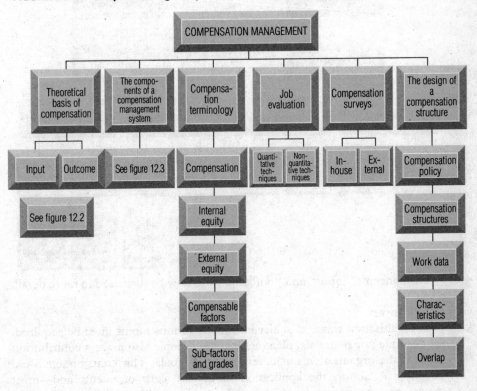

12.1.1 The theoretical rationale underlying compensation

Compensation in an organisation is based on two variables, i.e. *input* and *outcome*.

Input is the contribution made by people to achieve the goals of the organisation, while outcome is the compensation or reward received by people for the input they give.

The organisation (the employer) is the receiver of input and the source of outcome; the employee is the source of input and the receiver of outcome. Human resources management attempts to arrange the relationship between the employer and the employee in such a way that the goals of the organisation will be achieved.

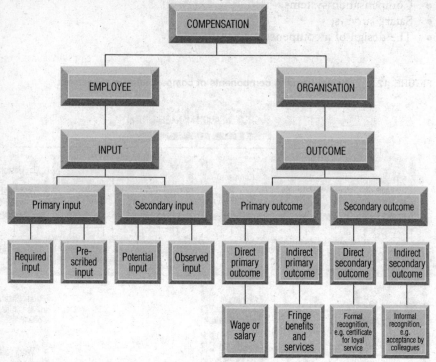

The concepts "input" and "outcome" will now be discussed in more detail.

12.1.2 Input

If an organisation wants to achieve its goals, various inputs must be acquired, for example raw materials, plant and capital. People also make a contribution towards the organisation's achievement of its goals. This contribution could be physical labour, the application of certain skills or talents and—most important—the manner in which people use their ability to think and to make decisions.

As far as the human resources function is concerned, we are only interested in the input made by people. Because this input is an indispensable element of the overall input, it is desirable and even essential that the organisation should have control over it. To achieve control over the input requires control over people as the source of input. Consequently, people enter into a formal relationship with the organisation: the employee-employer relationship. This relationship forms the basis of the exchange model approach to compensation.

Primary and secondary input

Primary input is an absolute requirement for the execution of a certain task. Secondary input is not an absolute requirement for executing the task, but it

232

makes an indirect or secondary contribution towards achieving the goals of the organisation.

Elements of input

We can distinguish between the following elements of input:

- *Required input*: Each job in the organisation has certain input requirements. These requirements of course primarily depend on the nature of the organisation and its aims, and secondarily on the nature of the job. One of the first tasks of the human resources function is to determine the required input for every job (job analysis, job description, job specification).
- *Potential input*: Every person has certain competencies, aptitudes, skills, experience, etc. that can be used as input. These abilities are initially latent and are only expressed as input in the work situation. Human resources management has the important task of determining the potential input of the employee (personnel selection) and to weigh up the potential input against the required input (personnel placement).
- *Prescribed input*: The required input must, of course, be prescribed to the employee by means of communication between the employer and the employee. Instruction, induction and initial training thus form another important part of the human resources function.
- *Observed input*: The observed input of the employee is expressed in the work situation, based on the required input and the prescribed input, and within the framework of his or her potential input. This does not, however, happen by itself and the employee must be persuaded, encouraged or motivated to realise his or her potential in the work situation.

Evaluation of input

One of the most important tasks of human resources management is the evaluation of input. The evaluation criterion is the extent to which the required input, potential input, prescribed input and observed input are in accordance with one another. If these inputs do not concur, the goals of the organisation cannot be optimally achieved. In such a case it is the task of human resources management to take corrective steps. The following examples serve to illustrate this statement.

Supposing that the observed input is much lower than the required input, such a situation can have a number of possible causes:

- The observed input might be equal to the prescribed input, but the latter deviates from the required input. In such a case it will be necessary to reformulate the task instruction.
- The required input might be unrealistically high and the employee (or any other employee) unable to meet the requirements. It might be expected of a salesperson to sell 500 units a week; later it may become clear it is beyond the ability of any person to sell more than 300 units per week. In such a case it is necessary to reduce the required input.

- The employee might perhaps be completely unable to deliver the required input. Further training might then be the best solution. Alternatively, the employee might be transferred to a job with a lower prescribed input so that he or she can meet the requirements. Maybe the only option is to dismiss the employee.

Supposing that the observed input is much lower than the potential input, this means that there is something preventing the employee from realising his or her full potential. The problem may either lie with the work situation (for example the supply of raw materials might be delayed and the employee cannot continue with his or her work), or with the employee (he or she might, for example, be in poor health, or not adequately motivated, or on a go-slow).

Supposing that the potential input is much higher than the required input, this means that the employee could be much better used in another job. Transfer or even promotion is then the solution.

12.1.3 Outcome

The employee is compensated by the employer for the input that he or she makes and, as already mentioned, this is known as outcome. No-one is prepared to make an input if there is no possibility of an outcome.

Primary and secondary outcome

Primary outcome is the monetary compensation received by the employee. One can further differentiate between direct and indirect primary outcomes. Direct primary outcome is the basic salary or wage received by the employee. Indirect primary outcome is the fringe benefits received by the employee (for example holidays at full pay, free meals, free medical treatment, interest-free loans).

Secondary outcome is the psycho-social satisfaction that the employee obtains from his or her work. This includes factors such as security, status, safety, possibilities for promotion and self-development and the degree of interest of the work. Furthermore, we can differentiate between direct and indirect secondary outcome. Direct secondary outcome is the psycho-social satisfaction that is formally awarded to the employee (for example a certificate for loyal service), while indirect secondary outcome is informal psycho-social satisfaction (for example approval by the employer or fellow employees).

Elements of outcome

A further differentiation can be made between the following elements of outcome:

- *Expected outcome*: Employees have certain expectations and set certain requirements with regard to the outcome they deserve as compensation for the input they are making. These expectations are based on numerous

234

factors, for example previous experience, prevailing wages in the occupation and how individuals rate their own competence.

- *Determined outcome*: Every employer determines what the outcome of employees should be. Once again, numerous factors are involved, for example the required input, the potential and observed input, the salary and wage structure in the organisation and the prevailing wages in the industry or occupation.
- *Prescribed outcome*: On the basis of the expected and determined outcome, the employee and employer agree on what the actual outcome should be. This agreement is often set out in a formal service contract or in conditions of service, but may also be informal.
- *Observed outcome*: Just like the input, the outcome is realised in the work situation. As primary outcome the employee receives a salary or wage and enjoys the fringe benefits. The secondary outcome is a function of the interaction between the employee, the employer and the work situation. Observed secondary outcome is highly subjective and there are great individual differences. One employee may be very "happy" in his or her work (high secondary outcome), while another may be very "unhappy" in exactly the same situation (low secondary outcome).

12.1.4 The relation between input and outcome

There is a direct relation between input and outcome. The outcome is a function of the input; in other words, the nature and extent of the input determine the nature and extent of the outcome. In some cases the opposite is true and the input is a function of the outcome.

If there should be a discrepancy between input and outcome, this leads to problems, as is shown by the following examples.

Supposing that the input is very high in relation to the outcome, this means that the employee makes an input for which he or she is not being compensated. In such a case the following reactions are possible:

- The employee reduces the input until it is, in his or her opinion, on the same level as the outcome (for example by a go-slow or by absenteeism).
- The employee demands a higher outcome (for example by means of a general strike).
- The employee withdraws from the work situation (for example by resigning).
- The employer reduces the input to bring it down to the same level as the outcome.
- The employer increases the outcome to place it on the same level as the input.

Supposing that the outcome is very high in relation to the input, this means that the employee is being compensated for input he or she is not making. This implies a loss for the organisation.

12.2 COMPONENTS OF A COMPENSATION MANAGEMENT SYSTEM

12.2.1 General

The management of the compensation process is both complex and sensitive. The best way to conceptualise the entire process is as shown in figure 12.3.

FIGURE 12.3: Compensation management model

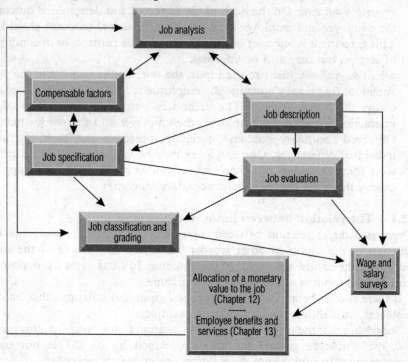

Three of the components of the model have already been discussed in chapter 5: job analysis, job description and job specification, which have many applications in human resources management and particularly in compensation management.

12.2.2 Delimitation of concepts

In its simplest form, compensation refers to the payment that employees receive in exchange for services rendered.

"Payment" in this context refers to all forms of monetary compensation received by an employee, whether this be a wage, salary, financial benefits, non-financial benefits or deferred benefits, but it excludes secondary outcome as discussed in 12.1.3.

Wallace and Fay (1988:397) define compensation as "the provision of monetary rewards in return for employment", while Burgess (1989:464) describes it as all forms of formal income, tangible services and benefits received by employees as part of a work relationship.

The *aim* of compensation is to attract competent employees, to retain them and to motivate them to achieve the aims of the employer (or organisation).

The employer's compensation package must be sufficient to attract competent employees from the labour market and to motivate staff to perform. Their services must be retained by keeping compensation packages market-related.

It is only by retaining the services of skilled staff that an employer will be able to achieve its organisational goals.

12.2.3 Factors that determine the levels of and differences in compensation

There are three factors that determine the levels and differences of a compensation package:

- Level of responsibility;
- Compensation levels in the market;
- Individual expertise.

Each factor will now be briefly discussed.

12.2.3.1 Level of responsibility

It is obvious that there are great differences between the responsibilities associated with various jobs in an organisation. Thus the responsibility of the managing director is much greater than that of the human resources director and that of the latter is in turn much greater than that of a clerk in the recruitment department. The responsibility levels of jobs in organisations are measured by the process of job evaluation (see figure 12.3). The result is a hierarchy of jobs to which a compensation structure can be linked. The level of responsibility determines the value of compensation, in other words what jobs are better paid than others. It does not, however, determine the *amount* of compensation.

12.2.3.2 Compensation levels in the market

In the labour market, supply and demand factors interact with one another. Both the basic compensation structure of an organisation and the structure of benefits and services must be based on market-related levels of compensation to enable the employer (organisation) to attract and retain personnel in a competitive market environment. The market determines the amount of the various compensation scales and the nature and extent of employee benefits and services.

237

12.2.3.3 Individual expertise

The last factor that influences the compensation decision is the particular expertise of the employee. The level of responsibility and market-related compensation levels determine the compensation scales. Within the limits of these scales, new employees must be appointed and the salaries of existing employees adapted. A new employee's previous salary will determine the point on the compensation scale at which such an employee is appointed, while the performance or period of service of existing employees will determine at what point of the compensation scale an adjustment will be made: the adjustment may be upward or downward.

FIGURE 12.4: Graphic representation of the factors determining compensation

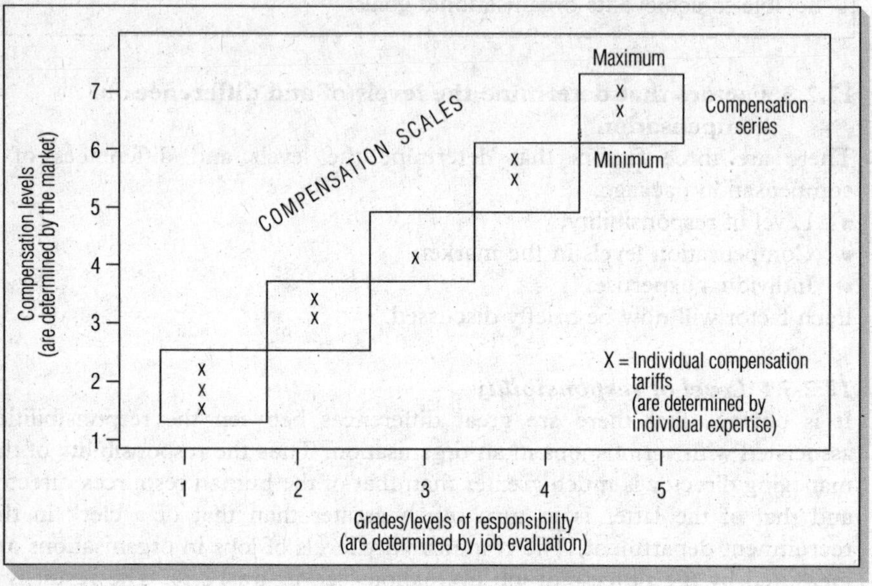

Source: Adapted from *IPM Journal,* June 1988

12.3 JOB EVALUATION

12.3.1 General

The first factor in the compensation management model (see figure 12.3) to be discussed in detail is job evaluation. Job evaluation is a method used by larger organisations (with 200 employees or more) to determine the relative levels of responsibility of jobs in the organisation.

Job evaluation implies that the job worth can be measured and that employees in jobs with more responsibility should receive more compensation. This approach is the result of a free-market economic system. For this reason, job evaluation is more common in capitalist countries than in socialist and communist-oriented economic systems.

In South Africa, most large organisations make use of formal job evaluation systems, either developed in-house or standardised systems supplied by consulting companies.

12.3.2 Explanation of concepts

Wallace and Fay (1988:404) define job evaluation as a formal process through which management allocates salary scales or grades to jobs in accordance with a predetermined method for the evaluation of the job's internal worth to the organisation. Burgess (1989:469) defines this as follows:

The formal process by which management determines the relative value to be placed on various jobs within the organization.

A principle known as *internal equity* is of particular importance and can be classified as one of the contemporary human resources management problems in South Africa. Internal equity indicates that the relative worth of each job in the organisation is fairly evaluated and that compensation tariffs are in accordance with this.

> Compensation structures in South Africa have in recent decades been characterised by the absence of internal equity. The basic right of equal pay for equal work is still being disregarded to a large extent. Discrimination in compensation against female and black workers cannot be tolerated in the new South Africa, and it may be expected that legislation in this regard will be promulgated in the near future.

The *aim of job evaluation* is to establish a logical hierarchy of jobs to which a fair and comparable compensation structure can be linked.

There are particular advantages for an organisation that makes use of a formal job evaluation system. These advantages will be of great importance to organisations, especially in the new South Africa. A distinction can be made between direct and indirect advantages (*IPM Journal* Fact Sheet 171).

Direct advantages include the following:

- It eliminates—in as far as this is possible—personal prejudices in the evaluation of the relative worth of a job.
- It establishes a fair and comparable compensation structure for all employees.
- It offers a logical job hierarchy to which a system of employee benefits and services can be linked.
- It provides an objective system on the basis of which negotiations with trade unions can take place.
- It establishes a sound compensation structure on which compensation reviews can be based.

Indirect advantages include the following:

- A hierarchy of jobs is established that can be used in organisational structuring and career planning.

239

- Job descriptions are developed that can be used for, among other things, selection, placement, performance appraisal, training and development.

The above discussion serves as a general introduction to compensation management. The theoretical basis of job evaluation methods will now be reviewed.

12.3.3 Theoretical methods of job evaluation

12.3.3.1 General

Any job evaluation system is based on what are called *compensable factors*. These factors, an overview of which was given in paragraph 12.2.3, will be discussed here in more detail. A distinction will then be made between quantifiable and non-quantifiable methods of job evaluation.

12.3.3.2 Compensable factors

The question here is: How can apples be compared with apples?

A compensable factor is any factor or combination of factors that is used as a basis for the evaluation of the job worth in comparison with that of all the other jobs in an organisation, and to which a common monetary value can be allocated by consensus.

The core of any compensation policy is the identification of certain factors that are common to all jobs in an organisation.

To be usable, a compensable factor must be present in a large number of jobs. This requires the compensable factor to be abstract. The greater the job universe covered by a compensable factor, the more abstract its definition must be.

Because job evaluation methods based on compensable factors cover a wide range of jobs at all levels, it requires the description and classification of compensable factors to be further subdivided. For this reason, compensable factors are subdivided into three main categories:

- Universal factors;
- Sub-factors;
- Grades or levels.

Universal factors are general, relatively abstract and complex characteristics that occur in all types of jobs. To make these abstract universal factors more understandable and to link them directly to what employees are doing, sub-factors within each compensable factor are used. *Sub-factors* are statements that exactly define the specific characteristics of a job. *Grades or levels* are determined from these definitions of the sub-factors and these form a scale of measurement to determine the specific quantity of the factor required in the execution of the job.

240

The subdivision of compensable factors into universal factors, sub-factors and grades or levels simplifies the comparative process, thus offering the parties involved in job evaluation a common basis for discussion. This subdivision also provides a way of linking job worth to indirect compensation.

The most acceptable universal compensable factors are:
- The knowledge that the position requires;
- Supervisor control;
- Guidelines;
- Complexity;
- Extent and effect;
- Personal contacts;
- Aim of contacts;
- Physical requirements;
- Work environment.

It must be emphasised that various job evaluation methods identify their own factors, which are however semantically the same as the above group. Each system also has its own definition of the compensable factors. However, they all have the theoretical basis described above.

12.3.3.3 Methods of job evaluation
As already mentioned, job evaluation is the use of job analysis information to determine in a systematic manner the value of each job in relation to all other jobs in the organisation. Job evaluation determines a ranking order for every job in the organisation. This is embodied in a hierarchy of jobs that reflects the relative value of each job in the organisation.

REMEMBER:
Job evaluation determines the value or ranking of jobs in the organisation and not those of the incumbents.

Traditionally a distinction is made between non-quantitative and quantitative methods of job evaluation.

Non-quantitative methods
Non-quantitative methods are subjective ways of determining the ranking order of jobs. These methods have been in existence for years and are discussed under compensation management in various books.
- *The job ranking method*: This simple and cheap method of job evaluation (also known as the job arrangement method) involves giving a committee of evaluators a short-list of job descriptions or even job titles. The evaluators then place the jobs in a ranking order according to their value, without taking into account the people who hold the jobs or the current salaries or wages they receive. The greatest advantage of this technique is

241

that it is simple, but the simplicity is also its greatest disadvantage, as the evaluation is very subjective and there is no predetermined value scale for each evaluation team. The subjective evaluation criteria make it difficult for job incumbents to understand exactly why their job is being evaluated in a certain way.

- *The job classification method*: With this method, a measure is developed according to which jobs are divided into groups. A value scale is drawn up according to which jobs and the associated job descriptions are compared with one another. The scale consists of gradings and the associated descriptions. As opposed to the job ranking order method, there is thus a predetermined standard evaluation scale.

  The job classification method has two important disadvantages. First, large-scale generalisations are used to define jobs. Second, it does not make provision for multiple definitions, which are necessary, particularly in organisations with widely diverging jobs. An example is that grade descriptions of production work will differ widely from, for example, the work of a clerk in an administrative office. These two types of jobs can thus not directly be compared with one another.

Quantitative methods

With quantitative methods, compensable factors are identified, as is the degree to which each of these factors is required for a particular job. If, for example, there are five degrees of responsibility in a job, points can be allocated for every degree of each factor. The points are then added up to obtain a total point value for the job.

- *The factor comparison method*: This method was developed by Benge in 1926 and involves comparing tasks (jobs) one by one with the aid of five benchmark compensable factors: mental requirements, skill requirements, physical requirements, responsibilities and work circumstances.

  An analysis of the benchmark jobs forms the basis for the scale of comparison. A monetary value is allocated to each factor instead of points.

  Benchmark jobs are then identified, after which the factors are arranged according to their relative importance in each job, and monetary values are allocated to the factors in each job.

  In the final step, the other jobs in the organisation are classified and compensated *in comparison with* the benchmark jobs.

  Table 12.1 is a simple example of such a process.

  This method is very subjective. In addition, it is difficult to find benchmark jobs which can be generally regarded as fairly compensated. Finally, there is too much reliance on benchmark jobs in terms of work factors and fair compensation. The latter, in particular, is highly subjective.

  The Hay method (see paragraph 12.4.4) was developed from this system.

TABLE 12.1: The factor comparison method

Factor benchmark job	Skills	Mental requirements	Physical requirements	Respon-sibilities	Work situation
Toolmaker	1	1	7	2	8
Machinist	2	3	8	4	7
Electrician	3	2	6	3	2
Forklift operator	4	4	5	1	3
Drill press operator	5	5	9	5	9
Inspector	6	6	10	6	10
Helper	7	7	2	8	5
Acquisitions clerk	8	8	3	7	6
Handyman	9	9	4	10	4
Labourer	10	10	1	9	1

- *The point allocation method*: This method is probably the most commonly used of all job evaluation methods. With this method, a number of compensable factors are selected for the evaluation of the jobs in the organisation. The factors differ in quantity and nature because organisations are unique. What is important, however, is that the factors selected should be representative of all jobs in the organisation, as well as relevant for all functions and levels in the organisation.

A series of points is then allocated to each of the chosen compensable factors. This may be the same for each factor or the points may differ, according to the importance of the compensable factors.

Every job in the organisation is then evaluated by adding up the points for each job factor. The points total for each job determines the place of that job in the job hierarchy. Some systems subdivide the points into more sophisticated series, with each series representing a notch on the salary scale.

Just like the factor comparison method, this system is vulnerable to the subjectivity of the evaluators. There are, however, some positive factors that may be regarded as advantages:

— When jobs are evaluated in relation to one another, the job evaluator must take a variety of factors into account.

— A clear distinction is made between the job evaluation and the determination of compensation: the conversion of the job's points total into monetary value takes place in a separate process.

— Structural discipline is provided for evaluators by establishing common standards according to which evaluators must do their evaluation. This promotes objectivity.

This method is useful in industries where trade unions are active, as the validity of the system can be proven. Trade union members can also be easily trained in the system and involved in the valuation process.

An important system was developed from this approach and is popular in South African organisations: the Peromnes method (see paragraph 12.4.3).

TABLE 12.2: Summary of points per job and factor for 10 selected jobs

Job	RESPONSIBILITY				SUPERVISION				
	Edu-ca-tion	Expe-rience	Com-plexity of duties	Mone-tary	Con-tact with others	Type	Ex-tended	Work situa-tion	Total points
Despatch clerk	40	25	40	10	10	—	—	10	135
Typist	40	25	40	5	5	—	—	10	125
Benchmark job operator:									
class A	40	75	40	10	5	—	—	15	185
Telephone operator/									
receptionist	40	50	40	5	20	—	—	10	165
Nurse: industrial	80	75	60	20	20	—	—	15	270
Tabulation machine operator	60	100	60	10	10	—	—	15	255
Secretary: class B	60	100	60	10	10	—	—	5	245
Interviewer	80	125	60	20	20	—	—	10	315
Supervisor: costing depart-									
ment	80	125	60	40	20	20	5	10	360
Sales engineer	100	150	80	60	60	—	—	15	465

Source: Adapted from Burgess (1992:171)

The most important systems in use in South African organisations will now be discussed.

12.4 PRACTICAL JOB EVALUATION SYSTEMS
12.4.1 General
A large number of job evaluation systems based on the theory discussed above are in use in South Africa and free-market economies. Only the most important systems in the opinion of the authors will be discussed, i.e. Paterson, Peromnes, Hay and the "Q" method of the National Institute for Personnel Research. All these methods are backed by compensation surveys (see paragraph 12.6). Methods such as Urwick-Orr, TASK and Castellion are not discussed because they are used by few organisations.

12.4.2 The Paterson decision-making band model
In the 1950s, Paterson, a professor of management, analysed the job evaluation systems in use at that time and came to the conclusion that their number of compensable factors (up to 20) made the systems too cumbersome and complex. He used statistical techniques to analyse the various factors and reached the conclusion that one factor, *decision-making*, has such a high forecast validity that it can be used as the only factor to determine job levels.

The result was the Paterson decision-making band model: a single-factor job evaluation system. The Paterson system is based on the assumption that the most important function of an employee is his or her ability to make

244

decisions. Decision-making is a general compensable factor present in all jobs, which enables jobs to be grouped into general, uniform categories.

In an organisation with diverging functions, different types of decisions are taken on the various hierarchical levels. The left side of table 12.3 shows the various decision-making bands that represent the various activities in the organisation.

According to the Paterson method, all jobs are grouped into six decision-making bands, which are then subdivided on the basis of a coordinating factor. For each of the bands, with the exception of unskilled workers, there are two grades: a lower grade for the mechanical execution of decisions and a higher grade for the supervisors who must take the decisions. The grades are further divided into sub-grades, usually limited to a maximum of two in the higher

TABLE 12.3: Paterson's job grading structure

Decision-making band	Job grades	Subgrades
F Policy formulating (Top management)	Higher F—Coordinating—11	F5
	Lower F—Policy formulating—10	F4
E Programming (Senior management)	Higher E—Coordinating—9	E5 E4
	Lower E—Programming—8	E3 E2 E1
D Interpreting (Middle management)	Higher D—Coordinating—7	D5 D4
	Lower D—Interpreting—6	D3 D2 D1
C Routine (Skilled workers and supervisory management)	Higher C—Coordinating—5	C5 C4
	Lower C—Routine—4	C3 C2 C1
B Automatic (Semi-skilled workers)	Higher B—Coordinating—3	B5 B4
	Lower B—Automatic—2	B3 B2 B1
A Defined (Unskilled workers)	Lower A only—Defined—1	A3 A2 A1

Source: IPM Journal (Fact Sheet 172)

grade of each band. The right side of table 12.3 is a representation of all 28 possible sub-grades (six decision-making bands, 11 job grades and 28 sub-grades).

The most common criticism of the Paterson system is that only one person is relied upon to analyse the jobs. In addition, decision-making bands and job grades are arbitrarily determined—six bands and 11 job grades, which are universal and rigid. Some flexibility is, however, permitted in the sub-grades.

The Paterson system is widely used in South African organisations, among others by the mining sector, the sugar and paper-making industries and by many large and medium-sized organisations. It is also used by organisations in Botswana and Zimbabwe.

A compensation consultancy, FSA (Pty) Ltd, has developed a derived Paterson system for South African organisations. The so-called TASK system (tuned assessment of skills and knowledge) makes use of a point system with four factors to sub-grade jobs. It is, however, not very popular; most organisations prefer Paterson to TASK.

12.4.3 The Peromnes system of job evaluation

The Peromnes system (Biesheuvel 1985:53) was developed by SA Breweries as a simplified version of the Castellion method. The system was later taken over by FSA, which now has the sole right to market it in South Africa.

Peromnes is a point system that evaluates jobs according to eight identified compensable factors:

Factor 1: Problem solving
Factor 2: Consequences of errors of judgement
Factor 3: Work pressure
Factor 4: Knowledge
Factor 5: Impact (influence) of job
Factor 6: Understanding
Factor 7: Educational qualifications or intelligence required
Factor 8: Training or experience required

All eight factors are inherent aspects or requirements of a job, and characteristics such as physical work circumstances are excluded, as these may vary from place to place and from time to time. Factors must thus be constant. During the job evaluation process, each compensable factor is placed on an exponential complexity scale according to prescribed "definitions". In each case the aim is to provide the best definition of the highest level of activity or the greatest requirements of the job. By evaluating all the compensable factors in this manner, a total point value is allocated to each job.

As soon as the total point value for a job has been determined, the job is graded in accordance with a predetermined conversion scale. The Peromnes system has 19 grades, of which 1 is the highest. Each grade has a series of points on the scale. The meaning of the grades is given in table 12.4.

TABLE 12.4: The Peromnes grade classification and description

Grades	Descriptions
1–3	Top executive management, most senior professional people and specialists
4–6	Senior management, high-level professional people and specialists
7–9	Middle management, superintendents and low-level professional people and specialists
10–12	Supervisors, high-level skilled workers and clerical personnel
13–16	Low-level workers and clerical personnel
17–19	Semi-skilled and unskilled workers

Source: IPM Journal (Fact Sheet 172)

One advantage of this system is external comparability. This means that a job on, for example, job grade 4 in one organisation has the same intrinsic value as a job on the same grade in any other organisation.

The Peromnes method is unique in that it does not use job descriptions for evaluation. Instead, a number of specialists on the panel of evaluators with an in-depth knowledge of the job under evaluation provide information about key aspects of the job.

TABLE 12.5: Peromnes cut-off point table—exponential score system

Assigned points	Job grade	Job level example
689–800	1	
481–688	2	Top management
369–480	3	
285–368	4	
225–284	5	Senior management and specialists
177–224	6	
133–176	7	
105–132	8	Middle management and superintendents
81–104	9	
62–80	10	
49–61	11	Junior management, supervisors and foremen
34–48	12	
29–37	13	
23–28	14	Skilled and semi-skilled workers and clerical
18–22	15	personnel
13–17	16	
10–12	17	
8–9	18	Semi-skilled (lower levels) and unskilled workers
0–8	19	

Some disadvantages of the Peromnes system are:
- It is subjective to an extent due to a lack of information, which can probably be ascribed to the unstructured evaluation process, the lack of a formal manual, training and standardisation exercises and because the cut-off points on the point scale are arbitrary.
- It is cost-intensive and time-consuming because the evaluation interview is unstructured and because of a lack of relevant information obtained in a systematic manner.
- The maintenance of the system is complicated because the evaluation process is not linked to job descriptions, and because the subjectivity of the system means that there is no definite framework for evaluation.
- The system is not acceptable to all line managers, which makes it difficult to establish a rational job and compensation structure.

12.4.4 The Hay method

The Hay method (also known as the Hay guide chart profile method) was developed in the early 1950s by the Hay group of consultants in Philadelphia, USA (Biesheuvel 1985:50–2). It is currently being used by more than 4 000 companies and organisations in about 30 countries. The method is based on three compensable factors and a total of eight elements summarised in table 12.6 (FSA information sheet).

TABLE 12.6: The Hay method

Factors	Elements
1. Know-how: the sum total of each type of skill necessary for acceptable work performance	1.1 *Performance procedures:* specialised techniques and knowledge in the occupational or commercial field or the professional or scientific discipline 1.2 Width of *management know-how* 1.3 *Human relations skills*
2. Problem solving	2.1 The *environment* in which thinking takes place 2.2 The *challenge* undertaken by the thinking
3. Accountability and its results: the measured effect of the work on the end results of the organisation	3.1 *Freedom to act:* the extent of personal procedure or systematic guidance and contol over actions in relation to the primary emphasis of the task 3.2 *Task impact on end results:* the extent to which the task can affect thinking that is necessary to render results within the primary emphasis 3.3 *Extent:* the portion of the total organisation that includes the primary emphasis of the task

Source: Biesheuvel (1985:50)

A further compensable factor, work situation, is used for tasks that involve obstacles, an unpleasant work environment or specific physical demands.

A complicated quantitative system is used to evaluate each factor and element of a task. Guide charts developed by Hay for clients differ from organisation to organisation. Biesheuvel (1985:50) maintains that

the relative importance of jobs is determined primarily by the purpose of the company or institution within which they operate, i.e. structure is a function of purpose, and guide is a function of purpose, and guide charts are built to represent the structure of the institution within which jobs are being measured.

Each of the three factors is analysed under two headings, which are, in turn, subdivided. A point value is allocated to each sub-section, which is read off the relevant guide chart in the form of a matrix specifically compiled for the user.

The compensable factor *knowledge* is measured in depth according to skill and education. Eight levels are distinguished, from primary education to total control over the principles and practice of a high-level job. Each level is again subdivided into three sub-levels. Eight levels are defined for breadth of management knowledge, subdivided into three sub-levels that vary from minimal to comprehensive knowledge of strategic functions and policy formulation. This structure is contained in a guide chart matrix of 24 by 15 for measuring knowledge.

A similar structure applies to the compensable factor *problem solving*. Eight levels, each divided into two sub-levels, are measured for limitations and practices set by the policy and procedures of the organisation, and five levels with two sub-levels each for the intellectual effort required for problem solving. This is contained in a guide chart matrix of 16 by 10.

For the compensable factor *accountability*, the two dimensions are the freedom to act (eight levels with a total of 24 sub-levels) and the extent of responsibility (16 levels) based on the monetary values involved in the risk, which in turn depends on how the freedom is used and the extent to which responsibility for action is shared with others.

One shortcoming of the Hay method is that there is no universal point system for all organisations, but that the point values must be individually developed for each user by the consulting company.

The aim of the Hay method is to place all the tasks in order of difficulty and importance. To do this, the following steps are followed:

- A benchmark sample is drawn from all the organisational levels, functions and units where jobs must be evaluated.
- Job descriptions are prepared and accepted for evaluation as soon as they have been approved by the job incumbent and one higher level of authority.
- A job evaluation committee is chosen to evaluate the benchmark sample.
- The committee is led by a Hay consultant who acts as trainer and coach.

- The committee evaluates each job once the job description has been accepted and classifies it as fair and credible.
- All the other jobs are then evaluated.

12.4.5 Comparison between the Paterson and Peromnes systems

The compensation manager may find it useful to compare systems with one another, as this facilitates salary investigations, scale determinations and scale comparisons.

The Paterson and Peromnes systems lend themselves to such comparisons, as is apparent from table 12.7.

TABLE 12.7: Comparison between the Paterson and Peromnes systems

	PATERSON		PEROMNES
Job level	**Band**	**Sub-grades**	**Grades**
Unskilled	A	A1 A2 A3	19/18 17 16
Semi-skilled	B	B1 B2 B3 B4 B5	15 14 13 12
Skilled	C	C1 C2 C3 C4 C5	11 10 9 8
Lower/middle management	D	D1 D2 D3 D4 D5	7 6 5
Senior management	E	E1 E2 E3 E4 E5	4 3 2
Top management	F	F1 F2 F3 F4 F5	2 1 1+ 1+ 1++

Source: IPM Journal (Fact Sheet 172)

12.4.6 The questionnaire method of the National Institute for Personnel Research

This system (also known as the Q-method) was developed by Biesheuvel and can be classified as a point system, although it also contains elements of the grade classification system. The system is based on the assumption that there is a direct link between the worth of a certain job to the organisation and the level of complexity of such a job.

Table 12.8 is a hypothetical example of job grades and cut-off points according to the questionnaire method of the National Institute for Personnel Research.

TABLE 12.8: Grade classification using the ranking order classification technique

Job structure	Total numerical ranking	Decision-making factor	Grades
Managing Director	158	135	Grade I
Technical Director	146	123	
Regional Manager	130	107	Grade H
Branch Manager	117	98	
Branch Secretary	112	89	Grade G
Chief Accountant	100	86	
Senior Technical Officer	95	73	Grade F
Accountant	82	72	
Personnel Officer	72	62	Grade E
Technical Officer	59	51	
Accounting Clerk	59	49	Grade D
Switchboard Operator	40	32	

Three principal factors are used to evaluate jobs according to this method. The key factor is the quality of decision-making necessary for the successful execution of a task. The second factor is that of control, which serves to qualify the decision-making competence. The third factor, contact with people, determines the extent of the job incumbent's influence.

The decision-making factor is divided into seven sub-sections with ten factor definitions, according to the logical steps in a typical decision-making process. In the case of contact with people, we differentiate between two aspects: the nature of contact within the organisation and the nature of contact outside the organisation.

Some disadvantages of the system are:
- It is difficult for a job incumbent to decide which aspects of his or her job are important and which are not.

251

- The examples of each grade description can be very confusing.
- The increase in the degree of difficulty in some grade definitions is difficult to perceive.

12.5 COMPENSATION SURVEYS

It is the task of the compensation manager to ensure that the compensation paid to employees by the organisation is as far as possible in accordance with that paid by similar organisations and jobs in the same branch of industry. This is known as *external equity*, which is defined by Wallace and Fay (1988:400) as

> *a fairness criteria that directs an employer to pay a wage that corresponds to rates prevailing in external markets for an employee's occupation.*

The aim of compensation surveys is to enable the compensation manager to ensure that the compensation system of the organisation has an acceptable degree of external equity. Compensation surveys can thus be used as a diagnostic instrument. A compensation system should attract, retain and motivate employees. High labour turnover or a high level of job offer refusal can probably be ascribed to inadequate compensation levels. Information supplied by compensation surveys is also useful for recruitment managers, as it indicates to what extent compensation contributes towards human resources shortages. It is also important for labour relations, particularly during negotiations.

When a compensation manager decides to make use of compensation surveys, he or she can follow one of two approaches: the organisation can undertake its own in-house survey, or it can purchase data. These two aspects will now be briefly discussed.

In-house systems

To develop an in-house system, the following steps must be carefully followed (Wallace and Fay 1988:153–63):

- Selection of the jobs to be investigated;
- Definition of the relevant labour markets;
- Selection of the organisations to be investigated;
- Determination of the information to be collected;
- Determination of the data collection technique;
- Administration of the system.

The first step is essentially an identification of key jobs. Wallace and Fay (1988:40) define a key job as follows:

> *A simple job used in wage surveys and job evaluation. Key jobs should vary in terms of job requirements, should exist in many organizations, should represent all salary levels in the organization, and should be technologically stable.*

A key job must meet the following requirements:

- It must be easy to define.
- It must be common in the labour market.

- It must vary according to job requirements such as qualifications, experience and other compensable factors.
- It must represent all salary levels within an organisation.
- It must not be in a process of change.

The definition of the relevant labour markets in which the compensation survey is to be carried out, is the next step. This implies determining the geographical area in which the organisation usually recruits all potential employees for such a job, and the geographical area in which employers usually lose employees in such jobs.

The relevant labour markets are determined by the source of supply. We can differentiate between the following labour markets:

- *Local labour market*: This is usually defined as the geographical environment that is easily and rapidly reached by commuters. A married working woman, for example, might not want to travel far.
- *Regional markets* are typical metropolitan areas such as the PWV area, the Durban-Pinetown area and Cape Town and surrounds. Most professional jobs are found in regional markets. People change jobs on the basis of the prevailing market price for a job in a particular region.
- *National markets* cover the entire geographical area of a country. There are few jobs in this market: these are usually highly successful executive officers, outstanding academics and medics and other highly professional people.
- *International markets*: Very few jobs are found here for the purposes of compensation management.

The next step is the selection of the organisations to be used in the survey. This is followed by determining the information to be collected. This must include:

- Identifying data: This consists of the name and address of the organisation, the contact person, the title and telephone number;
- Location of organisation: Where the participating organisations are situated;
- Type of industry: The main product lines marketed by participating organisations;
- Size: This includes sales volume and the total number of employees;
- Organisational chart: This indicates all jobs included in the survey;
- Working hours: The length of the work-week and the man-hours per day;
- Trade unions representing the employees of the organisation;
- Wage and salary policy: This includes the job evaluation systems used by participating organisations; the overall salary structure; merit adjustments in wages and salaries; general salary adjustments or increases; and other performance-based compensation;
- Employee benefit policy: This includes the policy on pensions, insurance, payment for time not worked, and other benefits;
- Individual work data of the job incumbent, such as average performance evaluation results and compensation scales.

The techniques usually used in such surveys are telephone interviews, job questionnaires and group discussions.

The last step, i.e. the administration of the system, is self-explanatory.

External compensation surveys

Most organisations use consulting companies that specialise in wage and salary surveys to obtain market-related compensation information. This is cheaper and does not tax the human resources department of the organisation. FSA (Pty) Ltd is the largest service provider in this field in South Africa. See Biesheuvel (1985) for more information on this subject.

12.6 THE DESIGN OF A COMPENSATION STRUCTURE
12.6.1 General

Now that the processes, methods and other important components of compensation management have been discussed, we can proceed with the last step, i.e. the design of a compensation structure for the organisation.

The aim of a scientific compensation system is to offer each employee of an organisation fair and just compensation. For this reason, this chapter emphasises the importance of thorough job analyses, the development of useful job descriptions and the implementation of an effective job evaluation system. Management must be able to explain internal compensation data to employees and to explain in practical terms why employees are placed in certain compensation categories. To ensure that the organisation is in line with the remuneration of similar employees in the same branch of industry or labour market (external equity) and to retain employees, it must pay competitive wages and salaries. With the internal and external compensation data at his or her disposal, it is the task of the compensation manager to draw up a scientifically defensible and understandable compensation structure for the organisation. This section deals with the establishment of such a structure.

12.6.2 Steps in the design of a compensation structure

The design of a reasonable and fair compensation structure requires the implementation of five steps that can also be described as the mechanics of a compensation structure. The five steps (Henderson 1985:263–300) are:
- Determining a compensation policy line;
- Deciding whether there is a need for one or more compensation structures;
- Displaying work data;
- Determining the characteristics of the compensation structure;
- Linking overlapping compensation structures.

The above determine the unique characteristics of an organisation's compensation structure.

Determining a compensation policy line

Determining a compensation policy line involves the establishment of a trend line or line of best fit which represents the average pay values of the jobs to be evaluated or classified. The trend line may be either straight or curved. Irrespective of how it looks, it must be the line that represents the average compensation value (i.e. the central tendency) of all the key jobs.

A practical and simple first step towards establishing a compensation policy line is to determine the lowest and highest compensation tariff in the organisation and then to draw a line to connect them, as shown in figure 12.5.

Another simple method to establish a compensation policy line is to obtain the market or prevailing compensation tariffs for the lowest and highest paid jobs in the industry and to connect these two points. This is known as the midpoint value (see figure 12.6).

However, the procedure followed by most organisations in the establishment of a compensation policy line for the organisation is to plot the market tariffs for the organisation's key jobs, from the lowest to the highest, on a graph (see figure 12.7). This is known as a scatter diagram.

Scatter diagram

A compensation scatter diagram plots the points on a chart where each point represents a job. Plotted job data provide a convenient way to see an entire array of relationships and identify natural groupings of jobs. The paired coordinates for locating each point are the evaluated score for the job and its actual pay.

Source: Henderson (1985:267)

Deciding whether there is a need for one or more compensation structures
The decision whether there should be more than one compensation structure in an organisation must be taken at an early stage. The decision is influenced by the nature and composition of the employees of the organisation and the occupational groups, but the scatter width of maximum and minimum wage and salary levels is the determining factor: if the scatter width on the scatter diagram shows large deviations, this indicates that more than one structure is necessary.

In practice, there are compensation structures for the following groupings of employees:
- Unskilled;
- Semi-skilled;
- Skilled: administrative or technical;
- Professional occupations;
- Management levels.

Displaying work data
At first glance, the use of multiple compensation structures to accommodate groups seems like the best solution. However, this is usually not accepted as fair by employees and is therefore not used. Through statistical procedures one compensation policy line can, however, be established in a number of ways.

FIGURE 12.5: Lowest to highest compensation tariff in an organisation

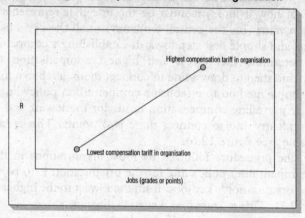

FIGURE 12.6: Lowest to highest compensation tariff in the industry

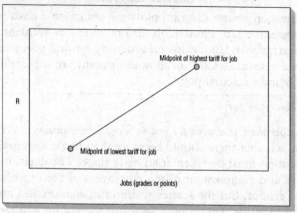

FIGURE 12.7: Scatter diagram based on market tariffs

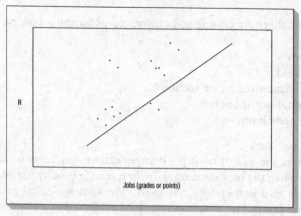

The skeleton compensation structure (figure 12.8) has three unlinked linear compensable factors, where y = a + bX. The same score X, with different gradients for each line b, gives three different compensation structures with three different compensation tariffs: Y1, Y2 and Y3.

In the case of a curved compensation structure (figure 12.9) where Y = ab, the equation curves upwards towards the right, which means that higher compensation tariffs are found for higher gradings for a comparable absolute increase in scores.

A curved compensation structure can also be shown on semi-logarithmic graph paper (figure 12.10).

These methods show compensation data in some form of curved relation, rather than as a straight line. Figures 12.8 to 12.10 show various mathematical procedures for establishing compensation policy lines.

Determining the characteristics of the compensation structure
This step pays attention to the progression from the lowest to the highest salary level on the compensation policy line. A central point or market rate for the organisation's compensation structure is determined, and acceptable progressive percentage salary increases between the central points—the so-called compensation grades—are developed. Compensation grades link job evaluations to job classifications and imply the allocation of a salary or wage to a specific job.

Linking overlapping compensation structures
In organisations using more than one method of job evaluation, multiple or overlapping salary compensation systems are often used. A basis for linking these overlapping compensation structures is, of course, essential. It is also important that there should be trust in the multiple compensation structures and particularly that it is justified to use more than one structure.

One approach to effecting this link is through the zero overlap compensation boxes shown in figures 12.11 and 12.12.

The diagonal line in figure 12.11 demonstrates the normal relationship, with compensation on the vertical axis and points on the horizontal axis. The line stretches from 0 to 800 points. The following procedure is used to plot the compensation overlap line:

- Use a pair of compasses to construct the chosen number of boxes (eight halves in this case).
- Construct the two zero boxes at the lowest and highest points of the compensation structure. (Boxes must be drawn so that the diagonal line runs through their centres.)
- To obtain zero overlap boxes, the top of the lowest box (at the left bottom of the figure) must be on the same compensation level as the lower part of the second-lowest box (bottom right).
- The same applies to the boxes at the top right of the figure.

FIGURE 12.8: Skeleton compensation structure

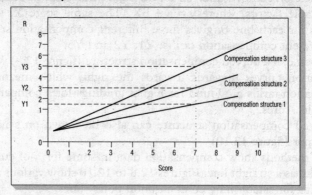

Source: Henderson (1985:278)

FIGURE 12.9: Curved compensation structure

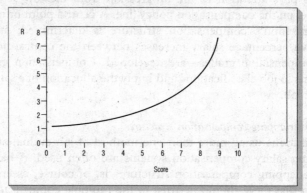

Source: Henderson (1985:278)

FIGURE 12.10: Curved compensation structure on semi-logarithmic graph paper

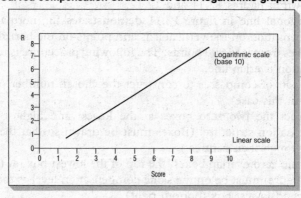

Source: Henderson (1985:278)

FIGURE 12.11: Drawing up zero overlap boxes

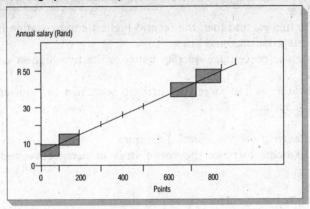

Source: Adapted from Burgess (1988:236)

The following step is the determination of the desired level of overlap on the top point of figure 12.12.

FIGURE 12.12: Determination of the desired overlap at the highest level of the compensation structure

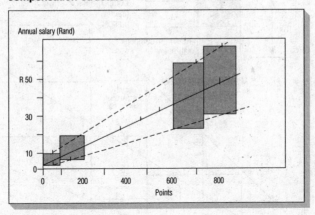

Source: Adapted from Burgess (1988:237)

On the left side of the structure, the dimensions of the lowest box (bottom left in figure 12.11) must be retained.

On the right side, a much larger box must be constructed as follows:

- Determine the midpoint on the right side of the previous structure (see figure 12.11).
- Arbitrarily make a dot somewhere above this midpoint.
- Make another dot just as far below the midpoint.
- Draw a diagonal dotted line that joins the top dot to the midpoint of the lowest box (see figure 12.12).

- Draw a second dotted line to join the bottom dot to the midpoint of the lowest box.
- Draw the highest and then the second-highest compensation boxes so that they overlap the diagonal lines.
- Calculate the percentage overlap between the two highest compensation boxes.
- If the overlap is too large, the highest box must be shortened and the process repeated.

Review the design of the compensation structure
Figure 12.13 helps to place the above steps in perspective and to simplify them.

FIGURE 12.13: The design of a compensation structure

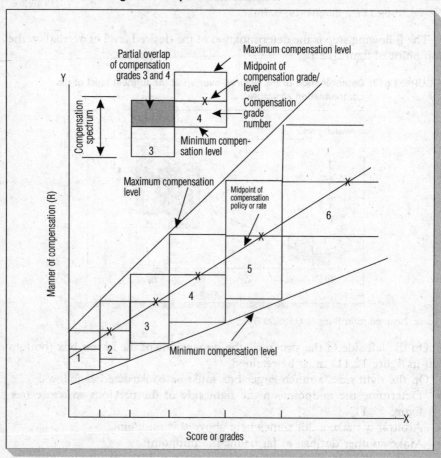

Source: Henderson (1985:299)

260

When designing a compensation structure, the following steps must be followed:

- Determine the minimum, centre-line and maximum compensation levels, including minimum and maximum tariffs for all compensation grades in the organisation.
- Determine the number of compensation grades, the compensation series in each grade, the extent of overlap permissible between adjoining compensation grades and the difference between the midpoints of grades.

When the compensation structure has been finalised, it has to pass its greatest test:

- Is it understandable?
- Is it logically defensible?
- Is it executable?
- Is it acceptable?
- Is it fair?

Finally it can be pointed out that compensation will certainly be an important subject of discussion in the new South Africa, second only to affirmative action.

12.7 CONCLUSION

The aim of compensation management is to establish and maintain a reasonable and fair compensation structure. Conflict about the compensation linked to each job may arise between employees, shareholders, consumers and other groups, and there may be a conflict of interests between individuals and groups. A successful compensation programme succeeds in balancing these conflicts and interests so that all those involved are satisfied, or dissatisfaction is limited to the minimum.

Compensation management is concerned with the financial aspects of needs, motivation and compensation. The starting point of a compensation programme is the compensation structure, where a price is linked to the job structure in terms of real earnings or wages. This excludes overtime pay, incentives, length of service and fringe benefits.

The various job evaluation systems that can be used to compare the value of jobs against each other have been briefly discussed in this chapter.

Questions

1. Discuss the steps that you would follow in establishing a compensation system.
2. Contrast the practical approaches to job evaluation with the traditional non-quantitative methods of job evaluation.
3. How would you design a compensation structure? Discuss.

Sources

Biesheuvel, S. 1985. *Work, motivation and compensation.* McGraw-Hill Book Company, Johannesburg.

Burgess, L.R. 1989. *Compensation administration.* Merrill, Columbus, Ohio.

Henderson, R.I. 1985. *Compensation management.* 4th edition. Reston Publishing, Reston, Virginia.

IPM Journal. 1988. Fact Sheets 171–3: IPM, Johannesburg.

Smit, P.J. & Cronje, G.J. de J. 1992. *Management principles: a contemporary South African edition.* Juta, Johannesburg.

Wallace, M.J. & Fay, C.H. 1988. *Compensation theory and practice.* PWS-Kent, Boston, Massachusetts.

Chapter 13

Employee benefits and services

P.D. Gerber

> **STUDY OBJECTIVES**
> After studying this chapter, you should be able to:
> - Motivate why employee benefits and services have increased in importance;
> - Differentiate between the various employee benefits and services;
> - Explain the management of an employee benefit and service programme;
> - Calculate the cost of employee benefits and services.

13.1 INTRODUCTION

Employee benefits and services have become such an important part of employees' compensation packages that it is almost unthinkable that some decades ago they were hardly considered to be part of an employee's compensation—they were really privileges and not rights. Today it is only the size and extent of the package that is negotiable, but not the "privilege".

Almost every organisation provides its employees with certain tangible benefits in addition to their basic salary cheque. These benefits are supposed to offer financial protection against contingencies such as illness, accidents, unemployment and loss of income as a result of retirement. Some benefits are also an attempt to satisfy the social and recreational needs of employees. Although benefits and services are not directly linked to higher productivity on the part of the employees, in most cases management nevertheless expects that such benefits and services should improve its recruitment, increase the morale

FIGURE 13.1: Principal learning components of employee benefits and services

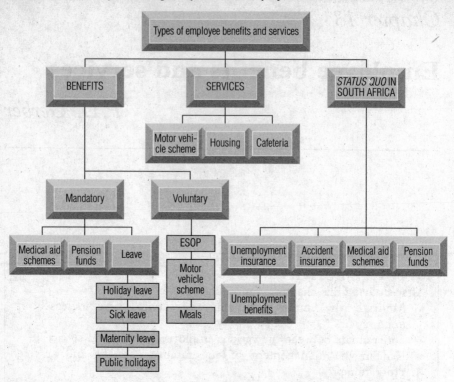

and loyalty of employees towards the organisation and reduce labour turnover and absenteeism.

Milkovich and Boudreau (1988:790) regard employee benefits as:

the indirect form of the total compensation: they include paid time away from work, insurance and health protection, employee services, and retirement income.

The increase in employee benefits and services has been particularly rapid since the Second World War. Reasons include the following:

- Changing attitudes among employers;
- Trade union demands;
- Legal requirements;
- Competition from other employers who offer improved benefits and services to attract or retain employees;
- Periodic wage control that regulates wages but then allows replacements to be appointed at higher wages.

One principle of the implementation of employee benefits should be: no employee benefit should be introduced unless there is an advantage to the organisation that is at least as great as the cost of the employee benefit.

Advantages to the organisation that arise from employee benefits are:

- More effective employment;
- Increased morale and loyalty;
- Lower labour turnover;
- Lower absenteeism;
- Better public relations;
- Reduced influence of trade unions;
- Reduced threat of government interference.

It is clear that these advantages cannot be directly measured and are mostly experienced as indirect benefits by the organisation.

Apart from the principle that the cost of an employee benefit must be at most equal to the benefit it brings the organisation, the following must be kept in mind:

- The benefit must meet a real need.
- The benefit must be aimed at activities in which a group is more effective than an individual.
- The benefit must be as widely available as possible.
- Any suggestion of paternalism in the granting and administration of benefits must be avoided.
- The cost of benefits must be calculated.
- Provision must be made for sound financing practices in the management of benefit programmes.

The following factors may influence the granting of benefits and services (Ivancevich and Glueck 1983:466):

- Government requirements as stipulated by legislation, for example unemployment insurance, accident insurance and pensions.
- Economic and labour market conditions: Under difficult economic conditions, organisations looking for the best employees will offer better benefits and services, which usually mean non-taxable income.
- The aims of management may affect these benefits and services. For example, management might strive for employee satisfaction or oppose trade unions.
- Competition can prompt an organisation to adapt or expand its benefit plans.
- The preferences or attitude of employees towards the programme: In order for benefits to increase employee satisfaction, employees must know what their benefits are and must prefer the benefits in their organisation to those offered by competitors. In addition, they must know that the benefits will satisfy their needs better than the benefits offered by competitors.

Now that these introductory remarks about employee benefits have been made, we can discuss the reasons for the growth in the number and types of employee benefits and services offered, as well as the cost and management of benefits.

13.2 REASONS FOR THE GROWTH IN EMPLOYEE BENEFITS AND SERVICES

The Depression of 1929 to 1933 was important in paving the way for the employee benefits that followed in the stronger economy of later years. Specific factors that more recently contributed towards the expansion of employee benefits include:

- *Taxation:* Most employees are only too well aware that an ever increasing part of their salary is going to the Receiver of Revenue. In addition, a rising inflation rate is pushing more employees into higher tax income brackets. This inevitably leads to employees being given an increasing number of tax-free benefits, while the employer subtracts the cost of the benefits from its own tax as a justified business expense.

- *Labour market conditions:* There is little doubt that relatively tight labour market conditions cause employers to emphasise benefits in order to attract new employees or retain existing ones. In such times, advertisements for vacancies place particular emphasis on the benefit package, which in many cases takes up half of the advertising space.

  It is important that benefits be expanded as the service period of the employee lengthens: longer holiday leave, better sick leave benefits, motor vehicle schemes, etc. This expresses recognition for service and seniority and, very important, represents a maintenance technique for retaining the services of the employee.

- *Insurance costs:* Increases in the cost of medical treatment, life assurance, disability schemes, pensions and other protection against loss of health or earnings have made it all the more attractive for employers to obtain insurance cover for all employees as a group. This is in any case cheaper than if individual employees acquired it themselves. The employer, and not the individual, is the logical buyer of this type of insurance service because of market forces. In most cases, insurance is offered as an employee benefit.

- *The influence of trade unions:* Trade unions undoubtedly make a contribution to improving existing benefits and introducing new ones. Their biggest contribution has been the improvement and increase in the number of benefits initiated by employers. In a country such as the USA, where trade unions are strong, their continued attempts brought about new forms of benefits, such as group motor vehicle insurance, dental services and pre-paid legal fees (Milkovich and Glueck 1985:584).

- *Changed employee needs:* As the living standard increased and the basic needs of employees were satisfied, greater emphasis was placed on alternatives such as more time to spend earnings and protection against financial losses. Employees also looked for more opportunities to satisfy their social, status and self-realisation needs. This meant more holidays, insurance of all kinds, etc. The satisfaction of higher-order needs by paying back study loans and giving bonuses and personal advice has also become more prominent.

13.3 THE VARIOUS TYPES OF EMPLOYEE BENEFITS AND SERVICES: A THEORETICAL VIEW

13.3.1 General

This section deals with the theory underlying employee benefits and services. First, attention will be given to the meaning of the two concepts, after which each will be discussed in turn.

It must be kept in mind that a compensation manager's job is only half done once wage and salary aspects have been determined. The other half is the creation of an employee benefit and service structure that will round off the total compensation package.

It must also be remembered that the benefits and service package has the same aims as the direct compensation package, i.e. it must attract potential employees and retain and motivate existing employees, but in the most cost-effective manner for the employer. The benefit structure must be complementary to the compensation structure and be planned in combination with it, with many levels of benefits. For this reason, a differentiation between benefit and service packages for ordinary employees, managers and professionals has been made for the past decade or two.

In simple terms, an employee benefit is a form of indirect compensation that is essentially financial, while services comprise employer or organisational services that are useful to employees and that can be quantified in financial terms.

To render a return for the employer, benefits and services must make a positive contribution to the employees. Benefits and services are often wrongly managed, which is why it is important that the organisation should determine what type of benefits and services the organisation's worker corps prefers and what is available. On this basis, management must decide what the organisation can afford. It must also be kept in mind that employee benefits and services are taxable.

13.3.2 Types of employee benefits

The most common benefits described in the literature are:

- Pension funds;
- Holiday leave;
- Sick leave;
- Medical aid schemes.

Some benefits are also legally compulsory. Each will be discussed in turn.

Pension funds
Pension funds have two principal aims:

- To ensure that after retirement employees have a continued source of income in order to maintain approximately the same standard of living as before;
- To delay the accumulation of income and its associated tax in order to realise income at a lower tax rate at a later stage.

Most pension funds are contributed to by both the employer and the employee. The employee's contribution is usually a percentage of gross monthly earnings. According to Wallace and Fay (1988:279) the employer's contribution is based on one of two approaches: the defined contribution plan or the defined benefit plan.

> Pensions are of particular importance in South Africa in these times. Uncertainties about a new government's policy in this regard have a direct influence on the security of thousands of employees.

In the defined contribution plan, the employer contributes a specific amount, i.e. a fixed percentage of the employee's salary. This contribution is invested monthly and on retirement, the employee receives the total amount realised. In a defined benefit plan, the employer's contribution is determined by the amount that will be necessary upon retirement. This amount is calculated by taking into account factors such as: present age of employee, years of service, present and projected compensation, expected retirement age, life expectancy and assumptions regarding expected interest rates.

Pensions are normally paid out upon retirement (for whichever reason) or death.

Payment for time not worked

Most people do not work every day of the month, but salaries are nevertheless calculated according to certain hours per day (usually eight hours) for each day of the month. This is an unwritten rule that applies in almost all countries, i.e. that employers pay employees for time worked as well as for time not worked.

In South Africa we differentiate between four types of benefits for time not worked: holiday leave, sick leave, maternity leave and public holidays.

Holiday leave

The number of days holiday leave to which an employee is entitled varies from organisation to organisation. Normally it is one day for every five days worked. It also varies between different types of industries and organisations. The "days" in question are a bone of contention. At some organisations, a weekend day counts as a holiday, while others exclude it. It may also vary according to the years of service and seniority in the organisation. In general, it may be said that it varies between 21 and 28 workdays of leave per year.

Sick leave

Organisations allocate a certain number of paid workdays as sick leave days to protect employees against loss of income. This applies to both hourly and monthly paid employees. However, each type of institution has its own policy, which has to meet the requirements of legislation in this regard.

Maternity leave
Every female employee, whether married or unmarried, is entitled to maternity leave. Once again the period and requirements vary from organisation to organisation. However, the law sets certain guidelines within which an organisation's policy on maternity leave must be formulated.

Public holidays
There are at present 11 public holidays to which employees are entitled. Employees who have to work on such days are usually entitled to overtime pay. The public holidays are listed in table 13.1.

TABLE 13.1: Public holidays in 1994

Public holiday	Date
New Year's Day	1 January
Good Friday	1 April
Family Day	4 April
Founders' Day	6 April
Workers' Day	1 May
Ascension Day	12 May
Republic Day	31 May
Kruger Day	10 October
Day of the Vow	16 December
Christmas Day	25 December
Day of Goodwill	26 December

There are other public holidays for certain religious groups. Organisations usually grant employees who belong to such religious groups their holidays.

Flexible benefit plans (cafeteria benefit plans)
Traditional benefit plans are not flexible enough to meet the present needs of employees. Traditionally employees received a single plan in which basic benefits such as pension and insurance are provided, irrespective of the career stage of the employees or of their different needs. During the past few years, however, organisations have begun to address the changing needs of employees. This led to the introduction of the so-called *cafeteria plans* or *flexible benefit plans* which grant employees a certain degree of freedom to select benefits that satisfy their specific needs.

ESOP (employee share option plan)
ESOP is a new employee benefit that has made its appearance in the past decade or two. According to Wallace and Fay (1988:280), there are two principal types of ESOP:

269

- *The share bonus plan*: In this case a trust is created for employees and the organisation transfers some of its own shares to the benefit of its employees. These shares grow and upon retirement the employee is entitled to the shares or their cash value. The employee makes a monthly contribution to the trust by buying company shares whose value may vary between 10% and 15% of the employee's monthly gross salary. The employee's benefit is not subject to tax until retirement, resignation or dismissal.
- *The lever plan* is similar to the above, except that the trust can incur debt to purchase company shares. The company guarantees the loan and also contributes cash to the loan.

There are a number of benefits for organisations that use ESOPs instead of the usual pension funds. The most important are:

- There is no decrease in working capital, as payment is made in company shares.
- Employee motivation and employee retention are promoted, as employees feel that they have a share in the company.

13.4 THE *STATUS QUO* OF EMPLOYEE BENEFITS AND SERVICES IN SOUTH AFRICA [1]

13.4.1 Introduction

Some employee benefits are controlled by legislation, such as unemployment and accident insurance. On the other hand, there are employee benefits that the employer can voluntarily offer employees. In this section we take a closer look at the various employee benefits that are mandatory in South Africa and at those that are voluntary.

13.4.2 Mandatory employee benefits

13.4.2.1 Unemployment insurance [2]

Introduction

The Unemployment Insurance Fund was established in terms of the Unemployment Insurance Act of 1946, which came into effect on 1 January 1947 and was then replaced on 1 January 1967 with the Unemployment Insurance Act, Act 30 of 1966. The income from the fund, which stood at R1 563 million in 1993, is primarily derived from the contributions of employees in terms of the Act. Contributions from some 193 000 employers and an annual contribution of at most R7 million by the state, plus interest on investments, are the other sources of income (Unemployment Insurance Fund 1993:7).

---

[1] This section has been adapted from Gerber, P.D. 1991. *Indiensneming: 'n praktiese handleiding*, pp. 44–82, Juta, Cape Town, with permission from the publishers.
[2] Based on Information sheets UP100 and UF25 and adapted, with permission from the Unemployment Insurance Commissioner of the Department of Manpower.

The law

The law makes provision for the insurance of employees who contribute to the fund against the risk of a loss of earnings arising from unemployment as a result of termination of service, illness or pregnancy. It also makes provision for payments to female contributors who adopt children and for payments to dependants of deceased contributors. Subject to the conditions, contributors or their dependants are entitled to the prescribed benefits. A married woman who becomes unemployed is entitled to benefits even if her husband is working.

The Unemployment Insurance Fund

The Unemployment Insurance Fund was established to make provision for the payment of benefits and grants to contributors, and for payments to dependants of deceased contributors, as well as to cover the necessary administrative costs. The law authorises employers to deduct employees' contributions from their earnings.

Unemployment benefits

When a contributor becomes unemployed, he or she must immediately register for work, irrespective of whether he or she is in possession of a contributor's report card. If the contributor cannot be placed in a job, he or she can apply for benefits by filling in an application form and handing in his or her contributor's report card.

Unemployment benefits are paid to contributors who are unemployed, provided they are both able to work and available for work, reside in South Africa and have been employed for at least 13 weeks during the 52 weeks before the beginning of the period of unemployment, with or without contributions to the fund. A maximum of one week's benefits is payable for each four-week period of service completed.

Sick benefits

Sick benefits are paid to contributors who are unemployed or who, although their service contracts have not been terminated, are receiving less than one third of their earnings, either in cash or in kind, from their employers as a result of any medically recognised illness, complex of symptoms or condition with regard to which the person in question requires medical treatment in the interests of his or her well-being. Alcoholism and drug dependence are only regarded as medically recognised for the duration of the period that the person in question is admitted to and treated for alcoholism or drug dependence at a recognised, registered rehabilitation centre or state psychiatric hospital. Alcoholics and drug addicts are therefore not entitled to benefits except during treatment at such centres.

Sick benefits are not payable to a contributor whose illness is the result of his or her own misconduct or who unreasonably refuses or fails to undergo medical treatment.

271

Military service

A contributor who is carrying out uninterrupted service or is receiving uninterrupted training in any part of the South African Defence Force (with the exception of the Permanent Force) or the Reserve, in accordance with the intention of the Defence Act of 1957, is regarded as a contributor who was employed for the qualifying 13 weeks referred to above.

Maternity benefits

Like unemployment benefits, maternity benefits are calculated at the rate of 45% of the weekly scale of earnings last received by the applicant as a contributor. Maternity benefits may be paid to a contributor who is unemployed during her pregnancy and confinement, but only for a maximum period of 26 weeks from the beginning of her period of unemployment, irrespective of whether she is able to work or available for work.

Payments to dependants of deceased contributors

An amount equal to a maximum of 26 weeks' benefits may be paid to the dependant of a deceased contributor, calculated at 45% of the weekly scale of earnings last received by the deceased as a contributor. The number of weeks payable depends on the period of service of the deceased as a contributor and on the benefits already paid to him or her.

Conclusion

Unemployment insurance is an important statutory fringe benefit which requires careful administration by the employer to ensure that it is used for the well-being of its employees. The extent of the activities of the fund illustrates the importance of this instrument, particularly in recent times.

13.4.2.2 Accident insurance

Introduction

In terms of the Workmen's Compensation Act (Act 30 of 1941), all employers operating a business are obliged to contribute towards the Workmen's Compensation Fund to make provision for mandatory insurance cover against loss of earnings as a result of the disability or death of an employee caused by an accident while on duty or by a contagious disease contracted during the execution of his or her duties.

Any person with employees (including female employees and minors) and with the aim to operate a business must contribute to the fund.

The law makes provision for the creation of a compensation fund controlled by the Workmen's Compensation Commissioner. Contributions are calculated on the basis of the risk of injury on duty in the industry in question. It must be emphasised that contributions to the fund are paid only by employers and not by employees.

Types of disability

There are three forms of disability for which a claim can be instituted against the Workmen's Compensation Fund:

- *Temporary partial disability:* This applies to employees who are able to work, but only part-time or in a job for which the compensation is lower than what they had received before the accident. If such a person is declared temporarily partially disabled, he or she will only receive a *pro rata* payment from the fund.

- *Temporary total disability:* In this case employees are entirely unable to work while they receive treatment for their injuries. After a period of convalescence, they will, however, be able to return to their normal work without being permanently disabled. Periodic payments from the fund are made to such temporarily disabled employees until they are able to return to their normal duties.

- *Permanent disability:* Permanent disability does not necessarily mean that an employee is declared disabled to such an extent that he or she cannot return to work at all. If he or she should, for example, lose a finger, compensation will be paid from the fund for the period in which he or she was absent from work. If he or she should return to work after a period of convalescence, the degree of disability will be determined. If the disability should be less than 30%, the employee will receive a lump sum to compensate for his or her disability. If disability is determined at more than 30%, such an employee will receive a life-long pension, apart from any other compensation that he or she might receive if he or she returns to work.

13.4.3 Voluntary employee benefits

13.4.3.1 Pension benefits

Introduction

An employer that makes provision in its conditions of service for the payment of pension benefits to employees when they reach the normal retirement age is making a meaningful contribution to the security and stability of the employee corps. The effectiveness of the organisation is promoted by the orderly retirement of senior personnel, thus creating opportunities for the promotion of younger, dynamic employees. In addition, the employer is absolved of its moral responsibility to care for the widow and children of an employee who has died before retirement, or an employee who becomes disabled during his or her period of service.

Pension benefits can be offered in the form of pension funds, provident funds or benefit funds.

Pension funds

There are two types of pension funds, i.e. private pension funds (or self-administered funds) and insured pension funds. In the case of private funds, the emphasis is on self-administration, which indicates that the fund makes its own investments. Insured funds are operated exclusively through insurance policies, which means that all the assets of the fund are kept by one or more registered insurers. It is important to note that this differentiation refers to the company that handles the investment of the fund's assets and not to the everyday administration of the fund.

- *Private funds* are administered by trustees, aided by specialists who supply actuarial, legal and investment expertise. Most of these trustees are normally appointed by the employer so that it keeps effective control.
- *Insured funds* function according to an agreement that details the arrangements between the employer and the members. The benefits are insured by life assurance policies. It has recently become common to issue a single master policy that covers the entire scheme. This policy is essentially a contract between the employer and the underwriting life assurance company. Contributions are paid in the form of premiums, and the benefits are payable in accordance with the agreement. The administrative functions are mainly carried out by the life assurance company.

13.4.3.2 *Medical aid schemes*
Introduction
The aim of a medical aid scheme is to establish a fund from member contributions and donations to make provision for assistance to members and their dependants in the payment of medical costs. These costs include medical, paramedical, nursing, surgical and dental services, the supply of medicines, and admission to a hospital or nursing institution. In this way provision is made for an important fringe benefit to employees.

The creation of a medical aid scheme
In terms of the Medical Aid Schemes Act, Act 72 of 1967 (as amended), a medical aid scheme can be established if a minimum number of 2 500 members are registered. In addition, the employer must deposit R500 000 in a bank account and provide a bank guarantee for a further R500 000. These financial requirements are set to ensure that the medical aid scheme begins on a sound financial footing.

Before a medical aid scheme is registered with the Registrar of Medical Aid Schemes, the employer is required to submit a set of rules according to which it intends to operate the medical aid scheme. Among other things, this set of rules must make detailed provision for the following (Registrar of Medical Aid Schemes):

- *Membership:* Membership of the scheme must be a condition of service and must be mandatory for all employees. A female employee whose husband is a member of a medical scheme with which she is registered as a dependant may not become a member of the scheme. A child under 16 may not be a member without the approval of a parent or guardian. A married female member will be regarded as a single member and can only claim benefits for herself, unless she nominates dependants who are accepted by the Committee of Medical Aid Schemes. Specific requirements are also stipulated with regard to pensioners and the widows of deceased members.

- *The liability of the employer and employee:* The liability of the employer is limited to the amount of its unpaid contributions or subsidies. The liability of an employee is limited to the amount of his or her unpaid contributions, together with any amount that has been paid on behalf of him or her or of dependants by the scheme, and which has not yet been paid back to the scheme by him or her. Any amount that the member owes the scheme may be deducted from the employee's salary by the employer.

13.4.4 Other employee benefits and services

In the *Guide for employers with regard to income tax on fringe benefits and allowances* of the Department of Finance, nine taxable benefits are identified, and it is detailed how to determine the cash equivalent of the value of each benefit. The benefits are briefly described.

Obtaining an asset at less than its actual value

Assets (with the exception of cash) are not regarded as taxable benefits under the following circumstances:

- An asset that has been received as an award for bravery;
- An asset that has been received for safe work in a dangerous occupation or for long-term service, provided this asset does not cost the employer more than R2 000;
- Fuel or lubricants used for a company vehicle, the private use of which has been calculated as a taxable benefit;
- Meals, refreshments, lodging, fuel, power or water that have been calculated as taxable benefits;
- Commercial stocks that the employee has obtained by exercising his or her rights to them.

The use of a motor vehicle

The value of private use by the employee of a motor vehicle that has been supplied to him or her by the employer is a taxable benefit if it is more than the compensation that the employee pays for the private use of the vehicle. The Income Tax Act gives various examples of how the tax is calculated on vehicles made available to employees, for example where the employee carries the full cost of fuel and the maintenance of the vehicle, or where he or she pays a portion of the purchase price.

Meals and refreshments

Meals and refreshments that are supplied free of charge by the employer, or at a price that is lower than their value, are regarded as taxable benefits. However, no taxable value is assigned to the following:

- Meals or refreshments that an employer supplies to employees in a canteen, cafeteria or dining room operated on the business premises that is mainly or entirely for the benefit of employees;
- Meals or refreshments that an employer provides for employees during business hours or on a special occasion;
- Meals or refreshments that the employee enjoys together with someone whom he or she is entertaining on behalf of the employer.

13.4.5 Conclusion

Employee benefits form an important part of the compensation package negotiated between the employer and the employee. It is therefore important that the employer be informed of the legal requirements with regard to mandatory fringe benefits such as unemployment insurance and accident insurance. The employer must also be aware of the legal stipulations regarding voluntary fringe benefits such as pension benefits, medical aid schemes and others that are made available to employees by their employers almost as a matter of course in the modern business environment.

13.5 THE COST OF EMPLOYEE BENEFITS AND SERVICES

When an employer wants to compare the cost of benefits and services with those of competitors or the industry as a whole, the following four aspects form the best basis for comparison:

- The total annual cost of benefits for all employees;
- The cost of benefits per employee per year (total cost divided by the number of employees);
- The cost as a percentage of the wage statement (total cost of benefits divided by annual wage amount);
- The cost per employee per hour (cost per employee per year divided by the number of hours worked).

Milkovich and Boudreau (1988:818) propose a mechanism for cost analysis using the following steps:

- The internal costs of all the benefits and services for the organisation are analysed for each wage statement classification and profit centre.
- The cost of benefits to the organisation are compared with external norms. For example, the cost of the entire benefit package to the organisation, or the cost of each benefit may be compared to average costs for the industry.
- A report is prepared for the decision-maker in which the previous two steps are compared to each other.
- The costs of the programme to employees are analysed. It is determined what every employee pays for benefits as a whole and for each benefit.

- The data in the previous step are compared with external data.
- An analysis is carried out of how satisfied the employees are with the employer's benefit programme and how they evaluate it in comparison with what competitors offer.

An analysis such as this should provide valuable information to enable management to take decisions that are of strategic importance as well as cost-effective. Management must consistently apply the principle of cost benefit analysis, particularly because the cost of benefits can be astronomical. Fiorello's anecdote (Ivancevich and Glueck 1983:484) emphasises this fact: a robber appears in the paymaster's office and demands: "Never mind the payroll, bud. Just hand over the welfare and pension funds, the group insurance premiums and the withheld taxes." With the cost of benefits increasing twice as fast as wages, the robber's words are perfectly understandable.

It is important that management should be aware of the various strategies available to counteract the rapidly rising costs of benefits and services. These strategies include sharing the costs with employees, self-insurance, the re-employment of employees, negotiation with regard to expenditure, and flexible benefits.

- *Part-payment benefit plans* require employees to pay part of the costs of benefits, for example a portion of the premiums of the medical aid scheme. Effective communication with employees is a prerequisite for operating such a scheme. An increase in the contributions expected from employees may be counterproductive for the long-term relations between the employee and the employer.
- *Self-insurance* involves the establishment of an own internal fund, for example to pay for medical expenses, instead of the employees belonging to an external medical fund. Organisations usually make use of reliable statistics to determine their budget for actual medical expenditure. By comparing this expenditure with the cost of membership of a medical fund, a well-founded decision about the best alternative can be taken.
- *The re-employment of employees* is a cost-saving strategy that can be of particular value for small organisations. According to this strategy, all the employees are dismissed and immediately rehired by a personnel agency. The agency then carries out the personnel functions of employment, training and compensation. This relieves the organisation of additional expenditure. Because the personnel agency renders this service to a large number of employers, it can offer a better benefit package to employees than the individual small employer could.
- *Negotiations for benefits* can take various forms. An increasing number of employers negotiate special tariffs with hospitals, laboratories and chemists on behalf of their employees.
- *Flexible benefits* are based on the principle that the preferences and needs of employees differ. Furthermore, this approach acknowledges that em-

ployees can best judge whether they are getting real value for their money and which benefits meet their personal needs. The strategy of management may thus be to make certain minimum benefits available, and then to provide additional benefits to employees who desire them and are prepared to pay for them.

It must be emphasised that an effective communication programme is a prerequisite for operating an effective benefit and service programme. Employees must be kept informed about how such programmes work and how the costs are calculated.

13.6 THE MANAGEMENT OF A PROGRAMME OF EMPLOYEE BENEFITS AND SERVICES

It is important to take the following facts into account when management takes decisions about the costs of fringe benefits:

- There is at present little proof that benefits and services really improve performance.
- There is also little proof that benefits and services necessarily increase the job satisfaction of employees.
- The cost of employee benefits and services is increasing dramatically.
- Employers are obliged by law to establish certain programmes (unemployment insurance, accident insurance, etc.).
- The voluntary programmes come under pressure from trade unions, competitors and industries constantly to make better benefits and services available to employees.

By keeping these aspects in mind, management can nevertheless institute an effective benefit and service programme by carefully following four important steps.

Step 1

The objectives and strategy are spelled out. There are three main strategies that can be followed in the benefit programme:

- The pacesetter strategy by which the organisation is the first to offer the benefits desired by employees.
- The comparable benefits strategy by which the organisation adapts its benefits to those offered by other similar organisations.
- The minimum benefits strategy by which the organisation only offers the benefits required by law, plus those on which employees insist and that are cheapest.

Before management decides what specific benefits and services to offer, it must first set objectives that tally with the envisaged strategy.

Step 2

Participants and trade unions are involved in decisions about employee benefits and services.

Apart from the specific strategy to be followed, it is important to ask those involved in the programme exactly which benefits and services they require. Top management must guard against deciding on its own what benefits employees desire: without their inputs, the benefit decision can never be effective enough. The so-called cafeteria approach can be meaningfully used here. All the employees are informed about the funds available for benefit plans after provision has been made for the programmes required by law and for minimum health benefits. The employees can then individually choose to receive cash or decide what services they would like to have. By involving the employees in this decision, the effectiveness of decisions about the implementation of benefit programmes is increased. The fact that employees know how much is spent on such programmes also has a positive influence in most cases.

Step 3
Communicate effectively about benefits and services. An effective communication programme is another way in which the effectiveness of the programme can be increased. It is very important that employees know to which benefits and services they are entitled and exactly how these programmes work. Numerous media can be used for this purpose, for example employee guides, newsletters, notice boards, annual reports, films, cassettes and meetings with supervisors and employees.

Step 4
The costs are carefully monitored. Apart from the consideration of the type of benefit or service to be offered, management must see to it that the chosen programmes are effectively administered. An example would be the conscientious handling of medical claims, or limiting wastage in the cafeteria through careful purchasing and control. The use of a computer for administrative procedures may result in savings and greater effectiveness.

13.7 CONCLUSION
Employee benefits and services offer employees financial protection against a variety of risks such as illness, accidents, unemployment and loss of income as a result of retirement. These tangible benefits are offered over and above the basic wage or salary. The management of these benefits requires particular knowledge and skill. Although these benefits and services are not directly linked to higher productivity, they nevertheless contribute towards increasing the morale, supporting the recruitment effort, increasing loyalty towards the organisation and decreasing labour turnover.

Questions
1. Write an essay about the various types of employee benefits known to you.
2. Describe how you would set about managing an employee benefit and service programme.
3. Why do you think employee benefits are so important in an organisation?

Sources

Ivancevich, J.M. & Glueck, W.F. 1983. *Foundations of personnel/human resource management.* Business Publications, Plano, Texas.

Milkovich, G.T. & Boudreau, J.W. 1988. *Personnel/human resource management.* 5th edition. Business Publications, Plano, Texas.

Milkovich, G.T. & Glueck, W.F. 1985. *Personnel/human resource management: a diagnostic approach.* 4th edition. Business Publications, Plano, Texas.

Registrar of Medical Aid Schemes: Internal manual. *Measures for medical aid schemes.*

Unemployment Insurance Fund. 1993. *Annual Report,* p. 7.

Wallace, M.J. & Fay, C.H. 1988. *Compensation theory and practice.* PWS-Kent, Boston, Massachusetts.

Chapter 14

Quality of work life and social responsibility

P.S. Nel and P.S. van Dyk

STUDY OBJECTIVES

After studying this chapter, you should be able to:

- Explain the course of development of the quality of work life;
- Motivate why organisations should be involved in programmes to improve the quality of work life;
- Describe what the quality of work life is;
- Explain the relation between social responsibility and basic human rights;
- Differentiate between various social responsibility projects;
- Show the nature of the interaction between human resources management and social responsibility.

14.1 INTRODUCTION

In modern society, people and organisations encounter rapid change which they have to take into consideration to achieve their goals. Today people are the focal point of an organisation, as we have stated repeatedly in this book. During the past few decades, people have increasingly become the centre of activities, to the extent that organisations today make people their main consideration internally and externally. Internally the quality of work life is enhanced to bring about job satisfaction and increased productivity. Externally social responsibility is the means for an organisation to give recognition to the people in the environment in which it operates and makes profits.

FIGURE 14.1: Principal learning components of quality of work life and social responsibility

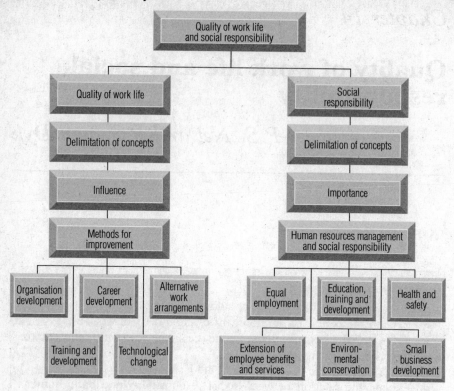

In this chapter the two facets of an organisation's focus on people are approached from a macro point of view. Quality of work life is analysed in the first section, and social responsibility in the second.

Enhancing the quality of work life and social responsibility are regarded as a maintenance function of an organisation towards its employees. In the job context environment it plays an important role in the creation of an achievement orientation among employees, and this also manifests itself in the job content environment.

14.2 INTEREST IN THE QUALITY OF WORK LIFE

To understand the present interest in the quality of work life, and to appreciate its significance, it is necessary to take a brief look at the historical development of human resources management, along with the parallel development of management philosophy, and therefore management styles.

Traditionally managers have been regarded as those people who knew best what employees had to do and what their needs and commitments were without expecting any questioning or interpretation on the part of the employees. Coleman (1979:439) provides an excellent example of this approach in his quotation of the President of the Philadelphia and Reading Rail Road in America, summarising his organisation's policy at the beginning of the century:

The rights and interest of laboring men will be respected and cared for . . . by the Christian men to whom God in his infinite wisdom gave control of the property interests of this country.

Employees had no say in the management of organisations. This attitude is also apparent in the management approach advocated by Taylor and his contemporaries later in this century, which regarded the employee as merely a machine in the organisation, who did not have to think at all. This management approach was adapted somewhat in the 1930s when the Hawthorne experiments showed that good human relations resulted in increased productivity, that people could be motivated and that pleasant working conditions could increase productivity. Management control was emphasised in the fact that, although labour unions were allowed in the public service, managements of state departments could still make operational decisions without consulting employees or their labour union representatives.

As for employees, for the greater part of this century they were expected to obey orders. Intensive training, strict supervision and even incentives were merely aimed at inducing submissiveness. Strict discipline and regimentation were the norm in the industrial environment, which functioned in accordance with a complex system of rules indicating exactly when an employee had to work, how fast he or she had to work and how much had to be accomplished within a set time. Consequently the work was narrowly defined and employees exercised few skills in the execution of their tasks.

The job as such was nothing but a means to earn a living.

One may therefore conclude that, under the traditional system, managers were in control and employees accepted this control unquestioningly. If an employee earned a reasonable salary, his or her living conditions, and therefore the quality of work life, were pleasant.

Little consideration was given to the causes of job alienation resulting in frustration and negative attitudes among employees. Alienation at work made employees feel powerless, without any means of questioning management's policy or the organisation's rules. Work lacked meaning because employees experienced no sense of fulfilment from the goods they produced or from the services they rendered. Employees were isolated because they had to work on their own and there was little social contact between them. The job itself was boring and gave little satisfaction.

However, these things came to be realised, and behavioural scientists concentrated on this field of study during the late 1950s and early 1960s. Maslow's work in this respect is of particular interest. He pointed out that human behaviour is motivated by physiological needs and the need for security, affection, esteem and self-actualisation. Herzberg's research indicated that work can result in personal satisfaction if it leads to a feeling of achieving one's objectives, development and self-actualisation. McGregor showed with his Theory X and Theory Y that traditional leadership styles in organisations needed to be adapted, that management should be based on employee participation, and that employees need challenging work. As a result of this research, much more serious efforts were made to make employees' work more interesting, to assist them in obtaining the right equipment to do their work, to provide more information on the work, to grant employees more authority in doing their work and to afford them the opportunity to learn special skills.

The present-day approach to the quality of work life advocates that work should be made more meaningful, that employees need to develop personal skills, that they should participate in the management process, and that the control of any system should be voluntary rather than mandatory. For this reason, methods such as quality circles and job enrichment are enjoying considerable attention today.

Interest in the quality of work life was therefore generated because employees are often frustrated in their work and experience little job satisfaction. They then begin to experience work stress and their health is affected. Various researchers have found that job satisfaction is essential if employees are to be happy and enjoy a long life. On the other hand, lack of recognition, uninteresting work, poor relationships with colleagues, poor working conditions and stress in the work situation cause job dissatisfaction (as indicated in chapter 24).

In the 1980s there was renewed interest in employees in their work environment, and in health and safety. This is particularly noticeable in the South African labour context, where a series of acts with regard to health, safety, training, and so on, were promulgated to improve the quality of work life. Furthermore, there has been a move towards improving career development (as discussed in chapter 9) because an increasing number of highly skilled employees are subject to stress, or face the possibility of retrenchment. As pointed out in chapters 21 and 22, training and development enable employees to experience greater job satisfaction, and this results in higher productivity, reduced labour turnover, reduced absenteeism and a better worker corps. It is thus clear why interest in the quality of work life has increased dramatically in the past few decades.

What determines the quality of work life? What characterises an organisation that does not merely pay lip service to the quality of work life? We shall now discuss these issues.

14.3 WHAT IS THE QUALITY OF WORK LIFE?

Chris Argyris, one of the best known authors on management science and human resources management of the past few decades, conducted in-depth research into the emotional state of employees in the work situation. He came to the conclusion that organisations that afforded employees more freedom and encouraged them to use their initiative functioned better and their employees experienced more job satisfaction. This formed the basis for improving the quality of work life in organisations. The quality of work life may be explained as follows: if a person wrote down the characteristics of the worst organisation he or she had ever worked for, and then the characteristics of the best organisation he or she had ever worked for, the differences would reflect his or her quality of work life in each organisation. The worst organisation would probably have been characterised by autocratic leadership, absence of team-work, lack of trust, lack of commitment, victimisation, discrimination and discourteous behaviour. The best organisation would probably have been characterised by good communication, team effort, challenging work and equal and fair treatment. From a behavioural point of view, job satisfaction is very important to the employee.

A definition by Kast and Rosenzweig (1985:652) of the quality of work life is as follows:

Quality of work life is a way of thinking about people, work and organizations. Its distinctive elements are (1) a concern about the impact of work on people as well as on organizational effectiveness, and (2) the idea of participation in organizational problem solving and decision making.

The core of this concept therefore is people and their work, and what management can do to create an environment for employees in which they can be both satisfied and motivated to perform well.

In view of this definition, Snyman (1990:96–138) maintains that the quality of work life is different at various levels in an organisation.

For low-level workers, it might mean a fair day's pay for a fair day's work, safe working conditions and possibly a supervisor who treats them fairly. Young managers, on the other hand, might see quality of work life arising from opportunities for development, creative tasks and a successful career from which they derive job satisfaction. In other words, in order to enhance the quality of work life, an organisation has to take into account each employee's needs and values, and the extent to which these needs are being satisfied and these values conformed to. The organisation will have to become involved in activities aimed at satisfying needs regarded as important by employees. At the same time, the goals of the organisation and of employees should be synchronised, for example through career development and training. Quality of work life can be high only if both the needs of the employee and the needs of the organisation are satisfied.

According to Walton (in Gordon 1983:658–61) the quality of work life has eight components:

- *Sufficient and fair compensation:* This means enough pay, fringe benefits and other remuneration to enable the employee to maintain an acceptable standard of living.
- *Safe and healthy working conditions:* These apply to the physical and mental work environment of the employee. In South Africa labour legislation has been drastically improved in this respect.

285

- *Development of human resources:* This includes training and development.
- *Security and growth in the organisation:* This includes the opportunity to acquire new tasks and skills, as well as a career within the organisation.
- *Social interaction:* The organisation should create the opportunity for social interaction among employees and should follow a policy of equal opportunities, disallowing discrimination on the basis of race, colour, etc.
- *Constitutionalisation in the work environment:* This includes the right to privacy and freedom of speech in the organisation, as well as the protection of all employee rights in terms of the Labour Relations Act. Employees are to enjoy dignity and respect, and are to be treated like adults in the work environment.
- *Total "lebensraum":* This depends on the balance between an employee's working time and his or her family life, that is, whether he or she has enough leisure time outside of work to spend with his or her family.
- *Social relevance of the job:* This is based on the principle that an employee's job should be to the benefit of all in the organisation and in the community, for example maintaining decent standards in the marketing and production of goods.

It is obvious, therefore, that the quality of work life is affected by all facets of the employee's functioning in the organisation. Effective utilisation of an employee and his or her satisfaction in the job are essential if a high quality of work life is to be maintained in an organisation.

The effect of the quality of work life on human resources management
Good quality of work life may influence human resources management in an organisation in various ways. The following are examples:
- *Job analysis:* Placing employees with the necessary skills and aptitude in appropriate jobs where they will be able to render their best performance.
- *Selection:* Placing the right person in the right job, so that employees will be satisfied and motivated.
- *Job evaluation:* Ensuring that wages are commensurate with jobs in the organisation, especially with regard to similar jobs.
- *Health and safety:* A safe working environment and consideration for the health of employees are vitally important to good quality of work life.
- *Grievance procedure:* Effective grievance and disciplinary procedures will protect the rights and dignity of employees, which will contribute to good quality of work life.

These are but a few examples of ways in which human resources managers can influence the quality of work life of their employees. The result is increased employee satisfaction and improved performance because of intrinsic motivation, recognition of worth, interesting work and opportunities for promotion and development in the work situation.

The benefits that an organisation derives from adopting this approach are a lower cost structure, higher quality employees, reduced labour turnover and reduced absenteeism. Benefits to be experienced by employees are growth in the organisation, more participation in decision-making, a feeling of self-actualisation, satisfaction, security and high self-esteem.

The methods to improve the quality of work life in an organisation are discussed below.

14.4 METHODS TO IMPROVE THE QUALITY OF WORK LIFE

Various methods may be used to improve the quality of work life in an organisation. These methods focus on aspects such as management and supervisory style, opportunities for decision-making, job satisfaction and a satisfactory physical work environment, safety, satisfactory working hours and meaningful tasks. This entails programmes in the task and work environment aimed at satisfying as many of the employees' needs as possible. A few methods are described below.

14.4.1 Organisation development

Organisation development as such is not a method to improve the quality of work life, but in its implementation various skills may be taught which contribute to the quality of work life, such as team building, sensitivity training and behaviour modelling, as discussed in chapter 22. Methods not covered in chapter 22 are now discussed in detail.

Quality circles

Quality circles consist of groups of employees who frequently meet with their supervisors to identify production problems and recommend plans of action for the solution of these problems. Recommendations are usually submitted to management and approved plans are implemented with employee participation.

Quality circles are a work team approach used in organisations to improve the quality of work life. A circle usually consists of between five and ten specially trained employees who meet with their supervisors for about an hour a week to solve the problems in their field. The members of the circle usually belong to a group that works together on the production of a specific component or product.

For a quality circle programme to succeed there must be clear objectives; the programme must be supported by top management; the organisational culture must accommodate participative management; employees involved must know the objectives of the organisation; when the programme is implemented for the first time, a section consisting of enthusiastic and co-operative employees should be used to form the quality circle; the programme must be strictly voluntary; participants must receive sufficient training; and the programme must be introduced slowly, with gradual progression.

Management by objectives

This method also emphasises participative management and has in the past been termed a management philosophy. Management by objectives employs the setting of agreed objectives by superiors and subordinates as the basis of motivation, evaluation and control. Management by objectives is based on three psychological principles, namely the setting of objectives, feedback and participation. The setting of objectives involves employees as well as supervisors, and this means that employees are well aware of what they have to do and how well they have to do it. Clear objectives also enable workers and supervisors to be compensated according to goal achievement. This is possible because there is feedback on performance which, if positive, in turn motivates employees. Timeous, relevant and specific feedback satisfies employees' need to know where they stand in their work and with their supervisors. Since this involves participation to some extent, employees experience job satisfaction and their higher-order needs are satisfied. This leads to improved performance and therefore increased job satisfaction.

Management by objectives may be regarded as the main predecessor of quality of work life improvement methods and techniques, since employees are afforded the opportunity to make job-related decisions; they then receive feedback on their performance and the extent to which they are attaining their objectives, while participating in decisions affecting them.

Management by objectives has six basic steps:

- Setting the goals of the organisation;
- Setting the goals of the department where the employee works;
- Discussing departmental goals with the head of the department;
- Specifying expected results, which includes the setting of individual objectives by the employee;
- Reviewing performance and measuring results;
- Supplying positive feedback from time to time between superior and subordinates.

Job enrichment

Job enrichment is aimed at satisfying the various psychological needs of employees. Job enrichment may be defined as the purposeful restructuring of a job to make it more challenging, meaningful and interesting for an employee. It is assumed that the employee is able to do the job at a higher level, at which he or she carries more responsibility, and will react positively to the opportunity of functioning at a higher level. An employee must however be motivated to function effectively at a higher level. Applying job enrichment programmes broadly in an organisation is an important adjunct to organisation development, and a way of improving the quality of work life. For an employee to react favourably to job enrichment, the following conditions are necessary:

- The job must offer variety, which means that a number of different skills will be used.
- Employees must understand the job in its entirety.
- The job must be meaningful so that employees feel they are performing an important task.

- Employees must have independence and freedom so that they can take their own decisions in the job.
- There must be feedback on the job they are doing.

Job enrichment may be achieved in various ways. First, work groups may be formed. Employees must feel that the section of the work they do is their own; they should be able to identify with it. Secondly, tasks may be combined so that one employee will be responsible for assembling a product from beginning to end. Thirdly, vertical loading may be instituted, which means that employees instead of an outsider will plan and control their own work. And fourthly, channels for feedback need to be introduced so that faster and better work methods can be communicated to employees without delay.

Do not confuse job enrichment with job enlargement. Job enlargement changes the scope of a job so that it offers the employee a greater variety of tasks. A problem is that employees may regard job enlargement as an attempt by management to force them to do more work without increasing their salary. This applies especially when new tasks are no more interesting or meaningful than present ones. In such a case job enlargement may have a negative effect on employees, impairing the quality of work life instead of improving it.

Participative management

This concept is widely applied in various parts of the world and has been extended to a point where employees participate in the management of organisations. In participative management, employees put forward their ideas, thus contributing to solving problems that affect the organisation. This means that employees have the opportunity to contribute to the decision-making process in the organisation. This approach is important, because managers do not have all the solutions to all problems, and employees are often better at solving problems in their own work environment.

The quality of work life of employees will be improved by participative management only if certain requirements are met:

- Employees must feel the need to participate in decision-making.
- The decisions in which they are involved should be related to their work environment.
- The organisation must be prepared to share information with employees to assist them in decision-making.
- Supervisors and managers must be prepared to allow employees to take decisions.
- There must be problems and situations that require decision-making.

Unless these requirements are met, participative management cannot be effective in the decision-making process.

Participation may be either *formal* or *informal*. When an employee participates in decision-making in his or her capacity as an individual, the term informal participation is used. Formal participation takes place when a manager and a group of subordinates participate in decision-making on issues affecting them in their specific situation.

Formal programmes in this category are quality circles, as discussed, and the process of collective bargaining, where the labour union and the organisation decide on issues. Service conditions, the promotion system, grievance procedures and disciplinary measures may be decided in this way.

Thus participation may contribute in various ways to the improvement of the quality of work life.

14.4.2 Alternative work arrangements

According to Ivancevich (1992:748–57), employers are continually trying to introduce more flexible work arrangements that will give employees more freedom of choice in their working hours. Three methods of improving the quality of work life are flexitime, part-time work and job sharing, and shorter work weeks.

- *Flexitime*: This is a method to provide flexible working hours. An employee chooses when to start and when to finish his or her jobs within the work schedule. Flexitime operates in two different ways. In the first case, employees may be expected to be at work for a certain set period of time, say from 9h00 to 15h00. For the rest of the day they may come and go as they please, provided they work the required number of hours in a working day. In the second case, employees may determine their own starting and stopping hours, for example an employee may work from 7h30 to 16h00, taking a 45-minute lunch break, which represents a full working day. In other words, each employee completes a compulsory working day of eight hours, but starts and finishes work as he or she chooses. The major benefits of flexitime are increased employee morale, reduced tardiness at work, the accommodation of working parents and a reduction in peak-hour traffic. The main disadvantages are that at times there is no supervision, key human resources are not always available and it is difficult to plan work schedules.

  Another system, termed flexiyears, is at present being developed in Europe. Under this system employees decide how many hours per month they will work for the following six months. During some months they may work much longer hours than during other months, but will still complete the prescribed average number of hours per month for the six-month period. In this way employees can plan an entire working year in advance so that it will fit in with their own programme, for example to accommodate a vacation of two months.

  Flexiplace is a further development. Employees may decide whether they would like to work at home or at the office, or at a satellite office in another part of town, or wherever it suits them best. This system is becoming increasingly popular in the USA.

- *Part-time work and job sharing*: Pensioners and working mothers, for example, who would like to work mornings only in order to have their afternoons free to attend to other matters, find part-time work attractive. If employees are able to arrange their work like this, their productivity will increase and their quality of work life will improve. Job sharing means that two people share a full-time job, with one working in the mornings and the other working in the afternoons. This may be applied especially in times of economic recession to prevent people from losing their jobs. Instead they would do less work, but would still receive an income and maintain some measure of quality of work life.

- *Shorter work weeks:* A four-day work week is becoming increasingly popular in Europe and the USA, during which employees work ten hours a day. (The concept of three-day work weeks consisting of 13-hour work days has also been mentioned.) The four-day work week is popular, especially in organisations with a major investment in capital equipment which must be kept going for as long as possible daily without stopping, for example paper and sugar mills. Shut-down time is very expensive and if the number of shut downs per week is reduced, an organisation can save considerable amounts of money. It also appears that companies with four-day work weeks show higher profit margins and reduced production costs, and employees have reduced travelling costs. There are indications, however, that a shorter work week may have a negative effect on employees' families over a long period, for example after two or three years, and causes more fatigue than a normal work week. Conclusive evidence is however not yet available.

14.4.3 Training and development
Chapters 21 and 22 contain a detailed discussion on training and development. If implemented effectively, training and development can make a significant contribution towards enhancing the quality of work life of employees.

14.4.4 Career development
Effective career development and planning are essential if employees are to experience job satisfaction and a feeling of fulfilment in their work life. Career development and planning make one of the most important contributions to improving the quality of work life (as discussed in chapter 9).

14.4.5 Technological change
As a result of rapid changes in the industrial environment, goods are produced and services rendered under increasing pressure. If pressure and the rate of technological change in an organisation are not controlled and coordinated, the quality of work life may suffer considerably. Individuals may be under stress mainly because of poor time management. This may lead to the burn-out syndrome, which is associated with stress (chapter 24 contains a detailed discussion of these aspects). It is also true that technological innovations, if

handled correctly, can contribute towards an improvement in the quality of work life.

14.5 THE EFFECTS OF QUALITY OF WORK LIFE PROGRAMMES ON AN ORGANISATION

Individuals derive great benefits from effective quality of work life programmes in an organisation, and such programmes certainly result in job satisfaction, increased productivity and reduced absenteeism. An organisation applying effective human resources management (i.e. effective recruitment, selection and maintenance of employees, as well as training and development) will of necessity provide a high quality of work life, especially if a participative and democratic management philosophy is adopted.

Just as the quality of work life is important to the internal situation of the organisation, social responsibility is important for maintaining good relations with its external environment. Aspects of social responsibility are discussed in the next section.

14.6 SOCIAL RESPONSIBILITY
14.6.1 General

Organisations have for a long time acknowledged their responsibility towards the community and the environment in which they operate. This responsibility does not end with the production of goods or the rendering of services of a high quality as required by the community, but extends into the social field. De Kock (1985:21) remarks in this respect:

> In the Middle Ages, Popes gave generously of their personal fortunes . . . In the Rotterdam era of the Dutch and in the Industrial Revolution of Britain we discern more direct, practical links between commerce as we know it and the welfare of society at large.

The social responsibility of an organisation is becoming even more important today. Organisations are expected to become involved in real social problems of the community within which they function. Therefore organisations are becoming increasingly involved in the community to show that they do not only want to use the community for personal gain, but that they want to give something back to it to ensure a better dispensation for both parties.

In the past, many organisations probably had maximum profits as their only goal. Today, however, organisations pursue multiple goals with emphasis on social awareness, social care and social commitment. Social responsibility is at present so important that the success of an organisation may depend to a large extent on it.

14.6.2 The importance of social responsibility

Various changes in applying social responsibility have taken place over the past few years, but real adjustments have been perceived since 2 February 1990, when an amended government policy was announced and organisations began to apply it.

Large organisations that had not previously had social responsibility programmes appointed full-time staff to administer funds in this regard. Social responsibility had formerly been regarded by most organisations as the task of the public relations department. Social responsibility now focuses on involvement in community programmes; separate programmes are usually launched by the public relations department. The emphasis has thus shifted to supporting an organisation's own employees and the impact that this has on the community in which they live. According to Nel (1992:27), organisations also encourage their employees to become involved in community projects by giving them time off or financial support to carry out community service. Larger organisations have also become involved in wider community programmes, as opposed to simply making available funds for some project with which they have only indirect contact.

Community upliftment programmes currently enjoy high priority in organisations. The emphasis is on community involvement and has thus shifted from corporate social responsibility to social investment, which indicates that organisations are more involved than merely making available funds. Organisations team up with the community to identify specific community needs that they want to satisfy instead of generally spending funds with only a distant involvement.

It can be expected that this approach will increasingly gain acceptance in future. In some cases, it even becomes part of the overall strategy of the organisation (Nel 1992:26):

A company's policy statement regarding social investment usually states its particular philosophy and areas of involvement, which is in accordance with the mission statement of the company. The social investment policy clearly defines the major objectives for its programmes, eg. "the creation of a just and equal society for all the people of South Africa", or "the improvement of the quality of life of all peoples of South Africa" etc.

Cronje *et al.* (1993:422–4) confirm that the social responsibility of business is increasingly coming to the fore. Nowadays the public expects an organisation to become closely involved in the social problems of the community within which it operates. One of the tasks of management is to initiate programmes to bring the corporate sense of social responsibility to the attention of the public. Management should also keep a watchful eye on any activities that might be construed by external groups as irresponsible, giving rise to resentment.

Long-term profitability cannot be attained if an organisation does not act in a socially responsible way.

Raymond Ackerman, chairman of Pick 'n Pay, says:

Profits are very, very important. They are the bloodstream of our whole economic world. But a businessman must realise his role is a much broader one and that this fabric of social responsibility is woven completely through a businessman's whole existence.

It is the duty of businessmen to make profits. However, this should not be at the cost of social responsibility.

The challenge facing management is how to marry the concepts of profit maximization and social responsibility.

Organisations determine their social investment budgets as a percentage of their pre-tax earnings. In practice, most organisations budget about 0,5% to 1% of their pre-tax earnings for social investment.

TABLE 14.1: Average social investment spending by type of programme (1990–91)

Programme	Rm	% Contri-bution
Education	554	66
Environmental conservation	59	7
Health	57	7
Welfare	51	6
General community projects	42	5
Small businesses and job creation	30	4
Arts and culture	27	3
Housing	13	1
Other	8	1
Total	**840**	**100**

Source: Nel (1992:28)

Some R840 million were spent on social investment programmes by the business sector in 1991 (Nel 1992:28). The actual expenditure is given in table 14.1. According to Cronje *et al.* (1993:424), organisations are usually reluctant to publish figures about the contributions they make to different social responsibility programmes, because there are always some people who will object to them and take offence. People who abhor boxing and wrestling, for example, will disapprove of an organisation that devotes large sums to the sponsorship of boxing, but of course boxing fans will take a different view. Shareholders are also apt to take exception to what they consider a "waste of money": they would naturally prefer a bigger dividend.

A budget is necessary for planning and control. There can be different budget allocations for the organisation's social responsibility programme:

- *Budget allocation for training of the underprivileged.* Most large organisations are well aware of the importance of training, since it is in the interests of virtually everybody. Productivity largely depends on educational levels. Since a high proportion of the population of this country is unskilled and ill-educated, training is generally regarded as a meritorious cause, and educational bodies are often supported by means of sponsorships.
- *Budget allocation for employees' welfare.* Good relations with employees are created by corporate support of educational, cultural, scientific and welfare

organisations serving employees. Housing funds, training programmes and bursaries for further studies are also offered. However, this type of financial aid is being dramatically reduced in favour of more direct support to specific community projects.

- *Budget allocation for community welfare.* Some organisations feel a social obligation to support health, welfare and cultural organisations.

The support of the community by an organisation fosters good morale and creates a higher standard of living for its staff, which can also lead to higher productivity. When it becomes known that an organisation has the welfare of its employees at heart, this creates goodwill in the labour market, and the organisation then has no difficulty attracting and keeping good workers.

Many organisations subscribe to the so-called Sullivan Code for their employees and working conditions. The stipulations entail additional expenses for the organisation, which should properly be financed from the social responsibility budget.

Most South African companies are sensitive to the criticism that they undertake corporate social responsibility programmes solely for the sake of publicity and are therefore unwilling to make details of such programmes known through the media. Two exceptions are:

- *Budget allocations for sponsorships.* Sport, recreational and community projects are often sponsored by large organisations. The object is not only to serve the community but also to get the name of the organisation mentioned in the media.
- *Budget allocations for charities.* Small sums are sometimes donated to charity out of sheer compassion, but such donations have little news value, and an organisation rarely gets any "free" publicity in that way. When the sums are very large and have news value, the cheque is usually presented to the recipient (say, the bursar of an orphanage) with a photograph of the presentation appearing in the press.

14.6.3 Basic human rights

In South Africa there can be no social responsibility without the recognition of basic human rights. With the changes that have taken place over the past few years, South Africa has also begun giving proper attention to the protection of the basic rights of the population. In this regard, proposals for a *Manifesto of basic rights* were published on 2 February 1993. South Africa has thus subscribed to internationally accepted norms, irrespective of race, colour, sex or religious conviction.

The *Manifesto of basic rights* contains three types of rights, which are briefly explained below to show how they pertain to social responsibility.

First-level rights (so-called "blue" rights)
These rights include the protection of life, freedom, property, freedom of movement, freedom of speech, privacy, the right to vote, the right to be

represented in government, to unite and to demonstrate, citizenship, not being arbitrarily detained and legal protection. These are the classic Western civil and political rights. These rights can be regarded as a primary democratic prerequisite for the ultimate effective application of social responsibility by an organisation.

Second-level rights (so-called "red" rights)

These include the right to medical services, food, housing, work, protection against unemployment, equal pay for equal work, education, free participation in the cultural life of the community and the protection of the aged.

These rights are universally known in the Western world as traditional socio-economic rights.

Organisations are already involved in correcting historical imbalances on this level. Poverty, unemployment, underdevelopment, housing and medical services are now being addressed as part of the social investment programmes of organisations; this may also be regarded as "democratic pro-active affirmative action". The South African Legal Commission (1991:13) says:

> There is not much point in telling the poor, the jobless or the illiterate that they have freedom of speech if they are dying of hunger or a treatable disease.

One must therefore begin with the basic upliftment of the disadvantaged in South Africa in order ultimately to apply social responsibility effectively.

Third-level rights (so-called "green" rights)

This is the lowest category of rights, the so-called people's rights. It includes minority rights and the right to a clean and safe environment. Organisations are also involved in this category to expand their social responsibility programmes.

Most South Africans accept that the country is undergoing a process of transformation and that the socio-economic system must be adapted. Social responsibility represents the striving of the business community for a system of equality before the law and in the workplace. For this reason the *Manifesto of basic rights* can be linked to the social responsibility of organisations.

Equal opportunities have been legally mandated by the publication of a Promotion of Equal Opportunities Draft Act in 1993, which also has an impact on social responsibility.

Equal opportunities are of vital importance because of the history of discrimination in South Africa. It can therefore be expected that organisations will be keen to redress these irregularities of the past through social responsibility and that the conventions of the International Labour Organisation will increasingly be applied.

The draft law recognises the following:

- The principle of equal value for equal work. Paragraph 3 of Convention No. 100 (ILO) determines that different rates for work of equal value is a contravention of the principle of equal compensation for equal work.

- The principle of non-discrimination against employees with family responsibilities. Paragraph 4 of Convention No. 156 determines that all possible steps should be taken to enable employees to meet their responsibilities without affecting their free choice of work, conditions of service or work security.
- The principle of equal opportunities and affirmative action. Paragraph 5 of Convention No. 111 determines that any member of the International Labour Organisation (ILO) may, after consultation with a representative employer and employee organisation, stipulate the special action to be taken to protect the needs of people with regard to gender, family responsibilities and social or cultural status in order to increase their quality of work life. An indication of differences that should not be regarded as discrimination must also be given.
- The principle of equal human dignity between people and non-discrimination on the basis of race, colour, language, sex, religious conviction, ethnic origin, social class, birth, disability and political or other convictions.
- The principle of equality between male and female employees. Special measures must protect female employees against discrimination in their dual role as economically active person and mother.

South African organisations are already moving in this direction and are taking these principles into account in their social responsibility actions. There is thus a deliberate ban on sexual harassment, discrimination against pregnant women, etc.

14.7 WHAT IS SOCIAL RESPONSIBILITY?

Social responsibility implies the utilisation of an organisation's resources in a way not required by law and not yielding direct returns. In practice it entails much more than a ritual cleansing of the corporate conscience. People in business strive for results—whether in the form of an improved image of the organisation or in the form of tangible benefits.

Definitions of social responsibility in the literature range from vague to specific. The definition preferred by the authors of this book is that of Ivancevich (1992:551):

> . . . *the awareness that business activities have an impact on society, and the consideration of that impact by firms in decision making.*

The responsibility of an organisation extends far beyond the internal maintenance of its human resources; it also has a responsibility towards human resources outside the work environment. These aspects are elaborated upon in another section of this chapter.

14.8 THE INVOLVEMENT OF ORGANISATIONS IN SOCIAL RESPONSIBILITY

Roy Pascoe, former managing director of Allied, answers the question why organisations become involved in social responsibility as follows: "Social responsibility is just as important to an organisation as the achievement of good profitability." There are also other reasons why an organisation would show social responsibility:

- *Relationship with employees:* A good relationship with employees is established if an organisation supports the educational, cultural, scientific and welfare organisations serving them. Such support results in high morale, increases the standard of living of employees and may lead to higher productivity. Rand Mines therefore believes that the quality of work life of its employees is of primary importance, and Volkswagen follows a policy of charity begins at home.

   The improvement of relationships with employees is also achieved by human resources management processes such as equal opportunities, affirmative action and health and safety programmes.

- *Relationship with the community:* An organisation cannot build a good relationship with the community on the basis of mere promises and propaganda. A good relationship is the product of responsible policy and conduct. Raymond Ackerman, chairman of Pick 'n Pay, states: "If we help the community, it will respond by helping us."

   An organisation therefore has a social commitment to support the health, welfare, educational, urban and cultural organisations in its area.

- *Educational relationships:* The low educational level of much of the South African population creates a huge educational task for all parties concerned. The social responsibility of organisations in this respect cannot be over-emphasised, but organisations realise that investment in human resources development will show a return in future. Examples of the involvement of South African organisations in education are: Burroughs makes contributions to the Urban Foundation and has launched Teacher Opportunity Programmes—a national scheme to improve the training of black teachers. Volkswagen makes contributions towards the training of apprentices, technicians, operators and managers. Anglo American continually allocates funds to secondary and tertiary education.

- *Relationships with consumers, dealers and shareholders:* By making contributions to social causes, an organisation fosters a positive attitude among consumers, dealers and shareholders.

Aspects on which organisations tend to concentrate
The social responsibility activities of organisations in South Africa focus on the following:

- Product types, for example dangerous products, product performance and standards, packaging and environmental impact;
- Marketing issues, for example sales practices, policy regarding consumer complaints, contents of advertisements, fair pricing;
- Human resources services, for example training, counselling and placement services;

- Organisation philanthropy, for example community development projects or the encouragement of staff to participate in social projects;
- Environmental activities and projects, for example control of pollution;
- External relationships, for example with various authorities;
- Employment of minority groups and women, as well as specialised career counselling;
- Health and safety of staff, including the working environment and medical facilities.

FIGURE 14.2: Social responsibility in context

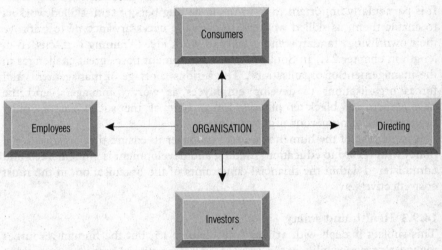

14.9 HUMAN RESOURCES MANAGEMENT AND SOCIAL RESPONSIBILITY

Many aspects of social responsibility in which organisations engage are in the field of human resources management, including human resources services, employment, safety and health. These and other aspects are now discussed.

14.9.1 Equal employment opportunities

During the past two decades this subject has come into prominence in South Africa. The principle has, however, been strictly applied in the USA for a long time. Equal employment opportunities imply that both an organisation's policy and its management practices ensure the employment, compensation and promotion of workers according to qualifications, merit, experience, performance and potential, irrespective of the worker's race, colour, creed, sex or language.

The distinction between the organisation's policy and its management practices is important, as there can be a vast difference between documented policy and practical implementation. Therefore we mean by management practices that the daily implementation of human resources policy in the organisation should also be free from discrimination.

14.9.2 Education, training and development
An example of involvement in this regard is what Pick 'n Pay began to do a decade ago (Ackerman 1983:4):

> *On the educational side, if an employee has a financial problem with a child or children, Pick 'n Pay assists with a bursary, and in this way we have helped hundreds of students through college and some through university.*

It is particularly important to train the large numbers of semi-skilled workers to enable them, as skilled workers, to earn the necessary income to improve their own living standards and quality of work life. (Training is discussed at length in chapter 21.) In South Africa, development poses great challenges to the management of organisations. The serious shortage of management staff forces organisations to develop employees as worthy managers, and the development of black employees forms part of the social responsibility programmes of numerous organisations.

It is the task of the human resources manager to ensure that organisational policy with regard to education, training and development is implemented and administered within the financial constraints of the organisation, in the most cost-effective way.

14.9.3 Health and safety
This subject is dealt with at length in chapter 15, but the human resources manager's responsibility in this respect is briefly outlined here. A safe working environment is primarily the responsibility of management. But safety also entails safe and responsible conduct by employees in their working environment. Organisations are obligated by law to ensure that all safety requirements are met. For example, the Occupational Health and Safety Act (No. 85 of 1993) covers all employees (including the owner of a business) in commerce, the public service, local governments, agriculture, housing, industry and construction.

Health as an area of social responsibility extends far beyond its traditional meaning in human resources management. It includes the provision of medical benefits to employees and their dependants. Traditionally only certain groups of employees qualified for these benefits, but social responsibility actions have ensured that these benefits are extended to all employees.

Health services are also gaining in importance and since 1987, organisations have gone out of their way to pay attention to them. Services are particularly being expanded in communities in those environments where organisations function. Preference is being given to services with regard to cancer, AIDS, tuberculosis and population development, as this is a way of increasing the quality of life of South Africa's people through social investment in these areas.

This also forms part of the guidelines set out in the government's Reconstruction and Development Plan (RDP), and in particular in the Health Policy, which was published in May 1994.

Numerous organisations have medical schemes for employees and their dependants. It is mainly the human resources manager's responsibility to ensure that such schemes are provided, maintained and managed effectively.

14.9.4 Extension of employee benefits and services to all employees

Employee benefits and services are discussed in detail in chapter 13, but a few remarks from the perspective of social responsibility are important. Organisations discriminated against certain groups of employees in the past by excluding them from the complete package of benefits and services offered to the average white employee, and by paying different salaries for the same work.

Pressure on organisations with international connections has increased to such an extent that they have been compelled to extend their benefits and services to all employees. For example, the Sullivan Code contains the following items:

- *Desegregate all eating, comfort, change-room and work facilities;*
- *Improve the quality of employees' lives outside the work environment in such areas as housing, schooling, transport, recreation and health facilities.*

Although the Sullivan Code specifically applied to American organisations based in South Africa, many organisations have instituted these actions voluntarily as they realise their social responsibility. Most organisations have provided, even at shop floor level, hygienic canteens, recreation facilities, and so on, and have opened these facilities to all employees.

Housing is probably the area in which social responsibility shows the most remarkable progress. This may be largely ascribed to the activities of the Urban Foundation. As far as transport is concerned, most big organisations today are sympathetic towards black employees, most of whom have to commute long distances between their homes and work. Organisations not only take the resultant fatigue into account, but also contribute on a large scale towards the transport costs of disadvantaged employees or provide their own transport service free of charge. Once again it is the human resources manager's task to ensure that these services and benefits are extended, maintained and administered effectively.

14.9.5 Environmental conservation

Much more effort, time and money than before are now spent on environmental matters. Organisations realise that concern about the environment is increasing all over the world and that this is an area on which they must concentrate to create goodwill. Just think of the *Exxon Valdes* that ran aground in Alaska and caused irreparable oil pollution. A great deal of publicity is given to aspects such as the greenhouse effect, the protection of endangered species and the conservation of natural water resources.

Involvement in environmental conservation projects is a contribution by organisations to the welfare of South Africa's communities and, as such, is an important social investment.

14.9.6 Small business development

Small business development is vital for economic growth in South Africa and for fighting unemployment because this type of stimulation of the economy creates many employment opportunities and is also cheap. Widespread support and publicity are therefore given to the development and promotion of the black business sector in particular, through organisations such as the Small Business Development Corporation (SBDC), the Urban Foundation, NAFCOC and FABCOS. Consequently, many organisations want to become involved and are allocating large sums of money to this type of development in South Africa.

14.10 CONCLUSION

The meaning and significance of the quality of work life have been clearly spelt out in this chapter. It was emphasised that organisations must improve their employees' work environment if their quality of work life is to be improved. This can be done by means of job enrichment, reduced work weeks and flexitime, for example.

With regard to social responsibility, organisations (and in particular their human resources departments) are faced with an enormous challenge, namely to join government and private institutions in making their rightful contribution towards the upliftment of the underprivileged in view of the principles contained in the RDP. By showing all employees that management is not only interested in obtaining maximum inputs from them, but is actively involved in their upliftment and support, a happy, satisfied and productive labour force can be created in South Africa.

Questions

1. Give your views on the effectiveness of quality of work life programmes in an organisation in improving productivity and employee satisfaction.
2. Discuss the advantages and disadvantages of flexitime and a four-day work week in the organisation for which you work.
3. Describe the effect of purposeful career planning on an employee's quality of work life.
4. Discuss quality circles, management by objectives and job enrichment as methods of improving the quality of work life in an organisation.
5. Is your organisation involved in social responsibility programmes? If so, why is it involved and what effect does this involvement have on your organisation?
6. You are the human resources manager of an organisation. The managing director has allocated R100 000 to you for a social responsibility pro-

gramme. How would you utilise and distribute these funds to get the best results for your organisation?

7. What is your opinion about the dependence of social investment on basic human rights? Motivate your answer.
8. Give your own critical evaluation of the involvement of organisations in social responsibility programmes.
9. Rate your own organisation's social responsibility compared to that of organisations discussed in this chapter.

Sources

Ackerman, R. 1983. Business facing challenges of social responsibility. *SA Forum*, Vol. 6, No. 21.

Coleman, C.J. 1979. *Personnel: an open system approach.* Winthrop, Cambridge, Massachusetts.

Cronje, G.J. de J., Neuland, E.W., Hugo, W.J. & Van Reenen, M.J. 1993. *Inleiding tot die bestuurswese.* 3rd edition. Southern Book Publishers, Halfway House.

De Kock, M. 1985. Corporate social responsibility: principle and practice. *Review: Gold Fields of South Africa.*

Gordon, J.R. 1983. *A diagnostic approach to organizational behaviour.* Allyn & Bacon, Boston.

Ivancevich, J.M. 1992. *Human resource management: foundations of personnel.* 5th edition. Irwin, Boston.

Kast, F.E. & Rosenzweig, J.E. 1985. *Organization and management.* 4th edition. McGraw-Hill, Johannesburg.

Nel, B. 1992. Social investment: recent trends. *People Dynamics.* July, Vol. 10, No. 9, pp. 26–9.

Republic of South Africa. 1993. *Government proposals on a manifesto of human rights.* Government Printer, Pretoria.

Republic of South Africa. 1993. *Draft act on the promotion of equal opportunities.* Government Printer, Pretoria.

Republic of South Africa. 1991. *The South African Legal Commission. Project No. 58.* Government Printer, Pretoria.

Snyman, C.M. 1990. Die rol van bestuur in die verbetering van werklewegehalte en produktiwiteit. Unpublished MBA thesis. University of Pretoria, Pretoria.

Chapter 15

Health and safety

P.D. Gerber

STUDY OBJECTIVES

After studying this chapter, you should be able to:
- Differentiate between the various forms of health;
- Explain ways to prevent accidents;
- Explain the Occupational Health and Safety Act (Act 85 of 1993);
- Explain the functioning of the National Occupational Safety Association of South Africa (NOSA).

15.1 INTRODUCTION

Although some occupational injuries and diseases might be the result of emotional and behavioural factors, most can be traced to the physical work environment. Those characteristics of the work environment associated with injuries are known as safety risks. To avoid accidents, these risks must be removed, for example by placing protective screens on dangerous machinery, wearing protective clothing or promoting greater safety awareness among employees.

Health risks refer to those characteristics of the work environment that are associated with diseases among employees. These risks are far more subtle than safety risks and also more difficult to perceive. It is often difficult to identify and eliminate a single causative factor for a disease. For this reason, governments have in practice paid more attention to safety by promulgating legislation to determine standards and to establish measures for protecting the employee. The field of occupational health has, however, been neglected.

While the consequences of safety risks primarily involve physical injuries, risks associated with occupational diseases do not only result in physical diseases but also in mental aberrations.

FIGURE 15.1: Principal learning components of health and safety

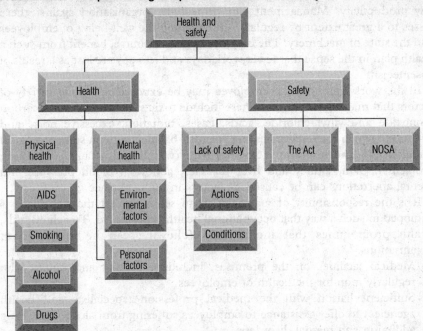

Who is responsible for health and safety in the work environment? In general: everyone in the organisation should be concerned with it. Formally, however, top management is responsible for instilling in employees an awareness of health and safety and for ensuring that the organisation meets the safety and health requirements stipulated by the government. This is particularly the case with small organisations. In larger organisations, this responsibility shifts to the human resources manager or to line managers. In most organisations, the direct supervisor is responsible for implementing safety regulations. The human resources manager or safety manager then has the function of assisting the supervisor. In this chapter, health and safety will be placed in an organisational perspective, as shown in figure 15.1.

15.2 HEALTH

15.2.1 Introduction

What does the word "health" mean? On the one hand it may be seen as a state in which disease is absent. On the other hand, "health" can be more fully defined as the physical, mental and social well-being of the individual. It thus has to do with the relationship between the body, the mind and the social patterns of the human being. An employee's health can be adversely affected by diseases, accidents and stress. This means that management must not only see to the physical well-being of employees, but also to their psychological well-being.

It is obvious that poor employee health will lead to high absenteeism and low productivity. Management can protect the organisation against these losses to a great extent by regularly investigating the well-being of employees and the state of machinery. The employee does, of course, benefit from such a health plan in the sense that fewer work days and less pay are lost as a result of absenteeism.

In the work situation, the employee may be exposed to a wide variety of factors that may lead to illness. These include toxic substances such as carbon monoxide and vinyl chloride, acids, gases, radiation, excessive noise and vibration (which may affect hearing, disturb balance and cause neurological imbalances) and extreme temperatures (which may cause breathing problems). Skin, kidney and liver diseases, abnormal blood pressure and mental aberrations can be caused by factors in the workplace.

It is the responsibility of management to see to it that the workplace is equipped in such a way that occupational health is promoted. To achieve this, health programmes that include the following can be instituted at organisations:
- Medical facilities on the premises, including doctors and nurses who regularly monitor the health of employees.
- Sufficient liaison with the medical profession (specialists and health agencies) to offer assistance to employees suffering from alcoholism, drug addiction and mental disorders.
- Special educational programmes that pay attention to nutrition, physical exercise, mass control, etc.
- Special attention to the cleanliness of the premises, including food handling, disease prevention, etc.
- Proper first-aid facilities for injuries and illnesses.
- Adequate and confidential medical records.

Physical health will now be examined.

15.2.2 Physical health
Human resources managers today have to deal with complex problems that threaten the health of employees. These include AIDS, smoking, alcoholism and drug abuse.

AIDS
As is well known, AIDS is a disease that undermines the immune system of the body, with the result that the individual is exposed to a wide range of diseases, usually with fatal complications. Employees in professions directly exposed to AIDS are dentists, dental assistants, nursing staff, medical staff, first-aid staff, police officers, laboratory technicians and personnel in the correctional services. In workplaces, attention should be focused on the dissemination of information about AIDS and the reduction of fear among employees, particularly those who have to work with employees suffering from AIDS.

Training in the workplace must disseminate information regarding the nature, symptoms and transmission of the illness, and prepare employees for the emotional problems they may experience when a fellow worker contracts this fatal disease.

Smoking

Until quite recently, smoking in the workplace was accepted by non-smokers. However, non-smokers have now begun to protect themselves by demanding from smokers and management a smoke-free work environment. This state of affairs leads to tension in the workplace, leaving managers with the task of protecting the rights of both smokers and non-smokers, which is not easy. Leap and Orino (1993:553) investigated the influence of smoking in the workplace on colleagues: 35% experienced nose irritations, 30% complained of throat discomfort, 25% were frustrated and rebellious because management permitted smoking in the workplace, while 19% experienced discomfort during meals.

Legislation is expected in South Africa in the near future to determine whether:

- Smoking should be permitted in public places;
- Smoke-free zones will have to be provided in restaurants and social places by the owner or organisation;
- Smoking should be prohibited on all public transport.

Alcoholism

Whereas alcoholism was previously regarded as a moral and criminal problem ("place the victim in a cell overnight to dry out"), the modern approach is to regard it as an illness that requires special treatment.

The most important components of a programme to control alcoholism are:

- *Policy document*: Top management declares the organisation's commitment to the programme and allocates responsibility to the relevant people. It confirms the willingness of the organisation to help those in need.
- *Cooperation of the trade union*: Where the employee is a member of a trade union, this aspect is important. If the trade union is involved at an early stage, this may play an important role in obtaining the support of the employee's colleagues.
- *Education*: An information programme and training covering all the dimensions of alcoholism and also spelling out the extent of the organisation's control programme is desirable.
- *Training*: Supervisors and managers at all levels must receive thorough training in how to handle alcoholism. They must also know their responsibilities in such a programme. The supervisor bears the primary responsibility for identifying the problem and for handling the alcoholic as an individual.

- *Professional services*: Provision must be made for nursing services, counsellors, human resources specialists, medical doctors and psychiatrists, as well as for medical outpatient treatment within the community.

Alcoholism has a drastic effect on employees and their work. The quality and quantity of work performed by an alcoholic are considerably reduced. It is interesting to note that alcoholics do not cause more accidents at work than other workers, as they tend to be more careful because they are aware of their problem and try to hide it. In addition, the labour turnover of alcoholics is not abnormally high, which is contrary to public opinion on the matter. It is a fact, however, that the morale of other employees is adversely affected because they often have to do the work of fellow employees addicted to alcohol.

There are two important misconceptions about alcoholics, i.e. that they are easy to spot and that they are primarily blue-collar and low-skilled employees (De Cenzo and Robbins 1988:511). No supervisor is a psychiatrist and therefore does not have specialised training to identify this problem. The four techniques according to which alcoholics in the workplace are handled are disciplining, dismissal, treatment within the organisation and referral to an agency outside the organisation. Disciplining to just short of dismissal is the most commonly used technique, followed by internal treatment and referral to agencies outside the organisation. Table 15.1 shows important warning signs of alcoholism at the workplace.

Drug abuse

Until now, drug-addicted employees have received much less attention than those who abuse alcohol. One reason for this is simply that drug abuse, despite its worrisome increase, has not yet assumed the proportions of alcohol abuse. Another reason is that alcohol abuse occurs among employees of all ages, while drug abusers are usually aged between 20 and 25 years and have usually been employed by the organisation for less than four years. Furthermore, drug abusers tend to attempt to persuade fellow workers also to take drugs, thus providing management with a good reason to get rid of them.

The programmes used for drug abusers follow the same approach as those for alcoholics. These programmes emphasise sensitivity on the part of the supervisor, so that he or she will be able to identify the problem at an early stage.

15.2.3 Mental health

Mental health may be defined as *a state in which an employee is well adjusted, has an accurate perception of reality and can adapt fairly well to the pressures and frustrations of life.*

Mental aberrations may be caused by physical illness, relationships with others outside the work situation and interaction in the work situation. Mental disorders may be the result of a poor supervisor-subordinate relationship, a poor motivational climate, pressure in the work situation, etc. Under certain

TABLE 15.1: Perceptible behavioural patterns of an alcoholic

Phase	Absenteeism	General behaviour	Job performance
1. Early phase of alcoholism	Tiredness Stops work early Absent from work situations "I drink to relieve stress"	Complaints from colleagues that he/she does not do his/her share Overreacts Complaints—"not feeling well" Makes untrue statements	Does not meet deadlines Often makes mistakes Lower job performance Criticism by supervisor
2. Middle phase	Often absent for days for vague or improbable reasons "I feel guilty for smuggling in alcohol" "I am shaky"	Noticeable changes Unreliable statements Avoids colleagues Borrows money from colleagues Inflates job performance Often hospitalised Less serious injuries on duty (repeatedly)	General decline Cannot concentrate Intermittent memory loss Warning by supervisor
3. Late or middle phase	Regularly absent for days at a time Sometimes does not return after lunch "I don't feel like eating" "I don't want to talk about it" "I like to drink alone"	Aggressive and contentious behaviour Domestic problems interfere with work Financial problems More regular hospitalisation Resignation: does not want to discuss problems Problems with the law and society	Far below expectation Punitive disciplinary action
4. Approach of final stage	Prolonged unpredictable absence	Drinks on duty Totally unreliable Repeated hospitalisation Serious financial problems Serious family problems: divorce	Unstable Completely incompetent Faces termination of service or hospitalisation

Source: Dessler (1988:676)

circumstances, illnesses such as alcoholism and drug abuse may partially be the result of stress, for example when too high workloads and problems with clients place an employee under so much pressure that a pathological reaction occurs, driving him or her to alcohol or drug abuse.

There are two primary causes of work stress: environmental factors and personal factors. *Environmental factors* that give rise to stress include the work schedule, the pace at which the work must be completed, the work quality, the route to and from work and the number and nature of customers per employee. No two people will, however, react to stress in the same way, because *personal factors* determine the tolerable level of stress. Employees who feel driven to give their best at all times place themselves under greater stress than others. Aspects such as patience, self-respect, health and exercise, sleep patterns and attitude to work will also influence the employee's reaction to stress in the work situation.

Whatever its source, excessive work stress has serious consequences for both the employee and the organisation. In the case of the employee, stress may lead to anxiety, depression, anger, cardiovascular diseases, headaches, accidents, alcohol and drug abuse, excessive appetite or poor interpersonal relations. In the case of the organisation, stress may lead to a reduction in the output of the employee, as well as to increased absenteeism and staff turnover and more grievances. It must be emphasised, however, that work stress and work pressure do not have to be negative or have a dysfunctional effect on work performance. Some employees, for example, work better under mild stress and work pressure, and are more productive if they know that they must complete a task within a given time.

The supervisor can play an important role in the identification and alleviation of work stress by carefully monitoring the work performance of subordinates.

Finally, some remarks on "burn-out": this means the individual feels that his or her physical and mental resources have been exhausted as a result of the continuous striving for a work-related objective. Burn-out is often the end result of too much work pressure and stress, particularly if the pressure arises from a striving for unattainable goals. Often dynamic, purposeful and idealistic people suffer from this syndrome as they tend to be excessively committed to their task (see chapter 24). These individuals are intense in everything they do, make high demands on themselves and usually aim their activities exclusively at attaining certain goals, which means that they often lead unbalanced lives.

By the time employees start working, their personalities are already well formed. Their ability or inability to handle various situations at work has, to a large extent, already been determined. Most employees can handle the work pressure and stress in a healthy, positive manner, but many employees have emotional problems at times. A small minority of these people—some 3%— are, however, so disturbed that they require psychiatric treatment (Sloane 1983:388). It is the task of management to pay the necessary attention to this group. The cause of this state can, in most cases, be traced back to pressure in the work situation.

15.3 SAFETY
15.3.1 General
Accidents at the workplace may be ascribed to two factors: unsafe working conditions and unsafe actions by employees. *Unsafe working conditions* include

defective equipment, inadequate mechanical protection, explosions, fires, unsafe machinery and unsafe placement of machinery and equipment. *Unsafe actions* include the wrong use of equipment and tools as well as failure to comply with safety regulations. Sloane (1983:381) refers to a study in which it was found that 50% of all injuries on duty are the result of unsafe working conditions, while 45% may be ascribed to negligence on the part of the employee. The cause of the remaining 5% could not be determined.

Data indicate that some employees tend to have more accidents than others. Employees who are accident-prone are usually younger than 30 years, have a lack of psychomotor and perceptual skills, are impulsive and often bored.

Like other human resources management functions, the success of a safety programme requires the support and cooperation of human resources management. Apart from the financial support necessary for the programme to run smoothly, it must also receive the necessary moral support. The success of the safety programme primarily depends on how well employees and supervisors cooperate in complying with safety measures and regulations. This relationship can be formalised in the creation of a safety committee that may consist of a safety specialist and representatives of the employees and management.

15.3.2 How to prevent accidents
Eliminate unsafe working conditions
It is primarily the task of safety engineers to eliminate the physical dangers that threaten safety. Supervisors and managers can also make an important contribution by paying attention to the following:

- General administration of the workplace: sufficient and wide passages; spare parts and equipment safely stored after use; even and non-slip surfaces; materials safety stacked; fire extinguishers easily reachable; work benches tidy;
- Materials handling: all means of transport safe; means of transport safely loaded; all materials safely stored;
- Ladders, benches, scaffolding and stairs; rails firmly attached and safe; footholds not slippery; equipment properly stored;
- Power supply: well anchored and earthed; adequate working space around machinery; safety goggles, gloves and protective clothing must be worn;
- Handtools: must be in good working order; must be properly stored; must be right for the task; protective clothing, goggles, etc. must be worn;
- Welding: proper protective clothing must be worn; equipment must be properly earthed; fire-fighting equipment must be within reach; adequate ventilation;
- Fire-extinguishing apparatus: must be properly maintained and identifiable; must be within easy reach; must be in working condition.

Eliminate unsafe actions
Unsafe actions by employees may be limited by the following conduct on the part of management:

- Proper selection and placement: By eliminating accident-prone individuals during the selection process, unsafe actions can be limited to a large extent. This can be done, for example, by using techniques to identify visual defects related to accidents in the workplace. Personal tests and measuring muscle coordination are other methods used to eliminate accident-prone individuals at an early stage.
- Information: Safety posters can be put up as a constant reminder to workers of the importance of safety in the workplace.
- Training can make an important contribution towards limiting unsafe actions. Recently appointed employees, in particular, must undergo intensive training. Older employees should also regularly attend refresher courses on the importance of safety.
- Positive reinforcement: Employees must not only be encouraged to comply with safety regulations, but employers should also give positive recognition to employees who maintain a high level of safety in the work situation. It is, after all, the organisation that benefits from a decrease in the number of accidents and from uninterrupted production schedules.
- The involvement of top management: Safety is primarily the result of the development of safety awareness among employees. It is necessary for top management to be involved in safety, otherwise such an awareness cannot be fostered among employees. This means that top management must visibly express its involvement (for example by insisting on regular safety investigations of vehicles) and by giving the safety officer proper status.

15.3.3 The Occupational Health and Safety Act

The new Occupational Health and Safety Act (Act 85 of 1993) was promulgated to make provision for: the health and safety of people at work and in relation to their use of operating equipment and machinery; the protection of other people against threats to their health and safety arising from the activities of people at work; the establishment of an advisory council for occupational health and safety; and related matters.

Each employer must, in as far as possible, establish and maintain a work environment that is safe and without risk to the health of its employees. In addition, each employer must, as far as possible, operate its organisation in such a way that people who are not employees and who are directly affected by the activities of the organisation are not exposed to threats to their health and safety as a result.

Each employee must take reasonable precautions at work for his or her own safety and health and that of other people who may be affected by his or her actions or failures.

The Advisory Council for Occupational Health and Safety
The Council established in terms of this Act consists of 20 members. It must advise the Minister on policy matters regarding the application of the Act and any matter concerning occupational health and safety.

The Advisory Council may, with the approval of the Minister, establish one or more technical committees to advise the Council on any matter concerning the activities of the Council.

Health and safety representatives
Health and safety representatives must be appointed in writing by any organisation with more than 20 employees, within four months after the Act has come into effect or after the organisation has come into being. In the case of shops and offices, there must be at least one health and safety representative for every 100 employees and for all other workplaces there must be at least one representative for every 50 employees. Section 18 of the Act specifies the activities of the health and safety representatives:
- To check the effectiveness of health and safety regulations;
- To identify potential threats and serious incidents at the workplace;
- To investigate the causes of incidents at the workplace in cooperation with the employer;
- To investigate complaints by any employee with regard to his or her health or safety at the workplace;
- To address representations to the employer or a health and safety committee regarding matters arising from the above or, if these representations are unsuccessful, to address representations to an inspector;
- To address representations to the employer regarding general matters that affect the health or safety of employees in the workplace;
- To inspect the workplace, including any article, substance, operating equipment, machinery or health and safety equipment at that workplace, with a view to the health and safety of employees, at the intervals agreed upon with the employer. The health and safety representative must give reasonable notice of his or her intention to carry out such an inspection to the employer, who may be present during the inspection;
- To take part in discussions with inspectors at the workplace and to accompany inspectors on inspections of the workplace;
- To receive information from inspectors as envisaged in Section 36 of the Act;
- To attend meetings with regard to any of the above activities.

A health and safety representative may, with regard to the workplace or section of the workplace for which he or she has been appointed:
- Visit the site of an incident and carry out an on-site inspection;
- Attend any inquest or formal investigation in terms of this Act;
- In as far as it is reasonably necessary, inspect any document that the employer must keep up to date in terms of this Act;
- Accompany an inspector during any inspection;
- Be accompanied by a technical advisor during any inspection, with the approval of the employer (which may not be unreasonably withheld);
- Take part in any internal health or safety audit.

An employer must provide the facilities, assistance and training that a health and safety representative will reasonably require, and that have been agreed upon for the execution of his or her duties.

Safety committees

One or more health and safety committees must be appointed by an employer where two or more health and safety representatives have been appointed. At each meeting, methods to ensure the establishment, development, promotion, maintenance and revision of the health and safety of employees at work must be discussed.

The number of members of a health and safety committee is determined as follows:

- If one health and safety committee has been appointed for a workplace, all the health and safety representatives for that workplace must be members of the committee;
- If two or more health and safety committees have been appointed for a workplace, each health and safety representative for that workplace must be a member of at least one of those committees;
- The number of persons named by an employer for any health and safety committee may not exceed the number of health and safety representatives on that committee.

Any incident must be reported to an inspector by the employer within the prescribed period and in the prescribed manner. The powers and competence of these inspectors are defined in detail in the Act.

A health and safety committee has the following responsibilities:

- It can make recommendations to the employer or, where these recommendations do not lead to a solution, to an inspector about any matter concerning the health or safety of persons at the workplace or a section of it for which such a committee was instituted;
- It must discuss any incident at the workplace in which any person was injured, became ill or died, and may make a written report to an inspector about the incident.

Victimisation prohibited

An employer may not dismiss an employee or reduce the scale of his or her compensation, or change the conditions of service to conditions that are less favourable to the employee or adversely change his or her position in comparison with other employees in the service of that employer.

Inspectors

Inspectors have the following powers in terms of the Act:

- To enter any premises used by an employer or on which an employee carries out work or uses operating equipment, or which the inspector suspects of being such premises, without prior notice at any reasonable time;

- To question someone who is or was present on such premises, either alone or in the presence of another person, regarding a matter covered by this Act;
- To require someone having control or supervision of a book, record or other item on those premises immediately to present such an item to the inspector at a time and place determined by him or her;
- To examine such a book, record or other item or to make a copy of or extract from it;
- To require such a person to explain an entry in such a book, record or item;
- To remove for investigation or analysis any article, substance, operating equipment or machinery that is or was present on such premises, or any work carried out on the premises or any article or part of it;
- To confiscate an article that, in the opinion of the inspector, may serve as proof during the trial of someone on a charge of misconduct in terms of this Act or of common law. The employer or user of the article in question may make copies of such an article before it is confiscated;
- To order an employer, employee or user to appear before the inspector at the time and place determined by the inspector, and to question such a person regarding any matter covered by this Act.

The Machinery and Occupational Safety Act of 1983 (Act 6 of 1983), the Machinery and Occupational Safety Amendment Act of 1989 (Act 40 of 1989), and the Machinery and Occupational Safety Amendment Act of 1991 (Act 97 of 1991) are revoked by this Act (Act 85 of 1993).

15.3.4 The National Occupational Safety Association of South Africa (NOSA)

The National Occupational Safety Association—known by its acronym NOSA—was established in 1951. It is a public body not for gain, with its own statutes and articles of association.

The original aims of this body were:
- The prevention of occupational accidents and diseases and the limitation of their causes;
- The handling of all matters of national importance regarding occupational safety, and acting as an advisory body in all such matters;
- The provision of training and guidance to management in the techniques of accident prevention.

The current aims of NOSA are:
- Guidance;
- Training;
- Providing motivation to management to prevent accidents and occupational diseases. This is done by implementing NOSA's management by objectives, by training programmes, the provision of publicity material and safety promotion activities.

NOSA is managed by a board of 17 directors. NOSA's income is generated from its own sources and from donations. Own income is obtained from training programmes, the sale of promotional products and the provision of various services. Among others, donations are received from:

- Federated Employers' Mutual Assurance (FEMA);
- The Commissioner of Unemployment Insurance;
- The Building Industries Federation;
- The Directorate of Civil Aviation.

In terms of the Compensation for Occupational Injuries and Diseases Act (Act 130 of 1993), a fund is managed by the Commissioner on the basis of an insurance fund. Most employers fall under the jurisdiction of the Commissioner and are assessed for a contribution to this fund.

FIGURE 15.2: Structure of the National Occupational Safety Association of South Africa

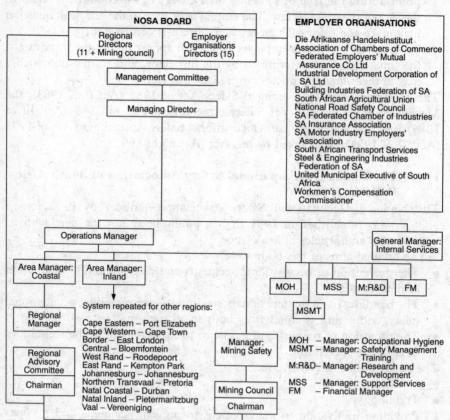

The assessment or premium is determined in accordance with the nature of a certain industry and its dangers and demands, which vary from industry to industry. For example, employers in a dangerous industry such as mining will pay higher premiums. When an employee is injured on duty, the Occupational Injuries and Diseases Fund (which came into effect on 1 April 1994) pays for treatment and hospitalisation, rehabilitation and compensation for income lost as a result of absence from duty.

A portion of the Occupational Injuries and Diseases Fund is made available to NOSA. These funds are primarily used for accident prevention programmes.

NOSA offers the following services to commerce and mining:
- NOSA ratings for health and safety;
- Auditing;
- Investigations;
- Consultation;
- Training.

15.4 CONCLUSION

The past 50 years have been characterised by a revolutionary change in the attitude of the public, employers and trade unions to the prevention and elimination of industrial accidents and diseases. It is no longer necessary to plead for legislation to help the victims of accidents and occupational diseases, nor to make most employers aware of safety. Nevertheless, the safety problem requires constant attention, as accidents and diseases still occur at work.

Questions
1. Discuss the various forms of health.
2. How would you limit unsafe conditions and actions at work?
3. What contribution does the Occupational Health and Safety Act make to promoting the safety of employees in South Africa? Discuss.
4. How do you see NOSA's contribution? Discuss.

Sources

Compensation for Occupational Injuries and Diseases Act (Act 130 of 1993).

De Cenzo, D.A. & Robbins, S.P. 1988. *Personnel: human resource management*. 3rd edition. Prentice-Hall, Englewood Cliffs, New Jersey.

Dessler, G. 1988. *Personnel management*. 4th edition. Prentice-Hall, Englewood Cliffs, New Jersey.

Leap, T.L. & Orino, M.D. 1993. *Personnel/human resource management*. 2nd edition. Macmillan, New York.

NOSA. 1993. *This is NOSA*. NOSA publication.

Sloane, A.A. 1983. *Personnel: managing human resources*. Prentice-Hall, Englewood Cliffs, New Jersey.

Occupational Health and Safety Act (Act 85 of 1993).

Chapter 16

Motivation

P.S. van Dyk

STUDY OBJECTIVES

After studying this chapter, you should be able to:
- Logically define the concept "motivation";
- Schematically illustrate the motivation process;
- Differentiate between content theories of motivation and process theories of motivation;
- Explain motivation in organisational context;
- Logically describe motivated employee behaviour.

16.1 INTRODUCTION

It is said that motivational problems today are much the same as those in the Industrial Revolution decades ago. Certain experts even say that the problem of motivation is as old as humanity itself. These statements are well-founded and acceptable, since the problem of motivation centres on humans as living beings. People's preferences, tastes and needs have changed through the centuries, and especially during the past few decades, but in essence they still remain human beings. Therefore one may safely say that motivation will remain a problem until the end of time.

In this chapter we will look at a general motivation model, and we will ask the question "Why do people work?" Content and process theories of motivation are then discussed. Motivation in the context of the organisation is examined, and the chapter concludes with guidelines for producing motivated employee behaviour.

Although this chapter deals with the job content environment as well as the job context environment, it should be clearly understood that motivation is influenced directly and indirectly by all the variables in the three environments.

318

FIGURE 16.1: Principal learning components of motivation

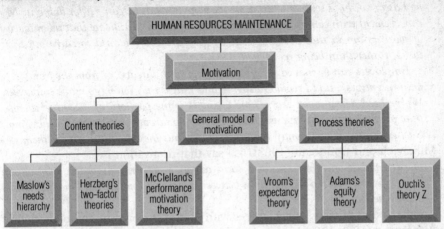

16.2 A DEFINITION OF MOTIVATION

The concept "motivation" is widely used, yet there is a great deal of ignorance about what motivation is and what it implies. Mol (1990:20) says:

At the outset it is important to define the concept of motivation accurately. When managers are asked what they understand by the term "motivation", the most common definition is influencing a subordinate to achieve the goal that the manager wants him/her to achieve.

Is that, however, a valid definition of motivation? I believe not, because it does not distinguish the difference between movement and motivation. According to Herzberg (1968:54), the difference can be summarised as follows:

When a person carries out a task for the sake of the remuneration (i.e. for what he can get out of it) he is being moved.

What then is motivation in the management context? What gives subordinates that extra commitment and dedication towards their work? The answer is relatively simple:

When a person carries out a task because he enjoys doing it, he is being motivated. That is the simplest definition I can think of, yet it highlights the fact that real dedication and commitment to a task can only come when the task itself is enjoyable for the individual concerned.

Much of the confusion over the issue of motivation is the fact that theorists do not always distinguish between "motivation" and "movement". Agreement on what is meant by the term "motivation" would cut out a great deal of misunderstanding. For example, the argument whether money motivates or not would become an irrelevant question. The more appropriate question would be whether money can get an employee to do something—and the answer is undoubtedly "yes"—or whether money can get an employee to enjoy his or her task more—and the answer to that is most likely "no".

That implies that even though an individual does not particularly like the task he has to do, he is willing to do it for the sake of what he can get for doing it. My involvement with commerce and industry would seem to indicate that the majority of workers are in that position, that is, they are being moved to carry out their tasks, rather than being motivated.

Employees can be moved from behind (e.g. with threats) or from the front (e.g. with incentives), and I would hasten to add that it isn't wrong to move employees. We've been doing it for years. One example is the plethora of incentive schemes that we find in organisations today. Do they motivate employees? I believe not. Such incentive schemes may move employees, but they do not motivate them.

Milkovich and Boudreau (1988:165) say that motivation is:

the drive that energizes, sustains, and directs a person's behavior. Motivation derives from perceived relationships between behaviors and the fulfillment of values and/or needs.

Another point of view, which agrees with that of the present author, is that of Armstrong (1988:120):

Motivation is inferred from or defined by goal-directed behaviour. It is anchored in two basic concepts: (a) the needs that operate within the individual and (b) the goals in the environment toward or away from which the individual moves. In its simplest form, the process of motivation is initiated by the conscious or unconscious recognition of an unsatisfied need. A goal is then established which, it is thought, will satisfy that need, and a course of action is determined that will lead towards the attainment of the goal. But, as goals are satisfied, new needs emerge and the cycle continues.

Therefore the concept of motivation has three clearly defined dimensions, namely stimulation of needs, human behaviour and goals or goal achievement. A person reacts to a need by behaving in a particular way, and the goal of this behaviour is the satisfaction of the need. The interaction between these intrinsic human activities will be clearly indicated in the general model of motivation.

16.3 A GENERAL MODEL OF HUMAN MOTIVATION

Two principles of human behaviour should be noted:

- Human behaviour is not incidental—there are reasons why people do or don't do things. This also applies to their behaviour at work.
- No two people are the same. Because people differ, they have different behaviour patterns. Even when people do show the same behaviour, it may not be for the same reasons.

Therefore all behaviour is motivated.

Human behaviour stems directly from human needs. If one or more of a person's needs are not satisfied, he or she acts in an attempt to satisfy such needs. An unsatisfied need makes a person feel that something is wrong and that he or she should try to put it right. In other words, the person develops an urge to satisfy the need.

This desire for need satisfaction prompts the person to release energy and spend time trying to rectify the situation. Babies release energy at random in trial and error. However, fixed behaviour patterns develop as a person learns to utilise his or her energy effectively.

Human behaviour is therefore directed towards whatever will satisfy a need (goal). This may be illustrated as in figure 16.2.

FIGURE 16.2: The motivation process

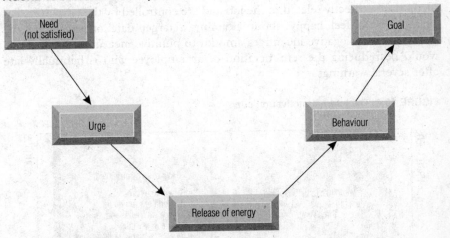

Figure 16.3 is a simple example of what can happen when a person experiences a need for food.

FIGURE 16.3: A practical example of the motivation process

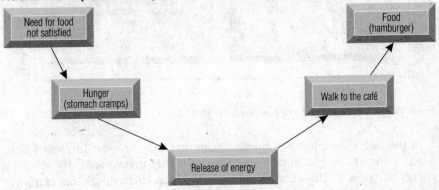

Most human behaviour patterns can be linked in this way to some need that has not yet been satisfied.

Motivation is thus the way in which urges or needs direct a person's behaviour towards a specific goal, and the intensity with which this goal is pursued.

The motivation process is not physically perceptible because it takes place internally. However, management can perceive the behaviour displayed by an employee and deduce the individual's motivation from it.

It is not easy to motivate employees, but management can use negative or positive incentives. Positive incentives may be subdivided into extrinsic and intrinsic methods. Extrinsic methods are external to the job and are administered by someone other than the employee. An example is a manager who may praise the employee and recommend a salary increase. Intrinsic methods are directly related to the job and are controlled by the employee. An example is to feel happy about attaining a target date or exceeding the standards set. Negative incentives amount to punitive measures. An example would be reducing the remuneration of an employee who is habitually late after several warnings.

FIGURE 16.4: The internal motivation cube

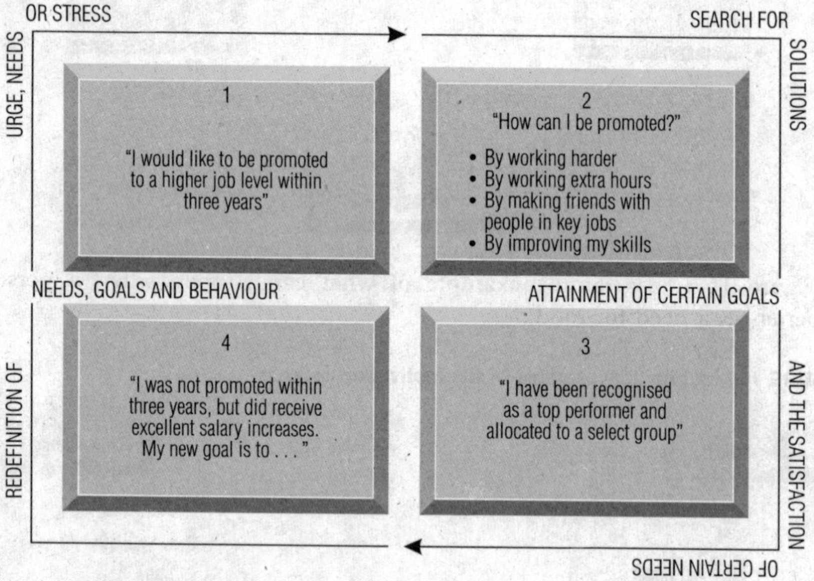

Source: Adapted from Skinner and Ivancevich (1992:339)

In the role of employee, a human being has many needs. In fact, human needs stimulate people to do something to satisfy these needs. By releasing energy at work in the execution of a task (work behaviour), an employee enables himself or herself to satisfy one of the most basic needs (in this case a goal), namely to earn a wage or a salary which enables him or her to satisfy other important needs by spending money. Therefore employees join organisations because they wish to satisfy particular and diverse needs. But is this the only reason why people work?

16.4 WHY DO PEOPLE WORK?

People work for several reasons. Whatever the reason for any particular individual, "working" seems to be the principal activity in modern society. People work not only for obvious reasons such as earning a salary, but because work plays an important role in the development of self-respect and a sense of identity. In modern society, people's jobs largely determine who and what they are. Their job determines their status in society, where they stay, with whom they associate and who is associated with them. Furthermore it is an important criterion by which people assess themselves and others.

A wide range of human needs is satisfied by working. The most important needs include a need for affiliation, a feeling of competence and success, authority, control, pride and status. Knowing employees' needs, and developing motivation strategies for their employees on the basis of these needs, is a major challenge for management. Therefore it is important for management to be aware of human needs and theories of motivation.

16.5 MOTIVATION THEORIES

Motivation theories are divided into three groups: content theories, process theories and reinforcement theories. Content theories have to do with needs and factors that incite behaviour; they focus on the "what" of motivation. Process theories have to do with the way in which human behaviour originates and is directed, maintained and discontinued; they focus on the "how" of motivation. Reinforcement theories focus on the manner in which desired behaviour can be learned and are discussed in chapter 22.

16.5.1 Content theories of motivation

Three content theories are discussed: Maslow's needs hierarchy, Herzberg's two-factor motivation theory and McClelland's theory of achievement motivation.

Content theories focus on the internal factors that influence an individual's behaviour and are based on the fact that the human being attempts to satisfy internal needs through unique behaviour.

16.5.1.1 *Maslow's needs hierarchy*

Maslow's (1954) theory has a twofold basis, namely:
- People are continuously wanting beings. As soon as one need is satisfied, another appears to take its place. People can therefore never be fully satisfied, and they behave in a particular way to satisfy a need or a combination of needs. A satisfied need cannot act as a motivator of behaviour.
- People's needs are arranged in order of importance, in other words lower-order needs must be satisfied before higher-order needs.

Maslow divides human needs into five main categories, in a hierarchy according to importance. The lowest level contains the most basic human needs which must be satisfied before higher-order needs will emerge and become motivators of behaviour. The levels of needs in Maslow's hierarchy are as follows:

- *Physiological needs:* The satisfaction of these needs is essential for a human being's biological functioning and survival (for example the need for food, water and heat). These are the most prominent needs; if they are not satisfied, human behaviour will be mainly directed at satisfying them.
- *Safety needs:* As soon as physiological needs are reasonably satisfied, needs on the next level in the hierarchy emerge and the importance of the previous level of needs diminishes. Humans now use energy to satisfy the need for safety, which also has a direct bearing on their survival.
- *Social needs:* Once a person feels safe and in control of possible threats, social needs are activated. These include the need for love, acceptance and friendship.
- *Ego needs:* Ego needs relate to a person's self-esteem and self-respect as well as the respect and esteem of other people. They include the need for self-confidence, independence, freedom, recognition, appreciation and achievement. These needs may be divided into two groups: self-respect and self-esteem, and respect and approval from others.
- *Self-actualisation needs:* If all the previously mentioned needs are largely satisfied or can readily be satisfied, people spend their time in search of opportunities to apply their skills to the best of their ability. Self-actualisation needs now become uppermost. Maslow (1954:92) describes these needs as "the desire to become more and more what one is—to become everything one is capable of becoming."

Human needs may be placed in a hierarchy according to their importance for human survival.

The importance of the various needs to a particular person at a particular time depends on the extent to which these needs are satisfied or can be readily satisfied. Figure 16.5 is a visual representation of Maslow's needs hierarchy.

This theory has many implications for individual performance. The most common strategy used by management to motivate people (among other things by means of money, service benefits and job security) is aimed at the continued satisfaction of needs on the physiological and safety level, while most employees in developed countries are easily able to meet these needs themselves. As Maslow clearly points out that, once satisfied, a need no longer acts as a motivator, this strategy is thus not an incentive to perform.

The first two levels of needs have been satisfied for most employees. (If they cannot satisfy these needs themselves, the community or the government will, in most cases, ensure that they are satisfied.) Social needs may be satisfied in the work situation to a large extent, but it is difficult to develop a strategy that

FIGURE 16.5: Maslow's needs hierarchy

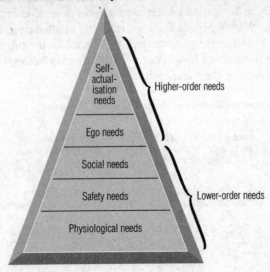

Source: Hodgetts (1979:264)

will translate these needs into an incentive for improved individual performance. The work people do, and the work environment, may be designed in a way that will increase interaction between employees. The disadvantage is, however, that this may have a negative effect on employees' work output.

The needs that probably provide the best opportunities for employee motivation are the fourth- and fifth-level needs of Maslow's hierarchy, i.e. the ego and self-actualisation needs. Self-esteem and self-respect (as well as the esteem and respect of others) are a function of the type of work people do rather than of working conditions such as free interaction and good remuneration. Interesting, challenging and meaningful work provides a solid foundation for the improvement of performance.

A further implication of Maslow's theory concerns the control function. People need to control their environment in order to manipulate it according to their needs. The opposite is also true, however. If people are controlled by the environment and thwarted in the satisfaction of their needs, they become frustrated and tense. If prevailing needs cannot be satisfied, the result is undesirable employee behaviour such as aggression, frustration and resignations, which can hardly be described as healthy or productive.

Further to the above: if a person's work is in itself a source of need satisfaction, that person becomes self-regulating and the role of external incentives, such as remuneration or punishment, as motivators becomes much less prominent. Systems relying on external mechanisms to motivate people usually also require a control system to ensure continued employee performance. The maintenance of mechanisms such as strict supervision, policy, and rules and regulations requires a great deal of effort on the part of the organisation. Where people are motivated by challenging, interesting and meaningful work, however, such control mechanisms are superfluous.

The question then arises how Maslow's theory may be applied in practice. Figure 16.6 provides a good indication.

FIGURE 16.6: Practical application of Maslow's needs hierarchy

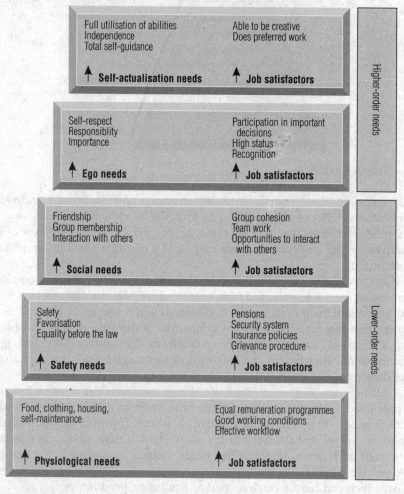

Source: Adapted from Skinner and Ivancevich (1992:340)

Smit and Cronje (1992:329) point out that although Maslow's theory cannot fully explain human motivation, his needs hierarchy is generally accepted and used in practice for the following reasons:

- The hierarchy is easy to understand and makes sense.
- Important categories of needs are pointed out by the theory.
- A differentiation is made between higher- and lower-order needs.
- The importance of personal growth and self-actualisation in the job context is pointed out to managers.

In most developed Western countries, organisations are particularly successful at meeting the lower-order needs of their employees. Physiological needs, for example, are met by paying good wages and salaries, safety needs are met through salaries and fringe benefits, and social needs through interaction and association between employees (see figure 16.6).

16.5.1.2 Herzberg's two-factor motivation theory

Herzberg (1954) found, after intensive and extensive research, a set of factors or working conditions that tend to motivate people to improve their performance, thus resulting in job satisfaction. These factors are closely related to the nature and content of the work done. Herzberg calls them motivators; they include:

- Achievement, for example successful execution of tasks;
- Recognition for what has been achieved;
- The job itself: how interesting, meaningful and challenging it is;
- Progress or growth;
- Responsibility.

According to Herzberg, a job will tend to generate high intrinsic motivation if it includes these factors. If the factors are absent, however, the result is not necessarily dissatisfaction. Herzberg states that dissatisfaction is caused by the absence of another set of factors, which he terms the hygiene or maintenance factors. These factors satisfy a person's lower-order needs and include:

- Organisational policy and administration;
- Supervision;
- Interpersonal relationships with colleagues, superiors and subordinates;
- Salary;
- Status;
- Working conditions;
- Work security.

Herzberg maintains that if employees regard hygiene factors as insufficient, they would be unhappy and dissatisfied and tend to be less productive. For example, if employees feel that their compensation is not on a par with that of other employees in the same occupation at other organisations, they will be unhappy and this will affect their performance. If, however, their remuneration equals or exceeds that of other employees doing similar work, it does not mean that they will be motivated, as a high level of motivation is ensured by the motivators, not by the hygiene factors.

These two sets of factors are very different. The core of the motivators is the nature of the job or task. Motivators such as achievement, recognition, responsibility and growth will not be readily present unless the job itself is interesting, challenging and meaningful. (The motivators correspond to Maslow's two higher-order needs, namely ego needs and self-actualisation needs.)

Hygiene factors are present in the job or work environment, are related to the job and are often known as the job context factors. Although, according to Herzberg, these factors do not provide motivation for improved performance, it does not mean that employees do not pay attention to them. If these factors are not present in the work situation, motivation is adversely affected. Individuals or groups who think that they are not receiving fair compensation or that they have to work under unpleasant working conditions, tend to reduce their productivity.

Herzberg sees the solution to the motivation problem in the design of the job itself, especially in job enrichment, to make the work more challenging, interesting and meaningful.

Herzberg was among the first theorists to recognise the importance of personal goals. According to Cronje *et al.* (1987:384) the need to do challenging, interesting and meaningful work, to execute it successfully, to receive recognition for this and to be able to develop in the process, may be regarded as *intrinsic goals* pursued by each employee. Further needs for pleasant working conditions, a good salary, security at work, and so forth may be regarded as *extrinsic goals* pursued by any employee. These sets of employee goals are represented in figure 16.7.

As illustrated in figure 16.7, motivation is intrinsic to the nature of the job itself, whereas certain conditions surrounding the job (i.e. extrinsic conditions) provide need satisfaction.

FIGURE 16.7: Intrinsic and extrinsic goals

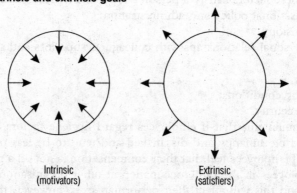

Intrinsic
(motivators)

Extrinsic
(satisfiers)

Although Herzberg's theory has elicited much criticism, his view that job satisfaction lies in the task itself is of value.

What contributes to an employee's enjoyment of the work? Mol (1990:21) maintains that it is pride in attaining a goal, irrespective of theory, and he expands on this as follows:

328

The common thread in all these theories is the idea that motivation results from the opportunities a job provides for increasing the achievement, responsibility, advancement, sense of personal worth, and individuality of a worker.

In other words, if the work itself is not a source of pride for the employee, he or she will never be motivated, but will only be moved. This statement is based on the assumption that most workers have a basic need for self-actualisation and personal pride.

There are, however, a number of theories that question this assumption. These so-called contingency theories emphasise the individual differences between employees and the necessity for managers to focus their approach to motivation on the individual characteristics of each employee. According to Mol (1990:15), the application of this theory holds certain inherent dangers—particularly in South Africa. One of these dangers is that it reinforces the negative behaviour of employees. Another is that it requires managers to be psychoanalysts who must diagnose the unique characteristics of each subordinate. Mol is convinced that most employees can be motivated to higher productivity levels because the majority of employees have a deeply ingrained need to feel good about themselves.

Mol (1990:12) says that his experience in South African organisations indicates that a large number of managers are very successful in motivating their subordinates, particularly at the lower levels. They do this by concentrating on the task or job itself. One of the greatest mistakes made by management and trade unions is to think that fair treatment, pleasant working conditions, above-average remuneration and outstanding fringe benefits will motivate employees. There is no doubt that these aspects are important, but they seldom give rise to an increase in productivity—for the simple reason that they do not contribute towards an employee's enjoyment of the job.

16.5.1.3 Herzberg's theory in management

Herzberg made the following important contribution towards knowledge about motivation (Smit and Cronje 1992:315):

- He expanded on Maslow's ideas and made them more applicable to the workplace.
- Herzberg focused attention on the importance of job-content factors when motivating workers.
- His insight gave rise to a growing interest in job enrichment and the restructuring of work.
- His theory offers an explanation for the limited influence that more money, fringe benefits and better working conditions have on motivation.
- He points out that if managers only concentrate on hygiene factors, no motivation would occur. Motivators must be built into a job.

There is much similarity between the theories of Maslow and Herzberg, as is apparent from figure 16.8.

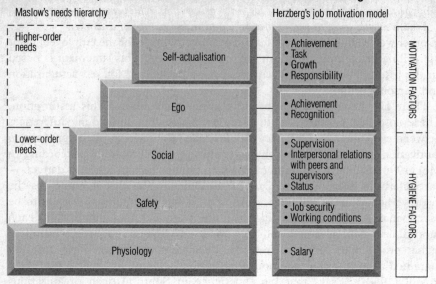

Source: Adapted from Skinner and Ivancevich (1992:346)

16.5.1.4 McClelland's theory of achievement motivation

McClelland (1961) bases his achievement motivation theory on the assumption that there is a relation between the achievement motivation aroused in individuals, entrepreneurship and economic growth of a particular cultural group. He asserts that culture and community play a definitive role in the achievement motivation of the members of that culture or community. His theory is that any person has the potential energy to show a variety of behaviours. How a person behaves, however, depends on the relative strength of his or her various motives, and the opportunities offered in the situation. Litwin and Stringer (1968:12) give the following perspective on McClelland's assumption:

> *A person's aroused motivation to behave in a particular way is said to depend on the strength of readiness of his motives and on two kinds of perceptions of the situation: his expectancies of goal-attainment and the incentive values he attaches to the goals presented.*

This theory may be represented as follows:

Aroused motivation = $M \times E \times I$, where

M = strength of the basic motive,

E = expectancy of attaining the goal, and

I = perceived incentive value of the goal.

The presence and strength of the need to achieve, the need for affiliation and the need for power, are tested by means of a projection test, known as the

Thematic Apperception Test (TAT), which consists of a series of ambiguous pictures. The person being tested is asked to write a story on each of the pictures. From this, McClelland identified three primary needs that are important to different individuals. People with a high need for achievement motivation have the following characteristics:

- They want and accept a high degree of personal responsibility;
- They set realistic performance goals;
- They take calculated risks;
- They show a need for concrete feedback on their actions.

Therefore McClelland found that some people have a significantly higher need for achievement than others, and that they make a greater effort to overcome difficulties in order to achieve their goals.

One shortcoming in McClelland's theory is the oversimplification of the complex composition of work motivation.

16.5.2 Process theories of motivation

Process theories of motivation are aimed at determining not only what arouses behaviour, but the relationship between variables constituting the motivation process. Two process theories are discussed: Vroom's expectancy theory and Adams's equity theory.

16.5.2.1 Vroom's expectancy theory of motivation

The assumption that individuals have expectations about outcomes that may manifest themselves as a result of what they do, underlies the expectancy theory of motivation. A further assumption is that individuals have different preferences for different outcomes. This means that individuals are regarded as thinking and reasoning beings who are able to anticipate future events. Consequently they are able to choose one course of action over another. Vroom (1964) suggests that individuals will be motivated to work well if they have the perception that their efforts will result in successful performance. Furthermore the individual must also expect or believe that successful performance will result in desirable outcomes. These desirable outcomes may be divided into two groups: *intrinsic outcomes*, which are directly related to the task itself, i.e. how interesting and challenging it is, and *extrinsic outcomes*, which are related to the job context environment, i.e. salary and working conditions.

Milton (1981:70) represents the relationship between the basic variables in Vroom's motivation process, namely expectations, outcomes, instrumentalities, valences and choices, as in figure 16.9.

Vroom's variables include the following:

- *Expectancy:* The effort a person makes to obtain a first-level outcome is influenced by his or her expectancy that the outcome will be realised. If the expectancy is that performance will be impossible or improbable, little or

FIGURE 16.9: Vroom's motivation process

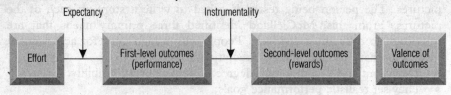

Source: Milton (1981:70)

no effort will be made. If the probability of achieving a specific performance goal is regarded as high, every effort will be made to achieve the goal. Therefore expectancy may be defined as the conviction that a particular action or effort will result in a particular outcome. For this reason expectancy may be regarded as an effort-to-performance relationship. The degree of conviction or expectancy may vary between 0 (a complete lack of conviction) and 1 (complete conviction that the outcome will be realised). However, expectancy is based on the individual's perception of the situation and not on objective reality.

- *Instrumentality:* Reaching a first-level outcome may in itself not mean anything to a person. It may, however, be instrumental in reaching a second-level outcome or reward. For example, reaching the production standard (first-level outcome) may be instrumental in an employee's obtaining a salary, security, recognition, and so forth. Instrumentality is the degree of conviction that the first-level outcome (performance) will result in attaining the second-level outcome (reward). Therefore instrumentality may be regarded as a performance-to-outcome relationship and can vary between −1 and +1.

- *Valence:* Valence refers to the expected satisfaction that will follow an outcome, rather than the immediate satisfaction it brings. The importance or value of second-level outcomes varies according to the degree to which the outcomes will satisfy the individual's needs. The strength of an individual's preference for an outcome is called valence. This may be positive or negative, and varies from −1 to 0 to +1; in other words, from minimal importance to very important. For example, if acceptance by the group has a positive valence for an employee, an increase in the volume of production may have a negative valence because it may result in the employee's being rejected by his or her peers.

Vroom's motivation process (figure 16.9) contains three variables which affect motivation: from right to left valence, instrumentality and expectancy. These are collectively termed VIE.

Calculating VIE

Each VIE variable has a numerical value and these values may be used collectively to calculate motivation or effort to perform.

332

Example of how to calculate VIE

Say a production employee expects that extra effort will probably result in a first-level outcome, namely higher production (expectancy 0,8). This employee is strongly convinced that such performance will lead to increased remuneration (instrumentality 0,9). The employee really wants a salary increase (valence 0,9). When these factors are multiplied $(0,8 \times 0,9 \times 0,9 = 0,65)$, it may be deduced that this production employee is strongly motivated to achieve. If expectancy, instrumentality or valence has a value of zero, the resulting motivation will also be zero.

The question is how management can use this theory to accomplish achievement motivation. An individual's *expectancy* of reaching a first-level outcome is influenced by a number of variables, including the work as such, previous experience in similar situations, the individual's self-esteem and self-image, and communication. Management can affect these variables by introducing training or by redesigning a task in order to change an employee's expectancy. In the same way management can affect *instrumentality* by introducing a compensation system and promotion policy (second-level outcomes) that are clearly linked to performance (first-level outcome). Management can thus readily change expectancy and instrumentality variables. The last variable in Vroom's theory, *valence*, cannot be manipulated as easily, as it depends on individual differences and preferences. In other words, the value attached to second-level outcomes (such as compensation) differs from one individual to the next. Therefore managers must take into account individual preferences in respect of salary, promotion, recognition and so on, and make an effort to satisfy individual preferences with the available outcomes.

This theory is complex, but it can be summarised by saying that individual performance orientation is determined by motivation, personal ability and the environment in which the individual functions. The expectancy theory assumes that motivation leads to a certain attempt and that the attempt, individual ability and environment will result in a certain performance (Smit and Cronje 1992:335). The individual attaches a certain value (preference) to each result.

Figure 16.10 is a simple example of the above.

At the core of the expectancy model is the expectation of individuals that an attempt will result in a certain performance and that this performance will lead to certain outcomes (results), each of which has a value.

16.5.2.2 Adams's equity theory of motivation

Adams (1975) bases his equity theory of motivation on the assumption that motivation is influenced by the degree of equity an employee experiences in the work situation. This boils down to a comparison of what one employee

333

FIGURE 16.10: Example of the expectancy model

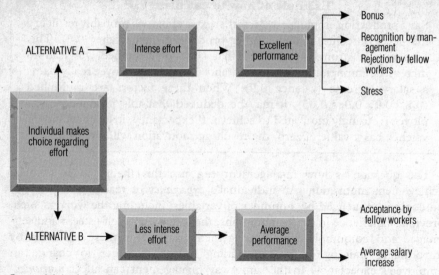

Source: Adapted from Donnelly *et al.* (1987:305)

receives on the basis of his or her effort with what other employees receive on the basis of their efforts. For example, if an employee feels that he or she is being paid less than one or more colleagues for the same quality and quantity of work, such an employee will be dissatisfied and attempt to reduce the inequity. The degree of inequity is determined by comparing the relation between an employee's outcomes (remuneration) to his or her inputs (effort) with that of a comparable employee. The comparative process is schematically shown in figure 16.11.

FIGURE 16.11: Adams's theory of comparison

Source: Adapted from Milton (1981:73)

If an employee sees that his or her outcomes and inputs are not equal to those of a comparable employee, feelings of disequilibrium will be aroused. Aspects of this theory are:

- *Input-outcome factors:* According to Milton, inputs include anything the employee regards as an investment in his or her work and that is worthy of a certain yield. Examples are skills, training, education, previous experience and effort. Outcomes are anything an employee may regard as a yield from the work situation. They may be positive or negative. Positive outcomes include salary, intrinsic job satisfaction, satisfactory supervision, seniority benefits and status in the organisation. Negative outcomes include poor working conditions, monotony, lack of security and other hygiene factors.

- *The inequity comparison process:* An employee's present position is compared not only with that of other employees, but with where he or she was or would have been in a previous or other organisation. This process of comparison is closely related to the psychological contract discussed in chapter 4. One of three things happens when an employee compares the relation between his or her inputs and outcomes with that of a comparable employee:
  - If these ratios are equal, the employee experiences *equity*. Mathematically, it may be represented as:

  $$\frac{Op}{Ip} = \frac{Ocp}{Icp}$$

  where O and I are outcomes and inputs respectively, p is the employee and cp the comparable employee, group of employees or position in previous or other organisations.
  - If the employee experiences inequity in the sense that his or her outcome-input ratio is less than that of the comparable employee, the employee experiences a state of *underpayment*. The mathematical representation is:

  $$\frac{Op}{Ip} < \frac{Ocp}{Icp}$$

  This situation causes dissatisfaction.
  - If the employee experiences inequity in the sense that his or her outcome-input ratio is more than that of the comparable employee, the employee experiences a state of *overpayment*. The mathematical representation is:

  $$\frac{Op}{Ip} > \frac{Ocp}{Icp}$$

  This situation may cause dissatisfaction.

How does this affect motivation? Inequity causes dissatisfaction or an unhappy emotional state. In the first place, a perception of inequity causes internal tension in the employee. This tension is proportionate to the degree of inequity: the greater the inequity, the greater the internal tension. Secondly, this tension will motivate the employee to attempt to reduce it. The employee will therefore make an effort to obtain equity or to reduce inequity. Once again the strength of the motivation is proportionate to the degree of tension generated and is therefore a function of the degree of inequity experienced.

Research has shown that inequity may be reduced in one or more of the following ways:

- *The employee may change his or her inputs* by reducing or increasing them, depending on the situation, in other words, depending on whether the inequity is ascribed to underpayment or overpayment. Increased inputs will reduce perceived inequity resulting from overpayment; reduced inputs (doing less work) will reduce inequity resulting from under-payment. This behaviour is consistent with a person's being a system in own right.
- *The employee may change his or her outcomes* by increasing them if the outcome-input ratio is lower than that of the comparable employee, or by reducing them if the outcome-input ratio is higher than that of the comparable employee.
- *The employee may distort his or her inputs and outcomes subjectively* by re-evaluating their use, relevance and importance. This boils down to the allocation of changed weights to both inputs and outcomes. For example, the employee may assign a lower weight to previous experience, thus reducing inequity.
- *The employee may withdraw*: This includes resigning from the organisation, requesting a transfer and other withdrawal behaviour such as absenteeism.
- *The employee may react to the comparable employee*: The employee may subjectively distort the inputs or outcomes of the comparable employee.
- *The employee may change the object of comparison*: This means that the employee replaces the comparable employee with another employee, with whom there is a more balanced comparison.

The equity theory implies that problems arise in employees' performance orientation if their perception is that they are not being equally remunerated. Therefore employees must be paid comparable salaries and wages. The real compensation an employee receives, however, is not as important as his or her relative compensation (what other employees receive in the same circum-stances). In terms of the equity theory an employee assesses his or her outcome-input ratio in accordance with that of relevant comparable employees.

16.6 OUCHI'S THEORY Z
According to the traditional approach to motivation, this theory cannot be regarded as a pure motivation theory, but can rather be categorised as a *special management style*, which combines Western and Eastern approaches to the management of people.

William Ouchi, a Japanese management expert, analysed the successful enterprises of both the USA and Japan and developed the so-called "Theory Z". Its characteristics are (Skinner and Ivancevich 1992:343):

- Life-long employment (to meet physiological and social needs);
- Individual responsibility (to meet social, ego or self-esteem needs);

- Careful evaluation and promotion (to promote self-confidence and self-esteem);
- Opportunities to use skills (to meet self-actualisation needs).

The Japanese approach to managing people is compared with Theory Z and the general South African management style in table 16.1.

TABLE 16.1: Comparison between management styles

Characteristics	South Africa	Japan	Theory Z
Employment period	Short- to medium-term, particularly among • unskilled workers • semi-skilled workers • middle management Large-scale redundancy under poor economic conditions	Long-term: life-long if possible	Keep employees under good and poor economic conditions
Performance appraisal and promotion	Mostly quarterly, based on serious dissatisfaction or previous promotions	Appraisal takes place with the future (long term) in mind and promotion is gradual	Assessment of skills and promotion are based on contribution and not on service period
Decision-making	Generally autocratic. Mainly done by person in control	Collective, with inputs from all interest groups	A democratic process striving for consensus
Responsibility	Strong personal responsibility	Group responsibility, i.e. shared responsibility	Responsibility lies with key individuals
Control	Policy, rules, regulations and standard procedure are strictly adhered to	Self-control	Informal but with the focus on objective facts and information
Involvement with employees	Focus only on the work itself	Focus on the whole life of the employee	Focus on the employee's life and family

Theory Z emphasises the principle of participative management. Employees participate in setting goals, solving problems, taking decisions and designing and implementing change. Participation or involvement is seen as a motivation factor—nevertheless it must be kept in mind that not all employees want to become involved in these activities.

Furthermore, some work situations require that there should *not* be participation: for example, a military commander who must take quick decisions during a battle cannot make use of participatory decision-making.

Theory Z can be particularly useful in a country such as South Africa, where there is a general need for mutual recognition within an ethnically or culturally diverse employee corps. Safety and physiological needs have enjoyed much attention in South Africa, especially in the past five years, and are now more important than ever before, for the following reasons:

- The official unemployment figure is now 46% (1994).
- Shelter and food are supplied to the population by numerous government and private institutions.
- Unrest and anarchy are the order of the day.
- The "brain drain" is the highest in the world.
- Capital outflow is massive.
- Personal taxation for the middle-income group is the highest in the world.
- As a result of taxation, company profits are the lowest in what are known as the first-group and second-group countries of the world.

16.7 GUIDELINES FOR PRODUCING MOTIVATED EMPLOYEE BEHAVIOUR

Milton (1981:80) makes the following comment on the problem hampering the achievement of motivated employee behaviour:

Unlike the physicist or chemist, the student of organizational behavior has no uniform formula(s) to apply for achieving desired results. This is especially true of motivation. Motives cannot be seen; they must be inferred from what the individual does or says. Such inferences are complicated because the employee may not be conscious of his or her needs or may not express them adequately. Also a single act may be an expression of several needs.

Although there is no magic formula for producing motivated employee behaviour, Milton (1981:80-1) suggests various guidelines for management:

- *Know the basic human needs and motivation processes:* Human needs arouse human behaviour. Insight into general and work-related needs and knowledge of the relation between the variables affecting motivation are the first step towards understanding the complexity of motivation.
- *Place the motivation process in the context of the organisation:* Motivation is more than human needs and personal characteristics. It is affected by job characteristics and organisational culture. Motivation is the result of numerous direct and indirect variables.
- *Bear in mind that individuals differ from each other:* No two people are the same. Something that motivates one person will not necessarily have the same effect on another, because the needs structures of people differ.
- *Know your employees as unique individuals:* Any person in a senior position spends time with subordinates, which affords him or her the opportunity to get to know their needs, aspirations and frustrations. Openness, mutual trust and two-way communication will enable any superior to discover which factors motivate his or her subordinates.
- *Be aware of things that threaten need satisfaction:* Many organisations are continually changing their work flow, job structures, policies, procedures and so on. These changes may threaten people whose needs are at present

satisfied. Sensitivity to these potential threats may lead to the development of alternatives that will eliminate negative effects.

- *Promote changes conducive to the satisfaction of human needs:* A manager may initiate changes that have the potential to satisfy human needs in the organisation. This should be done with circumspection, however, as change may also cause resistance among some employees.

How can employees in South Africa be motivated?

If Theory Z is applied to South Africa, this will entail acceptance of the following:

- Democracy in the workplace;
- The realisation that people are the most important asset of an organisation;
- The job satisfaction experienced by an employee is to the advantage of the organisation, the family and the community as a whole;
- Policies, procedures, rules and regulations are only meant to guide employees in their decisions, and not to be slavishly followed;
- Responsibility lies within the employee;
- Sound interpersonal and group relations in the workplace contribute towards motivated behaviour by individual employees;
- The esteem and respect of supervisors and managers for the employee as a human being, irrespective of his or her level of competence, is a basic human right;
- The employee, irrespective of race, sex, religious conviction, age and physical or mental state is a human being in his or her own right, i.e. a being created by God.
- Employees must be remunerated according to their real worth to the organisation they serve.

16.8 CONCLUSION

In this chapter motivation was discussed from various points of view. First a distinction was made between content theories and process theories of motivation by discussing the traditional theories of well-known authors. Cognisance should be taken of all these theories, as a single theory does not enable one to motivate employees. Therefore insight into the complex relation between variables that affect employee motivation negatively or positively is essential. One needs to remember that each employee has a unique personality, unique needs and unique preferences. It is therefore essential that employees be motivated on the basis of their unique characteristics.

Questions

1. In your own words, give a definition of motivation.
2. Draw a diagram of the process of motivation and discuss it from a practical frame of reference.
3. Compare and contrast Maslow's motivation theory with that of Herzberg.

4. Give a critical evaluation of Vroom's expectancy theory of motivation.
5. Discuss the behaviour an employee will manifest when he or she experiences inequity in the work situation.
6. Give a critical evaluation of Theory Z in organisations.
7. Based on your knowledge of motivation, compile a list of guidelines that you can follow to produce motivated employee behaviour.

Sources

Adams, S.J. 1975. Inequality in social exchange. In L. Berkovitz (ed.) *Advances in experimental social psychology*. Academic Press, New York.

Armstrong, A. 1988. *A handbook of personnel management practice*. Kogan Page, London.

Cronje, G.J. de J., Mol, A.J., Palmer, P.N., Vegter, E. & Van Dyk, P.S. 1982. *Business economics (study guide)*. UNISA, Pretoria.

Donnelly, J.H., Gibson, J.L. & Ivancevich, J.M. 1987. *Fundamentals of management*. Business Publications, Plano, Texas.

Litwin, G.H. & Stringer, R.A. 1968. *Motivation and organizational climate*. Division of Research, Harvard University, Boston.

Maslow, A.H. 1954. *Motivation and personality*. Harper & Row, New York.

McClelland, D.C. 1961. *The achieving society*. Van Nostrand, New Jersey.

Milkovich, G.T. & Boudreau, J.W. 1988. *Personnel/human resource management: a diagnostic approach*. Business Publications, Plano, Texas.

Milton, C.R. 1981. *Human behavior in organizations: three levels of behavior*. Prentice-Hall, Englewood Cliffs, New Jersey.

Mol, A.J. 1990. Motivating subordinates. *IPM Journal*. March, pp. 19–23.

Skinner, S.J. & Ivancevich, T.M. 1992. *Business for the 21st century*. Irwin, Homewood, Illinois.

Smit, P.J. & Cronje, G.J. de J. 1992. *Bestuursbeginsels: 'n eietydse Suid-Afrikaanse uitgawe*. Juta, Cape Town.

Vroom, V.N. 1964. *Work and motivation*. Wiley, New York.

Chapter 17

Leadership in organisations

P.S. van Dyk

STUDY OBJECTIVES

After studying this chapter, you should be able to:
- Pragmatically describe leadership;
- Differentiate between leadership and management;
- Explain leadership challenges in South Africa;
- Theoretically discuss the basics of leadership;
- Differentiate between the following leadership approaches and discuss them in detail:
  — The leadership trait approach;
  — The functional approach;
  — The behaviouristic approach;
  — The situational approach;
- Differentiate between the variables that influence leadership.

17.1 INTRODUCTION

The management of organisations is increasingly realising that *leadership*, not *management*, is the critical success factor for an organisation. The focus is increasingly on leadership and leadership development rather than on management and management development.

> *Leadership is unquestionably the crucial determinant of the success of any institution, be it one of the great industrialised nations of the late twentieth century, the Chrysler Corporation or a chestnut vendor in front of the Royal Ontario Museum on a brisk October afternoon. Focusing on leadership is going for the jugular.* (Dimma 1989:17)

Never before has South Africa had such a great need for effective leadership, in the country as a whole, the government at all levels, all economic sectors and other groupings. Leadership ultimately determines the quality of life of all citizens. The country depends on sound leadership.

FIGURE 17.1: Principal learning components of leadership

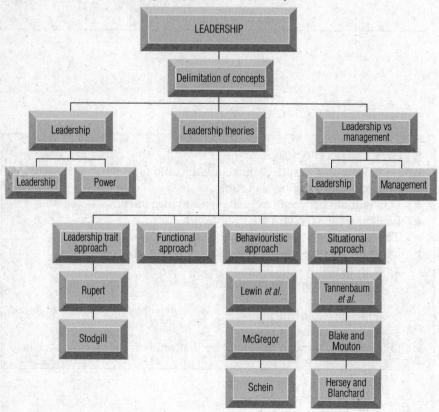

The performance of any organisation, large or small, is in direct relation to the quality of its leadership. Even if leadership is not the only important component of a company's success, it is an important one. Cronje *et al.* (1987:113) point out that the business world is full of examples where the success or demise of a certain organisation can be ascribed to a specific leader. The success of Sun International under Sol Kerzner, Standard Bank under Dr Conrad Strauss, Barlow Rand under Warren Clewlow, Rembrandt under Dr Anton Rupert, Sanlam under Dr A. Wassenaar and Toyota under Dr A. Wessels need not necessarily be ascribed to the competence of these leaders as managers. However, these successes can to a considerable extent be ascribed to the leadership of these people. In the case of organisations that are less successful, a relation may also be found between success or performance and the quality of leadership. The thought that comes to the fore here is that good managers will take their organisations to greater heights of performance, productivity and ultimately profitability if these managers are also good leaders.

The way in which leadership is practised is certainly one of the critical management functions determining the success of modern organisations in South Africa. Since modern approaches to leadership require superiors to act in a situationally diagnostic way towards individuals or groups in accordance with their particular traits, leadership in South African organisations is particularly complex. South African organisations are characterised not only by a disproportion between the number of skilled and unskilled workers, but by a large variety of cultures represented in their workers corps. This sets the scene for great challenges regarding effective leadership in South African organisations.

> *Leadership is one of the most important elements affecting the performance of organisations. Poor leadership is often cited as one of the key problems in floundering organisations and also in the downfall of governments. Conversely, good leadership is used to account for all kinds of success.*

Source: Cogill in Barling *et al.* (1986:473)

It may therefore be stated unequivocally that the practising of sound leadership is a critical factor in the successful management of organisations—especially in South Africa with its complex composition of human resources.

17.2 WHAT IS LEADERSHIP?

Leadership in general refers to the influencing of subordinates by a superior in order to persuade them to pursue the goals of an organisation actively and effectively.

A few decades ago, Stodgill (1950:1) provided an accurate definition of leadership: "The process of influencing the activities of an organized group in its efforts towards goal setting and goal achievement".

From an extensive investigation into leadership in South Africa, Schilbach (1983:18) concludes that leadership may be defined as follows:

Leadership is an interpersonal process through which a leader directs the activities of individuals or groups towards the purposeful pursuance of given objectives within a particular situation, by means of communication.

This view contains the following important aspects:

- Leadership is regarded as an activity that gives rise to active, visible conduct.

343

- It is an interpersonal process pursuing certain objectives by means of influencing people — individuals as well as groups.
- Inborn talents as well as acquired skills are applied when leadership is practised.
- Leadership is practised by means of communication.

Leadership is therefore a complex process directly aimed at achieving the goals of the organisation.

17.3 LEADERSHIP CHALLENGES FACING THE MANAGERS OF SOUTH AFRICAN ORGANISATIONS TODAY

Because of the complex composition of labour in South African organisations, the challenges facing managers in their leadership capacity are of particular importance for the survival of our society in a highly competitive international market. These challenges are summed up pertinently by Jopie van Rooyen (1991:8), Manager: Organisation Development of the HSRC. Her views are now discussed (with permission).

Organisations, as micro-representatives of the greater social environment, are confronted by "crucible challenges" in creating new workplace cultures. Creating new cultures is the responsibility of managers — they require unique leadership skills. New perspectives need to be developed on the nature, purpose and structures of organisations and the influence that change, particularly in available human resources, may have on organisational functioning, culture and ultimate effectiveness.

Fundamental questions to be addressed in developing new perspectives relate to economic and technological issues, such as:
- The nature of national and international competition and changing markets, and how this will affect the organisation;
- Uncertainties related to recessionary and inflationary circumstances and the organisation's ability to adjust in time;
- High-technology changes, particularly in communications and computer technology, and their educational implications;
- Changes in production and service due to changes in the workforce (skilled, unskilled, professional and managerial);
- The productivity and cost-effectiveness implications of worker skills and worker effectiveness, and the continued viability of the concern.

The socio-political changes confronting South African companies emphasise the need for managers to be aware of:
- Expectations that a redistribution of wealth must occur, and how this can influence workers' aspirations;
- Conflicts arising from changes in government policy (e.g. subsidisation) and regulations;
- Mechanisms and skills required to resolve potential disputes between the "haves" and "have-nots";
- Social responsibility and environmental management needs.

The development of power coalitions forcing change from a socio-political perspective can have important implications for the changes required in workplace cultures. Issues that may have to be confronted call for:

- Democratisation of the workplace and greater distribution of power;
- New definitions of equity and changes in employment practices;
- Eliminating differences in interpreting concepts such as work productivity and the work ethic;
- Addressing, in a work context, unemployment realities, political aspirations and expectations of freedom, power and riches among members of the younger generation.

Organisations, as social entities, maintain congruence and effectiveness in part through their cultures. Culture is often called the normative glue that keeps the organisation together. Such cultures are based on shared beliefs, norms and values of employees which create feelings of homogeneity and identification by individuals with the organisation and what it stands for.

A challenge faced by leaders in organisations is to reassess existing organisational cultures and to acquire the skills needed to develop new workplace cultures as they become necessary. If workers regard the existing culture as outdated, organisational effectiveness as a whole can be affected.

Inherent in the culture challenges lies a need for knowledge and skills to deal with potential disillusionment, frustration and dissatisfaction among professional, managerial, technical, skilled and unskilled workers because of the nature of change or the tempo with which change takes place or is being forced to take place. A further challenge relates to the accuracy with which managers at all levels of an organisation can assess environmental threats and opportunities facing their concerns. Assessing organisational strengths and weaknesses is a strategic team effort involving different competencies and skills at different levels of management. Assessment is needed to determine, for instance, whether the organisation's mission can be realised given its present resources. An assessment of a workable strategy, which identifies the manner in which the major organisational resources can be fitted together to accomplish the mission, is required. This is not merely a management function, but involves inputs of different kinds from all levels of the organisation.

Strategy implementation is not merely the mechanistic application of a predefined plan. It is a process involving team work on all levels of management. It requires new ways of thinking, solving problems, functioning as a team, communication and developing and motivating staff. It also requires reassessing the value of existing techniques because there is no blueprint for dealing with change.

An issue of particular importance in leadership is determining who should influence the actual strategic decision-making process at different levels of management. For instance, which managers should contribute specific inputs because of the functional or interpersonal influence they may have in implementing certain critical change interventions? Which questions should be asked to assist in translating vision into changed realities? Table 17.1 indicates critical role responsibilities inherent in different levels of management which can influence decision-making ability, particularly in times of change.

TABLE 17.1: Levels of management: key responsibilities in dealing with change

Global-strategic level vision and direction of organisation 6
Theoretical-abstract level creating new perspectives on adaptation, based on vision and direction 5
Conceptual-creative level creating or integrating a new or adapted visualisation of the organisation's direction and functioning 4
Conceptual assessment level determining the relationships of different organisational functions as a systematic unit 3
Concrete-conceptual level plan for achieving results in concrete terms 2
Concrete-direct level ensuring direct, concrete job outputs 1

Top management may have the power to conceptualise the necessary changes while senior management may have the power to convert the conceptualisation into potentially workable theories and strategies. Middle management may have the potential power to translate theory and strategy into workable realities. But some of the questions to be addressed are:

- Do managers, at all levels of functioning, have the insight to know how a change in the organisation's mission and functional strategy will impact on its existing culture?
- Do they have the skills to lead the changing of such workplace cultures when required?
- Can managers handle cultural changes which are influenced by external environmental realities and which can contribute to continued organisational effectiveness?
- Do line managers have the required skills to recognise and deal with value issues emanating from different cultural and socio-political expectations?

Effective human resources management is not only a staff function; it forms an integral part of a line manager's role. Human resources management is a responsibility built into the management process, but to discharge this responsibility effectively requires specific competencies and skills. Managing people is never easy and many managers' preferred style of management is more suited to functional supervision in stable conditions than functioning as leaders of multicultural groups in circumstances of turbulence, conflict and change.

Environmental changes confronting organisations with complex human issues also influence the functioning of human resources practitioners. Such issues now become important business matters to be addressed at the highest level because of the real and potential impact of worker effectiveness on productivity and the economic viability of an organisation. Effective handling of people-related business issues may therefore also require new roles, competencies, relationships and ways of operating from human resources managers. They must stop regarding their role as that of a professional individual contributor and realise that their job is to provide organisations with leadership on human resources.

Conclusion

South Africa needs managers who can ride the waves of change, who can function as leaders in the process of organisational and environmental adaptation to change. They must be able to read environmental signals and translate such signals into meaningful messages to be dealt with in various ways according to the requirements of the specific work circumstances.

Skills must be developed to scan the environment in anticipation of how, for instance, changed labour resources, changed economic circumstances and changed government policy can combine to create forces that are likely to influence each other, to gather momentum and to reshape the structure, culture and future of the organisation.

In analysing the leadership challenges faced by South African managers, certain themes become evident:

- Managers must be aware that in the "crucible process" confronting South Africa they, as leaders, will have no option but to change as well. They will have to learn to change from justifying what was done in the past to assessing strengths and weaknesses through a new perspective based on an awareness of the implications of the change that is taking place, and of how to deal with it. Managers will have to learn new skills, new competencies and new management styles.
- Managers are key actors in the creation and maintenance of the organisation's culture. Awareness of changes in workers' goals, values and expectations and how these need to be integrated to form a new workplace culture is important. Two elements that are closely connected with this are power politics and worker resistance. Strategic changes are influenced by ideological and personal issues. Successful leadership requires understanding of these dynamics, predicting the impact of

347

change and shaping situations and circumstances to make constructive use of change.

Finally, the art of negotiating is indispensable for all managers. An important aspect of negotiating is understanding how issues are interpreted, i.e. the ability to see circumstances through the eyes of other parties. Appreciating the views of others requires awareness of one's own perspectives—it requires knowing that some of the things managers may need to learn go well beyond "management" as it is commonly defined and practised. Managers need to develop skills that enable them to make sense and create new meaning out of change.

17.4 THE DIFFERENCE BETWEEN MANAGEMENT AND LEADERSHIP

There is some confusion about the meaning of or difference between management and leadership. A manager is a person who exercises daily management functions (planning, organising, leading, control) in an organisation and who holds a formal position of authority in the organisational hierarchy.

For example, a production foreman is a formal (first-level) manager who has been placed in charge of a number of production workers.

A leader, on the other hand, is any person capable of persuading other people (followers) to strive for certain goals (formal or informal).

One question that often arises is whether a person can be both a manager and a leader. The answer is yes, but a manager is not necessarily a leader, and vice versa.

For example, a production foreman is a manager because of the formal position of authority he holds and the legal authority he has. Whether the production foreman is a leader will depend on whether he has the ability to activate his subordinates to strive for the goals of the organisation.

The difference between management and leadership can be explained as follows (Cronje *et al.* 1987:115):

Managers are the bearers of authority allocated to them by the organisation—that is, they have the authority to enforce, order and direct the activities of others. This includes issuing orders and being responsible for their execution. A leader has the authority but gets results without having to use force. He is a leader by virtue of certain personal qualities that he possesses, including the ability to consult his followers and motivate them, enlisting their co-operation of their own free will.

Charlton (1992:33) defines leadership as the competencies and processes required to enable and empower ordinary people to do extraordinary things (outstanding performance) despite difficulties, and to maintain this to their own advantage and that of society.

He states that, just like leadership, empowerment is a term that is much used but with little understanding, and he maintains that organisations are *over-managed* and *under-led*. He defines empowerment as the action of investment and the allocation of authority through which organisations and people are able to reach their goals. This involves power sharing and allowing people to think and take decisions.

Furthermore, empowerment means giving people the authority to carry out their responsibilities, as well as removing factors that hamper personal and organisational development.

Table 17.2 sums up the difference between leadership and management.

TABLE 17.2: Leadership versus management

Category	Management	Leadership
Change	• Peacemakers: maintenance work, maintaining the present • Repeats and follows what is desirable and necessary • Administers • Maintains • First-degree (cosmetic) change	• Pacemakers: further change and create the future • Changes people's ideas about what is desirable, possible and necessary • Innovates • Develops • Second-degree (fundamental) change
People	• Depends on systems	• Depends on people
Attention	• Does things right	• Does the right things right
Planning	• Thinks of today	• Strategic thinking: forward planning
Thinking	• Focuses on the present • Focuses on getting things done • Reacts to events	• Vision of the future and strategy to attain it • Systematic structure: patterns underlying behaviour
Role	• Makes things happen; implementation • Tailor • Pupil • "You serve me"	• Influencing, guidance • Designer (vision, social architecture) • Teacher (more insight into reality; questions assumptions) • Server (attitude of serving others)
Attitude towards goals	• Impersonal, even passive • Goals arise out of necessity • External control • Reacts to change • Expectations ("You owe me")	• Active • Influences and changes the organisation • Internal control • Exercises personal choice and responsibility for change and the future • Aspirations ("I can create something")

Table 17.2 (continued)

Category	Management	Leadership
Worth (meaning)	• Reacts to worth	• High degree of personal worth • Controls and creates worth
Work	• Trusts in planning, budgets and other management instruments • Survival instinct dominates willingness to take risks	• Prepared to invest trust in others; excitement; prepared to take risks • Trusts the judgement of key executive officer • Focuses on value as the basis of motivation
Interpersonal	• Low level of emotional involvement; task-oriented	• Ability to empathise; gives and receives feedback
Self-image	• Regards self as conservative regulator of a *status quo* personally identified with	• Self-image does not depend on membership, job role or social identity • Seeks opportunity for change
Motivation	• Threat: "big stick" • Remuneration: "carrots"	• Develops intrinsic motivation • Creates goal or hope
Power	• Win/lose orientation • Counts on control	• Orientation that benefits can be extended • Gives power to receive power • Counts on trust

Source: Charlton (1992:33–4)

Good managers are therefore not necessarily good leaders, and good leaders are not necessarily good managers. From the point of view of organisational productivity, it is of course desirable that all managers should also be leaders — hence the constant search for people who are both managers and leaders.

Dimma (1989:19) identifies the following qualities of a leader:

- Leaders are often generous.
- Leaders often do the unexpected with excellent results; they often upset the *status quo*.
- Leaders are spontaneous and not reserved. They are seldom lazy.
- Leaders are professional; their behaviour is based on and guided by a set of honourable principles.
- Leaders are willing to tackle difficult problems. They are not afraid of taking decisions and do not avoid accountability.

17.5 AUTHORITY AND POWER: THE BASICS OF LEADERSHIP

There are almost as many theories and models of leadership as there are writers on the subject. However, all the theories contain two important concepts: authority and power.

17.5.1 Authority

Before the various approaches to leadership are briefly discussed, it is important to obtain clarity about the concept "authority" and its role in the leadership process. Cronje *et al.* (1987:114) say that every manager is, on occasion, also a leader who sees to it that subordinates co-operate in attaining the goals of the organisation, irrespective of the level of management. Without authority, no manager can manage. Authority thus has to do with obtaining the right to enforce certain actions within certain guidelines, and the right to punish failure.

According to Cronje *et al.*, authority is closely related to leadership. Authority is awarded to a manager by the management of an organisation. Unlike authority, power is not awarded to a manager, but is obtained in various ways. This difference between authority and power is important, because in practice there are many people who have authority (which has been awarded), but not the power (which must be earned) to exercise this authority effectively. Power is thus a basis of leadership.

17.5.2 Power

Power is awarded by the subordinates of a leader or manager. To have power, a leader (manager) must therefore have subordinates or followers. Leaders can influence followers and effectively assert their authority because a leader must have some sort of power to be called a leader. Without this it is maintained that a leader is not able to influence followers in such a way that they voluntarily aim their activities at the productive attainment of the goals. Power, i.e. the ability to influence the behaviour of others, has nothing to do with the hierarchical position held by a manager, and it is not obtained through a title or entry on an organisational chart—it must be earned by the leader. For this reason someone with authority and power, i.e. a manager with power, is much better than a manager who only has authority.

> Leadership is the ability to influence others to co-operate voluntarily.

French and Raven (in Griffin 1989:421) distinguish between the following types of power, which are generally accepted in management literature:

- *Legitimate power:* This is the authority allocated to a certain post by the organisation. According to this, a manager has the right to require subordinates to carry out their duties, and the right to dismiss them if they fail to do so. Legitimate power is thus the same as authority. Even if a manager has legitimate power, this does not mean that he or she is a good leader.
- *Reward power:* This is used to give or withhold rewards. Such rewards include salary increases, bonuses, recognition or interesting tasks. The greater the number of rewards controlled by a manager and the more

important these rewards are to subordinates, the greater the manager's reward power.

- *Coercive power:* This is exercised through fear, which may be psychological or physical.

Criminal gangs often exercise coercive power through physical violence.

- *Referent power:* This is also known as personal power and is a somewhat abstract concept. Subordinates follow a leader with referent power simply because they like or respect him or her or identify with him or her. In other words, the leader's personal traits make him or her attractive to others. Charismatic leaders such as Hitler, Yasser Arafat and even Idi Amin are examples.
- *Expert power:* This type of power is based on knowledge and expertise, and a leader who has this has a certain power over those who have a need for this knowledge or information. The more important the information and the fewer the people who have it, the greater the expert power of the individual who does.

Managers who want to be successful must exercise leadership in such a way that there is a healthy balance between their power and that of subordinates. Figure 17.2 illustrates this balance.

FIGURE 17.2: **Balance between managerial power and the power of subordinates**

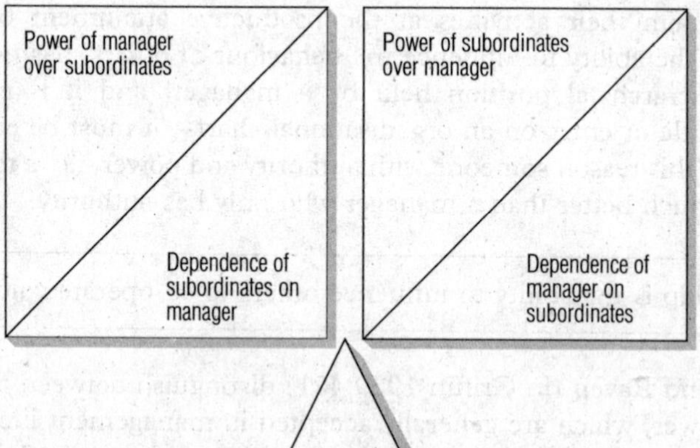

Power of manager over subordinates

Dependence of subordinates on manager

Power of subordinates over manager

Dependence of manager on subordinates

Source: Mescon *et al.* (1985:103)

A further essential differentiation must be made between position power and personal power. *Position power* points to formal leadership and is instituted by all organisations from the top to the bottom, while *personal power* points to informal leadership which is allocated to a leader, because of his or her personal qualities, by subordinates or followers.

Charlton (1992:ix) has a unique view of the power of a leader. He maintains that effective leadership is not about position power in an organisation's management hierarchy, but about personal power that enables the leader (manager) to create a bright future and the desired quality of life. Leadership is concerned with the creation of realistic expectations and balancing them against aspirations (see the psychological contract, chapter 4). It is the task of the leader to create the context in which both expectations and aspirations can be satisfied. Charlton (1992:ix) further remarks:

The challenge of leadership faces every person in every role in every society. An organisation's ability to survive is directly dependent on growing leaders and this in turn is dependent on meeting the cry of the human heart—of putting humanity back into organisations. An organisation's ability, skills and commitment to enable, empower and liberate human resources will be its only source of competitive advantage in the future. In this respect, it is a race—the Human Race.

FIGURE 17.3: Leadership and the quality of work life

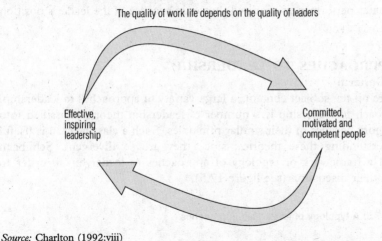

The quality of work life depends on the quality of leaders

Effective, inspiring leadership

Committed, motivated and competent people

Source: Charlton (1992:viii)

Hersey and Blanchard use position power and personal power to explain successful and effective leadership. According to them, any leadership effort will result in subordinate behaviour which may be classified as successful or unsuccessful somewhere on a continuum between the two extremes, as illustrated in figure 17.4.

Figure 17.4 implies that if the behaviour of subordinates is unsuccessful the leadership effort was inadequate. If the leadership effort is successful, however, it must be measured against a further criterion, namely effectiveness. For the leadership effort to be effective, subordinates must perform because they wanted to, in other words, their performance must tie in with their personal goals and needs, and be profitable to them. The leader therefore uses personal power, even though he or she has position power. On the other

FIGURE 17.4: Continuum of successful and effective leadership

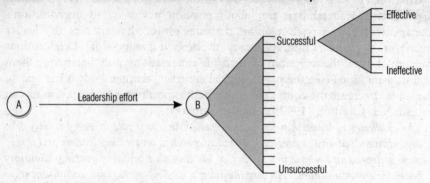

Source: Hersey and Blanchard (1982:104)

hand, a leadership effort may be successful but ineffective if the leader made use of reward or punishment to influence subordinates' behaviour. The subordinates performed as required, but only because of the leader's position power.

17.6 APPROACHES TO LEADERSHIP
17.6.1 General
Literature on the subject contains a large variety of approaches to leadership. An approach to leadership is a number of leadership theories classified into one category because of their similar principles. Such a classification is useful for understanding these theories, since they are so divergent. Schilbach designed a framework or typology of approaches to leadership in order to facilitate their discussion (see figure 17.5).

FIGURE 17.5: A typology of leadership approaches

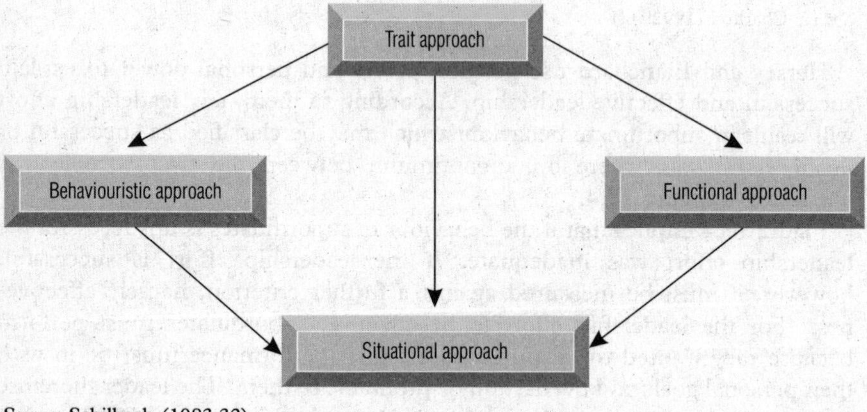

```
                    ┌─────────────────┐
                    │  Trait approach │
                    └─────────────────┘
                   ↙          ↓          ↘
┌──────────────────────┐  │  ┌─────────────────────┐
│ Behaviouristic approach│ │  │ Functional approach │
└──────────────────────┘  │  └─────────────────────┘
                   ↘          ↓          ↙
                    ┌─────────────────────┐
                    │ Situational approach│
                    └─────────────────────┘
```

Source: Schilbach (1983:32)

354

The approach of Schilbach (who conducted one of the most extensive investigations of leadership in South Africa) is now discussed in accordance with various writers' views of the different theories.

17.6.2 The trait approach to leadership

This approach derives from the so-called "great man theory". In the past, researchers tried to compare the traits of successful leaders (great personalities) in order to compile a list of ideal traits against which a person's leadership potential could be measured or predicted.

In 1965 Dr Anton Rupert conducted such an investigation in South Africa. He corresponded with some of the most prominent world leaders of the time in order to determine which traits they regarded as prerequisites for effective leadership. These people included Eisenhower, former President of the USA; Rothschild, a London banker; and Rockefeller, President of Chase Manhattan Bank. From this survey Rupert (1965:17–31) identified the following traits as prerequisites for effective leadership:

- Physical and mental health;
- A sound philosophy of life;
- A willingness to serve;
- Selflessness;
- Optimism, enthusiasm, inspiration and drive;
- Intelligence and knowledge;
- Languages skills;
- Will-power and purposefulness;
- Adaptability and flexibility;
- Understanding;
- Character.

Stodgill (1974:74–5) investigated the literature and found that researchers describe leadership traits mostly in the following categories:

- Physical traits such as height, appearance and energy;
- Intelligence and abilities;
- Personality traits such as adaptability and aggression;
- Traits relevant to the task, such as performance motivation, perseverance and initiative;
- Social traits, such as interpersonal skills, administrative ability and adaptability.

The trait approach to leadership has not made any worthwhile contribution towards understanding leadership. Although several investigations have been conducted in this respect, this approach clearly has little practical value.

17.6.3 The functional approach

The functional approach was developed as a result of the shortcomings of the leadership trait approach, and also because researchers realised that a leader cannot achieve anything in isolation, but that he or she is dependent on a group of followers.

355

The functional approach pays specific attention to the essential functions to be fulfilled by a leader, particularly in group context, in order to be effective. A leader's leadership traits are therefore irrelevant.

Under the functional approach leadership refers to what a person does in his or her capacity as a leader. These functions are, however, not restricted to the leader. Any member of the group may show leadership functions under specific circumstances and any leadership function may be fulfilled by any member of the group.

The functional approach was mainly experimental; in other words, it was developed under controlled laboratory conditions. Its validity when applied in practice may therefore be questioned.

17.6.4 The behaviouristic approach

Like the functional approach, the behaviouristic approach was developed because of dissatisfaction with the leadership trait approach. Followers of the behaviouristic approach emphasise the behaviour shown by effective leaders, or the behaviour that should be shown if a person wishes to function effectively as a leader.

In this chapter we will concentrate on work of Lewin, Lippitt and White; McGregor; Schein; and the managerial grid of Blake and Mouton.

17.6.4.1 The theory of Lewin, Lippitt and White

Lewin *et al.* (1939:280) define leadership in view of the way in which the leader provides guidance to his or her subordinates. They identify three leadership styles:

- *Autocratic leadership style*: The leader determines policy on his or her own and personally gives orders to subordinates.
- *Democratic leadership style*: Policy is decided by means of group discussions and the leader plays the part of facilitator only; in other words, he or she encourages group members and promotes interaction.
- *Laissez-faire leadership style*: In this case policy is virtually non-existent; the leader participates in group discussions to some extent.

Research shows that the democratic style is most likely to be successful, although it is also clear that different leadership styles are effective in different situations.

17.6.4.2 McGregor's theory

McGregor's (1960:53) theory, known as Theory X and Theory Y, is based on the assumption that although the workers and the management of an organisation are interdependent, there is always conflict between them. Subordinates depend on management for satisfying their needs and achieving their goals, while managers depend on their subordinates for the achievement of their own goals as well as those of the organisation. Leadership behaviour is based on the leader's assumptions about human nature and human behaviour.

McGregor compiled two sets of assumptions that leaders have concerning employees and that affect the leader's behaviour towards his or her subordinates.

TABLE 17.3: Leaders' assumptions regarding people, according to McGregor

Theory X	Theory Y
• The average person is inherently lazy and will avoid work if possible. • Because of people's laziness, most people must be forced to work, strictly controlled and threatened with punishment in order to persuade them to pursue organisational goals. • The average person prefers to be controlled, avoids responsibility, has relatively little ambition and rates security above any other need. • Most people have limited creativity in solving organisational problems.	• Physical and mental effort associated with work is as natural as relaxation. • People will exercise self-control to achieve organisational goals. Punishment is irrelevant. • People are mainly motivated by self-actualisation needs, although security needs and physiological needs are still present. • Creativity in solving organisational problems is common.

Source: McGregor (1960:147)

Because of his strong emphasis on the need to integrate individual goals with the goals of the organisation, McGregor implicitly advocates a "best style" of leadership.

In spite of criticism aimed at McGregor's theory, it has had a major effect on the modern concept of leadership. Especially its humanistic slant and the direct distinction between Theory X and Theory Y have had a remarkable impact.

17.6.4.3 Schein's theory of human assumptions
The human assumptions identified by Schein (1980:53) reflect the historical course of human assumptions. Each assumption is briefly discussed below.

(a) The rational-economic assumption
The rational-economic assumption is underpinned by hedonism, which claims that people's behaviour is aimed at obtaining the greatest advantage to themselves.

Assumptions of the rational-economic approach can be summarised as follows:
• People are motivated mainly by economic incentives and their behaviour is directed towards actions that will result in the greatest economic gain.
• Since economic incentives are controlled by the organisation, people are a passive factor that can be manipulated, activated and controlled by the organisation.

357

- People's feelings are irrational, therefore an attempt must be made to prevent these irrational emotions from interfering with people's work.
- Organisations must be designed in such a way as to neutralise and control people's feelings and their resultant unpredictable behaviour.

A supervisor who holds rational-economic assumptions will exercise control over subordinates by means of direct authority.

(b) The social assumption

Schein apparently formulated the social assumption on the basis of the well-known Hawthorne experiments by Mayo and his colleagues. Mayo found that work negates people's social needs. In this respect Schein (1980:59) says that "industrial life had taken the meaning out of work and had frustrated man's basic social needs."

The following assumptions are typical of this approach:

- People are motivated by social needs and acquire their basic identity in relationships with others.
- The meaning of work has been reduced by the Industrial Revolution and the rationalisation of work. Therefore people must find meaning in their social relationships at work.
- People will react to the social influence of their immediate colleagues (peer group) rather than to incentives and control from management.
- Subordinates will only react to management influence to the extent that a supervisor can satisfy their social needs.

The conduct and attitude of a supervisor with a social assumption towards subordinates will differ considerably from that of one with a rational-economic approach. Such a supervisor will pay much more attention to meeting the needs of subordinates, especially the need for social acceptance.

(c) The self-actualisation assumption

Schein (1980:68) maintains that several researchers, including Argyris, McGregor and Maslow, came to the conclusion that the meaning of work was lost in organisational life:

> many jobs in modern industry have become so specialized or fragmented that they neither permit workers to use their capacities nor enable them to see the relationship between what they are doing and the total organizational mission.

He emphasises the role of self-actualisation (1980:76):

> As the lower-level needs are satisfied, they release some of the higher level motives. Even the lowliest untalented man seeks selfactualization, a sense of meaning and accomplishment in his work, if his other needs are more or less fulfilled.

The following assumptions are typical of the self-actualisation approach:

- Human needs form a hierarchy, namely:
  — the need for survival, safety and security;
  — social needs;
  — the need for esteem (ego needs);

— the need for independence and autonomy;
— the need for self-actualisation.
- People strive towards maturity in their work and they can experience growth in the context of their work. This implies that they have to have independence and autonomy, accept long-term perspectives and develop special skills and greater adaptability.
- People are primarily self-motivated and can exercise self-control. External control measures and strict supervision are likely to make them feel threatened and reduce their maturity level in their work.
- There is no inherent conflict between self-actualisation and effective organisational performance. If an individual is given the opportunity, he or she will voluntarily integrate his or her own needs and goals with those of the organisation.

A supervisor who follows the self-actualisation approach will act in the same way as one who follows the social approach, except for a few important differences. According to the self-actualisation assumption, the supervisor will concentrate on making the work intrinsically more meaningful and challenging, rather than considering the social needs of subordinates.

(d) The complex person assumption

Organisational theories as well as leadership theories have in the past tended to produce over-simplified and generalised human philosophies. But people are more complex than the rational-economic, social or even self-realisation assumption would admit. Schein (1980:80) states:

Not only is he more complex within himself, being possessed of many needs and potentials, but he is also likely to differ from his neighbour in the patterns of his complexity.

The complex person assumption may be summarised as follows:
- People are not only complex, they are also highly changeable.
- Employees can develop new needs as a result of their experience in an organisation.
- Employees' needs may differ from one organisation to the next, and even in different departments of the same organisation.
- People may productively join in the activities of an organisation to satisfy different needs; ultimate need satisfaction and the ultimate effectiveness of the organisation are only partially dependent on the nature of employees' motivation.
- People may react positively to different management strategies (or leadership styles), depending on their own needs, goals, abilities and the nature of their work:

  in other words, there is no one correct managerial strategy that will work for all men at all times. (Schein 1980:80)

The most important implication of the complex person assumption for managers is that they must first be good diagnosticians and secondly be adaptable.

17.6.4.4 The managerial grid of Blake and Mouton

This approach by Blake and Mouton (1978:6) provided new perspectives on leadership behaviour, which are still enjoying great prominence. Their approach was developed from earlier research which indicated that a leader must consider both people and production in order to be successful.

The managerial grid and its accompanying theory constitute a useful instrument to enable leaders to identify their own assumptions about people and the job to be done. By knowing the styles of other leaders and their own leadership style, leaders will be better equipped to appraise themselves and others more objectively, to communicate better, to understand where differences originate and to assist and lead others in being more productive. Blake and Mouton (1978:6) describe the usefulness of their approach as follows:

> Learning grid management not only makes people aware of the assumptions under which they operate but also helps them to learn and to embrace scientifically verified principles for effectiveness in production under circumstances that promise mentally healthy behavior.

They identify three universal traits of organisations:

- Every organisation has certain goals to be pursued. These determine the jobs to be done.
- No organisation can function without people.
- Every organisation has a hierarchy of authority (in other words, employees in any organisation will hold different positions of authority).

The relation between these three traits forms the basis for the leadership matrix as shown in figure 17.6.

FIGURE 17.6: Blake's and Mouton's leadership matrix

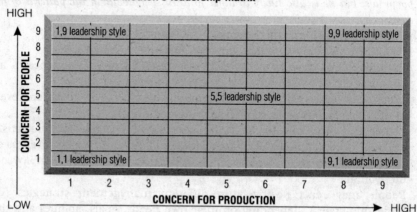

Source: Blake and Mouton (1978:11)

The managerial grid consists of two dimensions, namely concern for people and concern for production, each represented on a separate axis. "Concern" is explained as follows (1978:9):

Concern for is not a specific term which indicates the amount of actual production or actual behavior toward people. Rather it indicates the character and strength of assumptions present behind any given managerial style.

Concern for people is regarded as a leader's assumptions on aspects such as personal involvement with goal achievement, maintaining subordinates' self-confidence, responsibility based on trust rather than submissiveness, maintaining pleasant working conditions and maintaining satisfactory interpersonal relationships. *Concern for production* is regarded as a leader's assumptions on aspects such as the quality of business decisions, procedures and processes, creativity in research, the quality of human resources services, effectiveness of performance, and production volume.

Both dimensions of leadership behaviour are presented on the managerial grid in nine point scales from low (point 1) through average (point 5) to high (point 9). It must be noted that the different scale points do not allocate absolute values to leadership behaviour, but merely indicate varying degrees of concern for people and for production:

These numbers signify steps between low and high just as the gauge in an automobile indicates the amount of gasoline from empty to full, rather than specific quantities. (1978:10)

The third trait, *hierarchy of authority,* is deduced from the specific combination of a leader's concern for people and concern for production.

Although leadership behaviour represents different combinations of concern for people and concern for production, the hierarchy of authority within which a leader functions may affect the nature of his or her concern for people or production. The exact meaning of these concerns in different combinations may vary even if they are at the same level according to the grid:

For example, when high concern for people is coupled with low concern for production, the people concern expressed, that people be "happy", is far different from that when high concern for people is coupled with a high concern for production, that people be involved in the work and strive enthusiastically to contribute to organization purpose. (1978:10)

Concerns may therefore be regarded as a set of assumptions according to which the formal authority vested in a leader by an organisation's hierarchy of authority is used to obtain a particular combination of people and production in pursuance of the organisation's goals.

With due allowance for their position of authority, leaders must therefore be aware of alternative combinations of concern for people and concern for production according to which they may behave.

The following leadership styles are identified:

- *Autocratic leadership style (9,1):* An autocratic leader shows maximum concern for production (scale point 9) and minimum concern for people (scale point 1). Production is achieved by means of formal authority, and subordinates are controlled by enforcing submissiveness.

- *Democratic leadership style (1,9):* Unlike an autocratic leader, a democratic leader will show minimum concern for production (scale point 1) and maximum concern for people (scale point 9). Cultivating and maintaining sound interpersonal relationships with colleagues and subordinates will therefore be most important. This leader maintains that the job will be done automatically if interpersonal relationships are sound.
- *Impoverished leadership style (1,1):* A *laissez-faire* leader shows little concern for production and little concern for people (both at scale point 1). A *laissez-faire* leader does the absolute minimum required, in both the job and interpersonal relationships, to stay on as a member of the organisation.
- *Organisation man leadership style (5,5):* The "organisation man" leader tries to maintain a balance between production and interpersonal relationships. Blake and Mouton (1978:12) describe this style thus:

    This is the "middle-of-the-road" theory or the "go-along-to-get-along" assumptions which are revealed in conformity to the status quo.

    Such leaders try half-heartedly to pay attention to both aspects (both at scale point 5) but do not succeed.
- *Team leadership style (9,9):* A team leader integrates concern for production and concern for people at a high level (both at scale point 9). This style emphasises team-work, is goal-orientated and strives for excellent results through participative management, involvement with people and conflict management.

The managerial grid in figure 17.6 shows numerous possible combinations of concern for people and for production, but with the five general styles discussed, Blake and Mouton point out the most important differences between leaders' assumptions regarding people, jobs and the use of formal authority.

17.6.5 The situational approach

Dissatisfaction with the leadership approach, the functional approach and the behaviouristic approach gave rise to the formulation of the more contemporary situational leadership theories.

The main principle of the situational approach (Schilbach 1983:108) is that: *leadership is specific and always relative to the particular situation in which it occurs. Therefore, who becomes leader or who is the leader of a particular activity is a function of the total situation, which includes not only the leader and the subordinates and other groups to which the leader is related, but also myriad other human, physical and time variables as well.*

A wide variety of situational factors are mentioned in the literature. General factors are:

- The nature of interpersonal relationships in the group;
- The traits of the group;
- The organisational culture within which the group exists;
- The physical circumstances of the group;

- The values and attitudes of group members;
- Communication patterns in the group.

Although there are several theories, only Tannenbaum's and Schmidt's leadership continuum and Hersey's and Blanchard's situational leadership theory will now be discussed.

17.6.5.1 The leadership continuum of Tannenbaum and Schmidt

Tannenbaum and Schmidt (1958) advocate a leadership continuum which illustrates the situational and varying nature of leadership. The continuum contains a variety of leadership styles, from highly leader-centred (autocratic) to highly subordinate-centred (democratic), as illustrated in figure 17.7.

FIGURE 17.7: Leadership continuum of Tannenbaum and Schmidt

Leader-centred leadership ← → Subordinate-centred leadership

Use of authority by the leader

Area of freedom of subordinates

| Leader takes decision and announces it | Leader "sells" his or her decision | Leader suggests ideas and allows subordinates to ask questions | Leader suggests tentative decisions subject to change | Leader presents problem and obtains inputs from subordinates before decision is taken | Leader defines parameters within which decisions may be taken | Leader and subordinates make joint decisions within parameters set by organisation |

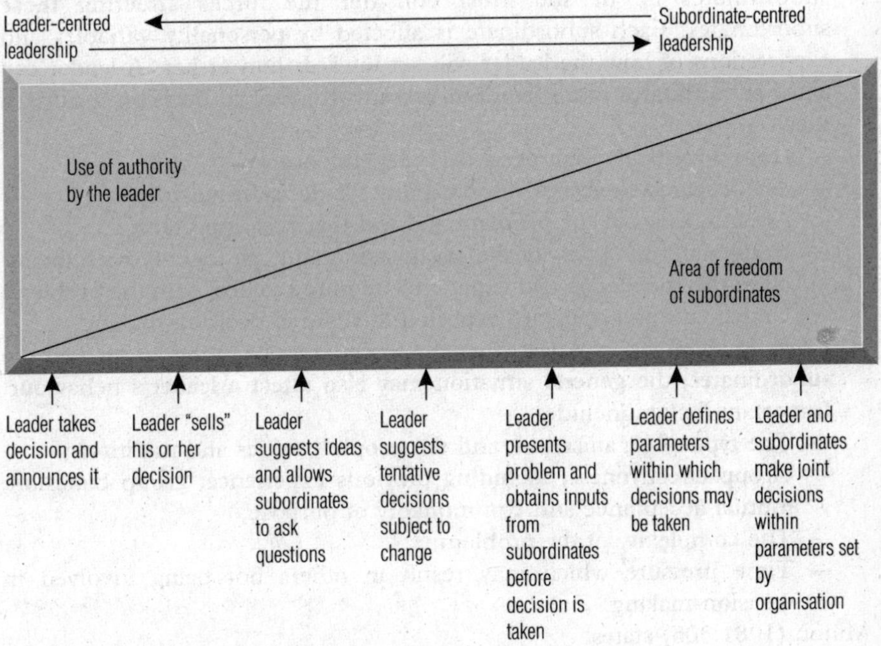

Source: Tannenbaum and Schmidt (1958:97)

The continuum illustrates that leadership varies according to the distribution of influence among the leader and his or her subordinates. The leadership style changes from left to right from leader-centred to subordinate-centred as the leader exercises less control (authority) and allows subordinates more influence and freedom to take decisions on their own. Leadership behaviour and the leadership style used by a leader will therefore depend on how much authority he or she delegates to subordinates.

Although possible leadership styles are indicated in figure 17.7, there is no indication which style is practical and desirable. The appropriate style is determined by three types of forces, namely forces in the leader, forces in the subordinates and forces in the situation.

- *Forces in the leader:* A leader's behaviour is influenced by his or her personality, background, knowledge and experience. Other internal forces are:
  — The leader's value system;
  — The leader's confidence in subordinates;
  — The leader's own leadership philosophy;
  — The leader's feeling of security in an uncertain situation, especially when he or she is operating towards the right of the continuum.
- *Forces in the subordinates:* Before a leader can decide how to guide subordinates he or she must consider the forces affecting these subordinates. Each subordinate is affected by personality variables and expectations of how the leader will act towards him or her. A leader can allow subordinates more freedom and involvement in decision-making if they:
  — Have a relatively high need for independence;
  — Are prepared to accept responsibility for decision-making;
  — Are interested in the problem and feel that it is important;
  — Understand the goals of the organisation and can identify with them;
  — Have the knowledge and experience required to deal with the problem;
  — Understand that they are expected to share in decision-making.
- *Forces in the situation:* Apart from the forces present in the leader and the subordinates, the general situation may also affect a leader's behaviour. Important factors include:
  — The type of organisation, and the people's values and traditions;
  — Group effectiveness, including previous experience, group cohesion, mutual acceptance and commonality of purpose;
  — The complexity of the problem;
  — Time pressure which may result in others not being involved in decision-making.

Milton (1981:305) states:

> *The successful leader is one who is aware of those factors that are most relevant to his or her behavior at any given time. He or she accurately understands himself or herself, the individuals and group being directed, and the broader organizational environment. Furthermore, the successful leader behaves appropriately in the light of these forces.*

Although the leadership continuum is a logical concept with practical application value, it does have some shortcomings, the most important of which is the lack of instructions on exactly how a situation is to be diagnosed. Furthermore it is not clear how leadership behaviour must be judged. Little empirical research has been conducted about the leadership continuum.

17.6.5.2 *The situational leadership theory of Hersey and Blanchard*

The point of departure of this theory can be explained by means of figure 17.8.

FIGURE 17.8: Diagram of Hersey's and Blanchard's situational leadership theory

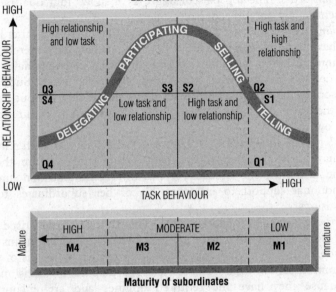

Source: Hersey and Blanchard (1982:152)

The following important concepts are contained in figure 17.8:

- *Task behaviour:* According to Hersey and Blanchard (1982:96), this implies the degree to which leaders are likely to organise and spell out the tasks of group members by indicating who should do what; when, where and how. Task behaviour is also characterised by a leader's instituting well-defined organisational patterns, channels of communication and procedures for the execution of tasks.
- *Relationship behaviour:* Relationship behaviour implies the degree to which leaders are likely to maintain interpersonal relationships between themselves and group members by providing open channels of communication, socio-emotional support, psychological stroking and facilitating of subordinates' behaviour.
- *Maturity levels:*
  — *Low maturity (M1):* According to Hersey and Blanchard (1982:154), this refers to subordinates who are unwilling or unsure how to execute a task, and do not have the neccesary ability to do it.
  — *Low to average maturity (M2):* This refers to subordinates who do not have the ability to execute a task although they are willing and confident enough to do it.

365

- *Average to high maturity (M3):* In this case subordinates have the ability to execute the task, but are unwilling or unsure how to do it.
- *High maturity (M4):* In this case subordinates have the ability and confidence to execute the task and are willing to do it.

- *Leadership styles:* The top part of figure 17.8 shows four quadrants, each representing a separate leadership style:
  - *Telling (S1)* (quadrant Q1): Hersey and Blanchard state that high task behaviour combined with low relationship behaviour is merely one-way communication: the leader explains by means of task behaviour to his or her subordinates what to do; how, where and when. Such a leader describes his or her subordinates' tasks thoroughly without explaining to them why a task has to be done or why certain procedures are to be followed.
  - *Selling (S2)* (quadrant Q2): High task behaviour with high relationship behaviour is characterised by a high level of guidance from the leader. The leader tries by means of two-way communication and socio-emotional support to influence his or her subordinates to accept decisions.
  - *Participating (S3)* (quadrant Q3): This style is characterised by high relationship behaviour with low task behaviour, which means that the leader and subordinate take decisions together by means of two-way communication. Subordinates can participate in decision-making because they have the required abilities and are encouraged to participate by means of high relationship behaviour.
  - *Delegating (S4)* (quadrant Q4): This style is characterised by low relationship behaviour with low task behaviour, which implies that the leader allows subordinates to take completely independent decisions by delegating authority to them. Therefore supervision is of a general nature, which means that subordinates' work is not checked continuously as they are fully capable of executing their tasks, they have the necessary confidence and are willing to do so.

According to Hersey and Blanchard, leadership behaviour is a function of subordinates' maturity. Schilbach (1983:169) says that a leader who wishes to determine which leadership style is appropriate for a given situation must first determine the maturity level of the subordinates, either individually or as a group, with regard to the particular task to be carried out.

Once the maturity level of subordinates has been identified, the appropriate leadership style can easily be determined by drawing a perpendicular on the continuum from the identified maturity level to where it crosses the bell-shaped curve in figure 17.8. The appropriate leadership style is indicated by the quadrant in which the lines cross.

According to Hersey's and Blanchard's situational leadership theory, a leader whose subordinates have a low maturity level (M1) should maintain a high level of task behaviour and a low level of relationship behaviour (the S1 leadership style: telling). As the maturity level of the individual subordinate or group of subordinates increases (to level M2), the leader should reduce task behaviour and increase relationship behaviour (the S2 leadership style: selling). When subordinates become even more mature (M3), both task behaviour and relationship behaviour must be reduced (the S3 leadership style: participating). When the individual subordinate or group of subordinates reaches a high level of maturity (M4), the leader should maintain a low level of both task behaviour and relationship behaviour (the S4 leadership style: delegating).

17.6.5.3 *Conclusion on the situational approach*
According to Schilbach (1983:183), the situational approach to leadership is most likely to result in effective leadership, as it makes provision for different leadership behaviours in different situations. No single leadership style, specific leadership functions or particular leadership qualities are recommended as being the best under all circumstances. This flexibility of the situational approach makes it particularly useful in the complex environment of South African organisations.

17.7 VARIABLES AFFECTING LEADERSHIP
The leadership process is affected by three sets of variables: the leader, the subordinates (group or followers) and the situation. The interaction between these variables determines the leadership behaviour of a superior and the resulting behaviour of the subordinates in terms of their performance and job satisfaction. It may therefore be stated that leadership is a function of the leader, the group and the situation. It can be presented as in figure 17.9.

FIGURE 17.9: Leadership variables

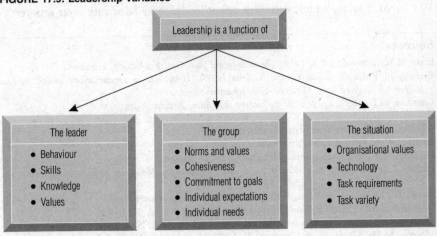

The interaction between these three sets of variables determines the leadership style to be used in a particular situation.

17.8 CONCLUSION

In this chapter it was emphasised that practising leadership in South African organisations is a complex and challenging task. Leadership is regarded as the interpersonal process in which a leader uses communication to direct the activities of individuals or groups towards actively striving for a specific goal in a specific situation. The causal relationship between leadership and power was discussed and five types of power were distinguished: legitimate power, reward power, coercive power, referent power and expert power. A further distinction was made between successful leadership and effective leadership. Schilbach's typology was used as a framework for the discussion of four approaches to leadership: the trait approach, the functional approach, the behaviouristic approach and the situational approach. Finally it was explained that leadership is a function of the leader, the group and the situation.

Questions

1. Describe in your own words what you understand leadership to be.
2. What is the difference between leadership and power?
3. What do you understand by the trait approach to leadership?
4. Discuss McGregor's Theory X and Theory Y as you experience it in your present work situation.
5. Distinguish between Schein's theories of human assumptions, and discuss each one briefly.
6. Discuss each of the five styles of Blake's and Mouton's managerial grid.
7. What is meant by the situational approach to leadership?
8. Draw and discuss Tannenbaum's and Schmidt's leadership continuum.
9. In no more than 500 words, give a critical evaluation of Hersey's and Blanchard's situational leadership theory.
10. In your view, which variables affect leadership? Motivate your answer.

Sources

Blake, R.R. & Mouton, J.S. 1978. *The managerial grid.* Gulf Publishing, Houston.

Barling, J., Fullager, C. & Bluen, S. (eds) 1986. *Behaviour in organizations: South African perspectives.* 2nd edition. McGraw-Hill, Johannesburg.

Charlton, G.D. 1992. *Leadership: the human race.* Juta, Johannesburg.

Cronje, G. de J., Neuland, E.W., Hugo, W.M.J. & Van Reenen, M.J. (eds) 1987. *Introduction to business management.* Southern, Johannesburg.

Dimma, W.A. 1989. Leadership. *Business Quarterly,* Winter.

Griffin, R.W. 1987. *Management.* Houghton Mifflin, Boston.

Hersey, P. & Blanchard, K. 1982. *Management of organizational behavior: utilizing human resources.* Prentice-Hall, Englewood Cliffs, New Jersey.

Lewin, K., Lippitt, R. & White, R.K. 1939. Patterns of aggressive behaviour in an experimentally created social climate. *Journal of Social Psychology,* no. 10, pp. 271–99.

McGregor, D. 1960. *The human side of enterprise.* McGraw-Hill, New York.

Mescon, M.H., Albert, M. & Khedouri, F. 1985. *Management.* Harper & Row, New York.

Milton, C.R. 1981. *Human behavior in organizations: three levels of behavior.* Prentice-Hall, Englewood Cliffs, New Jersey.

Rupert, A. 1965. Leierskap. Rembrandtgroep-ondersoek (In-house).

Schein, E.H. 1980. *Organizational psychology*. Prentice-Hall, Englewood Cliffs, New Jersey.

Schilbach, C. 1983. Die ontwikkeling van leierskapvaardighede by middelvlakbestuurders. Unpublished DCom thesis, University of Pretoria.

Stodgill, R.M. 1974. *Handbook of leadership*. The Free Press, New York.

Tannenbaum, R. & Schmidt, W.H. 1958. How to choose a leadership pattern. *Harvard Business Review*, vol. 2, no. 36, pp. 95–101.

Van Rooyen, J. 1991. Leadership challenges faced by South African managers. *IPM Journal*, March, pp. 8–12.

Chapter 18

Groups in organisations

P.S. van Dyk

STUDY OBJECTIVES

After studying this chapter, you should be able to:

- Discuss groups as systems in their own right;
- Differentiate between groups from various points of view and explain how groups are formed;
- Practically explain group functioning;
- Differentiate between interrelations within organisations.

18.1 INTRODUCTION

Organisations consist of individual employees who are officially divided into groups according to the unique work activities (functions) they carry out. Within these groups they attempt to achieve organisational objectives in the most efficient manner. The contribution that groups make to organisational success will become clear from the following discussion.

18.2 WHAT IS A GROUP?

There are as many definitions of groups as there are authors. Gray and Starke (1984:438) describe a group as follows:

In the broadest sense, a group is any collection of individuals who have mutually dependent relationships. This includes individuals who are in close physical proximity as well as those who have only a psychological attachment. While each group exhibits different behaviors, they do have much in common.

Robins (1989:226) simply states:

A group is defined as two or more individuals, interacting and interdependent, who came together to achieve particular objectives.

FIGURE 18.1: Principal learning components of groups in organisations

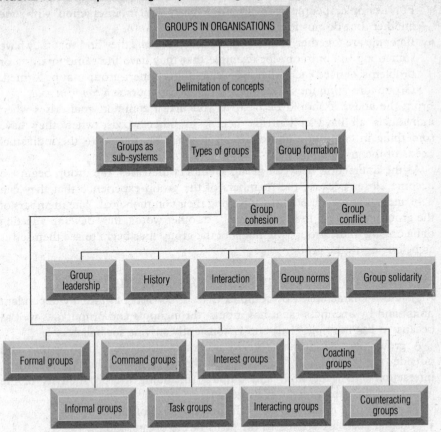

It is generally accepted that a group consists of a number of individuals who:

- Have a common goal or objective;
- Interact with one another to achieve this common goal;
- Are aware of one another;
- Agree that they belong to the group.

The following becomes clear from the definition above:

- A number of people together are not necessarily a group. People waiting at a bus stop, for example, are not a group, but rather a grouping of people. In the same way, a number of new first-year students in rooms along the same hostel corridor do not yet constitute a group.
- Before a number of people can form a group, there must first be interaction between them—in other words, they must talk to one another, get to know one another and become accustomed to one another.
- Interaction between a number of people can only take place if they are in each other's presence. Groups are therefore formed among people who are together, in other words among people who share a physical environment.

371

- Interaction alone does not, however, mean that a group will be formed. For example, people who attend a party are in interaction with one another, but do not form a group.
- If people are together, if interaction takes place *and* they find that they have something in common, for example that they have the same interests or problems, or need each other to get something done, a group may be formed. Group formation thus takes place when people pursue a *common goal.*

From the above it should be clear to you that a common goal arises when individuals all have concurring needs, in other words, when they have something in common. The common goal is thus related to the individual needs of the group members.

As the interaction between group members increases, the group begins to become closer because the members of the group experience that they can help and support each other in achieving their common goal. The members of the group then begin to speak of "us". In other words, they develop a feeling of belonging to the group. Members of the group thus begin to see themselves as belonging to the group.

18.3 GROUPS AS SUB-SYSTEMS OF ORGANISATIONS

A system is characterised by complexity (as it consists of mutually dependent units) and by openness (as it has inputs, throughputs and outputs, as well as because it has multiple goals and is constantly striving for balance).

A group also has inputs (including expectations from both within and outside the borders of the system), throughputs (including structure, interaction and leadership) and outputs (including the productivity of the group and the achievement of its goals).

The goals of a group can be both formal and informal.

- Formal goals are related to the goals of the organisation.
- Informal goals are usually not related to the formal goals of the organisation.
- The group also receives inputs from both the internal and the external environment.

The *internal environment* of a group is the physical situation in which the group functions, the authority structure within the group (both formal and informal), as well as the interaction patterns between individual group members.

The *external environment* of the group is twofold: the other groups (sub-systems) within the organisation, as well as groups outside the organisation.

The group constantly compares its functioning and the treatment it receives with those of other groups in the organisation. If, for example, the group thinks that a particular department receives more attention from management than itself, jealousy and conflict may arise, which may have an adverse effect on the functioning of the group. The external environment of the group consists of anything outside the group that can influence the group. Thus, for example, employees from another organisation in the same branch of industry could form the external environment of a group if they have the same training and do the same work.

In the throughput phase, the group finds itself in a structure, i.e. the organisation, where certain prescribed behaviour is expected. The group itself also develops a certain structure—either formal or informal—and acts accordingly. Groups show certain behaviours that they consider best as a result of previous experience. There is interaction between the group and others, both within and outside the organisation; in terms of the systems approach, the group's functioning depends on the other sub-systems.

> Workers in the production department, for example, cannot achieve their formal production goals without the necessary interaction with the purchasing and financial departments.

An important factor that influences group behaviour in the throughput phase is the manner in which the group is maintained, in other words whether the expectations of the group are being met. The group must be of the opinion that its work contributes towards achieving the goals of the organisation, that the group receives recognition for maintaining its performance and that it is compensated in accordance with its contribution. If this is not the case, the group will show behaviour that does not promote the achievement of the organisation's goals.

> What do you think is the cause of strikes, theft and internal sabotage?

The most important factor that determines a group's functioning during the throughput phase is the leadership or management of the group. The philosophy and style shown by the leader determine group functioning. A group will pursue organisational goals under the most adverse working conditions if its leader meets the most important needs of the group (higher-order needs—see chapter 16). On the other hand, the group will thwart the achievement of organisational goals even under the best working conditions if its leader does not treat the members decently.

The result of the throughput process is the manner in which or extent to which the group succeeds in achieving formally set organisational goals. This is an indication of the individual productivity and satisfaction of the members of the group. Many authors therefore regard productivity and satisfaction as measures of organisational effectiveness.

One of the characteristics of a system is a feedback process, the main purpose of which is to restore or maintain the balance of the system. Just as the individual as a system constantly uses the feedback process to monitor his or her progress towards the achievement of goals, the group as a system does the same. The formal feedback that the group receives from management about the way in which formally set goals are achieved, determines the functioning of the group.

If, for example, after a certain department has met an urgent request to supply X number of units, management does not give the department recognition for successfully carrying out its task, this will have an adverse influence on the motivation of the members of this department when similar orders are issued in future.

Positive feedback by management about the achievement of a goal does not take much effort, but it ensures positive group behaviour in similar future cases.

18.4 TYPES OF GROUPS

There is a variety of groups in any organisation. Gray and Starke (1984:437) distinguish the following types on the basis of Fiedler's leadership effectiveness theory:
- *Interacting groups*: the work (output) of one group is the input for another group, for example on a production line;
- *Coacting groups*: the work carried out by the various groups in an organisation is independent of that of other groups;
- *Counteracting groups* are in interaction with one another to gain knowledge or to solve differences, for example management and trade unions.

Fiedler conceptualises the above as in figure 18.2.

In 1957 already, Leonard Sayles (1957:47) identified four different types of groups: two are formal, whereas the other two may be either formal or informal.

A *formal group* is one whose goals and activities are directly related to the achievement of the declared organisational goals. Formal groups are part of the structure of an organisation and are formed during the organisational process. Formal groups may be departments, sections, task groups, committees and so on.

An *informal group* is one which, as a result of the daily activities, interactions and feelings of its members, develops so that it can satisfy their needs. The aims of informal groups are not necessarily the same as those of the organisation. The formal organisation does, however, often

---

exert a great influence on the formation of informal groups (for example because of the physical lay-out of the work and the leadership practices of the manager). At the same time, informal groups can also exert a great influence on the formal organisation. If, for example, the manager's leadership style is unacceptable to the workers, the informal group can offer resistance to him or her.

FIGURE 18.2: Diagrammatic contrasting of interacting, coacting and counteracting groups on the basis of three criteria

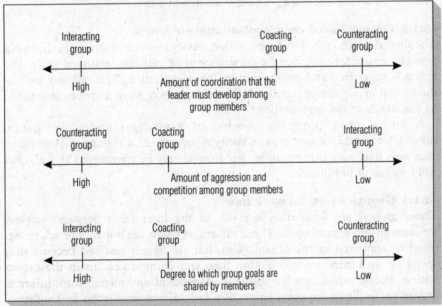

Source: Gray and Starke (1984:439)

Robins (1989:227) also identifies the following groups:

- *The command group*: This group is usually characterised by a formal organigram and a line of authority. Almost all businesses are formally organised into command groups, as the activities are carried out at the command of a manager. The "command" may take the form of a request, but it still remains a command due to the line of authority within the group.
- *The task group*: This group is created for a specific task or project. It is also a formal group. As soon as the specific project has been completed, the group disbands.
- *The interest group*: This group may be either formal or informal. The emphasis is on the needs of the group itself. There may be a line of authority and the group may have a task to fulfil, but the reason for the existence of the group is that the members all have the same interests.

18.5 GROUP FORMATION FROM VARIOUS PERSPECTIVES

18.5.1 General

As discussed above, there are various types of groups in any organisation. A group formed through the union of people in accordance with the organisational structure is known as a *formal group*, and a group that has been formed to complete a task or job is known as a *task or work group*. A group formed within the organisational structure but without official approval is known as an *informal group*, while a group formed for social reasons is known as a *social group*. The group classification of Huse and Bowditch (1977:216), which is generally accepted, is briefly discussed below.

18.5.2 Groups based on organisational structure

The formal group, which is found within an organisational structure, has as its primary reason for existence the pursuance of official organisational goals. The group is supported and maintained by the organisation. The tasks or goals of the formal group are well defined. The existence of formal groups is justified by the needs of the organisation.

A formal group normally consists of a manager and a number of subordinates, and the group as an entity is permanent, although the individual members may vary (for example, one person may be transferred and another will take his or her place).

18.5.3 Groups based on work flow

These groups are formed as a result of the interaction between workers throughout the organisation. These informal groups are not supported, recognised or approved by the organisation, but are largely justified because they speed up and improve information flow and communication in the organisation. People whose work is mutually dependent and related form informal groups to facilitate the completion of a task. Employees often find informal groups more pleasant than formal groups.

> Just try formally putting in charge of something a subordinate who creates many problems, is popular among his or her peers and always takes the lead when it comes to actions not approved by management. You will be surprised to see how quickly he or she will cooperate with management!

18.5.4 Groups based on human needs

Apart from group formation as a result of the needs of the organisation and mutual interaction based on the work flow, groups are also formed because people have certain needs that they can satisfy by forming a group. This type of group formation may primarily be ascribed to the fact that humans are social beings by nature.

As certain human needs such as giving and receiving affection, association with others and acceptance can be reasonably easily satisfied in a group context, people join groups. As members of a group, people constantly receive feedback about their behaviour, and in this way the group enables people to satisfy their higher-order needs.

An organisation without groups is unthinkable, and groups are important for any organisation because they have the ability to carry out critical organisational functions and to satisfy human needs. If management can succeed in reconciling group goals with organisational goals, this creates the possibility of maximum long-term organisational effectiveness and individual satisfaction of needs. This is the highest goal of any organisation.

18.6 GROUP FUNCTIONING

18.6.1 General

Not every collection of people satisfies the definition of a group. The internal functioning of a group (i.e. its goals, patterns of interaction, etc.) develops over time and largely determines the success of the group in achieving its goals and satisfying the needs of its members.

Effective groups have the following characteristics:

- The group knows the reason for its existence;
- There are guidelines or procedures for decision-making;
- There is communication between the group members;
- The members receive and render mutual assistance;
- The members handle conflict within the group in a constructive manner;
- The members diagnose their processes and improve their own functioning.

Without this, no group can be effective. The extent to which the group fails in one or more of these aspects determines how ineffective the group is. There are also various other factors that influence the effectiveness of a group, as will become apparent below.

18.6.2 Group leadership

It does not require much insight to realise that one of the most important keys to success is the type of leadership of a group. When a group (a department, section or even an organisation) is not successful, the cause is often ineffective leadership.

The decisive factor in the choice of a leader is spelled out in the question: What person will best lead the group towards achieving its common goal? The person who, in the opinion of the group, is most likely to succeed will be appointed the leader.

> The leader of a gang will be the one who is most aggressive, is physically the strongest and has the best "record" and the most impressive motorcycle.
>
> The leader of a group of bird-watchers will be the one with the most knowledge and experience of birds and the environment.

The most important point here is that each group has a leader at any given time, and that the person who is formally appointed is not necessarily the leader.

18.6.3 The history of the group
The historical background of a group influences the manner in which it functions, the nature of the interaction between its members and the manner in which they do their work. A temporary group that has been formed on the spur of the moment will not immediately meet the requirements for an effective group. It takes time for members to get to know and trust one another, to build up a healthy mutual communication pattern and to develop clear guidelines and norms for decision-making.

A well-established group, on the other hand, has already had enough time to develop a certain "climate" or group culture. As the members know each other's weaknesses and merits, they have clear guidelines for decision-making. Of course the group may also become extremely inflexible and unable to adapt to changing circumstances. It may be very tradition-bound—like some organisations—insisting that things are done in a prescribed manner, for example that all men must wear a tie on Fridays.

18.6.4 Interaction within the group
The activities of a group are the tasks the group must carry out. These tasks require that employees be in interaction with other groups or members during the work day. As the group members carry out the activities and interaction expected of them, other activities and interaction occur, in addition to those expected of them.

The interaction between group members and the leader may result in resistance against the leader, and in this process the group members may take counterproductive measures to fluster the leader or to "pay him back". In addition, interaction with other group members may lead to discord or conflict between individuals, and this can have a negative effect on the functioning of the group, harming group performance.

On the other hand, the interaction between group members can also lead to friendships: they can have coffee together, sit and chat for a long time, or play tricks on one another from time to time—all the things friends usually do. This may lead to greater cooperation within the group, which has a positive effect and improves group performance.

18.6.5 Group norms
Over time, the interaction within the group leads to the development of group norms. A norm is a generally accepted standard of behaviour that each member of the group is supposed to maintain. The strongest norms apply to the forms of behaviour that the group members regard as the most important.

Robins (1989:241) defines norms as "acceptable standards of behavior within a group that are shared by the group's members".

Do you know that golf players do not talk while a fellow player putts? Why?

Norms may be formal, for example taking the form of prescribed behaviour, or informal and based on interaction between group members, for example: "We do not tell tales about one another." Groups attach various values to various norms. Certain norms are valued more highly than others, and members of the group *must* adhere to them.

A student who does not attend the compulsory classes will quickly find out that he or she is not granted admission to the examination: an obligatory norm. There are also peripheral norms; although it is not obligatory for members to adhere to them, they are regarded as sound and worth the effort. A member of a soccer team, for example, will not gain the approval of his team mates if he misbehaves during the reception held after the match. A norm that is regarded as important by one group may be unimportant to another. A social club, for example, might prescribe that men who dine there should wear a tie and jacket, while another club might well regard this as a peripheral norm and permit its members to wear what they like.

The success and continued existence of a group may depend on whether the members adhere to the group norms. Groups that lack strong norms are unlikely to be as stable, long-lived or satisfying for their members as groups with well-developed norms that are strongly supported by the members.

A group member can react to group norms in three different ways (Dessler 1980:211): he or she may reject them, conform to them or only accept the important ones and ignore the peripheral norms.

When a group member *rebels* against the group's norms, he or she will experience considerable pressure to conform, as noticeable non-conformity constitutes a threat to the group's standards, stability and survival. This type of pressure may be particularly strong.

It has, for example, happened in organisations that pay workers according to a piece wage system, in other words according to the production of each individual, that the workers have a well-founded fear that if some of them were to perform at a very high level, the management would reduce the work tariff. The result was strong pressure on the workers not to exceed the group norms for work carried out.

Conformity takes two forms: subjection, in other words a change in behaviour; and internalisation, in other words a change in behaviour *and* convictions. Most work group norms are exclusively concerned with behaviour, although a declaration of conviction can be required for membership of certain groups, for example a church community.

Not all individuals conform to the same extent. Individuals with low status in the group, for example, will tend to adhere strictly to all the group's norms so that the other group members will accept them. People with little self-confidence also tend to conform to a greater extent, because they regard the group's decisions as better than their own. Individuals who feel that the group's goals coincide with their own, also tend to conform to a greater extent.

Creative individualism describes the behaviour of a group member who accepts only the most important norms of the group and ignores the peripheral norms. A member of a department may, for example, positively pursue departmental goals by doing excellent work, while at the same time ignoring the less important norm of visiting the local pub with "the boys" every Friday afternoon after work.

This reaction to group norms may, in the long run, be best for the group, as individual members will refuse to be intimidated or cast in a certain mould. In this way, this attitude may promote new thinking and innovation. Complete conformity, on the other hand, may counteract innovation, as the creative ability of a member will be lost to the group.

18.6.6 The impact of group norms on group behaviour

The knowledge of group behaviour we have today mainly arises from the experiments of the well-known Hawthorne studies. Earlier management theoreticians such as Taylor and Mayo also contributed to our understanding of this complex matter. From these early works, one important group norm has been identified that still exerts great influence on the outputs and performance orientation of groups, i.e. the norm of production standards.

> *While many work and non-work norms exist in small groups, the one most often referred to is the production norm (the group's perception of "acceptable" production behavior), which is often different from management expectations.*
> (Gray and Starke 1984:438)

For example, an organisation may set certain production standards that are not met by a specific group of production workers, out of fear that if they should meet them, the number of production workers will be reduced. The production norms set by a certain group may be the following:

- The non-adherence to production standards that, in the opinion of the group, are too high (out of a fear of staff cuts);
- The exceeding of production standards when there is a fear that action will be taken against group members as a result of too low inputs in the past;
- The maintenance of production standards when the group does not feel threatened and when there is a sound relationship between the group and its official supervisor.

The above can be explained with the aid of figure 18.3.

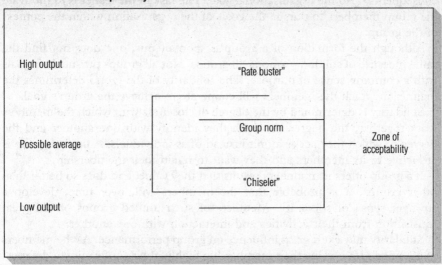

Source: Gray and Starke (1984:439)

18.6.7 Group solidarity and group cohesion
18.6.7.1 General
For any group to be successful in pursuing its formal and informal goals, high group solidarity and cohesion between group members are a necessity.

18.6.7.2 Group solidarity
Group solidarity refers to the influence that the group has on individual members. Groups with strong solidarity often experience less stress, fewer misunderstandings and less conflict between members than groups with weak solidarity.

> It is often the best technicians or workers who become managers. Nevertheless a person will not necessarily be a good leader simply because he or she is a good technician. An average technician with leadership qualities might be a much better leader than an excellent technician without the necessary leadership qualities.

A strong sense of solidarity may, however, cause problems if cooperation between groups is important, for example when the various functional managements are busy with strategic planning.

In the work situation, cooperation between individual group members is of vital importance. The better the workers in a department function as a group,

381

the greater is the possibility that they will achieve their common goal, and consequently also the organisational goal. The task of the leader is to motivate the group members to pursue the goals of the organisation within the context of the group.

Although the formation of a group is spontaneous, one does not find the same measure of solidarity among all groups. Not all groups pursue their goals with a common sense of purpose. The solidarity of the group determines the manner in which the members will cooperate to achieve the group's goal.

Solidarity is determined by the degree of closeness with which the members work together, the degree to which they identify with one another and the degree to which they act as a unit instead of as individuals. A unified group is attractive to its members and they want to retain their membership.

If a group offers its members results that they value, and does so better than other groups, it is probable that the members will, over time, develop a stronger sense of solidarity. Members of such unified groups obtain great satisfaction from their activities and interaction with one another.

Solidarity may exert great influence on group performance. As the members of a unified group value their membership highly, their conformity to the most important norms will be high. If, therefore, the group develops a norm of low job performance, the output of the members will be low; the opposite will of course happen in a group with a norm of high job performance.

The production norms of a unified group reflect its attitude to the manager. Dessler identifies six factors that influence group solidarity:

- *The size of the group*: The larger the group, the less solidarity there will be. This is easily explained. Interaction and communication between group members are essential for the continued existence of a group. We all know how difficult it is to talk to everyone at a large reception with many people. This is also true of an organisation in which the groups are large. Interaction and communication—the cornerstones of group formation—consequently suffer, which has an adverse effect on the success of groups.
- *Intra- and intergroup competition*: Intergroup competition is competition between various groups in the same organisation; intragroup competition is competition between the members of one group. The latter has an adverse effect on group solidarity. There are, however, indications that intergroup competition promotes group solidarity.
- *Group status*: Group status is reflected by many things, for example by the various levels within the organisation on which the group exists, the general performance of the group, its work and the degree of power it has to act at its own discretion. There is a direct relation between group solidarity and the status of the group: the higher the status, the higher the solidarity. There are, however, exceptions. For example, members of a group with low status (such as cleaners) who cannot easily leave the organisation (e.g. as a result of unemployment problems) tend to display a higher degree of solidarity because of their circumstances. On the other hand, a group with

high status may lack solidarity as a result of events in the past, for example if they could not succeed in achieving a specific goal. In general, however, it is true that groups with higher status have a higher degree of solidarity.

- *Group goals*: Workers join an organisation because they regard this as a way of achieving their personal goals while also pursuing the goals of the organisation. People also become part of a group whose norms, values and goals are reconcilable with their own. In other words, they join the group because they think that the group can help them achieve their goals. Consensus about goals promotes solidarity, while differences counteract it. Furthermore, if the group members do not agree on the manner in which the goals should be achieved, this can also prevent solidarity.
- *Job environment*: If the job environment complicates communication and interaction between members through factors such as noise or the type of work and its lay-out, this will have an adverse effect on group solidarity.
- *Lasting relationships*: A group should not be unnecessarily broken up, unless the needs of the organisations require it or the group members impede the achievement of the organisation's goals (for example because of rebels in the group). People who remain in the same group for a long time are more attached to one another than people in groups with a high transfer figure. It also promotes group solidarity if people know each other's strengths and weaknesses.

A group with a weak sense of solidarity is usually less effective than one with a strong sense of solidarity.

18.6.7.3 Group cohesion
Group cohesion indicates the extent to which a group (i.e. the group's goals and common interests) attracts individual members. The more the members of a group identify with the group's goals and see in them an opportunity to achieve their own goals, the more cohesion the group will have. This applies to both formal or official groups and informal groups. Irrespective of the nature of the group, research has shown that there is a positive correlation between group cohesion and output—in other words what the group has formally or informally undertaken to achieve.

18.6.7.4 The relation between group cohesion, productivity and other organisational outputs
Gray and Starke (1984:447) explain the relation between group cohesion, productivity and other organisational outputs as follows:

- Members of groups with high cohesion generally experience less work-related stress. Friction and conflict in interpersonal relations within a group upset group members. Groups with high cohesion are those in which interpersonal problems have been ironed out, and this promotes individual job performance.

- Groups with high cohesion experience lower job turnover and less absenteeism. Group members handle interpersonal problems in the work situation in a variety of ways. One extreme is to reduce the group's output, while another extreme is to withdraw from the work. As attendance at the job is a prerequisite for productivity, groups with high cohesion and strong conformity can promote high productivity.
- By placing employees with similar status, attitudes to life and cultural background together in work groups, the likelihood of high group cohesion is increased. Such group members generally experience a high degree of job satisfaction, have lower job turnover and cost the organisation less in labour and materials.
- The effect of cohesion on productivity changes in accordance with the source of this cohesion. High cohesion that is merely the result of a strong attraction between group members exerts only a slight influence on productivity. In extreme cases, personal attraction can even impede productivity, as group members are so active socially that it adversely affects their work. However, high cohesion as a result of a common goal can have a positive effect on productivity.
- The effect of cohesion on productivity varies in accordance with the leadership behaviour of the formal group leader. Managers who exercise supportive leadership towards a group with high cohesion usually succeed in increasing the group's productivity. On the other hand, managers who exercise a non-supportive leadership style towards a group with high cohesion will achieve less success in terms of group productivity.

> *The above comments suggest that it is impossible—and inappropriate—to make sweeping statements about the relationship between group cohesiveness and productivity. However, it should be clear that cohesiveness is a major input into productivity and that, because of the synergetic effects of group behavior, the cohesive group has inherently more energy than the uncohesive one.* (Gray and Starke 1984:447)

18.7 THE SOCIAL STRUCTURE IN GROUPS

In any group there is interaction between members. The result is the establishment of a social structure in which every group member has a certain group role (function) and the other members of the group have certain expectations about the execution of such a group role by that group member. Authors agree that the social structure of every group is comprised of a group leader, group members or followers and group norms:

- *Group leader*: As mentioned elsewhere, the leader of a group is not necessarily the formal leader or the officially appointed manager. The leader of a group may vary as the circumstances of the group change. A group member can emerge as leader if he or she, in the opinion of the group, is best able to satisfy a particular group need at a particular time.

- *Group members or followers*: The success of a group depends on whether the members or followers are prepared to accept the leader's leadership. For this reason managers and supervisors should also be effective leaders.
- *Group norms*: A group's norms are an extremely important aspect of its social structure. A sheet-metal worker who, for example, is part of a production team, has a high performance orientation and is therefore extraordinarily productive, will soon be admonished by the group. The reason is simple: such a worker exceeds the group's production norms, and if he or she continues to do so, the other members of the group will be expected to work to the same production standard. The group will therefore exert pressure on such a member to conform and maintain existing production standards.

It should be clear that the goals pursued by the so-called "deviant" differ from those of the group. This results in his or her displaying a different type of job behaviour. If the group does not succeed in persuading such a deviant to accept group norms, such a person is isolated from the group and rejected on both the psychological and social level. Such an isolated person will withdraw from the group in time.

People often make the mistake of thinking that a group rejects a member. The opposite is true, however: it is the member who rejects the group because he or she does not want to accept the existing group norms. The member is thus responsible for the rejection.

18.8 CONFLICT IN GROUPS
18.8.1 What is conflict?
When two or more parties have to work together to achieve a certain goal, conflict is almost inevitable. This does not mean that the two parties will necessarily fight with each other, but that they will have differences of opinion that could lead to a general breakdown in cooperation.

Conflict can be defined as *differences of opinion that influence the interaction between interdependent parties*.

18.8.2 What causes conflict?
Conflict in organisations has various causes, the most common of which are discussed below (based on Schein 1980:157 and Robins 1989:239).

Win-lose situations
It often happens that two groups pursue the same goal, which they cannot both simultaneously achieve. For example: two rugby teams playing against each other both want to win. The problem is that only one team can be the victor. In other words, the two groups (teams) are in a win-lose situation. This does not have any adverse effects, however, because the two teams are not interdependent.

The same type of situation is often found in organisations, and here it causes conflict because groups in an organisation are indeed interdependent.

The method by which the organisation's goals should be achieved
Conflict between individuals and groups about how the organisation's goals should be achieved is often more serious than conflict due to other causes. Conflict is particularly serious when the various groups (sections or departments) must compete for a larger share of the budget.

Serious conflict can, for example, arise if the production department attempts to increase the organisation's profits by reducing the range of products and increasing their quality, while it is the strategy of the marketing department—in pursuing the same goal—to market a greater variety of products.

Non-concurring status
From childhood onwards, people have a natural inclination to want to know where they stand in relation to other people. As a child you knew that you had to obey and respect your parents. As the eldest child in the house you may have had certain privileges and responsibilities. For example, you may have been allowed to sit in the front of the car when your family drove somewhere. You will also remember how you fought when your younger brother or sister took your place in the front seat. You had a certain status in the family hierarchy that you not only insisted upon, but were also proud of.

The same is true of organisations. For most people it is very important to know what their relative status position in an organisation is and where they stand in relation to other people. However, organisations have a variety of status hierarchies that are constantly changing. One can, however, differentiate between high-status employees and low-status employees.

Perceptual differences
Each person's perception of the world and of his or her environment differs from that of other people. A person acts in accordance with this perception. Perceptual differences come to the fore through, among other things, group membership and interaction between groups.

Members of the purchasing department may, for example, be worried about the price of a certain part, while the production department is more worried about its usefulness.

Where there are differences between people or groups, there is usually conflict.

Change
An organisation must be able to adapt to changing circumstances in order to survive and thrive. Its survival will be threatened if it persists with time-consuming and complicated production processes in a highly competitive marketing environment while better and more effective production equipment

is available. The organisation is therefore constantly forced to adapt, which may be to its own advantage as well as that of the workers.

Most people, however, tend to cling to the familiar and strongly resist new developments or change imposed on them from the outside. This happens because people know their present work. Change creates uncertainty which workers resent.

This normal human reaction causes conflict in an organisation, which nevertheless often gives rise to new ideas that are to the advantage of the organisation.

18.8.3 The consequences of intergroup competition

Not all conflict is undesirable. Constructively handled conflict may lead to valuable insights, new ideas and creative solutions. It does not fall within the scope of this chapter to discuss the various approaches to the handling of conflict. A manager should, however, be aware of what causes conflict, as well as of the effect this has on the behaviour of individuals and groups.

Schein (1980:163) divides the effect of intergroup competition into four categories, which will be explained below.

What happens in a competing group?
- The group develops greater cohesion and elicits greater loyalty from its members; the members form a close-knit unit and forget about internal differences.
- The atmosphere in the group changes from an informal, leisurely approach to the work to a formal, project-oriented approach.
- The leadership changes from a democratic style to a more autocratic style, which is accepted by the group members.
- The group becomes more structured and organised.
- The group demands more loyalty and conformity from its members to be able to show a unified front.

What happens between competing groups?
- Each group begins to regard the other as an enemy, and not simply as neutral.
- The group's perception of itself and other groups becomes distorted. The group tends to see only its own good points and to forget about its own weaknesses, while it sees only the weaknesses of other groups and ignores their strong points.
- Hostility towards the other groups increases while interaction and communication between the groups decrease. This further reinforces the negative perception of the other groups.
- If there is forced interaction between the groups—for example if they are forced to listen to representatives of the various groups—each group tends to listen more attentively to its own representative than to those from other groups. The group also tends to concentrate on the faults of the other

group's representative. Groups thus tend only to listen to what supports their own position and points of view.

What happens to the "winner"?
- The winning group becomes even closer.
- Subsequently, tension within the group begins to defuse, the group begins to lose its fighting spirit and becomes casual and playful. This condition is known as the "fat and happy" stage.
- The winning group strives for a higher degree of intragroup cooperation and becomes more concerned about the needs of the group members and less about achieving its objectives.
- The winning group becomes more complacent and thinks that the positive outcome (the fact that it has won) justifies its behaviour towards and perception of the group that has lost. There is little motivation among group members to evaluate their perceptions of themselves and the other group, or to take stock of the group's functioning. Consequently, the winning group does not learn much from the experience.

What happens to the loser?
- If the result of the competition is not crystal clear and leaves room for own interpretation, the group will display a strong tendency not to admit that it has lost and to ignore reality. The losers rationalise the situation with excuses such as "the assessor did not understand our solution", "the assessor was prejudiced", or "if fortune had not been against us, we would have won". Implicitly, the reaction of the losers is: "In reality, we did not lose at all."
- If the group gradually accepts that it has lost, it tends to blame something or somebody and go to much trouble to identify a scapegoat. If no outsider can be blamed, the group begins to look for internal reasons such as unsolved conflict or in-fighting—all in an attempt to find a cause.
- The group is more tense, ready to work harder and desperate. This is often called the "lean and hungry" state.
- The loser tends towards low intragroup cooperation, less concern with the needs of group members, and a determination to work harder in order to win the following round of the competition.
- Members of the group that has lost learn much about themselves, because the positive perception they had of themselves and the negative perception they had of the other group have been proved wrong by the fact that they lost. The group is thus forced to re-evaluate itself.

18.9 CONCLUSION
Groups in organisations can make positive or negative contributions towards organisational success. This poses a great challenge for the leadership of organisations. In modern society, where social interaction both within and

outside an organisation plays an important need-satisfying role, the leader must take careful note of the phenomenon known as group formation.

Questions

1. Define the term "group".
2. Differentiate between a formal and an informal group.
3. Identify and briefly describe the various types of groups in organisations.
4. Write an essay of not more than 300 words about the way in which groups function.

Sources

Dessler, A. 1980. *Organization theory: integrating structure and behavior*. Prentice-Hall, Englewood Cliffs, New Jersey.

Gray, J.L. & Starke, F.A. 1984. *Organizational behavior: concepts and applications*. Merrill, Columbus.

Robins, S.P. 1989. *Organizational behavior: concepts, controversies and applications*. Prentice-Hall, Englewood Cliffs, New Jersey.

Sayles, L.R. 1957. *Research in industrial human relations*. Harper & Row, New York.

Schein, E. 1980. The Chinese indoctrination program for prisoners of war. *Psychiatry*, Vol. 19, May 1956, pp. 149–72.

Chapter 19

Industrial relations: the role of the human resources manager in industrial relations

P.S. Nel

STUDY OBJECTIVES

After reading this chapter, you should be able to:

- Explain the importance and the complex role of industrial relations in human resources management;
- Describe the relation between the three participants in industrial relations in the business world;
- Explain the role of a policy on industrial relations in an organisation;
- Explain why industrial relations and human resources matters are interdependent and promote general human resources stability and progress in an organisation;
- Explain which policy components are essential to limit labour unrest and strikes;
- Indicate in which primary aspects of industrial relations the human resources manager must be involved;
- Explain the effect of general employment practices on industrial relations.

19.1 INTRODUCTION

Industrial relations form part of the throughput process and feature under the job context environment (see figure 3.1), where they have a direct influence on the utilisation and development of workers and management. In the job context environment they have an influence on the organisational culture, on management philosophy, on human resources and industrial relations policy, on working conditions and on intergroup and intragroup relations. In the external environment, industrial relations are directly influenced by the national human resources policy, by economic conditions and by trade unionism in South Africa.

The discussion on industrial relations is divided into two parts, which are presented in this chapter and in chapter 20. In this chapter the focus is on the human resources manager's involvement in industrial relations on the micro-level. In chapter 20, we describe the industrial relations system in South Africa on the macro-level.

In this chapter we focus on those general aspects of industrial relations with which a human resources manager should be familiar. Today industrial relations are so specialised that most organisations employ an industrial relations officer or manager to deal with industrial relations issues. The material presented in this chapter therefore presupposes that the human resources manager has access to an industrial relations officer or manager in the organisation. He or she should nevertheless be familiar with some industrial relations issues, specifically in the private sector in South Africa. This chapter is therefore not addressed to the industrial relations specialist, and specific "how to" information on industrial relations is not given.

FIGURE 19.1: Principal learning components of the role of the human resources manager in industrial relations

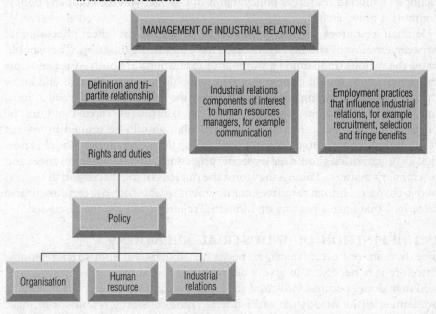

Industrial relations are of special importance for human resources managers in South Africa, particularly because of the rapid changes that are taking place at present. Human resources managers, particularly in large organisations in South Africa, have however handed over this new facet of human resources management to industrial relations managers. Industrial relations developments are so rapid that the task of the industrial relations manager may soon become as important as that of the human resources manager.

Not all organisations are lucky enough to have the services of an industrial relations manager or officer (particularly smaller organisations) and many do not have a separate industrial relations section or department. Here industrial relations are the human resources manager's responsibility. It will be detrimental to the progress of the organisation if he or she neglects this responsibility. He or she needs to know the functions of industrial relations, and should be willing to do the work of an industrial relations officer, should one not be employed by the organisation.Industrial relations are crucial in South Africa, and as more specialists in this area become available, human resources managers will become less involved. However, they should remain au fait with the general functioning of industrial relations in an organisation.

What, then, should human resources managers know about industrial relations and how should they go about integrating this function with the broader context of human resources management in an organisation?

In the modern business world it is essential that organisations have a company policy, a human resources policy and an industrial relations policy. An organisation that neglects to synchronise all three policies or draws up, for example, a human resources policy that is not in line with the company policy, commits a grave error.

Human resources managers should be aware of the effect that conflict between employees and managers could have on the organisation. They should know the various trade union groupings or federations in South Africa and how the organisation should cope with a strike, should it occur. They should know that collective bargaining is an integral part of the interaction with trade unions, that industrial relations training should be continually carried out in the organisation and that supervisors, in particular, should be trained in human relations to interact with employees on the shop floor. Finally they should know that an organisation should have specific procedures to deal with grievances and disciplinary matters. These issues form the nucleus of the discussion in the rest of this chapter. Human resources management issues (such as recruitment and selection) that have a bearing on industrial relations will also be discussed.

19.2 DEFINITION OF INDUSTRIAL RELATIONS

The human resources manager needs to understand industrial relations, therefore it is necessary to give a definition of it. Unfortunately this is easier said than done, because industrial relations is a complex subject. Even leading academics in the field, such as Flanders, Dunlop, Salamon and Clegg, have not been able to produce a definition of industrial relations that is universally accepted. It is difficult to define industrial relations for a number of reasons, primarily because a number of academic disciplines contribute to its subject matter.

Disciplines such as economics, anthropology, psychology, political science and, most recently, sociology, all have an impact on industrial relations. Industrial relations as a discipline describe the conditions under which employees attempt to satisfy their economic, sociological and psychological needs in their working environment.

The subject of industrial relations is further complicated by the fact that the industrial relations system in any country is largely determined by the ideology of its government, which is also the legislator. This means that the industrial relations system reflects the socio-economic and political ideological characteristics of the party in power. In South Africa this is a market-oriented ideology.

Each definition of industrial relations varies according to whether a country has a free-market, socialist or command economy. In addition employees, employers, the state, trade unions, political parties, employers' associations, and so on, all have an influence on the industrial relations system.

According to Bendix (1984:10), the general definition of industrial relations most readily accepted in South Africa regards industrial relations as the system of social relations in production, covering "all forms of economic activity or production and all forms of industrial relations regardless of the presence, absence or variety of formal organisations".

The Department of Manpower defines industrial relations in the Manpower Training Act (No. 56 of 1981, Section 1, xxi):

All aspects and matters connected with the relationship between employer and employee, including matters relating to negotiations in respect of remuneration and other conditions of employment of the employee, the prevention and settlement of disputes between employer and employee, the application, interpretation and effect of laws administered by the Department and the management of the affairs of trade unions, employers' organizations, federations and industrial councils.

These definitions of industrial relations can be applied as follows in the South African context: industrial relations can be formal or informal, and deal with institutionalised intergroup relations in the work environment between workers, management and the government. Decisions arrived at, for example by means of collective bargaining between workers and management through their various representative bodies (such as employers' associations and trade unions), are enforced by legislation or mutual agreement.

Industrial relations are a specialised and complex field and organisations would be wise to appoint specific industrial relations officers or managers to manage this function. It should, however, be stressed that the human resources manager still needs to understand the general principles and applications of industrial relations, since it is his or her task to integrate these activities in the business environment.

19.3 THE TRIPARTITE RELATIONSHIP IN INDUSTRIAL RELATIONS

South Africa subscribes to a free-market ideology, which implies that industrial relations have a democratic system and structure. A clearly defined role is ascribed to the various participants, i.e. workers, employers and the state. They form the tripartite relationship characteristic of the economic systems of democratic societies. According to Nel and Van Rooyen (1993:19), the three participants can be described as follows:

- *Workers* sell their labour to the producers of goods and services. Workers may be organised into trade unions which regulate all matters on their behalf, or they may be unorganised and operate by means of, for example, the works council system or on an individual basis in their organisations.
- *Employers* are compelled to ensure an acceptable return on investment for shareholders. This means that they must ensure the most effective application of the scarce resources at their disposal.
- *The state* is both master and servant of the other two participants. On the one hand the state holds legislative power, on the other it is expected to give assistance to both the other participants in satisfying their respective needs.

This tripartite relationship between the various participants in the industrial relations system is illustrated in figure 19.2.

FIGURE 19.2: The participants in the industrial relations system

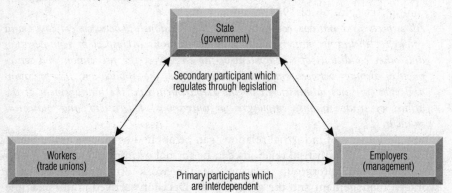

Figure 19.2 clearly shows that workers and management are the primary participants in the system and that the state is the secondary participant. The role of each participant is derived from its needs structure. Consequently, if participants wish to satisfy their respective needs, there must be some form of cooperation from each of them.

Because workers and management are the primary participants, they reach their own agreements whereby conditions of service, remuneration, protection of workers, safety and health, acceptable return on investment, and so on, are stipulated. This means that group interaction and interrelations form the bulk of the industrial relations activities of the various participants in the system in South Africa.

It is important for the human resources manager to recognise that all three participants play an important role in shaping and reforming industrial relations in South Africa. The *state* has the power to change the relationship dramatically, which it has done, for example by drastically simplifying procedures for the settlement of grievances. Furthermore, an industrial court has been instituted, as has action against unfair labour practices. All these factors can contribute to the reshaping of the relationship between employers and employees.

With regard to *employers:* only three South African conglomerates control 70% of the private economy in South Africa and these conglomerations handle their own industrial relations. The result is that employers' associations receive inadequate support from large organisations for reforms in industrial relations. One positive consequence of this situation, however, is that the industrial relations function of management has become established as separate from the operation of the human resources department in many South African organisations in the last few years.

Employees have also played a part in reshaping the industrial relations system. In an attempt to bring about fundamental change, plant-based *recognition agreements* were entered into because workers rejected the industrial council system (i.e. the formalised institutional system discussed in chapter 20). The extent to which the industrial council system has been rejected is clear from the approximately 3 000 recognition agreements that have been signed with employers by various trade unions in South Africa up to 1993. It certainly demonstrates the power of plant level (in-company) interaction between employers and trade unions.

Activities undertaken by any of the three participants can have far-reaching effects on the other two participants. Therefore, by respecting the role and activities of the other participants, each participant can ensure the continued survival and welfare of the other parties in South Africa. Human resources managers should take notice of those problems which directly influence their relationship with workers and the state.

Workers and organisations (employers) have definite rights and certain responsibilities towards each other, and mutual respect for these rights and responsibilities will contribute to positive relations between them.

19.4 THE RIGHTS AND DUTIES OF EMPLOYERS AND WORKERS

There is a division between the ownership (shareholders) and control (management) of capital, and management (or employers) need a certain amount of freedom in their management of organisations if they are to assure an acceptable return on the owners' investment. This means that they have certain rights (and responsibilities) in managing the organisation successfully.

Employers and workers are completely interdependent and need to cooperate if the running of the organisation is to be successful. Managers and workers, however, have different roles in the organisation and this, according to Nel *et al.* (1993:5), means that they have different rights and responsibilities.

19.4.1 The rights of management

Managers need freedom to manage an organisation. This means that they have certain rights to execute their task successfully. There are two kinds of management rights: exclusive and traditional rights.

Management has the *exclusive* right to determine the objectives of the organisation, determine product policies, plan and implement policies, provide financial and material resources, establish and expand facilities, determine the quality of products, determine work standards, determine the content of the workforce, direct and organise the workforce, belong to an employers' association and manage the organisation. Many attempts have been made by workers to take over these rights, but it has never been adequately shown in the Western democratic system that these rights should not be exclusive to management.

In South Africa these rights belong indisputably to management.

The following rights belonged *traditionally* to management, but in time have come to be shared with workers through the introduction of worker participation and in the spirit of industrial democracy. These are rights to recruit and appoint workers, assign them to jobs, promote or demote them, transfer them, increase or decrease their salaries or wages, discipline workers, discharge or lay them off, establish hours of work—i.e. starting and quitting times—grant or refuse leave of absence and determine overtime required.

What is important is not so much management's prerogative or otherwise regarding the exercising of the rights, but the way in which these rights are exercised. If these rights are exercised in a dictatorial or autocratic fashion, this is against the principles of industrial democracy and is completely unacceptable to workers. Today, even if the traditional rights are exercised in a one-sided way by management, this is unacceptable to workers as they wish to participate in decision-making processes.

Rights are never without obligations. Management represents the employers (and therefore the shareholders) of the organisation, and management's obligations to the organisation are:

- To take calculated risks;
- To render an acceptable return on investment to the shareholders.

The general duties of management towards workers

Management has the responsibility of facilitating contact with workers and their respective representative bodies. This means management should:

- Arrange regular meetings with the aim of establishing sound relationships with workers;
- Discuss matters of importance with all parties;

- Understand the real and legitimate needs of workers;
- Share important information, such as human resources statistics, human resources turnover, absenteeism, safety arrangements and production targets and achievements;
- Help worker representatives (especially works council members and shop stewards) understand their own responsibilities;
- Provide facilities for works council and trade union meetings, such as the meeting room, time off for meetings and secretarial services.

Other general duties of the employer are to promote the quality of work life, help with housing, etc.

The specific duties of management towards workers
The employer's specific duties include the following: employees must be retained in service as far as possible, and there should be no unnecessary appointments or dismissals. Employees must be paid for the services they render and no unlawful deductions should be made from their pay. There should be job-related benefits for employees, such as safe working conditions, vacation leave, pension, unemployment insurance and sick leave.

These aspects are usually left to the human resources manager or the industrial relations manager, who keeps relations between management and workers smooth by negotiating with unions or the works council or, in the absence of any formal worker representative body, with the workers themselves.

19.4.2 The rights of workers
Workers have six internationally recognised categories of rights, namely the right to work, the right to freedom of association, the right to collective bargaining, the right to strike, the right to protection and the right to training. According to Nel (1986:21) these rights are also generally applicable in South Africa.
- *The right to work:* In South Africa the right to work is not a legal right, but rather the democratic right of a worker to find employment and to perform the job willingly. Employment possibilities are determined by the free market economy which dictates the job market and the rate of remuneration.

    In its constitution and labour laws South Africa does not recognise either the right of a citizen to be placed in employment or the duty of the state to provide work. Section 46 of the Unemployment Insurance Act (No. 30 of 1966) makes provision for unemployment pay for a specified period, which is at most an indication of the state's interest in the continued existence of industrial relations between employers and workers.
- *Freedom of association:* This right is entrenched in the Labour Relations Act (No. 28 of 1956) and is discussed in chapter 20. It gives anybody in South Africa, irrespective of race or colour, the opportunity to join an association

(be it a trade union or a works council) which will protect him or her and negotiate on his or her behalf with the employer for fair and acceptable remuneration and conditions of employment.

- *Collective bargaining:* This right is also protected by the Labour Relations Act. It enables trade unions to represent workers and to bargain on their behalf with representatives of employers about all aspects of the employment contract.
- *Strikes:* This right is also protected by the Labour Relations Act. A strike is usually effective only if it is undertaken collectively regardless of whether or not workers are unionised. Unionised workers usually stage the most effective strikes.
- *Protection:* The right to protection consists of a number of components: the right to fair remuneration and conditions of service, the right to health, safety and security, and the right to protection from unfair labour practices.

  There are various laws to protect workers in the work environment, for example the Workmen's Compensation Act (No. 30 of 1941), the Unemployment Insurance Act (No. 30 of 1966) and the Occupational Health and Safety Act (No. 85 of 1993).
- *Training:* This right is of paramount importance in South Africa today, and the Manpower Training Act (No. 56 of 1981) gives training prominence. This right has two components, namely the right to vocational (or job) training and the right to industrial relations training (which relates to trade union training).
  - As far as *vocational training* is concerned, it is the duty of the state to provide the machinery for training in the form of training centres or tax concessions for employers who provide training for workers. The responsibility for training lies with employers and they have to see to it that all workers undergo the training necessary to qualify them adequately for their jobs. Workers, however, are obliged to ensure that, as far as possible, they have the necessary educational qualifications to benefit from vocational training, for example mathematics at matriculation level for training in electronics.
  - Regarding training in *industrial relations*, workers need to be trained in basic economics, sociology, psychology, business economics and labour law to give them a better perspective of their position, not only in the business environment, but in society. *Trade union training* should cover the philosophy, history, organisation and administration of all kinds of worker organisations. The reason is that knowledge of trade unions promotes an organised, responsible and well disciplined workforce. Workers then have a better understanding of what is required of them and of how to maintain their position in the industry in which they are employed. Workers who know what they are doing and striving for can play a responsible role in the industrial relations system of South Africa.

The general duties of workers towards management
Management is responsible for planning, directing and controlling the organisation's human resources. On the other hand, workers are responsible for the implementation of management plans. Without this shared responsibility, an organisation cannot be effective. If workers are to fulfil these responsibilities towards management, they need a workers' representative body which will undertake the following:

- To ascertain the views and feelings of workers towards the organisation and brief management on workers' customs and cultures;
- To investigate grievances and resolve them if this is within their power, and to make recommendations to management regarding these grievances (if a grievance is not resolved, a formal grievance must then be lodged with the human resources manager, the industrial relations manager or the supervisor of the worker, depending on how the grievance procedure operates);
- To maintain regular communication with workers, transmitting decisions and information from management to workers and explaining the reasons, and to communicate business results to other workers;
- To explain works council and trade union activities and representative procedures and methods; to make the responsibilities and limits of authority of these bodies clear; and to teach workers about the business they are in;
- To contact new workers and participate in their induction into the organisation;
- To help workers understand the importance of economic considerations and to convey to management how this has been understood, in order to ensure that workers make requests that are economically possible.

The specific duties of workers towards management
The workers' duty to work implies no unnecessary absence from work, not to be late for work, leave the work station without permission, work under the influence of intoxicating substances, indulge in bad behaviour in the workplace or strike for no good reason. Workers also have the duty to be subordinate: that is, not to ignore legitimate orders or stir up other workers. Workers must behave well, which means that they must not insult co-workers or become involved in a fight on the organisation's premises. They should never be dishonest or commit fraud. Workers must be loyal to their employer and not reveal the secrets or work methods of the organisation to the opposition.

It is clear from the above that industrial relations are a complex field of study and that the relationships between managers and workers are of cardinal importance to the goals of an organisation. Many attempts have been made to establish structures and procedures to formalise the relationship between managers and workers. This can be achieved by drawing up company, human resources and industrial relations policies. The contents of these policies and the relation between them are discussed in the next section.

19.5 THE RELATION BETWEEN COMPANY, HUMAN RESOURCES AND INDUSTRIAL RELATIONS POLICIES

19.5.1 Company policy and human resources policy

Management and workers have different interests, objectives and needs. It is essential, therefore, that there should be written documentation in the form of a policy to regulate communication and interaction between them. Company policy forms the basis upon which other policies and procedures in the organisation can be drawn up. The various levels of management in an organisation have different policies, and depending on its size, these could vary from simple to very complex. Should an organisation be fairly small, it may combine such documents for its own needs and purposes.

According to Prinsloo and Bruwer (1993), an organisation needs to formulate short-term and long-term objectives and strategies (corporate planning) to achieve objectives. After this corporate planning is done, the organisation can draw up formal policies.

The formulation of an industrial relations policy or a human resources policy is never done by the industrial relations manager or human resources manager. It is the end product of corporate planning and strategy formulation, and therefore it is a corporate responsibility, like corporate planning.

Policy formulation is top management's responsibility because the area of responsibility of the top executive team is the optimum application and integration of resources. Policy is dependent upon this integration and application of resources, and has at the same time a major effect on it. It must, therefore, be a top executive responsibility, although the human resources or industrial relations manager will assist in working out the details.

It is important once a policy is formulated and accepted, to put it in writing and make it public by perhaps publishing it in the in-house magazine. This step is in itself proof of commitment to the policy. It is easy to deny or reverse a "policy" that is merely part of the organisation's culture. Such informal policies are also open to manipulation or misinterpretation, either accidentally or intentionally.

The failure of many organisations to develop formal company, human resources and industrial relations policies could be one of the reasons why there is increasing labour unrest in South Africa. It is of cardinal importance for the human resources manager to ensure that his or her organisation has such policies and follows them.

A policy provides proof of commitment and of preparedness to declare views and attitudes and it sets limits of behaviour. It shows the intention of the parties involved to honour these declarations. It implies that there has been conscious and rational consideration of the relationship between management and workers. It recognises the security needs of workers and the interdependence of workers and management in the organisation. It acknowleges that workers are indispensable and that they are more than mere production factors. At the same time it recognises the rights of workers and the obligations of managers.

The company policy therefore forms the basis for the development of all other processes and procedures that determine the conduct of workers and management in an organisation. An effective disciplinary procedure, for example, can only be drawn up once an industrial relations policy has been formulated.

An organisation therefore needs a policy statement that indicates its approach and business philosophy. The company policy statement could contain the following (according to Fact Sheet No. 103 of the IPM, where the Barlow Rand Group is quoted):

> *The Barlow Rand Group's primary objectives are to maintain its record of growth and to increase its return to shareholders. At the same time it acknowledges its corporate responsibility to contribute to the prosperity and progress of the people in South Africa.*
>
> *The group recognises that the achievement of these two objectives will very largely be dependent upon the well-being, the training and the most effective use of its greatest single asset—its people.*

Other terms in the company policy statement could, for example, provide incentives to ensure maximum productivity and encourage worker participation in decision-making that affects workers; make provision for housing and for educational projects for employees; and there could be a statement of the organisation's right to manage these.

An organisation should also have a human resources policy. Its terms could include: the aim to assist each employee in developing his or her skills and enable him or her to use these skills to the full, thus ensuring the employee's job satisfaction and ability to contribute to the organisation; the intention to promote and preserve at all times the dignity and self-esteem of each employee; and to develop and maintain open lines of communication and personal contact between the organisation and each employee.

According to Swanepoel (1989), an organisation should also have an industrial relations policy, and it is important to draw a distinction between a human resources policy and an industrial relations policy. A human resources policy addresses the needs of the individual within the organisation; an industrial relations policy, on the other hand, is intended to regulate the relationships between management and the workers, between management and organised labour, and between management and the several external agencies that play a part in industrial relations.

In practice the distinction between these policies is not always clear, as many organisations combine them.

19.5.2 Industrial relations policy [1]

The industrial relations policy of an organisation is the expression of top management's philosophy towards the human resources of the organisation.

---

[1] Permission has been granted by the Institute of Personnel Management (Southern Africa) to quote in this and other sections in this chapter information that has appeared in various fact sheet supplements to the *IPM Journal*. Full source references appear in the bibliography at the end of the chapter.

It is a declaration of the fundamental values, beliefs, standards and philosophies (principles) that underlie the behaviour of the organisation, but it is detailed enough to provide specific guidelines for the relationship between the organisation's people.

According to the IPM Fact Sheet No. 103, the industrial relations policy statement of an organisation should contain the following:

- A statement of the organisation's responsibility to protect worker rights and to provide workers with the opportunity of participating in decisions that directly affect them;
- A commitment to the principle of freedom of association;
- Acceptance of the rights of workers to collective bargaining in industrial disputes;
- Acceptance of the principle of lawful withholding of labour as a result of industrial disputes;
- A statement of the organisation's attitude to the available machinery for collective bargaining; for example, support of industrial councils and willingness to consult with unregistered unions and the relevant employers' association.

It is important to bear in mind that a policy reflects values. Therefore the policy objectives should cover the following: development of mutual trust and cooperation; prevention of problems and disputes through agreed procedures; reduction of labour costs; strengthening of managerial control; development of human resources skills; and management of productivity. The policy standards should be universally acceptable to all departments or subsidiaries; they should be in writing, in broad terms and in clear language; they should be justifiable in terms of their impact on profit; they should be approved and authorised by the highest authority so that the policy carries the weight of a directive; and the terms must be inviolate.

Other important considerations in drawing up an industrial relations policy are:

- The policy must be unambiguous.
- The policy must be positively phrased and not contain negative statements; for instance it is preferable to say, "the organisation intends granting equal pay for equal work", rather than "the organisation will not engage in any discriminatory practices".
- The policy statement must not require interpretation.
- The rationale behind the policy must be explained.
- The boundaries within which individual discretion may be exercised must be clear.
- A distinction must be drawn between policies (for example equal pay for equal work) and procedures (such as grievance procedures).
- The use of such words and phrases as "may", "generally recommended", "in most cases", should be avoided as they have a permissive tone.

- No statement of policy that is contradicted by any other confidential policy should be included. It is better to ignore a subject than to say one thing publicly and another privately.
- The policy should meet the relevant legal and government requirements.
- Management should avoid expedient settlement of disputes that could prejudice long-term interests.
- Collective agreements must be for fixed periods and should set out prescriptions regarding disputes of interest (such as the percentage wage increase employees are bargaining for when they regard the employer's offer as too low) for the full duration of the agreement. During the period of an agreement there should be no dispute of rights (such as a common law requirement, legal issues or the interpretation of a clause in the agreement).
- The policy should contain a clause stating that management will not negotiate or make concessions under illegal or non-procedural economic coercion or the explicit threat of it.
- Management must state clearly that the company's industrial relations practices will be made known and comprehensible to employees and their representatives, and will always be consistent with the organisation's general human resources policy and company policy.

The industrial relations policy statement should contain procedures and guidelines that will provide operational structures in the organisation. Management can then consolidate and strengthen the organisation's position by utilising the procedures set down in the policy for settling grievances, disputes and disciplinary actions. This means that managers can distance themselves from the negative side of the relationship between employer and workers in the sense that they no longer need to be seen as the source of discipline in their personal capacity, but merely as officials carrying out policy prescriptions. It also eliminates many negative emotions associated with employer-worker relationships because procedures have been agreed to by the participants in the industrial relations policy. Conflict is reduced in the work environment because the implementation of policy is then seen as an integral part of the relationship between employer and workers because it is formalised in writing and known by everybody.

The procedures and structures in the industrial relations policy prescribe relations with trade unions, strike handling, grievance procedures and general industrial relations issues such as recruitment, industrial safety and training. These issues are discussed in the next two sections.

19.6 THE MAJOR COMPONENTS OF INDUSTRIAL RELATIONS OF CONCERN TO THE HUMAN RESOURCES MANAGER

An industrial relations policy is a document that is instrumental in formalising the relationship between employers and unionised employees, in particular, in any organisation. The structures and procedures in the industrial relations policy form a basis for the practical details that govern the day-to-day interaction between management and workers. Issues that need to be precisely spelled out in the industrial relations policy include trade union and works council relations, participation in employer associations, dispute-handling procedures, methods of collective bargaining, strike handling, grievance and disciplinary procedures and the channels and role of communication between management and workers.

These issues are discussed separately in the sections after the discussion on communication.

19.6.1 The essentials of employer-employee communication

Communication and the channels used for it are essential for the survival of any organisation. The communication methods and channels used in organisations usually determine the effectiveness of communication between the various groups such as supervisors and subordinates, employee groups and the employer. Effective communication at all levels in an organisation is therefore essential. In the industrial relations context the means of communication, such as telephones, memos or even personally delivered messages, are not the most important. What is important is not what is said, but how it is said. If communication between trade union members and the employer is hostile, unfriendly and based on incorrect assumptions, this will lead to conflict and the relationship between these parties will be strained. The human resources manager should therefore pay attention to those issues of communication that are important to employers and employees and which, if not contained, could lead to disputes and even strikes.

Communication is indispensable in organisations. It is generally accepted that people spend 70% of their day communicating, and of this 45% is spent listening. It is also known that people normally have only 25% efficiency when listening. It is therefore not surprising that something like 50% of all communication attempts fail. Yet, communication in any organisation is essential to reduce conflict to a minimum and to increase the effectiveness of employees in carrying out their daily tasks. Effective communication should therefore be a top priority of the human resources manager so that the full benefit can be derived from it.

Effective communication results in higher productivity and greater cooperation in an organisation. People can give of their best only if they understand what they have to do, why they have to do it and to what extent they are achieving their targets. If communication is not systematic, employees who are affected by change, for example, will not understand the reasons for these changes and will resist them.

So far we have dealt in this chapter with those issues that are important in effective communication between employers and workers. The industrial relations policy provides the means to specify the relationship between employer and worker, and provides a structure for communication between them. It also sets procedures for collective bargaining and for dealing with grievances and

404

disciplinary issues—it thus makes known aspects of industrial relations within the organisation. The grievance procedure is a form of upward communication from the worker to the employer concerning problems and work-related issues. On the other hand, the disciplinary procedure is a form of downward communication from the employer to the workers about issues that are regarded as unacceptable behaviour on the part of the workers. The organisation can gain several advantages from employer-to-worker downward communication:

- *Commitment to the job is improved:* The provision of information helps to build trust and motivates workers. Trust and motivation improve the commitment of the workers to the work group and cause them to strive to achieve the goals of this group and of their section, and ultimately those of the organisation.
- *"Grapevine" distortion is reduced:* "Grapevine" distortion is inevitable in informal communication. Regular formal communication serves to reduce such distortion since workers come to expect an official version instead of giving credence to rumours.
- *Feedback is elicited:* Formal communication usually elicits a response from the receiver. This response provides valuable information and feedback to the sender, which enables him or her to assess the opinions and reactions of the interested parties.
- *The status of supervisors is improved:* To possess and to impart information confer status. If management wants its supervisors to enjoy status in the eyes of the workers, one way to achieve this is to make supervisors the bearers of management information to workers.
- *Workers are involved in change:* It is human nature to resist change. Advance communication of a proposed or pending change allows workers time to evaluate it and prepare for it. They are then more likely to cooperate in the proposed changes.
- *The disciplinary system is more effective:* Workers accept the authority of management and see the disciplinary procedure as a means used by management to eliminate inappropriate (unacceptable) behaviour in the organisation.

The management of an organisation, in conjunction with the human resources manager, should evolve a definite policy as to what should or should not be communicated to workers. Not all the activities of the organisation should automatically be communicated to everybody. The rights and responsibilities of managers and workers should be taken into consideration when communication structures are established. The following serve as guidelines on what should be communicated to workers:

- *Progress of the organisation, branch or section:* Workers are directly concerned with the results, whether positive or negative, of their efforts in their immediate job environment (section) and they are concerned with the progress of the organisation as a whole. Such results should therefore be communicated to workers as it gives them feedback on their work performance, serves as an indication that management recognises their contribution to the results and confirms their job security, which is very important in the present economic climate.

- *Movements of people:* Not every appointment, transfer, promotion and resignation is relevant to every worker. But movements of people belonging to their work group, people to whom they report or people with whom they are in frequent contact should be made known to workers.
- *Policy or procedure decisions affecting workers:* All new or revised procedures affecting workers should be communicated to them. Industrial relations decisions arrived at between management and union officials or shop stewards, such as industrial council or works council decisions, are of direct concern to workers. Worker representatives (shop stewards or works council members) as a party to the decisions should, however, report back to the workers through their own channels.

It is clear that aspects of industrial relations are major contributors to effective communication. We now describe the most important aspects of industrial relations with which the human resources manager should be familiar.

19.6.2 The relationship between employer and trade union

In South Africa freedom of association is guaranteed by the Labour Relations Act. Whether employers or human resources managers like or dislike trade unions is immaterial, since it is a violation of the Labour Relations Act to oppose the efforts of a trade union to recruit members from among the employees of an organisation. However, the human resources manager can, via the industrial relations policy of the organisation, place certain reasonable restrictions on trade union officials regarding access to the premises, and so on. However, unreasonable restrictions will lead to claims of unfair labour practices or victimisation of employees, and this may result in an industrial court case against the employer. (Freedom of association and trade unions are discussed in chapter 20.) In this section the focus is on the general relationship that may exist between an employer (represented by the industrial relations or human resources manager) and the relevant unions.

Relationships between organisations and unions vary between two extremes. Organisations may be apathetic, yet remain within the limits of the law, or they may be patronising towards any trade union that represents their employees. Neither attitude makes for good relationships. It is important for the organisation and the union to develop a working arrangement whereby their respective goals can best be achieved.

The relationship between the employer and trade union entails an acknowledgement of their conflicting interests and an appreciation of the need to compromise. Earlier we described the relationship between the primary participants in the industrial relations system in South Africa. Further aspects of the relationship are now highlighted.

According to Nel and Van Rooyen (1993:143–7) the objectives of trade unions are to protect and promote the particular goals or interests of individual workers or groups of workers. That is why workers' reaction to trade union membership will indicate the degree to which they believe such membership will decrease their frustration and anxiety, improve their opportunities and lead to the achievement of a better standard of living.

It is in the employer's interest, on the other hand, to maximise return on investment for shareholders, which means making the maximum profit that seems fair and reasonable to all parties concerned (including workers).

Human resources managers need to know that there are two systems of trade union interaction in South Africa, namely statutory interaction whereby unions operate in terms of the Labour Relations Act, and non-statutory inter-action, the system of trade union recognition that operates outside of the Labour Relations Act. (In chapter 20 both systems of trade union interaction are discussed.)

The human resources manager should bear in mind that it is immaterial whether there is a formal relationship with a trade union operating in terms of the Labour Relations Act, or an informal relationship based on a recognition agreement. It is not so much the contractual nature of the relationship with the union that matters, but rather the development of an atmosphere of trust and cooperation between the parties and the establishment of a working arrange-ment to accommodate each other's needs. According to IPM Fact Sheet No. 106 there is an apparent contradiction in the fact that the acknowl-edgement of inherent differences between employers and trade unions actually increases their chances of achieving their respective objectives. In the day-to-day running of the organisation, the human resources manager should therefore ensure that all management and supervisory staff reconcile themselves to the reality of trade unions. Provision should be made for the accommodation of shop stewards. Their role in the organisation is of cardinal importance in the promotion of harmony between the organisation and the trade union. Nel and Van Rooyen (1993:150) point out:

The primary role of the shop steward is to ensure and maintain the equilibrium in relations between management and labour within the framework of existing rules, regulations and customs, since it is precisely this that creates efficient liaison across the age-old gulf between the interests of management and workers.

It is the shop steward who represents workers and acts as the link between the workers and the trade union when grievances are lodged or disciplinary action is taken. It could happen that trade union officials who are not employees of the organisation may from time to time wish to enter the premises to com-municate with workers. The human resources manager needs to be aware of this and know the organisation's policy on such visits. This should be spelled out in the industrial relations policy, which should also clarify further practical issues with regard to access to the organisation's premises. It may be stipulated trade union officials may enter the organisation's premises only if they meet certain requirements (unless they obtain prior consent from the employer to do otherwise). For example, trade union officials may enter the premises on condition that:

- They do not hold meetings;
- They speak to workers individually;
- They hand out only non-provocative literature (literature must be submitted to management in advance for scrutiny).

Management could consider granting unions other facilities under certain conditions, such as an office at the disposal of trade union officials at certain times, the use of notice boards, time off for the training of shop stewards (but subject to specific limits: normally five working days per year). Arrangements should be made for interaction with the union if a serious dispute should arise.

Concerning collective bargaining, it is generally not in the interests of management to conduct dual discussions and negotiations where more than one union represent the same group of workers. The unions should get together to define the issues that they wish to discuss, and should present a single submission to management where possible. The human resources manager should take note of all these issues and should formulate a policy on them which can be incorporated into the industrial relations policy.

19.6.3 Relationships with employers' associations

Whereas workers can belong to trade unions, employers can join employers' associations. This is briefly discussed in chapter 20. These associations also operate under the sanction of the Labour Relations Act. In this chapter only the philosophy underlying employers' associations is dealt with. Employers' associations can consist of any number of employers in any particular undertaking, industry, trade or occupation, who associate for the purpose of regulating relations in that industry between themselves and their employees or some of their employees.

An important consequence of membership of an employers' association is that as soon as an employer becomes a member of such an association, it is automatically bound by the provisions of any agreements or awards that are binding upon that association. Employers' associations usually participate in the industrial council system (discussed in chapter 20) and participate at this level in collective bargaining with representatives of trade unions in order to enter into agreements. Employers (and trade unions) remain bound to such agreements during their currency and even if an employer ceases to be a member of the association, it still remains bound to the agreement.

South Africa's industrial relations system allows for the participation of employers and employees so that they regulate their own affairs as far as possible. Human resources managers must be aware that employers' associations serve a useful purpose: they collect and maintain statistics regarding their members and represent their members in a variety of bodies, such as industrial councils, conciliation boards, medical aid societies, pension and unemployment organisations, insurance companies and apprentice boards, as well as other statutory and non-statutory boards, councils, commissions and organisations. Employers' associations also provide guidelines to their members on how to cope with contentious issues.

The human resources manager should assess his or her particular organisation's position in the industry and then decide whether or not to join an employers' association. The criterion may be the degree to which the relevant industrial council is representative of that industry. The organisation's relationship with the employers' association will have an influence on the organisation's industrial relations profile both in the industry and in the eyes of the various trade unions that operate in that industry.

Participation in the employers' association and finally in the industrial council system means that collective bargaining can take place on behalf of the organisation by means of employers' representatives, and that specialists in negotiation and collective bargaining can perform this task on behalf of the organisation. Collective bargaining at industrial council level is discussed in chapter 20.

19.6.4 Dispute-handling procedures

A dispute procedure is distinct from a grievance procedure. A grievance procedure provides employees with a channel for expressing dissatisfaction or feelings of injustice in connection with the employment situation. (Grievance procedures are discussed in a subsequent section.) If a grievance procedure runs its course without any agreement being reached between the affected employee and management, and the employee will not accept the decision of management, a dispute arises. Note that disputes can also arise during the process of collective bargaining at the industrial council or when a recognition agreement is being negotiated. The kind of dispute referred to here is a deadlock between management and the workers (or the trade union), which is sufficiently serious to threaten industrial peace.

A dispute procedure prescribes the action to be taken by both parties during the interval between the start of a dispute and a possible work stoppage or, even worse, a strike. The dispute procedures that are briefly discussed below all operate under the sanction of the Labour Relations Act. (They are discussed in more detail in chapter 20.)

- *Industrial councils and conciliation boards:* The duty of an industrial council is to maintain industrial peace between all employers and employees under its jurisdiction. It also endeavours to prevent or settle disputes between employers (or employers' associations) and workers (or trade unions). Where there is no industrial council with jurisdiction, the Director-General (who is represented by the Regional Director and then in turn by an official) can, upon application, establish a conciliation board to settle a particular dispute. The constitution of the industrial council or the stated terms of reference giving the powers and duties of a conciliation board, must set down the procedure for dealing with disputes within the area for which that body is registered.

- *The procedures for handling a deadlock:* Provisions are laid down in South Africa for the settlement of disputes through industrial councils and conciliation boards, but both unionised and non-unionised workers have at times bypassed the procedures laid down by legislation, and so disregarded the industrial councils, conciliation boards and the industrial court as well. In such cases the individual management has to settle the dispute. This happens mainly where recognition agreements have been entered into. Management must then maintain dialogue with employees itself or through a third party in order to prevent a work stoppage.

  Procedures for handling a deadlock can be combined. The steps contained in the legislation can be followed or both parties (management and workers) can decide in advance what should be done. In either case the idea is to initiate procedures aimed at resolving the dispute. Such procedures can range from mediation to voluntary arbitration or even compulsory arbitration.

- *Mediation:* A mediator, as an independent third party, examines the dispute, establishes how far the parties have gone towards meeting each other, points out where hostility has clouded the debate and suggests alternatives for resolving the differences. There is no obligation on either party to the dispute to accept a mediator's proposals. The role of the mediator is to restore the relationship between the two parties and to identify any irrational issues or unrealistic assumptions that might have led to the deadlock. It is therefore in the interests of management, and in this case particularly the human resources or industrial relations manager, to appoint a mediator who is acceptable to both parties and who will maintain his or her role as a neutral person.

- *Arbitration:* Arbitration can be voluntary or compulsory, and is discussed in chapter 20. When parties have reached deadlock, the dispute is referred to an arbitrator. He or she will make a decision and both parties are obliged to abide by it, whether the arbitration is voluntary or compulsory. The arbitrator is usually appointed with the consent of both parties. Disputes in essential industries are resolved by compulsory arbitration. The Minister appoints an arbitrator in terms of the legislation.

The human resources manager must know which avenues are best to follow in the interests of his or her organisation if a dispute with the employees of the organisation should arise. A mediator or arbitrator could resolve the case quickly or the situation could develop until the parties have to resort to a strike or a lock-out to settle the dispute, both of which are very undesirable. It is therefore of cardinal importance that the human resources manager knows how these procedures operate and what the qualifications and talents of mediators and arbitrators should be in order to resolve disputes in a way that will be in the best interests of the organisation and yet will satisfy the workers as well.

19.6.5 Strike handling

Strikes are a fact of life in South Africa and the world over. The human resources or industrial relations manager must therefore be prepared for strikes, know what they are and how to handle them when they occur (in other words, there should be a contingency plan), as well as what to do after a strike. (The more technical aspects of strikes are discussed in chapter 20.)

In its general preparation for strikes, management needs to obtain information about unions and strikes by asking the following questions:

- Who are the unions?
- How and where do they operate?
- Who are the leaders?
- How strong are they?
- What are their aims or strategies?
- How many members do they have altogether?

Management should then answer the following questions regarding the organisation:

- What are the organisation's labour costs?
- How lean is the staffing and how easily can workers be replaced?
- Which are the critical areas in terms of management and effectiveness, and the key performance areas in the organisation's overall operations?

Management and the human resources manager can use the answers to these critical questions to prepare for possible strikes by taking proactive measures.

Strikes contain four elements that the human resources manager needs to be aware of. First, a strike is temporary, because strikers plan to resume their work with the same employer. Employers, however, do not always view strikers in the same light. Many employers regard strikers as people who have cancelled their employment contracts in an uncalled-for and unseemly manner. For this reason many employers attempt to end a strike by hiring a completely new workforce. Secondly, a strike is a stoppage. Contrary to popular opinion, striking is not easily used as a weapon, since it entails deprivation for the strikers and their families. This means that striking is the final weapon in a trade union's armoury. Thirdly, a strike is carried out by a group of workers: it is a joint action taken by the workers, as opposed to resignation, which is the individual withdrawal of labour. Fourthly, a strike is a collective action by workers to express a grievance, which may have been disregarded by management for a long time.

In the event of the refusal by a significant number of workers to start or continue working, management should react in the manner most likely to resolve the issues that caused the stoppage:

- As speedily as possible;
- As near to the point of origin as possible;
- Without injury to personnel and damage to property.

To achieve such an objective necessarily requires planning, organising and decision-making in advance to ensure appropriate and uniform behaviour on the part of management. This means that a contingency plan must be drawn up that will cover most of the issues discussed below.

Human resources managers are advised by the IPM Fact Sheet No. 106 to adopt the following procedures in the event of a strike:

- Maintain a chronological diary of events.
- Allocate responsibility for the overall situation to one person (usually the managing director).
- There should be no police involvement if this is at all possible, since the arrival of the police often leads to an explosive situation. However, the police are responsible for law and order and it may become necessary to call them, but management should liaise with the police and reach agreement on what their respective roles would be. Management should call in the police only in the case of violence.
- A reliable two-way channel of communication should be opened with the striking workers. Mass meetings to negotiate the issues should be avoided and an attempt should be made to identify representatives with whom management can communicate. The options available to management are:
  — The existing channels of communication;
  — An acceptable and neutral party;
  — Elected representatives who can speak on behalf of the workers;
  — A body (such as a trade union) that claims to represent the interests of the workers.
- Report-back facilities and a time schedule should be agreed on. Where necessary, workers should be allowed to hold meetings with their representatives to facilitate the process of resolving the grievances. Management must listen to and address any expressed grievances or demands.
- The Department of Manpower should be informed. Its role is to provide advice and information on legal procedures and not to intervene.
- A single spokesperson should be appointed to liaise with the press. The media should be kept informed as much as possible regarding the developments and the information they receive should be factually correct. Incorrect reporting should be avoided.
- Normal facilities such as food, accommodation and transport should be provided where possible, and any form of confrontation should be avoided.
- A strike develops a personality of its own and management should acknowledge this and not immediately attempt to suppress the strike. A request for striking workers to cease striking before negotiations can take place constitutes a contradiction, as it implies that the workers must forfeit their bargaining power in order to bargain, and as such the request is highly unlikely to be successful.

Once the workers return to work, management should see to the following:

- The promises that were made must be carried out.
- Managers and supervisors must be carefully briefed and requested to be tactful, without relinquishing essential controls such as promptness.

412

Workers are to clock in, in recognition of legal and civilised norms. They must be treated tactfully yet firmly, otherwise all previous efforts may have been in vain and the strike may flare up again.

- Management should inform all non-strikers of what happened, commend them on their responsible decision not to strike and express appreciation for their loyalty to the organisation.
- Management should, at the earliest opportunity, give consideration to the following:
  - The time and cause of the strike;
  - The role communication played in causing and resolving the strike;
  - The role of shop stewards and members of the works council;
  - Current channels for handling grievances and for disciplinary action, as well as those used by line managers for communication;
  - Mistakes that were made and the lessons to be learned from them;
  - The adjustment of plans to handle strikes better in the future. This may include a change to the contingency plan.
- The industrial relations policy may have to be reviewed. It is therefore important that all workers should understand the following:
  - Current procedures for the handling of grievances and discipline;
  - The role of shop stewards and works councils;
  - The organisation's industrial relations policy as set out in the employment contract.

It is clear that the human resources manager can do a great deal to prevent strikes, and can do even more once a strike is in progress. This is contrary to the general belief that there is little that can be done while a strike is in progress. The biggest task, however, starts when the strike is over, when management has to re-establish relations with the workers and the trade union and investigate and eliminate the issues that caused the strike.

19.6.6 Grievance and disciplinary procedures

Grievance and disciplinary procedures are assuming increasing importance in South Africa. Although they are not prescribed by the Labour Relations Act, these procedures have been introduced in practice. This is not surprising, as labour legislation is by nature conservative and often social realities and demands are given legislative expression only some time after events have occurred that demonstrate the need for it. In the early stages of their existence, trade unions bargained with employers on basic issues they regarded as fundamental to their functioning. Today they negotiate pensions, medical schemes, greater security for their members, and so on. The drive for security for workers has brought about the establishment of grievance and disciplinary procedures and a mutually acceptable structure to deal with conflict in the workplace.

Procedures used to settle grievances or to take disciplinary action can spark off conflict within an organisation. If this is to be avoided, a human resources and industrial relations policy should be drawn up in written form and circulated among employees. Written grievance and disciplinary procedures obviate the need for management to become involved in skirmishes about procedure with labour, thereby allowing management to get on with the job of running the organisation. The grievance procedure will be discussed first, followed by the disciplinary procedure.

19.6.6.1 Grievance procedures

There is no doubt that the grievance procedures are the most important institutional system that can be used to support an organisation's industrial relations. This can be deduced from the definition of a grievance, which is as follows: *a grievance is an occurrence, situation or condition that justifies the lodging of a complaint by an individual.* In the usual context of an organisation's industrial relations activities, a grievance would constitute a real, perceived or alleged breach of the terms of the employment contract. While this refers in most cases to the formal collective contract between the employer and the employees, it could also include both the individual's conditions of employment and the psychological contract between him or her and the employer.

If a sound grievance procedure does not exist, managers will not be aware of grievances or sources of dissatisfaction. This does not mean, however, that there are no grievances. It only means that they simmer under the surface. When they eventually erupt, the effect on the organisation is usually out of proportion to the extent of the underlying causes. Managers who profess to "know the workers" and maintain that they follow an "open-door policy" that is adequate for meeting workers' needs, are living in a fool's paradise and will eventually reap the bitter fruits of this shortsighted policy.

Furthermore, managers who limit the scope of the grievance procedure to those grievances relating to the formal human resources policy, or to the items contained in the collective agreement, are ignoring the complexity and uniqueness of individual human beings. It should be recognised that because of the complexity of human nature and the behaviour resulting from it, many issues that could constitute grievances fall beyond the scope of a written company policy and industrial relations policy. Such issues need to be assessed on merit and management must be flexible.

The grievance procedure starts when the worker raises a grievance with his or her immediate supervisor and should end at the highest authority in the organisation: the managing director or somebody of a similar rank. The roles of the employee representative and of the human resources department must be specified, as should the time limits within which grievances must be lodged and appeals heard. Employees need to be taught during their induction how to utilise the procedure, and employee representatives and supervisors need to be trained in the performance of their respective roles. Furthermore, records of proceedings must be kept and the execution of the procedure must be monitored by the human resources department, which should provide advice and assistance (when requested) on its operation.

414

Human resources managers need to realise that the key to successful grievance resolution is prompt action. A delayed or neglected grievance is often the origin of a new grievance. If specific time limits are laid down in the procedure, workers will be prepared to allow the process to be completed, and will even wait longer if facts are difficult to establish. They must however be kept continually informed.

An effective grievance procedure is an integral part of the organisation's total communications system. It keeps both workers and managers aware of each other's needs, desires, attitudes, opinions, values and perceptions. However, more important than handling grievances is preventing them. Being sensitive to potential causes of dissatisfaction and taking steps to eliminate them will obviate the need to apply the grievance procedure. This means getting rid of poor human resources practices, adjusting managerial behaviour and improving worker morale.

Finally it must be noted that if no solution to a grievance can be found, external intervention follows, for example by an arbitrator. Various external sources up to the level of the industrial court may be solicited to solve disputes of this nature, but the process should be according to the prescribed dispute procedure as set out in the Labour Relations Act so that use is made of industrial councils, conciliations boards or the industrial court.

Grievance procedures can consist of various stages which will depend on the size and complexity of the organisation. However, their operation should be just and fair, from the employee's interaction with his or her supervisor (the first stage) to the point where the grievance is lodged with the managing director, which would be the final stage in the attempt to solve the grievance within the organisation. (Thereafter it is forwarded to external sources, as mentioned above.)

19.6.6.2 *Disciplinary procedures*

Any organisation, irrespective of its nature, structure or objectives, needs to have rules and a standard of conduct, and its members have to observe these if the organisation is to function successfully. These rules determine permissible behaviour for all the employees in the organisation. The rules should apply to all managerial staff if they are to have maximum effect, although there would be some exemptions, such as exemption from clocking in and out and working shifts.

Discipline can be defined as action or behaviour on the part of the authority in an organisation (usually management) aimed at restraining all employees (including managers) from behaviour that threatens to disrupt the functioning of the organisation.

Disciplinary action is usually initiated by management in response to unsatisfactory work performance or unacceptable behaviour on the part of workers. This is downward communication. (When a worker has problems and initiates a grievance procedure, this is upward communication.)

The principles and requirements for disciplinary procedures are:

- Management should have the right to take appropriate disciplinary steps against any worker who acts in a manner conflicting with the interests of the organisation.
- Workers should have the right to a fair hearing and to appeal against any disciplinary measure they may consider to be unjust.
- The emphasis in any disciplinary system falls on prevention, justice and rehabilitation. The disciplinary procedure is regarded as a guideline, and its interpretation should be flexible enough to be adapted to various circumstances. Where possible, informal attempts should be made to correct wrong conduct. Disciplinary steps should be taken only if the worker makes no attempt to improve his or her conduct.

Like the grievance procedure, the disciplinary procedure can also have a number of stages. For example, in the first stage the employee would be given an informal, verbal warning by the supervisor, and in the final stage a committee within the organisation might recommend the worker's dismissal. Once again, should the worker not be satisfied at this level, the formal system in terms of the Labour Relations Act could be instituted, i.e. the industrial council, conciliation board, arbitration or even an appeal to the industrial court, depending on the particular circumstances of each case.

Generally no disciplinary action is taken before an informal warning has been given. If such a warning has no effect, a written warning is handed to the person concerned, who is requested to sign this document for a number of reasons: to ensure that the employee understands the validity of what has been written; so that it can be used as evidence at a later stage if necessary; to notify the employee that the procedure has been set in motion; and to bring to the employee's attention that the document will be placed on his or her personal file. (If the employee reforms, this letter of warning should be removed from the personal file and destroyed after a certain period, usually six months to a year, so that after the disciplinary action the offence is not held against him or her.)

According to Kölkenbeck-Ruh (1991), the disciplinary procedure should not be confused with the disciplinary code. The procedure describes the method whereby discipline should be implemented, whereas the code describes the

416

reasons for which an employee may be disciplined. If there is a disciplinary code that defines the offences, disciplinary action cannot be arbitrarily taken by management. It also gives employees an idea of management's expected standards of discipline, and how the human resources manager would institute disciplinary action. However, the code should not be inflexible, since an employee's previous job performance, years of service and any possible extenuating circumstances should be taken into consideration. The disciplinary code would, for example, state that for theft (also called "unauthorised possession of company property"), even as a first offence, an employee would be summarily dismissed. The procedure could be, however, that the matter is reported to the supervisor and finally handed over to the departmental manager or even the general manager who would then decide whether or not the case merited special consideration and whether the employee should indeed be dismissed.

The advantages to an employer of a consistent disciplinary procedure are threefold: first, it contributes to the stability of the workforce; secondly, labour turnover is minimised; and thirdly, it promotes productivity. The advantages to an employee of a consistent disciplinary procedure are also threefold: first, the people who are able to dismiss employees are competent to do so; secondly, those who who are able to dismiss employees have a strong sense of responsibility; and thirdly, employees need not automatically distrust every manager and every dismissal and disciplinary measure.

Three components are necessary for the effective maintenance of a disciplinary procedure in an organisation, namely consultation or negotiation; communication with everybody concerned regarding the exact way in which the system operates; and training of the individuals involved in a disciplinary process.

Grievance and disciplinary procedures are primarily aimed at interaction between employees and their supervisors where they have contact most often, that is, on the shop floor. It is at that level that the foundations of a sound industrial relations policy should be laid. The fulfilment of the needs of both workers and management is made possible through the grievance and disciplinary procedures because these structures minimise conflict between the workers and management.

There have already been a large number of industrial court cases with regard to unfair dismissals, which have laid down guidelines in this regard.

In the following section, issues that the human resources manager manages and that have a pronounced influence on industrial relations are discussed.

19.7 GENERAL EMPLOYMENT PRACTICES THAT AFFECT INDUSTRIAL RELATIONS

In this section, human resources management issues are covered that are commonly considered to be general employment practices. The manner in which they are handled in an organisation can hamper harmonious relations between management and workers; therefore their handling must feature in the industrial relations policy.

19.7.1 Recruitment

Recruitment has two stages: the defining of requirements and the attracting of candidates. Both are affected by the industrial relations standpoint of an organisation. For example, if an organisation professes to offer equal employment opportunities to employees, it is unlikely that it will tolerate any prohibitions in the recruitment of certain employees.

Prejudices and preferences in an organisation show in the manner in which recruitment is conducted. An organisation also has an opportunity, through the recruitment process, to advertise its employment practices and state for individual employees its public relations policy.

There is a direct overlap of the industrial relations policy of an organisation and its recruitment practices in the case of a closed shop agreement. In such an instance, an organisation is bound to employ only those individuals in certain occupations who are members of the appropriate trade union representing that occupation. This means that the organisation's recruitment criteria for that occupation include membership of the union; therefore there is a degree of cooperation between the two organisations. There is even more overlap between an organisation's industrial relations policy and its recruitment policy if the organisation uses a trade union as a recruitment agent.

19.7.2 Selection and induction

The selection procedures practised by an organisation also reflect its industrial relations policy.

Typical policy statement on selection

The organisation undertakes to fill vacancies with the most suitable individuals, and such individuals will be selected in accordance with established criteria for each job. Each individual's suitability will be measured against the job requirements by means of tests, past performance, education and biographical data.

Selection practices may be specified in an industrial relations agreement with worker representatives. Organisations may make provision for shop stewards to witness any testing procedures so as to ensure that the process is objective and no labour group's interests are being promoted or prejudiced. Affirmative action will manifest itself in the selection procedure.

Selection and promotion are closely intertwined, especially if the organisation follows a policy of filling vacancies from within where possible. Worker representatives have an interest in such promotion of employees: unions might prefer seniority as a criterion for promotion rather than performance, since this furthers the interests of their long-term members. Other unions may attempt to restrict occupation of certain positions to a limited group of individuals defined in their constitutions and as such will oppose promotion from within of anyone who does not meet these requirements.

During induction, new employees should be informed of the industrial relations policy of the organisation. They should be trained in the use of industrial relations structures, such as grievance and disciplinary procedures. Furthermore, it is during the induction process that new employees are informed of all the specific conditions of employment. Many of these, such as working hours and holidays, have probably been negotiated by a union, and new employees will therefore be able to gauge the industrial relations climate in the organisation.

The induction process provides the employer, and specifically the human resources manager, with an opportunity to sow the seeds for a harmonious working environment, and therefore contribute towards the maintenance of industrial peace in the organisation.

19.7.3 Training and development

Training serves a dual role in that it helps management meet its human resources requirements, while at the same time increasing the market value or marketability of those being trained, and hence their bargaining power. Training therefore is a matter of mutual interest to both workers and management. Policy statements on training may include the following:

- Employees are encouraged to develop to their full potential in the best interests of both the organisation and themselves.
- In the event of technological changes, retraining will be provided for affected employees.
- Training and retraining affecting union members will be implemented with the cooperation and support of the union concerned.

Industrial relations training is necessary if the procedures and programmes outlined in the industrial relations policy are to be successfully implemented. Employees who are to use such procedures and programmes must be trained in the actions required.

Personnel at the appropriate management and supervisory levels need to receive training in the application of policies and procedures. Detailed information is provided in a manual on industrial relations training compiled by the National Training Board in 1984.

Representatives should be trained in the functioning of works councils, conducting meetings, and so on. Employees not on the works council should also be informed about its functioning and made aware that it is a medium for communication. If industrial relations training involves members of a trade union, management should consult with the union involved about training material, and where necessary should conduct joint training.

19.7.4 Job evaluation

Job evaluation is a formal system for determining the relative worth of jobs in an organisation. Steps must be taken to ensure that all employees are familiar with the job evaluation system and that members of the job evaluation committee (including the worker representative) have received the necessary training.

In the sphere of industrial relations, job evaluation provides information that could have a profound influence on an organisation's management style. This is because management decisions on things like remuneration can be assessed by employees in terms of the job evaluation structures available to them. This highlights the industrial relations issues subject to management prerogative.

In the negotiation process over salaries and wages, trade unions should acknowledge both phases in the job evaluation process. Phase 1 is the process of grading jobs according to a particular job evaluation technique, such as the Paterson or Peromnes systems. Phase 2 is the process of attributing a pay structure to the graded hierarchy of jobs established in Phase 1. It is only in phase 2 that there can be flexibility and negotiation.

19.7.5 Compensation

The following aspects of industrial relations are relevant to compensation, and in particular to salary scales:

- Whether there is a common pay structure, based on an accredited job evaluation system, which applies throughout the organisation;
- A corollary to the above is whether employees are paid according to the value of the job performed;
- Whether salaries of the lowest remunerated employees are pegged at the minimum living level or the supplementary living level;
- That an employee's race or sex is no factor in determining that employee's salary.

Issues such as the cost of living, productivity, the skills gap, seniority and minimum wages also relate to the salary scales applied by employers and are likely to be raised during negotiations with unions.

19.7.6 Fringe benefits

Fringe benefits are compensation other than wages and salaries. Some fringe benefits are mandated by law, such as unemployment insurance and workmen's compensation. In other cases benefits result from negotiations between management and labour, and are then specified in industrial council agreements, wage regulating measures, private employment contracts, and so on. Leave arrangements, for example, are a benefit specified in this way.

Some employers voluntarily introduce other fringe benefits with the object of maintaining a stable and contented labour force, such as a canteen, additional leave, parking, medical benefits or club membership fees.

19.7.7 Employee promotion

Promotion—assigning an employee to a job of higher rank—is an area of management where trade unions can actively promote the interests of their members. Examples of the manner in which trade unions can assert themselves are:

- Unions can press for seniority as the criterion for promotion.
- Unions can insist that employees be promoted from within the organisation before outsiders are hired.
- Unions can press for the promotion of a specific individual, subject to the grievance procedure.

19.7.8 Industrial health and safety

The health and safety of workers in the working environment are of cardinal importance. Trade unions, in particular, focus strongly on this point. If a union were to take an organisation to court on a matter of health and safety, the union would be on safe ground since there would be no question of the union's moral right to ensure that proper safety and health standards are maintained. Consequently, health and safety can play an important part in union-management relations.

On the other hand, showing concern for workers' health and safety is to management's benefit in industrial relations because it enhances the image of the employer. The IPM's Fact Sheet No. 232 (March 1994) contains information in this regard.

Issues that might be the subjects of union bargaining include the provision of protective clothing, protection from industrial diseases, first aid provisions and the appointment of a safety official who represents the union's interests.

19.7.9 Retrenchment

Retrenchment becomes necessary when there are redundant workers. It is the removal of an employee from the payroll because of factors beyond his or her control. Such factors might include loss of sales, shortages of materials, seasonal changes, economic fluctuation, production delays and technological change.

Trade unions can negotiate with management to minimise reductions in the workforce yet maintain the efficient operation of the organisation. Measures might include the restriction of overtime, training and retraining, transfers between departments, division of work, reduced working hours, rotation of appointments and dismissals, and spreading the retrenchments over a certain period.

Unions will also negotiate with management on the retrenchment procedures to be followed, and on the selection of workers for retrenchment. It is desirable that the criteria according to which workers will be selected for retrenchment should be established in advance, with the approval of shop stewards or employee representatives, where necessary. Such criteria should give due consideration to the interests of both the organisation and the workers. Considerations might include ability, skills, experience and occupational qualifications, length of service (for example, last in first out, but with retention of skills), age and family circumstances. Also to be considered are voluntary resignations and early retirements.

How to deal with, and assist, those workers who are retrenched may also be negotiated. Issues in this regard include redundancy payments, reappointment with or without the retention of seniority, putting retrenched workers in touch with other employers, offering potential employers facilities to interview on the organisation's premises, waiving the notice period of retrenched workers who have found alternative employment, assisting workers in obtaining unemployment insurance benefits, helping workers compile a *curriculum vitae* in order to find employment, and giving redundancy counselling. The IPM Fact Sheet No. 200 also contains information about retrenchment that readers may find valuable.

19.7.10 Termination procedures
The industrial relations policy usually contains a disciplinary procedure and a disciplinary code, and these structures make provision for dismissal as a possible disciplinary step. There are nevertheless certain constraints on termination, which may be highlighted in an industrial relations context. Proper legal procedures must be followed when a person is dismissed, and matters such as notice of the termination of contract, payment upon termination, payment in lieu of notice and commencement of the notice period must be handled with great care and preferably in consultation with the organisation's lawyers.

Readers should note that the Department of Manpower has made available, free of charge, a publication entitled *Unfair dismissal: guidelines on the termination of employment.*

19.7.11 Codes of employment
Various codes of employment have been designed to encourage organisations to promote the social and economic development of South Africa's people. They are a contribution to industrial relations outside of the law. (Employment practices are discussed in chapters 6 and 20.)

It must be noted that a code of employment is not an industrial relations policy in its own right. Subscribers or signatories to a code may well model their industrial relations policy on the objectives laid down in their code, but the code itself is a policy statement with a much broader base, which merely expresses the organisation's intentions with regard to its labour force. A code of employment is sometimes used instead of a human resources policy.

19.7.12 Quality of work life and social responsibility
In chapter 14 the quality of work life and social responsibility are fully discussed. In the application of industrial relations to these issues, quality of work life is discussed first and then social responsibility.

422

Quality of work life reflects an organisation's concern for its employees. It is usually indicated by whether or not:

- Recreation facilities are provided;
- Precautions are taken to protect the health of employees;
- Training facilities are provided;
- Opportunities are provided for career advancement and security of employment is regarded as a priority;
- Satisfactory working conditions are provided;
- Ethical employment practices are maintained.
- There is company commitment to the implementation of the RDP.

Whether they are motivated by altruistic intent or provided as a means towards increased profitability, such benefits contribute towards the fulfilment of employees' social needs.

If an organisation meets its obligations (as outlined above) to its employees, this will foster cooperation and trust, which are necessary for collective bargaining, as well as generally better relations between management and employees in the organisation. It may reduce mistrust and the threat of strikes, and increase both parties' chances of achieving their respective objectives.

Corporate social responsibility (now also called social investment): Both social conscience and expedience motivate the organisation in its concern for the external environment. It is expedient in that by maintaining environmental conditions at a satisfactory level, an organisation safeguards its own future. An organisation may show its social responsibility towards the external environment in the following ways: through concern for the effects of ecological imbalances and pollution; through sponsorship of public recreation and entertainment; through research; by providing housing and electricity; and by promoting community development and welfare in the communities in which its employees live.

Trade unions are showing increasing concern for community affairs and are likely to monitor organisations' commitment in this regard. Such issues could be included in collective bargaining. Taking this process one step further, management and worker representatives in an organisation could jointly determine the allocation of corporate resources for social projects through joint committees. This would lead to better relationships between the organisation and the trade union, with resultant better industrial relations.

19.7.13 The monitoring of industrial relations

There are two dimensions to the monitoring of industrial relations programmes and procedures: first, the assessment of whether employees are implementing the required procedures; and secondly, an assessment of whether the procedures that are implemented are effective.

To determine whether an industrial relations policy and all the procedures that accompany it are being effectively implemented, the human resources or industrial relations manager can circulate questionnaires to staff, interview staff or observe interpersonal relationships in the organisation. However, the responsibility for the practical implementation of industrial relations policy lies with line management. This should be included in their job description, and their effectiveness in its execution should be reflected in their performance appraisals. If this approach is not used, industrial relations procedures will not be effectively implemented. It should be remembered that the human resources or industrial relations manager performs a staff function in the organisation and therefore can only advise management on how things should be done with regard to industrial relations, but cannot mandate action.

It is equally important that grievances (their nature and number), written disciplinary warnings, etc. should be examined to determine whether the procedures and programmes that have been implemented are effective. Other indices of the effectiveness of the industrial relations policy in its totality are rates of labour turnover, rates of absenteeism, the number of hours lost through work stoppages, the production rate for a certain period, exit interviews and the attitudes of employees towards management and towards their employment conditions.

It is evident that the monitoring of industrial relations in an organisation is of cardinal importance if the human resources or industrial relations manager wishes to determine the effectiveness of this function. In fact, it is crucial to the survival of the organisation in the turbulent times South Africa is experiencing. The human resources or industrial relations manager can make or break his or her career by the way he or she manages industrial relations in the organisation, because of the direct effect it has on the profitability of the organisation.

19.8 CONCLUSION

In this chapter a review was provided of those industrial relations issues that pertain specifically to human resources managers and with which they need to be familiar in order to perform their job effectively. We stressed that human resources managers are subject to numerous pressures regarding industrial relations because it is a complex and rapidly changing field in South Africa's business environment. This area of human resources management is a daunting task, and human resources managers have to be au fait with all the rapid developments in trade unionism and legislation in South Africa.

Human resources managers need to know how components of industrial relations affect them, such as relations with trade unions, and dispute-handling procedures. They should be able to manage these critical issues confidently, particularly if they have to make do without the services of an industrial relations manager. However, human resources managers can manage these components of industrial relations effectively only if they understand the value of company, human resources and industrial relations policies. They also need to understand that the relationship between employers and workers is based on their various rights and responsibilities.

As far as general employment practices are concerned, if issues such as recruitment, job evaluation, remuneration and industrial safety are ineptly handled, this will have an extremely negative effect on the organisation. This will be compounded if the industrial relations elements contained in all general employment practices are disregarded or underestimated by the human resources manager. He or she should therefore give special consideration to those general employment practices that affect human resources management in the industrial relations context.

The human resources manager's role was here discussed at the micro-level. Industrial relations should also be discussed at the macro-level to complete the picture of industrial relations in South Africa. Aspects of the macro-level are discussed in chapter 20.

Questions

1. Describe the relationship between the state, employers and employees in South Africa. Pay special attention to the primary participants in the industrial relations system.
2. Give your views on the rights and responsibilities of managers and workers in your organisation. Do you agree with the statements made in this regard in this chapter?
3. Does your organisation have company, human resources and industrial relations policies? If not, draw up such policies to reflect your organisation's culture, while still being acceptable to both top management and the relevant trade unions.
4. Which general employment practices in your organisation have resulted in disputes? Why? What solutions have been suggested by the human resources manager?
5. Draw up a profile of the trade unions with which you deal. How would you describe your relations with these unions? How can you go about developing mutual trust and cooperation on common issues?
6. Read the following case study and answer the questions.

Operation work stoppage at Poweron electrical contractors

On Monday morning you arrive at work at 07h00 to discover that a thunderstorm over the weekend has caused a complete breakdown of the whole telephone system in your area. Enquiries reveal that it will only be repaired on Wednesday.

It is now Monday, 08h00, and you have just been informed by the head of security that the whole workforce is gathered in front of the administration building on the premises. They are very disorderly and everybody is talking at the same time.

The workers appear to be grouped in two factions, which could be either trade unionists and non-trade unionists, or Sothos and Tswanas. It appears that there is a difference of opinion between the groups, and both groups are determined to have a discussion with management.

6.1 How do you go about talking to them and calming them down?

At 09h00, when checking the worker clock-in cards, you discover that apart from workers on leave and sick leave, four workers are unaccounted for today. They are:

- Jo Dlala (a loyal non-unionist worker)
- Solomon Manpanje (works council chairman)
- Petrus Hendriks (union member—CEWU: Cape Electricity Workers' Union)
- Rex Tlopala (local union under-secretary—GEWU: General Electrical Workers' Union)

At 09h30 the workers demand the presence of the absent workers at the business premises immediately.

6.2 What do you do?

By 10h00 the workers have become very noisy and aggressive and threats are being made. There are periodic scuffles between workers.

A manager from ACE Electrical Contractors arrives at your organisation for a meeting on finalising a big contract. He informs you that he wishes to increase his company's business with you by 30% as a result of residential and commercial developments in your area. He notices the labour disturbances and wants to know:

- What is going on;
- How this will affect the signing of the contract and its execution;
- Whether this happens regularly;
- Why you are apparently not in control of your workers.

6.3 What do you do about the scuffles between the workers and what do you tell the manager from ACE Electrical Contractors?

At 10h30 about 200 workers confront one another with sticks, heavy copper wire, knobkieries and metal pipes, while the rest look on. The mob then spills into the street and workers from nearby businesses also down tools and join the mob.

There is the threat of damage to property, equipment and cars.

6.4 What do you do?

6.5 Reporters from The Star *and* The Sowetan *are taking photographs of the workers and also wish to speak to workers and management—what do you tell them?*

At 11h30 the fighting has stopped. The workers agree to form two committees to speak to management while the rest remain gathered outside the administration building. These committees make the following demands:

Committee 1:

1. The informer (management stooge) must be handed over to them, since he stirred trouble between the union members and non-union workers.
2. The non-union workers (mostly Sothos) want to be protected and they also want to go home.

Committee 2:

1. Trade union members have been victimised by the other group. The committee wants a public condemnation of this by management before 14h00.
2. The committee accuses management of preferring the works council system to trade unions and not wanting trade unions on the premises. For this reason management is trying to drive a wedge between CEWU and GEWU by spreading the rumour that only CEWU members may be employed in future. Management must now make its stand on the issue clear.

6.6 What are you going to do about these accusations?

You are informed that news teams from ABC and CNN have just arrived at the gate and want to film the conflict. They also wish to interview management and the local leaders of the workers.

6.7 What do you do?

It is now 14h30 and you learn from the police that Jo Dlala (a Sotho) is dead. He went to the wedding of one of your workers during the weekend, and at the wedding accused Rex Tlopala (a Tswana) of being disloyal to the organisation because he was a trade union member. He said Tlopala should stop persuading non-union workers to become trade union members. A fight broke out and Solomon Manpanje tried to break it up, but Tlopala stabbed Dlala to death before the fight could be stopped. The police jailed both Manpanje and Tlopala because they thought they were both responsible for Dlala's death. A post mortem on Jo Dlala's body revealed that his blood contained 0,30% alcohol.

6.8 How do you convey this information to your workers who are congregated in front of the administration building?

You also learn that Petrus Hendriks was on his way to a trade union meeting when his car was stopped by police at a road block. His car was not roadworthy and he was apparently intoxicated, and was consequently jailed. One of the police reservists is one of your supervisors, Gert Elsenze. Hendriks recognised him and accused him of deliberately misreading the intoxication level on the meter to prevent him from attending his trade union meeting. On Monday morning Gert Elsenze boasted in the workshop that he was responsible for "putting away" Hendriks, saying that he would be "out of the way for a long time".

6.9 How do you convey this information to your workers and how do you handle it?

It is now 16h00. The non-union workers want to go home. They requested that buses be provided by the organisation to prevent victimisation. You have not yet responded to their request and they are now becoming aggressive.

6.10 What do you do?

The union workers claim that this is not a strike and that they want full pay for the day or else they will become violent or will not come to work tomorrow.

6.11 What do you do?

It is now 17h00 and the workers have gone home.

6.12 What do you do now, apart from heaving a sigh of relief?

6.13 What are you going to tell the workers when they arrive at work tomorrow?

6.14 What is your attitude towards trade union members and non-trade union workers?

6.15 Do you think it is necessary to adjust your industrial relations policy?

Sources

Bendix, D.W.F. 1984. *Labour and society in comparative socio-economic systems.* IR Texts, Cape Town.

Department of Manpower (undated). *Unfair dismissal: guidelines for termination of service.* Government Printer, Pretoria.

Institute for Personnel Management (undated). *IPM Journal.* Fact Sheet Supplements Nos 103–7.

Institute for Personnel Management. 1991. *IPM Journal.* Fact Sheet Supplement No. 200.

Kölkenbeck-Ruh, R.K. 1991. An investigation within the mining industry into the effectiveness of line management chairing disciplinary enquiries. Unpublished M.A. dissertation. UNISA, Pretoria.

Nel, P.S. 1986. Vakbonde se rol in die opleiding van ambagsmanne. *IPB Journal,* Vol. 5, No. 5.

Nel, P.S., Erasmus, B.J. & Swanepoel, B.J. 1993. *Suksesvolle arbeidsverhoudinge: riglyne vir die praktyk.* Van Schaik, Pretoria.

Nel, P.S. & Van Rooyen, P.H. 1993. *South African industrial relations: theory and practice.* 2nd revised edition. Van Schaik, Pretoria.

Prinsloo, J.J. & Bruwer, A.J. 1993. Industrial relations policy. In Slabbert, J.A., Prinsloo, P. & Backer, W.A. *Managing industrial relations in South Africa.* 5th edition. Digma Publishers, Pretoria.

Swanepoel, B.J. 1989. Strategieformulering as vertrekpunt vir die bestuur van arbeidsverhoudinge. Unpublished M.Com. dissertation. UNISA, Pretoria.

Chapter 20

Industrial relations: South Africa's industrial relations system

P.S. Nel

STUDY OBJECTIVES

After studying this chapter, you should be able to:

- Explain the present industrial relations system in South Africa (in its historical context);
- Identify the various structures comprising the system and indicate how these structures can be used;
- Identify the appropriate structures to meet the needs of a particular organisation;
- Explain the latest amendments to the Labour Relations Act.

20.1 INTRODUCTION

This chapter forms the second part of the focus on industrial relations and provides an overview of the industrial relations system in South Africa. The human resources manager's role in industrial relations in the organisation is not discussed—this was done in the previous chapter. Here the focus is primarily on the way in which the Labour Relations Act (No. 28 of 1956) is structured and applied. A brief historical overview of the factors that led to the establishment of the present system is also given.

According to Nel and Van Rooyen (1993:54–94), any country's industrial relations system is formed by its history as well as by influences from other countries. In turn the industrial relations system shapes a country's history and also has an influence on the industrial relations systems of other countries. South Africa is no exception. Great Britain, in particular, had a major influence on South Africa after the discovery of diamonds and gold in the 1870s.

FIGURE 20.1: Principal learning components of South Africa's industrial relations system

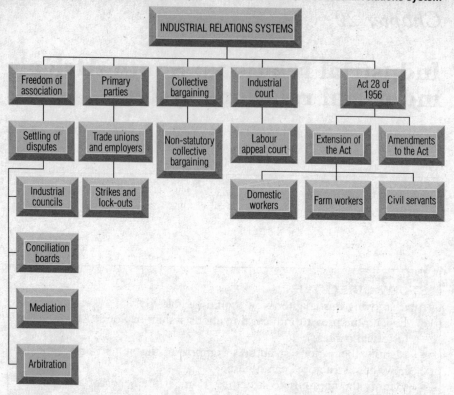

A new industrial relations system, which still contains many of the old components, is developing in South Africa. It is this system that is briefly described and analysed in this chapter. To obtain perspective, the individual employment relation is discussed first, followed by collective relations (i.e. interaction between employers and trade unions). The South African industrial relations system is shown in figure 20.2. The various elements are discussed in this chapter and represent the aspects (excluding recognition agreements) that form the subject of the Labour Relations Act (No. 28 of 1956).

20.2 THE INDIVIDUAL EMPLOYMENT RELATIONSHIP

The principles of common law were laid down before the 19th century, based on the old Roman Dutch Law. Only in the industrial revolution was the concept of "collectivity" introduced (i.e. where groups are involved). Common law was only applicable to the individual. It was left to industrial legislation to extend the collective aspect of the employment relationship as it applies today in industrial council agreements. The contract of employment serves as the foundation of the employment relationship and exists in every employment situation (even an illiterate worker enters into a tacit contract with his or her employer). This is the case whether the relationship exists in the private or the public sector or involves individuals or groups.

FIGURE 20.2: A visual representation of South Africa's industrial relations system

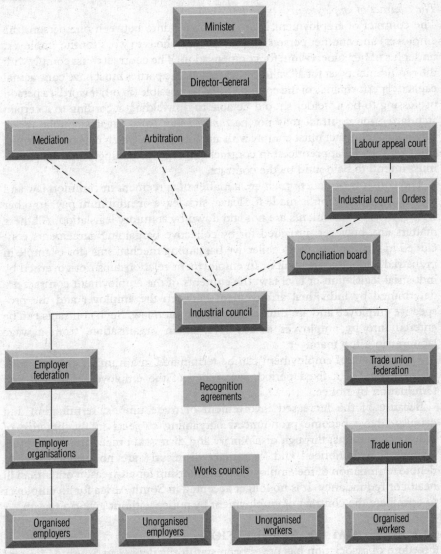

Source: Developed by P.S. Nel

The Labour Relations Act governs the most important aspects of employment relationships in the private sector, with the exclusion of, for example, the employment of domestic workers and employment relationships in farming operations. Individual employment relationships of employees such as domestic workers are mainly governed by the contract of employment, by relevant legislation (such as the Occupational Health and Safety Act, No. 85 of 1993) and by common law.

The contract of employment

The contract of employment is usually entered into between one person (the employer) and another person (the employee) who is to work for the employer, under his or her supervision, for compensation. The contract must comply with the requirements set for all valid contracts, i.e. the parties must have contractual capacity; performance of the contract must be possible (in other words, a person professing to be a welder should be able to do welding according to a certain standard); the contract may not be *contra bonos mores* (against public moral values); the contract must comply with any formalities which may be prescribed (for example, all apprenticeship contracts must be in writing); and the parties must intend to be bound by the contract.

The contents of the contract are a matter of agreement in common law and no statutory provision is made for leave, sick leave or minimum pay. In other words, these requirements are not laid down by statutory legislation. All these matters are, however, provided for by collective bargaining agreements concluded in terms of statutory collective bargaining mechanisms (for example in industrial council agreements). In employment relationships not governed by industrial legislation or civil law, the contents of the employment contract are determined by individual arrangement between the employer and the prospective employee and are thus subject to common law. Such contracts can be entered into by employees at any level in an organisation, from a wage labourer to a top manager.

The contract of employment can be terminated in a number of ways, such as the expiry of a fixed period, insolvency of the employer, dismissal and termination by notice.

Because of the increased involvement of trade unions, termination and dismissal have become pronounced bargaining subjects in the practice of industrial relations, through disciplinary and dismissal procedures. The terms "dismissal with notice" and "summary dismissal" are now understood to denote termination of the employment relationship for any reason other than ill health or redundancy. It is no longer accepted in South Africa for an employer to terminate the contract of employment by notice without giving a reason.

20.3 FREEDOM OF ASSOCIATION

Freedom of association has never been statutorily denied in South Africa and forms one of the main pillars of collective industrial relations. In other words, nobody in South Africa is precluded from belonging to a trade union.

In terms of Section 78(1) of the Labour Relations Act, no employer may require any employee not to be or become a member of a trade union or other similar association of employees, and any such term or condition in any contract

432

of employment entered into shall be void. Any employer that dismisses an employee for trade union membership or lawful trade union activities is guilty of an offence.

With regard to the right not to belong to a trade union, the position is vastly different. The right not to belong to a trade union or similar association of employees is not protected by law and is in fact non-existent. Before 1981 the system of closed shop agreements prevailed, whereby employees could be forced to belong to a trade union as a condition of employment. This system no longer applies, but agreements entered into before 1981 are still valid.

20.4 TRADE UNIONS AND EMPLOYERS' ORGANISATIONS

20.4.1 Trade unions

During the last few years trade unionism in South Africa changed considerably. The period has been characterised by the emergence of large trade unions and large trade union federations. They focused attention on the question of registration, and unions today operate as "registered" or "unregistered". The advantage of registration for a trade union is that only registration enables the trade union to use the collective bargaining machinery of the Act through industrial councils. Unions and employers are however not forced to utilise the machinery of the Act; they may also bargain without the statutory mechanisms, i.e. by means of recognition agreements. The advantage of using the machinery of the Act is, however, that bargaining is centralised and that the agreements reached become delegated legislation, which means they can be enforced by law as soon as they are published in the *Government Gazette*. Agreements concluded outside the scope of the Act are ordinary contracts, which can only be enforced in a civil court; recognition agreements are an example.

Registration also affects employers. Some unions prefer to bargain at the organisational level through recognition agreements rather than on a centralised basis through the industrial council. Although the majority of trade unions are registered today, many of them still prefer to bargain at organisational level and negotiate recognition agreements.

20.4.2 Employers' organisations

Employers' organisations are subject to the same registration procedure as trade unions. An employers' organisation usually comes into existence when employers who operate in the same industry form a group (for instance SEIFSA). They can be viewed as employers' "trade unions" but obviously do not have as many members as employees' trade unions. These groups usually come about when an industrial council is formed (see figure 20.3).

20.5 COLLECTIVE BARGAINING

A distinction can be made between statutory collective bargaining, i.e. that prescribed by legislation (such as industrial councils), and non-statutory collective bargaining (such as recognition agreements). This is discussed below.

20.5.1 Statutory collective bargaining

A number of statutes govern collective bargaining, but we shall discuss only the machinery created by the Labour Relations Act (No. 28 of 1956), because it is by far the most important. Although the term collective bargaining is never used in the Act, three collective bargaining mechanisms are created by it, namely industrial councils, conciliation boards and works councils. Industrial councils and conciliation boards operate on a regional (industry) level while works councils operate at a factory or organisational level. These three are briefly discussed below.

Industrial councils

Industrial councils are permanent bodies composed of registered trade unions and employers' organisations or employers (in terms of Section 20 of the Act) and they contain an equal number of representatives from registered trade unions and employers' organisations, as shown in figure 20.3.

The functions of industrial councils, according to the Act, are to endeavour by the negotiation of agreements or otherwise to prevent disputes; to settle disputes that have arisen or may arise between employers' organisations and workers or trade unions; and to take steps as they may deem expedient to bring about the regulation or settlement of matters of mutual interest to employers or employers' organisations and workers or trade unions.

FIGURE 20.3: The structure of an industrial council

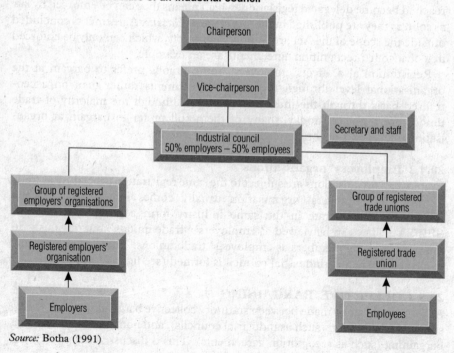

Source: Botha (1991)

434

The employers and trade unions who are parties to the collective bargaining process are also parties to the industrial council. Note that the members of the industrial council, who bargain an agreement there, are *not* the agents of the organisations they represent, but only carry out statutory functions. This means that a trade union member or an employer member of the industrial council executes the council's functions and does not represent his or her particular trade union or employer, but all trade unions or employers in the industrial council.

It is strange, but true, that the process of collective bargaining is not dealt with in the Labour Relations Act, but is left to the discretion of individual industrial councils through the constitutions of such councils. There is, however, some control over the outcome of the collective bargaining process. The authority of the state is required to give statutory effect to the agreements concluded in industrial councils, and this is achieved by publishing the agreements in the *Government Gazette*.

Apart from the formal aspects governing collective bargaining in the industrial council, the industrial council has certain notable characteristics.

First, membership of the system is supposedly voluntary. This is only true in the sense that an employer or registered trade union has a choice whether or not to apply for membership of an industrial council. Once the employer or union has obtained membership to such an industrial council, the voluntarism ends; an employer or trade union cannot refuse to bargain with a particular body in the industrial council, even if the body to which objection is made is no longer representative of the interests it claims to represent. Negotiation is compulsory with *any* trade union that is a member of the industrial council.

Secondly, membership of an industrial council is not automatic. Organisations wishing to join will not be admitted until all the parties on the industrial council agree to it in writing. (If an organisation is dissatisfied with the refusal of its application for admission to membership, it may appeal to the industrial court within 30 days of the date on which the industrial council declined the application.)

Thirdly, membership of an industrial council does not involve the members in one-to-one bargaining situations, because industry-wide issues are at stake. Therefore an employer that is a member of an industrial council negotiates on behalf of all employers and not only for itself. Note that where an unfair labour practice is concerned, individuals are usually involved and a unanimous decision is then required. Normal decisions on the industrial council require only a two-thirds majority.

Conciliation boards
Conciliation boards have much the same powers and functions as industrial councils as far as collective bargaining is concerned. Conciliation boards differ from industrial councils, however, in a number of respects. The differences and similarities are listed in table 20.1.

TABLE 20.1: Comparison of conciliation boards and industrial councils

DIFFERENCES	
Industrial council	**Conciliation board**
Permanent body	Temporary body
Prevents and settles disputes	Can only settle disputes
Participation is voluntary	Participation is compulsory
Only registered employers' organisations and trade unions may be parties	Both registered and unregistered employers' organisations and trade unions may be parties
Individual workers are not allowed	Individual workers are allowed
Can monitor agreements	Cannot monitor agreements
Has a constitution	Has no constitution
May have assets	Does not have assets
Is a body corporate	Is not a body corporate
Disputes must be referred to the industrial council before they may be referred to the industrial court	With the consent of the Director-General parties may bypass the industrial council and go directly to the industrial court

SIMILARITIES
Both may settle disputes
Agreements may cover the same matters
Agreements may be published

Source: Botha (1991)

Whenever a dispute is alleged by an employer or employee (or an employers' organisation or a trade union) to have arisen in any organisation, industry, trade or occupation in any area, any of the parties may apply to the Director-General (or his or her deputy, i.e. the regional director or the inspector) for the establishment of a conciliation board. This request must be acceded to if all rules have been satisfied.

A conciliation board consists of as many representatives as the Director-General determines in accordance with Section 37(2) of the Act, but 50% of the representatives must be appointed by the party representing the workers and the other 50% by the employers' party.

The conciliation board must then attempt to settle the dispute, and report to the Director-General:

- Whether the dispute has been settled and the terms of settlement;
- If the board has failed to settle the dispute, whether it is satisfied that further deliberations will not result in a settlement;
- Whether the dispute should be referred to arbitration; the conciliation board may then be disbanded by the Director-General.

Works councils

The industrial council and conciliation board system operates on a regional or industry level; works councils imply statutory bargaining at organisational level.

436

The industrial council system had been at the centre of South African industrial relations for many years; therefore organisational level bargaining did not feature in South Africa until recently, and many attempts were made to resist it. Plant or organisational level bargaining took place mostly outside the statutory framework, although provision is made for statutory plant bargaining through Sections 34(a) and (b) of the Labour Relations Act by means of works councils.

It is clear that works councils can be used as collective bargaining bodies in this system, but their functions are merely described as those agreed upon by the employer and the workers concerned.

Because legislation does not indicate specifically how works councils should operate or what functions they should have, the constitution or governing document of the works council is of paramount importance. Works councils today have consultative rather than negotiating powers, although in some cases works councils have *de facto* negotiating powers on procedural matters. They are also sometimes involved in decision-making in disciplinary and grievance matters. The part of the constitution that sets out the bargaining powers of the works council will have to be arranged by the parties within the guidelines of what they regard as fair and just.

20.5.2 Non-statutory collective bargaining

Statutory collective bargaining is the machinery established by the Labour Relations Act and is voluntary: organisations that do not belong to an industrial council are not compelled to bargain collectively with their workers, irrespective of whether these belong to a registered or unregistered trade union. During the last decade, a new type of non-statutory collective bargaining has manifested itself on an increasing scale in South Africa, namely the recognition system. It is not really a system at all, but a practice that has grown out of the needs of unskilled union members.

Recognition agreements are to a certain extent a reaction to the industrial council system, and can be regarded as an antipode to industrial councils. According to Nel *et al.* (1993), some of the reasons for wanting such an antipode were political, namely that the industrial council system had to be bad because it only accommodated certain trade unions (which were mainly white). Other, more technical arguments which carry greater weight are that the statutory system does not allow for effective plant level bargaining, whereas the emergent unions particularly address plant level needs such as job security; that the industrial council machinery is slow and cumbersome; and that membership of the industrial council is based on the premise that the union allows state interference in its internal matters through the registration process, which is unacceptable to many trade unions.

According to Piron (1990), recognition agreements have a great variety of styles. Because of the importance of recognition agreements in practice, human resources practitioners should take note of them; therefore they are discussed below.

437

The recognition agreement is an agreement whereby an employer undertakes to recognise a trade union as the representative of its workers who are members of the trade union, subject to the provisions set out in the agreement. Most recognition agreements are procedural agreements and seek to give structural expression to a behavioural relationship between the parties. Wages and financial matters, i.e. substantive elements, are normally not negotiated in a recognition agreement. The recognition agreement usually makes provision for a negotiation procedure whereby substantive terms can be negotiated.

Recognition agreements vary in length and complexity, but can cover such topics as the terms of recognition, the powers, functions and election of shop stewards, grievances and discipline, redundancy, negotiation procedures, mediation, arbitration and the peace obligation, industrial relations training, health and safety, and the administration of the agreement. Because recognition agreements are relatively new in industrial relations practice, there are no clear guidelines yet on the legal nature of the agreements, but as recognition agreements proliferate, guidelines will undoubtedly emerge. Legislation in this regard may be promulgated soon.

Recognition agreements developed spontaneously in practice, but certain characteristics of recognition have deep roots in the traditional South African industrial relations system.

The recognition process is in a sense a miniature plant replica of the industrial council system. The recognition agreement attempts to create permanent or semi-permanent relationships between the parties, on the basis of which substantive agreements can be negotiated. A recognition agreement therefore broadly corresponds to the institution of an industrial council.

In the settling of disputes, recognition agreements show marked similarities to the principles contained in the Labour Relations Act. Negotiations are often followed by a form of mediation or arbitration, and often the peace obligation is the common law equivalent of the strike provisions contained in the Act.

Although criticism has been levelled against the recognition process, it is clear that shop-floor bargaining in the form of recognition agreements and the substantive agreements concluded in terms of them will be a feature of the South African industrial relations system for some time to come, in spite of their being non-statutory.

20.6 THE COLLECTIVE AGREEMENT

Collective bargaining usually results in a collective agreement. There are statutory and non-statutory collective agreements. The agreements concluded in the industrial council, the conciliation board, the works council and in terms of the recognition process are separately discussed below.

20.6.1 Agreements concluded in the industrial council and conciliation board

When an industrial council or conciliation board negotiates an agreement, it is signed by the appropriate persons in terms of the Act and a copy is made avail-

438

able to the Minister. The agreement has no effect in public law until the Minister approves it and it is published in the *Government Gazette*. By notice in the *Government Gazette* the Minister may, in terms of Section 48(1), declare that all the provisions of the agreement shall be binding on all workers, employers' organisations and trade unions that concluded the agreement and on workers and employers who are members of the organisations or trade unions. He or she may also declare the agreement binding on all employers and workers engaged in the business, industry, trade or occupation to which the agreement relates, in the area or any specified portion of the area in respect of which the industrial council is registered or for which the conciliation board has been appointed. The Minister may also declare all the provisions of the agreement, or such provisions as he or she may specify, binding on employers and workers involved in or employed by an organisation operating in an area additional to that in respect of which the industrial council is registered. However, this last power of the Minister can be exercised only after interested persons have been given the opportunity to oppose it, and the power may not be used to usurp the jurisdiction of another industrial council. The same powers are usually held by conciliation boards.

Once the agreement has been promulgated in the *Government Gazette*, it becomes delegated legislation, and any contravention of a provision of the industrial council agreement is a criminal offence. The sanctioning of the agreement through the criminal law has obvious advantages: litigation on behalf of a wronged party under the agreement is undertaken by the state, which makes for speedy and inexpensive enforcement of the agreement. Furthermore, the threat of the criminal courts for non-compliance includes the possible social stigma attached to a criminal conviction.

20.6.2 Agreements concluded in works councils and committees
According to Sections 34(a) and 34(b) of the Labour Relations Act, works councils and committees may conclude a binding agreement with the employer. The question of the legal nature of such agreements was never answered and it is now of academic interest only. Presumably, any agreement concluded by the works council with the employer would have been regarded as an ordinary contract. Such a works council does not, however, automatically have a legal personality and the contractual nature of agreements concluded in the works council or committee would therefore have to be established on merit.

20.6.3 Recognition agreements
Recognition agreements are ordinary common law contracts, provided that all the requirements for a valid contract have been satisfied. Possible areas of litigation include conflict between the recognition agreement and the constitution of the trade union (see 20.5.2).

20.7 SETTLEMENT OF DISPUTES

Should a dispute arise (Section 24(1) of the Act describes the nature of a dispute) that cannot be resolved, there are various mechanisms that can be used, such as an industrial council, a conciliation board, mediation or arbitration, which are "peaceful" means of settling the dispute. The dispute settling procedures have been considerably amended by various amendment acts in 1988 and 1991. Further recommendations for amendments were made by the National Manpower Commission in 1993. All four these mechanisms are now discussed.

20.7.1 Industrial councils

The constitution of an industrial council must include a procedure for settling disputes. Industrial councils have generally been successful in settling disputes. The following steps are taken in settling a dispute by an industrial council:

- A dispute that does not involve an unfair labour practice does not have a deadline for referral to an industrial council. (It could therefore take, say, seven months from the time of the incident to the time when it is referred to the industrial council.) However, it is important that this period should be fair and reasonable.
- In the case of a dispute over an unfair labour practice, the referral must take place within 180 days from the date on which the unfair practice commenced or was terminated, as the case may be, or whichever later date the parties to the dispute may agree upon or may be determined by the Director-General, if he or she has been given good grounds for such a late referral.
- The dispute must be submitted in writing and signed by an office-bearer or official of the union or organisation concerned, as the case may be, and the referral must be accompanied by a certificate stating the reason for the dispute.
- A party that refers a dispute to the industrial council must send by registered post or deliver by hand a copy of the referral to the other party or parties to the dispute, or full details of the contents of the referral concerned must be sent to the other party or parties to the dispute by telegram, telex, telefax or some other printed form. The applicant must, if asked to do so by the industrial council, be able to prove to the council's satisfaction that either the copy or the full particulars of the contents of the referral concerned have been supplied to the other party or parties.
- The committee that has to settle the dispute must consist of an equal number of worker members and employer members.
- A dispute must be settled within 30 days of the date on which it was referred, or within further periods deemed suitable by the industrial council. The secretary of the industrial council must, however, report to the Director-General within 14 days after the mentioned dates have expired, whether or not the dispute has been settled.

440

- Should the dispute be successfully settled, a copy of the settlement must be sent to the Director-General.
- Should the industrial council fail to settle a dispute within 30 days of the date it was referred to it, a mediator may be appointed or the dispute referred for voluntary arbitration. (However, disputes in essential services must be referred for compulsory arbitration.) The industrial council may decide to refer the dispute to a single arbitrator, to an even number of arbitrators and an umpire, or to the industrial court. An arbitrator's decision is binding on the parties, whereas a mediator can only make a recommendation.
- Should the dispute not be settled, any party to the dispute may, within 90 days (or a longer period as per Section 27(a)) refer it to the industrial court for a decision.

20.7.2 Conciliation boards

A conciliation board will settle a dispute only if no industrial council has jurisdiction in respect of the dispute. Note that most of the dispute-settling procedures of the conciliation board are similar to those of the industrial council. Regarding the settlement of disputes, the following points are important:

- The conciliation board is an *ad hoc* body.
- It is appointed by the inspector.
- Unregistered trade unions may request a conciliation board via the inspector.
- The inspector has the power, if essential services are involved, to appoint a conciliation board on his or her own initiative.
- Conciliation boards can only act once a dispute exists.
- When a dispute is settled between the parties, even if an unfair labour practice is involved, the resultant agreement is binding on both parties.
- Should a dispute not be settled, a legal strike or lock-out may be called after all legal requirements have been met (except in the case of essential services, where arbitration is compulsory). There is also the option to refer the dispute to mediation or arbitration first, except in the case of an unfair labour practice, which must be referred directly to the industrial court for determination.
- The same time periods as for industrial councils apply for settling disputes (including cases of unfair labour practices), and also in the case of failure to reach a settlement.
- Conciliation boards became popular for solving disputes as a result of the amendments to procedure that came into effect in 1988 and 1991. This popularity is reflected in figure 20.4.

20.7.3 Mediation

Mediation can take place in terms of Act No. 28 of 1956 or in terms of a recognition agreement. Parties resort to mediation when they are polarised:

FIGURE 20.4: Conciliation board applications received, applications withdrawn, disputes settled

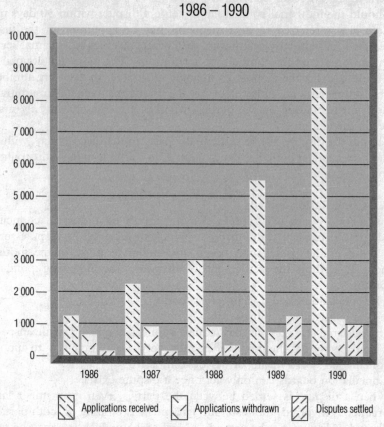

1986 – 1990

Applications received   Applications withdrawn   Disputes settled

Source: Department of Manpower (1991:59)

they appoint a person who is respected and trusted by both parties to act as go-between and to try to achieve a settlement by effecting a change in the position of one or both parties. He or she only makes recommendations and cannot make decisions.

In terms of the Act, an industrial council or conciliation board that cannot reach a settlement may apply to the Minister for the appointment of a mediator. Alternatively, the Minister may appoint a mediator without prompting if he or she is of the opinion that a mediator will be of assistance in settling the dispute. A mediator is not entitled to vote at industrial council or conciliation board meetings, but acts as the chair during the settlement of the dispute. The mediator reports to the Minister.

In recognition agreements with trade unions, mediation clauses are expressed in terms similar to those in the Labour Relations Act, but they do not have the sanction of the Act nor the involvement of the state.

The reasons for the increase in mediation are: the number of disputes is on the increase and there is renewed interest in dispute-settling mechanisms; the expertise of industrial relations practitioners is growing rapidly; and mediation is more attractive than arbitration to many employers and trade unions, because arbitration can enforce a solution that is unacceptable to both parties, whereas a mediator can only make recommendations, which the parties can reject if these recommendations do not suit them. It thus enables them to make another attempt at resolving the issue to the satisfaction of all the parties concerned.

The structures involved in mediation are less important than the person who is chosen as mediator, because the success of mediation depends on this person. Mediation *per se* is not a solution to industrial relations problems.

The Independent Mediation Service of South Africa is an organisation that provides mediators for parties to a dispute.

20.7.4 Arbitration

Arbitration can be undertaken in terms of Act No. 28 of 1956 or in terms of a recognition agreement. Where arbitration is undertaken in terms of the Act, it can be voluntary or compulsory:

- *Voluntary arbitration* is, in terms of Section 45, set in motion by an industrial council or conciliation board. If a council or board cannot solve a dispute, it may refer the dispute for arbitration and decide whether the arbitration is to be conducted by a single arbitrator, by an even number of arbitrators and an umpire, or by the industrial court. The industrial council or conciliation board also decides who the arbitrator or arbitrators and umpire should be. Should an industrial council or conciliation board decide to refer a specific dispute for arbitration but fail to appoint an arbitrator within 14 days after such a decision, the arbitration will be undertaken by the industrial court.

- *Compulsory arbitration*, in terms of Section 46, takes place in respect of disputes in essential industries that cannot be settled within 30 days by either the relevant industrial council or conciliation board. The procedures followed in compulsory arbitration are the same as those for voluntary arbitration. Where there is no industrial council and the parties to the dispute feel that a conciliation board would also not be able to resolve the dispute, they must report this to the Director-General and state that they have consented to submit the dispute for immediate compulsory arbitration. The decision made by the arbitrator is enforceable and all parties are bound by it.

In recognition agreements, arbitration clauses (except in essential services) can provide for arbitration according to the Labour Relations Act, the Arbitration Act or the common law.

20.8 *STATUS QUO* ORDERS

The dispute-settling mechanisms laid down by the Act are time-consuming. Meanwhile the dispute remains unremedied and may be causing hardship, inconvenience or hostility. Workers may have been dismissed and will continue to lose pay until the dispute is settled, or an employer may have introduced new work practices to the detriment or inconvenience of workers. Therefore, if any dispute involves the termination or suspension of workers, or a change in the established conditions of employment, or an alleged unfair labour practice, then the matter may be left with an industrial council, or the formation of a conciliation board may be requested. Any of the parties can simultaneously have the dispute referred to the industrial court so that a *status quo* order can be enforced (see Section 43 of the Labour Relations Act).

> A *status quo* order may be defined as an order made by the industrial court compelling the reinstatement of workers or the restoration of terms and conditions of employment, or abstention from an unfair labour practice.

This is a temporary order which is made pending the investigation and settlement of the dispute by negotiation at industrial council or conciliation board level or by arbitration.

Application for a *status quo* order can be made by:

- Any party to a dispute who has referred the dispute to an industrial council having jurisdiction;
- Any party to a dispute who has applied for the establishment of a conciliation board (if there is no industrial council having jurisdiction).

The application must be made simultaneously or within ten days of the date on which the dispute is referred to an industrial council or application is made for a conciliation board, or the date on which the parties report to the Director-General that in their opinion a conciliation board will not be able to settle the dispute. This must happen within 30 days of the date on which the action giving cause to the application (for example dismissal) occurred. If application is made after 30 days, the applicant will have to advance reasons to the industrial court for not applying within the 30-day period.

Any worker or employer covered by the Labour Relations Act, whether a member of a trade union or employers' organisation or not, may apply for a *status quo* order, subject to the conditions discussed in this section. The only persons excluded are those covered in Section 2.2 of Act No. 28 of 1956.

The procedures that must be followed

Application for a *status quo* order must be made to the industrial court. The application must contain particulars such as the names and addresses of the parties, the nature of the dispute and the nature of the settlement sought. The application must be signed by the applicant or his or her representative. The facts in the application must be verified on oath by the applicant or any other person who can swear positively to such facts.

444

The applicant must furnish proof to the satisfaction of the industrial court that a copy of the application has been sent or delivered to the other party and to the secretary of any industrial council concerned.

The party or parties and the industrial council (if any) may within 14 days of the date on which the application was posted or delivered by hand, submit an affidavit on the subject by registered post or delivered by hand to the industrial court, and shall send by registered post or deliver by hand to the applicant a copy of it. The applicant may, within ten days from the date on which the affidavit was posted or delivered, reply by means of an affidavit. The industrial court may change the time periods mentioned above as it sees fit.

Should the parties not follow the stipulations meticulously, the industrial court will probably declare the case invalid and refuse to hear it. The acceptance of a late application may however be requested, for example to allow the submission of written evidence. The various steps and the correct sequence are nevertheless crucial in obtaining a *status quo* order.

The content of the order

After considering the application, any further representations and any other matter it regards as important, the industrial court will order the employer (or employers' organisation):

- Not to suspend or dismiss the worker(s), or to cancel the suspension;
- Not to make the proposed change in conditions of employment or, if the change has already been made, to restore the terms and conditions of employment that existed prior to the change;
- Not to introduce the alleged unfair labour practice or, if the practice has already been introduced, to restore the labour practices that existed prior to such introduction.

The industrial court may also at any time, on the application of a party to the dispute, withdraw or vary any such order.

The content of the order must be carefully applied, since according to the Amendment Act of 1988, the industrial court is no longer compelled to reinstate the exact conditions of employment of the aggrieved person that existed before that person was dismissed, for example. The court may even grant less remuneration and less attractive benefits, or take into consideration the remuneration earned elsewhere during the period not worked for the employer. The exact circumstances will determine the content of the order.

An employer who pays workers the remuneration that would have been due to them during normal working hours, had their employment not been suspended or terminated, will be deemed to have complied with the order. The employer is, however, not obliged to give the workers work to do.

The duration of the order

The industrial court fixes the date from which the order is operative. This date may be retrospective to a date not earlier than the date of suspension or

445

dismissal, or on which the conditions of employment were changed or on which the alleged unfair labour practice was introduced.

Normally a *status quo* order remains operative for a maximum period of 90 days from its commencement. The industrial court may, however, of its own accord or on application extend the period by periods not exceeding 30 days at a time.

The industrial court may at any time vary or withdraw such an order on the application of a party to the dispute.

Within the maximum periods outlined above, an order remains operative:

- Until the dispute has been settled by the industrial council or conciliation board or by an arbitrator making an arbitration award or by the industrial court making a final determination;
- Until the industrial council or conciliation board informs the industrial court that it failed to settle the dispute and has decided not to refer the dispute to arbitration or to the industrial court for determination.

Costs

The industrial court may not award costs for a *status quo* order, except on the grounds of unreasonableness or frivolity on the part of a party to the dispute.

20.9 STRIKES AND LOCK-OUTS

A lock-out occurs when the employer prevents workers from doing their job by locking the gates to the premises. However, strikes and lock-outs are not the sole weapons of industrial action. Strike law in South Africa is quite complex because the definition of strikes and their legality or otherwise are governed by the Labour Relations Act and the Riotous Assemblies Act, but these statutes only govern the public law situation. The Labour Relations Act gives a detailed definition of a strike, which is summarised in the accompanying box.

> A strike is a certain act, done by two or more persons, with the purpose of enforcing a demand connected with the employment relationship.

The Labour Relations Act outlines a number of circumstances under which a strike is prohibited (see Section 65) and prescribes a procedure to be followed in order for a strike to be "legal" in public law.

Workers may not strike and employers may not lock out during the time in which any award, agreement or determination is binding on them, or if the workers or employers are involved in essential services, or if there is an industrial council with jurisdiction, unless the matter has been considered by the industrial council and the industrial council has not arrived at a solution within a fixed period of time, or where there is no industrial council (and application was made for a conciliation board and this had also been unsuccessful), or if the conciliation board could not arrive at a solution within a fixed period of time.

446

Workers and employers may not strike or lock out if an industrial council or conciliation board has referred the matter for arbitration. Even if these conditions have been met, registered trade unions and employers' organisations may still not strike or lock out if they are party to an industrial council whose constitution provides that disputes that cannot be settled by the industrial council shall be referred to arbitration, or, where this provision is inapplicable, unless the majority of the members of the union or organisation in good standing have voted by ballot in favour of such action.

Once all these conditions have been met, the strike is legal in public law. If the strike is legal, i.e. if the requirements of the Labour Relations Act have been met, and if the strikers are not in breach of the Riotous Assemblies Act, it merely means that the strikers cannot be prosecuted through the criminal courts.

Strikes and lock-outs can be further complicated by the so-called "peace obligation" clause in recognition agreements. In terms of some recognition agreements, parties regulate their common law position by making provision, for example, that the employer will not dismiss striking workers during the first 24 hours of a strike if the strike is not supported by the union, to enable the union to secure an injunction for the strikers to return to work. It is also possible for the "peace clause" to regulate the position of the parties in all forms of industrial action and not only the industrial action that is covered by the strike definition in the Labour Relations Act. Such industrial action could, for example, cover consumer boycotts, which have become very popular in South Africa during the last few years.

A trade union (whether registered or unregistered) may only call for a strike after the industrial court or conciliation board has failed to resolve the dispute, and after a secret ballot has been held among its members.

As far as the rights and powers of the industrial court with regard to strikes and lock-outs are concerned: the court has the power to issue an interdict or order in the case of illegal strikes and lock-outs. When the strikes and lock-outs are legal, the powers of the industrial court are curtailed: the court may not interfere with normal industrial actions, unless certain periods of time have expired. In Section 17(d) of the Act, specific periods are given for notices, etc., before strikes or lock-outs can be called. This can therefore be seen as a movement in the direction of total democracy in industry in South Africa.

20.10 INDUSTRIAL RELATIONS WITHIN THE ORGANISATION

According to Nel *et al.* (1994), industrial relations within the organisation have become a significant part of the whole field of industrial relations, and therefore industrial relations and human resources managers must be well qualified in this function to ensure that the organisation is successful.

Many organisations have developed industrial relations systems that consist of a policy plus grievance and disciplinary procedures and a works council constitution or recognition agreement. This is typically the area in which the human resources or industrial relations manager functions most of the day.

Recently many organisations have also agreed to a shift in decision-making functions by means of recognition agreements. Disciplinary matters are referred to disciplinary panels which may consist of two managers and one worker representative; recognition agreements thus operate very much like miniature industrial councils.

The typical consultation and communication mechanism used at organisational level is some form of works council. The collective bargaining functions of works councils have already been discussed. Because of the dynamic nature of South African industrial relations, works councils are continuously evolving.

A recurring problem regarding representation is that of clerical and administrative staff, i.e. salaried staff, who mostly have interests and problems that are different from those of hourly-paid staff. It is difficult to say whether both interests can be represented by the same body. How should clerical and administrative staff then be represented—by white-collar trade unions? This trend is now well established and at present a number of trade unions and one federation (Fedsal) accommodate such workers.

Another problem is the question of the relationship between a recognised union and a works council, if any such relationship exists at all. The existence of different cultures and interests on the same shop floor makes for complex, diverse and technically difficult shop-floor representation. New representation structures and mechanisms are however evolving in South Africa.

20.11 THE INDUSTRIAL COURT

The industrial court has to perform all the functions of a court of law with regard to a dispute or a matter arising from the application of the provisions of the laws administered by the Department of Manpower.

The industrial court is presided over by a president and a vice-president. It has the following functions:

- To decide on appeals with regard to the refusal of admission to an industrial council (Section 21(a));
- To provide urgent interim relief until an order has been made by the industrial court in terms of Section 43(4), i.e. in unfair labour practices;
- To issue an interdict or any other order in the case of any action which is prohibited by Section 65;
- To decide on appeals in terms of Section 26(2) of the Occupational Health and Safety Act (No. 85 of 1993);
- To decide on applications for *status quo* orders (Section 43);
- To decide whether or not a closed shop provision shall apply in respect of a person who has been refused membership or who has been expelled from a trade union or employers' organisation (Section 51(10)(c));

- To conduct arbitration in terms of the Act (Sections 45, 46 or 49);
- To advise the Minister whether certain employers and workers should be subject to compulsory arbitration (Section 46(7)(c));
- To rule on unfair labour practices (Section 46(9));
- To make a determination for an undertaking (organisation), industry, trade or occupation, or one in which a labour broker is engaged (Sections 76 and 77);
- To deal with any other matters which it is required or permitted to deal with under the Act;
- Generally to deal with all matters necessary or incidental to the performance of its functions.

The legal provisions as set out above lead to a number of interesting conclusions. The court has jurisdiction over disputes of right and disputes of interest. Individuals do not have automatic direct access to the court, but are first required to exhaust existing remedies, such as the mechanism of the industrial council, to solve their disputes. This has been a major criticism against the structure of the court. The jurisdiction of the court is confined to matters that arise out of the application of statutes administered by the Department of Manpower. This means that many individual employer-employee disputes do not fall within the jurisdiction of the industrial court. Moreover, the exclusion of jurisdiction in respect of alleged offences places another serious limitation on the court.

Access to the court as far as unfair labour practice claims are concerned falls under three jurisdictional headings: determination in terms of Section 46(9); *status quo* orders in terms of Section 43; and the court of law function in terms of Section 17(11)(a) which gives applicants speedy access to the court with regard to alleged unfair labour practices. The court may award costs according to the requirements of justice and the Act.

20.12 THE LABOUR APPEAL COURT

Since the institution of the industrial court it has become obvious that there should be a means of appeal to a higher authority. Amendment No. 83 of 1988 made possible the establishment of the labour appeal court.

The labour appeal court consists of sections that function throughout South Africa and can hold sittings in various cities. Each labour appeal court in sitting consists of a judge of the Supreme Court of South Africa and two assessors who have been appointed by the chairperson.

The powers and functions of the labour appeal court are:
- To decide any legal question set aside under Section 17(21)(a);
- To decide any appeal implied in Section 17(21)(a), i.e. an appeal against a decision of the industrial court;
- The proceedings of an industrial court can *mutatis mutandis* be brought for review before the labour appeal court on the grounds set out in Section 24(1) of the Supreme Court Act (No. 59 of 1959).

It is also possible to appeal against decisions of the labour appeal court. In such a case, except where the decision concerns an issue of fact, an appeal may be made to the Appellate Division of the Supreme Court of South Africa. An appeal can be laid before the Chief Justice, and after it has been heard, the Appeal Court can either endorse, amend or set aside the decision or order which is being appealed against, or give any other decision or order, as well as an order with regard to costs according to the requirements of the law and justice.

20.13 UNFAIR LABOUR PRACTICES

Legislation with regard to unfair labour practices was first introduced in 1979 and has been amended several times since then. The Labour Relations Amendment Act (No. 9 of 1991), which came into effect on 1 May 1991, has reverted to the position before 1988. The new definition of an unfair labour practice, according to the Amendment Act (pp. 2 and 4) is as follows:

"unfair labour practice" means any act or omission other than a strike or lock-out, which has or may have the effect that—

   (i) *any employee or class of employees is or may be unfairly affected or that his, her or their employment opportunities or work security is or may be prejudiced or jeopardized thereby;*

  (ii) *the business of any employer or class of employers is or may be unfairly affected or disrupted thereby;*

 (iii) *labour unrest is or may be created or promoted thereby;*

(iv) *the labour relationship between employer and employee is or may be detrimentally affected thereby; and*

The definition of "unfair labour practice" referred to in subsection (1) shall not be interpreted either to include or exclude a labour practice which in terms of the said definition is an unfair labour practice, merely because it was or was not an unfair labour practice, as the case may be, in terms of the definition of "unfair labour practice", which definition was substituted by section (1)(a) of the Labour Relations Amendment Act, 1991: Provided that a strike or lock-out shall not be regarded as an unfair labour practice.

According to this definition of an unfair labour practice, it is obvious that there have been radical changes since the previous amendment in 1988, and that a general definition now again applies. However, the industrial court still takes the principles contained in the 1988 amendment into consideration for its findings. This situation is summed up as follows by Landman and Le Roux (1991:53):

The effect of this provision is to neutralise the rule of statutory interpretation that the repeal of a provision is evidence of the legislature's intent to exclude the repealed provision. It would be absurd for the courts to be bound by the rule and obliged to decide, for example, that discrimination, boycotts and intimidation—all elements of the 1988 definition—are intended to be excluded from the "new" definition on account of the repeal of the definition introduced in 1988. When interpreting the definition introduced by the 1991 Amendment Act, the courts will ignore the fact of the 1988 definition, and its repeal. It will therefore be open to a party to contend that any of the specific elements of the 1988 definition, with the exception of strikes and lock-outs, constitute unfair labour practices for the purpose of the definition introduced by the Bill.

As far as procedure is concerned, an alleged unfair labour practice is first brought before the industrial council or conciliation board for a decision. If a decision cannot be reached, the matter is referred to the industrial court.

Acts by both employers and employees are covered by this definition. Although employers' organisations and trade unions are not specifically mentioned, the industrial court may make an order (a *status quo* order) requiring the employer or employers' organisation, or the worker or trade union, not to introduce an alleged unfair labour practice, or if the practice has been introduced, to restore the labour practices that previously existed.

Cases of unfair labour practice usually follow the same route through the mechanisms (i.e. the industrial council and conciliation board) as disputes that have to be settled.

An unfair labour practice need not necessarily involve the relationship between employer and employee. It can involve any other issue as well.

20.14 EXTENSION OF THE LABOUR RELATIONS ACT

Because of the rapid changes in industrial relations in South Africa, it is to be expected that labour legislation will be amended more often than before. The last general amendment to the Labour Relations Act took place in 1991, while several minor amendments have been made since.

The extension of the Labour Relations Act includes the Labour Relations Act for Civil Servants (No. 102 of 1993), which has been applicable to civil servants since August 1993. This means that civil servants are now fully covered by an own labour relations act, which corresponds closely to the Labour Relations Act (No. 28 of 1956). Various basic principles concerning collective bargaining and the right to disputes and strikes are also contained in the new law.

Farm workers are covered by Act No. 147 of 1993 (which came into effect on 17 January 1994), giving them access to the Labour Relations Act with certain amendments pertaining to their particular situation. Thus, for example, the law provides for an agricultural labour court for farm workers and employers in farming organisations to handle their own affairs in a unique industrial court.

It may be expected that the Act will be expanded in the near future to cover workers in the corrective services, the defence force, the police force and other semi-government organisations, taking into account their unique circumstances.

A draft labour relations act in 1994 applies to workers in the educational sector to cover schools, universities and technikons and to regulate industrial relations in these sectors. This follows on the Labour Relations in Education

Act (No. 146 of 1993), which has been in effect since October 1993 and pertains to educational and training personnel.

20.15 POSSIBLE AMENDMENTS TO THE LABOUR RELATIONS ACT

In August 1993, the National Manpower Commission published a notice in the *Government Gazette* containing proposals with regard to amendments to the Labour Relations Act. The most important proposed amendments are:

- A simplified system for determining unfair labour practices;
- The consolidation of regulations concerning urgent interim applications for legal aid in a single step to effect interim remedies until the industrial court can make a decision;
- That the definition of an employee be adapted so that dismissed employees and those who are reinstated can also initiate proceedings concerning unfair labour practices;
- The drafting of a code on unfair labour practices that may serve as a guide for employers, trade unions, employee and employers' organisations;
- That the Act be extended to include lecturing personnel at universities and technikons;
- That judgments of the appeal court or any section of the labour appeal court that create precedents should be binding on lower courts such as the industrial court and agricultural labour court;
- That employers' organisations and trade unions may become affiliated to political organisations and give monetary or other support to political parties. Monies collected for trade association safeguarding agreements (closed shop) may, however, not be used for political purposes;
- That only the labour appeal court can review decisions made by the industrial court;
- That the procedure for the referral and settling of disputes be simplified for industrial councils and conciliation boards;
- That costs recovered from other parties in civil suits be taken into account when a penal court issues an order on costs;
- That the indemnity against losses arising from a legal strike or lock-out be expanded to any offence related to a wage-regulating measure or a determination of the Basic Service Conditions Act with regard to wages and conditions of service;
- That unregistered trade associations could, by negotiating with employers, agree to subtract membership fees instead of having to obtain ministerial approval.

There will also be further amendments because of the changed political situation in the country. The ANC's industrial relations policy (1993:32) is currently as follows:

The ANC's Labour Relations Policy is aimed at fostering industrial peace and the settlement of disputes through:

- Recognising the rights of free association of workers and their rights to representation in all structures where their interests are affected, especially the extension of these rights to farm and domestic workers;
- Recognition of the right to strike for workers in all sectors;
- Maintaining the system of collective bargaining and underpinning collective agreements as legally binding on the different parties;
- Recognition of the right to paid maternity and paternity leave with employment security;
- The formulation and implementation of a Labour Relations Act which will protect the interests of all workers, including farm, domestic and public service workers;
- The transformation of the Industrial Court system to enforce the provisions of the Labour Relations legislation;
- The ratification of ILO conventions and the consequent respect of employer and employee rights and employment codes, as recognised by these conventions.

The ANC's current policy on employment (1993:32) reads as follows:

In implementing the development of productive employment opportunities with a living wage for all South Africans, the ANC is committed to fair and equitable recruitment and selection policies. There will be no forced labour, press ganging, or use of the apartheid migratory labour system and child labour and non-rehabilitatory prison labour will be abolished.

In ensuring the realisation of fair and equitable employment opportunities, legislation will be adopted which will outlaw all forms of discrimination in the workplace.

The ANC has proposed that a national labour commission be appointed, consisting of representatives of the state, trade unions, employers' organisations and other relevant community bodies. This central coordinating body for all labour matters can then make recommendations and draft legislation for parliament. Such a commission would also have a say in all labour laws and employment practices.

At the going to press of this book, all the possible amendments to labour legislation and policy had not yet been finalised.

20.16 THE POSITION OF FARM AND DOMESTIC WORKERS

As indicated in the previous section, the Labour Relations Act already applies to farm workers via Act No. 147 of 1993. Domestic workers do not as yet fall under this law.

Farm workers are covered by all labour laws (except the Wage Act), i.e. the Basic Service Conditions Act (via Act No. 104 of 1992), the Occupational Health and Safety Act (No. 85 of 1993), the Unemployment Insurance Act (via Act No. 130 of 1992) and the Compensation for Occupational Injuries and Diseases Act (No. 130 of 1993), which came into effect in March 1994 and replaced Act No. 30 of 1941.

It is clear that the legislator aims to include domestic workers in all labour legislation. It is expected that the Labour Relations Act will be made applicable to domestic workers before the end of 1994. As of 1 January 1994, domestic workers have been covered by the Basic Service Conditions Act (via Act No. 130 of 1993). However, domestic workers are not yet subject to the Wage Act and the Unemployment Insurance Act, but they are expected to be covered by these Acts in the near future.

20.17 CONCLUSION

It is clear that the South African industrial relations system is undergoing radical changes in both structure and application. Consequently, a detailed and durable description of the system is impossible at present. One can only point to some of the characteristics that are emerging and that will probably help shape the system in the near future.

The South African business environment is on the brink of radical changes in intergroup relations and particularly in industrial relations. The new South Africa is making itself felt on the factory floor and in everyday industrial relations. Industrial relations have broadened to include farm workers and, to a lesser extent, domestic workers.

The business sector and human resources managers, in particular, must carefully implement industrial relations practices and principles in order to manage their organisations with the minimum of conflict and optimal profitability. Human resources managers, in particular, have an almost impossible task if they are not well versed in the principles of industrial relations in South Africa. Readers are therefore advised to obtain more information than the limited material given in this chapter.

While the Labour Relations Act has been frequently amended and refined, large-scale amendments are likely in the near future. The Labour Relations Amendment Act (No. 9 of 1991) is already a milestone on the way to consensus negotiations between labour and employers. Landman and Le Roux (1991:57) put it as follows:

It is no exaggeration to say that the Amendment Bill represents the first piece of post-apartheid legislation. It was created by a unique extra-parliamentary process in which the key actors determined for themselves, by a process of negotiation, the rules by which they preferred to be governed.

Griessel (1991) also maintains that the agreement between SACCOLA, COSATU and NACTU is one of the first new-generation consensus decisions taken in the new South Africa and heralded a new era of cooperation and harmony in South Africa.

The Labour Relations Act, as the centrepiece of the South African industrial relations system, has been discussed in this chapter. It contains the legislation for statutory collective bargaining in South Africa. A number of other statutes together form the labour legislation in South Africa and cover labour, management and the state in the business environment. Training legislation is contained in the Manpower Training Act (No. 56 of 1981), the protection of workers by the Compensation for Occupational Injuries and Diseases Act

(No. 130 of 1993) and the Unemployment Insurance Act (No. 30 of 1966). These and other relevant Acts are discussed elsewhere in this book.

Questions

1. Why do you think the system of recognition agreements developed? What are the advantages or disadvantages of such an agreement for your organisation?
2. Critically discuss the present application of three collective bargaining mechanisms that form part of the statutory collective bargaining system in South Africa.
3. Discuss the use and application of the unfair labour practice in South Africa.
4. What is a *status quo* order? When and how would you apply for a *status quo* order? Discuss.
5. What is your opinion of the inclusion of domestic workers under Act No. 28 of 1956? Motivate your reply.
6. Do you consider that the Labour Relations Amendment Act (No. 9 of 1991) has made a significant contribution towards eliminating the uncertainty that surrounds unfair labour practices? Thoroughly motivate your answer.

Sources

ANC. 1993. *The ANC policy guidelines*. ANC, Johannesburg.

Botha, H. 1991. *Guide to the Labour Relations Act 1956*. Practition IR Publications, Pretoria.

Department of Manpower. 1991. *1990 Annual Report* (RP 51/1991). Government Printer, Pretoria.

Griessel, G. 1991. 'n Ontleding van die SACCOLA/COSATU/NACTU-ooreenkoms. Unpublished B.Com. Honours thesis. Rand Afrikaans University, Johannesburg.

Landman, A.A. & Le Roux, P.A.K. (eds) 1991. The Labour Relations Amendment Bill. *Labour Law Briefs*, Vol. 4, No. 8, pp. 49–57.

Nel, P.S. & Van Rooyen, P.H. 1993. *South African industrial relations: theory and practice*. 2nd revised edition. Academica, Pretoria.

Nel, P.S., Erasmus, B.J. & Swanepoel, B.J. 1994. *Successful labour relations—guidelines for practice*. Van Schaik, Pretoria.

Piron, J. 1990. *Recognising trade unions*. Southern, Halfway House.

Part 4

Human resources development

Training	
Management development	
Overview of human resources in South Africa	
Technology and the employee	

Overview of Part 4: Human resources development

AIM

To instil in the student or reader the theory underlying human resources development in a pragmatic manner in order to establish a basis for its scientific application among those who practise this sub-field of human resources management.

PRINCIPAL STUDY OBJECTIVES

Chapter 21: Training. To instil in the student or reader the importance of training as an input for increasing employee outputs in order to promote its scientific application in an organisational context.

Chapter 22: Management development. To instil in the student or reader the importance of management development as an input to increase employee outputs in order to promote its scientific application in an organisational context.

Chapter 23: Overview of human resources in South Africa. To demonstrate to the student or reader the problems surrounding human resources in South Africa as an organisational factor of production and to promote vigilance in this regard.

Chapter 24: Technology and the employee. To instil in the student or reader an understanding of the relationship between the human being and technology in an organisational context in order to manage it in an optimal manner.

Chapter 21

Employee development: training principles and legislation

P.S. Nel

STUDY OBJECTIVES

After studying this chapter, you should be able to:

- Explain the difference between training, development and education;
- List the benefits of effective training and the pitfalls to be avoided;
- Explain the principles of a national training strategy;
- Explain the value and basic functioning of the Manpower Training Act in South Africa;
- Describe the role and functions of training boards;
- Explain why adult learning and child learning are different;
- Show the value of training models in executing training effectively;
- Motivate why supervisory training in South Africa is a priority;
- Describe the principles of competence-based modular training.

21.1 INTRODUCTION

Once employees have completed their induction training (discussed in chapter 8), they must focus on the job for which they were employed. Able and motivated employees are an organisation's greatest asset, but these qualities do not come automatically. Effective training and development by the organisation are necessary to ensure that employees achieve the required level of competence. Training and development are the responsibility of the organisation.

In South Africa, human resources managers are faced with great challenges, because the employment situation in South Africa is unique: on the one hand there is a serious shortage of skilled employees; on the other hand, a high rate of unemployment prevails among unskilled employees. South Africa is also faced with the enormous challenge of increasing the productivity of lower-level workers. There is moreover a shortage of highly skilled managers in South Africa. It is essential that all training and development possibilities be fully exploited to alleviate this problem in the South African economy.

In theory, training and development form a unit, because they are totally interrelated. However, from a practical point of view, it serves the purposes of this book to discuss training and development as separate issues. We shall deal with training in this chapter, and development is discussed in detail in chapter 22. There are, however, a number of issues that apply to both aspects, such as training legislation in South Africa. These chapters should therefore be read as a single unit.

Training forms part of the job content environment and also of the through-put process, and has a direct influence on the job content environment (the nature of the job, utilisation and development), the job context environment (management philosophy and working conditions) and the external environment (labour market conditions, level of education, technology and national human resources policy).

FIGURE 21.1: Principal learning components of training principles and legislation

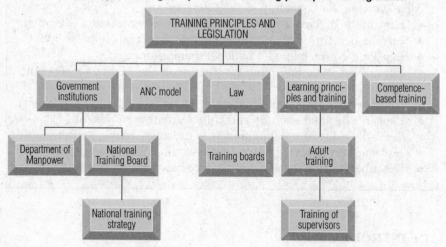

21.2 TERMINOLOGY

The terminology of training and development includes three major concepts that need to be distinguished if the subject is to be understood.

For the purposes of this book the most important aspect of training and development is that it is a means of making employees more valuable to the organisation by extending their skills and knowledge, modifying their attitudes to the job and adjusting their patterns of behaviour in the organisation.

The following definitions have been adopted in this book:

- *Education* refers to activities aimed at developing knowledge, moral values and understanding. Its purpose is to develop students intellectually and to provide them with a basis for further learning. Education is basic knowledge rather than applied skills, and has little or no immediate application to a specific job. Basic, preparatory education is received at high school, college or university. It is required in all walks of life and is of value throughout life.
- *Management development*, for the purpose of this book, is more specific than education. According to Ivancevich (1992) it is a process whereby managers gain experience, skills and attitudes to become or remain successful leaders in their organisations. Management development may take place for a variety of reasons ranging from the reorganisation of a managerial job to the improvement of the effectiveness of individual managers according to the present and future requirements of the organisation. It may therefore be regarded as a process whereby a manager learns to make increasingly important decisions under pressure, and to make the right decisions for his or her organisation. This is an important skill because many important decisions require the weighing of intangibles, and these intangibles are often linked to people's attitudes and capabilities, which play a role in the present and future welfare of the organisation. The term "management development" can refer to the improvement of the skills of a *person*—a manager—or to amendment of the management function in an organisation.
- *Training* refers to the use of specific means to inculcate specific learning and techniques that can be identified and continually improved. Training is therefore a deliberate effort to teach specific skills, knowledge or attitudes to serve a specific purpose. The purpose of training is to enable the learner to apply knowledge, skills and attitudes in order to achieve the objectives of the organisation and it should result in the trainee's being able to do a specific job effectively, either directly or soon after training.

From the above it is clear that education, development and training are interrelated, and that elements of each are involved whenever a specific activity is undertaken to improve an employee's performance in the organisation. The distinction between the three rests upon the purpose of the undertaking: whether it is for the general betterment of the employee, for improvement in a specific job or for better performance in the organisation in future. Camp *et al.* (1986:4) summarise the characteristics or key elements of training as follows:

Effective training is a learning experience activity—a planned business activity in response to identified needs—and is an attempt to further the goals of the organisation while simultaneously providing the opportunity for individual employees to learn and grow in the business.

Since training is of vital importance in South Africa, the main training institutions as well as training legislation in this country are important. This is discussed in the following section.

21.3 STATE INSTITUTIONS FOR TRAINING AND TRAINING LEGISLATION IN SOUTH AFRICA

Various state institutions are involved with training in South Africa to a lesser or greater extent. The most important are the Department of Manpower and the National Training Board. The Department of Manpower is the umbrella state department which coordinates and controls all training in South Africa. The Manpower Training Act is the instrument whereby all training is brought under statutory control.

As a result of the large-scale socio-political changes South Africa has undergone in recent years, state institutions have initiated adaptations in training. Thus, for example, a task team of the National Training Board proposed a new national training strategy in April 1994 (this is discussed in section 21.3.3). Together with other initiatives in the new South Africa, this strategy may help to correct the large-scale historical imbalance in training and development.

The proposed national training strategy will probably also make a valuable contribution towards economic and industrial growth, which will promote the availability of the necessary expertise.

In order to implement a national training strategy in South Africa, priorities need to be determined and attainable short-term aims and long-term objectives formulated.

Short-term aims may include:

- To design a national training strategy and formulate a structure for its implementation, and to revise this strategy regularly afterwards;
- To formulate a model for financing training by the state as well as by the private sector, so that training can be optimally promoted;
- To promote and support the privatisation, decentralisation and coordination of training;
- To promote the efficiency and effectiveness of training.

Long-term aims may include:

- To equip the workforce, including disabled persons, with the skills, values and attitudes required to support the development of the economy in the formal and informal sectors;
- To optimise the training capacity of employees by means of bridging training, the teaching of reading, writing, numeracy, job and learning skills, as well as further training;
- To design a qualification structure for training, to be administered by a certification body in order to ensure acceptable training standards;
- To promote the development of a competent, professional corps of trainers;
- To determine the needs and requirements of the working milieu, to formulate these clearly and submit them to the formal education sector;
- To create effective mechanisms for liaison between training and education so that they may complement and support each other.

In the light of the above, it would be meaningful to scrutinise the specific role and functions of the Department of Manpower and the National Training

Board, as well as the proposed national training strategy, before concentrating on training legislation.

21.3.1 The Department of Manpower

The mission of the Department of Manpower, the human resources policy of the state and the various objectives in the sphere of human resources are discussed in chapter 23. This section therefore focuses only on the Department of Manpower's involvement in training.

The Department of Manpower is involved in training in three areas, namely the training of artisans, the training of unemployed persons and the training of other employees. The Department of Manpower holds the view that the employer has the primary responsibility for the training and retraining of its employees and that the Department only has a supportive role. The mission of the Chief Directorate of Manpower Training is to improve the competence level of every member of the labour force by means of training and development.

The Department of Manpower only provides training for its own employees, which is what it expects of any other employer. The Department's support of training consists mainly of advice to employers on all aspects of training, providing a legal framework for a successful training relationship between employers and their employees and offering financial support and incentives to employers.

The functions of the Department with regard to training in South Africa are embodied in the Manpower Training Act (No. 56 of 1981):

- Providing a legal and administrative framework to promote orderliness, coordination and the maintaining of standards;
- Supporting and encouraging efforts at training in the private sector by, inter alia, some form of financial support;
- Supplementing the training efforts of the private sector by training certain categories of workers at technical institutions designated for this purpose.

Within the Department of Manpower the Chief Directorate of Training concentrates primarily on all training activities. According to Van Dyk *et al.* (1992), this directorate performs various functions, such as supervision of the training of artisans and administering the fund for the training of unemployed persons (also see chapter 23).

21.3.2 The National Training Board (NTB)

According to Section 3(1) of the Manpower Training Act (No. 56 of 1981), the National Training Board was established for the purpose of advising the Minister with regard to matters of policy arising from the Act, as well as any other aspect of human resources training. The NTB is committed to coordinating, encouraging, facilitating and promoting training at the national level.

The objectives of the National Training Board were considerably modified when the Manpower Training Amendment Act (No. 39 of 1990) came into operation. The main amendments are, first, that the NTB should concentrate more on research and investigations to promote training. Secondly, the NTB has to submit an annual report to the Minister, which the Minister can table in parliament. Thirdly, various aspects with regard to a series of committees, which are contained in Sections 7 to 11 of the original Act, are repealed. (However, certain of these functions are reinstated in the new Sections 5 and 6.) Finally, the NTB's direct involvement in the apprenticeship system is radically curtailed, since this has been devolved to the relevant training boards set up by the Amendment Act (also see chapter 23).

The mission of the NTB (National Training Board 1992:1) is as follows:

The NTB endeavours, by means of research, to give the Minister of Manpower objective advice on matters relating to training policy and to coordinate, facilitate and promote training.

In view of this mission, the general objectives of the NTB are:

- To coordinate, facilitate and promote training;
- To deliberate critical and strategic matters concerning training;
- To identify needs, deficiencies and problems regarding training;
- To help develop the training infrastructure of the country;
- To promote orderliness and the maintenance of training standards within the legislative and administrative framework;
- To serve as a clearing house for information on human resources training.

In order to achieve its aim, the NTB focuses mainly on the following:

- Advising the Minister and the Department of Manpower (DMP) on training;
- Undertaking research on human resources training;
- Working with the DMP, other government departments and statutory bodies on matters relating to human resources training;
- Taking steps for the establishment of uniform standards of training;
- Liaising directly with the training fraternity;
- Establishing a network of committees to ensure successful functioning and rendering of service.

The functioning of the National Training Board is shown in the organisational scheme of the NTB (figure 21.2). This figure clearly shows that the National Training Board is administratively linked to the Department of Manpower and performs a specialised function.

21.3.3 The proposed integrated national training strategy

Since the establishment of the first national training strategy in 1991, based on research led by the National Training Board, circumstances in South Africa have radically changed. It soon became clear that the national training strategy was in urgent need of complete revision and reformulation. Consequently, a task group of the NTB was established and began its activities in 1993 (National Training Board 1992:40). A provisional report of this task group was published by the NTB in April 1994. The principal recommendations of this report are summed up below.

FIGURE 21.2: Organisational scheme of the NTB as at 31 December 1992

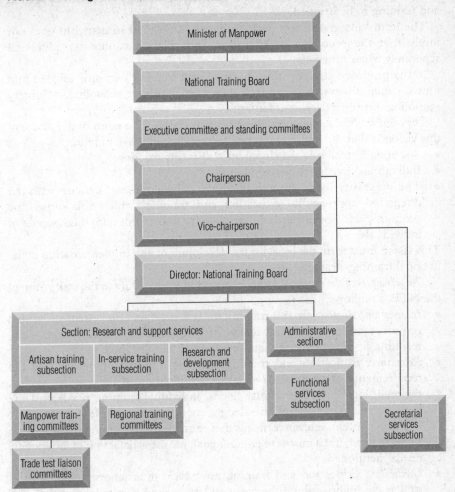

Source: NTB (1992:18)

It is clear that because of the new dispensation that came into being in South Africa in April 1994, there is a need for a common goal and core strategy for training, guided by a comprehensive government system and supported by the necessary infrastructure, funds and incentive measures. All these elements must be integrated into the national strategy.

The concept of an integrated approach to education and training forms the basis of the proposed national training strategy.

Such an integrated approach to education and training in one system requires a new pattern or paradigm of thinking in which education and training are no longer seen as separate entities, each with its own reason for existence, but as one life-long process, i.e. "learning". This requires the gap between education and training to be bridged.

The term "integrated approach" indicates an overall strategy but does not imply that the problems of education and training cannot be addressed separately when necessary.

In the proposed strategy, the education and training system is divided into four distinct sub-systems: pre-school care, compulsory schooling, voluntary schooling or pre-tertiary, and tertiary.

The context of the national training strategy is vision. The point of departure of this vision is that the national training strategy should take note of:

- Social and economic development and reconstruction;
- Individuals' needs for development;
- The necessity of a human resources development system with an integrated approach to education and training, which will satisfy the economic and social needs of the country and the development needs of individuals.

This vision must form the basis for the development and implementation of the national training strategy.

The principles of the national training strategy are, according to the task group of the NTB, as follows:

- *Integration:* Education and training must form part of a system of human resources development that makes provision for an integrated approach, resulting in qualifications that are accepted all over the country.
- *Relevance:* Education and training must be and remain relevant to the requirements of national development, industry and the services sector, regional, local and community needs, individual training needs and the need for the expansion of knowledge, science and technology.

   In this context, relevance means that education and training should not be a goal in itself, but a means to another goal, i.e. the satisfaction of the specific needs mentioned.

- *Credibility:* Education and training must have international credibility as well as credibility among the industrial and services sectors, suppliers and learners, satisfying them that the joint national goals can be achieved.

   No country can exist in geographic and economic isolation, nor can any country afford to be internationally regarded as incompetent. The education and training system of a country is an excellent way to obtain international credibility and must, for this reason, be of such a standard and type that it enjoys status in the international community.

- *Coherence and flexibility:* Education and training must encompass an interconnected framework of principles and standards that are valid on a national level but that are at the same time flexible enough to satisfy the needs of the industrial and services sector, suppliers and learners.

   Many educational and training systems were created piecemeal and at random, and do not clearly differentiate between the various qualifications and ways to qualify. In numerous cases the systems had been designed for an earlier era but are still being rigidly applied, rendering them practically useless. For example: in South Africa there is no way of determining the relative value of a qualification awarded by a university against one awarded by a technical college. Moreover, courses are often designed with more emphasis on academic value than on their usefulness to organisations, with the result that the qualifications have no practical value. However, the opposite is also true. The aim of this principle is to solve these problems.

- *Standards:* Standards for education and training must be contained in a nationally agreed upon framework with internationally acceptable results.

It has long been common (and legally required) to express the results of training in terms of competence. However, competence is differently interpreted by different organisations and must be defined more clearly. For this reason, the term "results" is preferred in this context. It has also become clear that there is no way to compare the value of various training qualifications with each other, just as it is impossible to compare those in the formal education sector with one another. The reason is an inadequate framework in which the results of education can be defined and evaluated and this inevitably leads to ineffectiveness and inefficiency in the system of education and training.

- *Legitimacy:* Education and training must make provision for involving all important stakeholders in planning and coordination in order to ensure transparency.

In the political climate in which South African organisations find themselves, the acceptability of any solution depends on a number of factors, with some being difficult to define. One of these is legitimacy, certain aspects of which are mentioned above.

- *Access:* All prospective learners must have access to the relevant levels of education and training, and must be able to make unhindered progress.

In South Africa, the majority of learners have not had sufficient access to formal education, and their access to training has been impeded by legislation and job reservation. This still poses an obstacle for many learners today, because development is only accessible to those who were able to overcome these circumstances. It is now essential to make easy access to the relevant levels possible, for example by removing the artificial barriers to education and training.

- *Articulation:* Education and training must make it possible for learners who have met the requirements to move from component to component within the training system.

It is well known that people who appear to have qualifications of an equal value, for example a three-year tertiary diploma obtained in the non-formal sector, may not enter the formal education sector at this level and proceed from there. They are forced to start from scratch in the formal sector. The aim of this principle is to remedy this shortcoming.

- *Progression:* Education and training must ensure that the framework of qualifications makes it possible for individuals to progress through the levels of national qualifications with various combinations of components of the training system.

  This principle, which is closely related to both articulation and portability, aims at ensuring that no learning is lost in an era in which a life-long learning process is essential for the survival of individuals and organisations. This allows the individual to obtain credits for learning acquired and set this off against learning needed in order to progress through the levels of national qualification.

- *Portability:* Education and training must make it possible for learners to transfer their credits and qualifications from one training institution or employer to another.

  This principle is related to articulation but also involves the transfer of knowledge, skills and attitudes from one organisation to another. For example: a motor mechanic remains a motor mechanic, irrespective of the type of vehicle on which his or her training was based.

- *Recognition:* Education and training must recognise, through a process of assessment, earlier learning activities whether formal, non-formal or informal, as well as experience.

  This principle accepts that no person who enters the learning situation has never learnt anything, and measures and recognises these earlier learning activities.

- *Guidance:* Education and training must make provision for guidance to learners by people who have met nationally accepted standards.

  The quality of learning is in direct relation to the quality of the educator or trainer who guides it. Although there are national standards for teachers, there are at present no such standards for people known as instructors, trainers, mentors, etc. This principle aims at remedying this shortcoming.

The national training strategy contains various core elements. It forms the core strategy that must be accepted as the basis for a national strategy in an integrated approach to education and training in South Africa. The core strategy accepts that suitable education and training:

- Empowers individuals by providing them with the necessary knowledge and skills;
- Improves the quality of life;
- Contributes towards development goals in a national plan of economic growth;
- Is implemented by a national qualification framework (NQF).

The core elements of this system are depicted in figure 21.3.

A national qualification framework (NQF) specifies learning activities in terms of nationally and internationally accepted results. This forms the basis of an integrated approach to education and training that empowers individuals and promotes the skills and learning culture required for a well-educated and

FIGURE 21.3: Core elements of a national training strategy

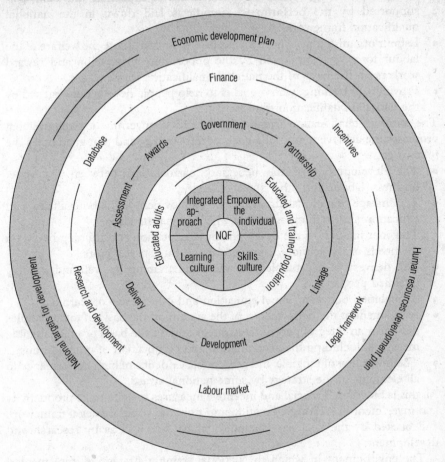

trained population that can contribute to its own economic welfare and that of the country as a whole.

The national qualification framework is supported by the following key stakeholders:

- The state.
- The community, whose need for development is met by access to basic adult education, linked to appropriate national education and training qualifications.
- The business sector, whose support of the education and training of workers is based on the realisation that this can improve productivity, organisational growth and profitability, and which offers an opportunity to make a contribution towards the community as a whole and specifically to that part of the community from which the organisation draws its human

resources. The business sector's investment in education and training is supported by the performance standards laid down in the national qualification framework.

- Labour organisations, whose main purpose is to promote the welfare of the labour force, are supported by the opportunity to develop and reward workers on the basis of the national qualification framework.
- Providers of training, whose goal is to help people develop, are backed by the national qualification framework.

The national qualification framework requires a government structure that promotes the achievement of the goals of this strategy and that guarantees the following:

- The development of the necessary partnerships between the state, business, labour and other stakeholders;
- The linkage of national structures for employment and labour affairs with education and training as well as with regional structures;
- The coordination of the development of education and training based on the needs of the services, commercial and industrial sectors.
- The delivery of acceptable education and training by well and suitably qualified people;
- Articulation between school education and other levels of learning;
- Assessment of the performance of the system on the basis of the principles that form an integral part of the strategy and on the basis of other suitable measures, including the accreditation and certification of qualifications;
- The rewarding of tangible and perceptible evidence of high performance in all elements of the strategy by some national award.

All this is based on financial and incentive measures to encourage productivity and investment in relevant education and training within the legal framework and backed by the necessary national database as well as by research and development.

The environment in which the national training strategy is implemented consists of:

- The national human resources and economic development plans, drawn up by the relevant multipartite forums and government bodies;
- The strategy derived from the plans to support and involve education;
- A series of national development objectives that have been jointly determined by stakeholders in order to base education and training on the results required for socio-economic growth in the country, which will include the education of adults within and outside the labour force.

Other aspects that have an effect on the national training strategy, but are not discussed here, include the rationalisation of legislation concerning the more than 200 institutions, boards, committees, directorates and other bodies to which authority with regard to education and training has been awarded.

The above makes it clear that as far as training and development, and specifically the national training strategy, are concerned, a shift in the paradigm of thinking will have to take place in South Africa. Many of the recommendations and concepts in the proposed strategy may appear revolutionary to those who have not been involved in their development. The integrated approach to education and training, the national qualification framework, sector-based rather than industry-based training organisations, results rather than competencies, and process-oriented decision-making rather than autocratic management may require adjustments that many people find difficult.

The paradigm shift mentioned is, however, easier said than done: it cannot be brought about by merely reading a report; attitudes must change, new methods must be developed and applied. All these are essential for the success of a new strategy. However, this does not take place by itself, and neither do the results become evident overnight. Planned intervention and time are therefore necessary for success.

21.4 THE MANPOWER TRAINING ACT (NO. 56 OF 1981)

The Manpower Training Act (No. 56 of 1981, as amended) governs all training in South Africa and consolidates all other training legislation. It is therefore important to all employers and trainers who carry out employee training of any nature, be it the training of apprentices or training in industrial relations.

The main points of the Act are now briefly discussed.

The aims of the Act

The Act provides an institutional framework within which the training needs of all employees in South Africa can be met. One of the explicit aims of the Act is to encourage and coordinate training, so that the best training is offered to the labour force. The Act also describes training facilities and opportunities. Indirectly, the Act is intended to ensure a flow of trained labour to meet the economic and industrial needs of the country. The Act created for the first time a basis for constructive cooperation between the private and public sectors in South Africa.

The Act aims at the better utilisation of South Africa's labour force, as is evident in the work of the Department of Manpower through the National Manpower Commission and the National Training Board. Projects undertaken include the drawing up of a national human resources audit, the supplementing and upgrading of the labour force by immigration and training, the increased use of female labour, the distribution of trade skills, and creation of a national training strategy and guidelines for competence-based modular training.

The Manpower Training Act was promulgated to structure technical and artisan skills in South Africa; it therefore combines Acts aimed at promoting skills at these levels. The Act is primarily aimed at training and the development of management expertise.

The Act is also designed to establish, coordinate and maintain an infrastructure for training by institutions and facilities such as the National Training Board and the Manpower Development Fund. The Act is administered by the Department of Manpower, assisted by the National Training Board as an advisory body.

The National Training Board has the following functions:

- Advising the Minister on policy matters arising from the Act, as well as on any other matter related to human resources training;
- Coordinating, encouraging, facilitating and promoting training at the national level.

The Board also has a number of standing committees which have tasks in specific areas, for example human resources training committees, specialist committees and a committee for in-service training. (The functions of the NTB are discussed elsewhere in this chapter.)

The Manpower Development Fund: This fund can finance private and regional training centres and schemes recognised by the Act by means of loans towards capital expenditure. The funds are derived from interest on loans, from donations by the private sector and from monies voted by parliament from time to time. The fund can also obtain money in the form of training levies, which the Minister of Manpower may exact from time to time from all employers, from employers in a certain industry or sector, or from all persons engaged in certain areas, skills, trades, occupations or categories. Funds for private training schemes may also be established with the consent of the Minister.

Training schemes are a feature of industrial training and came into being as a result of criticism of the apprenticeship system. The objective of training schemes is to give structure to training, to make it more cost-effective and to focus it on specific work-related needs. The control and financing of schemes were originally the responsibility of industrial councils or professional training boards, and the funds were created out of levies on all employers in a particular industry or area.

The Act makes provision for the compulsory registration of an employee training scheme by an employer that wishes to become eligible for subsidies. The Registrar of Manpower Training reports all applications for schemes to the National Training Board. A training scheme has to be registered according to its type of work, and registration depends on set conditions being met and specific standards being laid down.

Regional training centres: Groups or associations in specific industries, sectors or areas that have common or compatible training needs, may apply to the Department of Manpower to establish a regional training centre. Upon registration with the Department, the centre receives a legal personality. Registered regional training centres may apply to the Minister to impose levies on participating employers. Such centres may also provide training for workers whose employers do not participate in the centre. There is at present also an advisory committee which has been set up for regional training centres to advise the Registrar of Manpower on matters affecting the training of workers.

Private training centres are generally limited to a single industry, employer or training agent and usually supply training in a single skill, occupation or trade.

The terms and conditions for registration are the same as for regional training centres. Only the following may offer industrial relations training without being registered as a private training centre: trade unions, employers' organisations, trade union federations, industrial councils and educational institutions. Private training centres may be financed by personal funds or by a structure of fees: which of these is adopted must be specified when application is made for registration.

Training boards have accepted the responsibility for training apprentices, and any other training in the particular industry. (Training boards are discussed in more detail elsewhere in this chapter.)

Industrial training centres: Provision has been made for industrial training centres, which are established and operated by accredited training boards.

Competence-based modular training (CBMT): Because of the shortage of skills that impedes economic development in South Africa, the Act gives recognition to two issues: first, many workers are experienced and competent in tasks that require technical knowledge and skills, but are not qualified artisans. Secondly, many tasks in industry require a certain level of technical knowledge and skill, but not necessarily at the level of qualified artisans.

In order to accommodate employees with this type of background, they may, after completion of training, be issued with a certificate specifying the trade in which they have been trained. After training they may also sit for a qualifying test. This provides above-average trainees with the opportunity of becoming artisans, and so helps to alleviate the shortage of skilled workers in South Africa. This measure provides an alternative to the requirements of artisan training, by which an apprentice who is a major may write the test after less than the specified normal training period; for example after 18 or 20 months instead of the normal 36 months. If the apprentice passes the test, he or she will be considered qualified. See paragraph 21.11.

Apprenticeship (artisan training): The training of apprentices takes up a major portion of the Act, which indicates the chronic shortage of artisans in South Africa. The emphasis is on the availability of artisans and on their training. Only trades designated in the *Government Gazette* are recognised as such. The Act covers the following matters in detail: the employment of apprentices; contracts of apprenticeship; cancellation and amendment of contracts and conditions of apprenticeship (artisan training). This system is now implemented through training boards.

The training of work seekers: To relieve the human resources shortage in South Africa and to facilitate the placement of unemployed persons who seek jobs, the Act makes provision for the training of work seekers who meet certain requirements (age, level of education, and so on). They are trained to a level at which they can be placed in a job and may become eligible for more advanced training (see chapter 23).

Industrial relations training: The Act makes no specific or separate provision for training in industrial relations except to stipulate that only trade unions, employer organisations (or their federations), industrial councils and educational institutions may present training courses in industrial relations without the express prior approval of the Registrar.

The prescriptions for training in industrial relations include matters connected with the relationship between employer and employee, negotiations with regard to, for example, compensation and other conditions of employment, the prevention and settlement of disputes, the application and interpretation of the relevant laws administered by the Department of Manpower, and the management of trade unions, employers' organisations, federations and industrial councils.

This kind of training is important in the light of the prominent role played by trade unions in South Africa today, and because all interested parties must know enough about these matters to deal with them effectively.

21.5 THE MANPOWER TRAINING AMENDMENT ACT (NO. 39 OF 1990)

Training legislation in South Africa underwent dramatic changes with the promulgation of the Manpower Training Amendment Act (No. 39 of 1990), which came into effect on 1 July 1990. The most important amendments to the Manpower Training Act are:

- The establishment and accreditation of training boards by means of which industry accepts responsibility for apprenticeship training and other industrial training.
- The setting up of an advisory committee for regional training centres (formerly group training centres) by the Minister, to advise the Registrar of Manpower Training on the training of workers in general, and other related matters.
- The establishment of a fund for training unemployed persons, and thereby obtaining greater cooperation from the private sector with regard to mobilising funds and using the infrastructure for this purpose.
- A changeover from the existing time-based training system for apprentices to a performance or competence-based modular system.

These amendments represent an important milestone in the quest for more effective training in South Africa. The Amendment Act laid the foundation for a new training dispensation. An important result is that because of the Margo Commission's report on income taxation, tax rebates for training were phased out on 31 July 1990. In their place, the Minister of Finance instituted training subsidies as well as cash allowances.

The comprehensive changes in the field of training extend far wider than training legislation as such:

- The present time-based training system will gradually be transformed into a performance or competence-based system in which modular training will play an important role.

- Every industry will set up its own training board, which will replace the present Manpower Training Committee. The main functions of these boards will be in the structuring and control of the training of artisans in that industry.
- Greater emphasis will be placed on institutional training and trade theory will be taught together with practical training.
- All artisan training will be evaluated by means of skills tests, and artisan status will no longer be attained automatically after a certain period of time.
- The principles of accredited training and evaluation or testing institutions will be the basis of a revised training system.

In addition to this, the amendment makes provision for the principle of training boards to be extended to all forms of human resources training, i.e. training other than that of artisans.

The Manpower Training Amendment Act is based on the devolution of authority. For this reason, the control of the apprentice system, for example, has been transferred from the National Training Board to the Department of Manpower Chief Directorate, Training. Should training boards be established for an industry, however, the responsibility for training apprentices will be assumed by such a training board. The responsibility for training artisans is thus shifted to its rightful place, according to Haasbroek (1990:20):

> I believe we have now placed the responsibility for apprentice training where it should be. An industry which will eventually employ the trained artisans is in the best position to judge what the standard and the quality of the training should be.

It is clear that one of the most important changes of the Amendment Act is that most of the functions and powers of the Registrar of Manpower Training have been devolved to the training boards. These include:

- The registration of contracts;
- Exemptions;
- Issuing certificates to apprentices who have passed the trade test;
- Determining the conditions for apprenticeship and the conditions under which employees and apprentices have to work together;
- The obligation of the employer to ensure that the apprentice receives adequate training;
- Granting permission for an apprentice to serve for less than the usual period, and to make his or her services available to another employer;
- Suspension of an apprentice and other disciplinary steps;
- Adaptation of a contract of apprenticeship;
- To allow any person who has been trained or has not yet passed the qualifying trade test, but who has received training or gained experience in a suitable branch of the trade, to sit for the trade test in accordance with the standards set.

21.6 ESTABLISHMENT, ACCREDITATION AND FUNCTIONS OF TRAINING BOARDS

Industries wishing to set up a training board must contact the Registrar of Manpower Training in order to establish whether there is an existing training board for a related industry and area, with which they could readily link up.

Establishment: A training board can be established by any of the following:

- Employer, if the Registrar approves;
- Employers' organisation;
- Group of employers;
- Group of employers' organisations;
- Group of one employer and one or more employers' organisations;
- Group of employers and one or more employers' organisations;
- One or more industrial boards;
- Trade union;
- Group of trade unions;
- Group of employees.

A draft constitution, which has been drawn up in accordance with the provisions of the Act and which has been tested against circumstances in various industries, is available from the Registrar of Manpower Training. Industries that intend establishing a training board can also ask the Registrar for assistance, and therefore should not encounter any insurmountable problems with such an establishment.

The main objective of a training board must be the promotion of training, and its constitution must as far as possible make provision for the representation of all parties involved in that industry, including employees.

With regard to the training of employees in general, the establishment and accreditation of a training board is optional, although it is strongly recommended by the Department of Manpower.

Should an industry be training apprentices, however, it will be compelled to establish a training board and apply for accreditation in order to continue the training of apprentices in terms of the Act, since the Amendment Act transfers the administration and control of the apprenticeship system to training boards.

Although the amendment makes provision for a transition period during which industries may still, after the amendment has come into operation, establish training boards in order to take over the apprenticeship system, this period has now lapsed. Failure by industries that are already training apprentices to have their training boards accredited before the deadline or institute competence-based modular training conditions will have the result that the trades relevant to such industries will be excluded from their conditions of apprenticeship and consequently from their entire apprenticeship system.

Industries that are not training apprentices at present but still intend doing so are not subject to this transitional restriction, but will only be considered for accreditation with regard to the apprenticeship system if training is in the form of a competence-based modular training system.

Accreditation of a training board takes place as follows: its constitution, signed by or on behalf of the parties to the training board, and its application for accreditation must be submitted, and the Registrar must be furnished with all the information required.

In order to qualify for accreditation:

- The main objective of the training board must be to promote training;
- The training board's constitution must comply with the Act;
- The board must be financially capable of performing its function;
- If the board also trains apprentices it must:
  — Submit modular learning conditions and practical training schedules;
  — Submit relevant documents such as contracts, certificates and a log-book;
  — Determine standards for trade tests in consultation with the Registrar in accordance with Section 28.

Should there not be another accredited training board for the same industry and in the same region, the Registrar may accredit the training board and furnish it with a certificate of accreditation.

By accreditation the training board acquires all the powers and accepts all the duties that the Act accords to and imposes upon a training board.

Should the training board however fail to exercise its powers or fulfil its obligations, the Registrar has the right to repeal the accreditation and lay claim to the assets of the training board.

21.7 ANC INITIATIVES TO RESTRUCTURE TRAINING AND DEVELOPMENT

The ANC has published various documents with regard to education and human resources development, including a general policy framework for training and development.

A short summary of the salient points contained in three ANC documents is given below.

21.7.1 The ANC's policy guidelines

The ANC's policy framework document contains sections that specifically focus on education, development, scientific development and the development of human resources. From this, the policy and recommendations of the ANC in this regard may be deduced. It is said, for instance (1991:28):

Furthermore we believe that the right to education and training should be enshrined in a Bill of Rights which should establish principles and mechanisms to ensure that there is an enforceable and expanding minimum floor of entitlements for all.

The right to training and development must therefore, like basic human rights, be contained in legislation.

As far as an integrated human resources policy is concerned, the following is stated (1991:28):

The ANC is committed to the evolution of a coherently and nationally integrated strategy for the development of our country's human resources. Education and training policies will be integrated within the framework for economic transformation and with the strategy for the conservation of natural resources and with the objective of using the benefits of science and technology to the full.

A specific educational policy is also spelled out, which addresses, for example, the following aspects: pre-school education, school education and further education, adult education and a programme for the education of youths who previously had not had this opportunity. It is also stated that education must be regulated by a policy based on democratic principles as well as by a joint national education and training system. It is said that the democratisation of education and training can be best served by maintaining a balance between the role of the central government and that of regional and local authorities.

The proposed national development strategy for the training of human resources includes the following (1991:31):

- *Development programmes are sensitive to the specific needs of each community, particularly with regard to the needs of women, youth, rural people and the disabled;*
- *Allocation of resources in development programmes must redress deprivations and imbalances between and within different communities;*
- *The provision of education and training within development programmes should have recognition with the national education and training system.*

A national training fund is envisaged to finance the investment in human resources development. A levy on employers is proposed to back this fund. It is indicated that training must be linked to the economic policy of the new South Africa and that it must form an integral part of the restructuring of the economy. Therefore trade unions, employers and other organisations should play a central role in the planning, implementation and monitoring of training, as well as in establishing procedures for selection and testing according to national standards.

21.7.2 The ANC's reconstruction and development programme (RDP)

Various drafts of this programme are already in existence; the latest that was available when writing this section was the 7th draft of February 1994. For the purposes of this book we concentrate on chapter 3 of the programme, which deals with the development of human resources. The programme focuses on various aspects of training and development, as well as on their structuring in South Africa. The following aspects are discussed:

- Girls and women in education and training. It is emphasised that there must be equality for girls and women at all educational levels.
- An integrated framework of qualifications. The establishment of a national qualification framework that integrates all elements of education and the training system will enable learners to progress to various levels from any point of departure.

478

- Early child education is addressed.
- Basic education and training for adults is extremely important and must be a priority. There must be special education for handicapped adults.
- There must be compulsory schooling to satisfy everyone's needs. By the end of the decade classes should contain no more than 40 students and skills should be acquired as rapidly as possible. A new certification and qualification system should also be established.
- Further education and post-school training should lead to a National Secondary Certificate. There should also be parity between this certificate in industry and in community centres.
- The access of black and female students in particular to higher education and educational institutions must be considerably expanded. All post-secondary training should become part of general human resources development programmes.
- The restructuring of education and training should integrate various bodies, and new approaches to curricula, teaching and certification, as well as an integrated system, should be established. This also applies to career planning.

The restructuring of training into an integrated system is of vital importance to the ANC. The training system must also be considerably expanded and basic education after standard 7 must be integrated with higher education to involve disadvantaged communities in the educational process.

21.7.3 A policy framework for education and training

A discussion document on education and training policy was published by the ANC in January 1994. It deals with the following aspects:
- Part 1 focuses on a strategic perspective: objectives, policy procedures and policy initiatives that should be pursued for the following five years;
- Part 2 deals with a new structure and organisation for training and education that focuses on the evolution of a national learning system as well as on its democratic control;
- Part 3 focuses on the mobilisation of financial sources for educational reconstruction to ensure the efficient and effective management of educational funds.
- Part 4 focuses on a new policy for teachers, the professional development of teachers and an industrial relations policy for the teaching profession.
- Part 5 deals with a language policy for education as well as curriculum development, certification, types of learning and library information. The importance of the sciences, mathematics and technology is emphasised.
- Part 6 deals with various sectors, adult learning, general training, special educational needs and further and higher education.

The ANC proposes an integrated policy for the total reconstruction of all education and training in South Africa.

21.7.4 Conclusions from the ANC documents

The general conclusion is that the ANC has made proposals for training and education in South Africa at various levels and from various angles and that these will serve as important inputs for the future.

Note should be taken, however, that the earlier government initiatives (particularly those of the National Training Board—see 21.3.3) and the suggestions of the ANC largely coincide with and supplement each other. It is important to take note of both approaches and to regard them as complementary.

The above gives an indication of the direction in which education and training in South Africa will develop in the years to come.

21.8 REASONS FOR TRAINING, AND CONCOMITANT PROBLEMS

There are several reasons why training is necessary if an organisation is to achieve its objectives effectively:

- Training gives workers direction in their jobs and acquaints them with their working environment, thereby helping them to become productive quickly.
- Despite high unemployment, there is still a shortage of trained people in South Africa. Intensive training is needed to provide the human resources that are necessary for commerce and industry to be effective. Good training provides employees with information tailored to make them more productive. Training also serves to increase the loyalty and raise the morale of employees. A training programme with effective feedback and evaluation techniques enables employees to reach the required performance level in their jobs in a relatively short time.
- Training helps to improve the quantity and quality of an organisation's output. It reduces costs incurred through wastage and through maintaining inefficiently used machinery and equipment, and also reduces the number and costs of accidents. Good training can reduce labour turnover as well as absenteeism, and it promotes job satisfaction. Technological developments make continual training essential for new employees, as well as for employees who have been in the service of the organisation for some time.

Beach (1985:244) outlines the benefits of effective training for any organisation as follows:

- *Reduced learning time and cost:* With proper training, employees learn rapidly to do the job to the required standard; they become familiar with safety measures and learn how to avoid wastage of materials. There is a reduction in maintenance and repair costs of damaged equipment.
- *Improved job performance:* Training enables employees to raise their level of performance, and as a result, output increases and quality improves.
- *Less supervision is required:* Properly trained employees know what to do and therefore require less supervision, which saves the time of the supervisors.

- *The right attitudes are fostered:* Because employees are exposed to similar inputs in training programmes, they all tend to become more loyal and committed to the organisation.
- *Better recruitment and selection:* A sound training programme can attract new applicants and is an incentive to existing employees.
- *Human resources needs are met:* Training and development provide employees with the skills required to meet human resources needs.
- *Benefits to employees themselves:* Employees who acquire knowledge and skills increase their earning capacity and their value in the labour market. This increases their job security and creates opportunities for promotion to more responsible jobs.
- *Increased customer satisfaction:* Because training makes employees more effective, improved goods and services can be provided.

Training may look easy to a casual observer, but there are certain problems that may seriously complicate the trainer's task. The following are the major pitfalls to be avoided in training:

- *Placing the primary responsibility for employee training and development on training staff only:* The direct line supervisor and the employee should ultimately have the final responsibility for the employee's training and development.
- *Lack of experience on the part of the trainer:* This means that unqualified staff run programmes, which implies poor training that cannot be expected to be effective.
- *Training and development undertaken with no specific purpose in mind:* Training should be undertaken only when a definite need among individuals or in the organisation in general has been identified.
- *Substituting training for selection:* This might occur, for instance, when a manager tries to overcome an error in the recruitment of an employee by trying to train an unsuitable employee. Training seldom cures a poor recruitment effort.
- *Ill-timed employee assessment:* Employers and trainers often evaluate an employee very soon after he or she has begun a new job, when he or she has not yet had time to settle down. Trainers and superiors may in such a case recommend and undertake additional training and development, which may be unnecessary.
- *Regarding training and development as an activity limited to courses only:* Many trainers and employers forget that the work environment itself provides excellent opportunities for job-related learning by employees, and consequently fail to realise the value of on-the-job and vestibule training.
- *Inadequate evaluation of training:* When a training programme is undertaken but not properly assessed, further training programmes are jeopardised because there is no proof of the effectiveness of the programme.
- *Cost versus benefit squeeze:* Training and development programmes often prosper in economically sound periods, but are axed during recessionary times. This happens when top management believes that no actual monetary

benefit is derived from training and development programmes. It is up to training and development specialists to convince management that there is a constant need for training and development.

- *Management is too busy* or lacks the time and conviction to motivate and support training and development specialists in developing and implementing effective training programmes. The result is second-rate training.
- *Too much emphasis on the staff role of the instructor:* This results in training managers not being given sufficient authority to do their job properly. The problem stems from the failure of top management to assess the contribution of training and development to the objectives of the organisation.
- *Trying to change the personalities of the trainees:* It is practically impossible to change the personality of an employee by training and development. Too much concern with the trainee's personality, coupled with too little emphasis on his or her performance, may cause the training programme to fail.
- *Lumping together training and development:* Trainers often try to conduct both these activities simultaneously. This is impracticable, because training and development imply different activities, although they may sometimes overlap.
- *Random crash programmes with no continuity:* Here training is regarded as a panacea and is not based on a needs analysis, with the result that it does not work.
- *Failing to prepare trainees:* It is a mistake to assume that all employees are motivated to undergo training. The opposite is true—employees often do not understand why they should undergo training, and in such cases training cannot be expected to succeed.
- *Training with limited practical application:* Programmes are often devised with too much emphasis on theory and too little attention to on-the-job problems. For training to be effective, it must link up with the actual job the trainee does or will be doing.

From the above it is clear why training is important to any organisation, particularly in view of the benefits that can be derived from training.

21.9 LEARNING PRINCIPLES APPLICABLE TO TRAINING

The success of training and development programmes depends on the selection of the right programme for the specific trainees. A needs analysis is necessary to identify the staff members who need training and to devise a programme that will meet those specific identified needs. The course should be designed in such a way that both the content and the methods of the programme are tailored to suit the needs of the trainees. Some of the principles applicable to learning are discussed below:

- *Motivation* plays a decisive part in any training programme. There are two kinds of motivation and both are important in learning:
  — Intrinsic motivation is the enjoyment that the trainee finds in the learning itself, and the sense of accomplishment it brings. He or she

knows that the training will reward him or her with greater job satisfaction in future.

— Extrinsic motivation is derived from the expectation of the reward that will come to the trainee if he or she completes the learning task successfully. Such a reward might be a bonus, salary increase or promotion.

- *Guidance and recall:* Guidance early in the training process greatly facilitates learning, but it should be given in such a way that the trainee is allowed to learn from his or her errors. Developing the powers of recall is important because it helps trainees to remember what they have learned, and because it increases their alertness and involvement by requiring them to demonstrate or apply what they have learned.

- *Reinforcement* is closely related to motivation, and is sometimes called "the law of effect". It is based on the idea that behaviour is fairly easily learned and repeated if it clearly leads to a reward or satisfies a need. Trainees learn best if reinforcement of the appropriate behaviour takes place as soon as possible. They must be rewarded for their new behaviour patterns in ways that satisfy their needs, for example by increased pay or recognition. Standards of performance should be set. Norms provide goals which, when attained, reward trainees with a feeling of accomplishment.

- *Knowledge of results* is also related to motivation, because it gives trainees insight into the learning process. Employees given feedback on their performance and the opportunity to correct their errors learn a good deal faster.

- *Learning by doing:* In many cases trainees find it difficult to understand what they are learning unless they physically do certain procedures. This may involve sight, hearing, touch, smell and even taste—all reinforce learning by holding the learner's attention and concentration, and so speed up the learning process itself.

- *Learning motor skills:* In learning work that requires motor skills, certain movements are important, but these are under sensory control. Examples are carpentry, welding and setting up and operating machine tools. Training is more effective if the learners are shown the materials, tools and equipment while receiving instruction as to their nature and use. Trainees should also practise using these, to make learning really effective. However, periods of practice should be interspersed with periods of rest, since short, interrupted practice sessions are usually better for acquiring motor skills than prolonged, concentrated sessions.

- *Learning concepts and attitudes* is much more complex than learning motor skills. At one extreme there is rote learning, by means of which the trainee has to master, for example, the names of the parts of a machine or a computer language. At the other extreme are subjects intended to increase depth of understanding, change beliefs or impart attitudes. The important principle here is to encourage learners to explore problems and issues in depth so that they can discover relationships and principles for themselves. Time should also be allowed in this type of learning for trainees to work on exercises and problems related to the concepts to be learned or attitudes to be changed. It is also important for the trainer to adopt a democratic participative style of leadership, which tends to promote the learning of new concepts and attitudes.

- *Whole or part learning:* Which of these approaches is needed depends on the trainee's powers of comprehension and on the nature of the material. If the learning material is long and complicated, it is advisable to break it up into parts, to be learned section by section. However, if the learning material consists of subsections or forms a natural unit that is short and simple, trainees will have little trouble in learning it as a whole.

- *Learning curves and plateaus:* Learning does not always progress at the same rate during a training programme. According to Schuler (1981:338):

  > *Different rates of learning can be described by learning curves and plateaus, which illustrate the relationship between the time an individual spends learning the task for which he or she is being trained and the rate of success in acquiring that skill.*

  For example, people may find that they learn less per hour as the study hours pass. This pattern of learning is described as a *decreasing return curve*. An *increasing return curve* occurs when someone learns very slowly at first and then faster as he or she begins to understand and correlate the material. A plateau is reached when there is a temporary levelling-off in the learning process. It may happen when motivation and the initial excitement of learning decline for a while before picking up again. Another reason is that the trainee may have to synthesise what has been learned before he or she can proceed to the next step.

- *Transfer of training* may facilitate the learning process, for example when a particular learning activity can be applied to a new one which has similar components, although the new task as a whole may be different. The instructor can help in this process of transfer by pointing out the components in the old job that are similar to those in the new job.

- *Meaningful learning and rote learning:* Learners gain far more from material they understand than from material learned by heart, without understanding. Trainees should therefore be encouraged to find summaries or governing principles in their work that will enable them to organise what they are learning. They will then find the material more logical and will arrive at intelligent answers to problems, which is far less likely in rote learning.

- *Trainees learn best at their own pace:* People have individual and different learning speeds, depending on their abilities and powers of comprehension. This must be taken into account during training. Self-pacing is effective and indeed often essential, because it allows individuals to respond at rates that enable them to assimilate information at the speed that matches their abilities.

484

- *Different kinds of learning require different training processes:* Trainees learn better if learning materials and methods are suited to their particular learning activities. A wide range of learning material is available for training, and only the most appropriate material and processes should be determined and used.

The above shows how important learning principles are if instructors hope to train effectively. By applying the various principles of learning, trainers can ensure successful training, and trainees will learn more quickly and effectively.

Adult learning

Trainees in industry are mostly adults. Because the learning style of adults differs considerably from that of children, there are a number of additional learning principles that trainers should bear in mind. In this regard we also refer to Fact Sheets Nos 218–20 of the Institute for Personnel Management (1992), which deal with basic adult education.

During the learning process, adults experience episodes of reintegration in which concepts or principles learned earlier are re-evaluated in terms of personal experience. Knowledge that is of little practical value to the adult is apparently "lost" in these integrating episodes, while useful knowledge is rediscovered and integrated with practical experience. It seems that in adults, learning is related to personal experience and is less abstract than in children. But, like children, adults learn by doing. It also seems that for adults to learn new concepts or principles, they must first "unlearn" or reintegrate what they already know and then link the old and new information. This may appear to present an insurmountable obstacle to instructors, but techniques such as breaking down a task into small units can stimulate the learning process in adults. It helps them not to regard it as threatening—they gradually gain confidence as they become used to learning again. Learning units can then be increased and will be accepted with increasing confidence. Children generally learn from curiosity, while adults are more interested in gaining knowledge for its application in the near future. Adults are motivated to learn to enable them to solve problems at work, to prepare themselves for an occupation or to increase competence in some area with which they are already familiar. Therefore, while many adults tend to resist learning for its own sake, they will be eager to learn something that they regard as useful. Camp *et al.* (1986:89) state:

> The need to know and the readiness to learn are critical aspects in the success of adult learning programmes. The "need to know" refers to the value of the knowledge to the learner. "Readiness to learn" refers to the amount or prerequisite knowledge the trainee possesses and the trainee's subjective opinion of his or her ability to learn the material.

Adults also prefer to plan their own learning and to adopt a self-directed approach because they like to set their own pace, establish their own structure and keep their own options open to revise the training method. In adults the will to learn is however a prerequisite for successful learning. Adults want guidance and not grades; the emphasis should therefore be on development that adults see as beneficial to them in their work and their career. Adults will consequently judge their learning experience according to what they gained from it and not according to the grades they achieved.

Finally, anyone training adults should take into account his or her pupils' physical and mental aptitudes and should bear in mind that they will learn only what they deem desirable and necessary. The instructor should understand that adults try to integrate new information into their existing system of knowledge and that they react to new knowledge as they reacted in the past. If they fail to achieve satisfactory results, they do the same things over and over with increasing frustration. To overcome this problem, adults should be exposed to training which is related to actual problems rather than to predetermined theoretical and abstract notions. Different approaches could apply when identical learning material is taught to different cultural groups at supervisory and lower levels in organisations.

21.10 HOW TO IMPLEMENT EFFECTIVE TRAINING

In this section the whole field of implementing training is discussed, from identifying training needs in accordance with the objectives of the organisation to evaluating a training programme.

Organisational objectives and job performance: The effective achievement of the objectives of the organisation should be the ultimate aim of any training and development strategy. This means that the short-term and long-term objectives of the organisation and trends likely to affect these objectives must be analysed. It also means that organisational planning, which includes human resources planning, recruitment, selection and placement of staff in the organisation, must be effective. Only when strategic planning has been done, can the organisation's objectives be translated into specific demands for the human resources and skills required, and only then can programmes for supplying the necessary skills be developed and implemented. Training and development therefore play a prominent part in matching what employees have to offer with the demands of the organisation.

Training should be given only if it can help to solve specific problems in the organisation. This requires a needs analysis at three levels. First, training needs at the organisational level should be identified by analysing the organisation in its totality, as well as general weaknesses. Secondly, needs may be identified at the occupational level, and these refer to what employees require in terms of skills, knowledge and attitudes to carry out the various duties in their job or occupation. Thirdly, training needs at the individual level may be identified: specific deficiencies that prevent individual workers from operating optimally.

This discussion focuses on the identification of individual needs through assessment or appraisal. The assessor compares the standard of performance *required* from individuals with their *actual* performance standard. The difference reveals the performance gap and therefore the training needed.

486

It is important to note that training is not necessarily the cure for all the problems in an organisation. It may be that there are faulty materials, processes, equipment or engineering designs that prevent effective performance by employees. It could also be that quality or standards are set at an unrealistic level or that the workload makes high quality impossible, or that some workers sabotage the productive efforts of others. Training will not rectify these deficiencies in an organisation.

Identifying individuals in the organisation who lack particular skills, knowledge or attitudes can pinpoint specific training needs. There are definite steps to be taken in discovering training needs. First, pinpoint organisational and production problems, such as low productivity, high costs, poor materials control, poor production quality, excessive scrap and waste, conflict between management and employees, excessive numbers of grievances, high labour turnover, excessive absenteeism and failure to meet production schedules. Secondly, analyse jobs and employees by means of job analysis and performance appraisal. Thirdly, invite the opinions of both management and workers by means of interviews and questionnaires. Fourthly, anticipate problems that might arise with future expansion of the organisation, new products, services, designs or technology. Such an analysis could indicate possible training needs.

From the above it can be deduced that training can be either *reactive* or *proactive*. Reactive training applies to existing situations and problems, while proactive training is intended to anticipate future problems and expectations; it is therefore regarded as management development.

As we have stated, identifying training needs is done by assessing the difference between the required performance standard and the actual performance standard. This is the performance gap, which indicates the training need. Identifying training needs therefore entails a specific analysis of each worker's performance. The model proposed by Ivancevich (1992) can be used to good effect for this purpose. It is depicted in figure 21.4 and discussed below.

Step 1—Pinpoint deficiencies in performance (behavioural deficiencies): As we have said, the first step is to determine the performance gap. Only once this is done can one go on to the next step.

Step 2—Analyse the cost/benefit: The trainer now needs to determine the cost and the value of training an employee. In other words, will it be worth the expense?

Step 3—Is it a case of "can't do" or "won't do"? It is important to establish whether the employee could do the job if he or she wanted to. To establish this, three questions need to be answered:

- Does the employee know what standard of performance is expected?
- Could the employee do the job if he or she wanted to?
- Does the employee want to do the job?

To answer these questions, the trainer must carefully observe, listen and ask questions. (Steps 4–9 apply to "can't do" problems.)

FIGURE 21.4: Performance analysis: the analysis of training needs

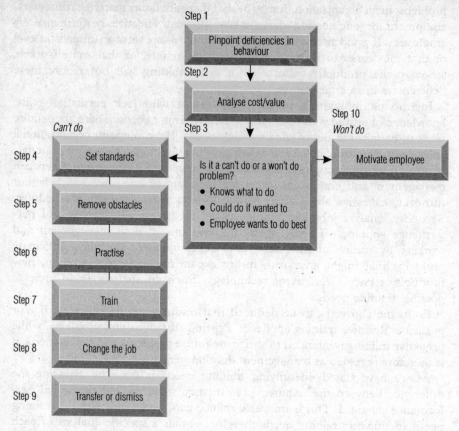

Source: Ivancevich (1992:490)

Step 4—Set the performance standard: If the employee does not know what the standards are, his or her work will probably fall below it. Once the standard is explained to the employee, his or her performance will probably improve.

Step 5—Remove obstacles: Try to identify and remove any obstacles the employee may be encountering at present, which may be impeding effective performance.

Step 6—Provide practice: When an employee has the opportunity to practise, his or her performance usually improves.

Step 7—Training: If training is necessary, then provide it (the rest of this chapter is devoted to this).

Step 8—Change the job: Redesign the job by means of job enrichment, job simplification or job enlargement.

Step 9—Transfer or dismiss: If all else fails, it may be necessary to transfer the employee or terminate his or her services.

Step 10—Create a motivational climate: It is often the case that an employee could do the job if he or she wanted to, but he or she does not want to. This is a motivational problem. In this case a motivational programme should be offered and, depending on the employee's behaviour after completing the course, he or she should be either rewarded or punished.

Performance analysis applies only to workers who are already employed. Training needs for new employees are identified by using *task analysis* and *job inventory* methods.

Methods used to identify the training needs of supervisors include questionnaires, the critical event method, exit interviews, performance reviews, check-lists and observation.

Once training needs have been identified, the next phase is to identify specific learner needs.

21.10.1 Identifying learner needs

Learner needs can be identified only if there is agreement on what an employee's job consists of and how it is to be performed. In other words, a job analysis should have been conducted. Nadler's (1982) model (figure 21.5) depicts the process of determining learner needs and implementing an appropriate training course.

Note that the first elements of the model have already been discussed. It is obvious that the needs of the organisation and those of the individual must be matched, for if individual needs and objectives are in conflict with the objectives of the organisation, the training will be a waste of time.

In order to establish the training needs of individual employees, the following sources can be consulted: production records, performance appraisal, other supervisors and the employee himself or herself. Methods that could be used are meetings, observation, questionnaires and various tests.

21.10.2 Determining training objectives

Objectives are statements of what is to be accomplished. A training objective is thus a specified level of performance the learner must have achieved once training has been completed. The objective must specify skills, knowledge or attitudes. Any learning objective must be expressed in the following terms: first, performance, i.e. what the learner ought to be able to do by the end of the learning experience; secondly, the condition, i.e. the limitations or constraints under which the performance is expected to take place; thirdly, the criteria, i.e. what the accepted level of performance is. According to Nadler (1982), if the correct decisions have been made, the following questions will have positive answers: Are the programmed objectives acceptable? Are the learning objectives acceptable? Are all the needs reflected in the objectives? Is the priority order of learning objectives acceptable? Do the objectives relate to specified job performance?

FIGURE 21.5: The critical event model

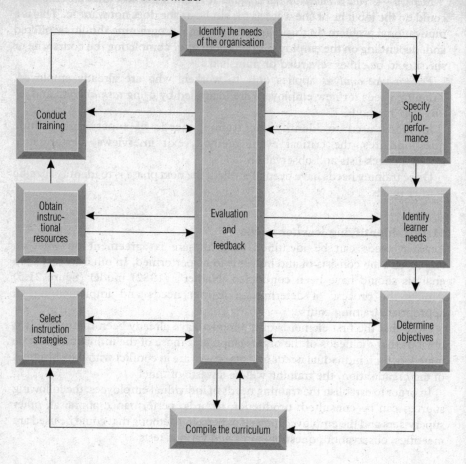

Source: Nadler (1982:12)

Training objectives should thus be defined in behavioural terms, specifying exactly what the learner will be able to accomplish after the successful completion of the training. They provide the focus of the efforts of the trainee and the trainer and are a bench mark for the determination of the success or failure of the training programme.

21.10.3 Compiling a curriculum
What the learner has to learn must be broadly formulated in a curriculum. Subjects are classified in one of four categories, namely essential, helpful, peripheral and unrelated. A list of specific items to be learned is then drawn up and prioritised. In other words, the curriculum lists both the subject and a sequence of the material to be learned.

Lesson plans must also be drawn up to guide the instructor in directing the learning of the learners. Lesson plans could employ the *job instruction technique,* which means that four steps are followed in presenting a lesson, namely preparation, presentation, application and verification. (This technique is discussed in detail in chapter 22.)

21.10.4 Selecting instructional strategies and obtaining resources
Various methods can be used in training. (Training methods are discussed in detail in chapter 22.)

The term *instructional resources* refers to the physical, financial and human resources necessary to offer the training. Physical resources are the equipment, buildings, films, overhead projectors, transparencies, and so on. Financial resources are the monies used for the training. In order to obtain financial resources the trainer needs to draw up a budget in advance. (Training costs are discussed in chapter 22.) Human resources need to be scheduled as well; the person or people who will conduct the training are selected. The organisation's own trainer or external trainers could be used.

21.10.5 Conducting and evaluating training
In this phase, the previously designed training programme is presented. Participants in the training programme are selected on the basis of the programme's learning objectives and the instructional methods used.

Evaluation of the training programme can only take place if objectives had been clearly defined in behavioural terms. (Evaluation is discussed in detail in chapter 22.)

If the process of training, from the assessment of job performance to the evaluation of the training programme, is tackled as we recommend here, it is easy for the instructor to rectify problems or to refine the programme if it is to be used again.

21.11 COMPETENCE-BASED MODULAR TRAINING
For decades South Africa followed a time-based system of skills training, especially in the training of artisans. The time-based apprenticeship system, however, had a braking effect on the flow of artisans to the labour market in South Africa.

The Manpower Training Amendment Act (No. 39 of 1990) effected the following changes:
- The changeover from a time-based training system for apprentices to a performance- or competence-based modular training system;
- The evaluation of artisan training by means of skills tests;
- The designation of trades and the announcement of the qualifying conditions for apprenticeship by the Minister on the recommendation of an accredited training board.

This amendment to the Act did not take place overnight, but developed gradually. The National Training Board (1991:30–68) issued various publications in this connection, including *The NTB/HSRC investigation into the training of artisans* (1985), *Guidelines for the institution of modular training of apprentices* (1987), *Further training and retraining of artisans* (1987), *Guidelines for the implementation of competence-based modular training: a guide for instructors* (1988); and *Decentralisation of artisan tests* (1990). All these publications ultimately contributed to the promulgation of the Manpower Training Amendment Act in 1990. These changes, especially those in artisan training, represent an important milestone in the quest for more effective training in South Africa.

One of the main advantages of the modular competence-based system is that training is soundly structured and based on the individual.

The NTB report, *Guidelines for the implementation of competence-based modular training: a guide for instructors* (1988:151), defines competence-based modular training as follows:

The training system is a modular system which has been designed, developed, implemented, controlled and evaluated so that trainees can achieve a definite level of competence in work-related tasks.

The term "modular" is defined as follows:

It includes the fact that the content of the programme is structured into definable modules, and that these modules are arranged in an interlocking progressive training system, in which progress is based on being able to comply with measurable criteria for achievement (competence) in certain modules before tackling further modules.

The information given below has been taken from the first few pages of *Guidelines for the implementation of competence-based training: a guide for instructors* (1988:1–6), which sets out the whole system in broad outline. Readers who require more information are advised to study the report in full.

21.11.1 Origin

Competence-based modular training may be regarded as a modern training method or system. The final objective, namely the mastery of certain prescribed skills, is however an age-old principle that has always been part of practical training to a greater or lesser extent.

Taking the traditional working method of a blacksmith as an example, the training procedure may be explained as follows: The craftsman first gave the apprentice a practical demonstration of how to make a chisel. The apprentice was then permitted to do the job on his own. The procedure for making a chisel was passed on to the apprentice orally and he had to translate the knowledge acquired in this way into a practical form. The training involved the repetition of a practical task until the necessary skill had been acquired and the completed chisel met all the requirements.

Any apprentice must also be informed in advance of the purpose of and necessity for the training and the conditions under which the job must be done.

Once all the aspects of the trade have been explained to the apprentice, he or she is familiarised with the duties, tasks and responsibilities required.

21.11.2 Description

Competence-based modular training focuses on the ability of the learner to master a specific skill. The training programme comprises a set of clearly defined learning objectives that are attained by carrying out specific actions or tasks. The training method is designed and structured as accurately as possible so that the learner will be able to attain the required level of mastery or competence. The most important characteristic of a competence-based modular training programme is that the learner is expected to master fully all the skills objectives set for a particular occupation in order to be regarded as competent.

A further characteristic of a competence-based modular training programme is that learners are individually held responsible for the successful mastery of a skills objective, while the instructor manipulates and uses external conditions in an attempt to ensure that the learner will attain the required level of mastery.

Competence-based modular training is based on the following principles:

- Competence is an internal and external condition that is chiefly personal in nature;
- To attain competence in a certain area, diverse training methods must necessarily be used;
- Competence is more easily acquired if the learner is positively motivated.

The attainment of the required level of competence during the training process means that the learner has to achieve certain prerequisites before he or she can qualify and be regarded as competent for the task.

Competence-based modular training may be regarded as a training technology that attempts to assess human performance on the basis of specified criteria or standards. It therefore largely deviates from the norm-based evaluation system which tries to explain and evaluate human performance on the basis of a normal distribution curve.

The differences between a competence-based modular training approach and the traditional norm-based system are summarised in table 21.1.

Because a competence-based modular training programme is chiefly aimed at making learners more competent for a particular task, individual differences have to be addressed. With this method of training there is consequently a shift in emphasis from the group to the individual, which means that training is more purposeful. The system is ideal for the training of apprentices in South Africa because its primary aim is to enable the learner to master predetermined skills objectives, which can be measured against specific standards or criteria.

The series of tasks that must be carried out to develop a competence-based modular training programme for effective skills training is contained in figure 21.6 on page 497.

TABLE 21.1: Differences between competence-based modular training and the traditional norm-based system

Traditional norm-based training or instruction	Competence-based modular training
Expectations linked to abilities and motivation	
1. Not all learners will be able to pass; the results will represent a normal distribution.	1. All learners selected for a competence-based modular training programme will be able to pass the course. Their results are based on the number of performance or skills objectives they have mastered.
2. The trainer regards it as his or her primary task to motivate the learner to achieve higher performance. The success he or she achieves in this may be ascribed to the training methods applied.	2. Learner success is a prerequisite for motivation: "Nothing succeeds like success." Because learners are kept informed of their progress, their performance and motivation are enhanced.
Final objective of the training	
3. The object of the training is to enable each individual to develop according to his or her particular abilities and to evaluate his or her performance in relation to that of other people.	3. The object of the training is to allow each individual to develop in such a way that he or she will be competent to master certain skills objectives at specified levels of competence. His or her performance is not compared with that of others.
The setting of skills objectives	
4. The idea of skills objectives is accepted but is not necessarily defined in measurable terms. Learners are permitted to discover for themselves and opportunities are created for them to express their drive for self-assertion.	4. The setting of skills objectives emphasises competence, and learners are informed as to: • What they will have to be able to do; • Under what circumstances the task will have to be performed; • How well the task will have to be performed (the minimum standards). The attainment of the required standards is left to the learner, i.e. he or she is dependent on his or her own progress.
Shift in emphasis during training	
5. Instructor-centred: the instructor remains the focal point. He or she decides what method is to be used to convey factual knowledge to the group. The emphasis is chiefly on	5. Learner-directed: each learner has to receive effective and efficient instruction or training to enable him or her to master the skills objectives. The trainer's method of presentation and

demonstration or instruction and not on mastery.	use of resources vary with each skills objective. Emphasis is on mastery and not on the method of instruction or presentation.

Purpose and basis of testing

6. The aim of measurement and testing is to determine the learners' acquired knowledge and compare their performance with that of others in the group in order to determine whether individuals are progressing satisfactorily.	6. The aim of testing after each module has been completed is to compare learners' performance with the standards prescribed by a particular skills objective. This testing takes place during and after completion of a specific training programme.
7. Remedial instruction is provided for learners experiencing problems in completing certain tasks according to particular requirements. The requirements that apply are not necessarily set at a particular level of mastery.	7. The results obtained after each learner has been tested against a particular skills objective indicate whether corrective measures are required. If the standards set have not been attained, the learner is not considered competent to progress to more difficult tasks.

The setting of certain entry requirements for the course and for learning units

8. Learners are permitted to start a new course or progress to higher units as soon as they have met the requirements for a pass.	8. Learners have to master all the basic modules of the unit or level concerned before being permitted to progress to a higher level. Their progress therefore depends on how well they perform at the various levels and whether they have achieved the prescribed levels of mastery.

Learning time versus mastery

9. The learning time and the number of practical tasks a learner has to perform are kept constant and the results are permitted to vary.	9. The learning time and the tests (criteria) are varied in accordance with the structure of the course, while the results are constantly fixed at mastery. If the learner has not attained the required level of mastery during his or her first criterion test, limited repetition of tests is permitted.

Results

10. The final evaluation marks obtained by most learners vary between 15% and 85%, with an average figure of 50%.	10. The results are described as "skills objectives mastered"; requirements are set at 100% for a particular level.

Evaluation	
11. The course and test content are determined in advance by experts in the particular field.	11. Skills objectives are evaluated against the requirements of a particular occupation. Criterion tests are evaluated through direct comparison with skills objectives. Performance testing is based on in-task training requirements.
12. Instructors are evaluated according to the syllabus completed in the time available and according to the marks individuals obtained in the tasks.	12. Instructors are evaluated on the basis of the degree to which each learner has mastered the prescribed skills objectives and how successful the instructor was in motivating learners to achieve higher performance.
Accountability	
13. Since there are no prescribed skills objectives in the training process, the instructors are obliged to follow a particular prescribed training schedule.	13. The trainer is held responsible for seeing that learners master the required skills objectives. The skills objectives are formulated and approved in advance.

Source: NTB (1988)

21.12 THE TRAINING OF SUPERVISORS IN SOUTH AFRICA

Supervisors control the activities of lower-level employees and through those employees in their charge they are responsible for carrying out the policy and achieving the objectives of management. For lower-level employees, supervisors represent management. The supervisor's attitude to the organisation affects the contribution workers are prepared to make to achieve the objectives of the organisation. Supervisors act as a model and example to subordinates. They are the link between higher management levels and lower-level employees, and for this reason it is essential that supervisors do their work effectively.

The Institute of Personnel Management (Fact Sheet No. 14) suggests the following questions to check whether a supervisor is doing his or her job effectively. The supervisor requires assistance if the answer to any of the questions is "yes", and he or she should receive training in the identified area.

- Does the supervisor fail to get the best out of the workers?
- Has he or she failed to tell them what they are doing and why they are doing it?
- Is absenteeism among people under his or her supervision high?
- Is discipline poor?
- Are workers often late?
- Is the labour turnover in his or her department high compared with other departments?

FIGURE 21.6: Sequence of tasks to develop a competence-based modular training programme

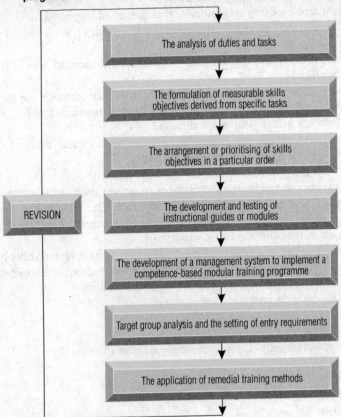

The analysis of duties and tasks

The formulation of measurable skills objectives derived from specific tasks

The arrangement or prioritising of skills objectives in a particular order

REVISION

The development and testing of instructional guides or modules

The development of a management system to implement a competence-based modular training programme

Target group analysis and the setting of entry requirements

The application of remedial training methods

Source: NTB (1988)

- Do new employees working under the supervisor leave within the first three months?
- Is the accident rate high?
- Does it happen regularly that management hears of accidents under his or her supervision too late to take effective action?
- Is the supervisor often overloaded with work while his or her subordinates are under-utilised?

Poor supervision may, however, be due to factors such as inadequate support from senior management, an ineffective organisational structure, a lack of proper guidance from management and poor working conditions. These issues cannot be rectified by subjecting supervisors to training.

It is important that supervisors be fully informed about the reasons for training. Before training needs are finalised, the instructor should take note of their comments in order to determine their specific training needs. Supervisors could be asked the following questions:

- Do you know of ways to improve the quality of supervision?
- Do you want to increase your own job knowledge? With regard to which aspects of your job?
- Do you understand the reasons for the work done and how it is done in your section?
- Do you understand the basis on which your subordinates are paid?
- Do you understand the organisation's human resources policy and other benefits that affect your subordinates?
- Do you understand the organisation's attitude to trade unions?
- Do you know the extent of your authority?
- Do you know enough about accident prevention?
- Do you encourage your subordinates to act on their own initiative?
- Do you know how the various workers' duties are defined?

Questions of this nature will indicate to the instructor the areas on which to concentrate in training a specific supervisor.

According to the Institute for Personnel Management (Fact Sheet No. 217), supervisors should have various levels of knowledge about the work they do:

- An understanding of their role in the organisation;
- Problem-solving and decision-making;
- Planning;
- Organisation;
- Time management (their own time and that of others);
- Delegation;
- Giving instructions;
- The empowerment of subordinates;
- Control;
- Leadership;
- Effective communication (both verbal and written);
- The bridging of communication barriers;
- Team work and the initiation of team leader strategies;
- The effective chairing of meetings;
- The management of change;
- The motivation of people;
- An understanding of how the organisation functions;
- Understanding employee behaviour;
- Handling conflict;
- Implementing quality procedures;
- Giving effective feedback;
- Effective cooperation with workers, peers and managers;
- Carrying out recruitment and making appointments.

These aspects will give supervisors an overall grasp of their work, which means that they will have an holistic understanding of their work.

There are also socio-economic changes that directly influence supervisors in their work environment and that should also be covered in training:

- *Understanding and implementation of the organisation's policies and rules:* Supervisors may be expected to know and understand the policies and practices relating to, for example, job evaluation, grading and wage deductions. However, many supervisors lack a basic understanding of policies, practices and structures. Training should therefore focus on these issues.
- *Job structure and authority:* Black supervisors are often accorded little status and authority by their superiors, and consequently their power to manage subordinates effectively is practically non-existent. These problems can be remedied if supervisors receive support from top management and the necessary training. The role of black supervisors is becoming increasingly important and it is therefore essential that they receive correct and effective training to enable them to do their job effectively and thereby contribute to productivity in South Africa.
- *Human resources policy:* After the recommendations of both the Wiehahn and Riekert commissions had been embodied in legislation, many changes in the labour policy were introduced, for example augmented training and the abolition of all discrimination in the work situation. Better training of supervisors can play a key role in influencing workers and the work environment positively to overcome resistance to these changes. This will be to the benefit of everybody in the work environment.
- *Industrial relations:* The recognition of trade unions through legislation has brought about changes in the power and authority of supervisors. Their authority has been modified, and often even eroded. Supervisors need to be trained to deal with trade union officials and shop stewards as well as with workers who are trade union members. Unacceptable behaviour on the part of the supervisor in dealing with these workers cannot be tolerated, as the risks of the consequences for the organisation are too great. Therefore training in industrial relations is of great importance in South Africa's work environment.
- *Intergroup conflict in the work situation:* Supervisors have long been recognised as key figures in socio-political problems and problems related to cultural diversity in South Africa. This is because the relationship between themselves and their subordinates is so significant. Supervisors' values and attitudes often shape the attitudes and behaviour of their co-workers and subordinates. Therefore, if supervisors received interpersonal relations training at this level, they could contribute significantly to peace and stability in the workplace. The effectiveness of a supervisor in minimising intergroup conflict depends on his or her values and knowledge of company policy and of other management aspects. (More detail is given in chapter 19.)
- *Interpersonal contact and social interaction:* It is well known that intergroup stereotyping and prejudice can be alleviated by contact between members of the different groups. Frequent informal and social events should be

organised within the organisation. Training in order to develop inter-personal skills and understanding between different race groups could also promote better relations in the work environment, particularly at super-visory level.

The above issues are some of the major focal points in the South African business environment, and supervisors, in particular, are exposed to their concomitant problems. Training in these areas will enable supervisors to reduce labour unrest and to contribute to productivity, profitability and understanding between different groups in the work environment.

21.13 CONCLUSION

Although training has taken place since time immemorial, it is now (often erroneously) regarded as a cure-all for a variety of problems, especially in the business world. In the South African business environment, training only gained momentum after the promulgation of the Manpower Training Act, which formally structured training and gave detailed guidance as to how it should be implemented.

The Manpower Training Amendment Act (No. 39 of 1990) brought changes in especially the training of artisans, by moving away from a time-based system to a competence-based modular system. Training boards were set up, through which each industry accepted responsibility for its own training, based on its own needs.

The functions of the National Training Board were reformulated, and at present much greater focus is placed on research and support for the Depart-ment of Manpower, as well as on advising the Minister on policy matters. The NTB is committed to coordinating, encouraging, facilitating and promoting training at the national level. This includes the creation of a national training strategy, which will probably incorporate the initiatives of the ANC for training and development.

Trainers need to be aware of the serious consequences of training not properly conducted; it is a waste of the organisation's money. Training should not be haphazard. Training needs should be properly identified and training principles effectively applied. If these requirements are met, training will be of great value to any organisation.

Because of the importance of training boards and competence-based modular training, special attention was paid to these subjects in this chapter.

Supervisory training in South Africa has many shortcomings, but if training needs are properly identified and appropriate training implemented, super-visors will make a greater contribution to productivity than at present. In the next chapter we shall examine the various training methods and discuss evaluation as well as the benefits of training and development.

Questions

1. What, in your view, are the differences between training, development and education?
2. Discuss mistakes trainers make in your work environment when they conduct training.
3. List and evaluate the learning principles that are important when you are designing a specific training programme.
4. Do you think the national training strategy published in January 1994 by the NTB will be successful? Motivate your reply.
5. How would you determine the training needs of individual employees?
6. Describe the steps in initiating and executing a training programme in terms of the models outlined in this chapter.
7. What shortcomings are there in supervisory training in South Africa? How do you think these shortcomings can be corrected by means of training?
8. Discuss the application of the Manpower Training Amendment Act (No. 39 of 1990). Was the amendment effective, or should there be further amendments? Motivate.

Sources

African National Congress. 1994. *A policy framework for education and training.* ANC Education Department, Braamfontein.

African National Congress. 1994. *Reconstruction and development programme.* 7th draft, February. ANC Education Department, Braamfontein.

Beach, D.S. 1985. *Personnel: the management of people at work.* 5th edition. Macmillan, New York.

Camp, R., Blanchard, P.N. & Huszcszo, V.E. 1986. *Toward a more organizationally effective training strategy and practice.* Prentice-Hall, Englewood Cliffs, New Jersey.

Haasbroek, G.D. 1990. Training boards must become the leaders in their field. *Human Resource Management Journal,* Vol. 6, No. 9, September.

Institute for Personnel Management. 1974. *People and profits.* Fact Sheet No. 14, August.

Institute for Personnel Management. 1992. *People dynamics: investing in supervisors.* Fact Sheet No. 217, July.

Institute for Personnel Management. 1992. *People dynamics: adult basic education.* Part 1. Fact Sheet No. 218, August.

Institute for Personnel Management. 1992. *People dynamics: adult basic education.* Part 2. Fact Sheet No. 219, September.

Institute for Personnel Management. 1992. *People dynamics: adult basic education.* Part 3. Fact Sheet No. 220, October.

Ivancevich, J.M. 1992. *Human resource management: foundations of personnel.* 5th edition. Irwin, Homewood, Boston.

Nadler, L. 1982. *Designing training programmes through the critical events model.* Addison-Wesley, Reading, Massachusetts.

National Training Board. 1985. *The NTB/HSRC investigation into the training of artisans.* Government Printer, Pretoria.

National Training Board. 1987. *Guidelines for the establishment of modular training for apprentices.* Government Printer, Pretoria.

National Training Board. 1987. *Further training and retraining of artisans.* Government Printer, Pretoria.

National Training Board. 1988. *Guidelines for the implementation of competence-oriented modular training: a manual for trainers.* Government Printer, Pretoria.

National Training Board. 1990. *Decentralisation of artisan tests.* Government Printer, Pretoria.

National Training Board. 1991. *Annual report.* RP 35/1992. Government Printer, Pretoria.

National Training Board. 1992. *Annual report.* RP 58/1993. Government Printer, Pretoria.

National Training Board. 1994. *National training strategy initiative: a concept for an integrated approach to education and training.* April. Government Printer, Pretoria.

Schuler, R.S. 1981. *Personnel and human resource management.* West, New York.

Van Dyk, P.S., Nel, P.S. & Loedolff, P. van Z. 1992. *Training management: a multi-disciplinary approach to human resources development in Southern Africa.* Southern, Halfway House.

Chapter 22

Employee development: management and organisation development

P.S. Nel

STUDY OBJECTIVES

After studying this chapter, you should be able to:

- Explain the training and development process;
- Outline the factors that determine which training methods should be used;
- Describe on-the-job and off-the-job training and development methods;
- Explain management development as a part of organisation development;
- Indicate the importance of evaluating management development programmes;
- Explain why cost-benefit analysis of training and development is important.

22.1 INTRODUCTION

Management and organisation development is part of the throughput process and features in the job context environment. The interaction of management and organisation development in the various environments has a direct influence on the utilisation, status, recognition, task guidelines and objectives in the job content environment.

In the job context environment, it has an influence on the organisational culture, human resources and industrial relations policy, working conditions and intergroup and intragroup relations. In the external environment, it is

503

directly influenced by the national human resources policy, labour market conditions, technology and level of education in South Africa.

FIGURE 22.1: Principal learning components of management and organisation development

In chapter 21 we focused primarily on the training of lower-level employees such as supervisors and workers. However, some of the issues discussed are also applicable to the management development aspect of employee development. In this chapter, the focus is primarily on the development of individual managers, on the role of managers in the organisation and on development of the organisation as a whole (i.e. organisation development).

There are various connotations to the term "management development"; consequently there is much confusion about what is really meant by it. To eliminate misunderstanding it should be noted that there is a difference between the process and the context of management development. The *process* is primarily concerned with helping individual managers change their ways in such a manner that there will be a discernible improvement in their management skills—an improvement that will continue into the future. The *context* of management development depends on an organisation's needs related to the achievement of its objectives. The needs of an organisation are, for example, the number and types of employees, as well as their skills and abilities, in particular those of the managers required to achieve the organisation's stated objectives. In other words, the organisation needs to have sufficient managerial resources available to meet its objectives, or alternatively, it needs to change the organisation's existing managerial style through modifications in individual and group behaviour. (This is career development, discussed in chapter 9.) This is known as the *top-down view*. Another way of ensuring that the organisation will be successful in achieving its objectives is to consider the development needs of individual managers. This is known as the *bottom-up view*.

Development is defined by the IPB (1994:318) as:

A progressive change leading to higher levels of differentiation and organisation. The connotation is one of progressive progress, increases in effectiveness of function, maturity, sophistication, richness and complexity.

From this definition it is clear that management development is future-oriented. The broad definition of management development given in chapter 21 is refined as follows by Skinner and Ivancevich (1992:383):

The process of developing and educating selected personnel in the knowledge, skills, and attitudes needed to manage in future positions.

Why, then, are managers so important to an organisation? It is because managers are responsible for the planning, organising and control of most of the organisation's activities. This means that they are ultimately responsible for the organisation's effectiveness in achieving its objectives. Managers are, for example, responsible for ensuring that lower-level employees have the knowledge, skills and positive attitudes to do their jobs effectively. If managers themselves do not have the necessary skills, knowledge and attitudes, it cannot be expected that the organisation will achieve its objectives. Management development thus addresses the question of how managers need to behave to ensure the fulfilment of the organisation's goals and objectives.

Management development is essential for two reasons: it is seen as a means of improving the approach of managers towards subordinates in general, and of improving industrial relations in the organisation. It must be realised that productivity is determined by industrial relations *per se*, and that managers are in a position to contribute effectively to increased productivity in South Africa by treating industrial relations responsibly.

Management development in this area needs to be handled carefully, because managers do not simply need to learn to deal with individual subordinates, they need to learn to interact with workers' representatives and trade unions too.

Management development should be a continuous process of goal-directed exposure to various inputs which will give managers the necessary knowledge, skills and attitudes to execute their managerial task effectively and achieve their organisation's objectives. This could be a difficult task, because the business environment in South Africa is becoming more and more complex. Managers need to cultivate better judgement and the ability to make better decisions under increasingly complex working conditions, while avoiding obsolescence.

Each manager appointed in an organisation must focus on achieving the objectives of the organisation. It can therefore be accepted that the expectations of top management exert considerable pressure on subordinate managers to perform effectively. In order to carry out the tasks allocated to them effectively, managers must constantly update their knowledge and skills in the field of new developments in technology, the economy, politics, legislation and related business activities. Work pressure and rapid changes and developments in the field of business have meant that it is not always possible for managers to remain up to date, frequently resulting in obsolete management methods. Obsolescence means that a person in a particular job lacks the skill and knowledge that are regarded as important by other managers and that are essential for effective performance. This usually has an adverse influence on the functioning of an organisation and leads to stagnation and—in extreme cases—to bankruptcy.

One of the general new aims of management development is therefore to prevent management obsolescence.

According to Van Dyk *et al.* (1992:48), it is essential for an organisation to avoid obsolescence and to develop managers who can face new challenges in order to survive in a highly competitive and developing world economy.

Management development plays a vital role in the achievement of an organisation's objectives, although it has only recently become internationally established. Silver (1991:175) says:

> It was only in the mid-1980s, that we came to the conclusion when we looked at our five-year plans—and the constraints to growth—and lo and behold the major constraint was going to be the availability of skilled trained people . . . and development and training has become not only the flavour of the month, but the flavour of the next decade or so.

The above is confirmed by research undertaken by the NTB (1990). What is more, good managers can only remain good managers with the help of effective management development.

What, then, are the attributes of a good manager? The criteria for management success are primarily effective performance, intelligence, self-actualisation, self-assurance, decisiveness and independence in the sense of not needing the approval of others. It is clear that each of the characteristics mentioned requires a strong element of individuality on the part of the manager.

Camp *et al.* (1986:276–80) also list a number of characteristics managers should possess in order to be successful in their job. First, administrative knowledge and skills, which include planning, decision-making, organising and controlling abilities. Secondly, technical knowledge and skills, which consist of, for example, marketing, advertising and direct sales skills and knowledge of consumer psychology. Thirdly, interpersonal knowledge and skills, which include leadership qualities and communication skills. Fourthly, intellectual abilities such as conceptual, analytical and diagnostic ability, and personality traits such as work-orientated motivation, career orientation and initiative.

From these requirements it is easy to deduce what the objectives of a development programme for managers should be if they are to manage their organisations successfully. The programme should:

- Improve the present functioning of managers;
- Increase managers' satisfaction in their present job or managerial position;
- Develop the latent abilities and potential of managers, equipping them for the future needs of the organisation;
- Ensure that managerial obsolescence is prevented, whether technological (the Peter principle) or physical.

What is the basic content of management development? Management development should be primarily done on the job, to equip managers to deal with particular issues in their organisation. However, the following areas should be given special attention:

- Matters affecting the organisation, such as policies and procedures, plant facilities and union-management relations;
- Management principles and techniques, such as management information systems, strategic planning, human resources management, risk management, cost analysis and data processing;
- Human relations, motivation, conflict resolution, communication, human resources management responsibilities, supervision, selection, training, compensation, counselling and grievance handling;
- Technical knowledge and skills peculiar to the organisation;
- Economic, social and political issues, such as business ethics, the economic system in which the organisation operates, social responsibility and consumerism;
- Personal skills such as report writing, conducting meetings and effective speech.

It is obvious that not all these skills will be required by all managers at all levels in an organisation, and that the development needs of a newly appointed manager differ from those of an experienced manager. An experienced manager would, for example, need only slight coverage of issues like policies and procedures, whereas a new manager would study these topics in detail. Top managers should be exposed to economics, finance, organisation theory, administrative control, international and local business operations, and so on, while middle managers should be exposed to issues such as data processing, production planning and control and sound human resources management practices. The course contents therefore depend on the needs of the organisation and the level of the manager concerned.

In view of the issues discussed above, it is obvious that before an organisation decides to undertake management development, a number of factors should be considered. Development methods should be decided upon, and organisation development, the evaluation of management development programmes and the cost and possible benefits to the organisation have to be considered.

22.2 FACTORS THAT DETERMINE WHICH TRAINING AND DEVELOPMENT METHODS SHOULD BE USED

A review of recent references on human resources management reveals a large number of training and development methods for training supervisors and developing managers. The result is that the determination of the actual methods to be used creates enormous problems for the planners and presenters of management development programmes. It is difficult to select the method or combination of methods most likely to fit the management development needs of managers in a particular situation. Nel (1977:95–6) suggests that the factors listed below could aid decision-makers in the selection of training and development methods for managers and other employees:

- *Development objectives* should be selected in such a way that they suggest learning objectives and the best means to train or develop employees and managers.

- *Responses of learners and feedback:* The design and methods planned for the course should be determined by whether they allow instructors to correct errors or reinforce the learning that has taken place, and by the extent to which managers or employees in the training situation can measure their own responses. The ideal training and development method gives the instructor the opportunity to observe the development of an employee or manager and correct him or her by giving immediate feedback on performance.

- *The instructor's knowledge and level of skill:* The instructor's level of competence is revealed in feedback to management on successes that are attributable to good teaching. When the success of a training and development programme is being assessed, management should be careful to disregard those results that are not due to the instructor's teaching. Instructors who use methods with which they are not familiar can spoil the learning experience and cause unpleasant consequences for the learners. It is extremely important to employ competent instructors.

- *The time available* for a specific training and development programme often determines the method to be used, because some methods require much time, while others can be completed quickly. Management games and case studies, for example, demand more time to be effectively used than lectures and brainstorming.

- *Adaptability of methods:* A particular method can sometimes be effectively used for different types of learning for employees and managers. Although supervisors and managers, for example, come from different environments in an organisation, specific methods can be used in a variety of activities. An example is programmed instruction, which is extremely adaptable. When selecting methods, management should bear in mind that some training methods are easier to use and are more readily adaptable with small groups of learners. For instance, the smaller the group, the easier it is for role-play exercises to satisfy all the learners' needs.

- *Costs* play an important role in the selection of a training method. Four important elements need to be considered here:
  - When training and development programmes contain a variety of methods, particularly sophisticated ones, they can be very costly—even too costly to implement.
  - Certain training aids may be too expensive to use, even if they are considered essential support for particular teaching methods. For instance, closed-circuit television is prohibitively expensive and its use is only justified where large groups of learners are continually involved. The cost usually rules it out for a once-off exercise.

508

— Payment for the instructors and the costs of facilities need to be considered, as well as tuition fees for learners who attend external off-the-job courses.

— Costs should be measured against the effectiveness of course strategies: if the gains expected of a particular strategy do not offset additional costs incurred by the use of that strategy, a less costly instructional method should be sought, even though it may be slightly less effective. There also need to be corresponding savings in time, human resources and facilities to justify expensive teaching methods. (Cost is discussed in greater detail towards the end of this chapter.)

If the selection of training and development methods is carefully considered by instructors and used as guidelines when developing training and development programmes, the benefits derived from the application and usage of new techniques could be extremely advantageous to learners and ultimately to the organisation itself. On the other hand, if a mistake is made in the selection and use of training methods it could have severe repercussions, not only for the learners and their morale, but also in terms of lost profit and a tarnished image of the instructor and the training department in the organisation concerned.

We now examine the various training and development methods that can be used.

22.3 TRAINING AND DEVELOPMENT METHODS

There are three categories of training and development methods:

- *On-the-job training*, which means that trainees receive training in their work environment. The training is usually directly related to the job.
- *Off-the-job training and development* consist of seminars or classroom activities which can take place at the work premises or elsewhere, for example at a training centre. The majority of these activities involve *simulation techniques* to provide trainees with experience that they can later use in their work environment.
- *Organisation development*, whereby improvement in the organisation's effectiveness is achieved through modifications in individual and group behaviour. These behavioural modifications are brought about by the use of applied behavioural science.

It must be stressed that a number of the methods discussed below can be applied equally to supervisors, lower-level employees and managers.

22.3.1 On-the-job training

On-the-job training methods usually fit the needs of a particular employee and suit his or her background, knowledge and skills. Trainees learn by doing; they learn continuously and over a long period. Trainees are extensively influenced by their immediate superior; superiors are usually directly responsible for the training of their subordinates. According to Ferrell and Hirt (1993:322), on-the-job methods are thus regarded as:

allowing workers to learn by actually performing the tasks of the job. New employees work under the guidance of an experienced employee who can offer advice and suggestions for performing the job efficiently and effectively.

On-the-job training can however prevent trainees from acquiring a broad perspective and can adversely influence their perception of their job and how it fits into the activities of the organisation.

The following methods are generally used for on-the-job training or development.

Coaching

This is also called counselling. It entails the instruction of a subordinate by his or her superior with the purpose of developing the subordinate's potential. It includes daily guidance by the superior to develop the subordinate in his or her present position and to prepare him or her for promotion. It is a continuous process of learning based on the face-to-face relationship between superior and subordinate.

Coaching is a low-cost means of improving employees' performance in the department where they work. Solutions to problems can be found and subordinates can be given the opportunity to make suggestions to superiors regarding the work they do. It enables a superior to set tasks and to check the standard of work done. It is, however, only effective if the subordinates understand the relevance and value of their work and if the coaching is systematic and purposeful. The relationship between the superior and subordinates must be based on mutual trust if the method is to succeed.

Job rotation

Job rotation is a method whereby trainees receive training and gain experience in turn, under close supervision. According to Skinner and Ivancevich (1992:383), job rotation means that "managers are transferred from job to job on a systematic basis. Job assignments can last from two weeks to six months." According to Nel (1977:110), it is used to develop generalists with wide experience of the organisation to enable them to make high-level decisions later in their careers. By rotating through various jobs, learners cultivate a fresh approach which will enable them to establish new procedures and make changes in their existing jobs. Trainees are moved into new jobs for short periods of time. They need to be extensively briefed as to what is expected of them and their progress must be carefully checked. This method enables trainees to acquire specific practical experience quickly, instead of having to wait for opportunities to present themselves over a period of time through transfers and promotions. Job rotation is also an invaluable method for inducting a young graduate.

Junior boards

This method, also called multiple management, is usually employed to give promising managers experience in analysing the overall problems of the organisation. These managers are given assignments by top management to study problems identified by top managers, and to propose solutions. The members of junior boards, mostly promising middle and junior managers, usually rotate to ensure the continuity of the board's work in the organisation. This is an effective development method only if the problems assigned to the junior board are genuinely company-wide and cut across all departmental lines. Junior boards are not usually granted authority to take decisions, but merely to investigate and analyse problems and propose solutions to top management.

Job instruction training

This is a precise method for teaching a trainee to do a specific job. It compels all trainees to learn in a standard fashion. It is a way of quickly expanding manual and psychomotor skills, and is particularly applicable to lower-level workers. A number of steps are followed. The trainer decides what the employees are to be taught and ensures that the right tools, equipment, supplies and material are ready and the workplace properly arranged. Once this is done, trainees are instructed by means of the following four steps (Institute of Personnel Management, Fact Sheet No. 141):

- Preparing the workers. The trainer puts the workers at ease, explains what the job is and finds out what the workers already know about it. He or she gets workers interested in learning the job.
- Presentation of the operation. The trainer now describes, demonstrates and illustrates the new operation. He or she questions the learners to be sure that they have grasped the facts. Only one step should be given at a time, and key points should be stressed. The operation should be summarised in a second practical demonstration.
- Performance try-out. The learners are asked to perform the task while the trainer asks them the why, how, when and where of the job. Instruction continues until the instructor can see that the trainees have mastered the job.
- Follow-up. Trainees now work on their own but their work is checked to ensure that they follow instructions. The learners work under close supervision until they are qualified to work under normal supervision.

Understudy

This method resembles coaching and job rotation in some respects. Understudy is the temporary assignment of a manager to a more senior manager in order to broaden his or her managerial viewpoints by exposing him or her to various aspects of managerial practice. During a short period of time, the subordinate manager closely observes the activities of the senior manager and helps him or her to perform duties, and at the same time is given the opportunity to be coached. The method usually provides a trainee with a broader perspective because the work he or she does during training is normally carried out by the senior manager. Giving junior managers understudy assignments provides the organisation with a pool of potential managers who have been carefully observed and evaluated and could, if they were successful as understudies, be promoted at a later date to a higher level of authority in the organisation. It is also a popular career development method. It is therefore a practical and fairly quick way of preparing designated junior managers for greater management responsibility. The motivation to learn is usually high because "learning by doing" is emphasised.

Learner-controlled instruction

This method allows trainees to decide on the pace at which they choose to learn, as well as the specific methods used and the sequence of learning steps. They also evaluate their own learning. Methods that could be used are, for instance, case studies, simulations, group discussions, books and films. The instructor only acts as a facilitator and offers assistance to the trainees. There are no set lesson plans and no examinations. The instructors set learning objectives with the learners' participation. The learners themselves are expected to be accountable for meeting these agreed-upon objectives. This method is usually used in conjunction with other methods.

Apprenticeship training

This type of training dates back to Biblical times. It is used to train workers in trades such as toolmaking, armature winding, electronics and diesel mechanics. The major characteristic is that the apprentice works under the guidance of a skilled artisan. Naturally he or she receives lower wages than the artisan. According to an HSRC investigation (1985:32) an apprentice enters into a contract which can be registered only if the trade has been designated and the conditions of apprenticeship have been prescribed. These designated trades and conditions vary from one industry to another in South Africa, since they depend on the needs of a particular industry. Contract conditions include qualification requirements for apprenticeship, periods of apprenticeship, remuneration, technical studies required, centralised technical training and the use of log books.

According to the Institute for Personnel Management's Fact Sheet No. 137, apprenticeships (in this case for school-leavers) are characterised in South Africa by the following:

- Programmes are usually jointly planned by employers, apprentices and trainers.
- Programmes combine on-the-job experience with related technical instruction, which is usually provided by a local technical college.
- Training is directly related to human resources needs (in relation to skills and numbers).
- Apprentices are carefully selected. Different industries require different school qualifications, the minimum usually being standard 7 or 8 or equivalent. Standard 9 is the minimum for apprenticeship as an aircraft electrician, radar technician and other advanced trades. Only those candidates are

accepted who show aptitude and manual skill in the area in which they want to qualify. The minimum age to start an apprenticeship is 16 years.

- All apprentices are paid on a graduated scale which is related to their progress in learning the work.
- On-the-job work and training experience are carefully planned and supervised by skilled personnel.
- Related and supplementary technical training is provided by professional vocational teachers.
- Work experience and related technical college instruction are coordinated in order to ensure maximum benefit from the programme.
- The progress of the apprentice in on-the-job training and technical college studies is reviewed periodically by a joint management and technical college committee, in order to ensure acceptable performance.
- Upon completion of training, apprentices are given certificates of qualification. They are usually employed by the organisation where they were trained, which eliminates the need for job hunting and placement services.
- Training boards will be closely involved in the training of apprentices in future.

The Manpower Training Act (No. 56 of 1981), which is discussed in chapter 21, contains more detailed information about apprenticeships. The Manpower Training Amendment Act (No. 39 of 1990) provides for apprenticeship training by training boards, which has resulted in a completely new dispensation in the field of training in South Africa. Apprenticeship training employs competence-based modular training, according to the NTB (1991). According to Nel (1986), South African trade unions also play a prominent role in the training of apprentices. This observation is confirmed by Slabbert *et al.* (1993).

Internship
This is a method whereby professional persons divide their time between attending classes and working for an organisation. Employees in this category include aspiring lawyers, accountants and industrial psychologists. Internship provides trainees with an opportunity to gain experience in practical situations which cannot be simulated in the classroom. It provides the opportunity for the employer to determine the suitability of the employee for a permanent position in the organisation, and is therefore a far better method than ordinary selection and placement. For the trainee, the oppportunity he or she has to integrate theory and practice is invaluable and cannot be replaced by any other means of training.

22.3.2 Off-the-job training
Off-the-job training is usually done in a classroom situation. It can be on the premises of the organisation but away from the learner's place of work, or it can be totally removed from the organisation, for example at a conference centre. These methods may also be classified as classroom or simulation methods since

they simulate real-life situations. They may be used to develop the ability, interpersonal skills and attitudes of the trainee.

Off-the-job methods differ from on-the-job methods in a number of ways:

- Training is usually given to mixed groups, and is not tailored to a particular manager's needs.
- Learning by doing is usually very limited, as the activities are removed from the actual job situation. (It may even happen that the knowledge gained is unacceptable to the trainee's superior, because it was not learned on the job.)
- Off-the-job training is usually over a short period of time, as work pressures do not allow for lengthy periods away from work.
- Attempts are made to teach trainees over a short period of time to change their behaviour, and there is limited or no follow-up.
- Off-the-job training methods allow managers to view their jobs and their organisations from a fresh perspective.
- Managers have the opportunity to learn new theories and practices which may not be available in the work situation.

Methods such as programmed instruction and vestibule training can be used for lower-level employees as well as trainee managers.

Case studies

The trainees read, study and analyse a hypothetical business problem that contains elements of a real-life situation. They are then required to choose the best solution and implement it. Learning is best if there is interaction between the learners and the instructor, because the role of the instructor is that of catalyst and facilitator. The method gives learners an opportunity to apply the knowledge and principles they have learned previously and to test their ability to deal with a simulated real-life situation. It also provides trainees with an opportunity to develop independent thinking and to exchange ideas. The experience is a trial run for business activities in the real world.

The incident method

This is a variation on the case study method. In this method trainees are given the bare outlines of a problem and are each assigned a role. Each trainee must then view the problem from the perspective of his or her role. Additional information is made available according to the questions they ask. According to Ivancevich and Glueck (1986:484):

> Each student "solves" the case, and groups based on similarity of solutions are formed. Each group then formulates a strong statement of position, and the groups debate or role-play their solutions. The instructor may describe what actually happened in the case, and the consequences, and then everyone compares their solutions with the results. The final step is for participants to try to apply this knowledge to their own job situations.

Role-play

This method is another variation on the case study method, because trainees physically act out a specific role, applying the theory instead of merely thinking passively about it. It becomes a dynamic learning process, particularly if closed-circuit television which films the trainees playing their roles is used to assess them. In role-play there are no rehearsals, because situations must be spontaneously acted out. A realistic representation should be allowed to develop, particularly when the topic deals with human relations. The instructor should first explain the human relations problem in a formal lecture. He or she then stipulates the roles that learners are to play, but *not how* they should play them. Learners then use their initiative and play the role as they perceive it ought to be played. The role-play starts with a given passage of dialogue and ends when the stipulated problems have been solved and the situation has been brought to a conclusion. At the end, the instructor comments on the observed actions. Role-play can be effectively used to give learners insight into inter-personal problems. It makes them aware of their attitudes towards others and it creates opportunities for them to improve their ability to deal with human relations issues. It is important for trainees to understand that this method involves serious learning and that each participant needs to be positive towards change, otherwise the exercise will not be successful.

In-basket training

This is also called the in-tray exercise. The trainee is given a number of letters, messages, reports and telephone messages that would typically come across a manager's desk. These items are presented in no particular order, but they require action ranging from urgent to routine handling. The trainee must act on the information contained in these items. He or she has to analyse each item and decide how to carry out the tasks. Afterwards the decisions are analysed and evaluated by the instructor. Trainees are normally not allowed to communicate with one another during this type of exercise; they are thus compelled to undertake independent thinking and problem solving. The method can be effectively used to analyse trainees' decision-making abilities in order to identify further training needs. It can also be used to develop their managerial skills and provide them with practice in decision-making. This method is often used in assessment centre training.

The Kepner-Tregoe technique

This variation on the in-basket method resembles the case study method in that material about an organisation is provided in writing ahead of time. It also involves role-play, and each trainee is assigned one, two or even five roles which he or she is required to play in the hypothetical organisation. Each trainee plays a role for approximately 90 minutes and then switches roles. Trainees are then evaluated on their performance in each role. Once again, some problems are more urgent than others and trainees have to sort out the important from the unimportant in order to make decisions. This method claims to make trainees better aware of the managerial decision-making process, and it also improves problem-solving skills if teams work together on the exercises.

Management games

Management games, also called business games, are a development of the in-basket and role-play methods. Trainees play various roles in an imaginary business situation over a period of time. A business game usually involves two or more hypothetical organisations competing against each other in a given product market, and participants are assigned the roles of managing director, marketing manager, etc. They are required to take decisions on price levels, production volume and inventory levels. Their decisions are manipulated in a computer to give results as in an actual business situation. The participants are then able to see how their decisions affect other groups, and vice versa. A lengthy business phase of, say, five to ten years can be played in a short time, for example three to five hours. There are usually six to eight participants in a group representing a specific organisation. Two to five organisations can simultaneously compete against each other. The groups normally start off by controlling identical shares on the market and they then have to react to various stimuli presented to them.

The feedback session by the trainers is an important aspect of this method because it enables individuals and groups to evaluate their performance. Participants' performance and decision-making abilities are compared with those of other groups representing other hypothetical organisations. The advantage of this training is that if a group makes a mistake that costs their hypothetical organisation a few million rand, they do not lose their jobs in real life. They will, however, learn to exercise caution when making decisions in the real-life situation.

Syndicate training

This is also a variation on the case study method, and combines lectures and group work in small groups of about five to ten trainees. Instructors formulate points that should be considered by their groups. After the groups' deliberations, each trainee writes a report which is then criticised and discussed by other members of the group. Finally, group decisions are arrived at and discussed by the instructor and other groups. This method gives each trainee a chance to participate in group discussions, especially in complex tasks. Problem-solving ability is improved by deciding what is relevant and what is irrelevant. This form of training can also bring about changes in attitudes and behaviour in individuals and groups.

Conference method

Group discussions are conducted according to an organised plan in which the trainer seeks to develop knowledge and understanding by obtaining verbal

516

participation from all the trainees. This method has advantages over the lecture method, because each trainee plays an active role. Learning is achieved by building on the ideas contributed by the various participants. Thus one trainee learns from another. Groups should be limited to 15 to 20 participants who should sit facing one another around a conference table, rather than in rows in a classroom. Responses of trainees are recorded on a chalkboard, and the discussion is summarised by the instructor. Interest tends to be high because this method stimulates talk about problems and issues which can be examined from different points of view. It can also be used to reduce dogmatism and to modify attitudes, because trainees participate in obtaining solutions and reaching conclusions, and because many different points of view are heard and expressed.

Brainstorming
This is also sometimes called "free wheeling". Brainstorming seeks creative thinking, rather than practical analysis. A small group of participants meet, with or without conscious knowledge of the subject, and submit any solution or idea that occurs to them, no matter how strange or impossible it may sound. Trainees do not consider the practicality of ideas. They list all ideas generated and place the list where all the participants can see it. Later all the ideas or solutions are examined and assessed to determine how practical or acceptable each might be. The time period for such an exercise is usually from five to 20 minutes. Brainstorming is primarily used to develop novel ideas to solve problems, and to encourage creativity and participation among trainees. Note that the number of ideas is more important than their quality, because the prerequisite for this method is the suspension of all judgement and of all evaluative or analytical discussion until the group has drained itself of ideas. To ensure the success of this method, participants should represent a variety of disciplines and management functions in the organisation. Brainstorming is a form of *synergism* because it produces a result that is better than the members could have achieved had they been working on the project individually.

University programmes not for degrees
University programmes give managers a new perspective on their organisations, helping them to change their outlook on events around them. According to Nel (1977:104), courses of this nature are ideal for middle and top managers with the potential to broaden their perspective, to prepare them for the highest positions in their organisations. Such programmes are aimed at adapting a manager's attitude to changing circumstances and providing him or her with up-to-date information on a broad front. Examples are the Management Development Programme (MDP) and the Senior Management Programme (SMP) of the University of Pretoria's Graduate School of Management. In these programmes the teaching staff act as equals rather than superiors and serve as moderators and discussion leaders rather than teachers. In this way

executives gain maximum benefit from these courses in an adult teaching environment. Managers expand their knowledge and learn about theories and procedures that they would not encounter on the job. University programmes are also popular for career development.

Sabbaticals

Sabbaticals provide managers with the opportunity for mind-stretching, particularly those who have been in business for a number of years. Managers should be granted one academic year (sabbatical) in ten years of employment. The sabbatical should be planned well in advance to give an assistant the opportunity to understudy the superior's position and gain experience in it while the superior is away. A variation is to allow top managers who are experts in certain fields to be assigned to academic institutions for a period of time to teach. This gives such managers an opportunity to refresh their knowledge, update facts in a different environment and advance their own development. It provides students with an opportunity to learn practical know-how from seasoned business people. Such an exchange programme could be of great benefit to South African students who need practical knowledge of the business environment, since many students are rapidly moved into managerial positions because of the dire shortage of managerial personnel the country is experiencing.

Vestibule training

This is training that takes place away from the production area but uses equipment identical to that used in the workplace. According to the Institute of Personnel Management (Fact Sheet No. 137) vestibule training is appropriate when the job to be learned involves the operation of one machine or repetitive processes, or is performed in an area too full of distractions to permit effective learning. An advantage of this style of training is that there are none of the production requirements and pressures of the real work situation. In other words, the trainee is not under stress to maintain a standard of production from the outset, nor is he or she held accountable for high reject rates in the early stages of training. Once the employees meet the standards, they move on to the job itself.

Programmed instruction

In using this method the material is presented in small, carefully sequenced fragments, usually called "frames". Each frame elicits a response from the learner who immediately finds out whether or not the response was correct. If the response was correct the trainee can proceed to the next frame. This method can be used at odd times and in odd places: trainees use books because machinery is not necessary and consequently the learners can study either at home or at work. A high degree of learner motivation is, however, necessary for this method to succeed because progress depends on the learner. The higher the learner's motivation, the faster and more effective the learning will be.

Programmed instruction provides knowledge rather than skills. The method is useful for learning concepts, particularly in relation to interpersonal behaviour.

Computer-assisted instruction

This is an extension of programmed instruction and takes advantage of the speed, memory and data manipulation of computers. The learner's response determines the level of difficulty of the next frame, which can be selected and displayed almost instantaneously. The speed of presentation and the limited dependence on an instructor are major advantages of this method. Computer-assisted instruction can be effectively combined with video and audiotape materials and the combination provides considerable flexibility in directing the student through various phases of learning. The major drawback is, however, that it takes a great deal of preparation time for even an hour's instruction by this method. If the numbers of trainees are sufficiently large, the method becomes cost-effective.

Assessment centres

Programmes at assessment centres are primarily used to assess the personal characteristics and potential of supervisory or managerial candidates. According to Ferrell and Hirt (1993:322), assessment centres are defined as:

> Internal programmes to identify employees who have managerial potential and provide them with specialised training.

Malherbe (1986:340) states that such a programme usually lasts from two to five days and that participants are involved in a variety of group and individual exercises, for example in-basket exercises, business games, role-play and tests. Each participant's behaviour is carefully monitored and evaluated by trained observers who are often line managers. On completion of the programme, each participant receives individual feedback on his or her behaviour and his or her development needs are identified and spelled out. This approach is used for the selection and development of managers and supervisors. Trainees are sometimes assigned to mentors who guide them through a phase of their career development, based on the written report on development needs identified during the assessment centre programme.

Lectures

Lectures remain an essential method for supervisory and management training and hold considerable advantages, particularly flexibility and economy. A good lecturer can achieve excellent results within a short space of time, provided lectures are carefully structured and presented. Lectures are seldom presented on their own; they are usually accompanied by a variety of audio-visual aids and tools. Some of these can also be used on their own. The most common training aids are:

- Films and video-tape recordings: These can be used to good effect in training, in particular to explain principles and theories, and to present case studies, etc. They should, however, be used in combination with other methods. For example, slides, tapes, flip charts and the chalkboard can enhance lectures and films.
- Closed-circuit television: Video-tape recordings of role-play situations are often used to give trainees direct feedback on their behaviour. They are often used in interpersonal skills training and team building exercises because they let trainees see a recording of their own behaviour. Trainees can use video-tape recordings to make detailed analyses of their skills.
- Other tools that can be used to supplement a lecture are overhead projectors, magnetic boards and flip charts.

22.3.3 Organisation development

A variety of problems occur in the daily running of an organisation that are not covered by conventional management development methods. These problems can be addressed through organisation development, since its focus is the total organisation and not the individual or small groups. Beach (1985:278) describes organisation development as:

> a planned process designed to improve organizational effectiveness and health through modifications in individual and group behavior, culture, and systems of the organization using knowledge and technology of applied behavioral science.

The objectives of organisation development are, first, to improve communication among managers and between the different managerial levels and departments in the organisation, with the purpose of establishing a process of performance feedback in the organisation; secondly to have decisions taken on the basis of information supplied by those managers who are closest to the point of action; thirdly, to bring underlying hostility and conflict into the open so that constructive efforts can be made to resolve it; and fourthly, to improve the ability of the organisation to adapt to change (Acton 1986).

A consultant or change agent is normally used as a facilitator or catalyst to effect change. Organisation development takes place in a number of phases:

- *Diagnosis:* In this phase the consultant or change agent seeks to determine what the problems of the organisation are.
- *Selection and design of interventions:* This step is closely linked to diagnosis since decisions about the programme that should be designed and implemented to effect the change are based on the diagnosis.
- *Implementation of intervention:* This is the process of working with the managers in departments where the change is to be effected.
- *Evaluation:* This is done by measuring the results against the objectives set for the organisation development programme.
- *Adjustment and maintenance of the system:* The information gained by evaluation is used to determine whether any changes need to be made to the

original process. The questions are asked: Were the intended results realised? If not, why not?

The most important organisation development methods are discussed below.

Behaviour modelling

This is also called interaction management. Behaviour modelling mainly involves identifying interaction problems faced by managers and supervisors, such as resistance to change and tardiness on the part of subordinates. The programme of learning follows a sequence of steps:

- Modelling: A film, model or demonstration of the skills necessary to solve the problem is presented.
- Role-play: Each trainee plays a number of roles in an attempt to solve the problem.
- Reinforcement: The correct behaviour is reinforced during practice sessions.
- Transfer of training: Planning is undertaken to enable each trainee to transfer the acquired skills to his or her specific job or situation.

Grid training

This method, based on the popular work of Blake and Mouton (1964), focuses on individual learning, team development and the strengthening of both intergroup relations and the structures of the organisation. The approach aims at altering the leadership style in the organisation. With grid training, managers come to understand the rationale of systematic change; they gain insight into the strategies of management training and how this can be used for better performance. The method can also be used to identify leadership styles and participation techniques that are most likely to produce good results, and to improve the skills of executives and supervisors in the organisation. A grid programme is presented in six phases:

- *Phase 1—A study of the grid:* This is designed to acquaint all the participants with the grid's concepts and material. This can be done by means of a laboratory seminar. Each manager then determines his or her position on the grid.
- *Phase 2—Team development:* Managers analyse their leadership styles and the group skills necessary for line management. In this phase trust and respect within the teams need to be built up.
- *Phase 3—Intergroup development:* The emphasis is on intergroup relationships and joint problem-solving, practised in simulation exercises. Thus an ideal model for intergroup relations is approximated.
- *Phase 4—Development of an ideal model for the organisation:* Management by objectives (MBO) is used to establish individual and organisational objectives. A framework is established to link top levels and lower levels of management.

521

- *Phase 5—Implementing the model:* A systematic reorganisation is undertaken to meet the requirements for the ideal strategic model. Human resources plans are also drawn up for use in the model.
- *Phase 6—Evaluation:* In this phase the previous phases are systematically measured and evaluated in order to determine whether any problems still exist, what progress has been made and whether there are any further development needs.

Team building

This is a popular method among human resources practitioners, and has seen significant development over the last two decades. The rationale of team building is that any organisation is dependent on the effective cooperation of a number of managers, and these managers are compelled to work together on a permanent or semi-permanent basis to perform their jobs effectively. A team-building programme is therefore a planned event with a group of people who have a particular relationship and common organisational objectives. The programme is designed to improve the way in which the group accomplishes its tasks, and at the same time to enhance the resourcefulness of the various group members. The crux of team building is a series of team-building exercises that take place at a location totally removed from the organisation. The programme usually lasts from two to five days. The objectives are to set goals and priorities, clarify roles, identify problems and conflicts, and improve communication and understanding in order to build effective teams. One of the major advantages of team building is that it encourages and sustains participation over a period of time. This results in improved communication and problem-solving between and within the different teams.

Laboratory training

Laboratory training is a generic term that covers both sensitivity training and T-group training (Van Dyk 1987:328). T-group training is based on the conference method, with the focus on small groups and individual participation. However, it is conducted in a laboratory environment and is therefore considered to be laboratory training. According to Byars and Rue (1984:185) the objectives of laboratory training are:
- To make participants aware of their own behaviour and to give them insight into its meaning in the social context;
- To increase participants' sensitivity to the behaviour of others;
- To teach participants to exercise diagnostic skills in social, interpersonal and intergroup situations;
- To increase participants' ability to analyse their own behaviour continually, in order to help themselves and others to build more effective and satisfying interpersonal relationships.

Transactional analysis

This is a method designed to help people understand their own ego states and those of others so that they can easily interact with others. According to transactional analysis there are three ego states: parent, adult and child. The *parent ego state* of a person comprises the judgemental, moralising, value-making and rule-making components of personality. It is expressed in advice and in prescribing "do's" and "don'ts". The *adult ego state* is reliable, direct and based on reality. It is rational, thinking, problem solving and truth seeking. The *child ego state* comprises emotional, creative responses, the spontaneous and impulsive components of personality. It should be noted that ego states are not tied to chronological age: during the course of a day a person may display all three ego states. A transaction is the basic unit of social interaction between two people and consists of their respective words and behaviour. The most important aspect of transactional analysis in training is examining the words exchanged between two people. The learner identifies the ego states of both the initiator and the respondent by analysing these words as they are spoken in the transaction. The objectives of transactional analysis are very similar to those of laboratory training. This method, however, generates less tension in learners and is experienced as less threatening than laboratory training.

Other interventions

The interventions outlined below preceded the emergence of organisation development as a process, but they are nevertheless included with organisation development programmes for management development purposes (they are discussed under the quality of work life in chapter 14):

- *Job enrichment:* This is the addition of decision-making responsibilities, challenges and other issues to enrich routine jobs.
- *Management by objectives:* This is a collaboration between superiors and subordinates in setting work objectives for the subordinates that are in line with the objectives of the organisation, and in evaluating progress.
- *Changes in the organisation's structure:* This introduces different designs, such as project or matrix organisation, or decentralisation.
- *Participative management:* This includes issues such as participative problem-solving, meetings, union management and cooperation.

The issues discussed in this section highlight the on-the-job and off-the-job methods that can be used to develop managers, supervisors and other employees in an organisation. Depending on the identified training needs of learners, various methods or combinations of methods can be used to improve their performance in the organisation. What is most important is that once a training and development programme has taken place, it should be evaluated in order to determine whether it was effective in terms of its stated objectives. Aspects of evaluation are now discussed.

22.4 THE EVALUATION OF TRAINING AND DEVELOPMENT

It is unimaginable that an organisation might not calculate its profit for the year or the return on its investment. Yet it is true that organisations often do not evaluate their training and development programmes. This is analogous to a person wanting to lose weight: no one would deny the importance to an obese person of losing weight, and many people try to do so. But unfortunately the results are rarely what one would have hoped for. And if one does not weigh oneself before and after the attempted weight-loss programme one has no accurate means of evaluating success or failure. Similarly, unless top management insists on the evaluation of training and development programmes, there is no possibility of determining their exact benefits. Training programmes should not be undertaken unless suitable criteria for their evaluation have been agreed upon by the instructors and the trainees and have been built into the programme. Evaluation can only be effective if it is based on clear and specified objectives which are determined beforehand and are qualified and quantified. Evaluation must be continuous, not a once-off exercise, and must be based on uniform, objective methods and standards.

Furthermore, to be effective the evaluation of training and development must be *reliable* and *valid*. A measure can only be *reliable* if its measurement is exactly the same every time it is used. In other words, there must be a high correlation between the first and subsequent tests of the same predefined material. To assess the reliability of evaluation, the test re-test method can be effectively used.

Validity means that a test measures what it is intended to measure. Validity has two components, namely internal and external validation. Internal validation is determined by a series of tests designed to ascertain whether the training programme achieved its behavioural objectives. It therefore measures changes in the knowledge, skills or attitudes of the trainees, whether the instructor conducted the course effectively, and whether the programme itself was effective. External validation is determined by tests and assessments that indicate whether the behavioural objectives of an internally valid training programme were realistically based on the training needs initially identified. External evaluation of a programme determines whether the objectives of the programme were reached within the specified time. This time could be during the programme, immediately after the programme or quite some time after its completion.

There is a multitude of methods for testing and evaluating training programmes, but these are unequal in value. While some are scientific, others are haphazard and restricted to a single criterion. The ultimate result of poor evaluation is that training is regarded as a fad or false panacea by top management, because it appears to be a waste of money. There have been efforts by a number of researchers to implement scientific evaluation of training, and notably by Kirkpatrick (1976), who designed a multiple criterion evaluation system. This is a valuable system, because it ensures that evaluation is scientifically done. Kirkpatrick suggests that the following be measured: participant reaction, extent of learning, behavioural changes and results. These can be measured according to levels ranging from simple to complex, or alternatively according to frequency, from popular to seldom used. These four evaluation criteria apply to all types of training programmes, irrespective of whether they are for supervisory or skills training. The four criteria are explained below.

Participant reaction
This focuses on whether the trainees liked or disliked the training programme, i.e. to what extent they are satisfied customers and feel they have gained from the programme. This information is usually obtained by means of a questionnaire. Questions are also asked about the course leader's presentation, for example whether he or she was friendly and kept the sessions interesting. The administration of the programme should also be examined, for example whether the accommodation was adequate, what trainees felt about the duration of the course, refreshments, notes and seating arrangements. These issues are important in determining whether the training programme as such was of the required standard.

   Reaction questionnaires are distributed at the end of a training course and are collected immediately. Experience shows that if they are taken home to be completed and returned, up to 80% of the participants will not complete and return them. The major drawback of this assessment method is that the enthusiasm of the trainees cannot necessarily be taken as evidence of improved ability and performance in the work situation. Another drawback is that trainees are usually unable to assess the methods used objectively and therefore their responses cannot be relied upon.

Extent of learning
This criterion is used to measure the extent to which trainees assimilated the material presented in the training programme. The skills, knowledge and attitudes of the trainees have to be tested to determine the degree of assimilation.
- *Skills* are usually easy to measure, especially in low-level work. Performance is measured before and after the training. The training of a machine operator drilling holes for valves in a vacuum brake system, for example, was successful if after the training he or she is able to drill as many holes per hour as the standard requires. The improvement can be measured because the number of holes drilled before and after the training can be counted. In other words, pre- and post-testing can be used. Other means that can be used include paper and pen tests. These could be essay-type tests, objective tests requiring some free response or tests requiring true/false responses or multiple-choice responses to questions. Once again a comparison of pre- and post-tests measures how much learning has taken place. Trainees could

525

also be subjected to role-play situations so that the evaluator can observe how certain skills have improved, for example some aspect of communication such as answering a telephone. The exercise will immediately reveal the learner's ability or inability because immediate feedback is received.

- *Knowledge:* It is assumed that in order to master a skill, a trainee requires a certain level of knowledge. Therefore in evaluating the trainee's skill, his or her knowledge is in fact also evaluated. Davies (1973:90) states:

  The main method of measuring the achievement of cognitive objectives is the use of a criterion-referenced performance test . . . A criterion-referenced test is usually given before and after instruction so as to assess gains.

  Pre- and post-test measurements should be objective. When a lengthy training programme is conducted to broaden the knowledge of trainees, it may be necessary to undertake interim tests to evaluate their changing knowledge so that adjustments can be made to the programme if the results are not on target.

- *Attitudes:* It is difficult to measure attitudes and use them as a criterion because they are an expression of people's thoughts and feelings. Two methods can however be used: trainees can either make their own judgement and say what they think of a new situation, or they can be observed and inferences can be drawn from their performance in a particular job. Observation to determine a trainee's attitude is however subjective and should be used with circumspection. Another method is to use a well-designed semantic differential test before and after the training to determine whether the trainee's attitudes towards given issues have changed. Once again it should be done with circumspection, because it requires specialist skills.

Behavioural changes

A criterion for evaluating the effectiveness of a training course is the degree of behavioural change discernible in a trainee. Differences in job behaviour are far more difficult to assess and measure than trainees' reactions and learning. Behaviour measurement can only be considered accurate if the training needs analysis and training objectives were described in terms of desired on-the-job behaviour. It is then possible to measure the difference between the trainee's undesirable pre-training behaviour and his or her new post-training behaviour. Performance appraisal before and after training therefore has to be done and the following persons or groups could be involved: the trainee, his or her superiors, subordinates and peers, or other people familiar with his or her performance (IPM Fact Sheet No. 47). The evaluation could be done approximately three months after completion of the training, to enable the trainees to put into practice what they have learned. The methods that can be used include questionnaires, interviews, on-the-job observations by the instructor or superior and voluntary feedback by the trainee. The latter is particularly important because assessment done by the trainee himself or herself is very valuable, provided it is objective.

526

Results

The degree of achievement of the objectives formulated for the training programme, based on the needs analysis, determines whether the training course has been successful. Achievement of objectives could manifest in improved profits, reduction of costs, lower staff turnover, reduced absenteeism or grievances, an increase in the quality and quantity of production, improved morale, or whatever was stated as training objectives. Some of these issues are easy to evaluate, but others, such as higher morale among employees, are practically impossible to evaluate accurately. A number of factors could affect a trainee's performance following successful training, but variables beyond his or her control may impair performance and distort training results. According to Mondy and Noe (1987:290):

a mild recession forces the lay-off of several key employees; a competing firm is successful in luring away one of the department's top engineers; or the company president could pressure the employment director to hire an incompetent relative.

These factors may have the result that the performance of the trainee is worse or unchanged, but the blame should not be placed on the training programme or on the trainee.

Achievement of the objectives of the organisation (as opposed to the trainee's objectives) also has to be measured at various times to ascertain the effectiveness of training. Evaluation should take place immediately after the training, to measure differences in the performance of employees; three months after the training, to evaluate behavioural change in particular; and approximately a year after training to determine whether the profits of the organisation have in fact increased, whether employee turnover has decreased or whether the morale of the employees is better. These changes may be due to other factors, such as a recession, but they should nevertheless be related to the training done. Other issues that could negatively affect the results of the training and development are jobs that change rapidly, new equipment, new techniques and changed environmental influences on the organisation.

22.5 THE COST-BENEFIT RATIO OF TRAINING AND DEVELOPMENT

The evaluation of the costs and benefits is crucial if training and development programmes are to receive any credit for improved performance in organisations. However, the costs and benefits of training are not always taken into consideration by instructors and top managers, who also neglect to define objectives and therefore cannot measure achievements against objectives. Many training programmes would have been far more effective, and many unsuccessful ones would not have been embarked upon, if the following basic questions had been asked and answered: "What will it cost if we do it? What will it cost if we don't do it?" The top management of an organisation for gain needs to know what the contribution of training is to profits. Put differently, the return on investment needs to be calculated. If instructors can guarantee a positive return on investment, they will never have a shortage of requests for training and development.

As for any other activity in an organisation, training and development have to be budgeted for. Although a budget is only an estimate of expenditure and not easy to draw up, it is important to make the estimate because this is necessary for effective training planning. By carefully weighing up each expenditure item, top management and the trainer can set accurate norms that will aid them in calculating the real costs of training. Later it would also be easier to evaluate the cost in relation to the benefits of the training.

Costs

Costs refer to the direct and indirect monetary outlay to plan, present and evaluate the training, as well as other costs that may be incurred when the trainee goes back to work. The IPM Fact Sheet No. 71 lists the following basic expense categories:

- Lost work time of the trainees. This should be estimated in hours for the duration of the training and multiplied by the hourly salary or wage. This will give the cost of the work time trainees lose while they are on the course.
- The time of planners, staff, instructors and others whose time is consumed by the training programme. It should be calculated by multiplying a standard cost by the number of hours estimated for preparation, supervision and evaluation of the training.
- Direct costs include materials, books, notebooks, meals, travelling, housing, telephones, visual aids and all other costs incurred in the preparation and presentation of the training programme.
- Unusual expenses peculiar to specific courses. Examples are fees for guest speakers and consultants, and special aids such as video tapes.

The total cost of the programme is determined by adding up these costs. The value of the training will only become apparent once the benefits have been calculated.

Benefits

There are four aspects that must be taken into account when assessing the benefits of training:

- Have the stated objectives been met in terms of increased productivity?
- Was the expenditure incurred for the training justified?
- Identify those areas with the most potential benefits to ensure that their objectives are given priority.
- Ensure that the training received is, in fact, being transferred to the workplace.

Various sources can be used to assess the benefits of training, such as departmental managers' reports, production reports, plant efficiency reports, quality control reports, sales reports, attendance records, earnings and recom-

528

mendations or proposals to senior managers, which might result in changes in techniques or procedures in the organisation.

The following direct benefits may result from training: fewer accidents, increased productivity, increased sales, fewer warranty claims because of improved quality, less down time, improved customer service, lower recruitment and labour turnover costs, less scrap and lower maintenance costs.

It is important to ensure that the improvements are attributable to training and not to new equipment, increased supervision or other factors.

According to Van Dyk and Nel (1989), the management of organisations must also bear in mind that training benefits cannot be evaluated in terms of money alone. There are other, intangible benefits, such as greater individual job satisfaction, improved communication, greater adaptability of employees in the organisation, fewer grievances, better capital investment decisions by managers, greater acceptance of training and a positive attitude among managers, supervisors and employees towards the need for retraining in the organisation.

22.6 CONCLUSION

Management development is aimed at preparing managers to perform their present and future jobs in the organisation effectively. Training, on the other hand, primarily aims at teaching lower-level workers the skills they need to perform their present tasks effectively. Training or development cannot be effective unless attention is paid to various factors, such as the skills of the instructor, which would affect the method to be used.

On-the-job and off-the-job methods can be used for the development of managers, on-the-job methods being more popular. There is a vast variety of methods, and specific methods can be chosen to suit the identified development needs, such as classroom training and role-play. In South Africa, particular attention should be given to advancement training for semi-skilled employees.

Organisation development is an approach that is gaining considerable ground and is of particular importance in modifying the leadership style of an organisation as a whole.

The evaluation of training and development is of cardinal importance if the training department of an organisation is to convince top management that training and development render an adequate return on investment in that they lead to an increase in the profitability of the organisation. The cost-benefit ratio can be used to evaluate the effectiveness of training and development.

Questions

1. What do you regard as the essential components of a comprehensive management development programme?
2. Describe the following on-the-job methods of management development: coaching, role-play, job rotation, management games and in-basket training.

3. Why are training and development programmes among the first items to be eliminated when an organisation's budget has to be cut?
4. Under what conditions do you consider organisation development to be an effective means of management development?
5. Which training methods can be used to train lower-level employees in motor skills?
6. Why do many organisations fail to evaluate training and development programmes?

Sources

Acton, C. 1986. Organisation development: a case study. *IPM Journal*, Vol. 5, No. 8, December.

Byars, L.L. & Rue, L.W. 1984. *Human resource and personnel management*. Richard Irwin, Homewood, Illinois.

Beach, D.S. 1985. *Personnel: the management of people at work*. 5th edition, Macmillan, New York.

Blake, R.R. & Mouton, J.S. 1964. *The managerial grid*. Gulf Publishing, Houston, Texas.

Camp, R., Blanchard, P.N. & Huszcszo, G.E. 1986. *Toward a more organizationally effective training strategy and practice*. Prentice-Hall, Englewood Cliffs, New Jersey.

Davies, I.K. 1973. *The organization of training*. McGraw-Hill, London.

Ferrell, O.C. & Hirt, G. 1993. *Business: a changing world*. Homewood, Boston.

Human Sciences Research Council. 1985. *The HSRC/NTB investigation into the training of artisans in South Africa*. HSRC Publishers, Pretoria.

Institute for Personnel Management. 1994. *Human resources directory & handbook: buyer's guide for human resource consultants & services*. B & G Publications, Randburg.

Institute for Personnel Management. n.d. *IPB Journal*. Fact Sheets Nos 47, 71, 137 & 141.

Ivancevich, J.H. & Glueck, W.F. 1986. *Foundations of personnel: human resource management*. 3rd edition. Business Publications, Plano, Texas.

Kirkpatrick, D.L. 1976. Evaluation of training. In R.L. Craig (ed.) *Training and development handbook: a guide to human resource development*. 2nd edition. McGraw-Hill, New York.

Malherbe, J. 1986. Improving supervisory performance: an integrated approach. In J. Barling, C. Fullager & S. Bluen (eds) *Behaviour in organisations: South African perspectives*. 2nd edition. McGraw-Hill, Johannesburg.

Mondy, R.W. & Noe, R.M. 1987. *Personnel: the management of human resources*. 3rd edition. Allyn & Bacon, Boston.

National Training Board. 1988. *Guidelines for the implementation of competence-based modular training: a manual for trainers*. Government Printer, Pretoria.

National Training Board. 1990. *Decentralisation of artisan tests*. Government Printer, Pretoria.

National Training Board. 1990. *The changing role of management over the following decade—a critical review*. Government Printer, Pretoria.

National Training Board. 1991. *Annual report of the chairman for the year ended 31 December 1990*. (RP 61/1990). Government Printer, Pretoria.

Nel, P.S. 1977. An investigation into management development in the Durban-Pinetown area. Unpublished MCom dissertation, UNISA, Pretoria.

Nel, P.S. 1986. The role of trade unions in artisan training. *Industrial Relations Journal of South Africa*, Vol. 6, No. 3.

Silver, M. 1991. *Competent to manage*. Routledge, New York.

Skinner, S.J. & Ivancevich, T.M. 1992. *Business for the 21st century*. Irwin, Homewood, Illinois.

Slabbert, J.A., Prinsloo, P. & Becker, W.A. 1993. *Managing industrial relations in South Africa*. 5th edition. Digma, Pretoria.

Van Dyk, P.S. 1987. 'n Organisasie-ontwikkelingstrategie vir 'n gemeenskapsdiensorganisasie. Unpublished DCom thesis, UNISA, Pretoria.

Van Dyk, P.S. & Nel, P.S. 1989. *Training management*. Only study guide for Training Management TRAIN-3. Honours BCom Business Economics. UNISA, Pretoria.

Van Dyk, P.S., Nel, P.S. & Loedolf, P. van Z. 1992. *Training management: a multi-disciplinary approach to human resources development in Southern Africa*. Southern, Halfway House.

Chapter 23

Review of human resources in South Africa

P.S. Nel

STUDY OBJECTIVES

After studying this chapter, you should be able to:
- Describe South Africa's human resources problems;
- Give South Africa's total population figures;
- Outline the population trends up to the year 2010;
- Explain why there are human resources shortages and surpluses;
- Explain the principles and philosophy on which South Africa's human resources policy is based;
- Explain how job opportunities are created in South Africa;
- Explain human resources policy as a prerequisite for the effective demand for and supply of skills in a country's economy.

23.1 INTRODUCTION

Human resources form part of the throughput process. In the job content environment, human resources exert a direct influence on the nature of jobs, the utilisation and development of workers, and on management. In the job context environment, human resources have an influence on management philosophy, interpersonal and intergroup relations as well as organisational culture. In the external environment, human resources are directly influenced by the national human resources policy, technology, level of education, economic conditions and labour market conditions. These and other related issues are focused upon in this chapter.

Associated aspects are the policy of the new, democratic South African government with regard to human resources, employment activities, unemployment and the job creation that will take place to counteract it, the training of work seekers and the unemployed, and affirmative action.

One of the most important problems currently facing the South African labour market is that there is a dire shortage of highly skilled people, but there is also large-scale unemployment among the unskilled. Counteracting unemployment while making sufficient highly skilled workers available for effectively running the economy is essential for a developing Third World country.

23.2 THE MOST IMPORTANT HUMAN RESOURCES PROBLEMS IN SOUTH AFRICA

Historical and socio-cultural development has resulted in South Africa's having a very heterogeneous population who speaks a large variety of European and African languages and dialects as well as various Asian languages. This is also the reason for the 11 official languages of the country. The prevailing socio-cultural differences remain enormous.

One of the consequences of the discriminating labour legislation of the past is that the range of control of managers in organisations has become too great to handle effectively. In addition, it has led to socio-economic and social problems. The most important problems in the South African labour market that human resources and industrial relations managers must be familiar with are outlined below.

Low productivity
South Africa, regarded as a developing country, has one of the lowest productivity figures in the world. This creates serious problems for human resources managers and organisations to maintain profitability.

There is much concern in South Africa because the utilisation of capital is increasing twice as rapidly as the utilisation of labour—thus leading to more unemployment. Warnings have already been issued about the increasing use of capital, while the productivity of capital per unit is actually decreasing.

In comparison with most Western countries, South Africa is certainly no longer a country with low labour costs. It has in fact become a country with very high labour costs, with the result that it has difficulty competing on international markets. The unit costs paid for labour in South Africa in 1989, for example, were six times more than in Japan, almost twice as much as in Italy and four times those paid in Germany. This means that human resources and industrial relations managers will have to pay serious attention to salaries, since increases will further lower South Africa's labour productivity and push up the rate of inflation. Consequently, South Africa's competitive position internationally is adversely affected, as are exports and the balance of payments, while at home, unemployment increases. Productivity is therefore one of the most serious human resources problems South Africa faces at present and will face in future.

The population explosion

South Africa's population increase is one of the highest in Africa, and has far outstripped job creation. This puts tremendous strain on the country's natural resources and will probably lead to unemployment figures of close to 10 million by the year 2000. Therefore population planning is of vital importance to counteract the problems that South Africa may have to face in future. This aspect is discussed in detail elsewhere in this book.

Too rapid mechanisation of the economy

Unfortunately many organisations are intent on mechanising their production and getting rid of labour. The reasons for this are: firstly, labour unrest and strikes are forcing organisations to provide more reliable production systems. Secondly, organisations are forced to mechanise because of the shortage of skilled human resources, and thirdly, mechanisation has become an attractive option in view of the enormous wage increases given to low-level semi-skilled and unskilled workers during the past few years. The result of this is increased unemployment: an example is that 70 000 employees were retrenched in 1991 in the gold mining industry alone.

A high level of unemployment

South Africa's unemployment statistics are extremely high for several reasons, including economic recession and the factors mentioned above. The unofficial unemployment figure is currently estimated to be some 50% of the economically active population. This puts the entire country under great strain. For example, the near exhaustion of the unemployment insurance fund means that contributions to the fund have to be increased.

A shortage of skilled workers

South Africa is experiencing an acute shortage of skilled workers as a result of rapid economic growth during the past two decades and restrictive labour legislation, which in the past placed an enormous strain on the economy as a whole. This shortage has resulted in reduced productivity because there are not enough skilled employees to cope with management tasks. South Africa is functioning at present with only 9% of the economically active population being highly skilled, while the figure for First World countries is 33%. Where managerial staff are concerned, the figure for South Africa is 2%, as against 7% for First World countries. The shortages are therefore acute.

A rapid rate of urbanisation

Projections based on 1990 figures estimate the total population of South Africa at 54 million in the year 2010, of whom 36 million will be living in the main metropolitan areas: the PWV, Durban, Cape Town, Port Elizabeth, Bloemfontein, Pietermaritzburg, Goldfields and East London. In 1990 Durban was the city with the fastest population growth in the world and it will take Durban only 10 years to reach a size comparable to that of cities such as Mexico City and Rio de Janeiro. According to figures published by the Urban Foundation in 1990, by the year 2010 more than two-thirds of the South African population will be living in metropolitan areas. The PWV will then, like cities such as Bombay, Calcutta and Jakarta, number among the 10 largest metropolitan areas in the world.

It is further estimated that 11 million people will move to the cities before the year 2000. The Urban Foundation urges that decisive steps must be taken right now to combat this problem. Should R750 million be set aside annually for the next five years, 500 000 informal, serviced housing units could be provided. This will have to form part of the reconstruction programme. However, there is a shortage of 820 000 housing units in South Africa at present, which means that some 250 000 formal units would have to be constructed every year to meet the demand for housing among the South African population by the turn of the century.

People will probably converge on the four main metropolitan areas, but these make up only 4% of the country's land area. This means that a city with a capacity of about 650 000 residents, with houses, parks, roads, schools, sewerage, water and other amenities would have to be built every year until 2010 to accommodate the increase in the population.

All infrastructure such as telecommunications and transport will have to be provided on a large scale. Job opportunities will have to be created and the socio-economic and other problems related to urbanisation will have to be solved, not only by the state, but also by the private sector. Human resources managers will therefore have to consider how they can assist South Africa's employees in the process of urbanisation, for example with housing, since it directly affects their organisations.

Violence

Violence has become a nightmare in South Africa, and human resources managers are under tremendous strain to keep their workforces productive and safe from violence as far as possible. This trend continues despite attempts by the new government and political parties to combat it. Millions of rands' worth of damage and production losses have already been caused by violence in the business sector.

The insecurity and tension which violence creates in the residential areas and industrial environment in South Africa have extensive local as well as international side-effects, and have a particularly negative effect on productivity and economic growth in South Africa. The syndrome of violence that has developed in South Africa since 1976 must be brought to a halt; social and moral values and the sanctity of life must be restored, both at schools and at the industrial level. This will put South Africa on the road to economic success once more. Human resources managers must regard it as one of their main tasks to combat and eliminate violence in South Africa.

Violence is obviously detrimental to organisations and prevents them from achieving their goals. Already in 1990 the then executive director of the Institute of Personnel Management commented as follows on the violence in South Africa (Crous 1990:3):

The IPM believes that a focus on the wider environment is essential in an attempt to understand and hence manage the problem of violence in the work place. The reasons for violence are manifold and include the non-existence of outlets for social and political grievances, poor quality of life in South Africa for the majority of the population, high unemployment, the shortage of housing . . . and the education system and general intimidation. High levels of political unrest and faction fighting also contribute to violence.

Crous states that violence can be solved as follows:

The key to the solution of the problem lies in the macro-level political and economic arena as well as within organisations. It is crucial for disparities in social, economic and political matters to be removed and the disadvantaged to be empowered.

He proposes the following strategy to stamp out violence in the workplace:

Prior to undertaking social-political actions on behalf of the employees, management must ensure that their work place is free from discriminatory practices. Management must halt unilateral actions and enter into meaningful consultation and negotiation on all issues which could effect employees' worklife. Consideration must be given to the democratisation of the work place—to such issues as worker participation and participative management.

If human resources managers would implement this, the vicious circle of conflict and violence in the workplace and the negative effect this has on the political and economic system in South Africa can be counteracted.

It is clear that South Africa urgently has to deal with socio-political problems at the macro-level. The serious human resources problems and the population explosion must also be dealt with to bring about efficient economic development.

23.3 AFRICA'S POPULATION STATISTICS
South Africa is an integral part of Africa. Consequently the population figures and the manner in which the population growth is being handled elsewhere in Africa and Southern Africa may serve as inputs when South Africa's population problems are discussed.

It is useful to look at the current population figures for Africa, population growth over the past four decades and expected growth in the following four decades up to the year 2025 (table 23.1).

TABLE 23.1: Countries in Africa with the largest population in 1950 and 1992, with forecasts for 2000 and 2025

1950		1992		2000		2025	
Country	Population (millions)	Country	Population (millions)	Country	Population (millions)	Country	Population (millions)
1. Nigeria	32,9	1. Nigeria	115,7	1. Nigeria	147,7	1. Nigeria	280,9
2. Egypt	20,3	2. Egypt	54,8	2. Ethiopia	67,2	2. Ethiopia	126,6
3. Ethiopia	19,6	3. Ethiopia	53,0	3. Egypt	64,8	3. Zaïre	99,4
4. South Africa	13,7	4. Zaïre	39,9	4. Zaïre	51,0	4. Egypt	90,4
5. Zaïre	12,2	5. South Africa	39,8	5. South Africa	47,9	5. Tanzania	84,9
6. Sudan	9,2	6. Tanzania	27,8	6. Tanzania	35,9	6. Kenya	79,1
7. Morocco	9,0	7. Sudan	26,7	7. Sudan	33,2	7. South Africa	65,4
8. Algeria	8,8	8. Morocco	26,3	8. Kenya	32,8	8. Sudan	59,6
9. Tanzania	7,9	9. Algeria	26,3	9. Algeria	32,7	9. Uganda	53,1
10. Kenya	6,3	10. Kenya	25,2	10. Morocco	31,7	10. Algeria	51,9

Sources: United Nations (1991 and 1992), *World resources* (1992–93:246)

From table 23.1 it is clear that Nigeria consistently has the largest population in Africa, both historically and in forecasts. In 1950, South Africa was the fourth largest, in 1992 the fifth largest—a position it will retain until 2000—but in 2025 it will occupy seventh position.

23.3.1 The total population of Southern Africa
The population figures for the countries around South Africa appear in table 23.2.

It is clear that, both in the context of Africa and of Southern Africa, South Africa is a country with a very large population. It is therefore understandable that the country has various cultures, languages, beliefs, races and community systems.

23.3.2 The economically active population of South Africa
The economically active population consists of people aged 15 years and older who are either working in the economy or would be working if they had the opportunity.

TABLE 23.2: Total population of countries in Southern Africa in 1992

Country	Population (millions)
Angola	9,9
Botswana	1,3
Lesotho	1,8
Mozambique	14,9
Namibia	1,5
South Africa	39,8
Swaziland	0,8
Zambia	8,6
Zimbabwe	10,6

Table 23.3 shows the number of economically active people in South Africa (and in what were known as the TBVC states) since 1960, with forecasts for 1995 and 2000.

TABLE 23.3: Economically active population of South Africa (millions)

Year	Total	Asians	Blacks	Coloureds	Whites
1960	5,83	0,13	3,93	0,58	1,18
1970	7,62	0,20	5,09	0,76	1,57
1980	10,17	0,28	6,97	0,99	1,94
1985	11,70	0,33	8,02	1,17	2,18
1990	13,42	0,37	9,38	1,34	2,32
1995	15,36	0,42	10,98	1,51	2,44
2000	17,61	0,46	12,98	1,65	2,52
Annual growth (millions)					
1980–1990	2,81	2,92	3,02	3,14	1,83
1990–2000	2,75	2,15	3,30	2,06	0,81

Source: Barker (1992:40)

Earnest attempts will have to be made to create job opportunities in South Africa to counteract unemployment, the economic and social decline associated with it, and violence and political unrest. This can only be done if education and training are effective and the demand for and supply of human resources are in equilibrium. These elements are discussed in the following sections.

23.4 DEVELOPMENTS IN EDUCATION AND TRAINING IN SOUTH AFRICA

Great strides have been made in recent years with the development of a joint strategy by business organisations and political institutions for meaningful change in the educational system in South Africa. The National Manpower Commission (1991:45) sketches the educational situation as follows (translated from Afrikaans):

The provision of adequate formal education of high quality forms the basis for the achievement of a competitive economy. This education must establish a sound point of departure for meaningful further vocational training, and the extent to which success is achieved in this respect will be of vital importance in increasing productivity and creating prosperity for all South Africans.

In September 1990 the Minister announced far-reaching changes in the field of national education and a team of experts was appointed to make recommendations on the possibility of changing ordinary education into career-oriented training, among other things. This is essential in South Africa's present situation since there are great shortages of career-orientated staff. Moreover, it is necessary to confer with the private sector on adapting education and training in accordance with human resources needs. The state, educational institutions, parents and the business sector have to work together as mutual partners in education. Career guidance is vital to make pupils aware of career opportunities and the requirements of the technical and technological fields. Human resources managers can play an important role in this by providing the communities in which they function with aid, advice and guidance for those who intend to enter the career market in the near future.

According to the National Manpower Commission, South Africa in the 1990s was characterised by:

. . . radical developments in the political arena in South Africa. The role of training with regard to these changing political, social and economic spheres will be particularly important for the changeover to a new South Africa in the next decade. Most observers agree that successful change is very closely linked to economic growth and prosperity, and that education, training and retraining of the available human material with regard to the knowledge, skills and attitudes demanded by the rapidly changing situation, will play an important role in the future.

With regard to further initiatives to adapt the educational and training system in South Africa to correct historical imbalances, note must also be taken of the ANC's (1993) policy guidelines in this regard. The ANC advocates 10 years of compulsory and free education for all pupils, in a schooling system that prepares individuals for participation in the economy and the community. There must be maximum flexibility and mobility between the various levels of both formal and informal education and training. The ANC will give special attention to the education and training of women and rural students, as well as the development and provision of adult education for literacy up to the level of a secondary school certificate. The ANC also contends that employers should regard it as their main priority to make literacy training available for employees in their service. A national system must be established for standards and certificates in adult education. As far as the control and management of the educational system is concerned, the education and training policy must be regulated by the principles of democracy within a national unitary system. This will also be brought about by equality between education and training by the central government and the regional and local authorities.

The policy document of the ANC contains a code for education and training. This reads as follows:

A code of practice in relation to training, education and adult education, as determined by the state, together with employers, trade unions and other organs of civil society, will promote the achievement of our policy objectives. It should encompass at least the following:

- *The integration of training, education and adult education into a national system of qualifications and accreditation which allows people to transfer credits between the different systems, which is recognised and accredited by employers, and also allows people full employment mobility;*
- *On-going employment advice, career guidance and counselling from basic schooling through to retirement;*
- *The training of trainers and educators in an integrated national strategy to meet the needs of all sectors of the society;*
- *The effective use and deployment of community members after the completion of training programmes on which they have been sent in consultation with their communities. They will feed back into the community the skills that they have gained. A data base of those who have been on such training programmes will be established and follow-up tracer studies used to enable the implementation of this;*
- *Prioritising the development of an appropriate technology policy and the training of technical specialists to ensure that our economy meets the needs of all South Africans within the context of the world economy;*
- *The adoption of a national policy on the importation of skills and technological know-how which will aim to lessen our dependence on these imports and increase our capacity to be self-reliant. We will actively seek the support of our international allies to achieve this goal;*
- *Prioritising strategies for employment creation programmes and employment security. Within these programmes, the training of youth and women will be prioritised. Such programmes and training will include safety and protection rights.*

The present situation in education must be seen against the projections for human resources trends in South Africa (Dostal 1989). This is discussed in the following section, together with the trends up to the year 2010.

23.5 HUMAN RESOURCES TRENDS IN SOUTH AFRICA UP TO THE YEAR 2010

In this section we mainly deal with estimates; therefore the statistics discussed will not necessarily be accurate. The implications of population growth and its accompanying problems are of vital importance, however, and the sooner more effective population planning is initiated by the government, the better it will be for the South African population.

The total population figure of South Africa is important in population planning and development for the country as a whole. Whatever the final population figure for the year 2010, now is the time to get to work to be able to feed, clothe and provide work for that population.

Before going into a detailed analysis of the demand for and supply of human resources in South Africa, a review of the future South African population is essential. The projections (table 23.4), which include the former TBVC countries and are based on various estimates, extend to 2010.

TABLE 23.4: Total estimated population of South Africa (millions)

Year	Total	Asians	Blacks	Coloureds	Whites
1995	45,10	1,03	35,29	3,53	5,17
2000	51,17	1,10	40,97	3,80	5,31
2010	64,38	1,20	53,38	4,27	5,53

Source: Barker (1992:27)

In the light of the massive population increase set out in table 23.4, it must be borne in mind that the number of pupils will increase proportionately. The increase in necessary infrastructure, such as schools, teachers, books and playing fields, will therefore also be astronomical. The resultant supply of labour and therefore the demand which has to be established by job creation must also be taken into account.

These projections serve as background to the analysis and discussion of the demand for and supply of human resources in order to calculate how the tremendous surplus of human resources can possibly be accommodated.

Labour supply refers to the economically active population, which is usually defined as persons aged between 15 and 64 who are prepared to work if the opportunity exists.

Labour demand is largely a function of the growth and structure of a country's economy. In order to solve unemployment problems and create jobs, economic growth is usually emphasised. On the other hand, structural characteristics such as changed technology, managerial skills and institutionalised processes, such as tax legislation, do not receive sufficient attention to absorb the supply. Normally labour demand cannot be changed by economic growth only. Therefore, for the next few decades South Africa needs structural changes in the economy, as well as significant economic growth, in order to counteract the small demand for labour and the resultant underemployment and unemployment.

Dostal's (1989) updated projections put these terrifying population figures into perspective and indicate what effect they will have on South Africa. The combined demand for and supply of labour according to skills and educational level are shown in table 23.5. Note that skills levels do not necessarily correspond with educational levels. Therefore the results in the table should be seen as a rough estimate of labour shortages and surpluses compared with demand in the various educational categories.

Table 23.5 shows that there has been a growing surplus of workers with an educational level lower than standard 8 since 1980, whereas a shortage was experienced at the higher levels. However, employees with lower qualifications,

TABLE 23.5: The supply of and demand for labour by skills and educational level for the years 1980 to 2000

	1980			SCENARIO 1—2000			SCENARIO 2—2000		
	Supply ('000)	Demand ('000)	Surplus/ shortage ('000)	Supply ('000)	Demand ('000)	Surplus/ shortage ('000)	Supply ('000)	Demand ('000)	Surplus/ shortage ('000)
Level 1/Degree	178	299	−121	433	414	+19	790	559	+231
Level 2/Diploma	425	758	−333	1 184	1 305	−121	1 666	1 763	−97
Level 3/Std. 8–10	1 964	1 958	+6	5 607	2 197	+3 410	5 738	2 969	+2 769
Level 4, 5/Below std. 8	8 227	4 479	+3 748	11 431	4 191	+7 240	10 461	5 663	+4 798

Notes
1 Scenario 1 is a conservative projection of educational improvements in the labour supply, while the demand is based on the assumption of an average annual economic growth of 2% between 1980 and 2000.
2 Scenario 2 presupposes educational improvements in the labour supply according to more recent trends in education, while the demand is based on the assumption of a 2% economic growth up to 1990 and a 5% growth thereafter.
3 The employment levels 1, 2, 3 and 4/5 correlate broadly with professional (level 1), highly skilled (level 2), skilled (level 3), semi-skilled (level 4) and unskilled (level 5).

Source: Dostal (1989)

for example standard 8 to 10, might have been doing work of higher qualified people. This means that the surplus in the standard 8 to 10 group was taken up in the diploma group, or even in the degree group. It may therefore be assumed that there was actually an even bigger shortage in the diploma and degree groups, while the surplus in the standard 8 to 10 group was in reality also bigger.

Certain deductions may be made on the basis of the forecasts for 2000. According to scenario 1 the rate of education among blacks and the explosion in education for blacks which started in 1975 are maintained. There may, however, be too many university students taking courses that are not career-orientated. The result will be a surplus of graduates in South Africa.

During the recession of 1990 to 1993, graduates with non-vocational qualifications were battling to find jobs, and even had to resort to jobs for which only matriculation is required. There is still, however, a disquieting shortage of people with diplomas. Vocational studies at technikons should therefore be encouraged. The surplus of people with standard 8 to 10 and lower than standard 8 keeps growing. The assumption can again be made that there are many standard 8 to 10 people who might be handling work for which a diploma or even a university degree is usually required.

Scenario 2, a more optimistic view, is based on the assumption that education will keep on growing at an accelerating rate. There will, however, still be a shortage of diplomas offered by technical institutes, technikons and training colleges. As a result of technical developments in South African industries there will still be a shortage of qualified people at this level by the year 2000.

Dostal's (1985) earlier projections estimated a surplus of 6 000 graduates in the year 2000; table 23.5 envisages an alarming 231 000 superfluous graduates.

There should therefore be more career-oriented education and career guidance for pupils at school right now, to encourage them towards more career-orientated studies after school. Human resources managers and vocational guidance officers can play an important role in this respect.

An alarming forecast in scenarios 1 and 2 is that the surplus in the group with an educational level lower than standard 8 will be 7,2 million and 4,8 million respectively; and the surplus in the standard 8 to 10 group between 3,4 and 2,8 million. An estimate of 10 million unemployed in South Africa by the year 2000 is therefore not far-fetched.

If the economic growth in South Africa is higher than the estimated 5% up to the year 2000, the surplus in the standard 8 to 10 group may be smaller. This is, however, highly unlikely. Political instability and the large-scale violence, coupled with an economic recession, make the 5% growth rate in scenario 2 unrealistically high. The authors of this book think that scenario 1 will come true. This means a catastrophe on a vast scale for the South African economy and people; and as for the claims to a distribution of wealth—there will be no wealth to distribute. The authors hope that their perception of the situation will not materialise because if it does, South Africa will sink into a Third World-type of morass from which it will be extremely difficult to emerge. Political unrest, instability and violence must therefore be brought to an end soon, so that large-scale foreign investment can take place and job opportunities can be created.

The figures given above also indicate the shortages already experienced in the economically active population of South Africa. These are discussed in the following section.

23.5.1 The demand for skilled human resources in the new South Africa

If South Africa wants future economic growth, serious attention will have to be given to obtaining and utilising skilled human resources. These aspects are discussed below in the context of the 1990 *Annual Report* of the National Manpower Commission (1991:39–43).

Structural changes, advances in technology and other developments have a continuous influence on the demand for human resources. This makes it possible for the authorities concerned and the private sector periodically to adapt their employment, education and training policies. South Africa is at present experiencing a double imbalance in its labour force. On the one hand there is an excessive demand for skilled workers, while on the other hand there is an excessive supply of unskilled workers.

According to the National Manpower Commission (1991:63–4), the various levels of human resources are identified as follows:

- *High-level human resources:* Engineer or engineering technologist; engineering technician; draughtsman; architect, quantity surveyor; natural life or agricultural scientist; natural or life technician; other technicians, doctor, veterinarian, chemist, nurse, careers in education, religion or law; accountant, auditor; careers in management, administration, the arts, sport or entertainment; and other professions.

- *Middle-level human resources:* Clerks, salespeople, miners, transport workers, workers in the various services, supervisors, technical assistants, artisans, apprentices.
- *Low-level human resources:* Semi-skilled and unskilled persons.

The shortage of high-level human resources leads, among other things, to reduced levels of productivity resulting in poor-quality products and services, delays in technical innovation and upward pressure on the rate of inflation on account of the large turnover of qualified staff, and eventually to a lower rate of economic growth. The inevitable result is a negative effect on the welfare of the population.

It is an accepted fact that men are almost fully utilised in the South African economy. The role of women, however, can be drastically expanded. In 1989 the proportion of women in the high-level category was 39,9% and 36,9% in the middle level. In total only 28,8% of workers were women—employed mainly in traditionally female occupations, such as nursing and teaching. If these two careers are excluded, women made up only 19,2% of higher-level human resources. This source of available high-level human resources will therefore have to be exploited and expanded to meet the needs.

The main factors that restricted female participation until recently were probably the human resources policy in many organisations, the tax system, as well as a lack of encouragement and inadequate career planning for women. As far as legislation is concerned, considerable progress has been made with eliminating discriminatory measures, for example by the amended Wage Act of 1983 and the Matrimonial Property Act of 1984, as well as by separate taxation.

Table 23.6 clearly shows that there are serious shortages, particularly in high-level occupations, and that urgent attention must be paid to making people available in these sectors. Shortages in various professional categories are also expected.

The following high-level and middle-level careers (not yet discussed) have been identified by the Department of Manpower as those in which a critical shortage is being experienced. (Because we are concerned here with the subsidisation of training, most of the occupations that require university qualification have been omitted.)

- *Apprentice:* metal and engineering, electrical and electronic, building, motor, printer, furnishing;
- *Technician:* engineer, draughtsman;
- *Engineer:* not registered (technologist);
- *Clerical:* bookkeeper and bookkeeping financial clerk;
- *Computer-related:* office machine and computer operator, computer system occupations including programmers;

TABLE 23.6: Projection of the demand for human resources up to the year 1995

Occupational group [1]	1985 [2]	1995	% growth
Engineer and engineering technologist	22 047	29 754	3,0
Engineering draftsman	42 575	60 852	3,6
Draftsman, topographer, cartographer	9 665	11 326	1,6
Natural and life scientist	7 946	10 721	3,0
Natural and life technician	24 444	34 631	3,5
Other technicians	5 243	6 586	2,3
Medical doctor, dentist, veterinarian	21 470	28 221	2,8
Paramedical occupations	19 736	28 557	3,8
Nursing occupations	15 963	23 148	3,8
Teaching occupations	92 958	130 466	3,4
Art, sport and entertainment occupations	256 559	360 504	3,5
Legal occupations	13 196	17 569	2,9
Accountant	6 891	8 625	2,3
Other professional occupations	29 557	36 599	2,2
Management and administrative occupations	33 578	47 784	3,6
	207 406	279 895	3,0
Total: High level	**809 234**	**1 115 238**	**3,3**
Clerical worker	820 331	1 033 286	2,3
Sales worker	324 517	440 921	3,1
Transport worker	243 774	287 208	1,7
Service worker	536 728	726 922	3,1
Foreman, supervisor	108 043	150 761	3,4
Artisan, apprentice	285 321	338 251	1,7
Technical assistant and trade-related occupations	28 703	37 918	2,8
Total: Middle level	**2 347 417**	**3 015 267**	**2,5**
Production and mine worker, labourer	2 740 300	3 142 665	1,4
Grand total	**5 896 951**	**7 273 170**	**2,1**

Notes
1 Domestic workers, the informal sector and agricultural workers excluded; former TBVC states included; based on a real economic growth rate of 2,7%.
2 Normalised figure based on the relevant growth rate over time.

Source: Barker (1992:121)

- *Production supervisor:* building and construction; preparation and manufacture of food, drink and tobacco products; chemical, petroleum, coal,
  rubber and plastic product manufacturing and processing; metal
  manufacture and processing; woodwork; manufacture of paper and pulp
  products; manufacture of clothing and textiles; mining and stone-
  quarrying.

It should be clear that human resources projections are vitally important for
human resources planning. Since the accuracy of such projections is dependent
on numerous factors, such as technological and political developments, they are
used to identify only broad trends up to the year 2000.

In line with developments in other countries, a sharp increase in the demand for high-level human resources is expected, particularly in occupations in the engineering, technological, scientific, medical and teaching spheres. At a projected real economic growth rate of 2,7% per year, the demand for high-level human resources is expected to increase by between 3% and 4% per year, or between 500 000 and 600 000 people.

For middle-level human resources, the expected growth in demand is between 2% and 3% per year, with particularly sharp increases in the demand for the occupations of foreman, supervisor, service worker, artisan and salesperson. Since the supply of people with school qualifications from standard 7 to standard 10 will increase even more rapidly, a significant oversupply of middle-level human resources is predicted, although probably not in all middle-level occupations. Occupations that require a fair amount of in-service training will still experience shortages.

The least growth will be evident in the demand for low-level human resources (between 1% and 2% per year), and this level will also have the greatest over-supply.

The National Manpower Commission conducted a survey among 25 organisations in 1990, which involved 363 000 workers, to identify the occupations in which there was a perpetual shortage. The following list of critical occupations has been compiled on the basis of the inputs of these organisations and in consultation with the Department of Manpower:

- *Engineer:* mechanical, electronic, electrical, chemical, metallurgical, civil and related, mining, transport, industrial;
- *Engineering or natural science technologist:* textile, mechanical;
- *Computer science occupations:* computer programmer, computer systems analyst, computer systems designer, computer systems co-ordinator, software systems engineer;
- *Artisans:* electrician—construction, telecommunication, engineering; instrument mechanic, tool-maker, instrument-maker, electronics mechanic;
- *General:* accountant (chartered), metallurgist, general medical practitioner, photolithographer.

The umbrella organisation for personnel agencies, APSO (Association of Personnel Service Organisations of SA), was asked to conduct a similar survey for the private employment placement industry. The results of this survey confirm to a large extent the data obtained in the National Manpower Commission's survey.

It is clear from the above that South Africa is experiencing acute shortages of high-level human resources in particular, and the prospects of overcoming these shortages before the year 2000 are bleak. Even at a growth rate of 2,7% annually up to the year 2000, enormous human resources shortages are envisaged in the skilled cadres. The problem is so acute that not even immigration will solve it. Educational institutions and human resources managers must take note of these trends now so that they can make the necessary adjustments in their human resources planning and demand for human resources.

23.5.2 General aspects that affect human resources in the new South Africa

Something to be borne in mind up to the year 2010 is that the industrial or modern economy can only accommodate part of the growing population, and that the informal and peripheral sector will have to carry a large section of the growing population. Dostal (1989) estimates that 30% to 40% of the total economically active population will have to be employed in the informal sector of the economy by the year 2000. In other words, 8 to 10 million people will not be accommodated in the modern economy and will have to be employed in the informal sector, or remain unemployed.

It is clear that the worst shortages will be experienced in the technical field: there will be a great demand for technical diplomas. At the same time, the surplus of people with standard 8 to 10 will remain. This points to a lack of coordination between educational planning and human resources development. It is clear that the economy will not be able to accommodate everybody holding this qualification, which could lead to frustration because people's expectations of the new South Africa are high. It is therefore advisable for South Africa to study international developments in educational strategies to solve these problems. For example, rapid technological progress could change as well as create employment opportunities.

Positive development activities involving the media in education, and computer-based training will have to be used to improve the skills level of the labour force. This is particularly important because technological development renders traditional tasks superfluous (see chapter 24).

Attention should also be paid to aspects such as decentralisation, self-employment, and extention of the small business sector. This will enable even persons with a standard 8 to 10 qualification to form part of the informal sector and start small businesses on an informal basis. Schools will have to adapt their curricula and concentrate more on the practical aspects of business development and business economics in order to pave the way for these developments.

When it comes to mobilising human resources, all human resources managers in South Africa who want to contribute towards the successful functioning of their organisations up to the year 2000, must meet the following seven challenges:

- They must be aware that human resources are strategically important to the organisation. All people, irrespective of colour, sex or creed must therefore be optimally mobilised to the benefit of the organisation for which they are working.
- A change will have to take place in the attitude and behaviour of all managers and employees to eliminate artificial obstacles in the decision-making processes in organisations and to institute affirmative action.

- The training of effective managers and the improvement of leadership practices will have to be expedited. Human resources managers must also actively cooperate in developing the potential of subordinates.
- A development dynamism and culture must be stimulated in organisations. Concern about quality and excellence, and a spirit of innovation must be cultivated among employees.
- A culture of freedom and candour must be encouraged, but in the context of realism and discipline in the organisation's human resources.
- Communication and training must be improved. Communication from the top down involves the organisation's mission, culture, strategies, results, environment, etc. Communication from the bottom up should focus on new ideas, suggestions and innovations. Training should take place continuously throughout the careers of employees, and focus especially on new technology, equipment and products, as well as the training of managers and supervisors in leadership, negotiation and participatory planning methods. This can only take place if the entire education system is adapted as proposed by various organisations, including the government, the ANC's policy guidelines for education and training, the Promotion of Equal Opportunities Draft Act (1993) and the Manifesto of Basic Human Rights (1993).
- Close attention must be paid to working conditions and remuneration systems. Employees as individuals and the various teams should be remunerated in accordance with their outputs and contributions to the organisation.

Note must also be taken of the ANC's (1993:31) policy guidelines for human resources development, which will influence the overall human resources policy in South Africa (see accompanying box).

Provision of education and training will be linked to the development of human resources within a national development strategy aimed at the restructuring of the economy, redistribution and the democratization of society.

Such a strategy will ensure that all development programmes are pursued in a systematic, coordinated and comprehensive manner to ensure that:

- *Development programmes are sensitive to specific needs of each community, particularly with regard to the needs of women, youth, rural people and the disabled;*
- *Allocation of resources in development programmes must redress deprivations and imbalances between and within different communities;*
- *The provision of education and training within development programmes should enjoy recognition within the national education and training system.*

23.6 HUMAN RESOURCES POLICY AND OBJECTIVES IN SOUTH AFRICA

South Africa's human resources policy is laid down by the government of the day and administered by the Department of Manpower, which is responsible for its implementation. As the Department of Manpower has been operational since 1 August 1924, it has had long years of experience in this task.

To understand the context in which the human resources policy is carried out in South Africa, it is important to note the task and functions of the Department of Manpower. The mission of the Department of Manpower (1991:16) is:

The Department of Manpower strives towards promoting and organising the rights and interests of all individuals in the sphere of labour, as best as possible, in an impartial manner and within the framework of government policy.

In the execution of the human resources policy of the government of the day, the Department of Manpower (1990:3–7) focuses on three elements, which are discussed below.

First, the department is responsible for the administration of the human resources legislation allocated to it:

- Legislation dealing with freedom of association, collective bargaining and service conditions: the Labour Relations Act (No. 28 of 1956);
- Legislation dealing with minimum standards, employment and social welfare: the Guidance and Placement Act (No. 62 of 1981); the Basic Conditions of Employment Act (No. 3 of 1983); the Occupational Health and Safety Act (No. 85 of 1993); the Wage Act (No. 5 of 1957);
- Legislation dealing with insurance and accidents: the Compensation for Occupational Injuries and Diseases Act (No. 130 of 1993); the Unemployment Insurance Act (No. 30 of 1966);
- Training legislation: the Manpower Training Act (No. 56 of 1981).

In the second place, the department must execute government decisions in the sphere of human resources.

In the third place, the department must report to the policy-making authorities and give advice with a view to possible policy and legislative amendments in the light of developments in the sphere of human resources, practical problems and the experience gained in the execution of policy.

The human resources policy of the country must be viewed against the background of the national economic objectives. These can be summed up as follows:

- Maintaining a satisfactory economic growth rate;
- Providing sufficient job opportunities;
- Distributing the national income according to socially acceptable norms;
- The geographical distribution of economic activities according to socially acceptable norms;
- Improving social welfare;
- Attaining an acceptable level of economic independence of external economic and political developments.

549

The following human resources objectives have been formulated by the Department of Manpower from the above policy:

- To research the human resources needs of the country and to plan the infrastructure in such a way that it will provide for the needs of the country both quantitatively and qualitatively;
- To make available various employment and information services in an effort to balance the demand for labour with the supply, and to help every worker to develop his or her potential;
- To maintain and promote industrial peace;
- To improve the utilisation and quality of the available human resources;
- To provide employment security for workers, which includes reasonable wage and salary levels, pensions, accident cover, medical aid and unemployment insurance;
- To integrate the human resources policy with the general economic policy of the country.

Three basic principles must be adopted to achieve these objectives:

- Maximal self-management must be left in the hands of the employers and employees to arrange industrial labour relations among themselves with minimal government interference.
- Safety, order and stability must be maintained in the sphere of labour.
- There must be consultation between employers, employees and the government.

The functions of the Department of Manpower are geared towards the fulfilment of its mission, and are divided as follows:

- Industrial relations;
- Occupational safety;
- Occupational services;
- Human resources training;
- Administration;
- Unemployment insurance;
- Accident insurance;
- Research.

Table 23.7 gives a schematic representation of the functioning of the Department of Manpower. The table shows that the Minister of Manpower holds the key position in the Department of Manpower. The department controls various statutory and other institutions.

If the structure of the Department of Manpower is analysed, it is indisputable that the department plays a vital role in all facets of human resources management in South Africa and that it is represented by various sections at numerous levels, for example by the National Training Board. The various sections of the department also reflect the main areas of effective human resources management. These tasks are emphasised in various chapters of this book, for example training undertaken by the National Training Board (as discussed in chapter 21) and the role played by industrial relations in the country (chapter 20).

23.7 THE APPLICATION OF HUMAN RESOURCES POLICY

Historically, South Africa's human resources policy has not only been formulated and applied as a result of government policy; it has also been influenced by the country's economic development. South Africa experienced rapid economic growth after becoming a republic in 1961. According to Nel and Van Rooyen (1993:72) this rapid economic growth and industrialisation resulted in a great increase in the demand for skilled labour. However, labour legislation mandated job reservation. Consequently industrial development outgrew the legislative structure as well as the human resources policy of the government.

This gave rise to widespread labour unrest in Durban during the early 1970s, followed by labour unrest on the Reef in 1976. The main causes were the country's inadequate labour legislation and its human resources policy. The formulation of a new human resources policy and the adaptation of labour legislation to changed circumstances therefore became most urgent.

The Wiehahn Commission investigated all aspects of labour legislation, the settlement of disputes and the elimination of restrictions in the entire field of labour in an effort to provide an improved foundation for industrial relations in South Africa. The Riekert Commission mainly emphasised the elimination of unjustifiable discrimination against certain population groups, the maintenance of internal security and industrial peace, the preservation and development of the free market system and the effective utilisation of all available resources (including labour). The Riekert Commission also dealt with policy regarding workers outside their work environment, housing, the mobility of labour, occupational mobility, the so-called free trade areas within South Africa's industrial centres, etc.

The result was that South Africa's human resources policy is now drastically different to that of a decade ago, and it will again change drastically in the following decade to keep up with political changes.

The present human resources policy may be regarded as a combination of schools of thought and developments. It is based on the following philosophy and principles:

- *Free enterprise and a free-market economy:* The point of departure is that the principles of free enterprise must apply also in the field of human resources. This implies freedom of association, freedom for workers to choose their work and for employers to engage in whatever business they regard as profitable. It implies belief in free and fair competition and in the promotion and remuneration of employees according to merit.
- *Maximum self-management and minimum government interference:* The free-market mechanism implies maximum self-management by employer and employee within the framework of a tripartite industrial relations system (i.e. government, employer and employee). Regulatory powers in labour affairs rest with employers and employees in the first instance, but with the

TABLE 23.7: Organisational structure of the Department of Manpower as on 15 May 1991

MINISTER

STATUTORY INSTITUTIONS

DIRECTOR-GENERAL

DEPUTY DIRECTOR-GENERAL

INDUSTRIAL COURT
PRESIDENT

Purpose: To settle conflicts of interests and rights in the labour field.

Functions

- To resolve and settle conflicts of rights and interests in the labour field.
- To determine whether labour practices in specific instances are unfair or not.
- To enquire into and report on any matters referred to it by the Minister regarding the objectives of the Labour Relations Act, 1956.

UNEMPLOYMENT INSURANCE BOARD
CHAIRPERSON

Purpose: To investigate and make recommendations regarding unemployment matters.

Functions

- The hearing of appeals against certain decisions and the consideration of recommendations by unemployment provident committees.
- Conducting investigations and making recommendations to the Minister regarding any matter pertaining to the Fund or the prevention or reduction of unemployment.
- Conducting any investigation or performing any other activities in terms of the Act or as directed by the Minister.

ADVISORY COUNCIL FOR OCCUPATIONAL SAFETY
CHAIRPERSON

Purpose: To make recommendations to the Minister on matters relating to occupational safety.

Functions

- To perform duties assigned to it by the Act.
- To advise the Minister on request or on its own initiative.
- To obtain and process technical information with the Minister's approval.

MANPOWER BOARD
CHAIRPERSON

Purpose: To advise the government on the utilisation of human resources in South Africa.

Functions

- The allocation of the human resources needed by the SADF for the performance of its task.
- Determining categories of persons employed in or practising any specific career, industry, business or trade who should be exempted from military service.

EXEMPTION BOARDS
CHAIRPERSON: CENTRAL BOARD

Purpose: To consider applications for exemption from or postponement of military service.

Functions

- Arranging meetings of the Military Exemption Board to consider applications for exemption from or postponement of military service.
- The provision of administrative auxiliary services to the Military Exemption Board.

BOARD FOR RELIGIOUS OBJECTION
CHAIRPERSON

Purpose: To classify certain persons as religious objectors.

Functions

- The consideration of applications for classification as religious objectors.
- To communicate decisions regarding the classification of religious objectors to interested parties.

NATIONAL MANPOWER COMMISSION
CHAIRPERSON

Purpose: To make recommendations to the Minister on all labour matters, including labour policy.

Functions

- The continual monitoring and analysis of the overall human resources situation.
- Keeping abreast of developments and trends on the international labour front.
- The continual evaluation of the application and effectiveness of labour legislation.
- Research into the design, planning and updating of human resources programmes.

NATIONAL TRAINING BOARD
CHAIRPERSON

Purpose: To advise the Minister on policy matters arising from or connected with the application of the Manpower Training Act.

Functions

- To perform the functions prescribed by the Manpower Training Act with a view to the coordination, encouragement and facilitation of training or its promotion in any other way.
- To perform any other functions prescribed by the Act or directed by the Minister.
- To advise the Minister on policy matters arising from or connected with the application of the Act and on any other matter related to training.

WAGE BOARD
CHAIRPERSON

Purpose: To investigate wages and conditions of employment in any trade as directed by the Minister and to submit to him a report and recommendations in this regard.

Functions

- To conduct investigations and submit reports to the Minister in terms of Section 4 of the Wage Act, 1957.
- To make recommendations in terms of this Act.

CHIEF DIRECTORATES

CHIEF DIRECTORATE OF MANPOWER TRAINING
CHIEF DIRECTOR

Purpose: To promote optimal human resources training.

Functions
- The creation of a legal and administrative framework for the achievement of orderliness and coordination and the maintenance of standards.
- Support for and encouragement of training efforts in the private sector, inter alia by way of financial assistance in some form.
- To supplement training efforts by the private sector through the establishment of public insitutions for the training of certain categories of workers.

CENTRAL ORGANISATION FOR TRADE TESTING
HEAD

Purpose: To test the knowledge and skills of prospective artisans.

Functions
- Conducting and controlling trade tests.
- Providing administrative auxiliary services.

CHIEF DIRECTORATE OF OCCUPATIONAL SAFETY
CHIEF DIRECTOR

Purpose: To promote the safety and health of workers within their sphere of employment and the safety of machinery in general.

Functions
- Preventing accidents and occupational diseases.
- Ensuring satisfactory working conditions.

OFFICE OF THE WORKMEN'S COMPENSATION COMMISSIONER
WORKMEN'S COMPENSATION COMMISSIONER

Purpose: To insure workers against pecuniary loss in cases of accidents at work.

Functions
- Maintaining the Accident and Reserve Funds.
- Dealing with medical matters in regard to accidents.
- Compensation of workers who suffer accidents at work.
- Accounting for trust monies.
- Rendering legal services and general office auxiliary services.

CHIEF DIRECTORATE OF LABOUR RELATIONS
CHIEF DIRECTOR

Purpose: To promote sound labour relations.

Functions
- The promotion of national, international and interstate labour relations.
- Overall control over the legal aspects of labour organisations and financial inspections.
- Achieving and maintaining industrial peace.

DIRECTORATE OF VOCATIONAL SERVICES AND PLACEMENT
DIRECTOR

Purpose: To promote optimal human resources utilisation.

Functions
- The establishment and provision of effective career guidance services.
- The promotion of optimal employment in the labour market.
- The collection and dissemination of information on human resources and unemployment.
- Control over exemption boards that consider applications for postponement of or exemption from national service.

OFFICE OF THE UNEMPLOYMENT INSURANCE COMMISSIONER
UNEMPLOYMENT INSURANCE COMMISSIONER

Purpose: To pay benefits to certain unemployed persons and the dependants of certain deceased persons.

Functions
- Collecting and making available fund monies and control over their disbursement.
- The registration of contributors and employers and the provision of office auxiliary services.
- The provision of legal services and general auxiliary services to the Unemployment Insurance Board.

CHIEF DIRECTORATE OF ADMINISTRATION
CHIEF DIRECTOR

Purpose: To provide administrative, clerical and other auxiliary services.

Functions
- Responsibility for staff and office administration.
- Liaison services for the promotion of the department's image.
- Control over training and work centres for the handicapped and the blind.
- The accomplishment of efficiency in organisation and work procedures.
- The financial administration of the department's budget.
- The administration of legislation regarding religious objection.

REGIONAL OFFICES
Regional directors
BLOEMFONTEIN, DURBAN, GERMISTON, JOHANNESBURG, CAPE TOWN, PORT ELIZABETH, PRETORIA, WITBANK

Purpose: To accomplish and maintain stability in the field of human resources.

Functions
- Ensuring the safety and welfare of workers within their sphere of employment.
- Promoting optimal human resources utilisation.
- Accomplishing and maintaining industrial peace.
- The promotion and regulation of human resources training.
- The provision of administrative auxiliary services.
- The payment of benefits to certain unemployed persons and the dependants of certain deceased persons.

Source: Department of Manpower (1991)

government in the second instance. For this reason there is minimum government interference, but maximum decentralisation of decision-making and autonomy for employers and employees in matters of mutual interest, and maximum consultation in matters of interest to all three parties.

- *Safety, order and stability:* Safety, order and stability depend on the responsible, disciplined and rational conduct of employees and employers towards one another and towards the South African community as a whole.
- *Consultation:* It is very important that changes in the private and public sectors should be orderly and evolutionary and should only be made after consultation and discussions with all the parties concerned. This requires the acknowledgement and protection of the rights of individual workers and employers, as well as of specific groups of workers and employers, irrespective of the basis of their group membership. There are, however, certain differences between employees in the private sector and those in the public sector, because they are subject to different legislation. The right to strike, for example, does not extend to civil servants.

South Africa's human resources policy emphasises the creation of sufficient job opportunities and the promotion of higher living standards. It aims at anticipating and planning to meet the country's human resources needs. Provisioning services must be introduced to synchronise labour supply and demand. Industrial peace should be maintained as far as possible. The utilisation and quality of existing human resources should improve. This means that training and retraining are extremely important. Workers must be provided with social security and wage and salary levels, pensions, accident cover, medical aid and unemployment insurance must be reasonable. The human resources policy must be fine-tuned to the economic policy of the country.

This human resources policy also mandates geographical freedom of movement for all workers, joint handling of all population groups regarding all functions that are not community-bound (for example employment services), and the execution of specialised functions on behalf of government departments on an agency basis, such as the payment of unemployment benefits.

The human resources policy is a tripartite system:

- *The government's role:* To provide the statutory framework within which the parties in the private sector can operate and through which the free-market system can function unencumbered.
- *The role of employers:* To implement the government's human resources policy effectively in several activities, such as the maintenance of standards in the selection, placement and training of human resources; consultation with employees and obtaining their cooperation in labour practices; the consistent maintenance of fair labour practices at all levels for all employees; serious attention to all labour matters; encouraging all workers to undergo training

and retraining; circumspect and patient action during strikes and, wherever possible, settling labour disputes between employers and employees peacefully; human resources planning to prevent problems and shortages of skilled workers in particular; and compliance with internationally acceptable labour standards.

- *The role of employees and trade unions:* The human resources policy recognises the right to work, freedom of association, collective bargaining, the right to strike, to be trained and to be protected. The basic rights of workers may be interpreted as follows: firstly, workers must be granted the opportunity of joining any organisation or trade union of their choice and also of working for any organisation. Secondly workers are expected to exercise their freedom of association with responsibility. Thirdly it is against the law for an employer to prohibit an employee from belonging to a trade union. Fourthly trade unions have a free choice to decide who their members should be. Fifthly employees are entitled to decide for themselves by collective bargaining what their service conditions, etc. with regard to an employer should be—workers may strike if negotiations fail. Sixthly any worker may ensure his or her future by making use of training and retraining facilities such as state training centres and group training centres made available by the government.

Unemployment and the creation of job opportunities are priorities for the government and are discussed below.

23.8 UNEMPLOYMENT

Unemployment is one of the greatest problems in South African society. Unemployment among economically active people increased from 7% in 1980 to 13,2% in 1989, representing an increase of 10% per year. The informal estimate of the unemployment rate is at present 50%, meaning that half of the people prepared to work have no jobs. It is estimated that from 1994 to the turn of the century only one out of 100 matriculants will be able to obtain work in the formal sector unless the economy shows drastic improvement.

Between 350 000 and 450 000 new jobs will have to be created every year merely to accommodate newcomers to the job market. This is disturbing, because unemployment is the background of the violence and political unrest from which the country suffers. However, these problems are interdependent and must be jointly addressed.

The two most important sources of unemployment statistics in South Africa are the Department of Manpower (registered unemployment) and the Central Statistical Services (current population census).

Unemployment can be defined in two ways:

- The strict definition, according to which an unemployed person has taken active steps to find work;
- The extended definition, by which people who have not actively sought work, but who would like to work, are classified as unemployed.

555

In South Africa, the difference between the estimated economically active population (12,5 million people) and formal employment (8,0 million) was 4,5 million people in 1990. According to the National Manpower Commission, this peripheral sector includes subsistence farming, other informal sectors and the unemployed.

The National Manpower Commission regards people as unemployed if they meet the following requirements:

- They have not been working, i.e. they have worked for less than five hours during the previous seven days;
- They have made an effort to get a job during the previous month;
- They are in a position to accept a job within one week;
- They are between 16 and 64 years old in the case of men; or between 16 and 59 in the case of women.

23.9 THE CREATION OF EMPLOYMENT OPPORTUNITIES

It has been mentioned in a previous section that the government regards increasing the general welfare of the entire population and combating unemployment as a top priority. However, the government feels that private institutions should assume co-responsibility in solving the unemployment problem. What is more, employment opportunities must be created within the framework of a market-oriented economic system, which is the system prevailing in South Africa.

There is no instant formula for the elimination of unemployment, but economic growth will counter it. Because South Africa aspires to a free-market system, the private sector also has to make a contribution: the government and the private sector should launch joint programmes to counter unemployment.

23.9.1 Guidelines for creating employment

The following guidelines for creating employment may be followed:

- *The role of the government and the private sector:* The creation of employment opportunities can only be successful if both the government and the private sector actively participate. The private sector can play an important role by, for example, using more labour-intensive methods whenever possible, instead of mechanisation or automation of work. The government can, for example, finance labour-intensive projects such as road construction and irrigation works. It may also play an indirect role by giving more direction in the creation of employment opportunities.
- *Economic growth:* The promotion of economic growth is one of the best ways of creating employment opportunities. Job creation is, however, dependent on steady economic growth, whereas sudden economic upswings and recessions are inherent to the free-market system. The active stimulation of economic growth should promote workers' vertical mobility and develop various occupational structures in order to create more employment opportunities. The government also needs to attend to matters that cause market distortion and ways to rectify them. This means the promotion of the

small business sector, optimal regional development, improved education and training and more effective utilisation of the country's available labour resources.

- *Formal and informal small business sector:* It is well known that small businesses and the informal sector of economies all over the world provide a significant proportion of the total number of employment opportunities in a country. They provide the necessities of life to a large number of people who cannot find employment as wage or salary earners in the formal sector of the economy or in sophisticated organisations. A sound regional development policy may contribute extensively to the creation of employment opportunities. South Africa has a large concentration of economically active persons in a few metropolitan areas; regional development can release the pressure in these areas by providing employment opportunities away from the metropolitan areas. This may also benefit the local populations in regional areas.

- *The development, utilisation and preservation of human resources:* These are active and effective means of providing people with more and improved employment opportunities. The training and development of human resources are discussed in detail in chapters 21 and 22.

- *A sensible population policy:* It is vitally important that the population growth rate should be reduced. A concerted effort has to be made right now to slow down population growth if the dilemma of 10 million unemployed by the year 2000 is to be avoided. Therefore the reduction of population growth is an important part of the government's human resources policy. On the other hand, the government is also trying to create as many employment opportunities as possible in order to provide every worker in South Africa's growing population with an income.

23.9.2 Review of employment creation
In 1987 the President's Council established a job creation strategy. Labour market programmes developed to address unemployment are an integral part of the wider economic policy framework in South Africa. Both the private sector and the work seeker are closely involved. Since 1990, the most important aims of government policy to relieve unemployment have been as follows:

- To make an optimal contribution over the long term to stable economic growth, with the emphasis on job creation and investment;
- To make a contribution towards easing the plight of people, and to equip them to compete in the economy on the basis of equal opportunities.

Van Dyk *et al.* (1992) in particular emphasise the urgency for addressing the socio-economic development problems of poverty, backlogs in housing, education and training, basic health needs and other factors that stand in the way of participating in the economy and improving the quality of life.

International sanctions and boycotts have had a negative effect on economic growth, but the harm that these steps have caused South Africa is hard to quantify.

The judicious curtailment of government restrictions on economic activity can play a fundamental role in promoting economic growth and job creation. Excessive deregulation can be counterproductive, however, since an economy cannot flourish in conditions of disorderliness, and therefore a healthy balance between economic and social objectives should be aimed at.

Smaller businesses are particularly important for creating employment, and they are relieved of the restrictions of labour legislation in a variety of ways. Various industrial councils, for example, exclude small businesses (normally those with fewer than five employees) from the terms of enforcement of certain agreements, or exempt them entirely. Examples are the clothing and furniture industries in the Cape and Natal, the Industrial Council for Motor Transport Enterprises (goods) and the laundry, cleaning and dyeing industry (Cape).

The importance of the small business sector for economic growth, and job creation in particular, cannot be stressed too strongly. The most successful and fastest growing economies in the world are characterised by an active small business sector. It is also regarded as an important instrument to counter poverty in South Africa.

If one considers that it costs an average of R4 300 to create one new employment opportunity in a small business as against R42 000 for the economy as a whole (excluding agriculture), there is no doubt as to the importance of the small business sector as a creator of jobs.

Various institutions are concentrating their efforts on the expansion of the small business sector. Among them are the Advice Bureau for Small Business Enterprises (ABSB) and the Small Business Development Corporation (SBDC). The ABSB also renders a variety of services to this sector, such as management consultations, planning sessions with people in small businesses, and training people in this sector. The SBDC gives financial help, accommodation and support services to people in small businesses.

Apart from the building of houses, and training and work centres, the government also initiated job creation projects such as nature conservation, the building of dams, combating soil erosion and laying on electricity and water for disadvantaged communities. One important advantage of these programmes is that this kind of government spending has little, if any, negative effect on the balance of payments. It is also one of the cheapest forms of short-term job creation (although the employment opportunities are usually of a temporary nature), and it can be aimed directly at disadvantaged communities.

23.9.3 Applying the Manpower Training Amendment Act to unemployment

The creation of job opportunities, together with the training of unemployed persons, has been accelerated by the promulgation of the Manpower Training Amendment Act (No. 39 of 1990) on 1 July 1990.

It makes provision for setting up a fund for the training of unemployed people, into which, in addition to funds granted annually by Parliament, contributions from the private sector can be deposited. This fund, which was put into operation on 1 October 1990, prevents training having to be terminated at the end of one financial year, only to be started again in the following financial year. The aim of the fund is to finance training which will equip unemployed people with the necessary skills to facilitate their entry into the labour market.

23.9.4 The scheme for training unemployed people

This scheme is the result of the Department of Manpower's special job creation programme. Among other things, training is given in the construction of low-cost housing to meet the needs of the informal sector. This type of training is important because there are not sufficient job opportunities in the formal sector, and people who have been trained only to work in the formal sector will therefore not necessarily find work. To provide meaningful training for the unemployed, particularly in building-related directions, they have been given nine-week training courses in construction since 1 April 1991, after which they are exposed to a minimum of three weeks' practical experience in a job creation project or with a building contractor.

The scheme for training unemployed people undertakes training in the following broad sectors:

- *Training to enter the formal sector:* There is greater emphasis on placing unemployed persons in jobs in the formal sector after they have been trained.
- *Development of the informal sector:* Training courses offered for the informal sector aim at providing people without work with the necessary work skills to enable them either to find employment or to identify an income-generating opportunity and pursue it, thereby functioning as an independent entrepreneur.
- *Training in building-related courses:* Training contractors are encouraged to cooperate with local authorities to integrate the provision of low-cost housing with the training of unemployed people. Before such a building project is approved, the local authority or owner must have made the plot and necessary material available. Because of the size of such projects, the funds for training are augmented with job creation funds so that the project can be completed.

As a result of the unrest in certain residential areas, several building projects have had to be scaled down or completely abandoned.

Specific problems encountered in the training of unemployed persons in building-related skills have led to new guidelines for this type of training being drawn up in cooperation with the Training Council for the Building Industry (TCBI). The most important requirement with which a training contractor now has to comply in order to offer building-related training in terms of the scheme, is that the contractor must be accredited by the TCBI. The training covers a period of nine weeks off the job, after which the trainee is accommodated for at least three weeks on a job creation project or in the service of a private building contractor. The TCBI monitors the training, which ensures that it meets the requirements of the industry and increases the chances of the trainees to find employment.

- *Training the handicapped:* The Department of Manpower is aware of the plight of handicapped people and special funds are made available for their training. The training courses for the handicapped are usually longer than other courses.
- *Training of entry-level computer programmers:* This training is especially aimed at those returning from compulsory or voluntary military service who are unable to find immediate employment. The training is intensive and takes 16 weeks. After completing the course, the trainees have to write an examination set by the Computer Users Council of South Africa.
- *Training in entrepreneurship:* People who show talent, skill or potential during the basic unemployment programmes may be given training in entrepreneurship. This training helps people to develop their management skills and to start their own businesses.

The Department of Manpower has made available a document, *Guidelines for training contractors,* to private persons who would like to train the unemployed. Obtainable at all offices of the department, it contains valuable information about the rules, regulations, financial assistance given by the Department of Manpower, etc.

Both the government and the private sector have shown that they are serious about programmes for job creation, and it may be expected that these programmes will gain momentum in future.

23.10 CONCLUSION

This chapter began with a review of the Southern African population. Labour problems such as low productivity, too rapid urbanisation and a very high population growth rate were then addressed. The nature and extent of the labour market were investigated and attention was paid to human resources surpluses and shortages up to the year 2010.

The human resources policy of South Africa and its effect on the labour market were addressed. The human resources policy is particularly aimed at job creation because by the year 2000 South Africa may well have to accommodate 10 million unemployed people. Consequently, large-scale job creation and the training of unemployed people have been undertaken by the government. Unemployment can be combated by launching practical job creation actions, seriously propagating population planning and encouraging the free-market system as far as possible in order to stimulate economic growth as a measure for creating job opportunities for the growing population.

It is clear that the composition and size of a country's economically active population and its human resources policy are completely interwoven, and that the synchronisation of these elements with effective economic growth may lead to full employment in South Africa.

Questions

1. What do you think are the greatest labour problems currently facing South Africa? How can these be solved?
2. How will the rapid urbanisation of the population affect human resources management in the future? What impact will this have and how can the problem be solved?
3. Do you think it is desirable to place strict limits on population growth by imposing legislation? Discuss your view.
4. What are your recommendations for eliminating industrial violence in South Africa? Also give attention to solving the issue of trade union-inspired labour unrest and the associated violence in the urban areas of South Africa.
5. Critically discuss the principles on which South Africa's human resources policy is based. Would you want to make amendments? Motivate your answer.
6. You are an advisor for the National Economic Forum (NEF) and have to compile an action programme for creating job opportunities. Present your suggestions in the form of a report with recommendations to the chairperson of the long-term working group (LTWG).

Sources

ANC 1993. *Policy guidelines*. ANC, Johannesburg.

Barker, F.S. 1992. *The South African labour market*. Van Schaik, Pretoria.

Crous, W. 1990. Violence in the workplace. *IPM Journal*, Vol. 8, No. 9. April, p. 3.

Department of Manpower. 1990. Guidelines for training contractors (a scheme for the training of unemployed persons). Unpublished document. Department of Manpower: Chief Directorate Manpower Training, Pretoria.

Department of Manpower. 1991. *Report of the Director-General for the year ending 31 December 1990*. (RP 51/1991) Government Printer, Pretoria.

Dostal, E. 1985. Manpower: supply and demand 1980–2000. *Industrial Relations Journal of South Africa*, Vol. 5, No. 3.

Dostal, E. 1989. The long-term future of education in South Africa. Occasional paper no. 15. Institute for Future Studies, University of Stellenbosch.

National Manpower Commission. *Annual reports*. 1980 (RP 39/1981), 1981 (RP 25/1982), 1982 (RP 45/1983), 1983 (RP 41/1984), 1984 (RP 46/1985), 1985 (RP 81/1986), 1989 (RP 45/1990), 1990 (RP 49/1991). Government Printer, Pretoria.

Nel, P.S. & Van Rooyen, P.H. 1993. *South African industrial relations: theory and practice*. 2nd revised edition. Academica, Pretoria.

Van Dyk, P.S., Nel, P.S. & Loedolff, P. van Z. 1992. *Training management: a multi-disciplinary approach to human resources development in South Africa*. Southern, Halfway House.

Chapter 24

Technology and the human being

P.S. van Dyk

STUDY OBJECTIVES

After studying this chapter, you should be able to:
- Define the concept "technology";
- Demonstrate the effect of technological change on the human being as an employee;
- Explain the socio-technical approach to technological change;
- Explain the demands and pressures that technological change exerts on the human being as an employee;
- Define and schematically illustrate a human resources management information system.

24.1 INTRODUCTION

Van Wyk[1] (1989:13) identifies technology as one of the macro-trends that will have a tremendous impact on human resources management in South African organisations during the 1990s. He refers in particular to the steadily widening gap between technological potential and technological literacy, as well as the rise of the so-called "techno-peasantry". He says (1989:16):

All of us have heard repeated descriptions about the rapid rate of advance in technology and the phenomenon of exponential growth. We are bombarded with information on technological phenomena such as Langmuir-Blodgett films, superconductivity, bio-electronics, super-magnetic-energy-storage and so on.

And yet we find very few of these significant events actively understood and debated by major corporate managements. Most companies do not have an overall technological guidance policy. The word "technology" hardly ever appears on a

---

1 Professor Van Wyk of the Management School of the University of Cape Town is considered a world expert on megatrends and their influence on societies and organisations.

boardroom agenda. And even major banks will incur investments with a high technological content without having an adequate grasp of the technology involved.
Because of the ever-growing importance of technology in the modern business environment, it is essential that the top management of organisations regard the development of technology as part of management training, and base board decisions on the results of technological analyses. Various guidelines have been proposed for human resources management in the 1990s. Van Wyk (1989:18) suggests that the overarching guideline with regard to technology should be the following:

Be alert to the growing need for technological understanding at the senior levels of management. Many companies are adopting training programmes, sending their managers on courses and appointing technology managers or secretariats. If your company has done so, monitor the activities of the technological secretariat carefully. What has it done to increase the capabilities of the board for grasping the unfolding technological frontier, to what extent has the technological secretariat created a skill base, to what extent have the soft managers been exposed to technological issues? Get to know the necessary resources available to increase technology capability of your corporation at the senior level.

In order to determine the effect of technological change on organisations and employees, one has to define technology, investigate the relation between technology and productivity from a macro point of view, study the reaction of organisations to technological change, and examine the reaction of employees to technological changes in the work situation. This approach is essential if one is to put the challenges technology poses for human resources management in the right perspective.

24.2 WHAT IS TECHNOLOGY?

Bedeian (1984:374) asserts that there is consensus, given certain conditions, that technology has to do with the way in which organisations transform inputs into outputs. This conception of technology relates to techniques or processes used to transform materials or information (for example labour, knowledge, capital or resources) into various outputs (goods or services). All organisations may be regarded as users of technology, whatever their nature. Porter *et al.* (1975:232–3) argue in support of this assertion as follows:

It must be emphasised that technology is a term that is applicable to all kinds of organizations, not just industrial or manufacturing. All organisations, whether production-orientated or service-orientated, are presumed to involve individuals in some sort of activities that result in the transformation of "things" (requests, raw materials, people, communication, symbols, etc.) coming in into things going out.

The Australian government appointed a committee to investigate technological change and its consequences. In its report (Australian Government 1980:3) the committee of inquiry into technological change in Australia defined technology as that amount of information or skills and experience developed for the production and utilisation of goods and services. It may include:

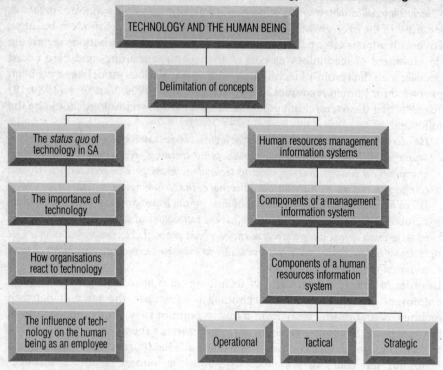

- Scientific and technical knowledge of specific products, processes and production methods;
- Engineering knowledge required to design, develop, manufacture, install, maintain or modify machinery;
- Management knowledge required to manage the labour force, utilise the plant and equipment, obtain and administer funds and identify and satisfy markets.

This indicates that technology includes every possible activity involved in the transformation of inputs into outputs in an organisation.

The same committee (1980:8) defines technological change as follows:

Technological change is change in processes, materials, machinery or equipment, which has an impact on the way work is performed in an enterprise or on the efficiency and effectiveness of the enterprise.

This definition fits the present author's view of technological change, i.e. that it should be aimed at building more successful organisations. Success can only be achieved by creating more efficient and effective organisations. We also think that change should never be brought about for its own sake, but only to increase productivity—particularly when the consequences of technological change are taken into account.

24.3 THE *STATUS QUO* OF TECHNOLOGY IN SOUTH AFRICA

It is remarkable to see the wide variety of different kinds of technology found in South African organisations in this last decade of the 20th century. Under-privileged communities, for example, are still using "traditional" technology (such as certain agricultural techniques), while somewhat more modern technology is used in the middle groups of societies (small business sector, informal sector, etc.). In both rural and urban areas we find a tendency towards labour-intensive industries rather than technology-intensive industries. This can largely be ascribed to the fact that these people lack the skills to make optimal use of more modern technology, and do not have sufficient capital to obtain it. At the other end of the scale we find large modern industries that are charac-terised by technological intensity in practically every sphere of production and services.

According to Cronje *et al.* (1990:54) an increasing amount is spent on research and development in South African organisations: such expenditure increased by about 22% per year in the 1960s and 1970s. The diffusion period—the time from the discovery to the implementation or commercial application of an innovation—has shrunk by 60% since the beginning of the century, and continues to shrink, which further speeds up the rate of innovation.

Another characteristic of technological innovation that management has to appreciate is that inventions and innovations are unlimited and will continue to affect the environment. Examples of possible innovations by the year 2000 (table 24.1), hint at the limitless opportunities and threats technology holds for organisations.

TABLE 24.1: Possible technological innovations by the year 2000

Strong possibilities	Less likely possibilities	Hypotheses
• Robots for domestic help • Genetic engineering to improve plant and animal strains through biotech-nology • New sources of food and energy • Three-dimensional televi-sion • Practical electric cars	• Small flying cars • Automated motorways • Artificial cultivation of new limbs and organs • Large-scale use of rockets for transport	• Complete genetic control • Space tours and space colonies • Lifelong immunisation against disease • The use of nuclear power in mining and civil engin-eering

Source: Cronje *et al.* (1990:54)

The question that now arises is how technological innovation affects the organisation and what implications it holds for management. According to Cronje *et al.* (1990:55), the most fundamental result is probably higher productivity. The ability to make more and better products threatens organisations with keener competition, compelling them to reassess such matters as organisational management, division of labour, appointment of staff, methods of production and marketing strategies. Another clearly discernible effect of technological innovation is the creation of complexities, for example complex consumer goods or production systems, which will make new demands on management. These demands will probably necessitate managers with a good background in technology or technologists trained in management. A third result of technological innovation, especially in industries with advanced technology, is an insatiable demand for capital. As capital is limited in South Africa, management will have to give constant attention to the use of labour-intensive technology not only to ease the pressure on demands for capital but also to provide more employment.

Improved technology: the key to prosperity
The essential aspect of economic viability in manufacturing is acceptance in the market. To a large extent, technology determines how competitively a product can be marketed. Improved process technology can improve quality and implies lower costs, which make lower prices possible. New product technology is the key to market entry. Technology is thus the key to increased market share with products of higher value.

Improved technology in all the industries of the economy implies a larger output with the same production factors (labour, capital and raw materials). The macro-supply in the economy is increased and more income is generated per worker. New product technology and the associated market creation and penetration improve the country's share in world markets. Various experts are of the opinion that the rate of and capacity for technological innovation in an economy form the basis of its dynamic competitive advantage in international trade.

Technological progress, therefore, affects the organisation as a whole, including its products, life-cycle, materials supply, production processes and even managerial approach, but more especially the employee who has to use such technology.

24.4 THE IMPORTANCE OF TECHNOLOGY
In general it may be said that the survival of a complex world with a growing population of divergent ideological leanings is impossible without accelerated technological change.

If South Africa fails to modernise, its competitive abilities in relation to its trading partners will decrease. (Hirschowitz 1990:12)

Technology is important for the following reasons:
- In the industrial sector, technology remains the primary source of increased productivity. Despite new approaches to the motivation of employees and various incentives to increase production, the consequent increase in productivity is insignificant in comparison with the increase achieved as a

result of technological advancement. For example, in the USA the index of manufacturing productivity (in output per hour worked) in the private sector increased by almost 34 points between 1961 and 1980. The greatest proportion of this increase can undoubtedly be ascribed to better technology.

- The exponential growth of technology has made the development of increasingly marginal resources economically viable, ensuring uninterrupted material benefits at acceptable costs. The limited and finite nature of national resources has become more prominent over the past few years. This resulted in recognition of the important role of technology in the recovery of resources.

This awareness of the necessity of technological progress and change gave rise to an international attitude that can be described as a continuous pursuit of increased innovation.

In the past few centuries the innovation of technological concepts took place over a number of generations. At the present rate of technological change several such innovations are introduced within the work life of an average employee. Bedeian (1984:375–6) provides a conjectural model of technological change (see figure 24.2). He explains his model as follows:

The solid line and its related ordinate scale at the left show intervals between preceding and succeeding technologies, that is the number of years that the preceding technology has survived before the advent of its successor. Thus, the scale reading for the point designated as circa 1450 is 2 000; this means that the technologies that preceded (e.g. manuscript writing, the distaff and spindle, and catapult) those introduced about 1450 (e.g. printing, the spinning wheel and flyer, the hand gun) had characterized society for about 2 000 years. Analogously, the reading for circa 1895 is about 90 years, the period of dominance of predecessor technologies introduced at the time of the Revolution.

The dashed line and its related ordinate scale at the right show index numbers for the increasing capital cost of each successive technology. The assumption of an index number of 100 for circa 1450 says, in effect, that the technology that cost 100 units then has been supplanted by the technology of 1960 (e.g. satellite communication and space travel) at a cost one million times as great.

Once the graphs have been studied and their implications analysed, one might ask what the picture would look like in the future. The logical conclusion, based on the knowledge at our disposal, is that technology will develop ever faster, accompanied by increasing costs. The pace of technological succession will therefore increase, while its costs will rise astronomically. The question therefore arises, in view of the nature and composition of the South African labour market, whether it would be economically sound for developing countries (such as South Africa) to keep abreast of technological change in all economic sectors.

In addition to the effect of technology on productivity, technology is important from a business economics point of view for another reason, namely

FIGURE 24.2: A conjectural model of technological change

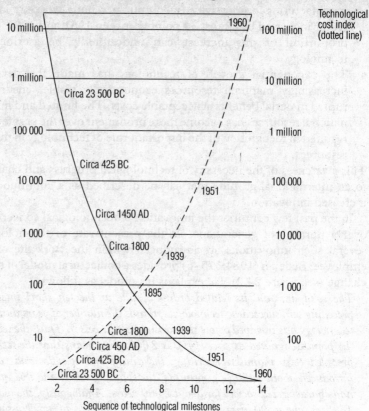

Intervals in years between preceding and succeeding technological milestones (solid line)

Technological cost index (dotted line)

Sequence of technological milestones

Source: Bedeian (1984:376)

that it is often a dominant determinant of task structures. Litterer (1973:280) substantiates this viewpoint with his statement that when technology and machinery change, tasks (jobs) change too. The truth of this statement is demonstrated by the evolution of technology, from the first elementary manual tools to the present use of computer-based manufacturing systems.

Another important reason is the effect of technology on employee attitudes and behaviour. Although the production line set-up springs to mind immediately, the effect of technology goes far deeper than the obvious subjection of humans to machines. Technology also affects the size and composition of groups, social interaction patterns and individual control over personal activities.

The last reason is the effect of technology on the structure of organisations. Researchers in this respect may be divided into two schools. One group regards technology as the main determinant of the structure of an organisation. This

568

group holds the opinion that different technologies require different organisational structures and that these structures are highly dependent on the technologies. This view is often referred to as the technological imperative. Members of the second group have a more moderate view: they regard organisations as open systems and acknowledge the mutual interdependence of technology and structure, i.e. that technology does affect organisations, but that organisations in turn affect technology.

Taking a systems approach to organisations we agree that there is a reciprocal relationship between technology and the structuring of the organisation.

24.5 HOW ORGANISATIONS REACT TO TECHNOLOGICAL CHANGE

The tempo of technological change is a clear indication of the continuing need for such technology. This need can easily be explained. In order to be competitive, organisations must always strive for the best input-output ratio which, as we know, is a function of the technological process. Although the usefulness of technology is not restricted to the industrial and public sectors, it may be assumed that these groups are the main users of technology. It may therefore be concluded that there is a critical link between technology (and technological change) on the one hand and the success of organisations on the other.

In an effort to survive in a competitive market environment, organisations are forced to adjust and to change. Greiner and Barnes (in Bedeian 1984:467) identify the purpose of change in an organisation as follows:

... on the surface, the purpose of organizational change is to facilitate the continued achievement of organizational goals; underlying the more obvious statements concerning greater profit and performance are two overarching objectives: (1) changes in the way an organization adapts to its external environment, and (2) changes in the behavioral patterns of its employees.

Researchers feel that organisations should pay more attention to the first overall objective mentioned above, and that the human subsystem is only taken into account after a decision has been made to implement new technology.

Organisations are continuously confronted with the need to adapt to changing circumstances and restrictions in the environment in which they function. As an organisation does not have complete control over its external environment, it is continuously forced to make internal organisational changes to enable it to deal effectively with new challenges arising from intensified competition, technological innovations, government policy and social requirements.

24.5.1 The effect of technological change on organisations

It has been mentioned that organisations need to accommodate changed technology in order to survive. The impact of technological change on a typical manufacturing organisation may be conceptualised as in figure 24.3.

FIGURE 24.3: The effect of technological change on an organisation

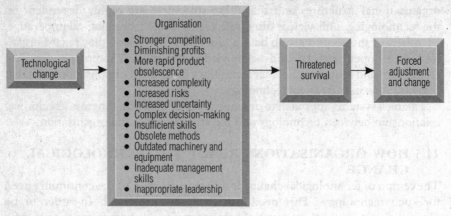

Source: Herholdt (1984:104)

Technological change affects all organisations, but particularly organisations for profit. New technology enables organisations to maintain higher productivity standards which enable them to market their products at lower prices. Organisations in the same industry that do not have such technology experience stronger competition because they cannot market their products at lower prices because of the cost factor. This results in reduced profits. New technology is characterised by new products, and organisations that have to make do without such technology find themselves in a market without a demand. (For example, the mass production of products with unique characteristics, such as the Cabbage Patch Kids dolls, by means of computer technology.) This results in increased management complexity, forcing organisations to take bigger risks in order to restore equilibrium. This leads to increasing uncertainty and more complex decision-making processes. The management of such an organisation will eventually realise that it has a serious shortage of skills. Obsolete production and other methods, as well as outdated machinery and equipment, aggravate the situation and managers are faced with a dilemma about the management skills and leadership styles required by the products, structures and technology outside the organisation. The survival of the organisation is thus threatened and it is forced to adapt and change (figure 24.4).

Herholdt (1984) and Bedeian (1984) corroborate our opinion on the way in which organisations react to technological changes, namely either proactively or reactively. Bedeian (1984:467) explains:

> *Organizational responses to such pressures may be characterised as ranging from reactive (changes introduced in reaction to unanticipated events) to proactive (changes introduced in anticipation of future happenings).*

Although a proactive attitude is more difficult, it is certainly a characteristic of organisations that try to influence their environmental outputs rather than react

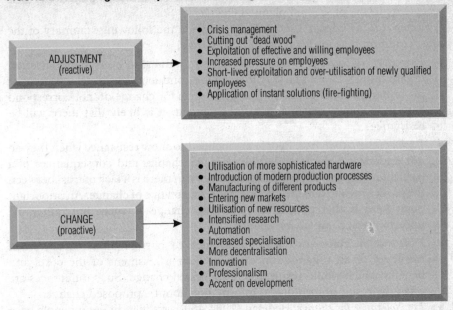

Source: Herholdt (1984:105)

to past events. This is the main difference between organisations that lead and those that follow.

As shown above, organisations do not really have much choice—they should all have a proactive attitude towards change. One might therefore ask why organisations resist change.

24.5.2 Resistance to change

Resistance to change is a subject on which volumes could be written. Although it is assumed that resistance to change usually comes from the workers, this is not always so: managements of organisations often display even more resistance to change. According to Peters (1978:35), managers have many reasons for avoiding change:

Talk to the managers and any number of reasons are given: We're just not ready yet. Our company is (is not) unionised. That would never work in our industry. That's all right in a high technology industry, but our people aren't that educated. The plant (company) is a lot larger (smaller) than ours. It might work in Japan . . .

Although change is universal and inevitable, it seldom takes place without problems. Resistance to change is a general, natural phenomenon; yet there is much difference of opinion on what the concept implies. Resistance to change is a big stumbling block in the way of successful innovation in organisations. There is also much disagreement on the extent to which people in organisations react positively or negatively to changes, and on the role played by their receptivity in the process of planned change.

Kotler *et al.* (Bedeian 1984:468–70) provide the following summary of the most common reasons for resistance to change:

- *Parochial self-interest:* It may be assumed that almost every member of an organisation will act in a way that will be conducive to the achievement of his or her personal goals. When suggestions for change do not correspond with individuals' personal goal achievement, it is likely that there will be resistance.

- *Lack of insight and trust:* People are inclined to show resistance when they do not understand the intended purpose, mechanics and consequences of a particular change. This usually happens when there is a lack of trust between the parties involved in the initiation and acceptance of change. An important point here is that people do not resist change as such, but rather the uncertainty accompanying change.

- *Difference in value assessment:* Resistance to change often occurs when members of an organisation differ in their assessment of the costs and benefits which would result from a suggested change. Such differences are often the result of insufficient information about a proposed change.

- *Low tolerance for change:* Bedeian (1984:469) says that different people have different capacities for absorbing change. Many people perceive the unknown consequences of change as a psychological threat to their feeling of competence and their self-esteem. Such people are usually scared that they will not be able to master the new behaviour and skills they may be expected to acquire.

These are only a few possible reasons for resistance to change. Bedeian provides a checklist that can be used to determine possible resistance to change. He suggests that the following questions be answered before change is introduced (1984:470):

- How much resistance will the suggested change cause?
- How will this resistance manifest itself?
- Is there a relationship of trust between the parties concerned?
- Do all the parties have the required information to understand the underlying reasons for the suggested change, as well as the benefits to be derived from it?
- Have the process of change and its consequences for individuals been spelt out clearly?
- Have real incentives been provided for the acceptance of the suggested change?
- What are the consequences of introducing or not introducing the suggested change?

The answers to these questions will determine how management should implement a particular change.

24.6 THE EFFECT OF TECHNOLOGICAL CHANGE ON EMPLOYEES

It is generally felt that much more time is spent on the non-human aspects of the development and implementation of technological change than on the employee, who is, after all, responsible for the operation of such systems. One of the main reasons for this is probably that people can think for themselves and can therefore not be directly controlled. Furthermore, although people are extremely adjustable, they can also be very headstrong when it comes to making their own decisions on how they want to go about things. Nevertheless, the role of the employee can be better integrated into the activities of the organisation by means of research into the behavioural sciences.

24.6.1 A socio-technical approach to technological change

A socio-technical approach is important in all organisations, since all organisations are characterised by the interaction between the human and technological sub-systems. In many cases, however, technology (including equipment, information and workflow) is developed first, and then people are selected and trained to fit in with this technology.

A socio-technical system is the fusion of the human (social) system and the technical system for a number of reasons to produce a desired result. These systems must therefore work in unison to produce the desired outputs. In addition, the social system has to deal with internal and external changes without disrupting the contributions of the technical system.

The nature of the work will therefore determine what type of organisation will develop among employees, and the socio-psychological traits of employees will determine how a particular task is executed. The interaction between an organisation and its environment is also important—not only should the demands and restrictions of the external environment (for example resources, capital and consumer preferences) be dealt with effectively, but also the expectations, values and norms of those who are responsible for the functioning of the organisation. These values, norms, preferences and so on of employees are not only relevant when they join the organisation, but are also influenced by the nature of the work and the structure of the organisation during an employee's career in a particular organisation. These values, norms and preferences are therefore subject to change. Schein (1970:107) says:

> Consequently, one cannot solve the problem merely by better selection or training techniques. Rather, the initial design of the organization must take into account both the nature of the job (the technical system) and the nature of the people (the social system).

Researchers such as Schein (1970) are of the opinion that any system exists within a threefold environment:

- A physical environment, for example the site, climate and layout;

573

- A cultural environment, represented by the values, norms and objectives of the community;
- A technological environment, consisting of the knowledge and the means available to the system for carrying out its tasks.

The environment prescribes certain activities and interactions for people in the system. These activities and interactions in turn give rise to the development of certain sentiments and feelings among employees and towards the environment. These interactions, sentiments and activities may also be regarded as the external environment. Schein remarks that increased interaction, and the accompanying new sentiments that are not necessarily determined by the external environment, go hand in hand with new norms and shared frames of reference generating new activities also not determined by the external environment. Homans (1950:76) refers to the latter as the internal system, comparable with what is generally known as the informal organisation. It also seems that the external and internal systems are interdependent: a change in one system will affect the other system. A change in technology will therefore result in a change in the patterns of interaction in the internal system. On the other hand, if the internal system has developed certain norms regarding the functioning of the organisation, these norms will often affect the way in which work is carried out, as well as its quality and quantity.

The underlying principles of the socio-technical approach need to be noted if this approach is to be successfully applied in order to convince groups and individuals to accept and accommodate changes brought about by new technology. Huse (1980:248) expresses its goal as follows:

The objective is to optimize the relationship between the social systems of the organization and the technology of the organization to increase quality of work life and produce output. When the systems are considered together, and arranged optimally, quality of work life is higher, output is greater, and the organization remains adaptable to change.

This is certainly a most desirable state in present-day environments and organisations in perpetual change.

Another important condition for the successful introduction of technological change in organisations is that the individual must be consulted. This is important, as the success of an organisation is the result of its efficiency and effectiveness and the efficiency of an organisation is the result of group performance, which in turn is the result of group efficiency and effectiveness. The latter is determined by individual efficiency and effectiveness. Individual performance is the smallest building block of successful organisations, and is the result of individual efficiency and effectiveness.

The above clearly indicates that technological change makes new demands on employees and places them under pressure. It also makes new demands on organisations and places them under pressure. One might therefore ask what kinds of demands and pressures affect individuals as a result of efforts made by an organisation towards adjustment and change.

574

24.6.2 Demands and pressures on employees as a result of change

According to Herholdt (1984:104) efforts to adapt (usually reactive) or change (proactive) result in increasing pressure on employees and drastically affect the demands made on them. These demands are often vague, obscure, conflicting, incomprehensible and characterised by limited guidance, unrealistic deadlines, too much information and irrelevant information. Employees are also faced with conflicting value systems, vague role expectations and a lack of accountability and permanence.

Employees react to these increasing demands and pressures in one of two ways: they either accept the situation as a challenge, or they perceive it as a threat. This behaviour is linked to the resistance to change mentioned earlier. Herholdt (1984:105) depicts the situation as in figure 24.5.

FIGURE 24.5: Nature of demands and pressures on employees as a result of adjustment and change by the organisation

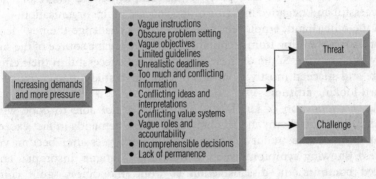

Source: Herholdt (1984:105)

If the employee perceives the increasing demands and pressures from management in the organisation as a threat, one or more of the reactions set out in figure 24.6 may be expected.

FIGURE 24.6: Employees' reaction to pressures and demands from the organisation

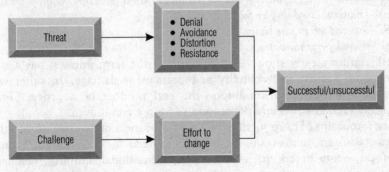

Source: Herholdt (1984:107)

An employee who indulges in denial, passing off demands as unrealistic in the belief that his or her ability, skills and knowledge are sufficient, will soon find himself or herself in a group of employees regarded as redundant by the organisation. Such an employee runs the risk of being demoted, reaching a dead end in his or her career or, at worst, being dismissed.

Similarly, employees showing avoidance are a burden to the organisation through their increased absenteeism, psychosomatic illnesses, avoidance of responsibility and tendency to drop out.

Distortion of demands and active resistance to change and adjustment are major problems in any organisation and seriously hamper efforts at development and renewal. Employees who react in this way are a burden to the organisation and contribute largely to the resistance to change syndrome (RC-factor) which affects the survival of the organisation at management level in particular.

Threat reactions on the part of the employee are therefore mostly unsuccessful and negative in terms of the success of the organisation.

On the other hand, employees who accept as a challenge the new demands and pressures resulting from technological change are the source of the survival of any organisation. Some of these employees are successful in their efforts to change and succeed mostly by means of continued study, perseverance and a forward-looking attitude.

A large proportion of employees are however not able to cope with the demands made on them, and in many cases these demands in fact exceed the human limits of adjustment and change. Such employees often become victims of stress, showing symptoms such as frustration, fatigue, insomnia, anxiety, reduced commitment, dissatisfaction at work, moodiness, guilt complex, absent-mindedness, concentration problems and physiological symptoms such as hypertension.

Continued pressure and repeated failure in an employee's efforts to adjust and change can cause depression and eventually culminate in the so-called burnout syndrome. Perlman and Hartman (1982:283) describe burnout in the context of the organisation as follows:

... burnout [is] a response to chronic emotional stress with three components:
  (a)   emotional and/or physical exhaustion,
  (b)   lowered job productivity, and
  (c)   over-depersonalization.

The literature clearly shows that burnout, as the term implies, has a strong element of finality, irreversibility and permanent damage. In other words burnout is an extreme condition—the end product of a process linking problems such as stress and depression to form a continuum.

The symptoms of burnout illustrate the seriousness of the condition: chronic fatigue, constant depression, an unrealistic need for recognition, cynicism, aloofness, acute boredom, withdrawal and emotional blunting, mechanical body movements, paranoia, disorientation and loss of contact with reality, muscle strain, psychosomatic illness, heart disease and self-destructive tendencies.

The most upsetting aspect of burnout is that the very employees who make an active effort to adjust, change and keep abreast of increasing demands may become its victims. Helliwell (1981) lists traits typical of potential burnout victims, which reveal them to be people who would generally be regarded as good and well-motivated employees. Potential victims are:

- Employees with an exceptionally full programme;
- Employees showing leadership qualities and giving guidance;
- Employees on whom others depend for support;
- Employees who would like to be accepted;
- Employees who are idealistic;
- Employees who enjoy leading others and readily accept responsibility;
- Employees who complete tasks faster than average;
- Employees who easily get impatient;
- Employees who have no problem in functioning under pressure;
- Employees who get bored easily and welcome change and variety;
- Employees who look for challenges;
- Employees who like being in the limelight;
- Employees who are proud of their achievements;
- Employees who cannot relax and do not want to be idle;
- Employees who are always emphasising the urgency of tasks;
- Employees whose performance is above average;
- Employees whose work is the most important thing in their lives;
- Employees who attach importance to their image and efficiency at work;
- Employees who are perfectionists.

No empirical evidence could be found to suggest that these extreme results of technological change in organisations manifest themselves more at any one specific employee level than another. One may therefore generalise by saying that employees at any level in an organisation who are continuously exposed to technological change are to a greater or lesser extent prone to burnout.

Technological change may thus exert a negative influence on productivity, progress, development and the survival of the organisation. This human restriction is particularly important if it is accepted that technological progress is responsible for 67% of the economic growth in the USA (Lewis 1982).

Herholdt (1984:109) points out that the effect of technological change on employees is becoming an increasing cause for concern in view of mental health in the community and the present emphasis on the quality of work life. (Quality of work life is discussed in chapter 14.)

24.6.3 Empirical research into technological change in South Africa

Little empirical research into technological change has yet been undertaken in South African organisations, and no publications on the subject could be found. In an investigation at a well-known building society conducted by the

Department of Business Economics of UNISA, Van Dyk *et al.* (1985) found that technological change affects employee functioning in three environments. They identify and define these environments as follows:

- *The psychological work environment:* Van Dyk *et al.* (1985:54) regard the psychological work environment as the primary environment, related to the psychological satisfaction experienced by the employee when doing the work for which he or she originally applied and was employed. Technological change disturbs this relationship and forces the employee to adapt to changed circumstances. The psychological work environment therefore refers to the intrapersonal work satisfaction experienced by the employee.

- *The social work environment:* The social work environment refers to interpersonal job satisfaction as well as intragroup job satisfaction experienced by employees because of their membership of organisations. In other words, it refers to the satisfaction an employee experiences in the context of the formal organisation. Intragroup job satisfaction is the satisfaction an employee experiences because of his or her membership of informal groups. Technological change affects both these relationships and forces employees to adapt to a changing internal social environment.

- *The physical work environment:* This refers primarily to the interaction between an employee and his or her physical work environment. More specifically, it refers to the environment affecting a person's senses and associated with his or her lower-order needs, which in turn affect his or her physiological functioning. Technological change has an effect on the physical work environment of an employee, who can adapt to this changed environment proactively or reactively.

Van Dyk *et al.* (1985:66) depict the effect of technological change on individual employees as shown in figure 24.7.

Figure 24.7 clearly shows that technological change forces organisations to adapt and change, and organisations may do this proactively or reactively. Organisations in turn pressurise employees to adapt or change proactively or reactively in accordance with those adjustments or changes made in the three environments within which employees function, namely the psychological, social and physical work environments. An individual adapts and changes primarily on the basis of the expectations contained in the psychological contract, which will eventually determine his or her attitude towards technological change. (There is a detailed discussion of the psychological contract in chapter 4.)

24.7 HUMAN RESOURCES MANAGEMENT INFORMATION SYSTEMS
24.7.1 General
Human resources management information systems are closely related to the above discussion of technology and the human being as an employee. The basic

FIGURE 24.7: The effect of technological change on the human being as an employee

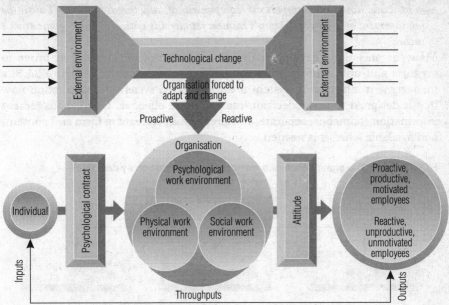

Source: Van Dyk *et al.* (1985:66)

aim of technology is to increase employee productivity. The scarcity of highly skilled employees in South Africa is well known; for this reason, the available employees must be used to the advantage not only of the organisation, but also of the country as a whole.

In most modern businesses and in the public sector in South Africa, practically all organisational functions have been computerised. Just think of the manufacturing process in the motor industry.

It is therefore important also to equip the human resources department of an organisation with modern information systems to increase the productivity of the employees of this department and enable it to render an effective service to the other organisational functions.

24.7.2 What is an information system?

Schultheis and Sumner (1992:469) explain the importance of a human resources management information system as follows:

An organization's human resources usually represent its largest operating expenditure, usually between 40 and 60 percent of total operating expenses. However, in service organizations, salaries and wages may account for up to 85 percent of total operating expenses. Cost alone would make human resources a very important element of any firm. However, the skills, knowledge, and attitudes of any organization's employees shape that organization in fundamental ways and

579

represent its human capital. It is important to remember that people are at once the most basic and most important component of any organization. Thus, the management of an organization's human resources is critical to the organization's success.

Many organisations develop management information systems in order to organise and utilise information more effectively. As shown in figure 24.8, a management information system is an integrated system of information flow that is designed to make decision-making more effective. Good management information is timeous, accurate, comprehensive, relevant in form and content, and available when it is needed.

FIGURE 24.8: The significance of a management information system (MIS)

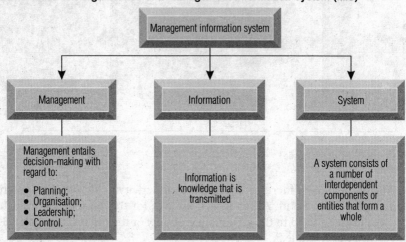

Source: Adapted from Murdick and Ross (1977:8)

Smit and Cronje (1992:161) interpret Murdick's and Ross's representation (figure 24.8) as follows. The first component of an MIS, *management,* requires no discussion in this section, as you are well aware of what it entails.

Before we define *information*, we must first clearly differentiate between data and information. Data are unprocessed facts, figures, opinions and forecasts, such as the stock records for car batteries at Volkswagen South Africa's Uitenhage plant. Information is processed data and is relevant for a manager during decision-making, such as: the stock of car batteries at the plant is sufficient for ten days, while the minimum stock ought to be sufficient for 30 days. Information thus tells the manager what a specific situation is. *Management information* is therefore information that is timeous, accurate and relevant and that represents the key factors of a certain situation. On the basis of such information managers can determine what they should do in the situation. The example of the stock cited above may be regarded as management information, as it implies that immediate action must be taken: increase the stock and determine how and why it was allowed to reach such a low level.

A *management system* consists of a number of interdependent components or entities that form a whole. These components are dynamically linked and have a mutual effect on one another in such a way that a goal is achieved. Examples of systems are all around us: the solar system, the education system, a car, an organisation and an information system (see chapter 3 for a further definition of the term "system").

A *management information system* (MIS) is an integrated approach that provides relevant information to assist managers in taking decisions. Similarly, a *human resources management information system* is an integrated approach that timeously supplies managers with sufficient information to improve the quality of their human resources management decisions.

24.7.3 Components of a human resources management information system

Schultheis and Sumner (1992:468) identify the following main and sub-components of a human resources management information system in accordance with the human resources management process:

- Operational human resources information systems;
- Tactical human resources information systems;
- Strategic human resources information systems.

They also provide a model of a human resources management information system (figure 24.9).

To a large extent, the components contained in figure 24.9 reflect the layout followed in this book. The management of an organisation must ensure that, just like other functions within the organisation, human resources management is also supplied with the latest technology to be more productive as an independent organisational function and also to render a better service to the other functional spheres of the organisation.

24.8 CONCLUSION

This chapter was aimed at highlighting the nature and extent of technological change, which affects both organisations and individual employees. The reaction of organisations to technological change may be proactive or reactive. Technological change affects employees, as they have to use this technology in the work process. Employees can react in various ways to technological change, but resistance to change is the most common. Employees are affected by technological change within three environments in an organisation. Employees, like organisations, can adjust reactively or proactively to technological change.

FIGURE 24.9: Model of a human resources management information system

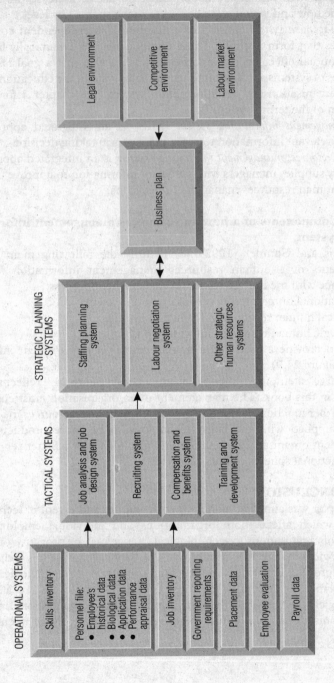

Source: Adapted from Schultheis and Sumner (1992:470)

Questions

1. In your own words, explain the concept "technology".
2. Identify the consequences of technological change.
3. In approximately 300 words, describe how organisations react to technological change.
4. Discuss the problem of resistance to technological change among employees, mentioning the underlying reasons.
5. What do you understand by the socio-technical approach to technological change?
6. Discuss the reaction of employees to demands and pressures from the organisation to adapt to technological change.
7. Briefly discuss the views of Van Dyk *et al.* (1985) on the influence of technological change on the human being as an employee.

Sources

Australian Government. 1980. *Report of the committee of inquiry into technological change in Australia.* Vol. 1. Canberra.

Bedeian, A.G. 1984. *Organizations: theory and analyses.* Dryden Press, New York.

Cronje, G.J. de J., Neuland, E.W., Hugo, W.M.S. & Van Reenen, M.J. 1990. *Introduction to business management.* Southern, Halfway House.

Helliwell, T. 1981. Are you a potential burnout? *Training and Development Journal,* October, pp. 25–9.

Herholdt, W. van der M. 1984. Die invloed van versnellende tegnologie op die mens as werknemer. In Du Toit, S.J. (ed.) *Menswees in die kollig.* NG-Kerkboekhandel, Pretoria.

Hirschowitz, R. 1990. Technological change and employment: some pertinent issues. *IPM Journal,* March, pp. 11–15.

Homans, G.C. 1950. *The human group.* Brace, New York.

Huse, E.F. 1980. *Organization development and change.* West Publishing, New York.

Lewis, J.D. 1982. Technology, enterprise and American economic growth. *Science,* Vol. 215, pp. 1204–11.

Litterer, J.A. 1973. *The analysis of organizations.* Wiley, New York.

Murdick, R.G. & Ross, J.E. 1977. *Introduction to management information systems.* Prentice-Hall, Englewood Cliffs, New Jersey.

Perlman, B. & Hartman, E.A. 1982. Burnout: summary and future research. *Human Relations,* Vol. 35, No. 4, pp. 283–305.

Peters, E.B. 1978. Job security, technical innovation and productivity. *Personnel Journal,* January.

Porter, L.W., Lawler, E.E. & Hackman, J.R. 1975. *Behavior in organizations.* McGraw-Hill, New York.

Schein, E.H. *Organizational psychology.* Prentice-Hall, Englewood Cliffs, New Jersey.

Schultheis, R. & Sumner, M. 1992. *Management information systems: the manager's view.* Irwin, Boston, Massachusetts.

Smit, P.J. & Cronje, G.J. de J. 1992. *Management principles: a contemporary South African edition.* Juta, Johannesburg.

Van Dyk, P.S., Gerber, P.D. & Nel, P.S. 1985. 'n Ondersoek na die invloed van versnelde tegnologie op 'n groep geselekteerde werknemers by Saambou Nasionale Bouvereniging. University of South Africa, Pretoria.

Van Wyk, R. 1989. Macro trends for HR management. *IPM Journal,* November, pp. 13–15.

Part 5

Human resources management in South Africa: *quo vadis?*

Strategic human resources management   Chapter 25

Overview of Part 5: Human resources management in South Africa: *quo vadis?*

AIM
To describe to the student or reader the theory underlying strategic human resources management in a pragmatic manner in order to introduce the newcomer to this sub-field to its importance.

PRINCIPAL STUDY OBJECTIVE
Chapter 25: Strategic human resources management. To instil in the student or reader the importance of incorporating strategic human resources management into the organisational strategy in order to improve the achievement of organisational success.

Chapter 25

Strategic human resources management

P.S. van Dyk

STUDY OBJECTIVES
After studying this chapter, you should be able to:
- Define the basic concepts with regard to strategy;
- Explain the human resources strategy;
- Demonstrate the integration of a human resources strategy with the overall organisational strategy;
- Schematically illustrate the approach of Rothwell and Kazanas.

25.1 INTRODUCTION

Each organisation should have a strategy, subdivided into sub-strategies such as marketing, finance and sales. Of all the sub-strategies, the human resources sub-strategy has thus far been mostly neglected by managements.

With the low productivity that characterises South African organisations and the great shortage of professional and highly skilled employees, management has realised that people are the only sustainable competitive advantage of an organisation. This shift in focus is being generally welcomed by human resources practitioners in South Africa, but the ball is now in their court to meet the expectations of top management in this regard.

This book deals with basic aspects of human resources management; strategic aspects are regarded as advanced subject matter. For this reason, strategy will only be briefly discussed on the basis of the principal learning components as shown in figure 25.1.

FIGURE 25.1: Principal learning components of strategic human resources management

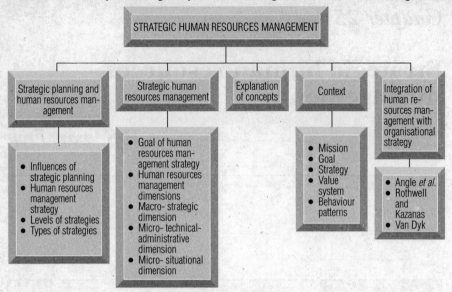

25.2 EXPLANATION OF CONCEPTS

The general concepts used in describing any organisational strategy are given in figure 25.2.

FIGURE 25.2: A pyramidical framework for strategic management

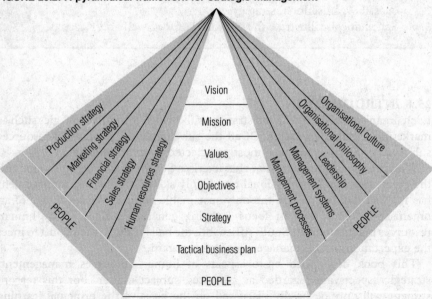

Source: Developed by Van Dyk (1994) for this book

> *Any talk about "vision", "mission" and "strategy" is nothing more than rhetoric unless the employees make it their own and learn to live with it.* (Plevel et al. 1994:62)

Only the concepts appearing on the front of the framework in figure 25.2 are briefly discussed here:

- *Vision:* This represents the goal or *raison d'être* of the organisation.
- *Mission:* This refers to the business in which the organisation is involved and represents a general plan of how the organisation aims to achieve its objectives.
- *Values:* These are expressed in the manner in which the organisation and its people handle customers, suppliers and each other.

Working definitions of different values

- *Respect for individuals* implies that people treat each other with respect and dignity, valuing individual and cultural differences. Communicate frequently and with candour, listening to each other, regardless of level or position.
- *Dedication to helping customers* implies truly caring for each customer. Build enduring relationships by understanding and anticipating customers' needs and by serving them better each time.
- *Highest standards of integrity* imply honesty and ethical behaviour in all our business dealings, starting with how you treat each other. It further implies to keep promises and admit mistakes. Our personal conduct must ensure that the organisation's name is always worthy of trust.
- *Innovation* is the engine that will keep the organisation vital and growing. It implies an organisational culture that embraces creativity, seeks different perspectives and risks pursuing new opportunities.
- *Teamwork* is a management philosophy that encourages and rewards both individual and team achievements. Freely join with colleagues across organisational boundaries to advance the interests of customers and shareholders.
- *Accountability* implies that each employee takes ownership of the success of the company. Rewards are determined by results.
- *Excellence* implies to be satisfied with nothing less than being the best in everything you do.

The purpose of values: to guide decisions and behaviour.

Source: Plevel *et al.* (1994:63)

- *Objectives:* The end result that the organisation wants to achieve is derived from its mission. Objectives generally represent the task that the organisation wishes to carry out.

- *Strategy:* The long-term plans developed by top management, usually for periods of two to ten years or even longer. These plans are used to evaluate and seize opportunities as well as to allocate resources. Strategy includes plans to create new products, to purchase other organisations, to sell unprofitable sections of the business, to make shares available and to enter international markets.
- *Tactical business plan:* Short-term plans to implement the activities and objectives contained in the strategy. These plans usually cover a period of a year or less. They keep the organisation on the course determined by its strategic plan. Tactical plans enable the organisation to react to changes in the environment, while at the same time concentrating on the overall strategy. Management should review and adapt the tactical business plan from time to time.
- *People:* These are all the employees of the organisation—from top management to the lowest level. They may be regarded as the power base for all the components of the pyramid. Plevel *et al.* (1994:59) rightly remark:

    People . . . an organisation's only sustainable competitive advantage.

The above confirms the main theme of this book, i.e. that the basic building block of organisational success is individual performance-orientation.

25.3 THE RELATION BETWEEN STRATEGIC PLANNING AND HUMAN RESOURCES MANAGEMENT

25.3.1 General

Organisations recognise that there is a critical relation between an organisation's human resources and their contribution to the achievement of its objectives. Managers are often confident that they will find human resources when business activities dictate it and the existing staffing appears to be insufficient. Key personnel in organisations tend to concentrate on financial and marketing plans and strategies, often at the expense of human resources. Human resources managers are often not informed of future business activities and expansions, and the critical relation between strategic business planning and human resources planning is ignored.

The need for a strategic perspective on human resources management is highlighted by Kochan and Barocci (1985:112):

As the company grows larger and more complex, we recognize a need to plan more systematically for the people needed to staff the business. A lack of adequate talent may be the single major constraint in our ability to sustain future company growth. This [process] is a practical step toward more comprehensive employee planning and development.

The following are the advantages of integrating strategic planning and human resources management:

- Improved understanding of the implications of strategic organisational planning for human resources;
- Proactive recruitment of the required and experienced human resources;

- Improved human resources development activities;
- Improved analysis and control of costs related to human resources, by providing more objective criteria for payroll, labour market, training and other expenses.

We believe that strategic planning should include human resources planning from the outset.

25.3.2 What is strategic planning?

In simple terms strategic planning may be described as a proactive process during which the key decision-makers in an organisation decide on the best business opportunities, based on opportunities, challenges and threats in the organisation's business environment. Objectives, goals and programmes are drawn up as a result of these decisions in order to implement the strategy. Kochan and Barocci (1985:113) give a definition of strategic planning which ties in with our view:

Strategic planning is the process of setting organizational objectives and deciding on comprehensive programs of action which will achieve these objectives.

The important elements of the strategic planning process, and their effect on human resources management and planning, in particular, are now discussed in terms of the views of Kochan and Barocci (1985:113–14):

- *Define the organisation's philosophy:* The first step is to answer basic questions about the nature of the organisation: What is the reason for the organisation's existence? What unique contribution does it make or can it make? What are the underlying motives of key persons in the organisation? Responses to these questions may vary from the creation of employment and promotion opportunities to making a contribution to the social well-being of a country and its people.
- *Analyse environmental conditions:* The question to be answered here is: What political, economic, social and technological changes are taking place that could hold threats or opportunities for the organisation? Labour provisioning and higher statutory requirements to be met by human resources management practices and policy have a significant effect on an organisation. Another question to be answered is: What are our competitors' strengths, weaknesses and strategies? Other organisations' human resources strategies could have a significant effect on those of this organisation.
- *Assess the strengths and weaknesses of the organisation:* The next question to be answered is: Which factors could promote or restrict future actions? Human resources factors such as an obsolescent worker corps, overspecialisation by key managers, a lack of promotable talent and a history of failure to develop general managers of a high standard could all have a negative influence on strategic planning.
- *Develop goals and objectives:* Other important questions to be answered are: What are the objectives for sales, profit and return on investment? What timescales have been set for the realisation of these goals? Existing

organisational structures and current management styles are often not conducive to the attainment of specific goals and objectives. Kochan and Barocci (1985:114) elaborate as follows:

Where commitment is difficult to attain, strategies suffer. Also, important qualitative goals give way to more easily defined and measured quantitative objectives even though strategic objectives frequently involve commitment to changes in quality of service, quality of management, quality of research and development, etc.

- *Develop strategies:* The last questions to be answered are: Which plans of action must the organisation follow to attain its goals while simultaneously achieving specific operational objectives? What changes are required in the organisation's structures, management processes and human resources? In this the emphasis falls on human resources management, and in particular planning, recruitment, development, utilisation and even termination of the services of employees for the effective staffing of the organisation. This phase of strategic planning in particular has a causal link with human resources management.

The relation between strategic planning and human resources management will now be discussed.

25.4 THE EFFECT OF STRATEGIC PLANNING ON HUMAN RESOURCES MANAGEMENT

Kochan and Barocci (1985:115) point out that the ability of an organisation to attain its strategic goals is affected by human resources in three ways:

- Cost economy;
- Ability to function effectively;
- Ability to establish new organisations and change operations.

Factors that contribute to these three areas of influence are set out in figure 25.3.

Kochan and Barocci regard the factors identified in figure 25.3 as useful because they force the executives of an organisation to think about the relevance of human resources planning. They (1985:116) comment:

Personnel costs are significant in many organizations, frequently ranking below the cost of financial capital or the cost of goods and materials. Costs of capital, equipment, and materials are increasingly difficult to control due to their scarcity and to inflation. Accordingly, control over staffing levels, compensation and benefits, and staffing mix are important focal points of management attention.

It can therefore be stated unequivocally that strategic planning cannot be effective without due consideration of the human resources in an organisation. After all, strategic planning is implemented by people, with their unique abilities. In South Africa, where there is a shortage of human resources at management, professional and skilled levels, managements of organisations should pay particular attention to this potentially restrictive factor. Figure 25.4 is a schematic representation of the relation between strategic planning and human resources management.

FIGURE 25.3: The strategic influence on human resources factors

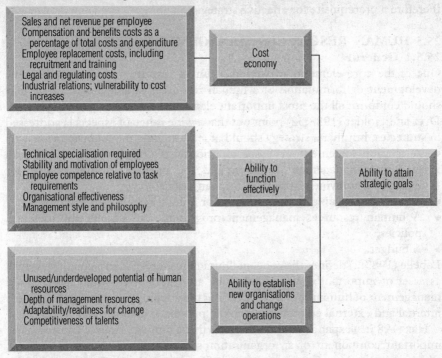

Sales and net revenue per employee
Compensation and benefits costs as a
  percentage of total costs and expenditure
Employee replacement costs, including
  recruitment and training
Legal and regulating costs
Industrial relations; vulnerability to cost
  increases

Cost economy

Technical specialisation required
Stability and motivation of employees
Employee competence relative to task
  requirements
Organisational effectiveness
Management style and philosophy

Ability to function effectively

Ability to attain strategic goals

Unused/underdeveloped potential of human
  resources
Depth of management resources
Adaptability/readiness for change
Competitiveness of talents

Ability to establish new organisations and change operations

Source: Kochan and Barocci (1985:116)

FIGURE 25.4: The relation between strategic planning and human resources management

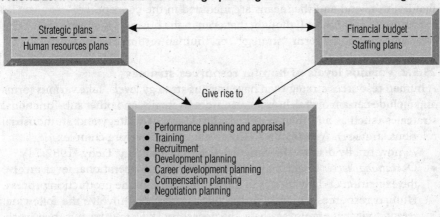

Strategic plans
Human resources plans

Financial budget
Staffing plans

Give rise to

- Performance planning and appraisal
- Training
- Recruitment
- Development planning
- Career development planning
- Compensation planning
- Negotiation planning

Source: Adapted from Kochan and Barocci (1985)

Figure 25.4 shows that in order to arrive at a feasible organisational strategy, the organisation as a system must consider all resources in its strategic planning. The strategic plan of an organisation represents financial, human and other resources. Taking into account all the resources available to an organisation is therefore a prerequisite for effective strategic planning.

25.5 HUMAN RESOURCES MANAGEMENT STRATEGY
25.5.1 General
One of the core elements of strategic human resources management is the development or formulation of a human resources strategy. Such a strategy should comprise all the most important elements of the management process. Dyer and Holder (1988:32) point out that a wide range of aspects is addressed in strategies, but that a strategy should at least include the following:

- A mission statement or a set of prioritised objectives for the human resources management function and the principal sub-functions (for example employment, training, compensation);
- A proposed organisational structure for human resources management;
- A human resources management programme to set out priorities and policies;
- A budget.

Labelle (1983:2) defines the concept "human resources management strategy" as a set of important decisions taken by an organisation with regard to the management of human resources, defining the adaptation to the organisation's internal and external environments in the pursuit of its objectives.

Hax (1985:1) expands on this and states that a human resources strategy is an important component of an organisation's corporate and business strategy, which includes a set of well-constructed objectives and action stages and which is aimed at ensuring a continuing long-term advantage over the organisation's competitors. From these definitions of a human resources strategy it is clear that both the end and the means are included in the concept.

It must be emphasised, though, that even in the business literature there is no unanimity about the term "strategy" or "human resources strategy".

25.5.2 Various levels of human resources strategy
A human resources strategy can have various strategy levels, take various forms and include certain overall human resources strategies and other sub-functional strategies (such as a human resources development strategy and an industrial relations strategy). A human resources strategy is therefore complex.

We now briefly discuss the various levels, as viewed by Tichy (1982:74):

- *Operational level:* Organisational functions at the operational level involve the execution of daily tasks, i.e. the maintenance of the production process. Human resources activities at the operational level involve the following: seeing to it that employees have the necessary skills to carry out their work, that they arrive at work every day, perform, are promoted and remunerated. At the operational level, the daily tasks of the organisation must be integrated with the human resources systems designed to facilitate this process, and it must be ensured that this process functions effectively.

- *Management level:* At management level, the organisational functions are determined by the strategic direction of the organisation. The focus is on obtaining the resources to carry out the strategic plans, and to develop processes for measuring and monitoring success. The human resources activities at management level involve the development of effective systems for the recruitment, selection, performance appraisal, compensation and development of the human resources necessary to achieve the strategic objectives. At management level, consultation on matters such as the following is of vital importance:
  — Is external recruitment taking place to develop the human resources that will be required in the medium term?
  — How will the internal need for human resources services be satisfied?
- *Strategic level:* At the strategic level, the organisational functions involve determining the businesses in which the organisation is involved or should be involved, the setting of objectives and their revision, the identification of priorities, the determination of important development programmes and the formulation of policies to carry them out. Human resources management at strategic level mainly involves the formulation of relevant human resources strategies to contribute to the ultimate success of the organisation in the long term, and includes the formulation of policy and programmes for the long-term development of human resources for future businesses, the development of the culture in which the business objectives can be achieved and the taking of relevant strategic industrial relations decisions. Liaison at the strategic level involves dialogue on the future plans of the organisation as well as on all possible human resources matters. There is also an evaluation of the alternative choices for all aspects concerning human resources, and the success of the organisation or business is always the final criterion. Achieving the objective of ultimate success may be regarded as the art of human resources management at top level.

When designing the various human resources systems, the overall organisational culture must be fully taken into account. In this context, Tichy (1982:75) remarks:

> If the corporate culture involves treating its employees as members of a family, then job security should be a key reward for performance. Such a value should be reflected in all of the human resources systems; it should be stressed as a recruitment criterion, tied to compensation, and built in as an assumption of development programs.

Factors that play a role here are (Fombrun *et al.* 1984:41):

- *The nature of the employment contract:* Two types of contracts can be entered into with employees: a pure *quid pro quo* contract with "a fair day's work for a fair day's pay" as the point of departure, or a contract that emphasises personal involvement with "challenging, interesting and meaningful work in return for a loyal, committed and self-motivated employee".
- *Internal versus external labour markets:* Organisations also differ as regards internal promotions versus external recruitment from the labour market.

Whatever the position, it influences the context in which the human resources systems are developed and function. In an organisation with a strong internal promotion strategy, the emphasis will be on the development of human resources. In an organisation with a primarily external strategy, there will be a strong recruitment function and a poor development function.

- *Group versus individual performance:* Human resources systems may be ordered according to collective, group-based performance or individual performance or a combination of the two. When the emphasis is on group performance, social adaptability must be taken into account during selection, the appraisal system must be group-based, and the compensation must provide incentives for the work group. Technology can also exercise an influence on the type of approach to be followed.

Strategic choices (top-level decisions) with regard to organisational culture are thus extremely important when human resources strategy is being formulated, because it is the "lubricant" that enables the final implementation phase of the human resources strategy to run smoothly.

25.5.3 Types of human resources strategies

There are various types of human resources strategies and various approaches to categorising them. There is, for example, the *organisational human resources strategy,* which applies to the entire organisation; *global human resources strategies,* which are more specific and narrow, but serve as sub-strategies for implementing the organisational human resources strategy and which can apply to the entire organisation or be delimited more closely, for example restricted to only one business unit; and *functional human resources strategies,* which are concerned with strategic (i.e. top management level) decisions about subfunctional areas such as compensation, training and development or industrial relations—but which may be either general or operational, as long as they are concerned with only one specific functional area of human resources management.

All decisions on these various human resources strategies ultimately involve a specific process that begins with mission formulation and internal and external environmental analysis, and ends in specific policy documents. Irrespective of the content of each strategy, its implementation thus involves a certain process.

Dyer (1984:6) developed a framework that differentiates between the two principal categories of human resources strategy, i.e. organisational and functional human resources strategies, and between two approaches to the analysis of these strategies, i.e. the content approach and the process approach.

In the *content approach*, the emphasis is on the core of both overall and operational human resources strategies, in other words on the essence of these specific strategies.

In the *process approach*, the emphasis is on the processes used to identify and analyse strategic information about human resources, and to make choices and take decisions about the content of the human resources strategies.

596

There are also more general approaches that can be followed or models that can be applied, which however also focus on the content of and procedures for the various human resources strategies (such as organisational or functional; operational or general). One such general strategic human resources model is that of Rothwell and Kazanas, which will be discussed later in this chapter.

The stages in the formulation of business strategies are summarised into three principal tasks by Dyer (1984:1–4):

- All human resources issues and the implications of the various alternatives or recommendations must be accounted for in detail (steps 1–4 in the model of Rothwell and Kazanas).
- It must be ensured that human resources objectives and strategies support business strategies (step 5 in Rothwell and Kazanas).
- Line managers must be involved as the main customers to ensure that human resources strategies are indeed well established (step 6 in Rothwell and Kazanas).

The model of Rothwell and Kazanas overlaps with that of Dyer in that both cover the important steps to be followed in strategic human resources management.

25.6 COMPONENTS OF STRATEGIC HUMAN RESOURCES MANAGEMENT

In a review of the literature, almost no acceptable definition of the concept "strategic human resources management" could be found. The reason for this may be twofold:

- It is an applied behavioural science that still has to be developed.
- The authors who write about it are hesitant to delimit the concept too quickly.

Miller (1987:360) states:

> there is little consensus in the literature about the meaning attached to the term strategic human resource management. The lack of definition of the subject matter is partially explained by the fact that, for many organisations, practitioners, academics, the human resource has not been thought of as a strategic one.

One of the earliest definitions found is that of Baird et al. (1983:15):

> Strategic human resources management identifies the organization's strategic goals and uses them as a basis for personnel practices and procedures.

Pansegrouw (1985:8) says:

> Strategic human resource management entails the deliberate alignment of human resource management plans and actions to the business strategy of the firm in order to ensure the human behaviours required by the business strategy.

He also points out the difference between the concepts:

> Strategic human resource management is a contextual approach to human resource management and assumes that different strategic types require different human resource management policies, plans and priorities. The main difference between

human resource management and strategic human resource management lies in the contextual or contingency approach deliberately adopted by the latter.

For his part, Tichy (1982:36) defines the concept as follows:

The concept of strategic human resource management tends to focus on organizationwide human resource concerns and addresses issues that are related to the firm's business, both short-term and long-term. It is particularly useful for designing specific human resource programs, policies, systems or management practices at the organizational or business level. It also suggests that the line executive is the most important constituent for the human resource function.

This definition supports the proactive approach advocated by the authors of this book. We hold the following view of strategic human resources management: [1]

- Strategic human resources management refers to the execution of strategic tasks and decisions such as:
  — Strategic human resources planning;
  — Strategic human resources marketing;
  — Strategic human resources selection;
  — Strategic human resources evaluation;
  — Strategic human resources training and development;
  — Strategic human resources compensation.
- Strategic human resources management further refers to the application of strategic techniques and instruments such as:
  — Scenario techniques;
  — Early warning systems;
  — Critical success factor analysis;
  — "Swot" analyses;
  — Assessment centres;
  — Human resources profiles.
- Strategic human resources management also refers to the development and implementation of human resources strategies from various points of view, such as culture, ethnic groups and political groups. The most important questions here are:
  — Which strategic options are available to human resources management?
  — How should human resources management strategies be designed and implemented to bring about the best fit between the overall strategy and human resources management strategy?
- Strategic human resources management further implies a philosophy, a new way of thinking, a new quality of human resources management. It focuses on characteristics of strategic thinking such as:
  — Proactive instead of reactive thinking;
  — Long-term instead of short-term thinking;
  — Systems-orientated instead of tunnel-vision thinking;

---

1 Based on a lecture given by Dr Ackermann from the University of Stuttgart, Germany, on a visit to the Department of Business Economics, UNISA, in 1990.

— Flexibility-orientated thinking;
— Opportunity and risk-orientated thinking;
— Innovation-orientated thinking.

The key question here is: How can strategic thinking be developed and implemented among human resources managers?

25.7 DIMENSIONS OF HUMAN RESOURCES MANAGEMENT

The aim of any human resources management strategy is to assist in executing the overall business strategy of the organisation.

Veldsman (1987:28) states that human resources management consists of three basic dimensions:

- A macro-strategic dimension;
- A micro-technical-administrative dimension;
- A micro-situational dimension.

His view is unique and is discussed below.

25.7.1 The macro-strategic dimension of human resources management

According to Veldsman (1987:28), this dimension consists among other things of the following aspects:

- The identification of the basic human resources needs of the organisation in the short, medium and long term;
- The formulation of a human resources management vision, mission and objectives to satisfy these needs;
- The development of an overall plan with its associated policy in order to achieve these human resources management objectives;
- The determination of the types and quality of human resources management services that must be rendered in accordance with the above plan;
- The provision, allocation and utilisation of these resources in order to render the services.

Finally he remarks with regard to this dimension (1987:28): "The human resource management strategy, in turn, has to be congruent with and supportive of the overall strategy of the organisation."

25.7.2 The micro-technical-administrative dimension of human resources management

This dimension is related to the traditional human resources activities such as human resources provisioning, human resources maintenance and human resources development. In this case, however, the focus is on the technical-administrative aspects concerned with the design, implementation, maintenance and evaluation of human resources systems. In the majority of South African organisations, attention is paid only to this dimension.

25.7.3 The micro-situational dimension of human resources management

Veldsman (1987:28) states:

The daily practice of human resource management by all superiors vis-à-vis their subordinates (also within the HR department) as an element of their management/ supervisory role makes up this dimension. In other words, the efficient and effective use of their human resources.

In this context, the human resources department must support both management and the supervisors by providing guidelines, advice, techniques and procedures to manage their human resources efficiently and effectively. A supervisor's success in this regard is a function of the quality of support and assistance provided by the human resources department and of the competent manner in which these inputs are applied by the supervisor.

Veldsman further remarks:

The macro strategic dimension naturally has a significant impact on the two micro human resource management dimensions, being a more encompassing dimension. It provides the framework within which the two micro dimensions are practised, and pre-determines to a large extent the content of both.

The two micro dimensions, however, also influence the macro dimension and thus provide inputs to the formulation and revision of the HR strategy. The macro strategy finds its implementation at the micro levels and in this way is tested continuously against the everyday human resources reality faced at the micro levels.

Strategic discrepancies are in this way highlighted, thus giving clues to areas requiring revision.

Whereas changes in the micro technical-administrative dimension obviously will have an effect on the micro situational dimension (e.g. the implementation of a new performance evaluation system), the latter dimension also impacts on the former.

Poor quality off-the-job training (micro technical-administrative dimension) will result in poor job performance and poor promotability and give rise to demands by superiors that this training should improve (micro situational dimension).

The interdependency of the three dimensions is illustrated in figure 25.5.

FIGURE 25.5: Human resources management dimensions

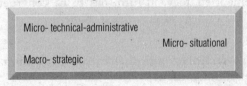

Micro- technical-administrative

Micro- situational

Macro- strategic

Source: Veldsman (1987:29)

From the above discussion it appears to be particularly important that the human resources managers in South African organisations should be both tactically and strategically innovative. They must also act as instruments of change, "selling" the importance of their function within the general context of organisational success to top management. Organisations in which they succeed in doing so are on the road to success, provided the human resources managers deliver what they have promised.

25.8 THE RELATION BETWEEN THE MISSION, GOAL, STRATEGY, VALUE SYSTEM AND BEHAVIOUR PATTERNS OF AN ORGANISATION

Campbell and Tawadey (1990:2) developed a definition of the concept "mission" that is much wider than the traditional one. They identify four elements, which they represent in the form of a figure (figure 25.6):

- Goal;
- Strategy;
- Organisational values;
- Standards of behaviour.

FIGURE 25.6: Elements of the mission of an organisation

Source: Campbell and Tawadey (1990:2)

In order to understand the relation between the elements, it is necessary to explain the concepts used in the figure.

According to Campbell and Tawadey, the *goal* of an organisation is the most philosophical part of the mission. It provides an explanation of the *raison d'être* of the organisation; in other words, for whom or for whose benefit the effort is made. Campbell and Tawadey (1990:2–3) state that "some chief executives dedicate their companies to the shareholders, arguing that the company exists to create wealth for the shareholders". This is probably true for small and medium-sized organisations, but according to the authors is not applicable to large corporations:

601

These multi-constituency companies believe in a stakeholder definition of purpose: that the company exists to serve the needs of all its stakeholders.

Strategy is the second element of the definition of a mission. It is the business rationale of an organisation. It relates behaviour and decisions to the goal of the organisation. In order to formulate a strategy, management has to describe and define the domain in which the organisation intends to operate and compete.

Campbell and Tawadey go on to say (1990:3):

It must also provide some rationale that identifies the competitive advantage or destructive competence that will enable the company to hold a special position in the chosen business domain.

A strategy serves no purpose unless it is transformed into behaviour patterns and decisions. A strategy should spell out what action and behaviour it requires if it is to have an influence on the organisation. Therefore the third element of a mission is standards of behaviour. *Standards of behaviour* are described by Campbell and Tawadey (1990:5) as follows:

Behaviour standards are therefore part of the organization's way of doing business. They are things that managers have come to feel are important to the effective running of the business. They are the ten commandments of the business.

These behaviour standards are defined not only by the company's strategy; they are also defined by its values. Our definition of mission recognizes that there are two reasons for doing something in an organization. The first is a strategic or commercial reason; the second a moral or value-based reason.

Organisational values are beliefs that support the organisation's management style and determine its attitude towards employees and shareholders, as well as its ethics. Campbell and Tawadey elaborate further on this aspect (1990:5):

In organizations with a sense of mission, values provide the emotional logic for managers and employees. They are the justification for managers and employees to say that their behaviour is not only good strategically but also good in itself: the right way to behave. Employees who have personal values similar to the organization's values find a sense of fulfilment and meaning in their work and behaviour standards. It is this sense of doing something worthwhile that gives them a sense of the company's mission.

According to the authors the mission will be healthy if all the previously mentioned components form a tightly knit whole. The question arises as to how important a mission is for human resources management. Campbell and Tawadey (1990:6-8) identify three advantages for employees who identify with the mission of the organisation.

First, employees are more motivated and will work more intelligently if they believe in what they are doing and trust the organisation for which they are working.

It is well known that everybody, including employees, seeks meaning in life. If an organisation can provide meaning for an employee, irrespective of salary and other circumstances, this will engender greater loyalty and commitment (a sense of mission) on the part of employees.

Campbell and Tawadey (1990:6) say:

The most powerful source of this commitment is the link between behaviours, the organization's values and the employees' values. If the behaviour standards in an organization are value laden (can be justified in value terms) they can have meaning for employees. Furthermore, if the values are those close to the heart of the employee, then the employee feels a sense of mission about the activity.

The benefits of creating a sense of mission are numerous. Inevitably they overlap with the benefits of clear strategy, such as better decision making, clearer communication, greater ease in delegation with its benefit of a lower need for supervision. But a sense of mission, enhanced by clear values, gives additional benefits. The main advantage seems to be the loyalty and commitment of the management and employees.

The second big advantage lies in staff selection and training. Organisations with strong values find it easier to recruit, select, promote, train and develop employees of the right calibre. It is implicitly a self-selection process, since prospective employees whose values and outlook on life do not agree with those of the organisation, will prefer not to join the organisation, or will resign at a very early stage. Campbell and Tawadey (1990:7) say further:

It is also a tool for helping managers make better decisions about selection, promotion and development. Training can be slanted to underpin the values and culture that the company is trying to reinforce, and an additional selection criterion can be used: does this person embody the values we believe in?

The third advantage of a sense of mission, and the one that the authors consider to be the most important, is better cooperation and mutual trust. Employees with a sense of mission find it easier to work together, to respect each other and to search for solutions that will benefit the organisation as a whole, and not just individual departments.

25.9 INTEGRATION OF HUMAN RESOURCES MANAGEMENT WITH THE OVERALL STRATEGY OF THE ORGANISATION: DIFFERENT VIEWS

25.9.1 The view of Angle *et al.*

Angle *et al.* (1985:51) make the following observation:

It would be fair to state that, in the typical U.S. organization's strategy-formulation process, the human element has taken a back seat to such other factors as logistics, economics, and technology. In essence, such organizations have tended to treat the human element more or less as "given" in formulating their strategic plans and in preparing to implement those plans. Often, organizations seem to assume that, when their strategies are implemented, the right mix of the right kinds of people, in the appropriate numbers, will be available; furthermore that they will possess the requisite knowledge and the motivation to carry out the organization's intended strategy.

The authors mention that great progress has been made during the past decade to incorporate human resources management, as a sub-strategy of the organisation, into the overall strategy. They state that it is especially typical of successful organisations, and give a critical résumé of this development (1985:53–4):

Stage 1
Organizational strategy formulation is based on such "hard" criteria as market position, technological advantage, capital structure and the like. Human resource issues are treated as an afterthought or a side issue in the corporate planning process. For the most part, the human factor is taken as "given" with respect to strategy implementation; i.e. it is assumed that sufficient numbers of the right kinds of people will be available, able, and willing to carry out the necessary steps.

Stage 2
Human resource planning is established as a staff responsibility. This planning is conducted, however, in relative isolation from line management and in a somewhat reactive manner—influenced by, but not influencing, the corporate planning process. Time horizons are fairly short.

Stage 3
Staff functioning within the human resource management organization adopts a "strategic orientation" toward the establishment and maintenance of human resource systems such as compensation, etc., but strategic human resource management is not integrated with the corporate strategic process. Fundamental barriers continue to exist between the legitimate subject-matter domains of human resource management and line management (or other staff agencies).

Stage 4
Strategic human resource management is somewhat elevated in status and is fully integrated into the corporate strategic planning process. The orientation of human resource managers and planners becomes proactive. Human resource managers operate from the perspective of the organization as a total entity (at their appropriate level). In the global strategic process, human system considerations are given co-equal status with economic and technical factors.

You can determine for yourself the stage that your organisation has reached in this process of development. What is undeniably true, however, especially in South Africa with its imbalance in the available human resources, is that top managements of organisations have to realise that the success of their organisations depends on the extent to which the overall human resources management strategy forms part of the overall business strategy.

25.9.2 The model of Rothwell and Kazanas
The various steps in the model of Rothwell and Kazanas are discussed according to figure 25.7.

The model of Rothwell and Kazanas consists of eight steps. The authors emphasise the various "roles" that must be played by a top-level human resources manager in carrying out these steps.

FIGURE 25.7: The strategic human resources management model of Rothwell and Kazanas

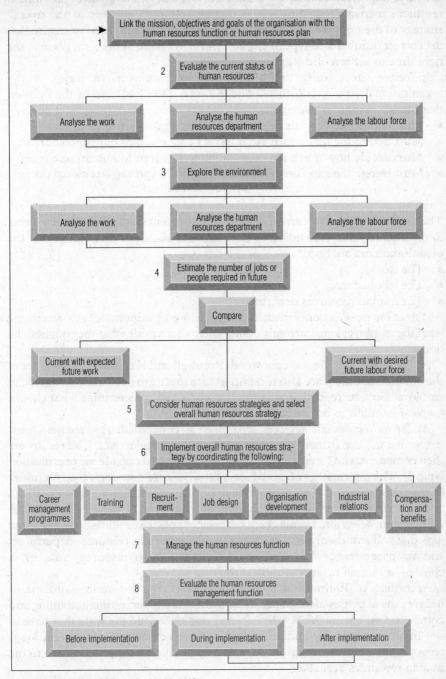

Source: Rothwell and Kazanas (1988:119)

Step 1

The first step involves linking the mission, objectives and goals of the human resources management function or human resources strategy to the overall strategy of the organisation. Among other things, this link helps to ensure that the correct number and type of employees are available in the right place at the right time to achieve the organisational goals.

In order successfully to link the human resources strategies to the organisational strategy, Rothwell and Kazanas (1988:44) are of the opinion that human resources managers:

- Must determine how the organisational strategy is formulated;
- Must determine how much attention is being given to human resources;
- Must decide how much attention ought to be given to human resources;
- Must bridge the gap between human resources and organisational plans.

Step 2

The second step involves an evaluation of the current state of human resources in the organisation. According to Rothwell and Kazanas, three aspects of the organisation are analysed:

- The work;
- The labour force;
- The human resources department.

As far as *the work* is concerned, two aspects are of importance: to determine what the employees are currently doing; and to determine what they ought to be doing.

As far as *the labour force* is concerned, Rothwell and Kazanas (1988:85) are of the opinion that there are also two important aspects: to determine what type of employees are currently carrying out the work; and to determine what type of employees ought to be carrying out the work.

As far as *the human resources department* is concerned: this analysis must determine the department's current strengths and weaknesses. The results are then compared with forecasts on conditions within and outside the organisation (step 3). The information obtained serves as a basis for a strategic plan for future human resources.

The analysis determines which human resources activities (for example recruitment, selection, training) are necessary to place specific employees in the jobs that will suit them best. In other words, the human resources department and its programmes are examined before a human resources strategy is chosen—a human resources audit is thus carried out.

According to Rothwell and Kazanas (1988:115), this audit is important because the activities of the department with regard to recruitment, training and compensation ensure the best fit between employees and the work they have to do. In other words, the audit determines which activity is a strategy for long-term change in its own right, which can help to link the work to be done to the human resources available.

Step 3

The third step in the model consists of exploring the environment in order to determine:

- How the work will change over a period of time;
- How the labour force will have to change over a period of time to adapt to the change in the work;
- How the human resources department will be influenced over a period by changes within and outside the organisation.

To determine the above, Rothwell and Kazanas (1988:141) suggest that the human resources planner should, by exploring the environment, achieve the following:

- Identify future trends within and outside the organisation (see chapter 20 for a discussion of the South African labour market);
- Predict the probable influence of these trends on the work, labour force and human resources department;
- Determine the desired influence of these trends on the work, labour force and human resources department, taking into account the future initiatives and plans of the organisation;
- Determine as specifically as possible the expected gap between what will probably happen in the future and what is desirable for the future.

Step 4

While in step 3 the principal focus was on the qualitative (content) changes with regard to jobs, the employees and the activities of the human resources department, Rothwell and Kazanas (1988:166) maintain that it is equally important to estimate the number of jobs and employees required in future. To be able to carry out this task successfully, Rothwell and Kazanas (1988:167–89) are of the opinion that the human resources planner should:

- Place the employees in clearly definable categories;
- Place the jobs in clearly definable categories;
- Determine the relation between output and number of employees (for example how many people are required to produce a certain quantity of goods);
- Predict demand for human resources by analysing current human resources needs and making a projection of future human resources needs with the aid of the plans and objectives of the organisation;
- Predict the supply of human resources by comparing current human resources inventories with the expected human resources that will be available both internally and externally in the future;
- Predict human resources needs by comparing the supply and demand forecasts.

Step 5

This step involves the selection of a single overall human resources strategy which will determine the initiatives of the human resources department.

The overall human resources strategy indicates the direction that the human resources department will take in the long term to support organisational objectives and strategy as effectively as possible. The overall human resources strategy is used to integrate the activities and outputs of the human resources department with each other in a vertical direction and with those of the organisation in a horizontal direction. Rothwell and Kazanas identify six overall human resources strategies, which indicate various long-term trends for the human resources department:

- A growth strategy when the external environment is favourable;
- Diversification when conditions favour the development of new organisations, products or services (in contrast with expansion by the organisation or the addition of new products and services);
- Integration when critical resources require closer ties with suppliers, competitors or distributors;
- Reversal when a strategy fails;
- A combination of strategies if circumstances require various strategies in various departments of the organisation.

Once the various overall human resources strategies have been identified, the one that will provide the desired outputs in the long run must be selected. The human resources planner must evaluate each overall human resources strategy on the basis of the information gleaned in steps 1 to 4 and must attempt to determine the possible results of each strategy. The advantages and disadvantages of each strategy must be weighed up against each other in order to select the most suitable strategy.

Step 6

This step involves turning the overall human resources strategy into a plan of action. According to Rothwell and Kazanas (1988:223), this step is known as human resources integration. The activities of the human resources department (recruitment, selection, training, handling of industrial relations, etc.) must be coordinated in such a way that they support the overall human resources strategy and that both employees and work change over a period of time so that the right people are available in the right place at the right time to support organisational plans.

Rothwell and Kazanas (1988:223) recommend the following steps for successfully carrying out this task:

- The development of long, medium and short-term human resources objectives for the organisation;
- The provision of leadership;
- The compensation of and control over employees' output;
- The development of a human resources policy to support the organisational strategy;
- The coordination of human resources activities;
- The linking of structure with strategy and vice versa.

Step 7

According to Rothwell and Kazanas, the effective management of the human resources function is essential for successfully implementing the above steps. This is the task of the head of the human resources department. Rothwell and Kazanas (1988:390–408) maintain that successful management involves the following:

- Setting objectives for the human resources department and its various spheres of activities;
- Developing a structure for the department;
- Obtaining staff for the department;
- Giving orders;
- Resolving conflict within and outside the department;
- Communicating with people within and outside the department;
- Planning resources for the department;
- Handling power and political matters.

Step 8

The last step in the model involves evaluation. The task of the human resources manager here is to determine whether the human resources strategy will work, is currently working or has worked in the past. Rothwell and Kazanas (1988:419) are of the opinion that evaluation must take place in three stages:

- Before implementation of the plans;
- During implementation of the plans;
- After implementation of the plans.

25.9.3 The view of Van Dyk

One deduction that can already be safely made is that South African organisations will not be able successfully to compete in the labour market for scarce human resources in all fields of specialisation. Furthermore, certain skills will be required that will not be available on the open labour market. This poses a great challenge to human resources management and—more than ever before—there will be a need for interaction between human resources managers and other functional and line managers in organisations. Figure 25.8 shows some of these interfaces, the most important of which are briefly discussed below, as well as the types of interaction and information that human resources managers will have to obtain at a strategic level.

It is clear from figure 25.8 that management with a view to successful human resources development is a comprehensive task. From a systems point of view, the macro-variables (megatrends) that have an effect on organisational strategy also have a profound effect on human resources. A proactive strategic approach implies that an analysis of the strengths and weaknesses of the available human resources must be done in order to adapt the strategy agreed upon for every sub-strategy (such as purchasing), both qualitatively and quantitatively. This must be done in the form of a human resources audit for every functional department

FIGURE 25.8: A strategic human resources management model

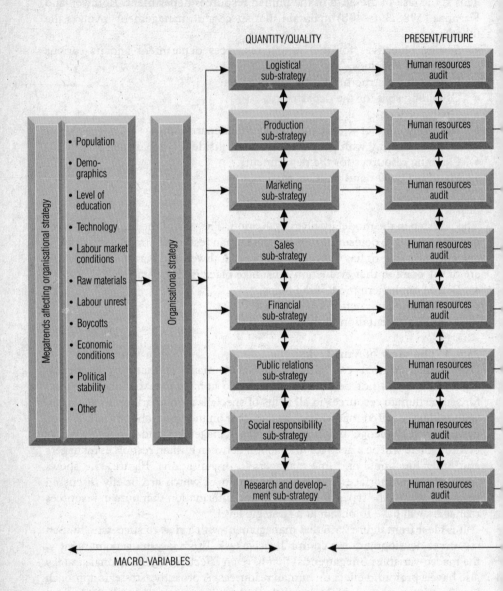

Source: Developed by P.S. van Dyk

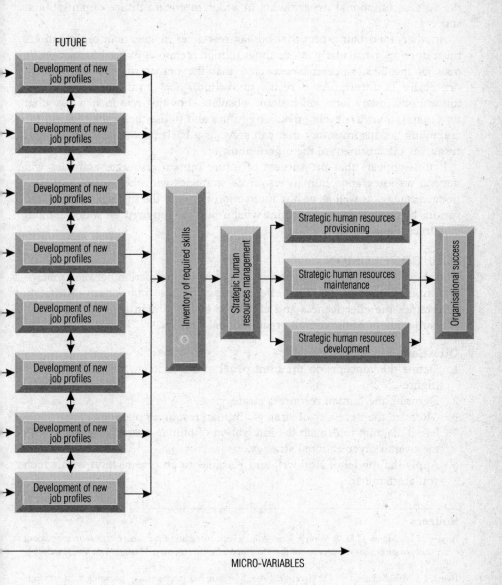

FUTURE

Development of new job profiles

Development of new job profiles

Development of new job profiles

Development of new job profiles

Development of new job profiles

Development of new job profiles

Development of new job profiles

Development of new job profiles

Inventory of required skills

Strategic human resources management

Strategic human resources provisioning

Strategic human resources maintenance

Strategic human resources development

Organisational success

MICRO-VARIABLES

and its sub-strategy to determine the current state of affairs and to extrapolate the figures for future requirements in the various labour categories (managers, professionals, skilled workers, semi-skilled workers and unskilled workers) for the various functional departments in order to ensure future organisational success.

Another important aspect that human resources managers of organisations must develop, particularly in our times of high technology and information, is new job profiles, since it is expected that the nature of jobs will change drastically in future. As a result of technological and other job-related innovations, many jobs will become obsolete. For this reason it is essential for organisations to develop new job profiles and to use them as a concept for compiling a skills inventory that can serve as a basis for the strategic human resources management of the organisation.

It thus appears that the success of future human resources activities will depend on integrating human resources strategies with the overall organisational strategy, as well as on the interaction between the managements of the various business units to determine what inputs are required for sound human resources management.

25.10 CONCLUSION

The above discussion clearly shows how necessary interaction between macro- and micro-variables is. The effectiveness of this interaction ultimately determines the effectiveness and efficiency of the human resources function as a sub-strategy of the overall organisational strategy.

Questions

1. Define the concepts on the front panel of the strategic framework (figure 25.2).
2. Describe the human resources strategy.
3. Motivate the necessity of strategic human resources planning.
4. Use a diagram to explain the integration of human resources strategy with the overall organisational strategy.
5. Apply the model of Rothwell and Kazanas to an organisation with which you are familiar.

Sources

Angle, H.L., Manz, C.C. & Van de Ven, A.H. 1985. Integrating human resources management and corporate strategy: a preview of the 3M story. *Human Resources Management*, Vol. 24, No. 1, pp. 51–68.

Baird, L., Meshoulam, I. & De Give, G. 1983. Meshing human resources planning with strategic business planning: a model approach. *Personnel* (American Management Association), Vol. 60.

Campbell, A. & Tawadey, K. 1990. *Mission and business philosophy: waning employee commitment.* Billings, London.

Dyer, L. 1984. Studying human resource strategy: an approach and an agenda. *Industrial Relations,* 23, pp. 156–69.

Dyer, L. & Holder, G.W. 1988. A strategic perspective of human resource management. In Dyer, L. (ed.) *Human resource management: evolving roles and responsibilities*. The Bureau of National Affairs, Washington.

Fombrun, C.J., Tichy, N.M. & Devanna, M.A. 1984. *Strategic human resource management*. Wiley, New York.

Hax, A.C. 1985. *A methodology for the development of a human resource strategy*. Assignment, Sloan School of Management, March, pp. 1–18.

Kochan, T.A. & Barocci, T.A. 1985. *Human resources management and industrial relations*. Little, Brown, Boston.

Miller, P. 1987. Strategic industrial relations and human resources management: distinction, definition and recognition. *Journal of Management Studies*, Vol. 241, No. 4, pp. 347–61.

Pansegrouw, G. 1985. Strategic human resource management—an emerging dimension. Part I. *IPM Journal*, Vol. 4, No. 5, pp. 22–30.

Pansegrouw, G. 1985. Strategic human resource management—an emerging dimension. Part II. *IPM Journal*, Vol. 4, No. 6, pp. 14–25.

Plevel, M.J., Nellis, S., Lane, F. & Schuler, R.S. 1994. Linking HR with business strategy. *Organizational Dynamics*, Vol. 22, No. 3, Winter.

Rothwell, W.J. & Kazanas, H.C. 1988. *Strategic human resources planning and management*. Prentice-Hall, Englewood Cliffs, New Jersey.

Tichy, N.M. 1982. Managing change strategically: the technical, political and cultural keys. *Organizational Dynamics*, 10, No. 2, pp. 59–80.

Veldsman, T.H. 1987. Human resources management should support the overall company strategy. *Human Resources Management*, May, pp. 28–30.

Index

618